Citizen Newhouse

Also by Carol Felsenthal

The Sweetheart of the Silent Majority
A Cry for Help (with Mary Giffin, M.D.)
Alice Roosevelt Longworth
Power, Privilege, and the Post: *The Katharine Graham Story*

Citizen Newhouse

PORTRAIT

OF A MEDIA

MERCHANT

Carol Felsenthal

SEVEN STORIES PRESS
NEW YORK / TORONTO / LONDON

FOR MY SON, DANIEL

In the U.K.: Turnaround Publisher Services Ltd., Unit 3, Olympia Trading Estate, Coburg Road, Wood Green, London N22 6TZ, U.K.

In Canada: Hushion House, 36 Northline Road, Toronto, Ontario M4B 3E2, Canada

Library of Congress Cataloging-in-Publication Data

Felsenthal, Carol.
  Citizen Newhouse: portrait of a media merchant / Carol Felsenthal. —A Seven Stories Press 1st ed.
  p. cm.
  ISBN 1-888363-87-8 (cl)
  1. Newhouse, Samuel I. 2. Publishers and publishing—United States—Biography. 3. Newspaper publishing—United States—History—20th century. 4. American newspapers—History—20th century. I. Title
Z473.N47F45 1998
070.5'092—dc21
[B]   97-52079
       CIP

Book design by Cindy LaBreacht

Seven Stories Press
140 Watts Street
New York, NY 10013

Printed in the U.S.A.

10 9 8 7 6 5 4 3 2 1

Contents

Acknowledgments

MY THANKS GO FIRST TO Patti Hagan, whose name I culled from a *Columbia Journalism Review* article in which she lamented the decline of the *New Yorker* since its purchase by Si Newhouse in 1985. Patti, a fact checker at the weekly during the pre-Newhouse era of William Shawn, arrived at our first meeting in 1994 shouldering tote bags stuffed with clips and with samples of stories that she had meticulously fact-checked. Once home, I came to anticipate her telephone calls filled with news of the latest coup or idiocy in the world of New York media; intelligence so useful to one working in Chicago and then not yet "on line." Even when I did get connected and no longer needed her fat packages of clips from the New York tabloids—both, to my surprise, fearless and enterprising in their coverage of the publishing scene—Patti remained essential to this project and among the most original people I have ever met. Her sole nod to technology was an answering machine, yet she seemed to have lodged in her brain her own kind of computer chip that spewed forth information on everyone connected in any way, at any time to the Newhouse empire. Her notes to me, typewritten on an aged Corona, were an incomparable roadmap to the mastheads current and past not only of the *New Yorker,* but also of such Newhouse properties as *House & Garden,* to which she had long contributed, Random House, and to an array of magazines owned by both Newhouse and his competitors.

When Putnam chief Phyllis Grann added Viking Press to her portfolio (Viking's parent company, Pearson PLC, purchased Putnam in 1996 and then she was handed Viking and Penguin to run as well) she decided, early in 1998, to cancel my manuscript, which I had finished late in 1997. The reason, she casually admitted, had nothing to do with the quality of the manuscript. It was wonderful, she said, but unfortunately a friend of hers appeared on nearly every page. Patti assured me daily, hourly even, that *Citizen Newhouse* was an important book and would find a publisher of principle and vision.

Al Silverman, while he was my editor at Viking, took an unwieldy manuscript and molded it into a book. Since our forced separation, I have thought of Al almost daily and missed his way with a pencil as news broke about the Newhouse empire—the sale of Random House and Tina Brown's exit from the *New Yorker* being the headliners—and as I added sections and an entire chapter.

To my agent, Flip Brophy, my gratitude and admiration remain undiminished. When Grann made her retreat, Flip hit the phones with her usual energy and nerve and found Dan Simon and Seven Stories Press. Dan quickly read the manuscript, admired it, and understood why it should be published. I also want to thank others at Seven Stories: Jon Gilbert, Ruth Weiner, Greg Ruggiero, Paul Abruzzo, professionals all. Flip's assistant, Nicki Britton, has always been smart, organized, and upbeat. She is also sweet, a quality not so common in New York publishing. Copyeditor Miranda Ottewell did an excellent job under a tight schedule.

Others who have helped along the way include *Media Industry Newsletter* editor Steven Cohn, maven of magazine numbers, who answered, day and night, my questions about circulation and ad revenue. Although undoubtedly busy at times, he never used that as an excuse. Thomas Maier, whose biography of Si Newhouse preceded mine, answered my questions and even suggested names of people I ought to interview. Ray Josephs, who knew Si's parents, Sam and Mitzi (he did public relations work for the company during Sam's heyday) has been generous with his time and papers.

David Fabish is the computer whiz who helped this klutz enter the interactive age. He tosses my incomprehensible manuals aside and simply makes my hardware and software go. He has answered my frantic pleas with patience and good humor. It is something of an exaggeration, but not that much of one, to claim that I'd be changing typewriter ribbons were it not for him.

My three children, Rebecca, Julia, and Daniel, wish, I'm sure, that I'd find a less consuming line of work, but they are always behind me, and follow my ups and downs, as I do theirs, with real interest, care, and maturity. My extended family—my mother Ruth, my brother Richard, my in-laws Eve and Jerry, my aunts Esther and Bette, as always, have helped in innumerable ways. Harriet and Rick Meyer, the best of friends, have offered advice and optimism when I sorely needed both. My friend, Charles P. Schwartz Jr., seemed never to tire of hearing my tales of *New Yorker* intrigue, and, as a shareholder of the magazine long before Si Newhouse entered the fray, he has been a font of wisdom, information, and brittle clips saved as if he knew that some day I'd happen along.

My husband Steve has nerves and principles of steel, and forces me not to retreat or to sell myself short when I undoubtedly would were he not there to remind me of my worth as a writer and reporter. When things looked bleakest, he insisted that all would work out. And they did, largely because of his ability to make them work.

Carol Felsenthal
September, 1998
Chicago, Illinois

I resent the fact that these men are fighting for a huge chunk of the "national estate" without there seeming to be any point to the fight. None seems to stand for a damn thing. This is the sort of thing that turns one against capitalism. I resent having these great companies owned by pointless men like these.—Henry Luce, as quoted by Richard Clurman in *To the End of Time: The Seduction and Conquest of a Media Empire*

I | Sam's Time

1 | The Self-Made Man

S. I. NEWHOUSE SR. WOULD HAVE BEEN horrified by
the utter extravagance of it. The elder of his two sons and his namesake
had purchased the *New Yorker* in 1985, six years after the father's death,
and by so doing had garnered reams of negative publicity—both for himself personally and for the billion-dollar media company that he and his
younger brother Donald had inherited from Sam, as S. I. Sr. was known to
friends and family. The founding father had always considered publicity an
evil to be avoided at all costs. His vast and byzantine empire was his business and no one else's, not his competitors', certainly not the government's.

Si, as his son was known, was flying home in 1992 on a private plane
from a *New Yorker* sales meeting in Florida. Aboard was Si's second wife,
Victoria Carrington Benedict de Ramel Newhouse. A fancily educated
Episcopalian—by then a devout convert to Catholicism—her extensive
surname reflected her failed marriage to a French count. Sam Newhouse
had married only once. And he had adored Mitzi Epstein from the day he
met her in 1923 until their marriage ended with Sam's death in 1979.
When the elder son left his first wife, Jane Franke, after eight years of marriage and three children, the patriarch was deeply disappointed, as was his
wife. Divorce, Mitzi always said, was not part of the Newhouse family. Sam
believed in lifelong marriages. He was a man of simple indulgences; to buy
still another newspaper—always one that had the potential to operate
unequivocally in the black—and to acquire for his Mitzi a still bigger diamond or a more lavish fur. The elder son's indulgences were more munifi-
cent; to pay $17 million for a Jasper Johns painting, or to lay out a few mil-

lion for *Details,* a downtown men's magazine filled with homoerotic stories and photos that his father would have found incomprehensible.

Also on board the plane carrying the Newhouses back to New York was Tina Brown, the British editor whom Si had imported to save *Vanity Fair,* a respected old magazine that had its heyday in the 1920s and that the son had resurrected in 1983. He had lost some $75 million on it until Tina seemed to staunch the flow, and he had since moved Tina to the *New Yorker* to work her magic there. But none of the tricks had clicked yet, and the magazine continued to post annual losses of as much as $15 million. Before the Newhouse purchase, it had run solidly in the black for more than fifty years.

Another passenger was the magazine's longtime art editor and cartoonist, Lee Lorenz. He and Tina Brown—the most celebrated magazine editor since *Vogue*'s Diana Vreeland—had been recruited to speak to and spark up the advertising sales force.

There was still another passenger on board—a nanny, though there were no children on the flight; Si and Victoria had none together. The nanny was there to tend to the needs of Nero, the black pug upon which the couple lavished the sort of attention usually reserved for a cherished only child.[1]

Four years later, in 1996, the results of such excess were there for the business and media worlds to see as they awakened to a front-page *Wall Street Journal* story reporting that nine of the fourteen magazines comprising Si Newhouse's Condé Nast were losing money. (The *New Yorker,* which itself might have been losing as much as all the Condé Nast titles combined, was not included in the article because it was then not yet officially part of Condé Nast.) The article was filled with the sort of delicious detail usually hidden inside this most private of companies: salaries in the half-million-dollar range, luxury automobiles, low or no-interest loans. Graydon Carter, Tina Brown's successor at *Vanity Fair,* which once again was said to be losing money, had received two loans totaling $450,000 to buy a country home in Connecticut and an apartment on Central Park West. Arthur Cooper, the top editor at *GQ,* also said to be losing money, had borrowed a million dollars for a country home in Connecticut.

Sam Newhouse, the founder, would not have been amused by a letter to the *Wall Street Journal* some weeks later, signed by a woman in Bellevue, Washington, and, although not naming the magazines, referring to two other Condé Nast titles, *Architectural Digest* and *Vogue:* "Condé Nast encourages its editors to live like pashas. No wonder they use their magazines to gush about million-dollar homes and absurd, ugly 'fashions' that are of no practical, aesthetic or affordable interest to mere mortals of the middle class."[2]

Sam was not opposed to the concept of interest-free loans to employees. He and his brothers, Theodore and Norman, regularly gave such loans to employees of his newspapers on Staten Island and Long Island and later in Newark, New Jersey; Syracuse, New York; Harrisburg, Pennsylvania; and Springfield, Massachusetts. These were modest sums to replace an ailing automobile or furnace or water heater, to pay for the care of a sick wife, or to send a son to parochial school or college. These were loans that Sam made in part out of benevolence, but also to discourage employees from joining unions. Because at many of his papers he offered no insurance or benefits, he understood that sometimes a working man's paycheck could not cover all necessities, much less the unexpected.

Sam Newhouse cared above all for his family. His sisters and brothers had helped him buy his first newspaper, and he later gave them and their children and their grandchildren jobs and opportunities.

Born in 1895, in a tenement at 53 Orchard Street on the Lower East Side of New York City, Solomon Isadore Newhouse was the eldest of eight children of Jewish immigrants. In the family he was called Sammy or Sam. In business he was called S. I. His father, Meier Neuhaus—he later Americanized his name to Meyer Newhouse—was an immigrant from Vitebsk, near the border of eastern Russia, and his mother, Rose Arenfeldt, was from Austria.

In better times in New York, Meyer Newhouse, who had studied to become a rabbi but had brought no practical trade with him from Vitebsk, operated the machine that made the leather ends of suspenders, and in worse times he was an invalid. He was not only weak bodied—suffering from severe asthma—but also weak willed. By the time Sam was twelve, his father was, in most every way, an invalid. It would later be written of Meyer that "he failed dismally at everything except procreation."

The burden of feeding her four daughters and four sons fell to Rose, who far outclassed her husband in determination. The family had moved across the river to Bayonne, New Jersey, in vain hopes of Meyer's finding business success. Rose awakened early every morning and headed to Manhattan, where she bought sheets, towels, pillowcases, napkins. Carrying her load over her shoulders, she walked the streets of Bayonne, peddling her wares door-to-door. "My father was a reflective man," Sam would later observe, "happier with words and ideas than with action. My mother, an unschooled farm girl, was the opposite. Impatient with too much talk, she was practical, energetic and clear of mind, concentrating always on the way to survive."

Sam, age thirteen, under five feet tall, his chubby cheeks giving him the look of a boy half that age, was filled with a determination even stronger than his mother's. He became, by default, the head of the household. For that year, 1908, his father moved out of the house to stay with his sister in Hartford, Connecticut, supposedly as a means of relieving his asthma. "Nothing had to be said when I became head of the family at so young an age," Sam later wrote. "Someone had to assume the leadership and provide the money; someone had to make the decisions, and it was obviously up to me, the firstborn." He vowed that he would make enough to support the family and to relieve his mother of her burdens.[3]

Although an excellent student, he quit school after the eighth grade, and that summer he enrolled in a six-week course in typing, shorthand, and bookkeeping at the Gaffrey School in Manhattan. (To save the three-cent fare for the ferry across the Hudson, he carried bundles of newspapers with him in both directions.) He soon found work as an office boy with a Bayonne lawyer, police court judge, and machine politician named Hyman Lazarus whose law office was situated above the offices of a weekly newspaper called the *Bayonne Times*. Sam landed the job by proposing that he work without pay until he proved himself worthy. After four weeks, he was making $2 a week for duties that included keeping the office books. He proved so adept a bookkeeper that two years later, when he was sixteen, Judge Lazarus promoted Sam to office manager of the law firm.

Lazarus also owned a 51 percent interest in the failing *Bayonne Times*. He had acquired the controlling share from a client who had no other means of paying a legal fee, but, to the judge, the paper seemed more trouble than it was worth. Lazarus, whom one relative described as a "big, popular political hack," had wider vistas in mind. He had close ties to political boss Frank ("I am the law") Hague, then mayor of Jersey City and a colossal power in Democratic politics, who was said to have promised to make Lazarus the next governor of New Jersey. With growing confidence in the boy, Lazarus instructed Sam, "Go down and take care of the paper until we get rid of it." He also told the sixteen-year-old that he would receive no increase in salary for adding management of the paper to his other duties, but he could keep half the newspaper's profits in the unlikely event that there were any. Lazarus fully expected that Sam would see no more success than any of the other managers who had failed to lift the paper into profitability.

At the time Sam had no particular interest in newspapers, but the challenge of making money was irresistible. If Lazarus had owned a chain of shoe stores and offered Sam the same incentive, the boy would have attacked the problem with equal zeal.

Sam quickly figured out that the paper was losing money because too few ads were being sold, so he began to sell ads himself and to devise ways to help merchants plan store sales and other merchandising schemes that they could then advertise in the paper. Within a year, Sam had made the paper profitable. Lazarus gave him a 20 percent interest in the *Bayonne Times,* which later grew to 50 percent. His salary was then $75 a week, and he had met his first goal of supporting his parents and his younger siblings.

And so Sam became the breadwinner of his family. When decisions had to be made about the younger children, it was Sam, not Meyer, who sat across the kitchen table from Rose to make them. Sam had started life sharing a bed with his brothers—one person who later worked for Sam says he slept on a board in the bathtub—but now he was given his own room. He had become almost literally the father of the household, sometimes referring to his brother Norman, eleven years his junior, as "son." Once, when Norman referred to their absent father as "the old man," the barely five-footer slapped Norman across the face. But Norman also became the first family member to go on Sam's payroll. That was 1911, and the five-year-old boy would stand on the street corner to hawk papers for a penny apiece. Sam would later say that his brother realized he could sell more papers if he held up a lone paper from his pile and pleaded, "Mister, please buy my last paper."[4]

On becoming overseer of the Bayonne paper, Sam decided to go to law school at night. (In those years neither a high school nor a college degree was a prerequisite.) By the time he turned twenty-one in 1916, he had graduated from the New Jersey Law School, later part of the Rutgers Law School in Newark, and had been admitted to the bar. That same year, with newspaper profits growing, his annual salary was $30,000, huge for its time.

His law career was brief. He tried one case, which he lost, and the defeat left him so embarrassed that he gave the client the $80 in damages he had sought in court. That was it for Sam, who never let go of his belief that the jury had been rigged. Anyway, he had found his home in the newspaper business, and he never looked back.[5]

In 1922 Sam was ready to grow. He used his own savings, borrowed what little he could from his siblings, and persuaded Judge Lazarus to join him in a new venture. For $98,000, Judge Lazarus and Sam bought 51 percent of a much larger newspaper—the *Staten Island Advance*. It had been losing money in a community of 160,000, but Sam could see its potential. He applied what he had learned in Bayonne, and the numbers almost instantly grew healthier.

Later Sam's sister Naomi became the inside "man" at the *Advance*, sort of the general manager, although the Newhouses were never much for titles. Brother Norman, with money flowing into the family from Sam, graduated from New York University and later became the *Advance*'s political reporter, city editor, and then managing editor.

Eventually, with economic times much better for Rose's family, Meyer returned home. And he too was given a job on the *Advance*. Although Meyer was still sickly—one Staten Island native, who as a boy delivered the *Advance*, recalls Meyer looking as if he couldn't blow out a match—he was installed by his son in a chair by the conveyor belt. Meyer, no taller than a schoolboy, sat watch attired in a jacket and tie, perhaps to lend dignity to what was inherently an undignified task—making certain that the delivery boys didn't steal papers. The boys, twelve and thirteen years old, would trick Meyer into turning his head, "so," one recalls, "we could grab a paper or two."

Meyer Newhouse, who would never understand where his son was headed or why, was a socialist, as were two of his brothers and a sister. But Meyer's radical politics did not touch Sam. "My father and his socialistic brothers and sister," Sam later remarked, "looked outward, away from themselves towards some kind of collective salvation and state control to meet their needs. I have always looked inward, toward individual responsibility and the potentials of the free marketplace." Meyer clung to his beliefs. When he was hospitalized with asthma in 1945—he would die later that year—one visitor was his son, who was so excited about his imminent deal to acquire a big newspaper, the *Jersey Journal,* that he rushed to his father's bedside to report the news: "Papa, Papa, I did it."

"Sammy, what did you do?"

"Papa, Papa, I bought it. I bought it."

"Sammy, what did you buy?"

"Papa, I bought the *Jersey Journal.* I bought the *Jersey Journal.*"

"Sammy, what do you need it for? You've already got a paper."[6]

In 1924, Judge Lazarus died suddenly after contracting poison ivy. And just as suddenly, opportunity opened to the judge's protege. Sam was eager to extricate himself from his share in the Bayonne paper; he wanted to devote himself to the *Staten Island Advance.* He paid Lazarus's widow for her husband's share in the *Advance* and soon bought out the remaining 49 percent that he and the judge had not owned. By 1932 Sam had enough capital to buy another paper, the *Long Island Daily Press,* for $750,000, and his incredible path to creating "the nation's richest family-owned publishing empire" had turned its first corner.[7]

Sam may have reached five feet, two inches in his prime; that was his claim. Old-timers at the *Staten Island Advance* recall that their boss, who often wore a fedora, was not quite as high as a counter in the lobby, so that one might see what appeared to be a disembodied hat moving swiftly along the counter's length. Sam had gray-blue eyes, a squat nose, a smile on his round, rosy face, puffy cheeks that gave him something of a chipmunk look, and always a suit and tie on his pudgy, next-to-neckless body.[8]

He could never be considered attractive, but he had money and energy, and now he wanted his own family, especially a son to carry on the business. Mitzi Epstein, at four feet, eight inches, seemed made to order for Sam (one acquaintance uses the word *Lilliputian* to describe them). Her first name reflected the Viennese origins of the maternal side of her family. She had grown up on the Upper West Side of New York in circumstances much more prosperous, cultured, and Americanized than Sam's, in a family that was decidedly upper middle class—so well fixed that a Hungarian woman was employed as the family cook.

Mitzi's grandfather, Emmanuel Fred, had emigrated from Austria, and with his first and second wives—the first died, and he then married his wife's cousin—had eight children. The home was a gathering place, but money was tight, and feeding, clothing, and housing eight children was a struggle.

Mitzi was the daughter of one of those children, Julia, a woman with a decided artistic and business sense, if not much education. When she married Samuel Epstein, she, he, and one of her brothers went into business together importing silk scarves and neckwear from France, some of it fine lace, through S. Epstein and Company on Eighteenth Street. The business opened in the early years of the century and ran prosperously until the crash of 1929. Besides being the owner/executive, Julia was also the designer. She had marvelous skills at knitting and needlepoint. She also loved foreign films and would go to the local movie house on Saturday afternoon, knitting in hand.

Julia and Samuel somewhat reluctantly accepted Sam Newhouse as the husband of their beloved and only daughter. When the two married on May 8, 1924—she was twenty-two and he almost twenty-nine—the Epstein neckwear business was still flourishing, and this diminutive proprietor of a paper on Staten Island seemed not quite so impressive to a couple who lived grandly in a big apartment on West End Avenue. But Mitzi, who had attended art school at the Parsons School of Design, loved Sam, and so they were married. They celebrated at Delmonicos, one of the most fashionable restaurants in New York. A younger cousin of Mitzi's, Ruth

Spaet, eight years old at the time, still remembers the piece of wedding cake sent home to her in a miniature white satin trunk. The newlyweds took a traditional but abbreviated American honeymoon at Niagara Falls. Having just acquired full control of the *Advance,* Sam had to rush home to be on the job.

When the stock market and the Epstein neckwear business collapsed five years later, Ruth Spaet recalls, "My uncle Sam [Samuel Epstein] was so overcome...that he had a stroke." Julia, undaunted, hired a round-the-clock nurse for her husband and went out to land a job as a designer of blouses and neckwear. According to her niece, Julia "commanded a marvelous salary for those years; she earned more than practically any man."[9]

The 1929 calamity did not stop Sam Newhouse. His wealth continued to grow. Sam wanted to live near his newspaper on Staten Island, and their first home was a model that had been part of an *Advance* advertising promotion. Soon after, Sam built a much more impressive home for Mitzi, an English Tudor on Staten Island's Ward Hill with a dramatic view of New York Bay. The Hungarian woman who had cooked for Mitzi's mother was handed down to Mitzi and would remain the family cook for years after. Cooking was a skill that Mitzi never cared to learn.[10]

On November 8, 1927, three and a half years after their marriage, Mitzi gave birth to Samuel I. Newhouse Jr., who was born by cesarean section. A second son, Donald Edward, followed two years later, also by cesarean. Her doctor advised Mitzi that subjecting herself to another cesarean delivery would endanger her health.[11] She would have no more children.

Mitzi had plenty of help with her boys, and she grew bored on Staten Island. As her honeymoon had taught her, she could not depend on Sam for companionship. He had told her before their marriage that he would devote himself to her. But he also told her that he would have to devote himself at least equally to his work. She longed for the distractions of the more sophisticated life of Manhattan. While he probably would have stayed on Staten Island had she not pushed them out, he finally did make the move to Manhattan, partly for its anonymity. One night in 1934, workers at the *Advance,* who had threatened to organize and met stiff resistance from Sam, picketed his house. All night long they marched back and forth, shouting anti-Newhouse slogans into megaphones and continuously shining a spotlight into his front windows.

And so the family moved to an apartment at 730 Park Avenue at Seventy-first Street—and not just any apartment. The fourteen-room duplex occupied the seventh and eighth floors of a building that was—and is—in terms of social status, one of the top buildings in Manhattan. It was home to composer Richard Rodgers and his wife, Dorothy, and to members of the Farkas family, who owned Alexander's department stores. John D. Rockefeller had lived in the building just to the north, 740 Park, which remained home to other Rockefellers. For the Newhouses, it was some twenty blocks below the line that Jews were then beginning to cross.[12] And those Jews were not of the Newhouse variety, but rather German Jews of education and cultivation whose families' arrival in New York antedated that of many of the board members who sat in such lofty judgment. Most buildings on Park and Fifth Avenues in the seventies and eighties did not want Jews of any origin, although the depression had forced some of their boards to hold their noses and accept them.

One thing was for certain. S. I. Newhouse could afford this luxury apartment, which his wife rendered even more luxurious by retaining a stable of society decorators to "do" the interiors to the hilt of glitter and gilt. Three years after buying the *Long Island Daily Press* in 1932, Sam bought the *Newark Ledger*. In 1939 he bought the *Syracuse Herald* and the *Syracuse Journal*, quickly merging them and turning their red ink to black. Two years later, he bought the *Syracuse Post-Standard*.

After the war ended, in 1945, Sam bought the *Jersey Journal*. In 1948 he bought his first paper in Harrisburg, the *News*. He would later buy the *Harrisburg Patriot*. In 1950 he bought the *Portland Oregonian*. (Eleven years later he acquired the competing *Oregon Journal*.) In 1955 he bought papers in Birmingham and Huntsville, Alabama (the *News* and *Times* respectively), as well as the *Globe-Democrat* in St. Louis. In 1962 he bought two papers in New Orleans, the *Times-Picayune* and the *States-Item*. In 1967 he bought the *Cleveland Plain Dealer*. The 1970s would bring him Booth, a highly profitable chain of eight dailies in Michigan. The deal also included the lucrative Sunday supplement *Parade*.[13]

He kept his eye fixed on newspapers—he resisted the temptation, for example, to buy the New York Yankees when that deal was offered him—and fixed specifically on bargain-priced papers in growing communities. He had no interest in starting papers. Later, as he had more money to spend, he looked for money-makers whose profits he could boost even further.

The best tonic for Sam's bottom line was to acquire a city's first newspaper, then get his hands on its second, thereby allowing him to set advertising rates as high as he pleased. He would promise to keep both papers in business and in competition. But he would eventually move in for the kill by merging the two, which generally meant closing the afternoon paper and keeping the morning. He thus created a monopoly money machine of the sort billionaire investor Warren Buffett likened to an "unregulated toll-booth." Buffett, an investor in a profitable monopoly paper, the *Washington Post,* has often observed that there are few better ways to make money than in a monopoly paper.

With Sam's wealth growing daily, Mitzi pushed for a country home. In 1942, they bought Greenlands, a working farm on what would come to encompass some 143 acres in Harbourton, New Jersey, in Mercer County, near Princeton.

But Sam was not the gentleman farmer type. A friend, Elaine Reiner, whose husband, Hal Eaton, was a theater critic and gossip columnist for the *Newark Star-Ledger,* remembers it as "an actual working farm because that was a tax deduction." Another guest calls it a "playground for people for the weekend."

A favored guest was public relations man and premier showman Ben Sonnenberg, an immigrant from Russia who presumably had much less money than Sam, but lived as if he had much more. He would drive to the farm in his vintage Rolls Royce from his thirty-seven-room mansion on Gramercy Park, which had been built for Mrs. Stuyvesant Fish. As Sam continued to swallow up newspapers and began to face hostility from the citizenry in the cities he targeted, he retained Sonnenberg's firm to upgrade his public image.

For his weekends at "the farm" (the family always referred to it as such), the patriarch had a set routine. When not eating Sunday lunch on the screened porch with friends and relatives who had been invited to drive down for the day, and when not playing an after-lunch game of poker with his brothers, he simply absorbed himself in his work. (He did enjoy informing visitors that the father of the farm's previous owner had invented the flush toilet.)

The main house, with its six-foot-thick fieldstone walls, dated to the American Revolution. The late James Michener, who had been introduced to Sam and Mitzi by friends, and who would go there occasionally for lunch, recalled most vividly Greenlands' his-and-hers swimming pools. There was also a tennis court, a riding stable, a five-car garage, and a full complement of servants.[14]

The elder son, Si, and his brother, Donald, grew up mostly in the Park Avenue apartment, with its series of decorators constantly redoing what already seemed done, its Louis XV and XVI furniture and decor tending to the overwrought; its doormen and elevator operators; its imposing two-story foyer that the visitor entered immediately on exiting the elevator; its curved, almost semicircular staircase; its wood-paneled, green-leather-furnished library that served as Sam's office. The hired help was expected to keep the whole show going and to make sure that these two boys—so tiny in stature that it was clear neither would much overtake their parents—were not lost in the shuffle.

It was a formal, rather lonely setting for childhood. There weren't many children in the building, and the few that were there did not appear in the Newhouse apartment for milk and cookies and an afternoon of play. The Newhouses did not socialize with their neighbors. Sam Newhouse once told an employee that he shared a elevator with a man for ten years before discovering it was Richard Rodgers.[15]

Mitzi loved her boys, but didn't have much of a sense of what to do with them. Had her doctors not advised otherwise, Mitzi, who adored clothes and jewels and fancy hairdos, would have loved to have had a daughter. That gap was partially filled by her brother Walter's daughter, Sue, the only girl in that generation on her side of the family. She was a pretty child whose father worked all his life on the business side of his brother-in-law's newspapers, most of the time in St. Louis. Starting at age eight, Sue would often come to New York and stay with Mitzi. Later she spent a couple of summers at the farm. Often it was just Sue and Mitzi. They dined at the big table, and Sue wondered how the servants knew when to appear, not realizing that Mitzi was pressing the buzzer on the floor with her tiny foot. Mitzi helped Sue style her hair, "and she would go through my clothing and show me what would go with what."[16]

In his privately published memoir, *A Memo to my Children,* Sam admitted that he had no time to do the conventional things that fathers do with sons. Anything outside his business life, he would later tell Calvin Trillin, then writing a cover story on him for *Time,* was Mitzi's domain. When Trillin asked Sam for a list of friends to interview, "He sort of told me that that was…Mitzi's department."

Perhaps because Sam himself never had a childhood, he had little patience with his sons, especially his namesake, who was by nature more withdrawn than Donald. By one report, Sam was "dreadful to Si, even when he was a little boy."

The boys, especially Si, on whose narrow shoulders the future of the business rested, grew up in awe of and even fearful of their father. Children unerringly sense when a parent favors one over the other, and Sam's clear preference for his younger son added to Si's feelings of inadequacy. Donald, although also far from perfect in his father's eyes, was more open, optimistic, well-rounded, and outgoing. He seemed tougher, more aggressive, and less acutely sensitive than Si. Donnie's round and smiling face resembled Sam's. Si's brooding eyes, heavy lips, and weak chin did not, in Sam's view, hold much charm or promise.

Despite Sam's preference for Donald, starting in his sons' childhood, there was always a doubt in Sam's mind that either boy had what it took to carry on. One might argue that it is unfair for a parent to judge the future ability of such small boys. But Sam knew what he had accomplished while not yet a teenager and probably could not help but judge his boys by similar standards. "I have always had a great deal of self-confidence, even as a child," Sam would later remark. The desirability of working to pass this quality on was not something that would have occurred to the patriarch.[17]

That Donald was lacking in any real creative or artistic sensibility made him easier for Sam to understand. Si, although he did not express his creativity in any obvious way, had an artistic bent, and for this ability he was Mitzi's favorite.[18] Still, for most of his school years, Si Newhouse didn't feel that *favorite* was a word that anybody would think of applying to him.

2 | The Education of the Heir

THE HORACE MANN SCHOOL FOR BOYS, where Si arrived in the fall of 1939 and Donald two years later, was a logical choice for the education of the Newhouse sons. Located on an ivy-covered campus in the exclusive section of Riverdale in the Bronx, it was small (approximately 400 students), private, wealthy, virtually all white, and lately, heavy (some estimate as much as 80 percent) with the sons of newly successful Jewish merchants and professionals. Aside from a few who received scholarships, mostly athletic, the only students whose parents did not pay full freight were children of Columbia University professors, who for a time received free tuition.

Horace Mann was one of the few private schools without a quota for Jews. Others, many within walking distance of the Newhouse apartment on Seventy-first and Park, were still unfriendly to Jews beyond the obligatory token or two. Old-line schools such as Collegiate and Trinity probably would not have embraced the Newhouse family, on the paternal side of which there was no tradition of any education, much less private education. There were Jews and there were Jews, and the Newhouses were decidedly not part of "Our Crowd."

Horace Mann was founded in the late nineteenth century as a coed training institution for Columbia University's Teachers College, but by 1914 it left the girls and Manhattan behind and moved up to its present site at 246th Street in the Bronx. By 1947 it left Columbia behind as well and became a totally independent school.

Organized along the British model of forms rather than grades—first form being the seventh grade and sixth form the twelfth—Horace Mann, during the years Si was a student there (1939–1945), was presided over by Charles Carpenter Tillinghast, who had held that position since 1920. (He retired in 1950.) The school was rigorously academic and highly competitive, with grades given in numbers rather than letters so as to reflect the smallest differences among students. Tillinghast dismissed the "child-centered" approach of progressive schools such as neighboring Fieldston as "an extension of the kindergarten methods into the upper grades."

Latin had only recently been dropped as a requirement, but most students took it. English, as taught by a popular teacher named Alfred Baruth, was heavy on Shakespeare, Wordsworth, Coleridge, and Browning, but devoid of such "modern" poets as T. S. Eliot and, presumably, even its own William Carlos Williams (Horace Mann, '03). Robin Lester, former headmaster at Trinity and before that head of the department of history at Collegiate, calls Horace Mann probably "the strongest academic prep school in the country, but it was up in the Bronx and that never gave it the social cachet that the Manhattan schools had."

At the first assembly of the year, Tillinghast would remind his charges that "a Horace Mann boy is a young gentleman," and that was all that needed to be said. Students addressed their teachers as "Sir"; they wore coats and ties, their hair was combed, and their nails clean and filed.

Except for the school librarian, there was only one female member of the faculty, A. Berdena McIntosh, who was also known as "Nail File" McIntosh. Her duties, in addition to teaching first-form Latin, included monitoring the boys' grooming—and that included surprise nail checks.

There was a religious cast to Horace Mann culture, with chapel every Wednesday morning—Tillinghast was a prominent layman in the Baptist church—but while the headmaster was said to know the Bible "inside out," his talks to the boys were more about personal responsibility than religion. Daniel Rose, a 1947 graduate of the school who wrote about life there during the 1940s, characterized them as "nondenominational moral pep-talks." Tillinghast liked to introduce his talks with a literary excerpt. His favorite reading was *Sir Galahad*—"His strength was as the strength of ten because his heart was pure."

The faculty was devoted, experienced, opinionated, and by today's standards wildly politically incorrect. One teacher tossed tennis balls and stubs of chalk at students who didn't know an answer or whose attention lagged. In a three-piece suit, his Phi Beta Kappa key dangling prominently from his vest, history teacher Harry Martin expressed outspoken contempt for Franklin Roosevelt (a faculty straw vote in 1936 gave Alf Landon 36 votes, Roosevelt 1). The intensity of this enmity was matched only by Martin's outspoken suspicion of the influence of Catholic priests on American history. Then again, he didn't think much of Zionism either, or—according to one of his students—Jews. This same student said that Martin believed Jews to be dishonest and blacks stupid.

Daniel Rose wrote that the values Tillinghast "assiduously cultivated" were high academic achievement, "'manliness'... and rugged determination in sports." Athletics were competitive and central to school life. Tillinghast rarely missed a school game and regularly practiced with the baseball team, playing first base.

With the encouragement of Columbia University, Horace Mann ran a program to boost the fortunes of its athletic teams beyond the level that its regular student body could achieve. Jack Kerouac, having just graduated from Lowell High in Lowell, Massachusetts, came to Horace Mann on an athletic scholarship during the 1939–40 year. Thus the school received the services of a player who led the football team to four victories and one loss before he moved on to Columbia with, in theory, his academic and athletic skills improved.[1]

It was probably the wrong school for Si Newhouse. He was notably unathletic, and unlike other boys who didn't participate much in sports, Si lacked a compensating forceful personality and leadership skills. Had he attended a school in which the arts were taken seriously—at Horace Mann they decidedly were not—his self-confidence might have been boosted rather than battered.

Still, the youngster did seek out others who shared his interests. He became friendly with a boy named Sandy Friedman who was from a wealthy family, flamboyant in his manner, and passionate about theater and acting. Si also had some ties to a group of boys who liked classical music. One of them, Si's classmate Joseph Bernstein, recalls that Si was good, although not the best in the group, at a game requiring the player to guess the name of a popular symphony after hearing only two bars.

Bernstein recalls visiting Si's home and marveling at the stacks of 78-rpm records in his bedroom closet and at the fact that he never put them back in the album jackets.[2]

Si did work for the school newspaper, the *Record*, and was a better than average writer. The experience gave him an opportunity to prepare for the family business. But probably an even stronger incentive was his desire to be near Allard Lowenstein, a charming, outgoing natural leader—later a political activist and U.S. congressman—who seems to have taken the hapless Si Newhouse under his wing.

Al Lowenstein loved newspapers the way other boys loved baseball. "He had a game where you'd formulate the front page of a newspaper," recalls classmate Samuel Heyman. "You took it to an impartial jury to see whose front page looked better. That was the kind of children's game he played." Newhouse had nowhere near that zeal for newspapers or for Lowenstein's other enthusiasm, politics—Al was voluble on the Spanish Civil War before his tenth birthday—but these passions did give Si's young life a kind of direction and excitement.

During the 1944–45 school year, when Lowenstein was editor of the weekly *Record*, he had the task of selecting a managing editor. In a move characteristic of him, he named two friends, Si Newhouse and Bob Carneiro, as comanaging editors. But Si did not throw himself into the task with the same intensity as Al and Bob did. Every Wednesday after school, those two would trek to Yonkers, north of Riverdale, where the *Horace Mann Record* was printed, to read proof. Carneiro, who is now curator of anthropology at the American Museum of Natural History, says he has no memory of Newhouse ever coming along.

Si was there at least once, however, when he wrote a subhead for an article about a baseball game between Halstead, a small private school in Yonkers, and Horace Mann in which his coeditor Carneiro hit a ball over the left center field fence. Si described it as the longest home run in Horace Mann history. In fact the record was held by George Washington Case, a student at the Peddie school who, in a game against Horace Mann circa 1933, set the record for the longest home run. (Case later played for the Washington Senators.)[3]

"Not remembering" Si having been there is a constant refrain among his classmates. Not remembered as an academic standout. Not remembered as a dropout. Not remembered as a prankster. Not remembered as an athlete or writer, or even as a spoiled rich boy. "I know he was my classmate, but nothing about him stands out" is a typical remark. Classmate David S. Maimin Jr. describes Si as "sort of like a stealth plane, he was there but I don't remember anything about him."

What stands out most about Si Newhouse in the memory of his classmates is his friendship with Lowenstein and, especially, with Roy Cohn. Cohn, who graduated from Horace Mann in 1944, a year before Si, was the son of an appellate division associate justice, Albert Cohn, who was also the power behind the throne in the Bronx Democratic organization. The source of the relationship was Mitzi's friendship with Roy's mother, Dora Marcus, an aggressive, insufferable, cartoonish version of the stifling mother, whose conversation consisted almost entirely of talk about her only child and who turned Cohn into a notorious mama's boy.

Dora Marcus's family had once had money. Her father, Joseph Solomon Marcus, had started the Bank of United States in 1913 on Delancey Street. Solomon Marcus served Lower East Side immigrants, then shunned by establishment banks, and his bank boasted more depositors, most of them Jewish, than any other in the country. It crashed in 1933 after crowds of depositors tried to withdraw their money, tens of thousands of them losing much of their savings. The government refused to allow the bank to reopen. Roy Cohn always claimed that the "WASP establishment" went after the bank "with a vengeance that was pure in its anti-Semitism." In major cities like New York and Chicago, Jews had become prominent in banking, and in general, the government did not allow the Jewish-owned banks to reopen.[4]

Most boys going to Horace Mann from Manhattan took the number one IRT train to the end of the line, 242nd Street, Van Cortlandt Park, and then made the long, steep climb up to the school. Roy Cohn and Si Newhouse were among those driven by a private car service run as a side business by their English teacher, Alfred Baruth. The driver would pick up Si and then head up to collect Roy, who lived at 1165 Park, at Ninety-second Street, and his across–Park Avenue neighbor Allan Newmark, another neighbor, Michael Loeb, and the late Generoso Pope Jr., Roy's classmate, whose father owned both Colonial Sand and Gravel and the Italian newspaper *Il Progresso Italiano*. (The son later bought the *New York Enquirer* from Hearst, turned it into the scandal sheet the *National Enquirer*, and came up with the revolutionary idea of distributing it in supermarkets.) For a time, Mayor Fiorello La Guardia's adopted son was also a regular in the car.

Talk en route to school was sometimes about politics, a subject the young Cohn adored and about which he would argue endlessly. Roy was then, like his father, a traditional democrat and supporter of the New Deal. He was also, like Si, someone who didn't quite fit in. But while Si sat silently in the car, Roy was noisy, often loudly disagreeing with a boy named Louis Brandeis Gilbert who was a nephew of the Supreme Court justice.

At Horace Mann, Cohn preferred a power-behind-the-throne role. In 1941 he ran Paul Sack's winning campaign for president of their sophomore class. But then Cohn turned around and managed the campaign of Anthony Lewis (now a liberal columnist for the *New York Times*) against Sack for president of the student body. Lewis won.

Si Newhouse also tried his hand at political strategizing, but less successfully. In his senior year he worked hard for Al Lowenstein, who was in a race for student body president against classmates John Haldenstein and Joe Bernstein. Schoolboy letters from Si to Lowenstein* show Si presenting various strategies for the coming contest: long lists of potential vote counts for primaries and finals; predictions of possible alliances and realignments; methods of channeling the "gentile vote"; and lectures about the importance of Al lobbying potential voters individually and often.

The result was a tie vote for the first two, who were truly the leaders in that class and serious rivals. Haldenstein persuaded Bernstein to throw his support to him, and he beat Lowenstein in the runoff. Al accepted the spot of vice president.

---

*Newhouse's letters to Lowenstein are among the latter's papers in the Southern Historical Collection of the University of North Carolina, Chapel Hill. Lowenstein apparently did not keep copies of his letters to Si, and because Newhouse did not cooperate on this biography, it's unknown to this author whether that side of the correspondence exists.

As Si's analyses went on, through page after handwritten page, he sometimes vented feelings of frustration, of being unappreciated; he also lashed out at Al for his idealism, which Si apparently considered a flaw in both politicians and statesmen. Churchill and Stalin became the men they were, Si lectured Al, because they were realists.

At the other end of the spectrum from Stalin and Churchill, Si consigned Henry Wallace, FDR's controversial vice president, who would be replaced in 1944 with Harry Truman. Henry Wallace is a brilliant politician compared to you, Si chided, knowing that Lowenstein vastly admired the progressive politician.

While Si enjoyed working for Lowenstein, he had his own ambitions. He told Al that he intended to run for president of the Speakers Club, an unlikely position for one who so feared public speaking, but the position mostly involved inviting speakers to the school. In one letter Si went along with Al's desire to run for vice president of the Speakers Club, but reminded his friend to leave the presidency to Si. He promised Al that he had plans galore for the club, but neither the space nor time to describe them just then. Si did become president of the club, a position held before him by Roy Cohn.[5]

In all his time at Horace Mann, the elder son never talked much about his father or what he did—not an uncommon situation. Classmate Paul Haberman, who describes Newhouse as "inauspicious," feels that far from flaunting his wealth, "if anything, I would say that he tried, maybe unconsciously, to conceal [it]." John Haldenstein is typical in recalling that while he knew Si's father "owned a bunch of newspapers somewhere, it didn't matter that much to a young boy."

But Al Lowenstein was different. He was quite aware of who Si Newhouse was. Paul Haberman recalls Lowenstein asking him, "Who do you think is the richest boy in our class?" When Lowenstein told him that Si took the honor, "I couldn't believe him at first because he simply didn't look the part."

Despite of or perhaps because of Lowenstein's own problems—he suffered doubts about his appearance and his sexuality—he was the one boy at Horace Mann who seemed to connect with the lost Si Newhouse. Lowenstein's sister, Dottie, vividly recalls middle-of-the-night phone calls from young Newhouse, "when Si would be so upset that Al would go over to be with him." Dottie says she thinks, but does not know for certain, that Si was threatening suicide, and in fact in a letter that Si later wrote to Al, he referred to his earlier talk of suicide and volunteered that the subject was once again on his mind.

From the bits and pieces she gathered from her brother, Dottie surmises that Si felt he "never could do enough, or anything to please his father.... I know Al was very worried about him. Al felt he was in a very tenuous position."

Si's letters to his friend carry a distinct quality of pleading. In one he suggests particular dates when they might meet, explaining that he has countless matters to discuss with Al. In another he implores Al to commit to a date, and that it be "as soon as possible!!!"

Permeating the relationship is the sense that Al was more important to Si than Si was to Al. Lowenstein was so easy in his social relationships, so quick to say the right thing, to offer the clever rejoinder. He was the very opposite of the withdrawn and awkward Si, a boy who repelled rather than attracted his peers. While Si knew he could never be like Al, that did not stop him from wanting to be around him. That Lowenstein was no one-dimensional glad-hander made him more attractive. Si likely sensed that Al suffered his own crises of identity, including his unhappiness with his Jewish roots—David Maimin recalls that in chapel Allard would sit the entire time with his hand "pushing up" the end of his nose, presumably to force a less semitic appearance—and his fear of homosexual longings: "The urge I get when I see certain boys is getting out-of-control," he wrote in his diary in 1943. "God, God, what will I do?"

Given the all-male student body and the almost all-male faculty, Daniel Rose's observation that "women were seen as social creatures for 'fun and games' rather than as 'real people'" rings accurate. The lack of school-sponsored social activities made things even more awkward for a boy like Si, who had such shaky self-esteem. Al Lowenstein started a club called the DCFMO, Diggers Club for Minors Only, which met on Saturday nights on the Columbia University campus with girls from the high school there. Joseph Bernstein and John Haldenstein cannot remember Si ever participating in the club's activities.[6]

As the time to apply to colleges approached, Si Newhouse figured that one of the schools in the Ivy League would accept him. In general, Horace Mann students were expected to go on to those elite schools. (At chapel, students sang the alma maters of several of the Ivies.) But Si ended up at Syracuse University, a large private school with a middling academic reputation and next to no social cachet.

Syracuse, in those years, was the quintessential "safety school," especially for students at an academic powerhouse like Horace Mann. (Syracuse did have its strengths. In political science, the Maxwell School of Citizenship was highly regarded, as was the school of radio, speech, and drama.) Paul Haberman, for example, says that he applied to Syracuse, the Wharton School at the University of Pennsylvania, where he ended up going, and a third school that he no longer remembers. "You tried for whatever other school you wanted to get into, and if you didn't get accepted there, well, you've already been accepted at Syracuse."

Many of the brightest students who attended Syracuse went there on scholarships. Bob Shogan and Mel Elfin, both of whom would work with Si on the Syracuse student newspaper and later enjoy successful careers in journalism, went to Syracuse on New York Regents scholarships, which paid tuition for four years. Those whose parents could afford to pay tended to be of the middle-of-their-high-school-class variety. Margot Goodman, who later married writer and syndicated columnist Nat Hentoff, applied to twenty-three schools and was turned down by all but Syracuse, which accepted her into its journalism school. *New York Times* television critic Walter Goodman, who also went to Syracuse, says that he can "only imagine that [Si] couldn't get into other schools, like Cornell."

Goodman is correct about Cornell, although Si's first choice was Harvard. He wrote Al Lowenstein a postcard, dated April 20, 1945, from the Hotel Statler in Boston. Si was full of praise for the school, which, in a phonily hearty tone, he referred to as his alma mater. Harvard, however, did not reciprocate Si's enthusiasm.

Jim Carleton, a former dean of men at Syracuse who rose through the ranks to become vice chancellor, speculates that after the apparent Harvard rejection, Si settled on Cornell because it was not as selective as some of the other schools in the Ivy League. So certain was Si that Cornell would admit him that he reported to the editors of the *Mannikin*, the Horace Mann yearbook, that he would be attending Cornell come September, 1945. His graduation blurb announced, "Cornell can look forward to Si's arrival in Ithaca." For a self-conscious young man like Si who had serious feelings of inferiority, how sad it must have been to broadcast to his world—a small world to be sure, but to him, the only one that mattered—that he was off to a school that in fact ended up rejecting him.

When Cornell turned him down, Si was furious. He wrote to Al Lowenstein that when a Cornell fraternity man, not realizing what had happened, called him to offer him the use of the fraternity house while he searched for a place to live, Si almost spit in his face through the telephone.

Si and Donald, who also went to Syracuse, apparently chose to blame Horace Mann for the humiliation of those Ivy League rejections. In the years since their graduation, Si hasn't given a dime to the school, and Donald limits his contributions to $500 a year.

When Si's Horace Mann class celebrated its fiftieth reunion in 1995, a small committee of his classmates was formed to call every member of the class. According to one person involved in the effort, no one on the committee called Si, so sure were they that he was a lost cause. When lists of distinguished Horace Mann alumni are published, Arthur Hay and Cyrus L. Sulzberger are featured, along with Anthony Lewis, Allard Lowenstein, James Schlesinger (secretary of defense and director of the CIA under, respectively, presidents Nixon and Ford), former congressman Bill Green, and writer Robert Caro. But the names of Si and Donald Newhouse are conspicuously absent—as is that of Roy Cohn, who did give money to the school, but is apparently one famous name that school officials believe is best left unmentioned.

As a Cornell reject attending Syracuse on the rebound, Si was not alone. The heavy influx of veterans starting or returning to school meant fewer spots for many applicants, even some who had achieved academic distinction. "There were any number of young men and women who were turned down at Cornell and came to Syracuse," says Jim Carleton. "And I was always amazed at how bitter they were against Cornell for having turned them down." Carleton, who finished his career at Northwestern University, says he saw students all the time who were at Northwestern because they had been turned down by the Ivy League, "but I didn't see the bitterness that I saw back then at Syracuse."[7]

Si did not find much comfort at home. Neither parent was much concerned about the boys' educations, knowing that they would be well fixed the minute they joined the business. Besides, sending his sons to Syracuse made sense to Sam Newhouse. He owned a radio station and both newspapers in town, and their success had contributed greatly to building the family fortune. The university offered a respectable, if not distinguished, journalism education to undergraduates and sponsored the *Daily Orange*, a better-than-average student paper that could give the Newhouse boys experience on both the editorial and business sides.

When Mitzi visited her sons at Syracuse, she would call on Frank Piskor—then dean of men—to ask how they were doing. "She was just as interested in their behavior as she was in academics," says Piskor, who rose to become vice chancellor and provost of the university.

Si took some consolation from the fact that Al Lowenstein had enrolled at the University of North Carolina. Al's father wanted his son to go to Harvard, which likely would have offered him a place. But Al wanted UNC and was deliberately late in mailing his applications to Harvard and Yale. His most recent biographer, William Chafe, as well as some friends and relatives, explain that Lowenstein saw Chapel Hill as a place where his liberal politics would make a difference and where he would stand out because of his progressive notions about civil rights, as opposed to Cambridge or New Haven or Morningside Heights, where his beliefs would be in danger of becoming clichés. Once at UNC, he came to admire Frank Porter Graham, then president of the university, later a member of the U.S. Senate.[8]

That summer of 1945, as the unpalatable prospect of Syracuse loomed, Si Newhouse was also dreading a commitment he had made earlier, at Lowenstein's urging, to go for the first time to a sleep-away camp in Waitsfield, Vermont, founded and run by Horace Mann English teacher Alfred Baruth. Al, Sandy Friedman, and several other classmates had gone to Camp MacArthur during previous years and would not return that summer. Baruth, the faculty adviser to the *Record* and the teacher who ran the car service that shuttled Si and Donald to school, had started the camp, which he named in tribute to General Douglas MacArthur, three years before. During the day, the fifty or so campers—male and, after the first year, female—worked on farms in the area to compensate for the lack of laborers who had been drafted. At night and on weekends campers would stage a play in various Grange halls and church sanctuaries for the towns-people. *Arsenic and Old Lace* was presented that summer.

MacArthur was hardly luxurious. The girls, who included Claire Cardozo, a niece of Supreme Court justice Benjamin Cardozo, slept in the house on a farm that Baruth rented from a doctor. The boys slept in the barn. Bathing was done in the Mad River, a fast-running stream, which the campers used only after the cows had crossed. There was never enough to eat, Si complained of the food, which in addition to being sparse was "grade A lousy," according to Si's Horace Mann classmate Louis Pulvermacher. (The camp's cook was, in real life, the dean of the Juilliard School.)

After a visit from his parents, Si wrote to Lowenstein, "There followed, as you might have imagined, the same sort of scrapping between us, and lecturing on their part which always occurs." Mitzi was likely horrified by the accommodations and the hard physical labor—haying and potato farming for the boys and picking beans for the girls—that was part of the regimen.

It was, indeed, a curious choice of camp for the pampered heir who had taken up smoking and whose muscle tone must have been seriously undeveloped. Yet it gave the lonely young man a surrogate family for the summer, a roster of activities, and the sort of social life he would not have found in Manhattan, and certainly not on the family farm in New Jersey. There was square dancing and ice cream socials—a favorite treat was maple syrup on ice—movies, pickup softball and basketball games, but nothing organized or serious.

Al Baruth was charismatic and flamboyant, especially when teaching Shakespeare. On the faculty since 1925, he had been a Ph.D. candidate at Columbia, a professional boxer and actor, a police beat reporter. Baruth's wife, Charlotte, while she could be cutting about the boys behind their backs, was lively and, although by then heavyset, earlier in life had been an actress and a beauty. There were also two Baruth daughters, the younger of whom, Pat, caught Si's eye. He pronounced her "very charming, not bad-looking and a lot of fun." Camper Sandy Gluck, a year behind Si at Horace Mann, recalls her as "very pretty, ...very blonde," and says that she and her older sister were both involved with other boys and that he doubts that she would have returned Si's interest.

Still, it was perhaps the happiest interlude of Si's young life. He wrote Al that he found MacArthur delightful, that he was doing things that he had previously only "dreamed of," like square dancing, becoming close to the Baruths, and attending church.

The latter was likely said to win Al's approval. During his summer at MacArthur, Al had encouraged his campmates to reach out to the suspicious townspeople by worshiping with them. Today a fashionable ski resort, Waitsfield was then, as Pulvermacher remembers it, "rural with a vengeance." That nearly all the campers were Jewish provoked some anti-Semitism. He wrote Al that in Waitsfield, one often heard the phrase, "MacArthur Jew." Si seemed untroubled, explaining that some of its targets deserved the designation.

Baruth briefed his charges that the townspeople had never seen a New Yorker or a Jew and that the combination might be overwhelming. According to Arthur Sprung, a member of Roy Cohn's class, Baruth, who was himself Jewish but "pretended he wasn't," advised the boys with the most obvious Jewish names to change them, so that one camper, Richard Katz, became Richard Keats. Another camper was assigned to a farm owned by the local undertaker. His wife, recalls Sprung, "happened to notice the name tag, which was a Jewish name...and said, 'Oh, you're Jewish. You can't work for me.'"[9]

Si returned home in an unhappy mood, dreading the move to Syracuse. He knew he wouldn't like it much, and he didn't.

3 | College, Marriage, and a Park Avenue Co-op

THE CAMPUS ON WHICH Si Newhouse arrived early in September 1945 was, like colleges all over the country, overrun by returning World War II veterans. During the war, enrollment stood at a low of 3,800; in the immediate postwar years it swelled, tripling in size by the early 1950s. Classrooms were so jam-packed that students sat on the floor and, typically, attended huge, impersonal lectures. All types of temporary housing, including trailers and barracks, were hastily assembled.

The elder Newhouse son started life at Syracuse in one of the university's many cottages. For the sixteen boys and a resident adviser who shared the cottage and one bathroom, this was home. Si described the rooms in a letter to Lowenstein at Chapel Hill as looking like a monk's "cubby hole." When his mother saw the accommodations she nearly fainted. To her it looked like a Lower East Side tenement.

Newhouse's housemates were not of the sort he mixed with at Horace Mann. One who hoped to make it to Hollywood as a stage designer, Si implied in a letter to Al, was homosexual. Another was severely crippled by polio. A third was a Jewish tough guy, a bruiser from Newark.

Si wanted out of the cottage, so he did what rich Jewish boys did on campuses all over the country—pledged Zeta Beta Tau (ZBT), where the accommodations were better and meals were sit-down affairs, with the "brothers" served by waiters who were mostly poor students scrambling to pay their way.

ZBT accepted Si as a pledge, but he soon wrote to Lowenstein that he had withdrawn from the fraternity. Later he admitted that just as the pledging period was drawing to a close, he had been called to the house and informed that he had been blackballed. The reason, he claimed, was that he had a bad attitude, was unwilling to accept the punishment and discipline that came with pledging, and was far too outspoken in his criticism of the brothers.

Si's bravado may have masked his emotional upset. But his father's response was unmistakably irate. Sam Newhouse had been delighted that his son had been asked to pledge ZBT. Newhouse was not one to live vicariously through his sons, but somehow membership in this most prestigious of Jewish fraternities struck a chord with him. It represented the social acceptance that had been so beyond his reach he wouldn't have even known how to strive for it. (Sam's brother Norman, whom Sam had put through New York University, had been a member of ZBT.) So he was furious—at his son, not at the boys who had blackballed him. Si claimed that his father would have been even angrier, would have "blown a gut," had Si withdrawn voluntarily.

Years later, after Chancellor William Tolley had persuaded Sam to give millions of dollars to improve the University's journalism school, he received both an honorary degree and initiation into ZBT. "The thrill of belonging to a college fraternity," Tolley wrote in his memoir, "and being one of the boys was priceless to him." That Sam would accept an honorary membership in a fraternity that had blackballed his son carries its own kind of message.[1]

Whether it was the rebuff from the Ivy League or from ZBT that bothered him, Si did not work as hard at Syracuse as he had at Horace Mann. Chancellor Tolley recalled both Si and Donald as "good students, but not outstanding students." Si would half boast to Al Lowenstein that he had done nothing in his first few months of college but fritter away the hours, stuck in a kind of hedonistic craze. When asked years later what he majored in, Donald replied, "In having a good time." Si felt the same. But Si would also confide in Al Lowenstein that "at the same time I have never had so many low periods (remember my old talk of suicide, well I was thinking of it again)."[2]

Still, Si picked himself up, and in his freshman year he applied for an editorial spot on the *Daily Orange*. To no one's surprise, he was accepted. Given that his father practically owned the city's journalism business and that Chancellor Tolley and other administrators had already targeted

Sam as ripe for tapping as a donor, it was a given that Si would have a chance to show his stuff.

Others found it tougher to win that chance. Murray Raphel, who would come to be considered among the most talented of the student journalists of those years and who would later become the paper's editorial page editor and, briefly, editor-in-chief, recalls applying for a position on the *Daily Orange* on the first day of his freshman year: "I was editor of my high school newspaper," he told the senior who was interviewing candidates. "Join the list," the senior replied. "There's 240 applications, and 235 were editors of their high school newspapers."

The *Daily Orange* was housed in a prefabricated Quonset hut, located next to and totally incongruous with the medieval-looking Yates Castle, home of the journalism school. (Graced by inlaid floors and paneling, Yates was designed by James Renwick, who had also designed St. Patrick's Cathedral and the Smithsonian Castle.) The hut was known unaffectionately as the Hell Box, in tribute to the hot lead type that was run off linotype machines and then, once used, discarded in a big box.

As was his inclination when working on the *Horace Mann Record*, Si did not live and breathe the *Daily Orange* or stay around to drink beer and socialize with his fellow editors. Paul Keil, Si's classmate and colleague on the paper, says that Si "had no friends on the paper that I knew of. He came and went."

It was the same for him socially, too, as at Horace Mann, except that he didn't have the humanizing influence of Al Lowenstein. "I don't know anybody who considered themselves friends with him," recalls Bob Shogan, later *DO* managing editor (during the 1950–51 school year), and a future Washington reporter for the *Los Angeles Times*. "I think people thought he was cold.... He was very serious, he was grim.... He was not easy to approach."

Shogan was a freshman when Si was a junior editor—so-called because he was in his junior year. One night every week the junior editor was required to put the paper out, from the beginning to end of the process, remaining at the plant while the paper was printed. As a mere freshman, Shogan was required to stay at the plant and assist the junior editor. That usually meant running errands, and Shogan remembers that Si would always send him out for the same items: two cream cheese and jelly sandwiches and four packs of Lucky Strikes. Shogan conjectures that Si's taste in food and his "constant" smoking showed "how little he cared about anything."

Si garnered mixed reviews on his contributions to the *Orange*. Some felt he was a competent young man; others saw him as "flaky."

Being Si Newhouse at Syracuse in those days could not have been easy. The Newhouse papers in Syracuse, the *Herald-Journal* and *Post-Standard,* were regularly ridiculed in journalism classes as representing much that was wrong with American newspapers. The sins they were accused of ranged from coddling the city's powerful to an archaic attitude toward national news to particularly ugly layouts. Journalism student Walter Goodman, who had completed a year at City College before serving in the navy and attending Syracuse on the GI Bill, calls the Syracuse papers of that era "terrible," and explains that "You had to read them in one course...and everybody would laugh about them, very shoddy." But because the Newhouse name was mostly absent from the papers, not many students were aware of the Si-Sam connection. Donna Cole, an undergraduate at Syracuse in those years and an occasional volunteer at the *Daily Orange,* grew up in Syracuse reading the local dailies and had no idea that they were owned by Si's father.

To Si, carrying the Newhouse name at this time seemed more a burden than a source of pride. Would others think that he, such an unprepossessing young man, was writing for the *Daily Orange* only because his name was Newhouse? Si took to bylining his stories with the name Si Mason—as in a mason builds new houses. Leonard Zweig, who was editor-in-chief of the paper in Si's time, says that he was always impressed by Newhouse's efforts to maintain his anonymity.

Si had mixed feelings about the *Daily Orange.* In a letter to Lowenstein he belittled it as incompetently managed, in part, he wrongly claimed, because it was run almost entirely by women. He lambasted it for a paucity of ideas, vision, and quality—both editorially and production-wise. He described its newsprint as looking and feeling like toilet paper.

In fact, the *Daily Orange,* which operated with a minimum of interference from the faculty, was among the better student dailies in the country. For those of Si's peers who put their all into the paper, it was an incomparable experience. They turned it into a kind of full-time job, and while they ended up with, essentially, a trade school education, they learned a lot about newspapering. According to Murray Raphel, "The students did everything except work the linotype machines.... It was a great learning experience for anybody who wanted to get into newspaper work." For Mel Elfin, who was the *DO*'s editorial director—he would later work for one of the Newhouse papers before going to *Newsweek*, where he became chief of the Washington bureau—the *Daily Orange* "was the real education.... It was a growing-up experience."[3] Si didn't give all that much to the paper, and what he took away was commensurate.

If the *Daily Orange* had one saving grace for Si, it was that he came to see it as a vehicle to convey his opinions on national and international affairs. His politics, which had been moderately liberal since high school when he founded the Wendell Willkie Award—Willkie was popular among liberals, especially when he ran for president in 1940, and was a particular favorite of Al Lowenstein's—were moving sharply to the right. In one of his last letters to Al—eventually their friendship simply petered out—Si warned that if Stalin were not stopped he would soon control the world and World War III would follow. He blustered that an editorial he wrote advocating a tough-guy stance toward Russia had provoked all the teachers and half the students to want to "lynch" him. He groused that professors were using their classrooms to "lecture" against the editorial and to make the point that Si's father owned the newspapers in Syracuse.

One night junior editor Si Newhouse had the assignment of putting the paper out. Late in the afternoon, he arrived for meetings with the staff and the managing editor to get together the news budget, to schedule the photos, to do the layout, and to go to the composing room in the plant where the paper was actually printed. Early in the evening *DO* editor-in-chief Paul Keil arrived to make sure all was running smoothly and asked, as was the custom, to see the layout of page one.

"I looked at it, and it seemed to be fine," Keil recalled. "However, at the same time Si had left the corner of another layout sheet sticking out from under some papers. I asked him what that was, and he fumbled

around...and I looked at it and it was another page one, the real page one."
The lead story, Keil says, was either proconservative or antiliberal, a
strongly slanted point-of-view piece that Keil believed had no business
running on page one. He was flabbergasted that Si would deliberately try
to mislead him.

"Si," Keil asked, "what are you trying to do here?"

"Well," Si said with a shrug, "I didn't think you'd approve of this, so..."

Keil, who alone among *DO* staffers considered Si a personal friend,
says that their friendship survived the incident. In fact Keil, recruited by
Si, would later work for several of the Newhouse papers. But he never forgot that Si had deliberately tried to deceive him; had it been other than a
student newspaper, he said, he would have fired him.[4]

While complaining to Al Lowenstein about the lack of political awareness
on campus, Si allowed as how the beautiful "set of coeds" was some compensation. In another letter he mentioned falling in love with a beautiful
girl from New York. Jane Franke—Frankenstein until her parents suggested that she shorten the name—was a fine arts major at Syracuse, and
soon she would fall in love with Si Newhouse. To Jane, Si's homely looks
and pint-size stature were not relevant. She found him cute and attentive,
and his neediness and sensitivity appealed to her.

Jane Franke came to Syracuse as a freshman two years after Si, in
September 1947. They were introduced that December by Doris Gottlieb,
an Alabaman whose family owned drugstores and who lived in the same
dormitory as Jane. Bamie, as Gottlieb was called, had met Si in a geology
class, and he was visiting her in her dorm, Griffin Hall, when he first saw
Jane. "It had a...tiny living room and I was seated on some boy's lap holding forth on some subject or other," Jane recalls, "and totally oblivious and
he saw me there and I guess the informality and the lack of inhibition to
be sitting on somebody's lap must have captured him, so he asked Bamie
to introduce us, and the next thing I knew I was dating him." By sophomore year Jane had moved into the Sigma Delta Tau (SDT) house, a sort of
female equivalent of ZBT—its membership entirely Jewish.

That Jane was, in those years, bold and outgoing certainly appealed
to Si. The fact that she was even shorter than Si also didn't hurt. But she

was more than those things; she was a person who drew others to her. She was cute and perky, with a blondish Dutch boy bob with bangs, big blue eyes, and an open and warm personality. Friends described her as fun and energetic, a girl who loved to dance. She also had an artistic side. Enrolled in one of Syracuse's distinguished divisions, the school of fine arts, she painted and was serious about it.

Jane did not immediately commit herself to Si. She dated other boys and recalls her dates with Si as being typical, except that Si was one of the very few students who had a car. They mostly went to movies, which they both loved—Si would develop a lifelong passion for movies—ate dinners at Chinese restaurants, and occasionally had a more posh night out at the restaurant in the Hotel Syracuse.

Unlike Si, Jane was always an enthusiastic student who embraced extracurricular activities. She was active in the student union and the French club, and she performed in a play and in the spring dance pageant, both of which Si attended as a spectator.

Jane was the middle of three sisters from an upper-middle-class Westchester County family. Her paternal grandfather, Samuel Isaac Frankenstein—coincidentally, another S. I.—was a lawyer who was friendly with Teddy Roosevelt and who, with his wife, whom Jane describes as a "world traveler," visited the president at the White House. Her maternal grandparents lived on the Lower East Side, but her grandmother, she says, had been brought up in a palace in Hungary. Her grandfather, Adolf Moscowitz, was a Tammany Hall politician who was so popular that, when he died, 5,000 people attended his funeral.

Jane uninhibitedly admired her father, who died in 1974—"a very strong, wonderful, very down-to-earth person," she says. "We still quote him today." Chester Frankenstein was originally in the cloak and suit business—he had, his daughter says, excellent taste—but he hated the business and, being mechanically inclined, borrowed money from his father and opened Port Chester Auto Parts, a business which brought him financial security.

According to Margot Goodman Hentoff, Jane's sorority sister and friend, Jane's mother was "a very cultivated and intellectual" woman. She had attended the Art Students League and in the 1920s worked as an illustrator for *McCall's*. She maintained an interest in design all her life, as reflected in her renovation of the family's carriage house in Purchase, twenty-five miles from New York City. The Frankensteins later sold that house and built a modern structure nearby, designed by the acclaimed architect Edgar Tafel. After her father retired, Jane's parents bought a house on Shelter Island, her father kept a boat, and they also kept a small penthouse in the city.

Growing up with doting parents, Jane's childhood was quite different from Si's. "Jane was a cherished child," says Shirley Schine, Jane's sorority sister and a fellow fine arts major. Jane would later remark in comparing her childhood to Si's, "I don't think he had a great, fond memory of his childhood like I had of mine." She says of her mother, who died in 1989, "She was a very good friend of mine."

Jane went to a progressive private school in Darien, Connecticut, and then she was accepted by Mills College in Oakland, California. But so close were mother and daughter that Jane ended up at Syracuse because, at the last minute, she and her parents couldn't face the prospect of a cross-country separation.

In the summer of 1949, when her relationship with Si had grown serious, Jane's mother encouraged her daughter and Shirley Schine in their plans to join a University of Chicago-sponsored tour of Holland, Belgium, France, Italy, and Austria, making them among the first group of American students to travel abroad since the war. They stayed with the group until Paris and then, unbeknownst to their parents, left to tour on their own, rejoining the group in Holland, where they participated in a program at the University of Utrecht, living in a sixteenth-century house with a group of Dutch students. When she sailed back from Europe, Si was there with her parents at the dock to greet her.

In Europe, Jane did date a bit, "innocently," says Shirley Schine, but "I knew that she was crazy about Si." Another sorority sister, Donna Cole, says that "they were very much in love."

A couple of Jane's friends saw in her then a bit of the bohemian. Shirley Schine calls Jane "as bohemian as a nice Jewish girl could be." For all of her perky friendliness, Cole describes Jane as "very arty" and a "little bit of a loner."[5]

Although meeting Jane had given Si a reason to stay in Syracuse, he soon tired of the *Daily Orange* and of school in general and decided that there was no point to his waiting around to earn a degree that wouldn't mean much to him. Chancellor Tolley writes in his memoirs that Sam wanted his boys to finish college, but that they were determined to drop out to join the business. But in an interview years later, Tolley put a different spin on it: "He didn't really care whether they got educated or not. He thought that the world expected it of them and it was probably a good thing for them. He was glad they were there, ...but I would say that he didn't have much interest in higher education."

Sam did, however, put one roadblock in the way of their quitting school, insisting that they first earn a B average. Si made his B average and left Syracuse in June 1948, one year shy of graduation. (Donald, who had enrolled in Syracuse at the same time as Jane, also stayed three years and left without a degree.)[6]

In Si's absence, Jane continued to catch the eyes of other boys, especially assorted *DO* editors. One of them was Bob Shogan, then managing editor, who recalls that after Si left Syracuse, Jane would hang around the offices of the *Daily Orange*. She was never on staff, but she volunteered to take phone messages for Shogan and to perform other clerical duties. Shogan wanted to ask Jane out, but he recognized that she was committed to Si and so he refrained. It didn't occur to him at the time, says Shogan, but "maybe she wanted to know something about the newspaper business" in preparation for marrying into the Newhouse family.[7]

Jane remained at Syracuse until her graduation in January 1951. Five months earlier, Jane and Si had made it official. He joined the air force with a two-year commitment and before leaving presented Jane with a six-carat, emerald-cut diamond engagement ring. Mitzi threw an engagement party for the young couple in the Park Avenue apartment. Although Jane felt completely comfortable with Sam, she would never feel that way with Mitzi, who liked Jane but didn't love her. Family friend Elaine Reiner speculates that Mitzi would have preferred that Si "marry some top society person."

The wedding on March 11, 1951, a month after Jane graduated from Syracuse, was held in the Jade Room of the Waldorf-Astoria, with 125 guests. Jane characterizes the affair as "very traditional." Mitzi's cousin

Ruth Spaet recalls it as "gorgeous," but in describing it talks only of Mitzi, who was dressed in a fashion so spectacular as to attract all eyes. Outfitted in a low-cut Elizabeth Arden gown designed for her, covered in pale blue paillettes, she wore an "exquisite diamond necklace," and her handbag had her name spelled out in diamonds. "She was just beautiful.... She looked as young as the bride." Si and Jane honeymooned in Havana, where they would continue to travel every year until 1959, when the Cuban dictator Fulgencio Batista was toppled and Castro came to stay.[8]

Si had then reached the point at which he had to figure out what to do next, and the role of budding newspaper mogul didn't feel right. He was by no means certain that he had what it took to run the family newspapers, and his undistinguished performance on both his high school and college papers hadn't boosted his confidence.

Nor had two short stints working in the real world. The summer before Si's senior year of high school, Sam had arranged a job for his son as a cub reporter on the *Long Island Daily Press*. The plan, Si wrote to Lowenstein, was to spend his first two weeks covering the courts and his last two at city hall covering Mayor Fiorello La Guardia—not bad for an inexperienced seventeen-year-old. But the next summer, rather than repeat the experience, he went to overnight camp, even though he was beyond the age of normal participation. He had nothing else in mind for himself, yet he simply was not ready to plunge into the family business.

Seeming to recognize that, Sam helped arrange an interim job for Si in that summer of 1948. Not a bad job either for a nineteen-year-old—reporting, from Paris, for International News Service.

In its time, INS was almost in a league with the Associated Press. Launched in 1909 by William Randolph Hearst, INS had employed such reporters and editors as James L. Kilgallen (father of Dorothy), Bob Considine, Irving R. Levine, Joseph Kingsbury Smith, Marvin Stone, Amy Vanderbilt (who had also worked for the *Staten Island Advance*), and Louella Parsons. By 1958, having fallen well behind AP, INS merged with United Press to become UPI.

Again, as if Si were somehow invisible, the men who worked in the Paris bureau at the same time as Si can't seem to place him. Si stayed under a year, handicapped by his indifferent French and by lackluster reporting skills. Sam next sent his son to Queens, where he was made the production manager of the *Long Island Press*.[9]

His air force service derailed that job, but it also gave him time to think more about how he might fit into his father's business. Now he had real responsibilities. After the honeymoon, Si and Jane had moved fifty miles from Syracuse to Geneva, New York, where Si was stationed at Sampson Air Force Base. There they rented the second floor of a private house until Si was transferred to Andrews Air Force Base in Washington, D.C., and the newlyweds moved to an apartment in suburban Alexandria, Virginia. It was there, in 1952, that their first son, S. I. III, was born.

After his discharge that year as an airman second class, Si, Jane, and the baby moved to Harrisburg, where Sam Newhouse, four years earlier, had purchased the *Harrisburg Evening News* and the *Harrisburg Patriot*. Si was expected there to begin in earnest his career in the family business.

Paul Keil saw the newlywed Si as essentially unchanged from the student. "I think his primary goal in life was to…have a good time, …to do the things he wanted to do and that publishing certainly or journalism was not driven by a passion with him. It was the second priority over living a full, happy life."

Donald, on the other hand, was said to be serious and focused and growing more impressive by the day. The young man who was energetically fulfilling family assignments at the newspapers was routinely described as a person of few words, serious, and absolutely devoted to learning this business. "Donald was perfect," says Geraldine Stutz, a former president of Henri Bendel's who knows the family well. "Donald always moved along, knew the right step, and Si was awkward in every way." When Donald, age twenty-one, left Syracuse University in 1950—he had been business manager of the *Daily Orange*—he moved happily into the *Long Island Press* as circulation district manager. He never looked back, and has devoted himself to the newspapers ever since.

Although also small, Donald was not so delicate of build as Si and much better looking, with regular, handsome features, "the best looking of the family," says one old family friend. Donald also had some charm and charisma. "The sons of the great carry a big burden," says Peter

Diamandis, who has worked for the Newhouses and knows them well. "Sam was great. Everybody liked Sam.... Donald's got some gregarious-ness, but you wonder how Si, where he came from.... He was like a horse. You'd say 'Hi,' and he'd paw the ground. Who knows what all those demons were that made him so inward?"[10]

When Si arrived in Harrisburg, the *Patriot* editors and executives greeted him with some trepidation, but not nearly as much as he felt. He and Jane had rented a small attached house and lived modestly. Leonard Zweig, who had known Si on the *Daily Orange,* was in the army, stationed at Indian Town Gap, near Harrisburg. He went to dinner at the Newhouses' and recalls that "Jane cooked the dinner, no servants, on their own, like any young couple."

Zweig's impression of Si in Harrisburg was that he was "beginning to get his feet on the ground and start to take responsibility." Another former *Daily Orange* editor, who knew Si in Harrisburg at that time, emphasizes that Si was learning "from scratch," but he says that Si was a quick study and was coming to know "what the hell he was doing.... He came into Harrisburg as a production manager and everybody said, 'Hoot, hoot, Sammy's son is coming.' And when he left there was a lot of respect."

Others disagree. Milton Jaques was then a police reporter on the *Harrisburg Patriot.* A key part of his job was to ingratiate himself with the cops on whom he depended for information. Every Saturday night he would rush to the newspaper's production department and, as the first edition of the Sunday paper rolled off the belts, hand-deliver it to desk sergeants at station houses throughout the region. One Saturday night he encountered Si Newhouse counting the papers as they came off. "When I grabbed a hand-ful," Jaques recalls, "Si said, 'Who told you to do this and why are you doing this and what do you do with them?' I said, 'Taking them out to the station houses.' We had quite a discussion."[11] The comparison between Si, the son whom Sam didn't quite know what to do with, and Meyer Newhouse, the father whom Sam didn't quite know what to do with, is irresistible— Meyer seated in a chair next to the conveyor belt at the *Staten Island Advance* making certain that the delivery boys didn't filch an extra paper or two, and Si performing essentially the same task in Harrisburg.

That Si was unhappy in Harrisburg was clear to Sam. But he was not sure what to do with Si, so he dispatched him to Portland, Oregon, for an assignment that was expected to take a few months—to assist the manager of radio station KGW, which the Newhouses had acquired along with the *Oregonian,* in applying to the federal authorities for a television license. (KGW was in stiff competition for the channel with radio station KOIN.) Robert Notson, then managing editor of the *Oregonian,* remembers it as a good time for Si, who brought Jane and baby Sam with him: "He seemed very relaxed and quite happy while he was in Portland." Notson says that his impression was that Si felt he hadn't yet begun to meet his father's expectations, "and he was a little disappointed and somewhat depressed by that fact.... But when he came here he was on assignment for the family, and he was free from pressure at least at the moment, to do things pretty much in his own way, and he seemed to blossom under that kind of situation." Si's assignment, as it turned out, didn't amount to anything because Sam Newhouse ended up buying a half interest in the company that owned KOIN and was forced to sell KGW.[12]

Next for Si was the *Star-Ledger* in Newark, where his assignment was to learn the business side of the operation, including production. Si was happy to return to the glamour of New York, but he was hardly headed for a glamorous newspaper. Nat Brandt, who worked for the *Star-Ledger* in the late 1950s, described it as "the worst newspaper in America.... We were housed in an old three-story building that had been condemned several times by the Fire Department. Leaky pipes circled the editorial floor. Windows hadn't been cleaned in years, if ever." He recalls the incongruity of seeing Si, his expensive shirts monogrammed at the pocket with the initials "SIN."[13]

It is said of the elder son in the 1950s that he was scared to death of his father. But the relationship was more complicated than that. Sam also feared Si, in the sense that he knew Si could simply drop out of the business and live off his trust fund while awaiting his inheritance. In some ways Si was beginning to behave like the spoiled heir. His taste for good restaurants had sharpened to the point that he frequented Manhattan's flashiest, most expensive spots. "Sam groaned to me," Jane recalls, "because he thought Si was spending too much money in restaurants.... So I said, 'Why don't you just tell him that he can't charge anymore?'... Well, he wouldn't do it.... He didn't have the guts. He didn't see that his son wasn't going to be leaving the business because he couldn't go to El Morocco or 21."

Donald seemed to have found his home on the business side, but Si didn't seem to be at home on either side—business or editorial. Sam worried that Si, especially, but Donald too, needed to be brought out a bit; to be tutored in the inner workings of power and influence. While the founder himself kept out of the limelight, he wanted his sons to see for themselves the kinds of doors that the owner of a chain of newspapers had open to him. And he wanted the people who mattered to know that his sons would one day be running things.

Sam turned to his public relations counsel, Ray Josephs—with Josephs's boss, PR impresario Ben Sonnenberg, working behind the scenes—for help. Josephs, who arranged to take both Si and Don to Washington, asked Clay Felker, then features editor at *Esquire,* to join them, the idea being that Felker could draw the Newhouse sons out, elicit the kinds of responses that Josephs could then use to sell another reporter on pursuing a story on the sons.

In Washington, Sonnenberg arranged a meeting for the three with Abe Fortas—then a young partner and blossoming power broker at Arnold, Fortas and Porter, and later a Lyndon Johnson Supreme Court appointee—and with then-senator Lyndon Johnson. The meetings went moderately well, Josephs recalls, but Si's extreme shyness made them a "little bit strained."

Washington did not hold much interest for Si. His friendship with Allard Lowenstein over, he lost interest in politics. Robert Hochstein, who worked in the 1950s in the Newhouse bureau in Washington, recalls Si and Jane occasionally visiting. Hochstein would be ordered by Andrew J. Viglietta, then the chief of the Newhouse bureau there, to make "arrangements" for the couple. That might include booking a hotel room or securing tickets for a tour of the White House. Si would stop at the bureau briefly, "but he had nothing to say."

Si did in this period take an international trip for the newspapers. Jules Witcover, now a columnist syndicated by the *Baltimore Sun*, but then representing Newhouse's Syracuse papers in Washington, recalls Si "wheeling in...with cameras, three or four cameras swinging.... He was supposed to go...to the then Soviet Union, and he was having trouble with his visa, so he came into the bureau to try to get Viglietta to help him.... Why he was going to Russia? He never wrote anything." Si later said that he toyed with the idea of writing for the Newark paper about these visits behind the Iron Curtain—he also visited Warsaw, Prague, Yugoslavia, Turkey, Greece—but decided that its readers would not be interested.

Witcover told Richard Meeker, then writing his biography of the father, that Si was known in the Washington bureau as Jerry Lewis. "He looked like Jerry Lewis. He acted like Jerry Lewis. They'd line him up with press credentials for these big foreign trips.... The kid was just ludicrous."[14]

Once it was clear that Si, like his father, would be based in Manhattan, Jane went looking for an apartment. Despite Sam's skyrocketing wealth, Jane was not interested in wasting money. Through the publisher of the Harrisburg paper, Ed Russell, who for years would figure prominently in the lives of members of the Newhouse family, Jane heard about the apartment for sale at 1185 Park. For Si, it was nearly twenty-five blocks up the avenue from where he had grown up, and miles down in social status. Mitzi was not pleased.

Nor was PR man Ray Josephs, who visited Si and Jane at the apartment. "I just thought, this is awful, that he should be living up there near Ninety-sixth Street, back in a courtyard."[15]

The apartment was soon home to two more children—Wynn, born in 1954 and Pamela, born in 1956. It was a tough time for Jane, who was busy with three small children and a demanding husband who insisted on going out nearly every night to Manhattan's most glitzy restaurants. Her husband was looking for something, Jane knew, but she did not quite understand that she could never provide it.

4 | Roy Cohn Takes Center Stage

IN THE BEGINNING, as the son struggled with his father's expectations, and as Jane struggled with the demands of having had three children in four years, Si and Jane's life together was sometimes tense. But it was also conventional. Their friends were other young Jewish couples with small children, although none was from a family possessing wealth anywhere near that of the Newhouses.

Most Saturday nights, Si and Jane dined and played cards with three of those couples, one of them the Rosses, as in Steve Ross, later of Time-Warner fame. (Ross, who then worked for his father-in-law's funeral business, would later amass enormous wealth and power as the man who made the mega Time-Warner deal that built the world's largest entertainment company.) The men played poker, and the women played canasta or chatted about their families.

Si made a decidedly negative impression on at least one of his poker companions, who says that Si showed no particular interest in or aptitude for anything, held no discernible opinions about politics or art or newspapers, and that his conversation was practically nil, "other than ordinary talk about the weather [or] where are we going to eat." So loath was Si to talk about his work that this man says he had no idea what Si did. He has vivid memories, on the other hand, of Steve Ross bouncing around ideas about buying parking lots and how those would relate to his father-in-law's limousine service or funeral business.

If Si was taciturn, Jane was the opposite. She loved to cook and sometimes prepared and served dinner to the card players. With his mother as the model for the social side of life, Si grew increasingly impatient with this domestic routine. He chafed against the ordinariness that life with three children under the age of five imposed on nearly anyone, even the very rich. Cream cheese and jelly sandwiches were no longer in his repertoire; neither were casual suppers with the kids, or a quick pickup from the local pizzeria. "He always wanted to go to a very good restaurant," recalls one of the women in the card-playing group. "He liked dining." One night at 21 when it was time to order dessert, Si took over: "There is no question about what to order for dessert. We're all having soufflés." (Si alternated 21 with El Morocco, where he had a regular table.)[1]

College friends who once detected in Jane a "bohemian" streak then described the young mother as down-to-earth. She liked to toss on a sweatshirt to run to the grocery store, cart her purchases home, and then make dinner. She also liked to stay home some nights to read or sew. Jane's priorities were different from her husband's. Most of all, she enjoyed her children. She was a loving, devoted mother who would have preferred to care for her children herself, despite the expectation in their social circle that children would be taken over by live-in nurses and nannies. Shirley Schine explains that Jane was a mother "in that earthy sense, in that very warm, nurturing sense, ...that sense of being connected to the world of touch and being in touch with the basic world."

This fundamental aspect of his wife's nature did not appeal to Si. He found it irritating, for example, that Jane didn't simply call to have groceries delivered. "She would have to go and select and schlep the groceries home," says Dave Morgan. Si wanted Jane to shop at Balducci's or Grace's Market, but Jane was happier at the A&P picking her own items off the shelf. Morgan describes Jane as "just not cut out for that [world]. She couldn't cope with it.... She hated to spend money."

One of the women in the poker/canasta group recalls the night when Si, who had begun to spend lavishly on his wardrobe right down to the finest silk underwear, took her aside and whispered, "You should be married to me. You would know how to spend my money."[2]

Jane gave in to Si's agenda. During opera season, she and Si accompanied Mitzi and Sam to the Met on Monday nights—the fashionable night to attend, to be seen. Naturally their tickets were front row center. Jane says that both she and Si "loved" the opera, but she suspects that Mitzi was partly motivated by the desire to show herself, "prancing down the aisle to the first row with whatever gorgeous outfit she happened to have on that moment." Sam could have been anywhere. His enjoyment of the opera, and theater as well, came from the pleasure he took in Mitzi's pleasure at being there.

After the opera came dinner at 21. Monte Sideman, then the maître d', recalls Sam as "a very lovely man," and Si as "the crowned prince" who was "nothing like his father. He knew he had wealth. He wasn't as nice, never as nice as his father."[3]

Despite her reservations about Jane, Mitzi certainly wanted the marriage to thrive. So she took Jane in hand, in the way Mitzi knew best: improving the way she dressed. According to one friend of Jane's, it was no easy task, for Jane was "what we called in those days more or less a beatnik.... She came up with odd combinations." On one trip to Paris, Jane accompanied her mother-in-law to such couturiers as Givenchy and Dior. They stayed at the Ritz, and Mitzi spent without limit on herself. "Mainly I was accompanying her," Jane recalls. "I used to wear a lot of clothes that she didn't want anymore."[4]

For Si, who was already having trouble keeping up with the accomplishments of his younger brother, there was the problem of constant comparisons between Jane and Donald's new wife, Susan, whom Mitzi adored. Susan Marley was born and reared in Syracuse, where her father, Harry, a lawyer and a Syracuse University graduate, was prominent in university and community affairs and very wealthy—the latter a result of his father's scrap metal business. Donald met and fell in love with Susan while he was at Syracuse; she attended Wellesley.

Susie, as she was called, was dark-haired, outgoing, social, and as Elaine Reiner puts it, "cute." Ray Josephs remembers that Mitzi "was enchanted with Susan." That her parents were rich, explains Dave Morgan, also helped, especially with Mitzi, who was impressed by them.

As if casting a seal of approval on the young couple, Mitzi and Sam invited Don and Susie and their growing family—they too would have two boys and a girl—to move into 730 Park, fittingly, one floor below the parents. The Donald Newhouses also kept a small house on the farm in New Jersey.[5]

In every sense Donald seemed the heir apparent, resembling Sam in many ways, but especially in his devotion to work. Donald didn't care about silk underwear or soufflés. He cared about the newspapers. Like Sam, he seemed genuinely unpretentious.

As her husband continued to acquire newspapers and net worth, Mitzi acquired airs. Having little interest in working for charities or performing good works, and having been given no role in the business, she was a lost soul. As she grew older and struggled to look younger, she could seem ridiculous, but there was also something sad about her. Jane recalls once talking to a prominent psychologist whom Mitzi had apparently consulted and who confirmed Jane's own feelings about her mother-in-law. Sam was "probably a very good husband," Jane speculates, but he "was busy so much of the time, and she had no daughters.... She didn't really do any charity work. I mean she didn't seem to do anything much except to create beautiful homes and buy beautiful clothes, and I guess there is something kind of sad about that. She may have been lonely."

Mitzi's concern about fashion and beauty, Jane explains, was tied to the fact that "she wanted to be noticed and admired, that was what I think she wanted most in this world. She was a very vain woman." The couture that came to preoccupy her so was her incentive to diet nonstop, even after she reached her goal of fitting into a size three. One woman who mixed socially with Mitzi observed that while Mitzi, who weighed about ninety pounds, put food on her plate and moved it around, she rarely let it pass her lips.

Sam's PR counsel, Ray Josephs, regularly took Mitzi to lunch to fill her time and her head with gossip. It was not quite an assignment from the boss, but Josephs understood that Sam appreciated his keeping Mitzi occupied. "The world of New York" was their subject, and Josephs describes himself as being "kind of like a [gossip columnist] Liz Smith to her," and before he would leave the office, he would ask his colleagues, "'What have you got good? I've got lunch with Mitzi.'"

Another favorite topic of conversation when Mitzi lunched with Ray Josephs was plastic surgery, of which Josephs had had his share. Mitzi, whose face showed evidence of many facelifts, had had much more than hers. Mitzi often wore gloves because, one friend explains, they allowed her to hide her hands, which otherwise would have betrayed her age. As Mitzi's hair grew thin—she overtreated it with dye—she covered it with a wig, always blond, "always perfect coiffed," says one acquaintance.

Even if Ray Josephs had devoted lunch every day to Mitzi, or even if there were 200 Ray Josephs, Mitzi's restlessness and insecurity would have required another outlet. She found one in serial decorating. The apartment, Jane recalls, "was always being redone. You could never be sure what you were going to find there because one of her activities was redecorating." John Gerald, Mitzi's charter decorator—he had been an acquaintance of Mitzi's mother and, early in his career, head of the decorating department at Altman's—told Sam's biographer, Richard Meeker, "When [Mitzi would] get bored, she'd bring in a decorator and demand, 'It's a mess. You know what I want. Fix it.'"

Within Sam's family Mitzi was the matriarch, but she did not wear the mantle graciously. She expected Sam's sisters and sisters-in-law, all of whom to one degree or another depended on Sam for their husbands' or children's livelihoods, to pay homage. "We had these family parties once a year," Jane recalls, "and she presided. Everyone had to come and kowtow a little bit to her."

Later in life Mitzi began to recognize the emptiness of her interests, and she regularly attended lectures on politics and international affairs, taking Elaine Reiner with her. Mitzi would not ordinarily socialize with an employee's wife, but she made an exception for Reiner, whose husband reviewed theater for the Newhouse papers. "I wasn't an ordinary employee's wife.... I was an actress, and Mitzi was crazy about the theater." Hal Eaton always saw to it that for every opening night of every hot show in town he delivered for Mitzi and Sam the best seats in the house—always first row, so that the tiny couple did not have to look over anyone's head. After the theater, Mitzi would depend on Elaine to accompany her and Sam to El Morocco or to the Stork Club for a drink and a light supper.

Mitzi longed to be close to the rich and famous—Estée Lauder, for one, a woman whose brains, guts, and vision built the family fortune. Mitzi once took over the Côte Basque for a party honoring the cosmetics tycoon. But Estée viewed Mitzi with a gimlet eye. She once advised a young female employee of the Newhouses not to be in awe of Si: "His mother didn't know how to set a table."[6]

Sam and Mitzi Newhouse would never be accepted into old New York German-Jewish society—a fact that irritated Mitzi but was immaterial to Sam. The Sulzbergers of the *New York Times* were the crown princes of this set; the Newhouses were not even in the court. The Sulzbergers nodded their heads toward the Newhouses only when they worried that Sam might buy a New York City newspaper.

Martin Duggan, then news editor at Newhouse's *St. Louis Globe-Democrat*, attended a dinner hosted by the *Times* in 1958 during the American Newspaper Institute at Columbia University. Duggan was cornered by Arthur Hays Sulzberger's son-in-law, Orville Dryfoos, soon to become publisher of the *Times*. Dryfoos started to pump Duggan about "what kind of man S. I. Newhouse was.... They thought he might be interested in launching or taking over one of the metropolitan papers."

It was this same year that Si told *Esquire* features editor Clay Felker, "Frankly, I could think of nothing more thrilling than to be publisher of the *New York Times*." He allowed, however, that the Newhouse method of running newspapers would not work at a paper like the *Times*. The Sulzbergers had nothing to fear.

The Blocks were another old-line Jewish newspaper family that worried, with better reason, that Sam Newhouse had his eye on their prized and profitable *Toledo Blade*. Their disdain for the Newhouses is reflected in a story passed down to John Robinson Block, today copublisher and editor-in-chief of the family's *Toledo Blade* and *Pittsburgh Post-Gazette*. His grandmother Dina, Mrs. Paul Block Sr., was living in Manhattan on Park Avenue. According to John Block, while she respected Sam's business prowess, "Part of her didn't like him and thought he was, I guess in relation to us, a cheap upstart." One evening at a party Sam approached Dina, then a widow, who was wearing a piece of expensive jewelry, given her by her husband. "Oh, that's beautiful," he exclaimed pointing to the jewels. "Is that for sale? Mitzi, come over here."[7]

Whatever outsiders thought of Mitzi, Sam always saw her as the most gorgeous, sophisticated, dynamic creature ever to grace the sidewalks of Fifth Avenue. Nothing he could buy for her was special enough. A publisher of one of Sam's newspapers remembers an emerald necklace—"really spectacular" with "seven or eight significant emeralds," one of which was the size of "a small postage stamp." He guesses that this creation, which also included diamonds, must have cost a million dollars. "Mitzi doesn't know how much money I have," Sam used to joke—out of Mitzi's hearing, and in recognition of the vast sums Mitzi lavished on herself. Yet Sam was never stingy with her. Whether it was giving the go-ahead to some "name" decorator for still another redo of the Park Avenue duplex, or for still another visit to the couturiere or the plastic surgeon, Sam seldom said anything but yes to Mitzi. Family friend Geraldine Stutz observes that behind Sam's genial face was an extremely demanding nature. "The only place that I have the feeling that Sam was absolutely permissive was with Mitzi. I think he probably took one look at her and said, 'Oooewww!' And spent the rest of his life, 'Isn't she wonderful?'"

The late Neil Walsh, whose family was in the insurance business in New York, was in Havana with Sam and Mitzi in the pre-Castro mid-1950s. "It was pouring rain and we were all going to dinner, and his wife came out and the car that we had hired was parked at the end of the driveway. Sam didn't want Mitzi to get wet.... He didn't have an umbrella, and he ran down in the pouring rain to get the car for his wife. I remember thinking to myself, 'Boy that's a guy who really loves his wife.' I mean, he could give the doorman a couple of pesos and he'd go get it. But he didn't want Mitzi to wait." When they arrived at the restaurant, he gave his suit coat to the waiter, who simply tossed it in a clothes dryer. That was just fine with Sam, whom Walsh calls "a very humble man."[8]

Despite their problems, Jane had every desire to stay married to Si, but she could see that after five years of marriage, he was not satisfied. He began, for the first time, to immerse himself in his work, traveling often with Sam or his uncles on on-site visits to the newspapers. On the days he wasn't on the road, he would usually leave the apartment early in the morning and return late in the afternoon. "He would take a nap," Jane recalls, "and we would always have our evening activity."

Being catered to by maître d's and fussed over by doormen and waiters seemed to give Si the sense that he mattered. He had no particular cultural or intellectual interests. He had no detectable spiritual side. He was a Jew without knowledge of or interest in his heritage. And in that disinterest, at least, he shared something with Jane.

The family in which Si grew up paid little attention to religion. Sam and Mitzi, after all, named their firstborn after Sam, thus ignoring the Jewish stricture against naming a child after a living person. They did belong to Temple Emanu-El, the large reform congregation on Fifth Avenue, although they were known to skip services even on the high holidays. Still, Sam was different from his father, the socialist who, despite having studied the Talmud in preparation to becoming a rabbi, was proud to call himself, if not quite an atheist, then certainly an agnostic. Sam simply had no time for religion, no interest, no emotional bond or calling. In Sam and Mitzi's home the focus was on family—no one could be more loyal to his family than Sam was—but it was also on the material, the here and now, the next chance; that was the religion they passed on to their son.

Jane's sense of her religious roots was also sketchy. Her grandmother was an Orthodox Jew who would bring her prayer shawl and candles when she visited, and who refused to ride on Saturdays. But Jane's mother had discarded all that and, says Jane, "just went in the other direction." Still, Jane had a basic knowledge of Judaism that Si lacked. When they were students at Syracuse, Jane recalls, Si told her, "I have to go home for my dead Aunt Aida's *bris*." As little as she knew, Jane says, she knew enough to tell Si that the unveiling of a tombstone is not called a *bris*.[9]

Si Newhouse seemed always on the prowl for the thing or the person that would give some center to his life. To Si at that time, center meant finding glamour and excitement. He found both in Roy Cohn, a lawyer/fixer par excellence who, if he had any values beyond power, hid them well. Starting in the mid-1950s, the two would become best friends.

If there was an aggressor in this relationship as adults, it was probably Roy Cohn. Certainly Cohn used Si, but then he used all his friends, which does not mean that he did not genuinely care for Si. The men who were close to Cohn, such as Bill Fugazy, a new friend of Si's whose family was in the limousine, travel, and investment banking business, and Neil Walsh, insist that the world has yet to see a better or more loyal friend.

Sally Obre, a friend of Si's who came to know Cohn in the late 1950s, says that he did some legal work for her and never billed her. He was, Sally says, "the most generous man I've ever met."

In the case of Si Newhouse, it wasn't simply Roy Cohn ingratiating himself with Si and Sam to collect legal fees from the Newhouses. More important were all those newspapers already owned and the new ones still to come. Cohn's growing roster of clients—mostly businessmen, some legitimate, some not, entangled in one way or another with politicians— were the sort who could benefit from the changed slant of an editorial, an endorsement made or withheld, a news story not pursued, an investigation squashed.

Although Sam Newhouse was famous for never ordering his editors and publishers to do anything except make money, Roy Cohn did seem a beneficiary of some of the Newhouse newspapers. In the early 1950s, the *Newark Star-Ledger*, for example, was one of the most staunch backers of communist-hunting Wisconsin senator Joseph McCarthy, for whom Cohn was chief legal counsel in 1953 and 1954, and about whom Roy would say in his autobiography, "I never worked for a better man or a greater cause." At the *Staten Island Advance*, reporters were surprisingly fearless in writing about the Mafia, but someone had imposed the unwritten but ironclad rule that Roy Cohn's name must never appear in its columns. (One reporter who wrote about Cohn's ties to a parking lot franchise in Staten Island said that the story found its way into the paper "by accident and we were pretty much told that would be the last time you'd see Roy Cohn's name in the paper.")

That Sam Newhouse was lending Cohn money is well known. According to Bill Fugazy, "The father loaned [Roy] a considerable amount of money." The money, adds Fugazy, was "to carry [Roy] over some very tough times." The reference here is to the period when Robert Kennedy was U.S. attorney general and relentlessly investigated Cohn. Cohn had been a bitter enemy of Kennedy's since the day he bested Bobby for the job as McCarthy's chief counsel. During the "vendetta" against him by Kennedy, Cohn later wrote, "There were periods of big trouble and I was lucky to have good friends who bailed me out with loans and outright gifts. The best of all was Samuel I. Newhouse, ...father of my best friend, Si. I remember going to see him, nervous as a cat, and he asked me what the trouble was. I said, 'I'm broke.' He said, 'Tell me how much you need.' Mr Newhouse smiled, 'C'mon, Roy, give me a number.' When I told him $250,000 he simply wrote out a check for the amount. I nearly fainted. I said I didn't know when I could pay him back. He said, 'You don't ever have to pay me back. You've already paid me with friendship.'"

Cohn never did pay back, but he did represent the Newhouses, both Si and Sam. He was not their main attorney, but he would handle some of the Newhouses' stickiest legal matters—ugly labor union disputes, for example, of the sort they would not have cared to send to their regular lawyers. "Roy Cohn played a substantial role in Newhouse's dealings with unions," says Sam's biographer Richard Meeker. "Roy took care of a lot of dirty business for the Newhouse family."

Neil Walsh put the relationship between Sam Newhouse and Roy Cohn in perspective by explaining that it was 98 percent personal and 1 or 2 percent business. Sam Newhouse set up an accounting and a law firm, which were for all intents and purposes in-house operations. His lawyer was Charles Goldman, and his accountant was Louis Glickman. Sam's family and his businesses were basically their only clients. Sam would bring in other professionals when needed, sometimes from the fanciest firms. But Sam needed Roy Cohn for special situations. "Sometimes some really tough cases that needed only the expertise that Roy had," explained Walsh, "which was tremendous, ...getting things done. Much more than most lawyers. He had great connections."

The late Erwin Knoll, who worked for the Newhouses in Washington, expressed his "feeling" that the Newhouses had people "who did certain dirty jobs for them, whether the dirty job was busting up a potential union or muscling their way on to the newsstands somewhere, ...there were people good at doing it who were totally loyal to them and who would get those dirty jobs done." In those instances, Walsh agreed, Sam would choose Roy over the most high-priced and high-prestige Wall Street lawyer.

Cohn biographer Nicholas von Hoffman insists that the most intriguing relationship was the one between Cohn and the father, not the son. So close were the two, agreed Neil Walsh, that "you kick one and the other squealed." The source of this closeness, said Walsh, was probably Henry

Garfinkle, whom Sam had years before set up in the newspaper distribution business and who later became an important client of Cohn's. (Distribution was the key to the success of Sam's newspaper and later his magazine businesses.)

Henry Garfinkle was, like Sam, very short (under five feet), and the eldest of eight children born to immigrant Russian Jews on the Lower East Side. From the time his father died when Henry was thirteen, he had supported his family—in his case by selling newspapers at the ferry dock on Staten Island. Sam, eight years older than Henry, befriended the boy, encouraged him, on occasion bought his entire stack, gave him a secret, interest-free loan in the 1920s, and continued, decade after decade, to help Garfinkle become dominant in the distribution business.

Garfinkle bought his first newsstand in the St. George ferry house on Staten Island, and, not surprisingly, gave prominent placement to the *Advance*. Out-hustling the competition, he soon had the largest stand in the terminal. Eventually, Garfield News Company, as he called it, expanded all over the New York metropolitan area. Another Garfinkle company dominated the northeast corridor. As his success multiplied, Garfinkle took over American News, through which he ran those companies and another, Union News, which had outlets coast to coast.

Reports popped up that Garfinkle's companies had ties to organized crime. Nicholas von Hoffman speculates that Roy Cohn was involved in this "very mobbed up" business. Soon after leaving Joe McCarthy, Cohn helped Garfinkle take over the American News Company, and in 1955 Cohn became general counsel to Union News.

As Cohn honed his reputation as a tough guy, a bully—Gary Marcus, Roy Cohn's first cousin once removed, who lived with Cohn for a while, says that his cousin "had no conscience" and that he "would use anyone at any time for anything"—he may have served Sam in still another way: "Cohn also played an active role in taking care of Si," claims Richard Meeker, "even though they were contemporaries.... Roy was at times on a retainer and would get as much as a quarter of a million dollars a year for just helping Si, ...just to be there to hold his hand." Roy served as a kind of protector, an inhibitor should anyone try to take advantage of Si.[10]

They were a study in contrasts: Si quiet and often morose, Roy bois-terous, always ready for a good time. Sally Obre explains Roy's appeal to Si as one of sheer brain power. "Si was a man...who was in awe of brain power." Geraldine Stutz, who through Si became friendly with Cohn, says that at heart Si was "a hero worshiper" and that Cohn's prominence and insider clout appealed to Si.

Si Newhouse was not a good storyteller, not adept at gossip, but he loved to listen, and nobody had more inside scoop than Roy Cohn. Way back, at age thirteen, Cohn had written a gossip column for the *Bronx Home News*, the seat of his father's political power, and he bragged, with justification, about feeding items to his friend Walter Winchell. Wherever Roy Cohn went, no matter how exclusive the restaurant or night club, he was treated like high royalty. The service was unparalleled, and the peo-ple who dropped by the table were the top gossip columnists, movie stars, politicians. "I think when he went out at night with Roy," says Sally Obre, "Si saw glamour, he saw excitement, he saw how it was with people who bowed and scraped.... I think he was just bowled over."

In some ways, Si and Roy were "as different as night and day," says Tom Corbally, a friend of Roy's, and a regular at 21. Corbally was typical of the group with whom Roy, and increasingly Si, mixed. He was a high liver, good looking—he had once been married to tennis player Gussie Moran—a "swordsman," said to be spectacularly well endowed, surround-ed by, in Neil Walsh's words, "every show girl, every model, every society girl in New York [who] wanted to be sure it was true."

Soon this group, which included Fugazy and Walsh, began to fre-quent the Stork Club, whose owner, Sherman Billingsley, Roy represented. Jane recalls that the Stork Club was not a restaurant that she and Si had ever particularly liked—he still vastly preferred 21—"but that's where Roy liked to go, so that's where we would go." They also began organizing parties together to go to the Copacabana, which, said Walsh, "was a hot spot in those days, Frank Sinatra, Martin and Lewis, and it was a hot table opening night."

Si also developed a new interest around this time when Bill Fugazy, who had ridden horses since childhood, persuaded him to give the sport a try. Fugazy had already won over Neil Walsh, who like Si had never ridden before, and the two of them went to work on Si until the unathletic, unco-ordinated Si Newhouse, who could barely kick a soccer ball or swing a baseball bat, found himself not only riding but also, recalls Fugazy, "riding the hounds and hunting." This was not a sport that appealed to Jane, and Walsh did not remember her ever participating.

The three men applied for membership at an exclusive riding club in Scarsdale. Admission was a given for Fugazy and Walsh, but Jews weren't allowed to belong, and it took some doing to finesse an exception for Si.

They would ride one or two nights a week, and Si kept his own horse at the club. According to Walsh, Si was not a natural rider, but "he worked hard at it," and went fox hunting with a group that, for the most part, had been born and bred to ride to the hounds. Fugazy recalls that Si had a couple of falls when he was learning, "but he was a very gutsy rider."

Si's new hobby and all the time he was spending with Roy Cohn was not helping his marriage. "I think that Roy Cohn was a very bad...friend-ship for Si," suggests Dave Morgan, "from the [perspective of his] person-al life." Jane was not the sort of woman to appeal in any way to Roy. She was not glamorous. She was not a celebrity-in-the-making like Barbara Walters, whom Roy said was his ideal woman, and whom he frequently talked about marrying. When Roy was not squiring Barbara Walters, he would bring a woman named Doris Hakim, whom, Jane recalls, was "crazy about Roy," or another woman named Joan Glickman.

Jane is uncertain whether she recognized back then Roy's apparent homosexuality. One of Roy's regulars once offered Jane the unsolicited confidence that she and Roy had had sex. But Barbara Walters, then a writer and producer for television stations in New York, once confided in her friend Sally Obre that she feared that Roy didn't find her attractive because he would always walk her to her door, give her a "peck on the cheek, hold my hand, and that's it. He never goes any further." Obre says that Barbara was in love with Roy Cohn and would happily have married him.

In those years Si's cultural interests were, like Cohn's, decidedly middlebrow. But Si was more intellectually curious than was Cohn, for whom high culture was the opening of a Broadway play. Jane recalls that as much as Si was intrigued by Roy's power, by "his dynamism as a person," Si once told her that he thought Roy was "one-dimensional, in the sense that he was really focused only on just that power of what he was doing. He didn't have interests, like he didn't really love theater or music or art. He didn't have any activities except his boat.... He wasn't broad in his interests."[11]

That Roy Cohn, no matter how one-dimensional, was having an effect on Si's feelings about his marriage was obvious when, in 1958, Si and Jane traveled with Cohn and with Dave and Alice Morgan to the Hotel Nacionale in Havana for the Christmas/New Year's holiday. Morgan describes himself and his wife as then "very happy and very exuberant.... We had adjoining suites in the hotel with Si and Janie.... Si came over to my room.... 'What is it that you do? I can see that you are so happy. You are having a good time. I just cannot do that with Janie. I'm just not quite happy.' He almost asked me for advice on how to handle life and marriage, ...searching for an answer.... It was very sad."[12]

Dave Morgan was not alone in witnessing Si's search for some change in his life. Others who knew him at this time said that Roy Cohn introduced Si to "girls." Given the revelations that came later about Roy's life—that he was gay and that his death in 1986 was from AIDS—there were the inevitable rumors that Si and Roy Cohn had an affair. But people who know them well remain entirely unconvinced. Two women who later had affairs with Si dismissed such talk as nonsense.[13]

When Jane is asked if Roy Cohn was an important reason behind what happened that year, 1959, when Si told Jane he wanted a divorce and moved out of the apartment, she says that it "probably would have happened anyway, but it surely didn't help. If it hadn't been Roy, it would have been somebody else. That's the way I feel about it. He was just ready for something else, that was it.... He was breaking away from the domestic scene at that time.... I don't know whether he would have stayed with another woman, but a lot of temptations were put in front of him, and Roy was like almost a Svengali figure."

Jane, now remarried, remains philosophical about her first marriage. "We married very young, and I don't think he had very much experience. I think it was the blind leading the blind in our marriage and our relationship."

It surprised no one, least of all Jane, that her husband retained Roy Cohn as his divorce lawyer. To battle Roy Cohn, Jane hired one of the most celebrated lawyers of the time, Louis Nizer. But one friend of Jane's suspected that "Louis Nizer was really in the pay of the Newhouse family. She was given an enormous amount of child support, ...and they talked her into taking a tiny permanent alimony. So here is Jane, married to one of the richest guys in America, [and she] really didn't get anything.... He dumped her with three kids and then took off."*[14]

As was the norm for that time, Jane was granted custody of their two sons and a daughter, Sam, Wynn, and Pamela, all under the age of ten, and Si was granted visitation rights. The divorce did not become final until 1962. It took so long, friends say, because the prospect of divorce had caused Si suddenly to become very interested in his children. "The irony," says Jane, "is that once we separated, he was up there all the time having little tête-à-têtes with the children." She speculates that he felt guilty about leaving the family when the children were so young.

Si wanted to codify this informal arrangement. "He wanted to come up every night to see the children," says one friend of both Jane and Si, "and she wasn't sure that she really wanted to give him that kind of agreement, in case she remarried, she wasn't sure how the next husband would feel about that."[16]

Just after he separated from Jane, Si began to date the glamorous Geraldine Stutz, who had trained at *Vogue* and then worked as an editor at *Glamour.* Stutz says that what she found most appealing about Si Newhouse was his attachment to his children. "I remember that Si used to come and pick me up about seven-thirty or eight, and he had been every day from five-thirty or six spending time with his children." As "uncomfortable" a young man as Si was, she explains, as plagued as he was by "an awkwardness in his dealings with people," he was "easier about his relationship with the kids."

---

*A letter sent to Nizer five months before his death in 1994 was answered by his secretary: "I have ascertained from our archives that, unfortunately, most of our files in the Newhouse divorce case have been destroyed. The attorney who worked on the case has passed away, and I regret that Mr. Nizer has no recollection of the case."[15]

Friends say that once Si Newhouse made up his mind that he wanted out of his marriage, he had not a second thought, no regrets, no apparent recriminations. Joni Evans, a New York book editor turned literary agent, was involved in her own painful divorce, from then Simon & Schuster chief Richard Snyder. She praises Si for being "emotionally supportive of this hideous divorce. He was extraordinarily good with me and testified on my behalf. Not that he wanted to; he was subpoenaed, but he was fantastic. I once said to him, 'Si, did you ever go through a divorce like this? It's such a nightmare,' and he told me, 'Oh, I went through a divorce once, but I would pay anything for my children, and I did.'" She then asked him about the emotional toll of the breakup, leaving his wife, "and he just shook his head in some way which made me know that whatever happened he didn't give a damn, he never looked back."

But Mitzi and Sam were unhappy about the divorce, and embarrassed. Those to whom Sam was close at his newspapers—top business and editorial side people—remember how "disappointed" Sam felt about Si walking out on his marriage. One editor working for the Newhouses recalls a lunch with Mitzi in which she confessed that she had gone through "a great deal" with her son.

In his biography of Sam, Richard Meeker writes that Mitzi was so upset by the divorce that for some time after she refused to receive Si in her home. "Of course that's not true," Jane says. "That is totally untrue.... Si was her favorite son. There would be nothing that would have allowed her not to be close to him. She was overly fond of him."

Jane did continue to see Mitzi after the divorce. "I was kind of protective in a way as she got older." As a grandmother Mitzi had a good heart, but, Jane says, sometimes Mitzi seemed to care more about how the children looked than how they felt, and they grew up closer to Jane's parents. Jane remembers the time, while she was still married to Si, when her mother was watching Wynn, who had been ill, while she and the other two children were out of town. When it came time for Jane's mother to send Wynn to Mitzi, who was then going to arrange for Wynn to join Jane, "My mother took all his clothes and wrapped each one individually in tissue paper. I mean she really knocked herself out, and Mitzi was so appreciative."

In looking back at her marriage, Jane shows little bitterness: "I have warm feelings about Si, and protective feelings."[17]

Si was, as he would remain, a man who seemed more like a boy, burdened with an adolescent's immaturity and insecurity. In certain woman, even an ex-wife who understandably might have felt badly used, he stirred the urge to want to help him as he navigated an adulthood for which he seemed so ill-prepared.

5 | "What Makes Sammy Run?"

ROBERT NOTSON, WHO WAS managing editor of the *Oregonian* at the time of Si Newhouse's separation from Jane, recalls Si as being "a little at loose ends." Like Si, Notson could see that Donald was moving ahead of his older brother. "He was becoming quite recognized for his work in rebuilding the *Newark Star-Ledger* and making it the dominant paper there, and I think he was quite in favor with his father, and I don't think S. I. Jr. was at that time."[1]

One thing is certain, and that was that Sam Newhouse was one hard act to follow. As an empire builder, there was no one like him. His business philosophy was simple, it was consistent, and it was so commonsensical that one wonders why more would-be press lords didn't steal his secrets, but perhaps the answer is obvious: Sam Newhouse was a man who lusted after profit, never power.

In running his newspapers, Sam held fast to a pocketful of principles. One of his bedrock beliefs was that a man who runs a profitable business ought to employ every relative who wants to work. In his prime, Sam had sixty-four Newhouses working for him. His brother Louis Newhouse, the least ambitious and personable of the boys in the family, supervised the composing room at the *Staten Island Advance* and became a skilled compositor. Louis's son Irving started as a photographer for the *Advance* and the *Newark Star-Ledger,* and became the production manager of the *Long Island Press.* Sam's brother Ted was the associate publisher of the *Press,* and brother Norman had been editor of the *Press* until Sam bought the *New Orleans Times-Picayune* and *States-Item* in 1962 and dispatched Norman down there. In Harrisburg, the circulation manager was Sam's cousin,

Harold "Pat" Newhouse. Caroline Harrison, the current publisher in Harrisburg, is the granddaughter of Sam's sister, Gertrude, and the daughter of Richard Diamond, Sam's nephew, who is the publisher of the *Advance.* And so on and on.

Sam filled his payroll with relatives not because he was a softy, but because he knew that it was smart business to have a Newhouse monitoring the cash register of every one of his "properties," as he called his newspapers. *Press* editor Norman Newhouse was, says Mel Elfin, who worked for him at the *Press,* both a newsman and "the family watchman." No member of the family would ever become so enamored of the former role that he would forget the latter. Newhouse relatives watched pennies in a manner reminiscent of Sam's father and his son, when they stood guard over the presses to prevent the filching of a few newspapers. James Roper, who worked for the Newhouses in Washington, remembers once asking if the late Mort Pye, the *Newark Star-Ledger*'s longtime editor, could have the paper mailed to the Washington office. Pye, who was married to Sam's niece, Florence Newhouse, said no. "Mort Pye won't give us the paper because he can sell it for a nickel," Roper's boss explained.

Sam balanced his belief in nepotism with a rule that no family member would receive special treatment. One publisher claims that Sam was a "stronger taskmaster where members of his family were involved than he was with nonfamily members." "Your name could be Sam Newhouse IV," agrees Saul Kohler, retired editor of the *Harrisburg Patriot-News,* "if you didn't know your rear end from third base, you didn't keep your job."[2]

The founding Newhouse never replaced editors and publishers with his own kin when he bought a new paper. On the contrary, he almost always retained the locals because they knew the community. Sam no more wanted to control the coverage of local politics in Portland or to call on the chairman of the leading department store in St. Louis than he wanted to run for mayor of New York City. When he bought both papers in New Orleans, he made a pledge to shareholders to retain management and announced that the paper's top executive could keep his job "for the rest of his life if he wants it."[3] Sam understood that bringing in an outsider, and a New Yorker to boot, would only weaken the bottom line and stir up opposition the next time he tried to buy a newspaper. And, he knew, there would always be a next time. This is not to say, however, that a Newhouse or two would not be posted full-time to that metaphorical cash register or assigned to visit it regularly.

Sam did not limit nepotism to his own family. He always encouraged his editors and executives to employ their own relatives, though sometimes with mixed results. One former reporter on the *Star-Ledger* recalls that the editor of the paper's sports section bestowed columns and "all the good assignments" on his sons. "It was total, outrageous nepotism. One of his sons was very talented, ...but [the other] was a fucking idiot."

A publisher of another of the Newhouse papers remembers the annual American Newspaper Publishers Association meetings, at which Sam would host a dinner for his publishers. He would rise and tell the assembled: "Now you all remember, we want members of your family in the business." Because unions were scarce at the Newhouse newspapers, part-time jobs abounded, and employees were urged to bring their children around for summer jobs or to work as they could during college.[4]

It is remarkable to consider that with so many Newhouses in the stable, all seemed to know their places. Sam paid his relatives well, but they were, at the end of the workweek, mere employees. None of them, not even Sam's brothers, had a meaningful ownership interest in the business. But of all the Newhouses, it was brothers Ted and Norman who were critical to the growth of Sam's fortune. (Those two were eventually given preferred stock, but Sam held all the common stock and voting rights.)

Because Sam kept his company private, he didn't have to answer to a board of directors, but he always consulted his brothers, each of whom had his own field of expertise. Norman's was the general business operation of the papers, especially the relation between editorial and business; Ted's was newsprint and labor relations. With no red tape, memos, or feasibility studies, it might take the brothers but one short get-together to agree to give the publisher in Syracuse the go-ahead for a $2 million wrapping system, or give the publisher in Springfield, Massachusetts, new presses.

Sam, a lifelong sufferer from insomnia—he always claimed he slept only a few hours a night, "and not on purpose"—would often call Ted and Norman in the middle of the night to compare notes or to flag potential trouble spots. "If I can't sleep, why should you?" he would say in greeting. (Sam had a theory that propping up the head aided sleep, and he used three down pillows, but admitted that he usually lay awake thinking about business.)[5]

While Ted held the title of associate publisher of the *Long Island Press*, he also visited Newhouse papers in Huntsville, Birmingham, Springfield, Portland (Oregon), and a chain of papers in eight cities and towns in Michigan. Because it was the bottom line that always interested him most, Ted kept his distance from editorial. Robert Notson recalls that when Sam bought the *Oregonian*, he and Ted decided that the "news and editorial departments were well run," and that was that. Ted was not interested in Portland politics except as they might affect business.

When Donald Sterling was editor of the afternoon paper, the *Oregon Journal*, Ted "would drop in to see me...for about three minutes, sit down, and say, 'What's going on?' I usually didn't have much very interesting to tell him, and he'd go away. He almost never made any suggestions or anything like that.... He never asked any questions about editorial policy."[6]

Ted Newhouse, eight years Sam's junior, was a man of very few words who never sought the limelight, and whose name sparks few warm memories or anecdotes. James E. Sauter, who had been president and CEO of Booth, the chain of newspapers in Michigan that Sam acquired in 1976, had been intensely opposed to the Newhouse takeover—both because he knew he'd lose his independence and eventually his job, as he did, and because he had studied the Newhouse papers and found them uniformly unexceptional.

Sam kept Sauter on, but he clashed repeatedly with Ted, who visited Booth headquarters in Ann Arbor, Michigan, every Wednesday, often with nephew Richard Diamond in tow. "Ted's a little guy," Sauter says, "and he comes stomping in my office...and doesn't even say hello and he says, 'There's a million dollars missing.' And I said, 'Well, I don't know where the hell it is, Ted, but I ain't got it.'... So I called my financial vice president.... He got Dick Diamond to go with him and they came back a couple of hours later and the financial VP...says, 'Well, there's not a million bucks missing,'... but to me it's a pretty good measure of a man. He doesn't say hello, he comes in and accuses you of stealing a million bucks."

Sauter recalls the week that he, Ted, and Dick Diamond were driving to one of the Booth plants when Ted said to him, "I can get you a better deal on newsprint." At the time, newsprint was Booth's number-one expense. Sauter agreed to take a look at the proposal. He also called the sales rep of the company from whom Booth had bought newsprint for thirty years and told him of Ted's offer. "My guy beat the price," Sauter recalls. "So the next time Ted comes up, he says, 'How about the newsprint deal?' and I said, 'I've talked with our supplier, and [he] gave me a price better than the one you have.' Ted tapped me on the arm and said, 'Will you do me a favor? I've already made a commitment.' And I said, 'Well, I guess I don't have a choice.'"

Ted's first wife, Bea, who was the one relative who declined to pay homage to Mitzi at annual family parties, died of cancer. His only child, a daughter, died early. Later Ted married Caroline, a German-born, Jewish, "very vibrant," according to Jane Franke, sculptor and painter who set up studios in their Park Avenue apartment and Connecticut country home. Ted was crazy about her and enthusiastically supported her work, and with her indulged his taste for travel and the opera.[7]

If Ted was the family disciplinarian, Norman Newhouse was the one with the common touch that endeared him to almost everyone. Leo Meindl, known at the *Press* as "Mr. Fixit," the man behind the paper's action-line-type column, remembers Norman as "brilliant" and caring. "More than one guy who had troubles...would go to Norman. You could talk it out with him, and he would be understanding."

Norman, who was three years younger than Ted, began his career as a political reporter on the *Staten Island Advance*, later became city editor, and then managing editor. When he moved over to the *Press* as night city editor, Jackie Gebhard, a *Press* reporter of the time, remembered him as a man who "really didn't know the newspaper business," but, she adds, he was "determined to learn." Paul Keil, then Sunday editor of the *Press*, fondly recalls Norman as "very much of a hands-on editor."

Norman was the flashy brother of the family. He would tool around in his Cadillac, and according to one woman who knew him well, he "always had some floozyish girl with him, a different one every time we saw him." Eventually Norman settled down, marrying Alice Gross of Queens, whom he met when she was a college student working at the *Press*. They had four sons, two of whom are key players at Newhouse today, and one daughter.

Norman had the sort of charming and colorful personality that was in short supply in that generation—and subsequent generations—of Newhouse men. He had served as a major in the Office of Strategic Services in Italy during World War II, and after the war remained in Italy to serve under General McNarney, for a time dating a woman whom the general was also dating. Norman was a fisherman, a baseball fan, and a bridge player who used to invite bright young reporters like Mel Elfin to his home in Great Neck for a game.

In 1967 Norman Newhouse left the *Press*, moving to New Orleans, where he switched to the business side. He had a wide-ranging job, overseeing the *Times-Picayune* and *States-Item* and taking over weekly visits to the family papers in Mobile, Birmingham, Huntsville, Alabama; Pascagoula, Mississippi; and Cleveland. Norman turned out to be as tough a businessman as he was an understanding editor. Murry Frymer, a former editor on the *Cleveland Plain Dealer*, says that on Norman's weekly visits to Cleveland, the bottom line was his sole concern. "He reminded me of a guy who collects rent in the old days."[8]

While the role played by the brothers was crucial to the founder's operation, his sisters, for the most part, provided husbands and sons to man the operation. Sam's youngest sister, Gertrude Diamond, married a physician, and produced *Advance* publisher Richard Diamond. Another sister, Estelle Miron, was married to a furniture manufacturer. Their son Robert would later head the Newhouses' cable TV operation.

Only Gertrude and Estelle's older sister, Naomi, who had no children, was in the business—as was her husband, Teddy Jablons, promotions director of the *Newark Star-Ledger*. Naomi was in fact, if not in title, publisher of the *Staten Island Advance*. One longtime Staten Islander calls Naomi the "inside woman there who just ran the show." He says that, unlike Gertrude, who was known to be very sweet and modest, Naomi was "as tough as nails, cursed like a sailor, and was often seen rushing to the pressroom to make certain the paper got out on time." Naomi told Ben Magdovitz, then advertising director at the *St. Louis Globe-Democrat*, that when Sam was about to appoint an outsider as publisher, "I went in and I turned on the tears and I said, 'Sam, you can't do that. You can't do that, favor anybody except a member of the family.'" He agreed—his only reservation about her would have been her sex—and she ran the show.[9]

Not only did the founder insist on the obligation to hire his relatives, he also felt pressured by Mitzi to hire hers. Mitzi's brother Walter Evans—he had changed the family name from Epstein—spent his entire career working semi-unhappily for Sam, first at the *Long Island Press,* then as circulation director of the Syracuse papers, and finally as circulation director at. the *St. Louis Globe-Democrat.* There he was regarded by one of the top people on the business side as lazy and lacking in ambition. And he was always insecure, fearing that not only he but every one else thought that the only reason he got that job was because his sister was married to Sam.

The *Globe-Democrat's* publisher, Richard Amberg, whom many found to be a frightening, blustering man, treated Walter with impatience and disdain. Amberg, who had risen quickly in the Newhouse organization—he came to St. Louis from the morning paper in Syracuse—was too smart and too ambitious to have mistreated Walter if he suspected that so doing would provoke Sam's anger. But Amberg was tough enough on Walter to cause the brother-in-law to complain to Mitzi, which caused Sam to appeal to another of the paper's executives to see what he could do about persuading Amberg not to be "mean and threatening to Walter."[10]

Only one man who was not a blood relation of S. I. Newhouse had a role as an insider in the newspaper operation. Philip Hochstein arrived from czarist Russia in 1907 at age six. His family was poor, and his school record in Bayonne, New Jersey, even poorer. "I had worn down the local truant officer into respecting my status as an incorrigible school dropout." He labored in Bayonne as an unskilled factory worker, and, in his spare time, honed his skills as a "radical soap box orator." In 1919, on his eighteenth birthday, he walked into the offices of the *New York Call,* a socialist daily, landed a job, and started to make a name for himself as a socialist journalist. When the *Call* went bankrupt, he moved to Hearst's *New York American,* and when that didn't work out, he returned to Bayonne and went to work for Sam at the *Bayonne Times.* It was Judge Lazarus's widow, then running the paper after Sam exited in order to devote himself to the potentially more profitable *Staten Island Advance*, who named Phil Hochstein editor.

The *Times* began to thrive under Hochstein, as it had under Sam. Sam took notice, and in 1925 he offered Phil $70 a week to be the *Advance*'s top editor. Hochstein accepted, later working his way up to be managing editor of the *Long Island Press* and editor of the *Newark Star-Ledger*.

The relationship between Sam and his one nonrelative seemed based more on respect than affection. "I don't think they were buddy-buddy," says one man close to Hochstein. "I certainly didn't get any feeling that they were...fond of each other." Mitzi, who wanted invitations to her home to mean something and was careful about who made the cut, was partly responsible for the fact that the business tie did not spill over into the social. She never invited Phil Hochstein, whose socialist Jewish roots and intellectual interests were too strong for Mitzi's tastes, to their home. Hochstein's wife, Leah, was sweet but far too plain and bookish to spark Mitzi's interest. Elaine Reiner describes the Hochsteins as "the most intellectual people in the whole world, their house filled with books because they read them," unlike Mitzi, who, Reiner says, was "not a real reader" and used books as a decorating motif.

Those who worked for Hochstein saw him as introverted, private, and imposing, but he was doing the job for his boss.

The Newhousian spin that each editor and publisher ran his own show was true as far as it went. But just as the brothers monitored every paper's financial bottom line, so Phil Hochstein kept his eye on every paper's editorial bottom line—i.e., was the editorial geared to producing the highest possible profit? Did the editorial fit with what the community (i.e., advertisers) wanted? Hochstein became the chainwide editorial brain for Sam, who came to call Hochstein the "newspaper doctor" of his organization.[11]

One of Hochstein's first and sickest patients was the *Newark Ledger*. Advertisers had been fleeing in droves from the tabloid scandal sheet, whose erratic publisher and owner, Lucius T. Russell, maintained a policy of hiring alcoholics and drifters as reporters because they would accept terrible pay and even worse working conditions. When Sam bought the controlling interest in the *Ledger* in 1935, he persuaded Lucius Russell to retire to California by offering to keep his name on the masthead, to pay him a $20,800 annual salary for doing nothing, and to make his son Edwin associate publisher. But the elder Russell, unstable and paranoid, soon decided that he had been swindled by Sam, and he came back a year later, threatening to sue Sam, whom he described as "a small, squat animal," and stirring up dissent among the paper's workers. A meeting with Russell, Richard Meeker wrote, "convinced" Sam that Lucius "had completely lost touch with reality." Sam canceled Lucius's contract, and Edwin Russell took Sam's side. There were more fights, and before it was over Newhouse, again with Edwin's help, stripped Lucius of his stock in the *Ledger* and helped to have him committed to a mental institution.

With Russell out of the way, Sam immediately dispatched Hochstein to fix the paper, which in a three-newspaper town ran third. During lunch at the New Jersey farm, Sam told the late novelist James Michener, "Everybody wanted to close the *Ledger* down, and I said, 'Wait a minute, this is a gold mine if it's properly run.'"

Hochstein targeted the editorial to the wealthier families who had left Newark for the surrounding suburbs and, especially, to housewives who were bored out of their wits at home. (The word "Newark" would be dropped from the masthead in the early 1960s, along with the last pretense that the paper would serve the city's increasingly poor and black population.) Hochstein saw to it that women readers, who, as any advertiser knew, were the ones who did the shopping, had editorial fare that interested them—household hints, movie gossip, news of weddings, clubs, teas, and charity events.[12]

Although Hochstein's aim was usually to enhance the bottom line rather than the quality of the writing or reporting, he differed from others in the top rung of the Newhouse organization. "He could," says one reporter, "think and he could write and there weren't too many people in the Newhouse organization in those days who could do both." In five minutes time, he would write letter-perfect editorials for what became, through a merger in 1939, the *Newark Star-Ledger*, the extremely profitable paper that served as Hochstein's home base.

When Sam quarreled with members of his family, he did so behind closed doors. But Hochstein was not family, and the disagreement that effectively ended their fertile relationship was played out in the pages of *Newsweek,* although the real reason for their estrangement never saw print.

In 1965 Hochstein founded in Washington a national paper called the *Jewish Week.* It was his paper, not Sam's, and Sam, who advised Hochstein against involving himself with it, admitted to a *Newsweek* reporter that he resented losing the time that Phil devoted to the paper, and that he told him that he must either give it up or retire. In fact, the problem lay even deeper.

Hochstein immediately named himself publisher and his son Joseph editor. (He had learned something from Sam.) Joe had been a reporter and an editorial writer at the *Star-Ledger,* and he later covered the state department and diplomatic beats for his father's brainchild, the Newhouse National News Service. Princeton-educated and highly intelligent, Joe had a strong interest in Jewish affairs and later developed a zeal for Zionism. (Eventually Joe Hochstein moved to Israel, where his son, a sergeant in the Israeli army, was killed in one of the Arab-Israeli wars.)

Phil Hochstein believed that it wasn't so much resentment of the energy he expended on his own paper that bothered Sam but, as Phil later wrote, "the thought that he might seem to be associated with an ethnic publication."

The crux of the discord had surfaced decades before, back in the early 1930s. Sam then worried that Hochstein was making too much of the threat of Adolf Hitler. "Newhouse asked me," Hochstein recalled, "if I wasn't devoting too much attention in the paper to the Nazi phenomenon. He wondered out loud whether I wasn't exaggerating the interest of our readers in Hitler's anti-Semitism. 'The great majority of our readers,' he pointed out, 'are not Jewish.' I assured him that I understood that fact, but I thought what was happening in Germany should not be ignored.... Newhouse argued that Hitler's extremism was a passing thing. 'He'll calm down after he gets power,' he said. 'He's a typical demagogue.' I disputed this view, telling him that I had been following the headlines in the German newspapers and was convinced what was going on in Germany would probably engulf the world. Newhouse concluded the discussion with: 'You're wrong, but have it your way.'"

It was when Hochstein left Sam in 1967 that *Newsweek* covered their dispute. In an interview that Phil gave the magazine, he claimed that their disagreement was about the future of the news service: "I was disappoint-ed in the lack of support I was getting. I think I've wasted a lot of my time." There was reportedly also a dispute over money—specifically Phil's pension, which Sam set at 70 percent of his annual salary of $92,000. Hochstein subsequently insisted that he had an understanding with Sam that he would "never be retired and that I would receive full pay and my wife receive full pay for the rest of her life if I were to predecease her. I was hardly pleased when Newhouse violated this understanding."

Ten years later there was some concern that Hochstein might become a source for Richard Meeker, a young Portland journalist who was, against the family's wishes, writing a biography of the founder. One man who was close to Phil Hochstein recalls that Sam wanted to show his old friend the consequences of talking. "I know that after [Phil] retired at one point he stopped getting [pension] checks.... He called [Sam] one day and said, 'What's up?' Newhouse said, 'I want you to know that I can do this anytime I want.'" The checks resumed, and Hochstein refused Meeker the requested interview.[13]

The falling-out between Sam Newhouse and Phil Hochstein offers a per-spective on Sam's complicated feelings about his religion. While Hochstein became a passionate supporter of Israel—at first he refrained because he was afraid of being seen as having dual loyalties—Sam Newhouse never came around to supporting the Jewish nation and never understood the fervor with which other American Jews did. Sam toyed with the idea of buying the *Jerusalem Post* in the mid-1950s, and even traveled to Israel to take a firsthand look. But on the advice of Phil Hochstein, he decided against making an offer. Hochstein advised Sam not to proceed because, according to one Newhouse editor who remains close to Phil, "ownership of Israel's only English-language daily would be an inappro-priate role for Newhouse as a non-Zionist Jew." To Sam, it could have been the *Jerusalem Post* or the *Rome Daily American,* another paper he consid-ered buying at around the same time. All Sam wanted was a paper with a healthy bottom line. Israeli officials wanted something much different: an advocate, a source of money and moral support. (The most compelling rea-son to Sam not to buy papers abroad was that neither he nor his brothers could conveniently make regular on-site visits. Some insisted, however, that Sam wanted the paper in Rome so that he'd have something to do while accompanying Mitzi on her shopping sprees abroad.)

In the 1930s the United Palestine Appeal, the precursor to the United Jewish Appeal, had been repeatedly rebuffed in its pleas to Sam Newhouse. In later years, after the state of Israel came into being, Sam regularly refused requests to contribute to the UJA. But if the person doing the asking was a valued employee, Sam usually gave, leaving the amount up to the employee's discretion, never begrudging the gift, but never taking the initiative.[14]

Oddly enough, the patriarch seemed more sympathetic to Francis Cardinal Spellman and Catholic charities than to his own heritage. It was Bill Fugazy who first took Mitzi and Sam to dinner with the cardinal. And, from that time on, says Fugazy, "They were very generous to the cardinal and many of the Catholic causes."[15] Sam's generosity was mostly an indication of his esteem for Roy Cohn, who was a close confidant of the cardinal.

6 | Building the Empire

WHEN IT CAME TO BUSINESS, the issue of Sam Newhouse's Jewishness never went away. Because he was a Jew, he quickly learned, certain papers were beyond his reach, no matter how much he was willing to spend. He wanted to buy the *Omaha World-Herald*, and some say, the *Denver Post*, but failed. The reason was clear: if at all possible, the owners preferred to sell to someone other than a Jew. Phil Hochstein once told a close relative that Sam "felt that he had lost out on a number of occasions...because of anti-Semitism."[1]

Bob Hochstein, a nephew who worked for the Newhouses in Harrisburg and Washington, recalls the time in 1962 when Sam was trying to buy Omaha, as he would have put it. "My uncle Phil had come into town, and I told him I saw this little squib in the *Wall Street Journal* that Sam was attempting to buy the Omaha paper...and Phil really turned ashen. He said, 'It's dead, the deal's dead.'" The nephew soon figured out the reason for his uncle's distress. "Apparently it was being bought through intermediaries.... When that piece surfaced, they put together a coalition of business leaders in Omaha to snap it out from under him."[2]

In some of these cities Sam was casually referred to as "Jewhouse," or by his initials, S.I.N.[3] In others the practice was to use his full name, Samuel Isadore Newhouse, or sometimes even his given name, Solomon Isadore, instead of the initials S. I., which he used for business. In 1955, when Sam acquired the paper in Huntsville, Alabama, one trusted Jewish editor who Sam dispatched there from the East overheard a group of executives in the men's room discussing the fact that Sam's accountant, Louis Glickman, was coming down to Huntsville from New York. One of the group referred to him as "Lou the Jew." Bob Hochstein observes that the "image of New York Jew was very much a problem for [Sam].... There was just a bad odor around him.... He wasn't radical, he didn't fit that stereotype, so I guess the stereotype that they chose for him was a little Jewish man who would burrow in before you realized and wind up owning you."[4]

But S. I. Newhouse was not going to be intimidated. His hunger to acquire more and more papers held sway over everything else in his life.

When Vance McCormick, the owner of the *Harrisburg Patriot* and *Evening News,* died in 1946, he left a widow who knew nothing about running a newspaper and was anxious to sell. McCormick had been a football star at Yale, he had accompanied Woodrow Wilson to the Paris peace talks after World War I, he was a civic leader in Harrisburg, a major owner of the Harrisburg Steel Company, mayor of Harrisburg, Democratic national treasurer, and owner of liberal-leaning newspapers. On paper he looked like a progressive, but in his will he specified that his papers were not to be sold to a chain, or to a Jew.

Sam devised a means to circumvent McCormick's wishes, which his widow, Annie, had every intention of honoring. Mrs. McCormick summered in Bar Harbor, Maine, and it was there that she hosted a wedding reception and met a spectacularly attractive young man named Edwin Russell. Russell was no stranger to Sam Newhouse, who in that acrimonious transaction, had bought the *Newark Ledger* from Russell's father, Lucius Russell, in 1935. Edwin Russell was everything Sam was not—tall, handsome, Princeton educated, a naval hero, an American who affected a quasi-British accent, and who was married to the real thing, Lady Sarah Spencer-Churchill, Winston's first cousin, daughter of the Duke of Marlborough, and granddaughter of Consuelo Vanderbilt. He was, says Saul Kohler, who arrived as a reporter in Harrisburg in 1949, "a perfect gentleman."

So taken was Annie McCormick with Russell that she confided in him that the papers were for sale and urged him to offer himself as a buyer. Unbeknownst to the widow, Ed Russell worked for Sam Newhouse, and he immediately called him to report the availability of these profitable properties. Late in the summer of 1947, Russell bought the papers, ostensibly for himself, but actually for Sam. He moved to Harrisburg and took the titles of president and publisher, and for a time the charade was maintained, although eventually what was long known to insiders became common knowledge.[5]

Sam again used Ed Russell as his front when he bought the sole remaining competition in town, the unrelentingly conservative *Harrisburg Telegraph,* owned by members of the blue-blooded Stackpole family and run by Brigadier General Albert H. Stackpole. Two months after the acquisition Sam folded the *Telegraph,* or as he would say, merged it into the *Evening News,* putting himself in the coveted position of being the only owner in town.

To help Russell run the expanded company, Newhouse imported his loyalists: a cousin, Pat Newhouse, to run circulation; Lou Glickman to oversee the books; Charles Goldman to oversee legal matters; Phil Hochstein to mold the editorial. The new top editor for both Harrisburg papers, Eugene Farrell, came from the *Star-Ledger* in Newark. Noting that the local citizenry had just approved movies on Sunday, Newhouse launched a Sunday edition, a move staunchly opposed by church and community leaders. The public loved it, and Sam sold more papers on Sunday than he did during the week, morning and evening editions combined.[6]

In 1960 Sam moved in on another blueblooded family, this one owners of the *Springfield* (Massachusetts) *Union, Daily News,* and *Republican.* The relatives and descendants of Sherman Bowles, the great-grandson of the papers' founder, were feuding with each other, as they had once feuded with Bowles, who had died eight years earlier. A disgruntled cousin offered Sam 42 percent of the stock. Sam snapped it up for $4.5 million in a deal that also included the option to buy, in 1967, an additional 45 percent of the company.

Although not a member of the family, the papers' treasurer, Sidney R. Cook, an employee of forty-five years, along with other managers, vowed to stop Sam from taking over. They wrote an editorial for the Sunday paper's front page lamenting that "the work and pride of four generations is at an inglorious end.... Principle, integrity, and courage are giving way to the lure of easy money.... Samuel I. Newhouse of New York is a stranger to this area. He is reported to purchase newspapers as one would 'collect objects of art.'"

Sam's lawyers were soon filing suits against the papers' directors and officers. Cook and his compatriots, as part of their strategy to keep Sam at bay, continued to publish hostile editorials, including one that charged that Sam was "determined to control, for personal ambitions, power, and profit, every means of communication he can acquire on the American scene." Nonetheless, in 1966, a year before Sam's option came due, the lawsuits were settled and Sam took control of the papers.

Ben Magdovitz recalls an American Newspaper Publishers Association meeting years later when Cook, whom Sam had given both a raise and the job of publisher, asked Magdovitz to join him for a drink that extended to three or four. "We really got loaded, and he started to talk about things he did...to [Sam] in the process of buying." Some of Cook's recollections, in Magdovitz's opinion, carried anti-Semitic overtones. But then Cook told his drinking companion, with amazement still apparent in his voice, "When it was all over, he offered me a job as publisher."

Sam was simply being true to himself. He had calculated that while Cook's hostility counted as points against him, his business acumen, his ties to the business and political leaders of the city, meant more. Ben Magdovitz explains that, to Sam, an employee's animosity was almost irrelevant. "He had the thickest skin on something that he had no control over. He couldn't help it if somebody was anti-Semitic. He wasn't going to solve the world's problems. He could tell if somebody was antiwork. He'd fire 'em."[7]

Another man might have said the hell with these owners and publishers who don't like Jews; I'll put my money where I'm wanted—like New York City. Not Sam Newhouse. With the exception of the *New York Herald-Tribune*, which he tried to buy in 1953, Sam never ventured to acquire a paper in Manhattan. Staten Island, Long Island, Newark, Jersey City, were all good fits, but not Manhattan, with its implacable unions and delivery problems.[8]

For the same business reasons that Sam avoided showing a smidgeon of sympathy for Zionism, he showed a strong devotion to anti-Communism. In some American cities, the words *Jew* and *Communist* were practically synonymous. Newhouse's uncompromisingly tough stand toward the unions—

especially the Newspaper Guild, which undoubtedly included Communist members—helped disabuse anyone of the notion that communism and Sam Newhouse had anything in common. Being tough on unions was good for Sam's bottom line. As a Jew of Russian extraction, it was also good for his image as a patriotic all-American.

That Sam courted the good opinion of FBI chief J. Edgar Hoover is not surprising, nor is it surprising that Hoover kept an active file on Sam, in which he is variously referred to as Samuel Isadore Newhouse, Samuel Irving Newhouse, or Samuel I. Newhouse. At first the Director, as he was almost always called in FBI documents, didn't seem to know what to make of Sam. At one point, as Sam's pace of acquisitions accelerated, a memorandum in his file stated, "The Director has inquired, 'What have we in our files on Sam Newhouse who recently bought newspapers in St. Louis…and Portland?'"

Apparently Hoover decided to give Sam the benefit of the doubt—a reasonable conclusion for Hoover to have reached. The S. I. Newhouse FBI file is stuffed with assurances by various FBI functionaries that J. Edgar Hoover couldn't ask for friendlier cooperation than that given by Sam Newhouse and his editors.

On February 3, 1939, according to an internal FBI memo, Sam Newhouse wrote a personal letter to Hoover "stating that the Editorial Council of the Newark Ledger had for some time been enthusiastic admirers of the work done by the Bureau. He requested that the Director send material which would be helpful in preparing editorials and news items." Others in the Newhouse organization also approached the FBI. A memo dated April 10, 1951, noted that "[Name blacked out], who represents several newspapers in the Newhouse chain, called" and that he is "very friendly to the Bureau" and "that the Long Island Press and the Long Island Star-Journal wanted to know if the Bureau would furnish answers to the following questions: How many Communists there are in Queens County, New York?... What part of Queens County has the greatest congregation of Communists? Who are the county and section leaders of the Party in Queens?"

In 1953, during the annual meeting of the American Society of Newspaper Editors, a "representative" of the Newhouse papers called to invite Hoover to a cocktail party for Newhouse editors at the Carlton Hotel in Washington. Hoover was out of town, so one of his top lieutenants, Louis B. Nichols, went in his place. Nichols, a public relations wizard who created the bureau's and the director's incorruptible, crime-fighting image, noted that he visited with Sam and also with Ted and Norman, and that Sam "asked that his regards be extended to the Director." Nichols concluded that he was "very favorably impressed with the Newhouse crowd. I was told by several of the editors that it was the policy of their papers to cooperate in every possible way. S. I. Newhouse told me personally if at any time he could be of assistance, he would like to be called upon."

Four days later, Hoover wrote to Newhouse at his Park Avenue apartment, regretting that he had been unable to attend the party. He offered Sam his "personal appreciation for the splendid cooperation which your various papers have extended our Agents in the field." He ended by inviting Sam to "pay us a visit" on his next trip to Washington.

When Hoover's agents noted that Newhouse had overtaken Scripps Howard to become the nation's second largest newspaper chain—after Hearst—they sounded almost like family as they also noted that in 1951 Sam's estimated worth was $40 million, and that by 1962 it had increased to an estimated $150 to $200 million.

The reassuring memos continued to accumulate in Sam's file. One described friendly approaches made to Hoover by Aaron G. Benesch, then head of the Newhouse Newspapers' Washington bureau, and by Edward O'Brien, Benesch's successor as chief of the *St. Louis Globe-Democrat*'s Washington bureau. Benesch sought permission to bring O'Brien to a meeting he had arranged with Hoover. The memo noted that both Benesch and O'Brien had "cordial relations" with the FBI, that O'Brien had shown a "cooperative attitude." Four years earlier, the memo writer continued, both men met with a top man in the Bureau, and Hoover wrote a "cordial" letter directly to Benesch. O'Brien, it was noted approvingly, "has contacted the Bureau concerning various matters.... On 7/26/55, O'Brien saw Mr. DeLoach [Cartha DeLoach was head of the FBI's Crime Records] and furnished information re Charles Grutzner of the *New York Times* and Grutzner's wife."

Another memo, written on the same day in 1958, noted that Benesch, in making his request to meet Hoover, had also "inquired concerning the possibility of obtaining news items from the Bureau" which he could then use in his column. "Benesch stated that he not only would be interested in light incidents of a human-interest type but should we have any serious current item which we can inject from time to time it would be helpful." An initial supply of such "items" was handed to Benesch on the day of his visit with Hoover.

As the years went on, the Newhouse notices became ever more enthusiastic: "Edward J. Mowery, a staff writer for the *Newark Star-Ledger*," one agent noted, "has prepared a series of articles dealing with the current attack against the Bureau and the Director." (The reference is probably to the *New York Post*'s fifteen-part series on Hoover and the FBI that ran in October 1959. Bureau officials tried to stop the series before publication by contacting the paper's advertisers and, later, by leaking derogatory information about the paper's publisher, Dorothy Schiff, and its editor, James Wechsler.) The Newhouse series, the agent noted, "is receiving prominent attention in newspapers affiliated with the Newhouse chain throughout the country." Mentioned particularly were Sam's papers in Harrisburg and St. Louis. A later memo noted that "Mowery is considered one of our closest newspaper friends and he frequently exposes various activities of the Communist Party and its officials in his articles." The memo also noted that in addition to "numerous cordial contacts" with Mowery, Phil Hochstein, "the number one man of the Newhouse newspaper empire," had also been friendly to the bureau.

Included in Sam Newhouse's FBI file are requests by various Newhouses for tours of FBI headquarters—in 1956 for Mrs. Norman Newhouse and her two children. It was routinely indicated on the memos whether or not a request was made to meet "the Director." "There was no request to meet the Director," it was noted that time. "In view of the importance of the Newhouse chain, it is recommended that an Agent from Crime Records handle this tour."

In 1962 Aaron Benesch called Cartha DeLoach to arrange a tour for Sam, Mitzi, and their ten-year-old grandson, S. I. III. DeLoach noted that Sam "has expressed a desire...to shake hands with Mr. Hoover," and that the Newhouse chain "is exceptionally friendly to the Bureau." Hoover's handwritten notation at the memo's end shows his agreement to meet Sam and his family as a prelude to what DeLoach described as a "very special tour." Hoover followed up by sending Sam photos of the event, and included an autographed photo for "young Sam."

At that meeting the Newhouses were accompanied by Andrew J. Viglietta, a former police reporter for the *Long Island Press,* then covering Washington for the *Press* and the *Long Island Star-Journal,* as well as running the Newhouse Newspapers' Washington bureau as Benesch's successor. Hoover sent Viglietta, who arranged many of the meetings between his boss and Hoover, an autographed photo, and Viglietta wrote a thank you note: "I assure you that it will be one of my prized possessions."

Two years later, Viglietta called again, this time with a request for a tour for Mitzi and ten-year-old Wynn. The fact that "there was no request to meet the Director" was duly noted. On the day of the tour, another memo was written, noting that Wynn "was furnished a silhouette target and some empty shells" and that "no request to meet Mr. Hoover was made today."

Unsubstantiated charges in Sam's file in the form of letters from people accusing him of using the Mafia as his bank and/or of being a Communist were not investigated. One might argue that Sam's eager cooperation might have dampened interest in pursuing these leads, although most were so zany as to defy serious consideration. One lead supplied by Joe McCarthy pal George Sokolsky—his syndicated column appeared in the *St. Louis Globe-Democrat*—linked Sam and Mitzi to a person who was attempting to "break down" wealthy people into developing pro-Communist and pro-Russian sentiment. This person, Sokolsky reported, "took Sam Newhouse and his wife to Russia in 1956 and currently was in Paris with Mrs. Newhouse, buying clothes for her and constantly using pro-Soviet, pro-Communist line."9

7 | Newspaperman?

THE PEOPLE WHO VIEW Samuel I. Newhouse most harshly are those who believe that a newspaper owner must care first about informing the citizenry and second about making money. Sam could never win the approval of this group because he believed first and foremost in making money. In reflecting on his nearly ten years as a reporter for the *Staten Island Advance*, Robert Miraldi, now a professor of journalism, says that when Sam visited the *Advance*, he asked only two questions: "One, Did we make more money last month than the previous month? Two, Is circulation up? What you did to reach those two goals was irrelevant as long as those two goals were reached.... If you had a good editorial product and that made you get there, that was fine, but if you had a lousy editorial product and you still got there, it didn't matter."

Sam Newhouse was not a news junkie. The newspaper business for him consisted of such tasks as personally negotiating ad rates for the Gertz department stores, the *Long Island Press*'s biggest advertiser. One of Gertz's children recalls that Sam was so relentlessly hard-nosed that every time he and Gertz met to negotiate, "My father came home with a migraine headache."

When he was working on the *Time* cover story, Calvin Trillin met one of Sam's grandsons. It was explained to the boy that Trillin was writing a story on his grandfather. "People are always doing stories on him," the boy said. "Why's that?" Trillin asked. "Because he's a newspaperman." Trillin remembers thinking to himself, "Of all the things that people called Sam Newhouse, nobody has ever thought to call him a newspaperman."[1]

S. I. Newhouse wasn't the only newspaper magnate who was indifferent to the editorial side of the paper, as the late Erwin Knoll—during a long career in journalism he worked, for five years, for the Newhouse Washington bureau—pointed out. Knoll called up the name of Frank Munsey, who owned newspapers all over the East Coast in the early years of the twentieth century—a "newspaper killer," Knoll said, who cold-bloodedly merged papers or closed them if their earnings failed to meet his expectations. When Munsey died, William Allen White, the famed editor of the *Emporia* (Kansas) *Gazette*, wrote, "Frank Munsey contributed to the journalism of his day the talent of a meat packer, the morals of a money changer, and the manners of an undertaker. He and his kind have succeeded in transforming a once-noble profession into an eight percent security." The same might have been said, Knoll insisted, about Sam Newhouse.

The reporters and editors who worked for S. I. Newhouse tended to think of him as a kind of bagman who grabbed the cash out of the register. "Once a week Newhouse would blow into town," said Knoll in recalling his colleagues' image of the owner, "walk into the publisher's office, sit down with the books, look at the bottom line, have them fill his suitcase with money, and take off."[2]

Journalists who had worked decades for the papers that constituted Sam's "paper route"—the phrase that Sam used to describe the list of newspapers for which each family member was responsible—hardly ever said more than good morning to him. Part of this was plain lack of interest on Sam's part; the working life of a newspaper reporter held little interest for him. Part of it was his natural reserve. Yet while Sam was not a social person, if approached, he could be perfectly friendly, if an eccentric conversationalist. Knoll remembered a reception in Washington at which he and his wife were introduced to the patriarch. Newhouse looked at Doris Knoll and said, "'You're 34 years old.' She said, 'That's right, how did you know that?' And he said, 'I'm very good at guessing peoples' ages.'"[3]

Sam's personal habits were for the most part austere; the routine of a first-generation Jew in business. He often ate breakfast alone at the counter of Schrafft's. When he visited his papers in Harrisburg, recalls editor Saul

Kohler, he ate lunch—hamburgers usually—in a "terrible greasy spoon" across the street. Mona Mills, who managed the Newhouses' Washington office, dropped a coin on the floor. She went to pick it up and almost fell over Sam. "He was crouched down there picking it up. I said, 'Good Lord,' and he said, 'Waste not, want not,' and he put it in his pocket."[4]

He had no pretensions, no affectations. He was simply a man who knew how to make money, enjoyed making money, hoped to pass that talent along to his sons, and hoped that they would never forget that his fortune was built on hard work. There was nothing magic about it, just hard work. When at 6:05 A.M. he stepped into a chauffeured Cadillac limousine, license SN—the car was, besides Mitzi, his one personal indulgence—he entered a gritty, tough, and decidedly unglamorous world.

The frugal patriarch traveled among his papers alone, never with an assistant or secretary. He kept no corporate headquarters. He took his front office with him, a battered black briefcase in which he'd stowed the latest financial reports from each paper and a pile of what he called "problems," knotty situations at one paper or another that he focused on until he solved. There were no files, no budgets, no corporate officers, no board of directors. It was always just Sam and his brothers, and, starting in the 1950s, his sons. Si would meet Norman in Cleveland every Thursday, and would accompany his father to St. Louis once a month. Donald started by accompanying his father on the Thursday visits to Harrisburg, and accompanying Ted to the papers in Birmingham and Huntsville.

Every month these Newhouses received reports covering all the numbers for all the papers. Sam would digest the contents and toss the paper. So flawless was his memory that, months later, he could regurgitate the columns line by line. He even memorized the financial facts of every newspaper in the country that he might, some day, want to own.

Then–managing editor Bob Notson realized just how flawless the owner's memory was when Sam visited Portland in May 1952, shortly after he bought the *Oregonian*. (The paper was on Ted's route, but Sam came on occasion.) The owner made the rounds of the various department heads, eventually stopping at Notson's desk. He began to ask Notson questions "rapid-fire." One of them was about the *Oregonian*'s role not only as a paper serving Portland but as a regional paper serving the northwest. "I indicated that in some cases we even competed fairly well in circulation with papers as far off as Vancouver. He said, 'Oh, is that so?'" Notson assured him that it was. Sam asked to see the figures.

"So I dug into my desk for the circulation figures and began trying to sort the thing out, and I was quickly embarrassed because the figures didn't bear me out." Sam, looking slightly impatient, but not angry, said, "'Well, never mind. The figures are this,' and he proceeded to quote out of memory what they were. So he knew already." Notson recalls vowing to himself, "I'll never give S. I. Newhouse a glib answer again. I'll be sure."

When his lawyers sent him memos, Newhouse senior would read and destroy them. And he rarely committed himself to paper. Ben Magdovitz, who worked for Sam for more than twenty years, said that in all that time he never received a single letter from the boss.[5]

In 1976, when the patriarch finally submitted to a cover story interview with *Business Week*, the reporter asked what titles his brothers held. "I couldn't really tell you," Sam replied. And so, declared *Business Week*, "The vast publishing and broadcasting empire of Samuel I. Newhouse seems to be run with all the managerial finesse of a family-operated corner grocery store." Once asked in a deposition to state his business address, Sam replied that he didn't have one. "I don't have an office. I just go from place to place. I use a desk, so I would have to give you twenty-odd addresses." He also worked in the back of the Cadillac. One Staten Islander remembers seeing him at the same time every Tuesday en route to the *Advance*, as his car pulled off the bridge. If Sam wasn't on the telephone—he had one of the early car phones—he had his head buried in his financials spread on the backseat.

When visiting that day's designated paper, Sam made the rounds of department heads, calling on them in their own offices, believing that the boss learned more when he went to the other guy. The department heads would talk, and Sam would take notes on little pieces of scratch paper, folded in quarters, using a stubby pencil that he pulled from his pocket. He might ask the executive a question, and if the answer required any research, Sam would be sure to bring the subject up at the next meeting. "When he said something," recalls Ben Magdovitz, "you put it in the bank. He never forgot what he said.... You could bet your last month's salary that he'd be asking you about that next time."[6]

As Sam walked into his newspapers, he seemed a figure of almost comic inconsequence. Paul Keil recalls one day in the city room at Newhouse's *Long Island Star-Journal* (Sam closed the paper in 1968) in Long Island City as deadline approached. Keil looked up from his work and noticed a small man sitting quietly on a bench in the back of the room. "I looked up fifteen minutes later and he was still there, and I was curious because I thought I recognized him from a distance. I walked closer and it was S. I. Newhouse." Keil asked a copy boy why Newhouse was sitting there, and didn't he know that he owned the paper. The copy boy replied that the paper's editor had given him strict instructions not to disturb him until the edition was finished. "I think it's all right in this case," Keil told him, "and I went up to him and I said, 'Mr. Newhouse, I have to apologize, the new copy boy didn't recognize you.'" Smiling shyly, the owner of the paper said, "That's fine. I just didn't want to disturb anybody."

This diffident quality stunned his staff. Donald Bacon, a reporter for the Newhouses in Washington, recalls that Sam would stop by the office and ask the secretary, without identifying himself, "Would it be all right if I used the telephone?"[7]

But those who thought that Sam's self-effacing manner signaled weakness were badly mistaken. Labor union organizers by the score could attest that Newhouse was as tough on unions as any owner in the business; maybe as tough as any owner in the history of American journalism.

When, as a college freshman in 1945, Sam's elder son described himself in a letter to Allard Lowenstein as having turned to the right, he gave no clearer evidence than his denunciation of the strikers who had closed down newspapers in New York: "While I'm on national events, thank god the news strike is over. There was as disgraceful a business as I've ever seen. Imagine 3,000 fugitives from a chain gang, keeping 17,000,000 people from reading newspapers. They all should have been thrown in jail." He worried about "CIO communists…grab[bing] control of the party and turn[ing] it into a [hotbed] of extreme leftish, communists and socialists controlled by labor."

Some of Si's attitude was surely acquired at home, just as some of Sam's hostility toward unions was likely a reaction to his own father's fervent and completely opposite belief in the right of workers to organize. For Meyer

Newhouse, unionism was as close to religion as he ever came. But Sam Newhouse went 360 degrees the other way and remained a foe of newspaper unions all his professional life. He believed that the unions were responsible for weakening and even killing newspapers, that on the production side especially featherbedding was notorious; that they made it impossible for an owner to make a decent profit and plow money back into the paper. Sam once wrote that "busting" unions was not something he enjoyed, but, "I refuse to stand by passively and allow any union to 'bust' me." He said that "to yield to others the controls that are vital to your own security is suicide."

The patriarch always tried to prevent his workers from organizing. And when he bought a newspaper that already had a union in place, he worked hard to emasculate it. His modus operandi on buying a paper was first to modernize the production facilities with labor-saving devices. He was, for instance, the first newspaper magnate to convert to cold type and, among his competitors, one of the first to automate mail rooms. Once all the innovations were in place, he would turn his attention to cutting the workforce. The unions, logically, resisted any cuts, and sometimes a walkout or a strike resulted; almost always the relationship between workers and management was poisoned.

One top executive at a Newhouse paper, the unionized *St. Louis Globe-Democrat*, still sounds angry when he describes newspapers as "the most featherbedded operations in America. The railroads were kindergartens compared to the featherbedding in the newspapers." He defends Sam as a man who wanted only "a fair day's work" and wasn't getting it. Ben Magdovitz agrees: "If a union...did their jobs, Newhouse was the easiest guy in the world to work with.... If they didn't, look out.... He was ruthless. He would just stomp 'em to death."[8]

Early in his career, in the 1930s, Sam showed just how ruthless he could be when he tried to prevent the newly formed Newspaper Guild, representing mostly editorial employees, from getting its foot in the door of his newsrooms on Staten Island and Long Island. By demanding the same contract for reporters on these essentially suburban papers as the contract they had insisted on at the metropolitan dailies, guild leaders were, Sam believed, deliberately provoking a fight. They were using him and his papers to establish their union.

The owner was particularly wary of forty-four-year-old Heywood Broun, a columnist for the *New York World Telegram,* and the guild's feisty, fearless president. Sam would later accuse Broun of making "a guinea pig of the *[Long Island] Press.*" Broun, coincidentally a graduate of Horace Mann ('06), went on to Harvard and then to the *New York Morning Telegraph,* the *New York Herald Tribune,* and finally to the *World,* where he wrote his increasingly left-leaning column, "It Seems to Me."

In 1934, a year after the guild's founding, and in one of its first attempts to organize, Broun and his lieutenants targeted the newsroom of the *Staten Island Advance.* Sam immediately fired the twenty-eight-year-old editorial writer Alexander Crosby, whom he considered the ringleader of the organizing effort—few believed Sam and Norman Newhouse when they denied that Crosby's guild activities had anything to do with his firing—and Sam held his ground, despite embarrassing picketing and harassment at his Staten Island home.

That summer he had taken Mitzi on the European honeymoon that he had promised her when they married ten years before. While he was away, guild members from other chapters passed out leaflets to Sam and Mitzi's neighbors, and picketed the *Advance*'s offices, as well as both terminals of the Manhattan–Staten Island ferry. Broun and Crosby took to the radio to urge readers to boycott the *Advance.* A sound truck traveled Staten Island's streets, presenting the guild's point of view and vilifying Sam Newhouse.

Broun proved relentless in his attempts to embarrass Sam, and he knew just how to get to Mitzi. As Cunard's *Aquitania* pulled into New York Harbor on August 24, carrying Sam and Mitzi back from their "honeymoon," it was met by a barrage of megaphone-amplified, Newhouse-bashing slogans. And there was Broun, in all his disheveled glory—Alexander Woollcott once compared the appearance of the messily groomed and dressed Broun to that of "an unmade bed"—approaching the liner in a pilot boat. Broun and a delegation were actually allowed to board the liner to ask Sam to reinstate Crosby, while above, a small plane flew the message, "Back the Guild." Other union men piloted their motorboat in circles around the *Aquitania,* shouting anti-Newhouse slogans through megaphones. Mitzi was humiliated in front of the well-heeled and -bred passengers she had been courting during the crossing.

Additional picketers awaited them on the pier, and that night, at Sam and Mitzi's house, a blaring sound truck and a spotlight trained on their windows prevented sleep. But Sam Newhouse won his fight, and the union never took root. Having failed to start a competing daily, the union slowed the picketing and in a matter of weeks stopped it altogether.[9]

It wasn't until the 1960s that another attempt to organize at the *Advance* was made, but that too was derailed. Robert Miraldi remembers an encounter with publisher Richard Diamond just around that time that brought home to him just how antiunion the Newhouses were. Diamond had stopped by the coffee machine that was located alongside the newsroom. Miraldi and another reporter were talking about a newspaper strike in New York City. Not wanting to be rude, Miraldi briefed the publisher on their conversation and wondered aloud if, when the strike was settled, they would take back the strikers. Diamond narrowed his eyes, "looked at both of us, and said, 'Never. You never take them back. People strike, you never, never take them back.' He just walked away, and that was the end of the conversation."

The paper's unwritten policy, Miraldi claims, was even tougher. "If you left the paper and wanted to come back and had gone to a union newspaper, it was simply not possible." Miraldi and others did at times leave the *Advance* to go back to school. They were always welcomed back. But one reporter who left to join the *New York Post,* a union paper, and then decided he wanted to return was not allowed to, even when he offered to accept a lower salary.[10]

On some of Newhouse's nonunion papers, salaries were kept at levels comparable to those offered by union papers. That was not the case at the *Advance,* where salaries were ludicrously low. Miraldi remembers *Advance* managing editor Les Trautmann whispering in the ear of a reporter, "You'll find five dollars more in your check next week, but don't tell anyone what your raise is." On receiving a similar confidence from Trautmann, Robert Keeler shouted across the newsroom, "No, I won't find five dollars more; I'll find a hundred dollars more because I'm leaving for *Newsday.*"[11]

In 1934 Heywood Broun turned his charismatic presence to the *Long Island Press.* This time Sam lost, and he felt betrayed when the editorial staff voted to affiliate with the guild. He thought that he had made life relatively better for its reporters since buying the paper two years earlier.

Harry Selden, then a reporter at the *Press*, enjoying his first newspaper job, says that Sam had a point. Although Selden joined the union, he didn't like what happened next. "Broun came in and started throwing his weight around, demanding higher pay.... Before I knew it, we were on strike. I couldn't understand the rationale. Before Newhouse bought the paper, it operated with a minimal editorial core, and a large contingent of young stringers. [Stringers, or people who work for space rates, are paid on the basis of copy published, no matter how long they work to write the copy; if their copy isn't used, they are paid nothing.] Newhouse hired more regulars and cut out the stringers." Not surprisingly, adds Selden, Newhouse's response was, "Fine, you want the guild, we'll go back to the old stringer [system]. I'll fire more than half the staff."

The guild's appeal to the *Press* reporters was simple, as expressed in a guild flyer: "Lineotypers get $60 to $80 a week because they are organized. Reporters get $15 to $30 because they are not. Lineotypers work seven hours a day; reporters nine or ten or more."

Phil Hochstein, then the *Press*'s managing editor, assumed the role of controlling the unions at all Sam's papers. During one acrimonious meeting, Hochstein called members of the editorial staff ungrateful, given his efforts to eliminate sweatshop conditions. In a report in the guild *Bulletin*, Hochstein was described as "a friend of the workers and has plugged hard for organization rights in other fields." When Broun, who knew of Hochstein's socialist past, asked him whether "he would sacrifice his job rather than carry out orders against which he was opposed in principle and belief," Hochstein refused to answer. (He did, however, on a hot day on the *Press* picket line, send Broun a pitcher of cold beer.) So although Hochstein maintained his role as the chain's editorial guru, he also came to be seen as Sam's "hatchet man" to keep the unions down.

In July 1934 eight of the nine women on the society pages of the *Press* joined the guild. They were the first and, for a time, the only employees to publicly affiliate. May Spencer Vecsey, society editor from 1933 to 1939, recalls that it was a reporter and union booster named Jack Ryan who persuaded the society writers to join. The strategy, apparently devised by guild activists, was to sign up the women first because it was thought that they would be less likely to fall victim to Sam's wrath and retribution.

The strategy backfired when the women—"the most helpless people," says Vecsey—were informed that their jobs would be eliminated and their section placed on a space basis. Hochstein informed their male colleagues that they could save the jobs of these "fledglings" by resigning from the guild. If they disbanded the guild chapter, Hochstein promised the *Press*'s older, male newsman, they could "protect the innocent lambs...they had led to slaughter." The men voted to disband.

The society women were out for only a day, but by then Newhouse had seized the momentum, hardening in attitude and resolve, and the union backers had lost their nerve. The guild picketed for four days, but used volunteers from other chapters, because, as Daniel J. Leab, a Columbia University professor who wrote a history of the formation of the guild, wrote, "a picket line composed only of *Press* guildsmen would have been an unimpressive sight." The guild charged Newhouse with "terrorist opposition" and observed, "Of all the New York newspapers on which the organization movement has taken place—and virtually all have experienced it good humoredly—only one has openly challenged this right and coercively opposed it."

By the middle of that month, 1934, Mayor Fiorello La Guardia called Sam Newhouse and Heywood Broun to City Hall, where after meeting for three hours, the owner agreed to recognize the employees' right to form a guild chapter and Broun agreed to recognize that pay scales at suburban papers could not match those at the metropolitan dailies. Although Newhouse promised not to fire employees for union activity, few believed him, and employees stayed quiet for the next few years.

But Heywood Broun had not finished with Sam Newhouse. Four years later, in 1938, the guild struck the *Long Island Press* with ferocity. Josephine Phillips and her late husband Bill, then a reporter and rewrite man at the *Press*, spent part of their courtship on the picket line. She claims that when the strike ended, "management began firing active Guildsmen wherever possible. On May 21, 1938, when I had got myself tenured [as a teacher in New Jersey] and Bill still had a job, we were married. On May 23 he was fired. 'Newhouse' was never a nice word in our household."

May Spencer Vecsey says that both she and her husband were fired after the strike. Her pregnancy, she claims, was used as an excuse to get rid of her. Norman Newhouse gave her a letter of recommendation that merely confirmed that she had worked from such and such a date until such and such a date—"no praise for me at all," she says, bitterness still clinging to her voice nearly sixty years later. Her husband, a sports reporter—their son, George Vecsey, is a sports columnist for the *New York Times*—was transferred to Newark, where he lasted a short time.

Another weapon Sam Newhouse tried to use against the Newspaper Guild was the assertion that its membership was riddled with Communists. Even those like May Vecsey, who in time supported the guild wholeheartedly, agree that Newhouse was partly correct on this point. She says that her own husband "joined the Communist party while he was at the *Press*, but he went to one meeting, he never did any work. It was the thing to do at the time." She describes herself as having started out "not very enthusiastic about the Newspaper Guild or communism or anything of that sort. I was a graduate of a Catholic college.... I was conservative." For the neighbors to see her on a picket line, Vecsey says, "was a disgrace."

What changed her mind about the guild, she insists, was Newhouse's treatment of her and her colleagues. It was when the paper's managing editor "put out a notice of all the terrible things we had done, ...none of which were true, and when I read that, I was furious, and I can remember walking on a picket line and shaking my fist."

Jackie Gebhard, who later went to work at *Newsday*, was May Vecsey's successor as society editor. Gebhard recalls that when she joined the picket line, her mother, a "Catholic boarding school graduate," disowned her. "For somebody, her daughter, to be picketing was just a family disgrace, ...plain bad manners."[12]

On Long Island, even though the union was entrenched, Newhouse did what he could to emasculate it. Employees who showed the slightest interest were punished so swiftly and severely that the connection could not be missed. One talented reporter, working for the *Press* in the mid 1950s for $54 a week, plus a Christmas bonus of $12.50 (after taxes), recalls making "the mistake of going to a guild meeting.... I just went to find out what it was all about, and the word got back and I was then in purgatory." He has no hard evidence but remains convinced that it was Newhouse's brother Norman, then editor of the *Press,* who assigned him "to the desk on nightside." He soon left the paper and newspaper journalism, and calls his exit "not a pleasant parting."

Newhouse and his brothers tried any and all angles to avoid having to pay reporters union scale. They operated the ABC News Service, located above a butcher shop on Jamaica Avenue around the corner from the *Press.* Presided over by the popular Barney Confessore of Floral Park, Queens, whom Karl Grossman describes as "an absolute angel," ABC seemed to have no purpose other than to bypass the union. John Maher, who was hired to open a news bureau in Suffolk County, calls it "a subterfuge to avoid putting people on the *Press* payroll"—i.e. to avoid paying them union scale, and also to avoid giving them pension benefits.

Maher recalls his own hiring: "I talked salary with [*Press* editor Dave] Starr, and about hours and duties and everything else as though the *Long Island Press* was hiring me. And then Starr said, 'Oh, by the way, you have to go across the street and around the corner and talk to Barney Confessore at ABC News.' And I thought that was radio or television. I never heard of ABC News." So he went over to talk to Confessore, "and it turned out that I was actually being hired by the ABC News Company and of course that meant we were not members of the guild and we were paid at a lower scale."

When Maher became Nassau/Suffolk editor, he was put on the *Press* payroll, but reporters working in Nassau and Suffolk were routinely hired by ABC. It was only the Queens reporters—Karl Grossman estimates them at 25 percent of the total—who were on the books as working for the *Press* and who received guild wages. ABC reporters could not get their byline in the *Press*'s Queens edition, Grossman adds, "partly because of the union regulation."

Grossman went to work for the *Press* in 1964 as a police reporter for Suffolk County. He was hired by ABC at $98 a week plus a sixth day of overtime, but was paid at the straight rather than overtime rate, bringing his weekly pay to around $128. Eventually Grossman also made it to the *Press* payroll and a substantial salary boost. He had won some journalism awards, and it became awkward for the paper to identify him as an ABC reporter. He remained the only Nassau/Suffolk reporter on the *Press* payroll.[13]

Until the government forced the Newhouses to offer some benefits, pensions and medical insurance were scarce at Sam's papers. Employees at the *Long Island Press,* for example, learned to their horror in the mid-1970s, in a memo from management, that the paper had no real pension plan but rather "an understanding based on the St. Louis [*Globe-Democrat*] plan." According to Leo Meindl, a thirty-year veteran of the *Press,* the purpose of that "legally worded" note to employees was to inform them that they could contribute to the government's just-launched IRA program, "because we do not have a pension plan, we have an understanding based on the St. Louis plan."

But outside official channels, the Newhouses could be generous. Leo Meindl remembers reporters going to Norman for help. Almost always Norman would reply, "Hey, listen, I'll give you a loan, no interest." The same was true at the *Advance,* where reporter Terry Golway asked Dick Diamond for an interest-free loan to buy a car, and Diamond okayed it. The loans, observes Robert Miraldi, were a means, in effect, of buying loyalty.

In another case, the widow of a longtime *Advance* employee was left financially strapped because her husband had no pension. According to a former Newhouse employee who knows the family, "She called the Newhouses and they immediately deposited some grand sum on her." At another of the papers the publisher died suddenly, and at his funeral Sam asked the man who was to replace him how the widow was "fixed financially.... I told him I didn't think she was very well off." Sam told him to "take care of her, as long as she needs it, and if she needs money for those children to go to school, you pay it, and if she needs money to live, you pay it." (Typically, the deceased's son-in-law and his son were both given jobs at Newhouse papers.)

It is this behavior that Sam's admirers cite again and again—the generosity to employees or widows in need. They tend not to focus on the reason for the need. The owner may have had a soft heart, but not necessarily when it came to providing all his employees with the basic protections of life.[14]

One of the fiercest fights Newhouse had with labor came in the city of St. Louis. Jack Flach, who arrived at the *Globe-Democrat* in 1951, four years before it became a Newhouse paper, recalls that "St. Louis was a real intense labor town in the 1950s," and the guild was firmly in place. The owner's reputation as a union-hater had preceded him and, says Flach, "The Newspaper Guild started warning everybody, 'Be prepared.'"

Newhouse was greeted with mixed feelings, however, because the paper, under its aging, ailing, and heirless owner, E. Lansing Ray, was in such poor shape that the betting was on the *Globe-Democrat* dying with its owner. That would give the Pulitzer family, which owned the *St. Louis Post-Dispatch*, the gift of a monopoly paper. When S. I. arrived in 1955 with the cash to buy the *Globe*—he paid a mere $6.5 million for the paper and its building—the paper's executives saw him as a savior, "a strong, financially secure owner," said one, whose presence would keep the paper alive.

Four years later, in 1959, any feelings of gratitude gave way to concern about the lack of a pension plan. The result was a bitter strike. Ominously for the paper's future, one week after the strike started, Newhouse sold the *Globe*'s building, presses included, to the *Post-Dispatch*. When the strike ended ninety-nine days later, the guild won a vested pension for its members but lost a great deal more. The remaining *Globe* employees—the services of the pressmen and printers were no longer needed—returned to work in vastly inferior quarters, a couple of floors in a bedraggled railway exchange building. The paper was no longer printed on its own presses, but rather on a fee-per-page basis by the *Post-Dispatch*. (The papers thus kept one set of presses going full-time, instead of two going part-time.) Reliance on its competitor's presses meant that the *Globe* had to discontinue its Sunday paper—traditionally a paper's profit center due to its outsized advertising revenue—because one set of presses could not have handled the printing of two Sunday papers.

Meanwhile, Newhouse was making back far more than his $6.7 million investment. Not only did he realize a fat profit when he sold the Globe's building and presses to the *Post*, but when E. Lansing Ray died of a heart attack in 1955, the same year Sam bought the paper, Ray left a life insurance policy worth a million dollars, with the *Globe-Democrat* as its sole beneficiary. Richard Meeker estimates that Sam netted "approximately $15 million during his first six years of ownership of the *Globe*."

On buying the *Globe*, Newhouse's goal, as usual, was to buy the *Post-Dispatch*, keep it alive for a time, and then fold it into the *Globe-Democrat*.

But, says one *Globe-Democrat* executive, the stock, "was so closely held in the family, he couldn't make any headway."

When the owner realized that his usual route was blocked, he devised an alternate plan and executed it under the table. Not even the guild, so suspicious of Sam Newhouse, figured it out until years later.

In 1960 Sam made a deal with Joe Pulitzer that all but guaranteed that St. Louis, like so many other cities, would eventually have one newspaper. Under the agreement, effective at the start of 1961, the papers would share not only presses but also profits and losses. Robert A. Steinke, who became executive secretary of the St. Louis Newspaper Guild in 1968, discovered the deal a year or two later and obtained copies of the original agreement and subsequent amendments. He put the word out to the guild's underpaid members at the *Globe-Democrat* that because the two papers were pooling profits, *Globe* employees were entitled to the same pay as their counterparts at the *Post-Dispatch*.

That the profit and loss-sharing deal was deliberately kept secret, said Erwin Knoll, was "particularly despicable." J. Kenneth Beaver, who had been a reporter for the Newhouses's *Harrisburg Patriot* before leaving in 1958 for the *Globe-Democrat*, refers to the agreement—eventually described in Senate hearings held by the late Democrat Philip A. Hart—as "shenanigans between the two papers" completed "under subterfuge."[15]

The agreement lessened the incentive to compete, but that did not stop Newhouse from striving to be the survivor in St. Louis. Publisher Dick Amberg came in determined to let the sleepy town know that he had arrived, and that he had a team of excellent reporters. Amberg took a paper that, according to Morton Mintz, who worked there in the 1950s before leaving for the *Washington Post*, was "essentially an arm of the Catholic church," and transformed it into a paper that, in Mintz's opinion, "beat the crap out of the *Post-Dispatch* on local news."

Newhouse's admirers at the St. Louis paper, and he had many, particularly on the business side, remain convinced that he would be able to persuade Pulitzer to fold. At dinner once with Ben Magdovitz, Sam responded eagerly to Magdovitz's desire to "kill" the competition. "I've never seen him get so excited, he hit his knee and said, 'That's the way I like to hear you talking.'"[16]

But no matter how well the *Globe-Democrat* performed, forces beyond the control of its excellent staff would lead, inexorably, to the *Globe*'s death. It is no exaggeration to observe that by going on strike and prompting Sam to make these deals with Joe Pulitzer, the *Globe-Democrat*'s employees had, in a sense, signed their paper's death warrant.

In 1959, while Newhouse was outmaneuvering the unions in St. Louis, his employees at the *Portland Oregonian* went out on strike. Not only was this strike as bitter as the one in St. Louis, it was also violent. It started with management's insistence on installing a labor-saving machine to cast plates for the presses—the first at any American newspaper. Union leaders insisted that once the machine was installed, staffing levels remain the same. Negotiations went nowhere. Newhouse hoped that the other unions, the guild especially, wouldn't support the stereotypers' demands, but they did. S. I. was determined to continue publishing even if all the unions walked out.

Officials at the *Oregon Journal,* which Newhouse would buy two years later, agreed—strangely, many thought—to support the *Oregonian* in the event of a strike. Together they published under the name *Oregonian-Oregon Journal,* with the help of some outsiders, but mostly with supervisors in the advertising and circulation departments who had been surreptitiously trained, late at night, to operate the equipment. Getting the paper out was difficult at first but, as time passed, became almost routine. The credit went mainly to Don Newhouse, a younger first cousin of Sam's, who was the *Oregonian*'s production manager and as such had trained the strikebreakers to print the paper.

Then, one Sunday afternoon in October 1960, someone—never apprehended—fired a shotgun through Don Newhouse's window as he worked in the basement shop of his house. The shot pierced his hip. Slowly, he recovered most—but not all—of the use of his leg. The surgeon decided not to remove the pellets lodged in his hip because some were so deep that removing them would damage muscle. (Don remained at the *Oregonian* for a while, but at Sam's request moved to Springfield, Massachusetts, to help build a new plant for Newhouse's papers there. While there, he died suddenly after some of the pellets worked their way into his bloodstream and to his heart.)

The wounding of Don Newhouse and the blowing up of several delivery trucks caused the union to lose sympathy and support—two-thirds of guild members, for example, eventually came back. According to Bob Notson, "the strike just simmered down to a holding operation, and they kept on picketing for five years before they gave up."[17]

S. I. Newhouse always put his toughest people in charge of keeping the unions in check. To Cleveland, where the Newspaper Guild local was very strong and proudly sported the badge of being Guild #1, Sam dispatched a tough Newark native named Leo Ring. Ring had worked for Sam in Newark, St. Louis, and Birmingham, accumulating nearly forty years of service to the family. He was a small, unassuming-looking man, ostensibly in charge of the physical plant. But he had more to do. In an FBI document obtained under the Freedom of Information Act, a "source" informed an FBI agent that every month, for several years, Leo Ring handed one thousand dollars in cash to one Carmen Parise, a local official of the Teamsters union, allegedly a "kickback" from the *Plain Dealer* for "concessions made" in negotiations between Parise's union and "the publishers" of the *Plain Dealer*. The paper's publisher, Tom Vail, denied the above in an interview with a reporter from the *Washington Journalism Review*.

Thomas van Husen Vail, an Episcopalian and a cum laude graduate of Princeton, was a member of the Cleveland WASP establishment— White sewing machine money on his side and Standard Oil of Ohio money on his wife's—and of the family from which Sam bought the paper in 1967. A fixture on various boards in town, Vail was the public face of the paper, a figurehead with little power. He had the title of publisher and editor, but the Newhouses didn't bother much with him, while Leo Ring, a convert from Judaism to Catholicism and a graduate of grade school, had all the power and access to Sam and to Norman, with whom he was particularly close. According to Jim Neff, a former investigative reporter for the *Plain Dealer*, Ring was known as "Tom Vail's boss," the man who ran the unions, the money, the contracts.

Vail was known as a pompous man who used his title to hobnob with governors and presidents and who coveted having his picture in the society pages. Many of his reporters and editors saw him as a "gadfly," and, in his column, as a terrible name-dropper. But Sam had closed the deal with the Vail family by promising that Tom Vail could keep the title of publisher and editor as long as he liked. The patriarch reportedly also had to agree that the *Plain Dealer's* Washington bureau could remain in its old National Press Building offices, that it would never have to move into the Newhouses' Washington bureau.[18]

As always, Sam did what he needed to do to break down the barriers to his buying a particular paper. In the case of the *Plain Dealer*, it was promising Vail a job for life. Besides, retaining a member of an old Cleveland family with ties to the city's top echelon was good for business. Sam Newhouse displayed his iron discipline when it came to putting up with the likes of a Tom Vail. He maintained that discipline by never taking his eye off the one thing that, to him, mattered most—the bottom line.

8 | The Secrets of Sam's Success

IN THE MID-1970s *More*, a respected and spunky journalism review, published a list of the ten worst papers in the United States. Three of them belonged to the Newhouses: the *Cleveland Plain Dealer*, the *New Orleans Times-Picayune*, and the *St. Louis Globe-Democrat*.

But veterans of the Newhouse organization had their own choices as to the worst paper in the chain. *The Jersey Journal* got Erwin Knoll's vote. "It was so bad as to be record-breaking bad." Jimmy Breslin, who started his career at the *Long Island Press* ("the worst paper in the world," he said), once described a bookie who set up shop every afternoon in the newsroom of the *Jersey Journal*. He came in, sat himself down at a desk, used the phone, and took his bets. That, Breslin concluded, said more about the state of the newspaper business in America than a whole year's subscription to *Editor & Publisher*, the trade magazine for people in the newspaper business.

The *Newark Star-Ledger* had its own alumni group who argued loudly, even proudly, that its paper was the worst in the chain. When Nat Brandt worked there in the late 1950s, he interviewed the governor and, on orders of the city editor, asked about a pending highway referendum bill. The governor told Brandt that he supported it. On returning to the newsroom, the city editor asked Brandt the governor's position, and when he found out that he was in favor of the bill, ordered Brandt to "write that he's against the bill." The city editor explained, as if it were a legitimate reason, "We've got an editorial in galley already that knocks him for being against it, and we're running it tomorrow." Brandt did as he was told, and the governor never spoke to him again.[1]

That S. I. Newhouse's papers were mostly mediocre should have surprised no one. At most Newhouse papers, the editors worked for the publishers. The line between church and state was blurred. Sam's biographer, Richard Meeker, observes that Newhouse's editors "recognize themselves for what they are, which is delivery people for advertising." The goal was to employ the minimum number of editors needed to deliver that advertising.

Frugality—cheapness really—was the chain's byword. Mel Elfin recalls once turning in an expense report at the *Press* for an interview he did with a student at Queens College. The 60-cent total covered round-trip bus fare to the college and two cokes, one of which he bought for the student. He was reimbursed for 45 cents and given the explanation, "You always have a Coke in the afternoon." Things were so tight, says Elfin, that when the great liner the *Andrea Doria* went down, "You had to get permission to call Montauk Point." When a passenger plane crashed on Long Island, the *Press*'s city editor pointed to a reporter and ordered him to rush to the scene, specifying that he could take a taxi.

Jules Witcover worked for the Newhouses in Washington at a time when the Christmas bonus amounted to about $5 a year for every year of service. Then a case arose in which an employee of another company had received a bonus over a number of years, until the employer decided one year not to give a bonus. The employee took his boss to court, arguing successfully that bonuses had been given for so long as to form a pattern, so that the employee could logically see the bonus as part of his pay. Witcover's next Christmas bonus carried a disclaimer printed on a little white card, the essence of which Witcover recites from memory: "It is not to our taste in this season of the year to wish you anything but the most joyous greetings of the season. However, our attorneys advise us that we must inform you that this is a one-time expression of our gratitude, not to be construed as a part of your salary."

What Newhouse editorial people lacked in salary was not made up in perks or comfortable working conditions. In the early days, says Witcover, the Washington reporters from five Newhouse papers "felt like inmates, ...tiny office in the National Press Building," presided over by Andrew J. Viglietta, the man who had brought together Sam and J. Edgar

Hoover, and who also covered Washington for Sam's Long Island papers. Each reporter, recalls Witcover, was expected to produce five or six stories a day and then put them on the teletype themselves, working until 7:00 or 8:00 P.M. Viglietta would take each one aside and say, "You're gonna find an extra $5 in your pay check this week. Don't tell the other fellas."[2]

The one area that the Newhouse newspapers covered completely was local news. "Local" was a Sam Newhouse watchword. Even the *Newark Star-Ledger*, the largest paper in the chain, devoted a massive number of columns to local sports and clubs and boards. James Warren, a reporter for the *Star-Ledger* from 1974 to 1977 (he now heads the *Chicago Tribune*'s Washington bureau), says that the paper rarely covered anything outside the state of New Jersey, including New York City.* But the *Staten Island Advance* was perhaps the most parochial of all. "If you had sewerage backing up into your house," recalls Robert Miraldi, "the *Advance* would send a photographer and a reporter because it was a city sewer line."

That several of his papers were the biggest, most dominant in their states—the *Star-Ledger* in New Jersey, the *Times-Picayune* in Louisiana, the *Plain Dealer* in Ohio, the *Oregonian*—was beside the point. Sam Newhouse cared little about exerting influence on issues of statewide or national importance. He kept his papers so local, so parochial, that not even the people back home, much less the powers that be in the state capitals or in Washington, knew who owned them. None of Sam's papers carried a company logo. "Newhouse had a real aversion to putting his name on anything," Erwin Knoll explained. "The newspapers were never referred to as the Newhouse papers, and unless he had a relative on the masthead, there was no way of telling. You can tell the Scripps Howard papers by the lighthouse that's part of the logo, and Hearst was never shy about identifying his newspapers, but Newhouse tried to keep his name hidden."[3]

*Warren notes that Sam Newhouse was "way ahead of the curve" in this focus on local news. Today "elite" papers such as the *Washington Post* and his own *Chicago Tribune* are "scrambling to follow suit, ...harnessing more resources to cover their own backyards, zealously zoning editions, ...and using armies of stringers to handle prep sports."

Newhouse preferred secrecy about his chain for several reasons, among them, as will be shown later, a desire to keep the Internal Revenue Service out of his complicated financial affairs and a desire not to pique the interest of senators and congressmen in the question of whether he might own too many newspapers for the public's good.

Through their Washington correspondents, the Newhouses courted members of congressional delegations representing districts in which the family had newspapers. One former *Long Island Press* reporter goes so far as to call the paper's Washington bureau during his years at the *Press* in the mid-1950s, a bureau of "hacks, liaisons with the local congressmen if Newhouse needed a favor. That was the point of having the Washington bureau." Bill Howard, who worked in the Washington bureau, charges that the Washington correspondents for the Newhouse papers were in collusion with congressmen and their staffs. "They used to write absolute valentine stories"—stories changed little, if at all, from the congressmen's press releases.

When Paul Keil left the newspaper business to go into public relations, one of his first assignments was to boost the scandal-scarred image of single-family home developers on Long Island. He planned a meeting between the developers and the members of Congress representing Long Island, and sent out invitations to the congressmen. When not a single one accepted, Keil asked Norman Newhouse to help. Norman called the *Press*'s Andy Viglietta in Washington and told him, "You tell them I want them all there." Promptly, they all accepted the invitation.[4]

Most men who own major newspapers or newspaper chains, and especially those who build rather than inherit them, become public and public-minded figures. If the newspaper is a public trust, then its owner is a man who is somehow answerable to the citizenry, who is expected to care about and comment on the issues of the day. No part of the above description fits Sam Newhouse. "I have no temptation to express my political views," he once said. "I'm not trying to save the world." He studiously avoided the spotlight. Indeed, he used the flashy Mitzi to divert attention from himself.

Sam easily could have become a leader in the newspaper industry, but he didn't want to be a leader. During his long career, he gave one, maybe two, public speeches. And at the most likely forum, the American Newspaper Publishers Association meeting, he never once addressed his fellow owners, nor did he attend any of the organization's sessions. It was enough for him to greet the publishers of his own papers, exhort them to hire their relatives, and sit down.

Sam was exactly the opposite of the Grahams of the *Washington Post,* the Chandlers of the *Los Angeles Times,* and the Sulzbergers of the *New York Times.* These were articulate people who had built impressive public personas. Sam was tongue-tied, awkward with strangers, inept at small talk, and completely lacking a public image.[5]

Over the years, Sam routinely refused requests for interviews from such mass-circulation magazines of the time as the *Saturday Evening Post* and *Collier's.* But there did come a time when he began to realize that his invisibility might hinder him in his primary goal in life—buying newspapers—and that his image needed editing. So in 1948 he turned to public relations man Ray Josephs.

A. J. Liebling, who wrote a column for the *New Yorker* called "The Wayward Press," had described Newhouse as having "no political ideas; just economic convictions." He also called Sam "a journalistic chiffonnier," or ragpicker, and the image had stuck. Sam could not afford to be thought of as a man who bought second-rate papers, turned them into third-rate papers, and stuffed his pockets with profits.

In the early press releases Josephs prepared, he highlighted Sam's policy of not changing the "editorial course" of the papers he bought. Two years later, in 1950, Josephs claims to have persuaded Walter Winchell to mention on his famous Sunday night radio broadcast that Sam was set to acquire the *Portland Oregonian.* "That brought Sam's name to millions of people who never heard of him," says Josephs.

But Sam always remained extremely wary of publicity. He had become friendly with the gossip columnist Leonard Lyons, whose column, "The Lyons Den," appeared in the *New York Post* as well as in some of the Newhouse papers. Most media moguls would have massaged that relationship in hopes of regular mentions. Sam's approach was the opposite. He offered Lyons companionship—Mitzi and Sam would often meet Lyons at Sardi's after opening nights—and an occasional lead, but the deal was that Lyons was to keep Sam's name out of the column.

It was twelve years after the Winchell broadcast, in July 1962, that Sam next went "live" to a national audience, this time via *Time* magazine. (The weird but fitting cover illustration featured a head-and-shoulders drawing of Sam beneath a press, off of which rolled a sample of his newspapers, which in turn appeared to be spitting out an endless supply of dollar bills.) Calvin Trillin, who reported the story but, in keeping with *Time*'s procedures back then, didn't write it, spent ten days with Sam, much of it in the backseat of his Cadillac, shuttling from one paper to the next. The owner showed no personal interest in him, Trillin recalls, made no effort to ingratiate himself, and engaged in no "image polishing." In fact, it was clear to Trillin that Sam "hated doing [the interviews].... He dropped me near *Time* in his limo and I started to get out and I was on the street side, and I guess he probably saw a car coming and he put his hand on my arm, 'Wait a minute,' he said. 'I'd hate to have to go through this again.'"

Trillin, himself the son of a Jewish immigrant from somewhere near Kiev, understood Sam and appreciated that he was neither a grandstander nor a phoney, and that admiration peeked through the finished story. But there was also implied criticism in his profile of a man who had risen from harsh poverty to amass a nationwide chain of newspapers and to realize the huge profits that eluded most other newspaper owners, but whose complete devotion to the bottom line meant that newspapers could have been eggs or underwear. Any business to which Sam Newhouse turned his singlemindedness and energy would have prospered. The cover boy emerged as mechanical, uncreative, lacking in intellectual curiosity—"He has no interest more consuming than the solvency of his properties"—and suspect because someone who buys newspapers ought to care about their editorial content.[6]

The *Time* cover hit the stands just as Phil Hochstein was launching for Newhouse in Washington a national news service that promised to offer behind-the-headlines analysis and in-depth reporting of the sort that no individual paper, save perhaps the *New York Times,* could afford. It was Hochstein's idea to start the Newhouse National News Service (NNNS), and he sold it to Sam as a means to address a very specific and looming menace, described, incidentally, in the *Time* piece: the increasing grumbling in Congress about the impact on the public's right to know of newspaper mergers and chain ownership.

Most ominous for Newhouse—and the reason he gave Hochstein the go-ahead for a national wire that was in many ways inimical to his dedication to local control—was the threat by New York congressman Emanual Celler, chairman of the House Judiciary Committee, to hold hearings on the subject. The Federal Communications Act then provided that no company could own more than five broadcast outlets, and the word was that Congressman Celler was looking at a law that would similarly limit ownership of newspapers. "I was told that Newhouse was just petrified about that," recalled Erwin Knoll.

A Washington bureau that would serve all the newspapers, that would hire first-class correspondents, would allow Sam to justify his ownership by telling members of the committee, "Look, because we have all these papers, we can afford to give them a kind of coverage that they couldn't possibly afford on their own." Eventually Celler was persuaded that regulating newspaper ownership could be regarded as an intrusion on First Amendment rights, and he dropped the issue.

In the meantime, out of this fear that he would have to sell some newspapers, which was in opposition to his most basic tenet—"I never sell; I only buy"—was born the Newhouse National News Service. It survives today, hobbling along in that peculiarly invisible Newhousian manner.

The hope back then was that not only would the Newhouse papers want to use the service, but that other papers would buy it as well—a nice plan, but then Sam refused to allow his name to be attached to the service. So it was launched under the name Advance News Service, or ANS, after the Staten Island paper. When Newhouse's people set up a lunch during the American Society of Newspaper Editors meeting in Washington to announce this new service, and to pique the interest of the editors in buying it, "They had a brochure printed out," Erwin Knoll recalled, "and on the cover were the letters ANS for Advance News Service. One of the editors walking in picked up the brochure and said, 'ANS, Another News Service.'" Eventually Sam agreed reluctantly to give it his name.

A charter reporter for the service who was as close to Phil Hochstein as anyone says that Hochstein "had a whole bunch of thoughts about what was lacking in daily news coverage." He wanted to "break new ground in our field and perform a real service." Spot news would be left to the AP;

the Newhouse service would offer perspective, interpretation, second-day stories, investigative reporting. It would delve beyond the breaking news that then monopolized the daily press. Bonnie Angelo, who had worked in the Washington bureau of *Newsday,* joined the NNNS in 1963. She calls it an "outstanding, prescient concept, they were ahead of their time."

Phil Hochstein and Arthur Laro, the dynamic man he selected to be the service's first bureau chief, assembled a four-person staff to cover science, including one man whose beat was medicine, at a time when science and medicine were largely not covered. He also hired a reporter to cover education at a time when nobody else did. Joe Hochstein, Phil's son, who came to the service at its inception, was assigned to write a series examining the concept of due process of law. Jules Witcover did a ten-parter on the AMA's involvement in politics, another on the farm problem. Erwin Knoll wrote a series about the antiwar movement on American campuses—one of the first reporters to note its importance as a national story.[7]

The NNNS office was a hodgepodge of thirty or so reporters, half of them hired specifically for the national service and the other half what were called "regionals"—the reporters who were in Washington to represent a specific Newhouse newspaper. In typical Newhouse fashion, there was no camaraderie or training beyond repeated warnings, undoubtedly with an eye toward Congressman Celler and his Judiciary Committee, to refer to the papers as a "group," not as a "chain." "They made a big point of that," says Angelo. "It was... [the] Hearst chain, Gannett chain, the Newhouse group."

Sam could not have it both ways. The NNNS limped along precisely because Sam's papers were so autonomous, so local. None of the editors wanted anything to do with a national anything; they saw it as the very sort of centralized control that Sam Newhouse rightly shunned. They already had the AP and UPI, and the better papers had the Los Angeles Times/Washington Post service and the New York Times service. Who needed another? An editor of one of Sam's largest papers showed his disdain by stuffing the Newhouse teletype printer in a closet.

Whether they wanted it or not, Newhouse demanded that his publishers pay, proportionate to their profitability, for the service. (In 1967, for example, the *St. Louis Globe-Democrat* was charged $50,000 for the

Newhouse service, estimated to be about ten times the amount the paper would have had to pay for the New York Times New Service.) To lessen Sam's tax liability, all the expenses of the bureau were billed to the individual papers. Presumably for the same reason, paychecks for all Washington reporters came from the *Staten Island Advance.*

The editors paid, but they still mostly shunned their own service. A secretary was charged with clipping all the Newhouse papers. In some cases a reporter's story was sent out over the wire, and not a single newspaper picked it up. "We should do what the Soviets...would do," one charter reporter for the service once suggested to Erwin Knoll. "When these editors come to Washington, we'll get them drunk and get them in compromising situations and photograph and blackmail them into running our stories. Erwin knocked the whole idea down by saying the obvious: 'It would never work because anyone who would publish one of those newspapers clearly wouldn't be embarrassed by anything else he might do in public.'" Jules Witcover, who had started to write for the national service and was assigned to the Pentagon, would spend a month or two on a major series. "If you got it in three or four papers you were lucky."

Erwin Knoll called it a "rudderless operation. You had the feeling that nobody much cared whether it worked or didn't. If you got the world's greatest story and put it on the wire, nobody much would give a damn, no feedback, and very little from within your own organization." Frustrated, Knoll started freelancing for magazines, and eventually left to become editor of the *Progressive.* Bonnie Angelo had the same sinking feeling. She left Newhouse in 1966 to go to *Time's* Washington bureau, and in 1968 she was named London bureau chief.

When Arthur Laro, the strongest leader the bureau would ever have, left to become president of the Chicago Tribune–New York News Syndicate, Hochstein returned to Washington to run the bureau. Laro, a former executive editor of the *Houston Post,* had brought from Houston as news editor a fellow Texan, Travis Dean Reed. Hochstein made the mistake of installing him as bureau chief, and, from all accounts, he was a disaster.[8]

After Hochstein's falling out with Sam in 1967, Sam had anointed a new editorial brain, David Starr. Sam gave Starr the NNNS to oversee. Starr had started with the Newhouse chain in 1940 as a copy boy at the

Long Island Press. Like Phil Hochstein, he was decidedly left-wing in his youth. After graduating from Queens College in 1942, he went to work full-time for the *Press,* covering, as he once put it, "the cops and the courts." No one disputes that Starr was smart. One top *Press* editor called him "probably the brightest man I ever met" and "unquestionably the best copy editor I ever saw." But, says this same source, he was also "a real thoroughgoing bastard" who was much feared within the organization. He was seen by some as a Newhouse apparatchik and enforcer. In the early 1970s, *Press* reporter Karl Grossman quoted columnist Jimmy Breslin in a story, which resulted in a call from an agitated David Starr. "You're never to mention Breslin," Starr warned him. Grossman was puzzled until he learned that Breslin had not only slammed the *Long Island Press* and the *Jersey Journal,* he had also described the Newhouse organization as the Sing Sing of American journalism.

At the NNNS, Starr was strictly an absentee overseer, so absentee that he apparently didn't realize how bad Dean Reed was. It wasn't until Donald's daughter went to the bureau as an intern and reported back to her father that the place was a mess, that Starr was asked to get rid of Reed. He did, but he replaced him with an old army buddy who, as impossible as it seemed to those in the bureau, was even worse.[9]

The next major story about the Patriarch ran as a *Business Week* cover in January 1976. Josephs claims that it was he who arranged the story by "cultivating" the editor, who was "fascinated" with the Newhouse story and who promised him, "If you could get me [interviews with Sam and his sons], I'd guarantee that it would be a cover story." Josephs assured Sam that the editor was "sympathetic," that the magazine was not the sort to take pot shots, and that the family would like the result so much that they would reprint it and use it as a weapon in their next acquisition battle. (He was right, they did.)

Sam had another reason for agreeing to the story. Although he was still healthy in 1976, he was beyond his eightieth birthday. The cover story would introduce his sons, both of whom were interviewed, and show, says Josephs, that this was "not just a one-man enterprise," and that another generation was on its way.[10]

Throughout his life, the owner made his share of bitter enemies—mostly people whom he had outsmarted in the race for a new property, or people who believed that the Newhouse way of doing business was bad for journalism. But he was, by most accounts, an honest man. One of his publishers insists that Sam was a man of "immense integrity." Phil Hochstein, who except for Sam's brothers, knew Sam the businessman longest and closest, wrote, after their falling out, that he respected Newhouse for "his convincing affectations of modesty, ...for an evident preference for honesty over trickiness.... In the somewhat ruthless business of piling up an incredible fortune in newspapers, he was often surprisingly and nakedly truthful."

Hochstein is correct in writing that Newhouse was not tricky; he was, in many ways, remarkably predictable. He had certain tried-and-true techniques on which he consistently relied. For example, he knew that the best hunting ground for newspapers was what he called a disrupted family; one in which lurked death, suicide, mental illness, scandal, difficult divorce, squabbling siblings, heirs—typically third generation—whose numbers were unwieldily large and/or contentious. He was like an ambulance chaser with a gruesome instinct for honing in on newspaper-owning families in the kind of turmoil that would cause them to turn over to him the next coveted property. He had open lines to newspaper brokers across the country who did nothing but look for families and newspapers ripe for the picking.

Calvin Trillin remembers Sam mentioning that he was monitoring one paper in which "they had something like six branches of the family and when they wanted to make a decision they had to call around to everyone. It was a very inefficient way of doing business."[11]

S.I. had the Block family in his sights since 1939 when he bought the *Newark Star-Eagle* from Paul Block. Sam bought the paper not because he wanted to run it, but because acquiring it was an important first step toward reaching his goal of a monopoly in Newark and ownership of the state's largest newspaper, the *Star-Ledger*. The Block paper Sam lusted after for its own sake was the family's *Toledo Blade*, already a monopoly paper. (Toledo was one of the first major American cities to have only one paper.) And it was that undisguised desire, according to John Robinson Block, today copublisher and editor-in-chief of the *Toledo Blade* and the

Pittsburgh Post-Gazette, both owned by his family, which caused his father, Paul Block Jr., to refer to Sam as a "buzzard." Family stories have it that after Paul Block Sr.'s death in 1941, Sam started to work on his widow, Dina. "There were times right after grandfather died," says John Block, "and for several years in the 1940s when the estate was probably strapped for…cash, …that she felt a Newhouse presence and somewhat threatened by it because it was a vulnerable time."

Sam failed to pierce Dina Block's resolve to keep the *Blade* in the family, but he never gave up. He could always hope that Paul Block's grandsons would somehow give way to him. John Block recalls an incident in his youth that shows the Newhouse determination. In the fall of 1969 John Block was sent to the all-male Gunnery School in Washington, Connecticut. It was his first time away from home, and as a ninth grader weighing in at under one hundred pounds, he was, he says, "an automatic target for some of the bigger guys." S. I. III, Sam's grandson and Si's son, was, says Block, "one of the brashest and…most domineering seniors…. 'What does your father do?' 'My father's a newspaper publisher in Toledo, Ohio.' 'Have you ever heard of the *Cleveland Plain Dealer?*' 'Yes, that fellow Newhouse has run it down.'… Well, he [S. I. III] was beside himself. And all I heard was how big they were and how small we were…. And he was going to call his dad and find out who we were." Presumably young Sam called home and was told to let John Block alone. From that time on, S. I. III couldn't have been nicer to the heir to the *Toledo Blade.*[12]

The Washington Post was another paper Sam wanted, correctly predicting that it had the potential to enjoy monopoly status. He believed he had a good chance there because the suicide in 1963 of the paper's owner and publisher, Philip Graham, had left control in the shaky hands of his shy and insecure widow, Katharine. She writes in her memoir of being "descended on" by people trying to buy the *Post* in the wake of Phil's suicide. CBS was one suitor, Times Mirror was another. But "the most persistent," she recalls, was Sam Newhouse, who offered $100 million for the paper. "We turned this down emphatically, but Newhouse never took no for an answer and kept reappearing with better offers. Every time I shut one door, he would enter through another."

In another book about the *Washington Post,* Newhouse was described as "a graveyard superintendent [who] goes around picking up bones, preying on widows and split families" and "the leading volunteer family counselor to troubled journalistic households." Graham herself had called him a "vulture" for his practice of swooping down upon grief-stricken families.

When Sam found his direct offers to Kay Graham summarily rejected, he began to use socially acceptable intermediaries. He hired Clark Clifford, the Washington power broker/lawyer, as a go-between. "He said that he would like to come and see me," Clifford recalls, "and talk to me about a business matter. He came and...said he was interested in acquiring *The Washington Post.* He knew that I knew Mrs. Graham.... We discussed this for some time and I said I would be glad to talk to Mrs. Graham about it and see if she had any interest, so within a few days thereafter I talked to her about it and she said they had no interest in it at all.... It wasn't for sale to anyone at any price."

When Clifford failed, Newhouse tried still another angle. Within months of Phil's suicide, Theodore C. Sorensen, John Kennedy's special counsel and speechwriter, took Kay Graham to lunch. He told her that he would like to work at the *Post* and she, taking him at his word and eager to have him at the paper, offered various positions, all of which he rejected. "The only job I really want is yours," he admitted. "Why don't you move over and let me run the company for you?" She rejected the offer. A few months later, Sorensen was back. "I am empowered to offer you a hundred million for the *Post* alone. I would run it, and you can keep the rest." Graham describes herself as "truly nonplussed." She then asked Sorensen, "Ted, is this from Newhouse?" Sorensen admitted that it was, but reassured her that he, not Newhouse, would run the paper. Kay was skeptical and disdainful: "You don't really think Newhouse would let you run it, do you?" She dismissed the offer by expressing her "surprise [that] he would participate in such an offer."

Kay Graham saw Sam as the polar opposite of her father, Eugene Meyer, who had bought the *Post* at a bankruptcy sale in 1933. His primary goal was not to make money but to give Washington first-rate editorial and op-ed pages, no matter how much money it took to do so, and for years the paper posted large annual losses. She described Sam Newhouse as an altogether different sort, a man, she wrote, who "operated his papers extremely tightly, with small newsholes and large profit margins."[13]

Kay Graham's other major print property was *Newsweek,* which her husband had bought from the Astor Foundation in 1961. Sam Newhouse had also put in a bid that year, but he didn't have a chance against the team of Phil Graham and Ben Bradlee—the latter then a reporter in the magazine's Washington bureau—who outdid each other in charming Vincent Astor's widow, Brooke. In her memoir Kay Graham implies that Sam had behaved dishonorably during the *Newsweek* bidding process but that, fortunately, Brooke Astor and her people had the character to withstand the dollars dangled before them. "Phil had triumphed over about a half-dozen other bidders. Sam Newhouse made a higher bid after the deal was closed, but the Astor Foundation honorably stuck by its word."

By the time Phil Graham won the race to buy *Newsweek,* he was already sick with untreated manic depression. Just after his suicide two years later, Newhouse tried again to buy *Newsweek,* hoping that Katharine wouldn't have the guts to run it. He offered $100 million for the magazine, more than ten times what Phil had paid for it two years earlier. Again, Kay Graham wasn't interested.[14]

If "disrupted family" was a phrase close to Sam's heart, so was "owning the town." New Orleans was one of those cities in which Sam in 1962 bought up all the papers in town with an eye toward merging—a euphemism for closing—the afternoon paper into the morning, creating a one-newspaper town, with ad rates set at whatever level the family pleased. (The unprofitable afternoon *States-Item* disappeared into the dominant morning *Times-Picayune* in 1980.)

Sam bought the unprofitable afternoon *Oregon Journal* in 1962. In order to close the deal, he signed a contract promising to keep the *Oregonian*'s only competitor open for at least twenty years. The "consolidation" occurred precisely twenty years later. Despite the fancy word, the *Journal,* for all intents and purposes, simply disappeared, and Portland too became a one-newspaper town.

In Harrisburg, Sam bought and then closed the *Harrisburg Telegraph* and thereby rid himself of a pesky competitor. Richard Meeker claims that on the day in 1948 that the merger was announced, Sam ordered the

Telegraph's presses destroyed—an apparent effort to prevent a group of locals from starting a competing paper.

In Newark, in 1939, Sam bought Paul Block's *Newark Star-Eagle*, an afternoon paper, merged it with the morning *Ledger* to form the *Star-Ledger*, then waited for the owner of the *Newark Evening News* to fail, which Sam correctly predicted was inevitable. In 1971 Sam bought the *News*'s plant and its Sunday paper. A year later he shut the paper down, and then sat not only on a monopoly gold mine but on the biggest paper in New Jersey. With the *News* gone, the *Star-Ledger*'s circulation more than doubled.[15]

En route to "owning the town," Sam understood that quibbling over price was a loser's strategy. When he paid $18.7 million for the Birmingham and Huntsville, Alabama papers, one television station, and three radio stations in 1955, the deal was characterized as the "biggest transaction in American Newspaper history." When he bought the *New Orleans Times-Picayune* and *States-Item* for $42 million in 1962, that became the top price ever paid for newspapers in one city. (*Time* reported the sale as "more than three times what the Louisiana Territory cost the U.S. in 1803.") In 1967 he again broke his own record by paying $54.3 million for the *Cleveland Plain Dealer*.[16]

When Sam Newhouse first met with James Sauter, then president and CEO of Booth, about acquiring the chain of newspapers in Michigan, he volunteered a simple philosophy: that every dollar he took out of the business was taxed by federal, state, and city income tax, and so he had a lot of money he needed to do something with. Having a lot of cash on hand was another of Sam's secrets of success. At the end of his career, he could count on one hand the number of times he had borrowed money—always from the Chemical Bank—to buy a newspaper. He didn't like banks, he explained, because "banks can make you sell." And as much as anything else, Sam Newhouse was proud of the fact that he had never sold anything.

Among the advantages of shunning banks was that he could make quick-draw decisions and he could keep his records secret, giving him a leg up on his competitors, many of which were public companies. He almost always knew more about his competitors than they knew about him. He could outbid those lacking such basic information about the company as outstanding liabilities and current assets.[17]

There were those who believed that Sam could not possibly have made the acquisitions he did without relying on banks. And so his FBI file contains the occasional speculation that the Newhouse bank was the Mafia—that, as one memo writer phrases it, he "may be connected with underworld interests." The writer concludes, however, "From the information available there is no indication in Bureau files that he has underworld connections." (Aides to presidents Kennedy, Johnson, and Nixon would request a "name check" on Sam—presumably a routine prelude to Sam's visiting the White House—and FBI functionaries responded that Sam's name appeared on the Christmas card list of Morris Barney Dalitz, "an executive of the Desert Inn Hotel and the Stardust Hotel, Las Vegas, ...and an associate of Samuel M. Giancana, who was described as 'head' of the Chicago...criminal element.")[18]

Sam had long vowed never to take his company public. While other media companies were going public—Dow Jones, Time Inc., Gannett, the New York Times Company, Knight Newspapers, Ridder Publications, the Washington Post Company—Sam held fast. Remaining private meant that Sam didn't have to report earnings or issue quarterly reports. He didn't have to report salaries or deal with inquisitive or demanding stockholders, or bring outsiders on to the board to keep watch over the family's dealings, or give the SEC a look at his books, or seek the board's permission before he bought an expensive piece of equipment or seemingly overpaid for a newspaper or a chain of newspapers, as in the case of Booth. He never had to explain himself to Wall Street. He didn't have to face demands from directors or stockholders that he sell properties that were losing money or that showed anemic profits, those inevitable "underperforming assets." He explained to Peter Diamandis, who once worked for the family before starting his own magazine company, "I tried to sell things when I was a young man so I could buy these expensive newspapers and nobody would give me what I thought they were worth.... Five years later, I suddenly realized that they were worth five times what I was trying to sell them for."[19]

He didn't have to defend the fact that there was no corporate staff or that whatever corporate headquarters existed was maybe in Newark, or was it in Staten Island, or could it really be, as everyone knew it was, in Sam's back pocket? He didn't have to justify his company's unique organization, that the top people had no discernible titles, that while Sam obviously had the last word, his two brothers and, in later years, his two sons were increasingly involved.

9 | The Last Hurrahs

THERE WERE GLIMMERS HERE and there that Sam Newhouse, still the master of a huge, self-made company, was getting older, more vulnerable. In 1967, after closing the deal on the *Cleveland Plain Dealer*, Sam, then seventy-two, downed a couple of scotches at the airport (he was a Johnny Walker Black Label man) while waiting to board his flight to Paris, where he was to meet Mitzi. He was intent on leaving the country because he didn't want to reveal the record price he had paid for the *Plain Dealer*.

Also about to board was Najeeb Halaby, financier, lawyer, once head of the Federal Aviation Administration and later of Pan Am World Airways, as well as father of Lisa, the American beauty who married King Hussein of Jordan and became Queen Noor. Halaby introduced himself to the older man, who, he noticed, was almost in a stupor. (Sam, who normally held his drinks very well, was apparently taking some kind of medication that didn't mix well with alcohol.) Halaby walked Sam on to the plane and settled him in a seat. An hour later Sam woke up, disoriented.

"Did I tell you how much?" Sam asked in a panic. It was only after Halaby assured him that he hadn't mentioned any number that Sam blurted, "Where am I? Where am I?" Halaby told him, and then reintroduced himself. Sam's terror that he might have talked in his sleep and revealed the price he paid for the *Plain Dealer* took some time to subside.[1]

As Sam grew older, he began to look toward the day when his sons and his grandsons and his nephews would run things. He wanted to leave something behind beyond record acquisition prices and booming bottom lines.

Besides, if he did it right, he figured, that legacy would bolster rather than bleed the bottom line.

The patriarch had Si and Donald in mind when he decided to give $15 million to Syracuse University. With that money he could help turn the middling journalism school that his sons had attended into a major program that, it was hoped, would eventually rival programs at Columbia, Northwestern, and Missouri.

That he selected Syracuse University for his largesse was almost preordained. William Pearson Tolley, a 1922 graduate of the university and its chancellor since 1942, was an uncommonly persuasive and persistent man. If the school hadn't been the Newhouse boys' first choice, and if they hadn't even stayed long enough to graduate, still the city of Syracuse had, without question, been very good to Sam Newhouse. He owned not only both newspapers in town, but also the important radio and television stations. S. I. Newhouse was known for his media monopolies, and Syracuse was the most impressively, profitably concentrated of all.

Those properties brought Sam to Syracuse regularly, and Tolley, who realized long before his peers that his most important job was to raise money, saw his opportunity. First he made Sam a trustee, then he saw to it that Sam was awarded an honorary degree, and then, in a rather strange gesture, he arranged for Sam to be initiated into the very chapter of ZBT that had blackballed his son.

Sam could not step foot into the city of Syracuse without Chancellor Tolley or one of his top people rushing over to see him. Frank Piskor, then the university's vice president of academic affairs, calls himself Tolley's "number two legman.... I would get the assignment of really keeping up contact and talking about our interest in a communications center bearing his name." Piskor described himself as the "emissary on the Newhouse vision," which more accurately could have been called the Tolley vision.

Sam Newhouse was a man who had never made philanthropy a part of his life and Tolley, the master teacher, had to show him how to be philanthropic. As Tolley put it, Sam "had to learn to give."[2]

Sam's initial gift was a sum much more modest than $15 million. In 1960 Chancellor Tolley broached a specific amount to Newhouse—$2 million for one journalism building. But no sooner had Sam agreed than Tolley decided that $2 million, given Sam's wealth, was not enough. Two years later, according to Newhouse biographer Richard Meeker, the brash chancellor named the amount he really wanted, $15 million, which would represent the largest gift the university had ever received: "'Sam,' Tolley said. 'I know you don't give to Israel, and the people in the Jewish community don't like you too well for that reason. But it's time for you to move up to the big leagues. You ought to make a major gift.' Tolley then described his proposal, focusing on a special point: it would constitute a 'living monument.'... Syracuse would be able to dedicate the world's most up-to-date center for the study of communications in Newhouse's name in less than two years, when the first building, for which he had already committed $2 million, was completed."

The owner came to see the point of Tolley's proposal, but Mitzi didn't, and as Tolley reported, she "was scared to death that I would take too much money from Sam."[3] For Sam, whose accountants and lawyers devised clever ways of funneling the money to the school, the gift, he knew, would be money well spent. The Samuel I. Newhouse School of Public Communications, as the complex would come to be known, not only would be dedicated during Sam's lifetime, but would make it possible for him to be remembered as someone whose vision reached beyond the bottom line.

Because the school would carry his name, Newhouse involved himself in the design of the first of a planned three-building complex. It was Sam who recommended the architect. "I'm going to invite Mr. I. M. Pei to think about this building," Sam said, referring to the highly regarded Chinese-born, MIT- and Harvard-educated architect for whom this would be, not his first, but an early commission.

Sam did not have much interest in architecture. Still, he wanted Pei, whom the New York real estate developer William Zeckendorf Sr. had introduced to him twenty years before. There was some opposition at Syracuse to Pei, but Sam wanted him, and in light of the $15 million, no one would have thought to question that choice. (Pei designed the first building—a concrete structure, shaped like the Red Cross under a flat roof, in association with King & King, Syracuse architects—the master plan for the eight-acre site, and the plaza.)

The first building, Newhouse I, as it was called, devoted to print journalism, was opened and dedicated in 1964, and Newhouse II, devoted to television, radio, and film, was opened and dedicated ten years later.

Plans for the third building were scrapped, as costs ran higher than expected and Sam refused to increase his gift to cover overruns.[4]

Once committed to the university, Sam took an endearing interest in its culture, as if he were making up for the fun he had missed as a young man. He especially liked to gather his family around him and sit in Chancellor Tolley's box at Syracuse football games. He enjoyed the spectacle of the bands and the marching, but, said Tolley, he knew little about the game. "But he would be scandalized if he heard me say that," Tolley said in an interview shortly before his death in 1996 at age ninety-five. "He thought he knew a lot." Mostly Sam sat at the games in silence, a look of contentment on his round face. Tolley, a world-class extrovert, recalled that Sam "would make you do most of the talking. You could sit next to him for hours and barely get 30 words out of him," Tolley wrote in his memoir, calling Sam "remarkably shy and reclusive.... I could remember every sentence I ever said to Sam, and every sentence he ever said to me. These exchanges could barely fill seven pages."[5]

Just as it was Newhouse's idea to hire I. M. Pei, so it was his idea to invite President Lyndon Johnson to Syracuse for the dedication of the first building in August 1964. Sam understood that there would be no better way to garner national publicity for the newly named Newhouse School than to have the still popular Lyndon Johnson on the podium. Sam was, incidentally, a supporter of Johnson's.

To deliver the invitation to Johnson, the patriarch called on Abe Fortas, the power lawyer whom Johnson would nominate the next year for a seat on the Supreme Court. Sam also worked through the Washington correspondent for the *New Orleans Times-Picayune*, Edgar Allen Poe, who was close to the late Louisiana congressman Hale Boggs, who in turn was close to Johnson. (Poe, no relation to the poet, had worked for the paper since 1930, when Huey Long was governor. The consummate southern gentleman, he was courtly, soft-spoken, and proud of the fact that he had never written anything bad about anyone.)[6]

Sam could have approached Johnson on his own. The men were hardly strangers. Johnson had just moved into the White House when he began to court Sam in the inimitable Johnson way, with smothering personal attention and frequent invitations to the Oval Office.

In his book about LBJ, Johnson aide Jack Valenti writes that on Friday, March 13, 1964, five months before the dedication, Edwin L. Weisl Sr., a Wall Street lawyer who had close ties to President Johnson and even closer ties to Roy Cohn and, through Cohn, to Sam Newhouse, arranged a lunch at the White House for Sam and the president. According to Bill Fugazy, Weisl, urged to do so by Roy Cohn, agreed to help Johnson lobby Sam for support in the pages of his newspapers.

On arriving, Weisl and Newhouse were informed by Valenti that the president was about to depart on Air Force One to inspect flood damage in the Ohio Valley. The two men were invited to join the president on his tour. Also on board were governors, several congressmen, senators, and Orville Freeman, then secretary of agriculture. "All during the trip," writes Valenti, "the president kept Sam Newhouse perched next to him," talking to him, directing Sam to peer through the clouds to see flood damage, the president almost never moving his attention from Sam, who was undoubtedly feeling a bit woozy by then, given his aversion both to flying—he was a lifelong queasy flyer—and to chatter.

Finally they landed, and after a helicopter ride from Andrews Air Force Base, they reached the South Grounds of the White House after 7:00 P.M. Valenti writes that Sam had been "the recipient of presidential implorings and urgings and declarations. He had been literally at the President's elbow all the time.... Inside the White House, the President was still not through. 'Why don't you call your wife, Sam, and tell her you are going to spend the night here with me at the White House?'" Not surprisingly, after his telephone conversation with Mitzi, Sam told the president "that he ought to get in his car and head home.... Again the president cajoled and again Mr. Newhouse...demurred."[7]

On Johnson's part, this had been a brilliant move. Sam was a captive audience, there being no way of exiting the plane or of extricating himself from Johnson's huge grip. The president was smart enough to hold back from asking Sam for specifics. There would be plenty of time to do that the next August, when the president had agreed to do Sam the big honor of appearing at the dedication in Syracuse.

Once the president had accepted the invitation, Sam wanted everything to be perfect. Hearing rumors that the event would be picketed because of his antiunion reputation in general, and a strike by printers in Portland in particular, Sam assigned Phil Hochstein to ask President Johnson to use his influence to see that there was no picketing. Hochstein was referred to an assistant to the president, who got George Meany, then president of the AFL, on the telephone. "Meany assured me," Hochstein wrote, "[that] he could and would stop any picketing on the simple ground that Newhouse was at peace with organized labor in all his cities but one."[8]

The festivities began on the evening of August 4, 1964, with a tribute to the newly minted philanthropist by Governor Nelson Rockefeller, who praised Sam for this "act of profound imagination and public responsibility." Then it was Sam's turn. He had worked and reworked his speech—the first public speech he had ever given. (Six years earlier he had given what he characterized as "my first speech" to mark the retirement of the publisher of his Syracuse papers. "It lasted three minutes, and no one will ever get me to do that again.")

Sam had tossed out drafts written by Phil Hochstein and edits by PR man Ray Josephs. The text of the speech, which he ended up writing himself, was prescient. At a time when the cold war was intense and Lyndon Johnson was escalating the Vietnam War with enthusiastic support from the American people, Sam observed, "Policies of nations and peoples alter too quickly for journalists to make inflexible judgments. Today's so-called enemy is tomorrow's friend. Indeed, we have no lasting enemies so much as we have ill-informed peoples." The end of the cold war, the American loss in Vietnam, the fact that Robert McNamara, the architect of the war, would one day visit his old enemies in Hanoi looking for forgiveness, showed just how prescient.

The text was impressive, but Sam's delivery was not. He confided in Ben Magdovitz that his knees were shaking, that he "was scared stiff.... He just couldn't hack it." He vowed never to give another speech.[9]

That same evening, at 11:36 P.M., Lyndon Johnson, still in Washington and scheduled to arrive in Syracuse the next morning for the official dedication and ribbon cutting, was on television addressing the American people—the first emergency press conference of his tenure as president. Looking grim, he told the nation that hostile vessels of the government of North Vietnam had attacked American ships in the Gulf of Tonkin that day and two days earlier, and that airplanes from the U.S. Seventh Fleet had fired on the North Vietnamese vessels.

The next morning, August 5, Lady Bird and Lyndon Johnson arrived in Air Force One at Syracuse's Hancock Field. A scheduled speech at the airport was scrapped, probably so as not to dim the drama of the war speech the president would deliver at the dedication—a speech that were it not for events in Southeast Asia probably would have focused on some Great Society program.

The mood in this city, which had last seen a president when Franklin Roosevelt visited, was a mix of carnival and crisis. Johnson was greeted by a representative of CORE presenting a stack of petitions dealing with Mississippi voter registration. High school bands played as forty young women billed as the Johnsonnetes cheered the president, who was not only commanding the forces in Vietnam but also running for the election that would save him from the fate of being remembered as an accidental president.

Security was heavy. On the runway were air force rescue equipment, crash crews, the fire department. Overhead flew two Marine Corps helicopters and a third, equipped with a sling, should the president be a casualty. Lining the route from airport to campus were police, plainclothesmen, secret service agents, state police, sheriff's department police. A solid throng of spectators lined both sides of the street, the crowd estimated at 10,000, rooftops covered with secret service men. There were people watching from the businesses en route, but, one reporter noted, none were hanging out of the windows, on specific orders from the authorities. The Dallas Book Repository was too fresh a memory.

Barely off Air Force One and a telephone conversation with Defense Secretary Robert McNamara, the president was rushed into a car in which Sam and Chancellor Tolley waited. The First Lady passed up that car and entered one that stood two to the rear.

Johnson would have preferred to be alone with Newhouse, so he simply ignored Chancellor Tolley. Members of the national press, many of whom had rushed to Syracuse as a routine dedication had turned suddenly into a major foreign policy speech, had portrayed the president as a man bowed under the weight of events in the Gulf of Tonkin. They would have been surprised by his quick change of agenda and attitude once inside the car.

Johnson had one thing on his mind. He wanted Sam to promise the endorsement of every one of his papers. He didn't care if the paper was Republican or conservative; he wanted them all. "Mr. Newhouse was very much antagonized by the president," remembered Chancellor Tolley. "He gave him no break at all. The minute we got in the car...the president turned to Mr. Newhouse and said, 'I want both the Syracuse papers.' And Newhouse said, 'You may have them.' 'I want the Harrisburg paper.' And Newhouse said, 'No problem.' Mr. Newhouse began to retreat [from his position of staying out of editorial] because he realized that he was up against a very tough guy in the president. The president went right down the list and finally Mr. Newhouse just said, 'I've given you enough. I don't need to give you anymore.' 'No,' he said, 'I want them all.' 'I've told you, I've given you enough.'" Left unsaid by Johnson, but understood between them, was that if some of these editors would no sooner endorse Johnson than vote for him, they should be at the least ordered to withhold an endorsement from his opponent, Barry Goldwater.

That international events had overtaken the best-laid local plans, and in a sense diverted attention from Sam and his new building to Washington and the hostile waters of Vietnam, was one thing. But the president's obnoxious lobbying, which in Sam's mind had sullied the dignity of the day, was another.[10]

The notion that Sam was apolitical because so being was better for business was only partly right. Sam considered it unbusinesslike to dictate endorsement decisions to his editors because those editors were in tune with their readers, and those readers were the source of circulation and thus advertising revenue. Although Sam personally opposed segregation, he would never have imposed that view on his editors in Alabama. Thus, his papers were all over the political map. The *Long Island Press* was a relatively liberal paper; the *St. Louis Globe-Democrat* was quite conservative. In cities in which Newhouse owned two newspapers—Harrisburg, Syracuse, Portland, and New Orleans particularly—the editorial stances of the sister papers often clashed. (Sam would claim to be delighted to hear that rival editors were not speaking.) He had cast his vote for Dwight Eisenhower in 1956 because he considered Adlai Stevenson too softheaded, but he was a registered Democrat who voted for John Kennedy in 1960.[11] In 1964 Sam Newhouse, much more moderate than many of his editors, was eager to support Lyndon Johnson wholeheartedly, which in Sam's case meant that he would vote for him. Now his enthusiasm for Johnson had been cut in half.

As the Ninety-eighth Infantry Division Band of Fort Dix, New Jersey, played Beethoven's Ninth Symphony, the honored guests, including Si with his children, and Donald and Sue with theirs, took their seats. Frank Piskor served as MC. In his remarks, Chancellor Tolley repeatedly referred to Sam as Dr. Newhouse and to the building being dedicated as the first of three.

Tolley then called upon "Dr. Newhouse" to introduce the president. Sam did that in one sentence.

As LBJ, in a size 44 dark gown and a mortarboard, gold tassel on the cap, took the podium, he returned to the subject of Vietnam: "Last night I spoke to the people of the nation. This morning, I speak to the people of all nations so that they may understand, without mistake, our purposes in the actions that we have been required to take." He called the attacks "deliberate" and "unprovoked," and when he said, "The attacks have been answered," the audience erupted in applause. He insisted that "peace is the only purpose of the course that America pursues." His warning that "the world must never forget that aggression unchallenged is aggression unleashed" brought another burst of applause. He ended to a standing ovation and the award of an honorary Doctor of Law degree, including the assurance by Chancellor Tolley that the president was well prepared for the degree by his graduation from Southwest Texas State Teachers College.

Next the ribbon cutting; Mitzi first, then "Mrs. Donald Newhouse," and then the president and Lady Bird, completed the task. Inscribed on the front of the building was a quote from Sam, "A free press must be fortified with great knowledge of the world and skill in the arts of expression."[12] Si, because he had no wife to perform these ceremonial duties, remained in the background.

Unwilling to subject himself to further presidential abuse, Sam refused to ride back to the airport with the president. He asked Alexander

"Casey" Jones, then editor of the *Syracuse Herald-Journal,* previously managing editor of the *Washington Post,* to make the return trip with the president. Chancellor Tolley also went along for the ride. "When we got ready to go back on the return trip," Tolley recalled, "Mr. Newhouse said, 'You take him over. I can't stand the SOB.'"

George Reedy, who was then Johnson's press secretary and accompanied him to the Syracuse dedication, explains that Newhouse's aversion to the "full treatment" from LBJ is understandable. "When Johnson sought to persuade somebody to do something the intensity of his operation could be fantastic. Only those who had seen it up close could get the full picture. It was an incredibly strong mixture of flattery, cajolery, badgering, threats that few people ever survived." In Reedy's mind, Johnson had a bewildering "obsession with...getting publishers to endorse him. I did not share that obsession, as I thought endorsements could be embarrassing at a later point when the publishers would put the heat on him to go along with some of their ideas on how the government should be run."[13]

When Sam returned to his paper route and his routine, he was stuck with a promise he surely wished he hadn't made, but one he felt he had to keep.

Most of Sam's papers did end up endorsing Johnson. But they would have done so in any case, without prodding from the owner, given Johnson's popularity at that time, his incumbency, the loyalty accruing to him in the aftermath of the Kennedy assassination, and the perceived extremism of Barry Goldwater, including the fear that he might trigger a nuclear war. But in a couple of cases, in which Sam's editors could not hold their noses tightly enough to endorse LBJ and ended up making no endorsement at all, they did so after a "nudge," as Tolley describes it, from Sam. (A few endorsed Goldwater, the *News* in Birmingham, Alabama, for instance. Sam, one associate says, would not have pushed an endorsement in Birmingham, and not even a man as obsessed as Lyndon Johnson would have expected it.)

St. Louis Globe-Democrat publisher Richard Amberg and Barry Goldwater would have seemed to be made for each other. The paper's political editor, Jack Flach, remembers Amberg telling him at the time that "he would never back Johnson and that Johnson does not deserve to be president." Many people could only scratch their heads when the paper broke its tradition of always endorsing, and almost always endorsing Republicans, and issued no endorsement. Instead, the editors issued what Flach calls a "wishy-washy" editorial "point[ing] out the negatives of both people." Flach calls it "the first time I think in the paper's history that we didn't endorse. We endorsed all the way down to dogcatcher."

Flach claims that he was told by a top executive at the paper that, Sam's policy of noninterference aside, "this was one case where he said he had to intervene." Flach recalls that Amberg "was very meek about the thing.... He didn't want to talk about it very much."

After that aberration, Flach says, the paper returned to its endorsement policy. "When we endorsed a Democrat, believe me, the Democrat would put it on the front page of his flyer because that was news."

Between the *Oregonian*'s founding in 1850 and that election of 1964, the paper had always endorsed Republicans in presidential races and generally Republicans in any race. (On its masthead, until 1936, it called itself a Republican newspaper; for four decades thereafter, it called itself an independent Republican newspaper.) Thus it came as a surprise when in 1964 the paper chose to make no endorsement, although it was known that the paper's publisher, M. J. Frey, favored Goldwater. The *Oregonian* then resumed its almost unbroken record of endorsing Republicans until 1992, when it endorsed Bill Clinton. (By then the Newhouses had closed the more liberal *Oregon Journal*, and the *Oregonian* moved a bit to the left.)

Robert Notson, the paper's managing editor in 1964, insists that the decision was entirely a local one and that there was absolutely no prodding from Sam. "Our editorial board at that time was unanimously opposed to endorsing Goldwater," he explains. "They didn't think very much of Johnson either, so they finally made no endorsement."[14]

Meanwhile, President Lyndon Johnson, his popularity plummeting as support for the war in Vietnam plummeted, was not through with Sam yet.

In 1968 the president again called on Sam—this time for editorial support for his nomination of Abe Fortas to succeed Earl Warren as chief justice of the Supreme Court. The nomination of the then associate justice was stirring up opposition and anti-Semitism. Johnson asked lawyer Edwin Weisl to lobby Sam to direct his editors to run favorable editorials and to persuade—or, better yet, order—the editor of the *New Orleans Times-Picayune* to reverse an already published editorial opposing confirmation.

The pressure on Sam was relieved when the nomination collapsed amid charges that Fortas had taken money from a foundation controlled by a man then under government investigation for securities violations. A year later, Fortas resigned from the court.[15]

By 1976 the patriarch, eighty-one years old, had other problems on his mind—the one looming largest, preparing his sons to take over the business. Donald was easy. He was at home in the newspaper world. The elder son was harder. Si had little natural bent toward newspapers. He had in fact become alarmingly attached to a relatively unimportant offshoot of the family business—a chain of glossy fashion magazines called Condé Nast that Sam bought in 1959. The father had to use what time he had left to sort things out between his two sons.

That year Sam Newhouse made his last hurrah: the hostile takeover of Booth, the then eightyfour-year-old chain of eight monopoly newspapers in Michigan, plus *Parade* magazine. The chain was such a moneymaker, says Bob Lewis, who worked as a reporter for Booth for twenty years, that "all you had to do was walk in in the morning and the money just flowed in."

Sam had insisted that Si and Donald join him for the initial meeting at the offices of Goldman Sachs with then Booth CEO James Sauter, whose manner made it clear that the acquisition would not be easy. Sam later described the scene in his car as he and his sons left the meeting.

"What do you think?" he asked. They both replied that this deal was trouble; it would be very difficult to do. "It's a public company, and there's got to be something else we could do with your money. Let's drop it," the sons advised.

Sam was likely disappointed at the ease with which his heirs were willing to give up one of the few "prime properties," as he called Booth, left to buy. He knew, and wished that his sons did also, that the third generation of Booths, then in control, was the easiest to crack.* "Look, you've

---

*The chain's founder, George Booth, a Canadian metalsmith, along with his wife, Ellen Scripps, whose family owned the *Detroit News*, used profits from the newspapers to found the Cranbrook School in suburban Detroit, famed for its devotion to the study of arts, crafts, architecture, and design.

got to learn in life," he told them, "that nothing worth getting ever comes to you without having to fight for it."

Sam forced his sons, then in their late forties, to learn this lesson by insisting that they be involved in the negotiation. At the Goldman Sachs meeting, Sam did the talking; Si and Donald said next to nothing. In subsequent meetings, Jim Sauter recalls, the sons "played second fiddle" to Sam's in-house lawyer, Charles Sabin. But as the fight for Booth continued, Donald began to emerge; Si remained in the background.

The Newhouses' competitor was Times Mirror, the parent company of the *Los Angeles Times,* which had entered the fray because Sauter and his colleagues, horrified by the prospect of being owned by Sam Newhouse and making no secret of it—they issued public statements blasting the Newhouses—appealed to *Los Angeles Times* publisher Otis Chandler to assume the role of white knight. Sam feared all along that Booth, in collusion with the establishment Times Mirror—Otis was the third generation Chandler in charge—would double-cross him. His usual confidence waned, especially on the day the Booth board met to make the final decision. But he stuck to his schedule and was in St. Louis making his regular visit to the *Globe-Democrat* on the day that he would learn whether he or Times Mirror would be the next owner of Booth Newspapers. One of the paper's executives recalls Sam as "so agitated, he was hardly able to sit still." Ben Magdovitz remembers talking to Sam while publisher Duncan Bauman pestered editors on the business desk for news coming across the wire about the Booth sale. "You see this tie I've got on today?" Sam said to Magdovitz. "I paid $50 for it. It's not worth $50. It's worth $20, but I wanted it, so I paid $50 for it."

"Do you think they'd double-cross me?" he kept asking. "I'm afraid they're going to double-cross me." He told the executive that he had made the best offer, $305 million, $9 million more than Times Mirror, and, if accepted, it would be the most ever paid for an American newspaper company, but he feared that Times Mirror, in a good-old-boys game, might be allowed to skirt the rules by slipping in a late bid.

As the wait continued, Sam told Ben Magdovitz, his voice full of pride, that it was his younger son, Donald, who had advised him, "'We don't have to answer to any board of directors. Let's kick it up, $5 a share,

$7 a share over the *Los Angeles Times*,' so we did." From his conversation with Sam, Magdovitz learned that Donald had been "tremendously involved." Sam said nothing about Si, who had let his younger brother take the lead in the deal that turned out to be a gold mine for the Newhouses. To no one's surprise, the Newhouses have kept all those papers open. "They were all the only paper in the market," says Jim Sauter. "Losing money on one of them is like screwing up a one-car funeral."[16]

In 1974 Duncan Bauman, Walter Evans, and several other *St. Louis Globe-Democrat* executives had pooled their money to commission a prominent local artist, Gilbert G. Early, to paint Sam Newhouse's portrait. It was time for such an honor. With the possible exception of Mitzi's brother, Walter, these men revered Sam Newhouse, and Sam returned the favor. Their paper had become his favorite.

At first the patriarch, who had never before sat for a portrait, declined to pose; he was too busy, he said. So one of the group asked Mitzi to intervene. She did, and Sam consented reluctantly, but only after the artist agreed to photograph him and work from the photographs.

"I went down to the newspaper," Gilbert Early remembers, "and got all my equipment set up and I was expecting a giant because he was such a huge success in the newspaper business. And this very small man walks in." By then Sam Newhouse was white-haired, clear-eyed, his suit jacket appearing boy-sized. His facial features were regular and appealing, with the exception of pouches beneath his eyes and, most noticeably, on the lower part of his cheeks, giving him the look of an aged, tired chipmunk.

At the unveiling dinner, Sam was so full of mixed emotions that he broke down and cried. "This was one of the very few times that something was given to him," says Ben Magdovitz, "with no holds barred."[17]

In the twilight of his life, Sam was becoming more approachable. And every once in a while he would uncharacteristically open up to his editors and publishers. "Good things come hard," he confided one day to one of his St. Louis people. "Sometimes things don't have a neat solution," he volunteered another day.

One night during that period, *Oregon Journal* editor Donald Sterling, along with three of his colleagues, had dinner with Sam. "He just kind of told us his life story," Sterling said, about the challenges of his childhood, about Judge Lazarus and his role in propelling Sam into the newspaper business. "He was a little bit frail," Sterling says, but he was certainly "in complete possession of himself."

In 1977 Sam became quite frail, and stopped visiting his newspapers. He did attend the 1977 American Newspaper Publishers Association meeting in San Francisco. Ben Magdovitz and his wife had dinner with Sam and Mitzi, and Magdovitz noticed that Sam "had lost a lot of his touch by that time.... He could move around but his speech got a little halting, and he just wasn't himself."

The trip to San Francisco had been taxing. Sam fell asleep in the waiting lounge at Newark Airport, and he and Mitzi missed their flight. Donald had to scurry to book them another. Meanwhile, Mitzi's million-dollar jewels had departed on the earlier flight. "Don't tell him I put my jewelry in one of the bags," she whispered to the Magdovitzes.

When S. I. III, Si's son, the eldest of Sam's grandchildren, and the first to marry, wed in 1977, Mitzi attended, but Sam stayed in Palm Beach, where Mitzi and he retreated with increasing frequency. In a matter of weeks his mental capacity seemed to have disintegrated.

"Donald told me," Magdovitz recalls, "that [Sam] started undressing in the barber shop in New York. He thought he was home in his bathroom." Saul Kohler, editor of the *Harrisburg Patriot-News*, had heard from the papers' publisher, Ed Russell, about Sam's illness, but he was warned by Russell, "We were not to publish anything about it. We didn't.... They didn't want him being held up to ridicule." Mitzi tried to maintain appearances, while watching over her husband with tender care. Florence Shientag, Mitzi's Park Avenue neighbor and friend, remembers how Mitzi "almost carried him across the street, getting him to exercise."

In 1978 Sam suffered a debilitating stroke, but he still had moments of lucidity. He was visited in New York by Rabbi Ronald B. Sobel of Temple Emanu-El who asked him why he didn't escape the cold weather by going to Florida. Sam mumbled a reply that the rabbi interpreted to mean that he wanted to avoid being wheeled through a hotel lobby and letting people see how sick he was.

"Why don't you buy a house?" Sobel asked him.

"I'd rather buy a newspaper," Sam is said to have replied.

Mitzi rented a house in Palm Beach that gave them the privacy they sought. Florence Shientag, who owned a house there, remembers Mitzi "entertaining, always entertaining," while Sam was kept out of view upstairs in the care of a private nurse.

One day Mitzi told Florence, "'I'm building a house for a million dollars.' So I said, 'But your husband's so ill.' She said, 'Well, I'm going to have that house.' And she did build it." (The house was at 106 Chateaux Drive.)

In July 1979 Sam suffered a totally disabling stroke. He was hospitalized at Doctors Hospital in New York. He died there, age 84, on Wednesday, August 29. The following day his obituary appeared on the front page of the *New York Times*. Sam would have had conflicted feelings about that kind of attention, yet it was undeniably a major accomplishment for a man who had started life so poor.

That Friday, August 31, his funeral, presided over by Rabbi Sobel, was held at Temple Emanu-El on Fifth Avenue. Sam's coffin was covered in orange flowers. The temple, said to be the largest in the free world, was packed with a thousand mourners, including Vice President Walter Mondale—President Jimmy Carter sent his condolences—Governor Hugh Carey, and Senator Jacob Javits.

The first eulogy was delivered by Ashton Phelps, president and publisher of the *New Orleans Times-Picayune* and *States-Item*. Phelps was a member of the old Louisiana family that had sold out to Sam Newhouse in 1962 and who, typically, was allowed to remain and run things his way. "My friend referred to his group of newspapers as a family," Phelps told the congregation, "and that is how we felt—as a family. [Sam] began the tradition of editorial autonomy. I have never known him to attempt to dictate editorial policy. He was a great defender of the First Amendment and a great believer in the challenge of responsible editors."

The second tribute came from Syracuse's Chancellor Emeritus Tolley: "The ultimate test of the man is that when he spoke with people, it was with care, interest, and energy that made them feel important. We give thanks for his integrity and character, his sense of fair play, and his magnanimity." He paid tribute to Mitzi, calling her "his first real love. At the end, she was the angel always at his side."[18]

Seven weeks after the patriarch's death, Mitzi and Si, carrying photographs of Sam, met with Andy Warhol and commissioned him to do Sam's portrait. Warhol later noted in his diary that Mitzi was eighty-two—she would have been mortified; she was actually seventy-seven—and that "she might want her portrait done, too."[19]

Mitzi, of course, felt the death most of all, but she tried to continue her life's work—getting groomed and dressed, entertaining, being entertained, and being seen, whether in a grand hotel in Europe or in the aisle of a Broadway theater.

But in her late seventies she began showing signs of frailty, both physical and mental. An old friend of Mitzi's and Sam's was vacationing with his wife in Capri in the early 1980s when he unexpectedly encountered Mitzi, who was traveling with her male hairdresser as her paid companion. The couple was shocked by Mitzi's deterioration. She was, as always, "ever so smartly dressed." But she seemed confused, by turns friendly and rude, and wherever she went, she carried with her a bag of jewels.

Mitzi invited the couple for drinks at her hotel and then to dinner. When the bill arrived, she announced that it would be "dutch treat." The hairdresser/companion, looking embarrassed, quietly apologized, and discreetly handed the waiter Mitzi's credit card. As the couple was about to say good night, Mitzi asked if they would help her to straighten out charges she had accumulated with a local tailor. The hotel bill was another stumbling block, and Mitzi confided that she had been arguing about it with the proprietor. Her friend finessed a settlement between Mitzi and the tailor and also paid the hotel bill, using Mitzi's credit card.[20]

By this time it was clear to her sons that Mitzi needed a paid companion, a woman trained in the art of caring for wealthy widows. Mitzi auditioned several such specialists, but none lasted more than three weeks because, says one of them, Mitzi was "difficult" and "spoiled." Then, in 1982, Mitzi found Dorothy Lay, who had worked for Anita Young, the sister of Georgia O'Keeffe and the widow of Robert Young, a railroad magnate, once considered one of the richest men in America.

At first it must have seemed to Dorothy Lay, who was then in her fifties, that the reports she had heard about Mrs. Newhouse were all too accurate. Mitzi, reportedly, would insult her; Dorothy would cry, run to her room, and then find notes of apology from Mitzi slipped under her door. With time, Dorothy came to like and understand Mitzi, as the widow came to appreciate Dorothy. Underneath it all, Dorothy told one acquaintance, Mitzi had a good heart.

For the final seven years of Mitzi's life, most of it spent at her house in Palm Beach, Dorothy was in attendance seven days a week, twenty four hours a day. She took over Mitzi's life, buying, selecting, and laying out her clothes, making all the arrangements for and accompanying Mitzi on trips to Europe, running her house in Palm Beach, paying all the bills, arranging parties, buying tickets for every charity event so that Mitzi could see and be seen. Nearly every day Dorothy would usher her charge out of the house to shop, to have lunch, to go to cocktail parties.

Through all of this, the sons did not neglect their mother. "They were wonderful," says one woman close to Mitzi in her final years. They called her frequently and they came "whenever they could." Asked once by Joni Evans why he was going to Palm Beach in July, Si Newhouse replied, "Because my mother is there."

"Good night, my angel," Mitzi would whisper to Dorothy every night at bedtime. Whenever she woke from a nightmare, Mitzi would call out Dorothy's name and tell her that she had dreamed that Dorothy had left her. "I'll never leave you," Dorothy would assure her, and she didn't, until June 29, 1989, when Mitzi, age eighty-seven, died at home in Palm Beach, alone except for Dorothy.[21]

II | Si's Time

10 | Si Finds a Home

SAM NEWHOUSE NEVER TIRED of telling the story of asking Mitzi what she wanted for a thirty-fifth wedding anniversary gift. She replied that she wanted *Vogue.* So in 1959 her husband bought her not only *Vogue,* but all of Condé Nast, the old-line company that also published *Glamour, House & Garden,* and *Young Bride's.*

In fact, the patriarch bought Condé Nast because he recognized that the $15 million he would spend to acquire 100 percent of the company's stock was a bargain, and that the magazines were chronic underperformers, just waiting to be whipped into profitability. Peter Diamandis, a former Condé Nast publisher who later bought and sold his own magazine company, recalls Newhouse once telling him that in buying the company, his personal goals and his business goals converged. "He wanted to do this for Mitzi, but...if it hadn't been a good deal, no way, no way," would he have bought it.[1]

Still, according to Ray Josephs, many in the industry who had never heard of Sam Newhouse dubbed his buy "Sam's folly." In 1958 Condé Nast had lost $534,528. And in the years before Sam's involvement, not even its flagship magazine, *Vogue,* made money. According to *Glamour*'s then editor-in-chief, Kathleen Casey Olds, that magazine too, now known as the cash cow of Condé Nast, was losing money and Olds worried that it might be shut down.[2]

Once Condé Nast was his, Sam sent Phil Hochstein and Harrisburg publisher Edwin Russell to Condé Nast's offices, then located in the Graybar Building on Lexington Avenue above Grand Central Station, to coax the lazy small company from red to black ink. Sam himself never took much interest in the day-to-day running of the magazines. This upper-crust, WASP bastion of elegance and elan—its longtime owner was an English lord—differed vastly from the gritty newspaper world that Sam knew. One writer has described *Vogue* of the 1950s as "a kind of trade magazine for titled Europeans and the Social Register set, with a regular column on royalty, a circulation of only 250,000, and an editorial staff drawn largely from the highest reaches of its readership."[3]

The company's founder, Condé Nast, was born in New York in 1874 and grew up in St. Louis. Although trained as a lawyer, in 1900 he took a job in New York as advertising manager of *Collier's Weekly.* In 1909 he bought *Vogue,* which had been founded seventeen years earlier as the "authentic journal of society, fashion and the ceremonial side of life." One of its many backers had been Cornelius Vanderbilt, and virtually all the others were members of Mrs. Astor's 400. At the time of the 1929 stock market crash, Nast had been worth $17 million, but he lost most of it. Still, he managed to keep up appearances in a thirty-room duplex penthouse at 1040 Park Avenue and, during the Great Depression, threw parties for two hundred in his Chinese Chippendale ballroom. He wore a pince-nez, despised FDR and the New Deal, and believed that if people were poor, it was their own fault. Helen Lawrenson, a writer and one of Nast's many mistresses, once described him as "consistently display[ing] the vivacity of a stuffed moosehead." But Lawrenson insisted that Nast was a businessman through and through and that his "shrewdness"—he was not a genius, she specified—was in choosing the right editors for *Vogue, House & Garden,* and *Vanity Fair,* and in letting those editors "put their own stamp on the magazines." He recognized that advertisers would flock to a magazine that offered a class, not mass, group of subscribers.[4]

Many Condé Nast people mistakenly believe that Sam Newhouse paid next to no attention to them. Not so. Every Thursday, battered briefcase in hand, the tiny mogul, looking decidedly out of place in this world of tall, elegant men and attenuated women, came to meet with Iva Sergei Voidato-Patcevitch.

Patcevitch, known as "Mr. Pat," had been running Condé Nast since Condé Nast's death in 1942, and Sam kept him on as the company's president and publisher. Tall, silver-maned, theatrically handsome, aristocratic, charming, Patcevitch was a White Russian who had escaped the revolution just in time—his father, an admiral, had held a high position in the czarist government. He had magnificent manners, and fascinating stories to tell, including one about his failed love affair with Marlene Dietrich. He also had a large share of social snobbery, which included, almost by definition, anti-Semitism.

The writer Francine du Plessix Gray knew Patcevitch well through her stepfather, the Russian-born Alexander Liberman, who, since arriving in *Vogue*'s art department in 1941, had become a major figure at Condé Nast. "I think anti-Semitism was absolutely bred into the White Russian milieu," du Plessix Gray says. "I think Uncle Pat was too much of a gentleman to talk about it, but I'm sure there had been that kind of attitude."[5]

One thing is certain: Patcevitch could not warm to this plain peanut of a man, whose weekly stops at Condé Nast were no different than his journeys to Jersey City to check on the *Jersey Journal*. And his wife Mitzi, so obvious in her social ambitions, was, to Patcevitch's tastes, beyond the pale.

Mitzi, uninvited, had begun to involve herself in the magazines. She took to entertaining Condé Nast editors, often at formal dinners, currying favor with those she thought important, some of whom would never view her as anything but an arriviste. When Kathleen Casey Olds married, Mitzi threw a wedding party for her, the Park Avenue apartment filled with "well-known people." Yet years later Olds dismisses her hostess as "kind of fakey with new money."[6]

If Mitzi sensed what these people thought of her, she acted as if she didn't care. They were, after all, employees of her husband's. She never hesitated to impose herself on Condé Nast editors—especially those at *Vogue*, whose style and wares she most admired. In the 1960s, a grandmother many times over, Mitzi still took to dressing in the plastic and metallic designs of Courrèges and Rudi Gernreich. It was questionable whether these clothes flattered an eighteen-year-old, but on Mitzi they looked ridiculous.

Mitzi was soon put in the hands of a *Vogue* editor named Baron Nicolas de Gunzburg, who was assigned the task of teaching her to dress more appropriately. "He knew the French couture," says Nancy White, then editor-in-chief of *Harper's Bazaar*, "knew all the designers here in

America." The authenticity of his title was the subject of much debate and gossip, but no one disputed the title that Nicky, as he was called, carried at *Vogue*, where he was senior fashion editor and grand arbiter of taste. Under Nicky's eye, Nancy White recalls, Mitzi "became considerably more...simply dressed, more elegant than she had ever looked before." At the Paris collections, Mitzi would often be seated next to Nicky. In New York, he or some other *Vogue* editor would be at her side. Nicky oversaw Mitzi, "A to Z," says White.[7]

Mitzi developed the unsettling (to editors) habit of calling *Vogue* and requesting various products, which she would have assembled into gift bags and then distribute at her dinner parties. When Valorie Griffith Weaver was working in *Vogue*'s beauty and fashion copy department, she remembers Mitzi calling as often as four times a month to request various beauty items. The unlucky editor—often Weaver herself—would have "to call up and get the perfume or makeup or sunscreen and put together twenty little giveaway bags for a dinner party or house gifts."

All *Vogue* editors, including Diana Vreeland, leaped to attention when Mitzi called. "They were afraid of her," Weaver explains. "She had enormous influence if she wanted to wield it, and they were there to wait on her as far as she was concerned."

Edith Raymond Locke, editor of *Mademoiselle,* one of several titles that Sam acquired to expand his Condé Nast stable, remembers finding it amusing rather than intimidating when Mitzi would call about some inexpensive little item that had appeared in the magazine. "She would call up and say that she loved such and such blouse or belt or whatever and could we get it for her wholesale?"[8]

But what Mitzi seemed to want most of all was to be in *Vogue*. Chessy Patcevitch insists that it was only because her husband was such a "terribly nice man" that he agreed. He turned Mitzi over to then society editor Margaret Case.

Mitzi couldn't have asked for more than the tribute that appeared in the June 1964 issue, accompanied by a full-page Cecil Beaton photograph showing her bejeweled, bewigged, and complexly made up, under the headline, "People are Talking about...Mrs. Samuel I. Newhouse." The embarrassingly overheated text mentioned nowhere that she was the wife of the magazine's owner. Mitzi has the "look of Belleek porcelain" with "a major delight in...opera," as well as Dixieland jazz, abstract paintings by Americans, and French furniture. The writer borrowed a phrase from Jane Austen to describe Mitzi as having "an open pleasantry," as well as a "furious curiosity" and a "gaiety of spirit."[9]

The patriarch might have shown more interest in Condé Nast had he not quickly concluded that a monthly magazine, no matter how fat with advertising, could never be as profitable as a daily monopoly newspaper. None of these magazines enjoyed a monopoly, and realistically, Sam understood, they never would. The magazine business was much more competitive than the newspaper business. In any given city or town, newspaper competition could be taken care of; not so in the magazine business, in which competition was generally national, not local.

The elder son, on the other hand, just as quickly concluded that Condé Nast was where he wanted to go to work every morning. Separated from Jane at the time of the purchase, still making little impression on anyone in the newspaper industry, painfully aware that his younger brother Donald, then carrying the nondescript title of general manager of the *Jersey Journal,* was the second-generation Newhouse who everyone in the know was betting would take over when Sam retired or died, the thirty-two-year-old problem child would come to see the magazine acquisition as his main chance. He could make his mark apart from his father and brother, while inhaling the glamour and glitz for which he had a growing taste.

The father, however, considered Condé Nast an appropriate perch for some cousin or nephew. He did not buy the magazines thinking they would come to preoccupy his elder son. According to Peter Diamandis, then a space salesman at *Glamour,* Sam still hoped that Si would adapt himself to where the money was—the newspapers.[10]

By the late 1950s Si did seem to have gained a more serious perspective on newspapers. He went to work most mornings in Newark at the *Star Ledger,* meeting his duties as general manager, but with plenty of backup from others. He visited the papers on his route, he took notes, he reported back to his father, he participated in family meetings, although he brought to the tasks little creativity and less passion. He had resigned himself to the newspapers, but it didn't seem to go much beyond that. Yet *Globe-Democrat* advertising director Ben Magdovitz recalls that in those years, the late 1950s, when Si visited, "you had to be prepared for a lot of questioning.... He would be very quiet except when he got me off in the corner and I was dead meat for the evening."

Si would fire questions at Magdovitz about his end of the business—which strategies were working in the battle to pull some of the higher-tone advertising away from the *Post-Dispatch;* how the particular strengths and the weaknesses of the *Globe*'s editorial mix were affecting ad revenues. And he would go further, asking Magdovitz about areas outside his expertise—distribution and the printing process and the union workers who controlled it.[11]

When his father reluctantly gave Si the okay to go to Condé Nast to learn the business, the privilege did not come without strings. Si had to agree to continue regular visits, with his father, to the *St. Louis Globe-Democrat,* and it wasn't until 1962 that the thirty-five-year-old general manager of the *Star-Ledger* traded his daily destination of Newark, New Jersey, for that of Manhattan's East Side. When in 1967 Sam bought the *Cleveland Plain Dealer,* he insisted that his elder son meet Uncle Norman in Cleveland every Thursday. "Every single Wednesday night Si flew to Cleveland," recalls Peter Diamandis. "It was like a pact. 'You're not going to avoid the newspaper business. If you're going to work in the fashion business with all of this froufrou, that's okay, but you're also going to learn the newspaper business.'"

Si had found his home, and there was no turning back. The newspaper side, says Diamandis, was "tough guys, printer's ink, bullpens and noise, deadlines." While Si was stuck in Newark or in Cleveland, his friends Roy Cohn, Bill Zeckendorf, Jr., and Bill Fugazy "all had limos, ...went out at night to these fine soirées. Si would go to the *Star-Ledger,* that was like...going to a steel mill for God's sake. I think the day he walked into Condé Nast, he said, 'These are my people.'"[12]

The father had calculated correctly that his new magazines could be brought quickly into the black. According to Richard Meeker, within nine months the company's losses had been "transformed" into net profits of $1,627,252.

Sam's first move was characteristic—try to cut down the competition. Shortly after the Condé Nast deal closed, he acquired an old publishing firm called Street & Smith. For $4 million he bought *Charm, Living for Young Homemakers,* and *Mademoiselle.* (Also included were five sports annuals, which he ignored, allowing them to continue to operate with a minimal staff and low-overhead offices—separate from Condé Nast's—and to earn a small but steady profit.) He ordered that *Charm* be folded into *Glamour. Living for Young Homemakers* became *House & Garden Guides. Mademoiselle* was allowed to survive because its audience was younger and better educated than *Glamour's; Mademoiselle* was aimed at the college girl, *Glamour* at the secretary. He also shut down the Condé Nast Press in Greenwich, Connecticut, which printed not only its own magazines but also the *New Yorker* and *Scientific American.* He leased Condé Nast's sewing pattern house to the Butterick Company, and got rid of a subscription fulfillment service.[13]

Still, Sam remained inclined to stay aloof from the company's day-to-day affairs. Harriet Burket Taussig, then editor-in-chief of *House & Garden,* recalls once seeing him at a cocktail party. On being introduced, he said, "'I have no worry about your book [i.e. magazine].' My book was doing very well." Then he said something that struck Taussig and her husband as odd, only because they didn't understand his devotion to the newspapers. "It was sort of a cold day before Christmas, and he kept saying, 'It's snowing in Syracuse, good for business.' We didn't know what he meant. Would they be selling more papers in the snow?"

Some at Condé Nast tended to underrate the patriarch, but not all. Kathleen Casey Olds, a *Vogue* editor whom Patcevitch had appointed editor-in-chief of *Glamour* in 1959, recalls asking Newhouse what he wanted in the struggling magazine, and Sam answered, "Make the magazine like you." That she did, turning *Glamour* into a magazine written for "a girl with a job.... A how-to magazine for young women." It started to make money, and Sam left it and its editor alone.[14]

There was, however, a distinct fear throughout the company, based on his chain of mostly mediocre newspapers, that S. I. would push Condé Nast downmarket and destroy it. The chief worriers were those who viewed the Newhouses as inimical to New York society. No one worried more than Iva Patcevitch, Condé Nast's handpicked successor. It got so that he didn't want his editors to associate with any Newhouse. When Patcevitch discovered that Harriet Taussig, who had worked at *House & Garden* since 1937, had had lunch with Mitzi Newhouse, he became "furious." Taussig remembers him saying, "How did you happen to meet Mrs. Newhouse, and did you invite her to have lunch?" When she assured him that she had not, and that they hadn't "talked shop," he snapped, "I don't like to have people going behind my back."

"I'm going to have to decide what I'm going to do about...this whole Newhouse thing," Taussig remembers Patcevitch saying. He was, Taussig recalls, very resentful. Dodie Kazanjian and Calvin Tomkins, in their biography of Alexander Liberman, attributed Patcevitch's stunning miscalculation of Sam Newhouse partly to garden-variety anti-Semitism, exacerbated by his second marriage to Chessy Amory, "a stylish...very beautiful woman... [who] tended toward the sort of prewar, unthinking anti-Semitism that had begun to strike many educated Americans as somewhat crude." (Chessy was short for Chesborough, as in the face cream.)[15]

When thirty-five-year-old Si Newhouse finally settled down to work at Condé Nast, he felt both happy and terrified. He guessed that Manhattan and slick magazines would suit him much better than Newark and the *Star-Ledger*. But as little natural affinity as he had for the newspaper business, at least he knew something about it. He knew nothing about magazines, and he feared that he'd be out of his league in every way, especially in the areas of looks and glamour. He had not grown out of his homeliness or his excessive shyness. The weak chin, the thick lips, the expensive but conventional clothes worn with little flair were still what even the most nonobservant stranger would notice first. And if the denizens of Condé Nast were anything, it was hyperobservant of style, a quality with which they were so well endowed that they seemed a breed apart.

Almost immediately, *Glamour* editor Kathleen Casey Olds was summoned to see Patcevitch. He had one question and it was about Si: "What should I do with him?"

"You can put him in my office," the English-born, Oregon-bred, Chicago educated Olds told Patcevitch, "I have nothing to hide, and lots of things go on there." She didn't expect Patcevitch to take her up on the offer, but the next day there was Si literally about to plant himself next to her desk. "Now, there may be times when I'll be doing personal things and will have to ask you to leave," she warned him.

"That's okay with me," he said, and for more than a year the unusual arrangement continued. If Si, who was officially assigned to *Glamour*'s promotion department, had a title, no one remembers what it was.

As Olds came to know Si, she found him "very smart" and eager to learn. He asked good questions and obviously loved Condé Nast. And, also unlike his father, he read every line of *Glamour*. In that year with Olds, he learned more about the magazine business than he had learned about the newspaper business in ten. While at the newspapers he had been seen as passive, at Condé Nast he came to life. He was a live wire, constantly moving and questioning.[16]

Miki Denhof, then *Glamour*'s art director, found herself frequently barraged with questions from the "extremely shy" Si about *Glamour* and, increasingly, about *Vogue*. "He wanted to absorb as much as possible," she recalls. On the first of every month, Si would come to Denhof with copies of *Vogue* and its main competitor, *Harper's Bazaar,* and say, "Analyze it for me."

"He wanted to know what made the magazine tick," Denhof explains. He wanted her to "point out what the differences were and how the editorial worked."

One of the differences that Si, with Denhof's help, came to see, was that *Harper's Bazaar* looked more stylish. The credit, he was told, went to its fashion editor, Diana Vreeland, and to its fashion photographer, Richard Avedon. Si decided that he wanted to hire both.[17]

But he would not have known how to get them without the help of the tall, handsome, graceful Alexander Liberman, a man of flawless taste who would become Si's true mentor—a father figure in a way Sam could never be. Some saw Alex as superficial; Si saw him as stunningly stylish. It was Alex's vision that defined how all the magazines, covers and beyond, looked, how their design interacted with editorial, who might be the next editor of *Vogue* or art director of *House & Garden*.

Peter Diamandis attributes the growth of Condé Nast to the working relationship that the elder son developed with Liberman. A brilliant, ambitious, intuitive man, Alex instantly grasped the fact, in a way that Patcevitch couldn't, that his prospects lay in the hands of this diffident lit-

tle man, utterly lacking in style and grace, the very qualities that so pre-
occupied the elegant Liberman and that so epitomized Condé Nast. As
Chessy Patcevitch puts it with much bitterness in her tone, Si "knew nothing, absolutely nothing, and Alex grabbed him." She claims that Alex
"never left [Si's] side," and shifted his loyalty "overnight" from her husband to the Newhouses.[18]

Liberman also remembered to pay close attention to Sam and, equally important, to Mitzi. Alex and his wife, Tatiana, a Russian-born, stat-
uesque beauty who designed hats for Saks Fifth Avenue but was also a
renowned figure in New York artistic and social circles, would never have
considered turning down one of Mitzi's frequent dinner invitations. When
Alex was named editorial director of Condé Nast in December 1962, it was
understood that the decision had been approved not only by Si, but by his
father too. Both father and son trusted Alex Liberman, but the son fell in
love with him. Within months of arriving at Condé Nast, Si came to see
Liberman as a genius in calculating what makes a magazine work.

One evening Si took his father and mother, James Michener, and Roy Cohn
to El Morocco for dinner. Si also brought along a *Harper's Bazaar* editor
named Barbara Slifka. When Si tipped the doorman, Slifka remembers
Sam quipping, "You must have a rich father." But the date was not all ban-
ter; she says Si pumped her all evening for information about Diana
Vreeland.

Diana Vreeland was an original, the likes of which the magazine
world would never see again. By her own telling, she landed her job at
Bazaar after its then editor, Carmel Snow, saw her dancing at the St. Regis
Roof. Vreeland was wearing a white lace Chanel dress, a bolero jacket, and
roses in her hair. Snow was so intrigued by Vreeland's style that she hired
her. Until then, as one writer put it, "she was a young New York matron
who had never seen the inside of an office." (Vreeland protested to Carmel
Snow, "I'm never dressed until lunch.")

That year, 1962, Alexander Liberman, with Si watching in fascination, went after Vreeland to replace *Vogue* editor Jessica Daves, whom
Liberman considered too dowdy and prudish for the times. Liberman was
definitely the mover in public, but Si was intrigued with the prospect of

landing the brilliant but eccentric editor and, according to *Bazaar*'s Nancy White, played a supporting role in persuading Vreeland to come to *Vogue*.

Selling Vreeland on *Vogue* was not difficult. She was offered, in her words, "an endless expense account…and Europe whenever I wanted to go," in addition to a large salary—a relief after, at Hearst, having her salary stuck for twenty-eight years at $18,000 until 1958, when she was given a $1,000 raise. "Can you imagine?" she complained, "Would you give your cook that after she'd worked for you for twenty-eight years?" More important, she knew that she had been passed over for *Bazaar*'s top job, and was particularly offended that it went instead to Nancy White. "We needed an artist and they sent us a housepainter," Vreeland sniped about White, who was the niece and successor of the legendary *Bazaar* editor Carmel Snow and the daughter of Tom White, who had run the magazines and then the newspapers for Hearst. (Carmel Snow had warned the "money-men" at *Bazaar* that Vreeland lacked the temperament to be editor-in-chief.)

Si and Alex assured Vreeland that not only would she have the editor-in-chief's job, but under Newhouse ownership, *Vogue* would become much more powerful than *Bazaar*. (What they didn't tell Vreeland was that Alex's recent promotion to editorial director of Condé Nast was done specifically so he could keep tabs on the unorthodox editor.)

Vreeland arrived at *Vogue* in 1962 and became editor-in-chief in January 1963. She was an inspired choice. "She used her authority to remake fashion journalism in her own image," Liberman's biographers write, "and in doing so she catapulted *Vogue* into its period of absolute dominance." She was sixty-three when she moved to *Vogue*—she had been at *Bazaar* since the 1930s—but more than any other editor she celebrated the youth and sexual revolution of the 1960s, featuring miniskirts and bikinis, which during Daves's regime would never have seen print. Vreeland is credited with discovering Halston, Lauren Bacall, Twiggy, and the Italian thong sandal, with popularizing the turtleneck sweater, and with coining the word *Pizzazz*.

The change at *Vogue* couldn't have been more striking. During the Daves years, hats and white gloves were required office attire. Daves, like her predecessor Edna Woolman Chase, the magazine's first editor, was partial to veils and in a now famous gaffe once forgot to lift her veil before eating a deviled egg at one of Alex Liberman's cocktail parties.

Vreeland's mother was American—Diana's great-great-uncle was Francis Scott Key—her father English. To their house in Paris, where Diana was born, came such visitors as Isadora Duncan, Nijinsky, and Diaghilev. At the start of World War I, the family moved to New York, where Diana was sent to the Brearley School. After three months she was asked to leave; her mother was told that Diana didn't fit in. In America, the family's circle included such exotics as Buffalo Bill, whom, Vreeland claimed, taught her to ride.

Raven-haired, beak-nosed, her lips and cheeks painted scarlet, her office walls painted scarlet, her newspapers and dollar bills ironed by her maid, Vreeland was an editor like none the industry had ever seen. Her signature became such eccentric pairings as couture gowns with combat boots and high-fashion models with green hair and bodies so free of flesh and curves that they would have looked at home at Auschwitz.[19]

Once Vreeland was his, Si turned his attention almost exclusively to *Vogue,* and, with Alex Liberman at his elbow, went poaching again at *Bazaar,* this time for the world's foremost fashion photographer, Richard Avedon. Nancy White recalls running into Si and Mitzi at a restaurant in Paris. Mitzi looked on approvingly as Si told the dumbfounded editor-in-chief that he wanted Avedon to leave *Bazaar* for *Vogue,* and that, as White interpreted it, "They were prepared to do anything to get him."

What was White to make of this apparent effort to strip her magazine of its stars? She had come to *Bazaar* from *Good Housekeeping,* and her wholesomeness and lack of flamboyance made her an editor unlikely to catch Si's eye or Alex Liberman's. But according to White, so intent was Si on having Avedon that he once told her, "We're determined to get Avedon even if we have to have you." Avedon moved to *Vogue* in 1965. White stayed put, and watched as the raids continued.

In 1966 Si hired Vreeland disciple Polly Mellen, who had joined *Bazaar* in 1950 and who considered Vreeland "my mentor, my best friend, my life." Nancy White tried to retaliate by hiring Vreeland's number two at *Vogue,* Grace Mirabella: "I wanted her very badly," White recalls, "but they were paying her a great deal more than we could afford."[20]

Mostly, though, Si was operating on a more modest Newhousian plane. He spent time with *Vogue* publisher Ed Russell. The Churchill-connected shill whom Sam had used to buy the Harrisburg papers had kept his title as publisher and president of the Harrisburg papers, but Sam, in 1960, had given him the added title of publisher of *Vogue*. One man who was later publisher of a Condé Nast magazine claims that Si sat behind Russell for two years, taking notes and saying nothing.

Through all the descriptions of Si Newhouse, who would turn forty in 1967, runs the image of the heir to the empire as an untutored, unformed boy. Some women found something charming, even slightly sexual, in Si's innocence and eagerness. "There was this little, unfashionable boy from like nowhere almost," says Pat Miller, who was the editor of a short-lived Condé Nast magazine called *Woman*, having his "little Jewish nose pressed against the WASPy bastion of Condé Nast." There was a code there, says Sally Obre, who dated Si just after his father bought Condé Nast—between 1959 and 1961, before his divorce was final—and later went to work for *Glamour*. That code applied even to the owner's son, so determined to learn. Trying to break it, Obre remembers, sometimes seemed like "a futile fight." The code was Condé Nast as an elitist cadre, a high fashion, artistic, exclusive world. Anthea Disney, later editor-in-chief of Condé Nast's *Self* magazine, describes the company as "the kind of place where you went into a meeting and people would be speaking French or Italian or Russian."[21]

Yet for all its WASPiness, says Obre, Condé Nast was run "like a Catholic girls boarding school, girls who came in little sweaters or black dresses in their fathers' limousines.... I think it was probably very hard for Si at the beginning to get in and learn what that business was all about." Geraldine Stutz, who was educated in private Catholic girls' schools and worked at *Vogue* and *Glamour*, agrees that life at Condé Nast was "like being in another convent school."

The mother superior was Mary Campbell, a former gym teacher and devout Catholic who had been Condé Nast's personal secretary, "his left and right hand," says Stutz. Campbell was suspected of favoring any girl who had been to a Catholic boarding school. According to Sally Obre, Campbell, then head of personnel, "was probably one of the strongest women in American business at that time. Even the damn editor-in-chief trembled with Mary Campbell because she knew where all the bodies were buried.... You couldn't do diddly without that woman knowing about it. She knew what time you got in, if you didn't pay your rent on time. She knew everything."

One of Mary Campbell's expectations of select editors was that they must serve as advertisements for the magazines; they were to go out and mix in society, not sit home at night, limited by an insufficient bank balance or wardrobe. "We were given charge accounts everyplace," says Geraldine Stutz. "We were introduced all over town as a Condé Nast editor," and the company gladly paid the bills.

The Condé Nast "culture," as it was called, clashed with nearly every aspect of the Newhouse culture. "It really wasn't about hard business," says Sally Obre. "It was about grace and elegance and it was about major expense accounts and looking wonderful and having important last names and everybody on the staff either had to be a deb or had to be related, you couldn't believe the secretaries at *Glamour* and *Vogue*—Mr. Paley's daughter, the daughter of the Slocums of Newport, everybody's daughter made $85 a week at Condé Nast and then they went over to 21 for lunch and charged it to Daddy." Obre remembers one British editor on *Glamour:* "You'd run by her office and pick up her ringing phone and...it would be Henry Ford."

When Val Weaver, from Kentucky, fresh out of college with no money, interviewed for an assistant's job at *Vogue* in 1968, it wasn't until the last minute that the issue of salary was raised, as if it were bad form to talk about money. "They said to me is 85 okay?" Thinking they meant $8,500 a year, she replied, "Yes, that's great." When she received her first paycheck, she realized with sinking spirits that they had meant $85 a week. Her take-home pay was $58, and she had to arrange loans in order to live. "It was assumed that most of the women there did not really have to work, they were absolutely up-front about it." But as early as the late 1960s, Weaver adds, the first signs of change were apparent. "They were...beginning to say, 'We need to have some smart people here at the assistant level.'"[22]

It did become a different game once Si Newhouse showed up. The more savvy people recognized that it was Si's company now and he would run the place anyway he cared to, and they flocked to his side to help him learn. Typical was Mary Jane Pool, who had arrived at *Vogue* in 1946 and worked her way up to executive editor. (Later she became editor-in-chief of *House & Garden.*) But among Si's most important influences was Richard Shortway. A tall, handsome, much-married man—at last count, five wives—he had come to Condé Nast as an ad salesman for *Glamour* in 1946, worked his way up to advertising manager, and then, in 1963, moved over to *Vogue* as ad director. In 1964, when Si officially went to *Vogue,* taking from Ed Russell the title of publisher, he and Shortway, as one Condé Nast publisher put it, were "joined at the hip." Shortway taught Si the advertising sales side of the business. Titles to the contrary, Shortway did the publisher's job, which at Condé Nast means selling ads, directing other ad salesmen, courting, and closing the big deals. In 1970, when Si traded up to the title of publishing director of *Vogue,* he named Shortway publisher.[23]

Si Newhouse would appear not to have much in common with Dick Shortway, but they did share a strong work ethic. In later years Si would become known for arriving at his office at 4:00 to 4:30 a.m. But even then, according to one editor at *Vogue,* "He was there at five or six in the morning before anybody got in, and he was working all day and he was still there in the evening." Sally Obre remembers occasionally having dinner alone with Si, "and we would talk the magazine business and the fashion business forever, for four or five hours...because literally that was his passion." Years later he would pay the highest tribute to an employee who had died by saying that, to him, "Magazine journalism was high culture."[24]

Although Shortway expressed it in different ways, he had the same passion for *Vogue.* One editor then at the magazine recalls Shortway as "a workaholic the way Si is, he lived and breathed the magazine." "Dick had one thing that was better than anybody I ever saw," says Peter Diamandis. "He had an absolute rhinoceros hide. He could get thrown out of a guy's office and call him up the next day and say, 'Hey, Joe, good to talk to you.' 'What are you talking about? I threw you out of here.' 'Ahh, well, come on, I want to talk to you.'... It just rolled off his back like a duck. He had that tenacity, stick-to-it-ness that great salesmen have."

Shortway was said to have been helpful to Si in social areas too. One former publisher calls Shortway at that time a kind of "baby-sitter" for Si. Others use a less respectful term. Val Weaver claims that Shortway would arrange dates for his boss. There was "a fair amount of grownup double-dating between Si and one or two of the publishers who would date members of the *Vogue* staff and maybe other staffs as well." (*Vogue* was considered the staff with by far the most desirable women. The best pickings, specifies Val Weaver, would have been in the fashion and beauty departments.) Shortway labels such descriptions "ridiculous, utter nonsense." He never served as Si's baby-sitter, he insists, and he never arranged a date for Si. As for "double-dating," Shortway adds, they went out together twice.[25]

Si much preferred to date where he worked than to meet women, say, through family connections. An aspiring actress whose parents were friendly with Sam and Mitzi recalls her one arranged date with Si. He picked her up in a limousine, cast an icy glance her way, and continued to read his newspaper. There was no second date.

Despite Si's dependence on men like Alex Liberman and Dick Shortway, the Newhouse hand was gradually coming to the fore. It was Si, for example, who in 1968 moved *Vogue* executive editor Mary Jane Pool over to *House & Garden*, in order to position her, two years later, to replace Harriet Taussig as editor-in-chief. Pool fondly remembers working with the Newhouse son at both magazines. "If you wanted to get something done, you'd go and say, 'Si, what do you think about this and that?'.... He was very receptive to ideas."

Those who worked with Si came to respect him in a way not often accorded the boss's son. "He really did his homework," says one *Vogue* editor. "He was always on top of things, always moving around, always asking questions, always learning." His style, she says, was to pull out of people as much information as he could, and then make up his mind. She says that sometimes his decisions surprised her because he "came at them from a different point of view. I remember somebody complaining that one of our people was ordering things wholesale and...then not paying for them and I was asked to tell management about it because the manufacturer was quite upset, and so I felt I had to mention it to Si.... Instead of getting upset at that person, he looked at me and said, 'We're obviously not paying them enough.'"

Glamour art director Miki Denhof remembers those early years under Si's leadership as a time when "one could do anything, one never had to ask, using the best photographers, the best materials, the best of everything."[26] Diana Vreeland was famous for spending whatever it cost to achieve the look she wanted. According to Grace Mirabella, "Vreeland liked to do retakes—two, four, ten—the cost was immaterial. 'I'm looking for the *suggestion* of something I've never seen,' she'd say.... She was willing to hold up an issue, rack up thousands and thousands of dollars in models' overtime, photographers' fees...just to get a look she thought was 'duhvine.'" Vreeland would send a photographer to India to photograph white tigers, Mirabella writes, for a layout that never ran. Si didn't seem to care, giving permission for all that and more.

Alex Liberman grew completely confident that Si would pay the bills without a word of question or recrimination. When Louis Oliver Gropp, former editor-in-chief of *House & Garden,* once suggested to Liberman that they could save money by altering a certain procedure, Alex just looked at him. "Never talk to me about money. Only talk about doing a good magazine. No one is ever going to thank you for saving money."[27]

While the culture of Condé Nast naturally bred a never-to-worry-about-money attitude, there was a reason beyond style or tradition for perks that included an unlimited flow of petty cash in the form of advances against expenses that the employee might or might not actually accrue. There had been, off and on, attempts by the Newspaper Guild to organize a union at Condé Nast. Picketers had even congregated outside the Condé Nast building. A year or so after her arrival in 1980 as an editor at *Glamour,* Kim Bonnell was summoned to a meeting. Gathered in the room were Si Newhouse, the managing editor of *Glamour,* a couple of "corporate types," and a lawyer or two.

"I was really baffled as to why I was asked to this meeting," Bonnell recalls, "but it turned out that it was about unions, and I had come from the [*New York*] *Daily News* where I was a member of the union. And I heard...that Si was absolutely terrified and concerned that the union would try to come into Condé Nast and they thought that I might be organizing."

One of the men, not Si, questioned her about the guild and whether she was still a member. It may have been naive of her, she says in retrospect, but she didn't feel particularly intimidated, and she heard no more on the subject of unions, from Newhouse or his lawyers or anyone else. Si really had little to worry about, Bonnell adds, because her colleagues "had no sympathy for the union, even though they were getting terrible salaries and terrible benefits and no one cared because their parents were supporting them anyway."

Still, Si wasn't going to take any chances, and it was after this union scare, Bonnell adds, that the company upgraded its salaries and benefits to bring them in line with those given to newspaper reporters.[28] The perks continued, both as a matter of style and as a kind of insurance policy against organizing.

By the mid-1960s Sam Newhouse came to accept that his elder son would never love newspapers, that he had fallen in love with magazines. The father gave the son a vote of confidence by buying the Borden Building at 350 Madison Avenue and moving the magazines there. Like the sale of the company itself, the $20 million purchase from the Borden dairy company, a bargain in retrospect, was initially dubbed "Sam's folly." The move was, in a way, symbolic of the new regime. The historic, art deco Graybar Building really did have the atmosphere of "a lady's finishing school," says Sally Obre.[29] The new building was much more corporate, a signal of where the company was headed. There were plenty of remnants of the past, but the days of a small staff of well-bred and like-minded people turning out magazines for readers just like themselves were over.

11 | Si Finds an Image

DURING THIS PERIOD of the elder brother's education, learning all he could about the magazines from the maestro, Alex Liberman, Si Newhouse was also busy assembling an image to present to the world. After leaving Jane and his three children behind—Jane reared the children in the old Park Avenue apartment and, to this day, lives there with her second husband—Si eventually found a duplex, penthouse apartment in a nondescript building at 235 East Seventy-third Street between Second and Third Avenues—and commissioned society decorator Billy Baldwin to redo it. Displaying just the opposite of his mother's taste for antique French furniture and gold decor, Si wanted a minimal look for his apartment.[1]

It had also occurred to him that he would need art for his walls, but that was not a subject that had ever engaged his interest. While they were married, Jane recalls, Si showed no interest in art. At the time she dated him, says Geraldine Stutz, they never went to a museum or gallery. Their "major activity" was going to dinner. Stutz calls Si at this point "really unformed, and I had no notion that he would turn out to [have]... what is known as one of the best eyes about modern painting."

With Alex Liberman and all those art directors to guide his purchases, he decided to buy contemporary paintings. "How do you buy pictures?" Si asked Miki Denhof straight out. He took Denhof, then art director of *Glamour,* with him when he made his first two purchases, both circle paintings by Alex Liberman, who in his time away from the office was a serious painter and sculptor.[2]

Soon Si became passionate about collecting art. It seemed to provide him with the sense of identity and self-worth that so long had eluded him. "This was one place where he had autonomy," says a former *House & Garden* editor in speculating that Si felt so eclipsed by his father.

Mitzi's artistic bent would be cited as the source of Si's inspiration to collect. But Mitzi was as conventional in her selection of art as she was in her selection of Louis XV and XVI furniture. One New York dealer remembers the time Mitzi visited his gallery, "followed by a rather swishy young man from the decorator's office carrying this pink pillow. She wanted the painting to match the pink of the sofa." Art dealer André Emmerich sums up Mitzi's approach to art: "She used art very effectively as a form of decoration."

The most important person in Si's forays into the modern art market was, of course, Alex Liberman. "Alex taught Si everything he knows about art," says one former publisher. In Si's early days at Condé Nast, says Peter Diamandis, Alex "dragged him around" to see art, to go to openings, to meet artists. Before that, adds Diamandis, "He wouldn't go anywhere."

Sally Obre remembers that when she was dating Si and he was just beginning to collect, she would meet Si for dinner and he would often greet her by exclaiming, "Oh, my God, I'm so excited. I just left Alex and we bought this wonderful thing."

In her memoir, Grace Mirabella, whom Si would later appoint and fire as *Vogue*'s top editor, describes with much residual bitterness why Liberman was so important to Newhouse. Si "didn't really move with the 'right' crowd. In fact, one of his closest friends was Roy Cohn. He hadn't had the 'right' sort of first wife. Or the right clothes. Or manners. That was where Alex Liberman came in."

Liberman's stepdaughter, Francine du Plessix Gray, herself married to an artist, Cleve Gray, offers perhaps the subtlest analysis of the relationship: "Si seems to enjoy having paternal role models.... I think that Alex became a mentor of sorts in the way of acquiring a veneer of urbane manners. Alex was not a member of the aristocracy, but he's born into the Russian Jewish intelligentsia, a milieu far more cultivated and gracious than the Russian nobility, who were mostly a bunch of philistine bores." (Born in Kiev in 1912, his father a businessman with close ties to Lenin, his mother a theater aficionado, Alex was educated in England and France.)

Gray describes Alex as always "very at ease with himself in the world and I think it may be that ease in the world which Si needed the most."

Another woman who knew both Si and Alex long and well describes Si as being "not in his own skin," a man who felt uncomfortable with himself and the world. "It's some kind of inferiority complex about not being as polished as the people he has to hobnob with.... That's what he maybe loved the most about Alex, his sense of being totally in his own skin."

It was Liberman who introduced Newhouse to the esteemed artist Barnett "Barney" Newman, who became a close friend, a frequent dinner companion, and another important teacher about art. The introduction to Newman, Si told Alex's biographers, "opened up the whole field for me. I started to absorb the culture of painting through Barney."

Si also began spending time and doing business with the late Harold Diamond, a private dealer who sold art from an apartment filled with wonderful paintings, and his wife, Hester. David Whitney, the freelance art curator, collector, and companion of architect Philip Johnson, was another person who honed Si's taste and offered advice.[3]

But as close as Si was to Liberman, his real love affair was with the late Condé Nast editor Leo Lerman, a grand guru of all things cultural, who nurtured scores of younger people in whom he detected an artistic bent or appreciation. *New York Times* style editor Holly Brubach, a former fashion writer for the *New Yorker* and fashion copywriter for *Vogue,* called Lerman "the greatest *appreciator* I have ever known. He fostered other people's talents with ferocious pride." Lerman's natural sweetness, generosity, and colorful eccentricities made his tie to Si warmer, more affectionate, "truly a family kind of relationship," says Amy Gross, who in 1964 became Leo's assistant at *Mademoiselle.*

Since his arrival at *Mademoiselle* in 1948, Lerman had directed all the arts coverage at the magazine and had showcased a long list of serious writers, among them Truman Capote, whom he was the first to publish. Twelve years later, when Sam Newhouse bought the Street & Smith magazines, including *Mademoiselle,* Sam's biggest payoff may have been the acquisition of Leo Lerman.

While Alex Liberman projected an aura of strength, Leo Lerman seemed, at times quite vulnerable, despite, in later years, his full white beard and godlike visage. Those were qualities that younger people responded to, as if they could protect this lovely gentleman who, behind the wit and sparkle, suffered for decades the progressive loss of his eyesight from glaucoma and constant pain from injuries that would eventually leave him crippled. (He was thrown through the windshield of a taxi in 1942 after its driver fell asleep.)

Si might not have been the kind of "kid" to whom Lerman's attention would have been naturally drawn, but Si was the boss's son. So when the boss's son came to worship at Lerman's altar of literature on theater and film history and criticism, Lerman became Si's prime teacher. Si appeared often in Leo's office, which with its wonderful library of books served him as a kind of perpetual classroom. Si would just sit there and listen to the grand master of culture.

Lerman did not go unrewarded for the attention he paid Si. In 1972, after twenty-six years at *Mademoiselle,* he moved to the Newhouses's royal magazine, *Vogue,* where he became feature editor with the assignment to cover culture. Culture included movies, one of Si's fervent loves. He and Leo often discussed those that Si had seen or planned to see or wondered about, some of them old or extremely obscure. Lerman would also arrange screenings, with Si the most eager viewer. During another meeting, Lerman might tell Si about the day in Paris in 1977 when he and Gray Foy, Leo's lover of forty-eight years, spent the afternoon with Maria Callas in her apartment—they had come to know her twenty-four years earlier after hearing her sing an aria from Verdi's *Traviata*—and the evening of the same day with Marlene Dietrich, who cooked dinner for the two men.

When Si first came to know Leo, he and Gray were living in a brownstone on Lexington Avenue and Ninety-fourth Street. In 1968 they moved to the Osborne, circa 1885, on the West Side, just off Carnegie Hall. Here they continued to conduct regular salons that drew a nonpareil gathering of intellectuals and artists. On a given night one might encounter Henry Green, Edith Sitwell, Evelyn Waugh, Cecil Beaton, W. H. Auden, Callas, Dietrich, Truman Capote, Paul and Jane Bowles, Marcel Duchamp, Anaïs Nin, Diana and Lionel Trilling, Julie Harris, Hal Prince, or, in much later years, Emma Thompson.[4]

Coming home to his six-room apartment after one of Lerman's soirees, Si came to realize that it was sorely lacking in character. He stepped up his acquisition of art in an attempt to add weight and interest.

Shortly after Si's friend Mary Jane Pool became the top editor at *House & Garden,* she featured his penthouse without mentioning that its occupant was an heir to the company that owned the magazine. In the article, "Art Everywhere You Look," datelined New York City, 1969, and one of several under the grand theme "Living With Art," Si is quoted as saying that his orders to Billy Baldwin were to decorate around the paintings and sculptures and to select "comfortable furniture, but nothing with too strong a personality of its own." The article contains a veritable inventory of Si's collection at that time—works by Alex Liberman but also by Morris Louis, Clyfford Still, Helen Frankenthaler, Kenneth Noland, and Jules Olitski, and sculptures by David Smith, Anthony Caro, Ruth Vollmer, Mark Di Suvero, Isaac Witkin, Morio Shinoda, and Paul Feeley. The unidentified writer dwells on Si's master bedroom, with its brown velvet walls and ceiling and the feel of a "beige and brown cave." The caption notes that the view from Si's bed is of "a huge, mysterious Mark Rothko, a black and white Barnett Newman lithograph, a darkly luminous Morris Louis.... Another Rothko hangs over the bed and a Julius Bissier over each table lamp."

The apartment became a venue for business. Si gave a cocktail party there in December 1968 to welcome Mary Jane Pool to *House & Garden.* He entertained designers and advertisers whose wares appeared in *Vogue* and the other fashion magazines. Si frequently invited *Vogue* publisher Dick Shortway for dinner. "Pedro [Si's Filipino houseboy and cook] would greet me at the door," Shortway remembers. "I'd have a scotch and soda.... We would sit, have dinner alone, and kind of plot strategies."[5]

Si's days had developed a seamless quality that they had previously lacked. His art and his magazines were his life; his companions were, with the major exception of Roy Cohn, magazine, fashion, and art people. To his admiring guests, the host was not merely Si Newhouse. He was the man who was heir to the ownership of the magazines they worked for or aspired to work for or in whose pages they wished to appear. He was also a man who was spending huge sums as fast as he could decide whose art to buy.

As early as the early 1970s, Si showed signs of tiring quickly of certain artists, whose work might be there one cocktail party and gone the next. (He would soon show a similarly short passion-span for editors.) Because his knowledge of art and its history was shallow, and because he was on the prowl constantly for the latest sensation, he could fall out of love with an artist and sell his or her work as quickly as he had fallen in love in the first place.

With women, he seemed similarly inclined. After leaving Jane in 1959, Si promptly began to date Geraldine Stutz, a glamorous figure in the fashion business, who was then, while still in her twenties, president of Henri Bendel's. Stutz liked Si from the start and particularly found his devotion to his children "endearing." When he picked her up for dinner, more often than not, he had just come from having spent time with his sons and daughter.

Dinner, often at 21 or Le Pavillon, usually included Roy Cohn, whom Stutz calls Si's "best buddy," and Cohn's then girlfriend, Barbara Walters. The columnist George Sokolsky—the man who secured Roy Cohn his job with Joe McCarthy—was frequently in attendance. Stutz remembers them all listening to Sokolsky's "rabid right-wing" views. Roy Cohn agreed with most everything he said, but Si would say nothing, no matter how extreme the view. Even in those days Stutz felt that Si stood back from politics. In fact, despite their intimate relationship, Stutz claims to have had no notion what his politics were, and she says today, "I still don't." She attributes this detachment, in part, to his difficulty in expressing himself. Had he tried, he wouldn't have done so effectively, as he was remarkably inarticulate.

Stutz, who considered herself a liberal Democrat, remembers that she and Barbara Walters would fight with Sokolsky. "I'd sit and listen to George's outrageous points of view.... I can remember a couple of times saying, 'Bye, I'm going home.'" She disagreed just as vehemently with Roy Cohn, but says that she couldn't help but like him. "I disapproved of everything that Roy stood for, but I liked him.... He had this enormous loyalty to people that he cared about."

During the year they were together, Si took Stutz on vacation, often with Cohn and Walters, to an island off the coast of Florida that Cohn either owned or held a lease on. There were getaways too on Roy's yacht.

But then Stutz and Si called it quits. "We just kind of drifted apart," Stutz explains.

Si soon had another girlfriend, this one more serious than Stutz. Sally Obre, then Sally Allen, was from Boston, and like Stutz, she had modeled as a teenager. She had recently arrived in New York with a twenty-one-month-old baby to support—her husband had abandoned them without child support or alimony—and $200 she had borrowed from her mother. She was living in a rent-controlled apartment on Central Park West. "I didn't have a dime to my name." Then in her twenties, she worked in sales on Seventh Avenue.

She met Si in 1959 at a dinner party given by a friend of hers from one of New York's "grand old families," a Guggenheim on one side and on the other an old upstate family of "great WASPy provenance, but no money." Around six one weeknight, Obre received a "hysterical" call from this friend, who had invited another friend to be Si's dinner partner. That woman was ill; would Sally fill in? Obre, who had never heard of Si Newhouse, was promptly informed that his father had just bought Condé Nast. So she went.

She hired a baby-sitter, threw on her black, spaghetti-strapped cocktail dress, her pearls, her black Capezios, and her Filene's camel hair polo coat, and rushed to her friend's duplex in the East Sixties. "I was trying to be very prim and proper, and Si was extremely shy," Obre recalls. She was sitting lightly on a chair when "I leaned back, and the back of the chair fell off." (She later called her hostess to apologize. She said not to worry: "It came from Aunt Peggy's [Guggenheim's] palace in Venice and it's 300 years old.") Obre figured that Si would see this as "the klutz move of the year," and she'd never see him again.

But Si was apparently amused by her good humor and easygoing nature, and attracted by her preppie good looks—she describes herself then as having "shiny scrubbed cheeks" and straight hair. As the dinner party broke up, he asked her to join him for a "nightcap" at the Stork Club. They danced, drank champagne, and had a "lovely" time. The mix of her extroverted personality and his "very introverted" one worked: "You both can't be screaming for air time at the same time," she explains. (They were joined at their table that night by newspaper columnist Jack O'Brian. A fervid anti-Communist and part of Roy Cohn's clique, O'Brian wrote a gossip column for Hearst's *New York Journal-American* and, at the Stork Club, was a regular tablemate and pal of Walter Winchell.)

Obre suspects that Si also liked her because she was "very, very simple. I think I was quite different from most of the girls that he was accustomed to going out with." On her side, she found Si "incredibly sweet, incredibly shy, and very interested in who I was and what I was all about." He had, she says, "a certain respect for women." While he was not handsome or even good-looking, she found him "cute.... He had a weenie boyness about him."

For Obre, the romance opened up a side of New York she might otherwise never have seen. One day Si informed her that they would be meeting Roy Cohn for dinner. She knew and detested the name from having watched the televised Army-McCarthy hearings in 1954. She gasped, "'Oh, my God, not that Roy Cohn!' I was absolutely beside myself. I went on and on about the McCarthy hearings." She told Si that she'd rather not have dinner with him. Si answered, simply, "He's one of my best friends.... I have dinner with him two or three times a week and I think you're going to like him, so do it for me."

She did, and like many others who came into Cohn's orbit, "I fell madly in love with him.... What I saw was a charming, funny, gossipy, dishy—oh, the biggest gossip in the world—charming guy." She describes how Cohn would "eat off everybody's plate," Si's included, "and you were deemed only a friend if you would let him eat off your plate, and the more he liked you, the more he had to eat from your plate."

Cohn was still seeing Barbara Walters, and at least twice a week the couples double-dated. On Monday nights they went to the opera, on another night to 21, on another to the Stork Club or El Morocco, on Saturday night to Le Pavillon with chef Henri Soule hovering over the table.

On some weekends the four of them would head for the beaches and casinos of San Juan, Puerto Rico. On other weekends, Roy would issue irresistible invitations. He once chartered a plane, packed it full of his friends, and took everyone to Miami to see a title fight with Ingmar Johansson preceded by a formal dinner.

Like Geraldine Stutz, Sally Obre admired Si's caring relationship with his children. On weekends in the city, he would take his children as well as Sally's son out for the afternoon and for dinner. Obre sums up Si as a man who "was passionate about his business, about art, and about his children."

When Si brought Sally home to meet his parents, Obre felt next to no warmth from Mitzi. "I was nobody at the time, so she wasn't exactly charming and warm." One evening Obre was at the Park Avenue apartment for dinner, looking pretty with a new haircut. "And where did you get your hair done?" Mitzi asked her.

"I said, just as bright as a button because I was absolutely guileless, 'Oh, I had it done at Lord & Taylor's, Mrs. Newhouse.'

"And she said, 'Oh, ha, ha, ha, can you imagine anyone having their hair done at Lord & Taylor's?' I thought to myself, 'Oh boy, there's a problem here. This woman is that insecure that she has to pick on the likes of little me.'" That was Sally's tipoff that Mitzi was a bully, and unlikely ever to accept her.

Still, she hoped that Si would propose marriage. As she explains her reasons for wanting to marry him, security, not passion, takes precedence: "I'd had one lousy, short, horrible, abusive marriage, and I was really anxious to get married. I never, ever had any desire to be a major career person." She also had plenty of financial worries. Looking good on Si's arm, she claims, cost her "untold thousands of dollars.... You have to have clothes where you can walk into 21 and look terrific." Si, she says, was simply oblivious to her plight. "He really didn't understand money.... He didn't know what it was like for a woman like me who made a lousy salary to support myself and my son."

Mitzi, Obre feels, was probably an obstacle to Si's proposing marriage, but there was more to it than that. "Si developed crushes on people left and right," she admits. She remembers being "terribly hurt" when Si called her and confessed, "I don't know how to tell you this, but I want to break our date Saturday night.... I've met someone. I've developed something for her. I've got to find out. I don't know whether it's serious or not." Obre said fine, and Si spent that evening and many others with Alex Mayes, a recent college graduate, an editor at *Glamour*, later managing editor of *Seventeen,* and the daughter of Herbert Mayes, who had been the top editor at *Good Housekeeping* and was then editor-in-chief of *McCall's.* Obre describes her as "bright, ...very attractive, a terrific gal.... They had nothing in common. She was a baby and he was a father of three."

Then Si came back to Sally. "I'm sorry," he apologized, "would you please go out with me again and I'll explain it all to you." They did, but without marriage in the offing the relationship ended after two years, in 1961. Si arranged for Obre to be given a job as a merchandise editor at *Glamour.* She stayed there for five years, later leaving Condé Nast for *Ladies Home Journal.* Shortly after the breakup with Si, she married someone else.[6]

There are some people who worked for Si, both male and female, who insist that all this dating was a ruse, that Si was in fact a closet homosexual, perhaps a bisexual. They point to his closest friendships with Roy Cohn and Allard Lowenstein as evidence of Si's sexual orientation. But the friendship with Lowenstein did not survive high school graduation, and those who knew Roy Cohn well insist that there was nothing sexual between Roy and Si. Roy's friend, the ladies' man Tom Corbally, puts the chances at "less than a thousand to one." Gary Marcus, a young cousin of Cohn's who for a time lived in his Manhattan townhouse, says of Si, "If Si were gay, Roy would have said so. He loved to expose closet gays.... Whenever Roy talked about [Si], he talked about him the way you would talk about a suburban neighbor." Marcus describes Roy's townhouse as the scene of "orgies" nearly every night. "They'd start going at it around ten o'clock and wouldn't quit until three in the morning." Not once, says Marcus, did he see Si.

Nicholas von Hoffman, Cohn's biographer, says that if Newhouse had an affair with Cohn, "I found no evidence of it." Syndicated gossip columnist Liz Smith maintains unequivocally that there was nothing between Roy and Si but a friendship marked by unlimited generosity and loyalty. "Roy Cohn lived his life in...divided compartments. He mostly lived his life in a very heterosexual world.... And he kept all of this gay thing all compartmentalized, something that happened at one in the morning."

Taki Theodoracopulos, who writes for the *Spectator* and for the *Sunday Times* in England, and for the *Post* in New York—he has also written for Condé Nast magazines—agrees completely with Liz Smith. "Newhouse trusted Roy Cohn," he says, because Roy was a "fixer." One kind of fixing he did, according to Taki, was to arrange for Si to have access to girls. He claims that Cohn and Si and Tom Corbally were often on the prowl together.

One woman who dated Si told others that a handshake was as intimate as he ever got. "I promise you, there was more than a handshake. He was totally heterosexual," says Geraldine Stutz about her relationship with Si. "There was nothing about Si that I felt was gay," says Sally Obre. "He was very sensual in his own little wee way." She judges him "a terrific lover, a passionate lover."[7]

In 1962, his divorce from Jane just official, Si proposed marriage to Rachel Crespin, known as Ray, who then worked for *Harper's Bazaar* as editor of a section within the magazine called "Junior Bazaar." Ray, who had been married and divorced before, appeared one day in the office of her boss, Nancy White, to announce that she was going to marry Si Newhouse.

Well regarded by her peers—her friend Edie Locke, an editor on *Mademoiselle,* later the magazine's editor-in-chief, calls her "brilliant"—Ray Crespin was a woman of independence and ambition. Even those who didn't like her much admit that she was, in Sally Obre's words, "quite stunning" and always beautifully dressed. Her looks were exotic—black hair, black eyes, resembling an American Indian or a Mexican Indian, straight out of a painting by Frida Kahlo.

According to Nancy White, Ray was Jewish, came from "a very fine family," would have looked wonderful on Si's arm, and would have elevated his social standing. Mitzi agreed, was much impressed with Ray, and showed her approval by making a lavish engagement party. Edie Locke recalls Ray suddenly sporting an "enormous rock on her left hand." The announcement of the engagement appeared in the *New York Times*.

Just three weeks after Ray told Nancy White of her intention to marry Si, she returned to her boss's office, this time to tell her that she needed to think and wanted to go off on vacation alone. On her return, she confided in White that "there was no sparkle" and called off the engagement.

Sally Obre says she could understand Ray's decision, that she also used to get a "hollow feeling" in the pit of her stomach contemplating what marriage to Si would be like: "It was too claustrophobic, it was too laid out, it was too Monday night we do this, Tuesday night we do this. There was absolutely no room left for any kind of spontaneity. You know that you would be puppets on a string to the family. I just think it would be horrible for an independent woman." And so, for the moment, Si remained single.[8]

November 22, 1963, was Wynn Newhouse's ninth birthday. Jane had planned a party. Si was there, and, Jane says, it's lucky he was. He could watch the magician performing for the few children who showed up, while she stood in front of the television set watching the news coverage of John F. Kennedy's assassination, tears streaming down her face. Si showed no emotion. That's the way he was, Jane says, "kind of a locked-up person."

He was as indifferent to President Kennedy's death as he was to politics in general. Jane thinks Si was basically a Democrat, but she isn't sure.

Jane worked during those years as a volunteer for Al Lowenstein in his races for Congress. (He served one term, 1969–71, as a Democrat from Long Island.) According to members of Lowenstein's family, his childhood friend never gave any time or money to the campaigns, or to Lowenstein's many political causes, including his successful effort to block Lyndon Johnson's reelection bid in 1968.

There were those back then who did hear Newhouse express political opinions on occasion, and he could be quite forceful. Francine du Plessix Gray remembers having "the most violent arguments" with him about the war in Vietnam. *New York Times* reporter Harrison Salisbury, playwright Arthur Miller, du Plessix Gray and her husband had just returned from Washington, "another demonstration, and Si launched into us with opinions like, 'You peaceniks, you're giving in to Hanoi.' I was thinking, 'Oh my God, there's no basis of conversation with [him].'"[9]

In 1966, departing from the family tradition of never talking to the press unless there was an extremely good reason to do so, Si Newhouse agreed to be interviewed for a *New York Times* feature on bachelors living in

Manhattan. The result was an article that made Si look so ridiculous that it probably accounts for his extreme reluctance ever since to be interviewed, especially about anything personal. He told the reporter that he had seen a movie the year before that had in it "a marvelous bachelor apartment," and that he decided he wanted to live in such a place. It's "very much me at the moment," he explained, adding, "It's all new," because when he moved he took with him only three paintings. The reporter described Si as "sliding his black espadrilles over the jackal fur rug (50 skins imported from Greece)" and described his bedroom as "tobacco-brown" and, on the bed, a "pale fox bed throw." The accompanying photograph, which must have triggered some gloomy thoughts in the father, showed Si, cigarette in hand and abstract paintings in the background, waiting for Pedro, the uniformed houseboy, to finish pouring tea.

Si soon acquired a wardrobe to match his apartment. Val Weaver recalls that after the move to the Borden Building on Madison Avenue, soon known as the Condé Nast building, she started to notice Si in the corridors. "He was the young, single guy in pretty good shape in very tight Italian suits." Chessy Patcevitch remembers Si in those years in what she calls "funny clothes.... A little, tiny fellow all done up. He wore black patent leather raincoats that went down to the floor."[10]

Fur rugs and espadrilles aside, Si seemed weary of changing girlfriends so often, and began a six-year commitment to a *House & Garden* editor named Nadine Bertin. Divorced from a fashion photographer, Nadine became, in the words of one former Condé Nast editor, "more or less his official hostess."

12 | The Man Almost in Charge

AS USUAL, WHEN ALEX and Tatiana Liberman dined with the Newhouses, Sam would ask Liberman, "How are things?" referring to the magazines. One night, Alex's biographers report, Sam went one step further, asking him whether Patcevitch was doing a good job. Alex replied that Patcevitch—once Alex's closest friend and the man to whom Alex admitted he owed his career—was not. Alex later explained that he felt that Patcevitch was "damaging the company by the way he treated Sam Newhouse. It was becoming a kind of open warfare between them, and I thought it was rude and grotesque on Pat's part."

Sam would let Patcevitch keep his job for the time being, although he had become, in fact, increasingly irrelevant. He would arrive at the office in the late morning, hours after Si. In 1968 Iva Patcevitch, seventy-two years old, committed a social gaffe that sealed his fate at Condé Nast. That summer Mitzi and Sam went to the Portuguese resort of Estoril for an extravaganza of parties and balls thrown by "Bolivian tin tycoon" Antenor Patino, in celebration of his marriage to a Spanish Bourbon princess. "Every European with a title, real or bogus, seemed to have wangled an invitation," write Dodie Kazanjian and Calvin Tomkins, "along with Greek shipowners, American trophy wives and reconstructed German arms merchants." Other guests included Henry Ford and Douglas Fairbanks Jr. The Newhouses were invited to most of the events, and Mitzi had turned heads by wearing a green Dior pants suit to one party, at a time before women wore pants at such occasions. But Mitzi's happiness was shattered when she learned from her hairdresser that she and Sam had been left off the invitation list of a cocktail party given by Iva and Chessy Patcevitch at the very hotel at which the Newhouses were staying.

Mitzi was livid, and to appease her Sam called Alex Liberman and asked him to see to it that a picture of Mitzi was included in *Vogue*'s coverage of the Patino ball. A photo of both Newhouses ran.

Shortly thereafter Sam ordered Patcevitch kicked upstairs and named Perry Ruston president. Ruston, whom Peter Diamandis calls "a clever, intelligent, ...no-nonsense businessman," was a holdover from the days before Sam bought the company. After promptly moving into Patcevitch's office, Ruston never forgot that he was there to listen to Sam and, increasingly, to Si, and to carry out their orders.

For Patcevitch, the final insult came when Sam asked him to give up not only his corner office but also his house. Some years earlier, grieving over the end of his love affair with Marlene Dietrich and still as close as a brother to Alex Liberman, Patcevitch had moved into a townhouse on the north side of East Seventieth Street, some three buildings off Lexington, a few doors west of Alex's house. Alex had helped him find the house. Condé Nast paid for it, but Patcevitch apparently imagined himself living there indefinitely, and when he married Chessy, she assumed that her new husband owned it.

Even Sam Newhouse, who throughout his life focused his energies on buying the next property, never on settling personal scores, must have taken some pleasure in informing Patcevitch that he must vacate the house so that *Vogue*'s new publishing director, Si Newhouse, could move in. According to Harriet Burket Taussig, the Patcevitches were "horrified." Taussig claims that they were given "just a minute" to move out. Si considered the Patcevitch interiors hideous, confiding to one friend that he "could just not wait to get rid of any semblance of what was there before."[1]

Now it would be the son's turn to live down the block from Liberman, who would be closely involved in the total renovation and merger of the Patcevitch house, and the one next to it, which Si bought. Si hired architects who worked for Condé Nast to merge the buildings, both built in the late 1800s, but began to worry that the architects did not share his and Alex's vision; that they were so focused on linking the two houses—the buildings were very different, with plenty of odd relationships to create difficult design and structural challenges—that they were not thinking deeply enough about how the spaces would flow and provide a backdrop for Si's evolving, risk-taking art collection.

Si had befriended a writer for *Glamour* and *Vogue* named Alexandra Penney, who was then married to industrial designer Richard Penney. Penney had apprenticed in Europe and then returned to New York to work for pioneering industrial designer Henry Dreyfuss. In the late 1960s the Penneys were Si's frequent dinner guests, and Si missed no opportunity to grill Richard about all things design related, including *House & Garden:* "Did I feel that they were doing a good job not only for the general readership but for the design community?"

Si liked the earnest young man who was so serious about the design of everything from the sofa in the guest room to the faucet in the master bath. Si confided to Penney that he was growing "very disenchanted with the process that [the architects] were using with regard to his home, his life, and his art, which were all so wonderfully homogenized in one man's spirit.... They were paying attention to how you build a building, not how you live in a building and how you and the building are a homogenous entity."

Penney was intrigued when, after dinner one evening, Si asked him to work on the project. The architects continued to handle structural concerns, but Penney assumed control over all matters of design.

Si was on the brink of another makeover, in which he would retire the swinging bachelor image in favor of that of a publisher and a collector, with an emphasis on the latter. He was determined to create a house worthy of a serious, intellectual, important collector of modern art. As intrigued as he continued to be with editors and art directors, he had in a sense reached one rung beyond them. Those invited to his small dinners and his big cocktail parties—guests to the latter would sometimes number as many as 150—would not be only the habitués of Madison Avenue but, more and more frequently and exclusively, the lions of the art world. They were the artists themselves, their dealers, the critics, the art historians, the top names at museums and auction houses.

A penthouse with terraces, fur rugs, chocolate brown walls, and Billy Baldwin was all wrong for that level of ambition. This time there would be no decorator. Instead, Si and his industrial designer would select the furniture, and cotton-covered and overstuffed would give way to sleek, hard, and Italian leather.

Geraldine Stutz lived across Seventieth Street from Si's houses— which took the address 157 East Seventieth Street. She marveled at the change in this man, who, she insists, when he first arrived at Condé Nast, lacked the confidence to undertake a project of this scope. Under the care of Alex and Leo, Si "had emerged to the point where he was able to decide what kind of house he wanted."

Si intended that this house serve as a long-term venue for his collection. He told Penney that he had much more art than the two houses could hold and that the space must be "defined as a place where art moves through and evolves, ...that it will not stay there for the rest of your life." Si took Penney to the studios of artists who were doing work for him or whose pieces he had recently purchased. "He really wanted me to know these people so I could get a sense of who they were and what we were going to do to accommodate their work."

And Si wanted to be involved in every detail of his new home, down to the selection of the door handles. He looked to Penney to teach him. When Si decided that he wanted to learn more about the design of Italian furniture, he took Penney to Milan for a week. "I'll put all my resources at *Casa Vogue* at our disposal," he promised.

Money was never an object. Si, for instance, wanted tables for card playing in the library. A search launched for the perfect granite ended in South America. The heavy slabs were shipped to New York, where they were transformed into tabletops.

Si kept his parents apprised of the house's progress, but Mitzi was mystified why anyone, especially a Newhouse, would want to live off of Lexington Avenue, when he could have had almost any co-op he wanted on Park Avenue. Pedro took the wife's role in expressing opinions on the design of the kitchen and the bathrooms.

For the building's exterior, Penney used stucco to achieve a modern feel and a simple facade without bringing it into "diametric opposition" to a block full of federal houses. For security reasons, Si did not want the house to appear opulent from the outside, and at a quick glance it looked anything but. One art book publisher says that the exterior reminded her of "a cement fortress."

As visitors entered they looked through the low-ceilinged dining room, which featured a large window facing the garden. Off the dining room were the kitchen, the breakfast room, and, says Penney, "very discreet" servants' quarters.

At the top of the next level was a gallery space in which large pieces of art were hung. To the right was the library, with a window looking into the garden, which was full of massive pieces of sculpture. Bookcases built into the half cylinder of what had been a bay window that had looked into the brick wall of the next house held a huge television. To the left of the library was a forty-foot-long living room, a showcase for the art, furnished with Italian leather furniture.

The next level up contained Si's bedroom, situated in the rear of the house, overlooking the garden. The walls were covered in textiles, the bed was big and Italian, the bookcases were "high polished lacquer," the television the biggest then available. At the front of the house on that level was a guest bedroom.

On the fourth level—there was an elevator in the building—were three bedrooms, one for each of his children, and a terrace. At the top of the house was a screening room, with large-screen projection. Here Si had the state-of-the-art surroundings to indulge his passion for movies.

Art dealer Leo Castelli pronounced the house "beautiful, ...just perfect, everything just so." But many—interestingly, those in the word and business ends of publishing—said that the house was cold, not homey, too beige, like being in the Museum of Modern Art. One frequent female guest calls the interiors "clinical...There is not much sign of life anywhere.... There wasn't a touch of humanity in it."

Si soon discovered that adjustments would have to be made to prevent his guests, after a couple of drinks, from behaving as if they were indeed in a public building. In the penthouse, guests had brushed against his art because the rooms were small; here the rooms were large, but the problem persisted. At a cocktail party he hosted just after moving in, Si watched in horror as the group of mostly magazine people leaned against a wall-to-wall, white-on-white canvas. Before the next party, he had a railing installed and lined it with geranium pots, which kept people away from the canvases. Some years later he hosted a party—this one attended mostly by book publishing people and writers—for which he hired uniformed guards to stand in front of the paintings.[2]

In listening to Richard Penney recall the process of building this statement of a house, it sounds as if it were a full-time job for both designer and client. In fact, Si Newhouse was paying close attention to Condé Nast and becoming, with Alex Liberman whispering in his ear, the man almost in charge.

Early in 1971 Si was central to the decision to fire *Vogue* editor-in-chief Diana Vreeland and to replace her with her deputy, Grace Mirabella. Vreeland's first five years at the magazine had been brilliant, but her next five had brought skyrocketing expenses, slumping newsstand sales, and in the last year, plunging revenues. The first three months of 1971 saw ad pages in a free fall of nearly forty percent.

Si agreed with Alex and with Condé Nast president Perry Ruston that Vreeland, then in her early seventies, was becoming a caricature of herself. Alex had been complaining that he could no longer control her. "I think at the beginning Si was totally enchanted with Vreeland," says one former editor at *Vogue,* who confirms Sally Obre's observation about Si's tendency to develop crushes. "Si is one of those people who when he's in love with someone is totally supportive," says this editor, "totally behind them, and he turns off the same way. When for whatever reason in his mind they're finished, they're just gone, done.... He began to feel that Vreeland's take on the magazine was not going to improve circulation and she was coming in very late in the day and the magazine was always behind schedule, and we're going to have to get rid of her."

The truth was that Vreeland was decades ahead of her time, but few on *Vogue,* editors included, recognized that, and advertisers certainly did not. "If you look at *Vogue* in 1968, '69, and '70," says Val Weaver, "everybody was topless and had blue eye shadow from their cheekbones to their eyebrows. It was very avant-garde, very dramatic, very visionary, very exciting.... It was wonderfully creative and out there and on the edge, but did it have anything to do with 98 percent of women in America? Absolutely not."

Liberman, much as he detested talking about money, felt that while this was the company's flagship and, in the interest of being cutting edge, must be allowed to spend massively and lose moderately, Vreeland had gone too far. "The problem was," Grace Mirabella later wrote, "Vreeland's *Vogue* was losing so much money that even a Condé Nast cash cow like *Glamour* couldn't sustain it anymore. And *Vogue* wasn't on the cutting edge, Alex thought, as the back-to-basic 1970s dawned. It was simply decadent."

Si was petrified at the prospect of doing the dirty work himself, of pushing a reluctant, stubborn, and terrifyingly dignified Vreeland into a consulting editorship. So Si left it to Perry Ruston, who in the spring of 1971, fired Vreeland. She said she would not accept the verdict until she heard it from Si's lips. Si would later recall for Kazanjian and Tomkins, "We just sat there for what seemed to me like about 10 minutes, each waiting for the other to say something. Finally I said that it wasn't working out, and that we were going to ask her to retire. She just watched me deal with her, perhaps in amusement, perhaps in shock. She was very cool. That night I had a very bad dream about it, a wild nightmare."[3]

Si was generous to Vreeland, keeping her on the payroll for seven months so that she'd be eligible for full retirement benefits. But he was not sensitive. She was moved into an office—its walls painted red in anticipation of her arrival—that had belonged to society editor Margaret Case. Case, who had been an enormous power at *Vogue*—a "five-foot terror," Val Weaver calls her, "the only person who I've ever been afraid of"—had recently committed suicide. Kazanjian and Tomkins suggest that the fact that Case was suffering from terminal cancer probably contributed to her despair, but they also write that "some of her friends, including Vreeland, blamed it on *Vogue* for taking away her office and asking her to work at home."

Mary Cantwell, who worked for Case at *Vogue*, described her as "a friend to the rich, a brute to her researchers," but so much and so consistently a type that "there was something noble about her," whether writing a letter to the consort of the king of Belgium, arranging a photo shoot for the archbishop of Canterbury and demanding that he wear his robes, sailing to Greece on Onassis's yacht, borrowing sapphires from Clare Boothe Luce because Case was, after all, a working girl, "struggling into a girdle and an evening gown night after night and smearing orange lipstick across her thin, impatient mouth."

According to one former *Vogue* editor, Case awakened one morning in her "grand society apartment and her maid, as always, brought her breakfast on her tray.... Margaret may or may not have eaten breakfast. She then got up and opened the French doors and walked out of them into a stone courtyard down below, and that was the end of that." According to Mary Cantwell, Case jumped fourteen stories, "naked under the plaid raincoat that was her all-weather uniform."[4]

Once moved out of her office—which was redecorated in wall-to-wall beige for Mirabella—Vreeland was prohibited from visiting her old haunts, and only a select few were approved to visit her. But she recovered quickly and took a job as consultant to the Costume Institute of the Metropolitan Museum of Art. There she achieved a resounding and public success with spectacular, theatrical exhibitions that reinvigorated the drowsy department.[5]

Alex's choice as Vreeland's replacement, Grace Mirabella, couldn't have been more different. A native of Newark, New Jersey, with all-American good looks, a designer sportswear rather than Parisian couture type, she was competent but hardly visionary, smart but not brilliant. Compared to Vreeland, she was conventional, predictable, and pragmatic, but then again, when compared to Vreeland, almost anybody was. Mirabella brought *Vogue* down to earth, insisting that the clothes in its pages be available in stores and within the realm of purchasing possibility for its readers. She recognized that increasing numbers of *Vogue* readers were working and no longer viewed fashion as fantasy or theater. For these women, fashion was becoming a tool for succeeding in the world of business or for expressing their striving for equality. Mirabella saw the absurdity in Vreeland's offering them "purple vinyl raincoats, see-through blouses, silver ankle boots."

Under Mirabella, says Val Weaver, *Vogue* seemed to change overnight into "an American magazine for the modern American woman.... At least twice a year [there were] major nods to Europe, but it was an American magazine."[6]

Vreeland's ouster made headlines in the States and abroad, and generated much quotable criticism of the Condé Nast bean counters, the men whom Vreeland had long dismissed as "the men upstairs." Andy Warhol's comment that Vreeland had been fired and Mirabella hired because "*Vogue* wanted to go middle class" was typical.[7]

Vreeland was the first major publishing figure, but would hardly be the last, to lose a job at the hand of Si Newhouse. In the years to come, Si would sentence to the ax editors with nearly as much renown, and the stories of their demise would sometimes make page one of the *New York Times*. As *Vogue*'s numbers improved and the magazine, for a time, seemed on track, Si saw that firing was as powerful a tool as hiring in shaping his sphere of the family empire. He felt, for the first time in his life, fully engaged in his work, and when he left the office, he also felt for the first time that he was returning to a house that expressed who he was.

13 | Victoria and Nero

ON FRIDAY, APRIL 13, 1973, in a civil ceremony, Si Newhouse, forty-six years old, married Victoria Carrington Benedict de Ramel. The name's final installment came from her first marriage to a French count, Regis de Ramel, which ended in divorce and produced no children. An American raised in Manhattan, she had remained in France after the divorce and worked as an editor of art and architecture books in the Paris office of New York publisher George Braziller.

She had recently returned to New York—she remained with Braziller as a senior editor—where she met Si at a dinner party. He was instantly intrigued. Victoria was nothing like the other women he had dated. There was not a hint of the commercial or glossy about her. She was the genuine article, a coolly cerebral product of Manhattan's elite Brearley School* and a magna cum laude graduate, with a major in French, of Bryn Mawr (class of '59), the most brainy of the Seven Sisters colleges. A life-long Francophile, after graduation she had moved to Paris. It was there that she met the count, who in real life was a banker.

Unlike the typical editor at *Vogue*, who seemed so much of the moment, Victoria was linked, from her first marriage and from her manners, to a time of elegance and culture. She was a woman who would look as at ease as the hostess of a formal dinner as she would in the corridors of Columbia University, where before long she was taking classes en route to earning a master's degree in architectural history.

---

*The same school that had asked Diana Vreeland to leave after three months.

Having corrected his image from swinging bachelor to serious collector, Si would now, with his attachment to Victoria and her circle of friends, add the dimension of the intellectual.

Francine du Plessix Gray attributes to Victoria a "natural style," imbibed, Gray says, from her mother, "a very well-bred woman with very beautiful manners." The mother was English, by all accounts lovely, and devoted to Victoria, her only child. Victoria's father, John C. Benedict, was a retired investment banker, an American. Although some people who knew Benedict say he was Jewish, her mother certainly was not, and Victoria was raised in the Episcopal church. (John Benedict died shortly after his daughter's marriage to Si.)

Given her own French roots, Francine Gray says she understands perfectly why Si, whom she describes at that time as still a "rough diamond," was so entranced. Victoria was "absolutely bilingual, and she offered Si a terrific cosmopolitan polish. As the former wife of a conservative French aristocrat, she can entertain in several languages, she knows how to seat people, what the order of seating people is. She is very much like an ambassador's wife—which is just what someone in Si's position of power needs; what every man with that kind of power needs."

Ten years younger than Si, several inches taller (at five foot seven), with short salt-and-pepper hair and the appearance of little or no makeup, she was a woman for whom the word "handsome" seemed coined. Robert Lang, who taught in the graduate film division at Columbia and later went to work at Condé Nast, describes Victoria's walking shoes, her tweedy suits—Armani though they are—as making her resemble "sensible English women who tramp the moors with their dogs." Writer and art historian Franz Schulze describes her as "not the kind of person who's going to stop you dead in your tracks, but she decorates the arm of Si Newhouse much more elegantly than he does her arm." She was, in a phrase, no trophy wife.

"I daresay that the thing that attracted him about Victoria," says Robert Lang, "is her intelligence." Mary Jane Pool guesses that Si enjoyed Victoria's "strong point of view, because she's an educated woman and I think that would be of interest to Si."

One person who wasn't so keen on Victoria was Roy Cohn. "Roy was trying to get Si not to be so involved with her," says a woman who was close to both men. "Roy didn't have a very fond name for her." To Cohn, Victoria was too intellectual, too serious, not impressed with the moguls and tough guys who formed Cohn's circle.

Another person who had reservations about Victoria was Si's mother. In Mitzi's eyes, Victoria had little to recommend her. She wasn't Jewish, she had no role in the fashion business, and she had no discernible compensating qualities. Her style, to Mitzi's eye, would hardly register as style. Still, Mitzi did want Si to settle down again; it worried both his parents that he was taking so long to find the right second wife. By this time Si had reached middle age, apparently beyond the point at which Mitzi could veto his choice.

What made Mitzi feel better about Si's marriage was that it meant that Nadine Bertin was out of the way. Mitzi had never much liked Bertin, the *House & Garden* editor who had been Si's girlfriend for six years, and who wanted nothing more than to exchange the role of official hostess for that of wife.

When it became clear that Si was not going to ask for Bertin's hand in marriage, she was "crushed," recalls Peter Diamandis. "She thought...this was a done deal."

Others say that the relationship with Bertin would have fizzled anyway, with or without Victoria. "I heard," says an old friend of Nadine's, "that she tried to meddle with the way he was bringing up his children...and he resented that." A fellow editor on *House & Garden* says that Nadine also trampled on his other passion in life. She made the "terrible mistake of demanding to be involved in the choice of the works of art that he bought. She said, 'After all, I live here too.'" He as much as replied, "Not anymore, you don't."

Some with close ties to Condé Nast claim that Nadine received a substantial consolation prize from Si—a promised job-for-life at Condé Nast. At *House & Garden* she was eventually put in charge of a unit called House & Garden Color. "It turned out to be losing a lot of money for the company," says another editor. "It was expensive to have and it wasn't paying off, and the advertising department was afraid to stop it because it was Nadine's." Later Nadine was moved out of the Condé Nast Building into the building on Broadway that houses the company's international division. She remained there until 1997, when Si told her it was time for her to retire.[1]

As eager as Si was to marry Victoria, it was, reportedly, no grand passion. One former employee speculates that the marriage was a "front." A major figure in the art world reports that the couple, on their honeymoon in the Caribbean, had a suite with separate bedrooms. But others saw a marriage that while it may have lacked passion—these are not, after all, twenty, thirty, or even forty-year-olds—was full of bonds of interest and commitment, foremost among them an interest in intellectual pursuits. Victoria opened for Si new friendships and opportunities and added a more serious tone to his personal life.

There were, as well, lighter pleasures that they shared—a consuming interest in movies, for example, which Francine du Plessix Gray describes as "intense and almost fetishistic." Perhaps reflecting Victoria's influence, Si brought to the hobby an academic bent, collecting an impressive library of books on the history of the cinema and developing a particular passion for early German expressionist film.

Two of Si's recent birthdays were celebrated with private screenings, arranged by Victoria, of old favorites, one at Juilliard and another at the Museum of Modern Art theater. One year it was *Pandora's Box*, a silent film starring Louise Brooks; the next it was the 1932 classic, *Love Me Tonight,* starring Maurice Chevalier and Jeanette MacDonald.[2]

Although the marriage produced no children, it did produce a pug called Nero, who until his death from kidney cancer in the summer of 1997 was at the center of the couple's life. Before Victoria, Si had shown no interest in dogs, yet Nero captivated him, and he became as demonstrably affectionate to Nero as Victoria was. In a 1996 *Wall Street Journal* page-one feature on Si, a reporter described Si's office, in which "the only visible personal memento is a portrait of his dog, Nero." One former Condé Nast publisher says that Si was known to get down on the floor at dinner parties to play with the dog. Not unusual for the average dog lover, but for Si, this woman says, it's "the only time that most people have seen him really playful. It's not a word one usually uses to describe Si Newhouse."

When Victoria visited the offices at Condé Nast, Nero was almost always tucked under one arm. "When my son had a party," recalls Jane

Franke, "Victoria came and she brought her dog with her, and her dog just stayed on her lap the whole time." Jane speculates that Victoria "would have loved having children," and that the dog was obviously a substitute. In 1996 Victoria lobbied for legislation to permit dogs to visit their owners or other patients in the hospital.

After a suitable mourning period and what one friend and fellow dog lover calls "the equivalent of a state funeral," a Manhattan veterinarian accompanied Si and Victoria to Wisconsin to inspect a would-be successor pug, but the dog's temperament didn't pass muster. By early 1998, a replacement had been found in England, and the lucky pug was named Cicero.[3]

Victoria and Nero were so often seen in the Condé Nast offices because Si had given her space there, out of which she ran the Architectural History Foundation—a not-for-profit publisher that provided grants for authors writing books on architecture too serious or obscure for commercial presses. Paul Gottlieb, who runs Harry Abrams, a premier publisher of art books, says he sometimes sent Victoria book projects "because the nice thing about having that kind of money is that you can support things which may not be economically viable, but are worth publishing.... She published some very distinguished works, prizewinning books, very beautifully designed, works of considerable distinction." An official high in the museum world says that Victoria "has really done a very special thing.... She's made some architecture in America come alive, which would not have come alive if it hadn't been for her."

Victoria, whose interests range from classic to modern architecture, has herself written two books—the first on American architect Wallace K. Harrison, who worked on the Rockefeller Center and the UN headquarters, and who also coordinated the designs for the Lincoln Center buildings. The book was published in 1989 by Rizzoli and without ties to her own foundation. Franz Schulze, who has written books on Mies van der Rohe and Philip Johnson, pronounces it "a solid, knowing piece of work." A woman who knows Victoria well and who writes in the same area seemed surprised when asked if Victoria used a ghostwriter. "Oh, heavens no, not at all, not at all." She is impressed by both the style and content of Victoria's work, and insists that "she's a very diligent scholar, ...not a dilettante." Victoria's second book, *Towards a New Museum*, on the subject of art museum architecture, was published in 1998 by Monacelli. *New York Times* architecture critic Herbert Muschamp pronounced it "a shrewd, biting account." He praised Victoria for reviewing more than one thousand art museums built in recent decades in both the United States and Europe, from the Guggenheim in Bilbao, Spain, to the Getty Center in Los Angeles. Muschamp pointed out that this is no paean to the museum establishment; that Victoria is tough, for example, on recent architectural forays made by both the Metropolitan Museum of Art and the Museum of Modern Art.[4]

If Si wanted seriousness, Victoria certainly delivered. At the dinner parties that she and Si hosted, her influence was evident in the mix of guests. One such party included Francine du Plessix Gray, critic and scholar Robert Pincus-Witten, and Yale professor Vincent Scully, who for decades taught and wrote about art and architectural history. Another guest describes a party that featured Philip Johnson, his companion, curator David Whitney, and Dutch architect Rem Koolhaas. Dinner conversations at the Newhouses', says Francine Gray, don't necessarily end when the guests leave, but can result in "a correspondence with Victoria and an exchange of books about personalities like Simone Weil."

Victoria has also developed an intense interest in religion. For years she has been taking courses in comparative religions at Columbia and has herself organized a course to which she invites friends for regular meetings throughout the year. She gave up the Episcopalian religion of her childhood to become a Catholic, and according to Francine Gray and other friends, "a strikingly intellectual but very devout Catholic" who attends mass regularly. She is extremely interested in Judaism as well. When Joni Evans was publishing a translation of the Talmud, Victoria would come to Evans's house every time the author, a rabbi, was in town.

About her husband's art, Victoria displays some caution, but according to friends, she is not shy about expressing her distaste for the more extreme examples of Si's collection. Miki Denhof, the former art director at *Glamour*, recalls that when Si first introduced her to Victoria, he said, "'Miki was there when I selected my first modern painting.' And she said, 'Oh, so you are responsible for all this madness.'"

While Victoria sometimes accompanies Si on his Saturday morning rounds of galleries, always with the dog in tow, more often she doesn't, say both André Emmerich and Leo Castelli. "I think," says Castelli, "that she just accepts his choices, doesn't interfere with anything that he wants."

But Victoria has broadened Si's tastes. She has made him realize that there is more to antiques than Mitzi's French furniture. With her, he collects classic architectural illustrations and enjoys touring Palladian houses. Mary Jane Pool remembers seeing them at "a little antique show," full of "old clutter.... I said, 'Why Si, I'm so surprised to see you here.'... He said, 'Oh, well it's all so interesting.'" She describes him as smiling with pleasure and looking as excited as a little boy in a wonderful toy store.[5]

About one thing Victoria was certain when she married Si; and she didn't spare his feelings. She hated his townhouse. To her, it was cold, forbidding, uncomfortable, and in need of immediate modification. And it was this that ruined Si's relationship with Richard Penney, which had been so good that Penney was designing Si's office suite at Condé Nast.

For a time the three worked together. Si and Victoria assigned Penney the task of creating separate bedrooms for them by turning the guest suite, which shared the master-bedroom floor, into Victoria's bedroom/office suite. Under Victoria's direction, Penney also undertook a redesign of the kitchen. Pedro soon retired, and Victoria hired a new cook, a woman.

Penney quickly recognized that both his tenure and his friendship with Si were shaky. Victoria was "very caught up and interested in some of the early postmodernist architectural forays," he says, "and had begun to develop certain associations...with other architects who were practicing in that vernacular, something that I was not interested in terribly." Soon Si and Victoria began to discuss with Penney the possibility of other designers being brought in to do certain aspects of the house. Would he mind? Penney decided that he would, and that it was "time to let go and let them live their own lives."[6]

While Richard Penney, long divorced from Alexandra, retreated from the Newhouses, his ex-wife took his place and then some. Alexandra, who over the course of her career was both a writer and editor for Condé Nast magazines, became a frequent visitor to Si's oceanfront, Spanish-style house in Palm Beach. She knew that there were no friendships more important to cultivate than those with the boss and his wife, and she took excessively good care of them. Although Alexandra did not own a dog, she threw annual parties for pugs—the late Nero as guest of honor one year and his successor, Cicero, another year—at which the canines lapped up Evian water and special food while the humans in attendance, including Si and Victoria, lapped up caviar and other delicacies.

When Victoria's book on Wallace K. Harrison was published, Alexandra hosted a book party at the Newhouses' newly acquired apartment at the United Nations Plaza, where they were living while awaiting renovation of the townhouse. One of Alexandra's underlings—a person whose credentials were as impressive as anyone's at Condé Nast—was assigned to tend to the details, and he spent hours at the apartment consulting with Victoria, organizing the guest list, talking to caterers, ordering flowers, designing T-shirts, and arranging for a cake to be baked that would be shaped and decorated to match the book's cover. He was momentarily stunned when Alexandra, whom he considered a personal friend as well as employer, informed him that while he should continue to plan Victoria's party, he should not plan to attend. He describes Victoria as "kind of haughty, a little bit frosty, a little bit aloof." Compared to her, he says, Si would be "relaxed" and "at ease" and attentive to anyone whose interests matched his. It wouldn't matter if that person were a professor of art history or the elevator operator.

Franz Schulze suggests that Victoria's imperious manner might be a function of marriage to one of the world's richest men. "I would imagine that Victoria Newhouse might have her hands full daily just fending off people who are looking for money.... The wife of the man who owns North America is a natural magnet for all kinds of people."

The other side of Victoria, friends insist, is enormous generosity and compassion. "I know when my friends, writers Andrew Sarris and Molly Haskell, were both sick in different hospitals," says Francine du Plessix Gray, "she would have entire meals brought to each of them every day." Jane Franke, who sees Victoria at family gatherings, recalls the time a few years ago when "my daughter was taking a trip to Europe with my mother. I think while they were in Paris, Si and Victoria joined up with them and they all went out to dinner together and then, later on, after my mother died and I saw Victoria, she said, 'Your mother was so lovely.'.... That was nice of Victoria to say that."

While she is often described as "the perfect hostess," people invited to the house on Seventieth Street for Condé Nast parties never entertained a doubt that, for Victoria, this was strictly business. But she made those parties work. Another former Condé Nast publisher recalls a "lovely" buffet dinner for fifty for a senior company executive. Victoria was "cordial and lovely and made an effort to talk to everybody and see everybody.... They had enough seating for people to sit around in small groups and talk. Victoria would come around and say, 'Okay, let's mix up this group,' and people would move around."

Victoria's friends insist that she is a lively companion, with a sense of humor often hidden behind her very formal demeanor. She needed every ounce of humor she could muster when she crossed paths with Taki Theodoracopulos, who had attacked her husband in the various columns he wrote, once commenting, "He's the only man I know who buys two tickets to go to the zoo, one to come in and one to come out." Taki was attending a dinner party and, he says, "Many people I had savaged were there, including Si and Victoria Newhouse.... She couldn't have been more charming, laughed like hell at my stupid jokes. I guess it's the best way to treat someone who's been savaging you for no good reason.... She was really charming and nice," even when, affecting a thick German accent, he pretended to be a brownshirt and started dropping German military terms and speculating on who would replace the führer at Condé Nast, the führer being Si Newhouse. Taki claims that she just laughed, and so did Si. "At the end I said to her how wonderful she was."

And yet, maintains Francine du Plessix Gray, behind Victoria's infinitely more polished manners, she is "just as inscrutable as Si is."[7]

14 | Doing the Dirty Work

HAD SAM NEWHOUSE been able to write his own epitaph, it would have been, he once told Peter Diamandis, "I never sold anything." That ringing watchword applied in another way too—he never closed anything, or almost never. Two Newhouse newspapers were, however, shut down; in the first case, when Sam was too ill to notice; and, in the second, five years after his death.

At the *Long Island Press*, Si and Donald could see no prospect for improvement, not so long as *Long Island Newsday* dominated. So in 1977, three years before their father's death, they killed the paper that Sam had bought in 1932. It would have been difficult for him to have done that, but the father never let his sons think that sentiment was a good business practice.

Despite its name, the *Press* had not much to do with Long Island, where the growth was, and too much to do with Queens, where it was headquartered and where the demographics were changing and the advertising base eroding. "The paper was very representative of the borough of Queens," says reporter Karl Grossman. But that was in the 1950s, when the population was a mix of Irish, Italians, and Jews. As African Americans, people from the Caribbean, Latinos, and Asians replaced the old crowd, the paper never learned to speak to its new audience.

Most damaging of all was Sam Newhouse's fatal underestimation of his competitor, Alicia Patterson, who owned and ran *Long Island Newsday* and who saw very clearly that the future and the money were in the suburbs. Daughter of *New York Daily News* founder Captain Joseph Medill Patterson, Alicia Patterson started *Newsday* in 1940 in a former auto dealership showroom in Hempstead, sold to her for $60,000 by none other than Sam Newhouse. Sam had tried to publish a paper serving Nassau County in that very spot but had given up too quickly, selling the space and some old presses to Alicia, thus launching the woman whose paper would prove his undoing on Long Island.

Sam thought he was humoring this cute redhead who wanted to start a newspaper. He was certain that she would tire of her new "toy," as he called it, and promptly fail or, at the worst, sell out to him. Instead, *Newsday* thrived. Alicia stuck it out in Nassau and soon owned not only that county but Suffolk as well. Bill Woestendiek, a veteran of *Newsday* and later the top editor at the *Cleveland Plain Dealer*, notes that the *Press* "just got way behind." So while *Newsday* was vacuuming up advertising in Nassau and Suffolk Counties by covering the communities closely, the *Press* relied on stringers, relegated one page to Nassau and Suffolk coverage, and didn't even hire an editor to run things in Suffolk County until 1967.

Curiously, Sam never engaged in hand-to-hand combat with Alicia. Perhaps he was too chivalrous to play hardball with a woman, or too sexist to think he had to. Jackie Gebhard, a reporter for the *Press*, and later for *Newsday*, who had to beg to be allowed off the *Press*'s society pages and onto its news pages, argues that Sam and his men had the terribly mistaken notion that Alicia was "just an older debutante playing around." Sam was sure she'd fail, and, Gebhard says, Alicia sensed this and "was determined to prove [him] wrong."

Over the years, as *Newsday* prospered, Patterson stubbornly rebuffed Sam's offers to buy her paper. (In *Newsday*'s infancy, he offered her a million dollars.) Later, she was said to be ready to sell to Sam because, according to Robert Keeler, who wrote a history of *Newsday*—he left Sam's *Staten Island Advance* for *Newsday*—Alicia wanted to use the proceeds to buy the *New York Daily Mirror* and "go into New York and beat the crap out of [her father's] *Daily News*." Captain Patterson had refused to back her financially when she started *Newsday*, and this was her chance to get even. When the call was made to Sam, he was in Europe, and, by the time he returned, says Keeler, she had second thoughts.

On Alicia's death in 1963, Harry Guggenheim, her husband and cofounder of the paper, took control. Heir to the Guggenheim fortune, he was an ardent conservative—he had served as President Hoover's ambassador to Cuba—and fretted that *Newsday* was becoming too liberal under its new publisher, Bill Moyers. In 1970 Guggenheim sold *Newsday* to Times Mirror, whose flagship paper, the *Los Angeles Times,* was still conservative. But what Guggenheim really feared, much more than the paper's liberal drift, was that Sam would see Alicia's death as his opening, buy *Newsday,* shut it down, and ride a monopoly to huge profits. Guggenheim was determined to keep *Newsday* out of Newhouse's hands.

The actual closing of the *Press* on March 25, 1977, was handled without finesse and sensitivity. The shutdown was to be kept a secret until the last possible moment, in order to prevent angry workers from damaging the presses. The *Press*'s editor, Dave Starr—he had arrived at the *Press* in 1967 to take over for Norman Newhouse, then just dispatched to New Orleans—arrived at the plant at 4:45 that morning, and ordered the night news editor to clear a space on the front page for the *Press*'s boxed obituary, which he had written earlier. This official farewell cited three years of losses, for which he largely blamed the unions. The paper's owners and managers, Starr wrote, had appealed to the production unions five years before to abandon "their featherbedding make-work rules" and to allow use of automated machinery. "Unfortunately, the unions could not see the wisdom of our appeal." Union officials countered that its members had been working for two years without a pay increase. In the wake of the Booth acquisition by a company flush with cash, Starr's lament rang hollow.

When John Maher, a top editor on the paper, reached the *Press* building in Jamaica, Queens—he had learned about the paper's death in an overheard conversation on the commuter train—he pushed through the throngs of TV reporters and cameramen and fled upstairs to find guards posted to prevent employees from walking off with those "god-awful typewriters."

In the newsroom, there were no scenes, as in the deaths of other papers, of the editor breaking the news to the sobbing troops from atop a reporter's desk. Starr stayed in his office, and people were invited in individually to talk to him. Starr already had his new assignment—running the Newhouses' papers in Springfield, Massachusetts. He took a few people with him. Everyone else was pretty much on his own. Six hundred people lost their jobs.

None of the Newhouses went near Queens that day.[1]

In Springfield, Massachusetts, Dave Starr, who allegedly had changed his name from Sinovitz, replaced publisher Sidney Cook—the man who allegedly had so much trouble accepting the fact that the Springfield papers would be owned by a Jew. Starr became the new Phil Hochstein, a kind of editor-at-large of the Newhouse papers whose title in Springfield didn't begin to describe his responsibilities. Mel Elfin calls Starr "the guy who used to run all the newspapers out of the Springfield operation."

He also oversaw the Newhouse National News Service, visiting five times or so a year. Si and Don had asked Starr to base himself in Washington and run things from there, but he declined, explaining that he wanted to be attached to a real newspaper. Starr, just like one of the family, later had his own newspaper route, sometimes, for example, visiting the *St. Louis Globe-Democrat* with Si and then visiting by himself, as Si, following his father's death, withdrew as much as he could from the newspaper side of the business. After Sam's death, Si also stopped accompanying his uncle Norman to Cleveland. Donald, meanwhile, considerably lengthened his route, adding papers in Newark, Syracuse, Harrisburg, Jersey City, and Staten Island. When Uncle Ted became too ill to visit Portland, Donald added that stop to his route as well.[2]

In 1978, a year after the closing of the *Press*, Si and Donald made a business decision that raised eyebrows and left some wondering whether they really were their father's sons. As Carol Loomis wrote in *Fortune*, the sons "disposed" of "a few minor masterpieces," meaning five television stations that Sam had acquired over the years in cities in which he also owned newspapers. They sold them to Times Mirror for $82 million. The selling price, she wrote, "was considered low when it was announced. Today, considering how TV station prices have soared, it seems downright bargain-basement."

Sam had recognized that cable was a "cash cow," Maggie Mahar wrote in a cover article on the family published in *Barron's*. Before his illness, he had purchased more than twenty cable systems. But the sons were slow on the uptake, and although they used part of the proceeds from the sale of the five television stations to buy cable, Mahar quotes one cable broker as criticizing them for not having moved into cable more quickly and aggressively. "The father built the base for the cable division," Mahar reported, "but the sons...failed to capitalize on it when cable was cheap." Eventually they would become active cable operators and programmers, but they missed a good buy. Sam would not have.[3]

Si and Donald might not have been as shrewd as their father, but, Si especially, soon showed that he could be every bit as tough—and, some said, quite a bit more unscrupulous.

In Cleveland, the Newhouses' people at the *Plain Dealer* were doing everything they could, legal and otherwise, to push the financially ailing *Cleveland Press* out of business, which would then give the Newhouses a monopoly. Longtime *Plain Dealer* watcher John Ettorre charges that the paper's publisher, Alex Machaskee, "was actively trying to encourage the Teamsters to give the *Cleveland Press* a hard time."

The FBI's file on then Teamster vice president Jackie Presser includes the following notes from an agent: "On November 21, 1980, source advised that several months ago when the *Cleveland Press* was in financial trouble Jackie Presser...received a visit from Alex Macheski [phonetic], Assistant to the Publisher [Tom Vail] of the *Plain Dealer*. Macheski wanted the *Cleveland Press* to close down and requested Presser's assistance inorder [sic] to accomplish this end. Macheski asked Presser if he would see to it that the *Cleveland Press* has 'problems' with contract negotiations with Teamster Locals representing employees of the *Cleveland Press*. Supposedly, Presser informed Macheski that he would not be part of this and felt strongly that there should be two newspapers in Cleveland. Source further advised that the *Plain Dealer* was using Carmen Parisi [sic], IBT [International Brotherhood of Teamsters] Union Local Official, to undermine negotiations between the *Cleveland Press* and [blacked out]." (Parise is the same man who, an FBI document alleges, received a $1000 a month "kickback" from Leo Ring at the *Plain Dealer*.) Machaskee denied the allegations.

The *Cleveland Press*, a Scripps Howard afternoon paper, had once been the dominant daily in town. But by the 1970s it trailed the

Newhouse's *Plain Dealer* in circulation and advertising revenue, and in October 1980, about the time Machaskee was allegedly meeting with Presser, Scripps sold it to a local businessman, the late Joseph E. Cole— a man bursting with political ambitions and a love for the limelight. Cole paid only $1 million in cash for the *Press* and its downtown building and land, and a $7 million promissory note that was to be paid out of future profits, if any.

The talk in town was that the paper was an ego trip for Cole, a self-made man who started as a street-corner salesman of keys and made millions manufacturing display racks for them. A Democratic party stalwart who had served as the party's national treasurer, Cole, it was said, fancied the idea of meeting with presidents and senators. "Joe had no newspaper background," says former Ohio senator Howard Metzenbaum, "and I think many of us thought [he] was just acquiring the paper for the purpose of enhancing his own prestige and stature.... I don't think anybody thought he was particularly interested in running a great paper." The paper's former editor, Herbert Kamm, saw Cole as "a political animal [who] felt he could have stronger clout in the Democratic party if he had a paper."

That said, Cole did seem to take his role as publisher seriously. He spent $2 million on new equipment, and he added color and, most important for the paper's future, a Sunday edition, which had never existed under Scripps Howard ownership. He hired pros to run the production and advertising ends.

Not much more than a year after the purchase, Joe Cole came to Herb Kamm, who had just retired and taken the title of editor emeritus, and showed him "written evidence that the *Press* was losing large sums of money." Some weeks later, his eyes filled with tears, Cole informed Kamm of the paper's imminent shutdown. The *Press* published its last edition on June 17, 1982.

There was an important piece of news that Cole didn't share with Kamm, but which would soon become public and create shock waves in journalism circles nationwide. Si Newhouse had agreed to buy the *Press*'s subscriber list for $14.5 million. For an additional $8 million, Newhouse signed to buy Delcom, a few-month-old, debt-ridden company owned by Cole and a partner that produced a shopper's guide newspaper insert.

Cole would thus pocket $22.5 million, less his partner's share and the considerable cost of improvements made to the *Press*. Peter Phipps and Dan Cook, who covered the closing of the *Press* for the *Akron Beacon Journal*, estimated that Cole and his partner walked away with about a million dollars from their brief ownership of the *Press*, but they stressed that did not include the piece of prime downtown real estate that housed the paper and that Cole acquired for the mere million he paid Scripps Howard for the *Press*.

Charges were soon flying that Si Newhouse had, in effect, bribed Cole to close the *Press*, paying millions for arguably worthless assets and leaving the *Plain Dealer*, as the monopoly paper, free to set advertising rates however high it pleased. Those who backed this theory pointed to a threatened strike by *Plain Dealer* reporters and drivers that would have put the *Press* in an enviable position, at least for the short term. The *Wall Street Journal* would later report that the *Press* closed "even as its circulation and advertising linage were increasing at the *Plain Dealer*'s expense."

The *Plain Dealer*, as expected, never touched this startling local story, but Phipps and Cook ran with it, and it was their reporting that prompted the Justice Department to empanel a grand jury, after first rejecting a plea from local Justice Department antitrust officials to do so. Phipps and Cook reported that the subscription list was considered next to worthless because in a two-newspaper town, when one paper closes, those subscribers who want a local paper have no choice but to sign on with the survivor.

Cole did have his defenders; or, at least, there were credible people who believed that he closed the *Press* because he had no other choice and that the $22.5 million had nothing to do with it. "My feeling has always been that he made a valiant attempt to keep the paper going," insists Herb Kamm. He suggests that if Cole "hadn't been sincere about perpetuating the paper, he never would have installed the improvements that he did."

Newspaper expert John Morton calls it "ludicrous" to believe that the circulation list payment was, in effect, a bribe. First of all, he argues, "Why would they have to bribe Joe Cole to shut it down? It was a dead newspaper." He calls Cole "basically ignorant about the newspaper business. If he knew anything at all about [it], he wouldn't have bought [the

Press]. It was a calamity, it was a disaster, it was a dead newspaper when Joe bought it."

While he wonders a bit why Si "bothered" to buy the list—and a case can be made that Si simply doesn't think much before spending millions of dollars—Morton sees nothing sinister about him having done so. When a second newspaper in a city dies, he explains, experience teaches that a certain, seemingly immoveable, block of readers signs on with the surviving paper. But "somewhere between 40 and 50 percent of the circulation of a dead newspaper just disappears," he adds. "The remaining newspaper is lucky to get somewhere between 35 and 45 percent of the circulation." He speculates that Si was trying to "improve that percentage by buying the circulation list and trying to capture more of that."

Si Newhouse had cut himself a very good deal. *Cleveland* magazine reported that in an eighteen-month period the *Plain Dealer*'s advertising rates increased by about 33 percent and circulation by 23 percent. "The joys of owning a monopoly newspaper are illustrated by some *Plain Dealer* statistics," Carol Loomis reported in *Fortune* in 1987. "Since 1982 its daily circulation has risen by nearly 50,000 to 455,000. Its rate of a page of local display advertising was $7,878 just before the *Press* closed, $10,504 a year later. After years of earning little or nothing, the *Plain Dealer* is quite probably now the second most profitable Newhouse paper."

If Si Newhouse had paid Cole multimillions to go out of business, that would have constituted a breach of federal antitrust law. Government attorneys, spurred by the intensive *Beacon Journal* coverage, launched a criminal antitrust investigation. If indicted and convicted, Newhouse and Cole could have faced three-year jail terms.

Some, including a federal judge, thought that the government had a persuasive case. In a related civil suit brought by *Press* printers—about 900 people lost their jobs—against Cole and dismissed on a technicality, U.S. District Judge Ann Aldrich pronounced the value of the paper's subscription list "negligible or non-existent" and its grocery shopper "debt-ridden." She also urged the government to pursue the investigation: "The record is replete with facts from which a jury could conclude that the Plain Dealer, Press Publishing, and Cole 'conspired together in restraint of trade for the purpose...of creating a monopoly.'"

Si spent three days in Cleveland before a federal grand jury in May 1985. (Donald was also called, as was Norman Newhouse.) Much to the disappointment of C. Russell Twist and Marilyn A. Bobula, senior trial attorneys in the antitrust division of the U.S. Department of Justice, after more than a year of deliberation, the grand jury disbanded without issuing any indictments. A spokesman for the Justice Department announced in June 1987 that it had "insufficient evidence to proceed."

Bobula and Twist were outraged, and to this day remain intensely angry about an investigation that, they charge, was stymied at every turn by their superiors in the Justice Department's antitrust division—a direct tribute, they argue, to the power of Si Newhouse.

By September 1986, Bobula and Twist, the only prosecutors pursuing a case, were no longer with the antitrust division, their disputes with their supervisors at a peak. Thereafter, the investigation quickly disintegrated. Bobula, who transferred to the Justice Department's U.S. Attorney's Office, tells of roadblocks in the way of subpoenaing documents and calling various people to testify. "Every step along the way, they stopped us from getting the evidence. It was not a matter of exercising prosecutorial discretion after reviewing the evidence. They attempted to prevent us from even obtaining the evidence in the first place. I think we frustrated them by developing the proof we did, in spite of them." Twist, fired from the antitrust division at the same time Bobula transferred out and now in private practice in Washington, puts it even more strongly: "I think the reality is that the Justice Department impeded an investigation...from being properly conducted and basically obstructed a federal grand jury."

When Twist, who had come to the government from the American Bar Association, where he was the director of the Department of Professional Standards, was fired, he was charged with being disrespectful to his superiors—the chief and the assistant chief in the Cleveland office. Bobula characterizes that charge as "the biggest lie." He was fired, she says, because "he reported them to the [Justice Department's] Office of Professional Responsibility for fixing the investigation. He kept saying, 'They're fixing it and they won't let us prosecute it.'" The real story, Twist concurs, was that "they were retaliating against me for telling the truth about the way they were conducting the grand jury." He charges that

"Their conduct was designed to shut [the grand jury] down without any prosecutions," without getting to the grand jury all the evidence it needed. He also charges his bosses in the Cleveland office with "inappropriately" granting people immunity. He claims that he and Bobula were being told to call witnesses and give them immunity "before the grand jury had all the documents from their discovery process."

Twist refuses to say whether Si Newhouse was immunized before his appearance, explaining that grand jury proceedings are secret and that it would be a serious breach of federal rules for him to make any aspect public. But James Neff, a former investigative reporter for the *Plain Dealer* and current director of the Kiplinger Public Affairs Reporting Program at Ohio State University, says that he "know[s]" that Bobula and Twist were told by their superiors, 'Let's bring in Newhouse and Joe Cole, immunize them and bring them into the grand jury,'... and this order, as I understand it, came from Washington, and so the lawyers are saying, 'Well, wait a minute, these are the targets. You don't immunize the targets, and you don't bring them in at this point. If these are the targets, you build and build and build up to them, and then you call them into the grand jury and you don't give them immunity. You ask them to testify and then they take the Fifth [Amendment against self-incrimination] and then you decide whether there's some kind of indictments or some sort of actions you can bring, so it was clearly just sort of very improper." (A reporter for the *Akron Beacon Journal* quoted from a document filed by Twist in which he charged that some of the "actual targets" of the probe were given immunity from prosecution. A month later, a reporter for *Crain's Cleveland Business* quoted from an internal Justice Department memo written by the head of the antitrust division in Washington, referring to the meeting attended by Bobula and her Cleveland boss that authorized the grand jury investigation. This memo reminds the investigators that they were directed, before the grand jury was impaneled, to forego prosecution of both Newhouse and Cole as individuals. Bobula and Twist call this the "smoking gun memo" because, they claim, it shows that the investigation was fixed in that the head of the division decided in advance not to prosecute the targets.

Others, like Herb Kamm, who was interviewed by Bobula, say that she "seemed to be groping. My conclusion is they dropped it because their investigation was leading them nowhere." (Bobula expressed surprise at

Kamm's remarks: "[After the interview,] Kamm wrote me a...note, which I still have, that read, in part, 'Marilyn, you asked all the right questions.' He's either protecting someone, or he's afraid of these powerful people, even now.")

Twist sued the government, alleging that he was fired for charging his superiors with obstructing a grand jury investigation. (His suit was later dismissed.) In 1987 the counsel for the Office of Professional Responsibility of the Department of Justice, Michael E. Shaheen Jr., issued an internal report concluding that every one of Twist's allegations— among them that his supervisors had "improperly sought to immunize certain subjects of the investigation" and "ignored relevant evidence"—was "without merit." The actions of Twist's and Bobula's bosses, Shaheen wrote, constituted "appropriate exercises of prosecutorial discretion intended by supervisors...only to advance the case." In a stinging rebuke, Shaheen concluded, "In the history of this Office, we have not seen charges of misconduct leveled by Departmental attorneys against other Departmental attorneys that were so utterly devoid of substance. The only aspect of management's conduct during the *Press/Plain Dealer* investigation we found troubling was the supervisors' failure to insist that Mr. Twist...either conduct the investigation expeditiously and within the constraints of the Division's limited resources and focus...efforts on developing direct evidence of criminality, or get off the case." (Bobula and Twist characterize the OPR inquiry as superficial and "nothing more than a whitewash.")

If Twist's and Bobula's allegations have any validity, the question remains: who stopped the investigation? Some claim that the Newhouses were big financial backers of President Reagan—Si was an occasional guest at the White House—and that he or Edwin Meese, who became Reagan's attorney general in 1985, ordered the probe derailed. Jim Neff suggests that the investigation was called off because "the Reagan Justice Department said, 'Take care of this.'" The fact that Si walked away unpunished, Neff adds, shows "what great power someone like Si Newhouse can have, where he could, through friends and influence, quash a Justice Department investigation into his businesses, or just make it go away." Howard Metzenbaum says he too believes that the antitrust case was "squashed...because I always had the feeling—I don't know this—I always had the feeling that there was some very strong political pressure."

Some saw the hand of Roy Cohn, who remained Si's closest friend. Sam had given Roy money when he needed it, and so did Si. To rid himself of the IRS, which, Cohn claimed, tortured him with a twenty-three-year open audit, he offered in 1981 to settle for $1 million—the million to be supplied by Si Newhouse. "He wanted me freed from all this madness," Roy wrote in his autobiography. The IRS ultimately declined the settlement offer because, for openers, in 1983 Roy had appeared on the cover of the Newhouses' *Parade* magazine, informing its huge and national audience, "You Can Beat the IRS."

Cohn was close enough to members of the Reagan administration, including Nancy Reagan, and did enough favors to give him some influence. In his autobiography, Cohn tells of having lunch with Edward J. Rollins, then running President Reagan's 1984 reelection campaign. Rollins mentioned that he and others were concerned that Reagan's age and health might prove to be an issue in the campaign. Cohn saw a way to neutralize that issue: a cover story in the Newhouses' *Parade,* which then had a circulation of 50 million, showing the president engaged in strenuous physical activity. Cohn called the magazine's editor, and the deal was done. Millions of people saw the photographs of the president diving into a swimming pool and chopping wood at his California ranch, looking the epitome of physical health.

"I don't have any evidence of that," Russell Twist says, referring to the Cohn tie, "but something happened." Twist, however, pursues another angle when he adds to the mix Douglas H. Ginsburg, head of the antitrust division between 1985 and 1986, currently a judge on the U.S. Court of Appeals in Washington, and in 1987 a short-lived Reagan nominee to the U.S. Supreme Court. Ginsburg withdrew his nomination after allegations surfaced that he had used marijuana while a professor at Harvard Law School. The real reason Ginsburg withdrew, Twist claims, was that his alleged role in quashing the antitrust investigation of the *Cleveland Press* would have been made public, and the affair would have looked so dirty that he would have had to withdraw eventually anyway. Implying that Ginsburg was pressured to withdraw by some unidentified person or people who did not want the closing of the *Cleveland Press* rehashed before the

Judiciary Committee, Twist calls it "much more probable that [Ginsburg's] nomination got pulled because they didn't want to be focusing on this grand jury than on whether he smoked some marijuana." Howard Metzenbaum, then a member of the Senate Judiciary Committee, had said at the time that he planned to question Ginsburg about his role in the probe of the *Press*'s closing and about his decision to fire Russell Twist. (Ginsburg did not respond to a request for an interview.)

Suzanne Garment, a former Washington columnist for the *Wall Street Journal*, writes in her book *Scandal: The Culture of Mistrust in American Politics* that after the marijuana controversy exploded, "Ginsburg was also charged with serious conflicts of interest dating from the time when he headed the Justice Department's antitrust division. Justice Department attorneys began investigating, to see whether an independent counsel should be appointed. They decided that the charges did not meet even the law's accommodating standards and that the case should not go forward."

There were other allegations—all more ammunition to those who believed that Newhouse had bought off Cole. Cole reportedly dodged the phone calls of at least one potential buyer, an Illinoisan named John Malone. But John Morton calls Malone a "gadfly," not a serious buyer, and implies that if Cole dodged Malone's calls, he was smart to do so. Malone "was going to buy and start at least fifteen newspapers in the last twenty years," says Morton. "Nobody takes him seriously anymore, doesn't have any money." Marilyn Bobula, for all her fervor for the payoff theory, says of Malone, "He said to Cole, 'I'm here to offer you millions of dollars to buy the paper. Send me the air fare so I can come to Cleveland to discuss it with you.'"

A second allegation in support of the theory that the last thing Cole wanted was a buyer to disturb his deal with Si was that his paper's press room was quickly and clumsily dismantled. That theory has it that the mess would deter potential buyers of the *Press* or, for that matter, anyone interested in starting a paper to compete with the *Plain Dealer*. According to a report in *Business Week*, when John Malone's representatives toured the *Press* building a month after the paper closed, they found "all the equipment dismantled, wires ripped out of the walls, and the print facilities useless." Malone told the magazine's reporters that "the plant was made absolutely inoperative so that there could be no continuing operations there."

Eventually the building, with what was left of the equipment still inside—the presses were sold and shipped to Florida—was demolished to make way for the $34 million office complex that Cole had built on the site. Herb Kamm says sadly that when it came time to demolish the building, Joe Cole "let himself be talked into the notion of sitting in the seat of the tractor which swung the cement ball that began to demolish the building."

The story of what happened in Cleveland may never be known, but one thing is certain. Ted Newhouse was right when he once boasted to Ben Magdovitz, "We're gonna own Cleveland one of these days."4

Shortly before the *Cleveland Press* died, two reporters at the Newhouses' *Cleveland Plain Dealer* were researching a story alleging that Jackie Presser, by then planning to run for president of the Teamsters union, took kickbacks and served as an FBI informant. According to Jim Neff—the former *Plain Dealer* investigative reporter who wrote *Mobbed Up*, a book about Presser—when Presser learned of the reporters' probing, he pressured publisher Thomas Vail to kill the story. Vail in turn talked to David L. Hopcraft, then the paper's executive editor. Neff claims that Vail worried that if Presser were sufficiently angered he would prompt the Teamsters, which represented the newspaper's drivers, to strike the paper and, because the union was so strong, to shut it down. That would provide the *Press* with the reprieve it needed, and perhaps with the wherewithal to at the least delay the Newhouses' dream of a monopoly in Cleveland.

Vail seemed to withstand the pressure, and the two-part story ran in August 1981. Presser then threatened the paper with a libel suit. He feared that the allegations that he had been a government snitch would destroy his chances at the Teamsters presidency. He demanded that a retraction be printed and that it run on the front page of the Sunday paper. At a different paper with a different owner, a libel suit like the one Presser threatened would have been dismissed as empty bluster. As Neff writes, "Presser knew he could never sit still for the exhaustive discovery of a real libel suit."

According to Neff, the action was taking place behind the scenes. New York mob boss "Fat Tony" Salerno, a Presser ally, called his lawyer, Roy Cohn, to see if he could help finesse the retraction. Cohn told the delighted Salerno that he represented the owner of the *Plain Dealer*, Si Newhouse. Cohn then took the matter to Si, and Si allegedly ordered that a retraction be published. "I was just stunned," Neff recalls. "It was a real eye-opener for me.... This is a story about how power really works in America."

Upon hearing of the proposed retraction, one of the reporters pleaded with Hopcraft not to run it. The reporter insisted that their story was unassailable. According to Neff, Hopcraft responded that it didn't matter how well documented their story was: "The orders are coming out of New York." One Sunday in October 1982, Hopcraft published the page-one, unbylined retraction, which infuriated and demoralized the paper's reporting staff. In April 1983 Presser was elected Teamster president.

When an excerpt of the Neff book appeared in the *Washington Journalism Review*, Vail was asked for his side of the story. He claimed that there was no pressure applied; that the page-one piece was not a retraction but simply a news story reporting that the government had dropped its investigation of Presser. That was true, as far as it went, but the reporters insisted that the government did so because the seven-year statute of limitations had expired on bringing charges based on the kickback allegations. They had pleaded, in vain, that the retraction include that information.

Like their father before them, Si and Don did not often interfere on the editorial side of any of their properties. When Roy Cohn needed a favor, however, that, it seems, was another story.[5]

The second newspaper that had to be attended to was the *St. Louis Globe-Democrat*. It had become, almost by design, a certifiable money loser. By cutting a deal in 1959 for the *Post-Dispatch* to print his paper, Sam had sentenced it to six-day publication and thus to the also-ran position. The *Post-Dispatch*'s Sunday edition was an advertising bonanza. According to one *Globe-Democrat* executive, "That Sunday *Post* had more advertising in one issue than we had all week."

When, a year later, Sam made the secret deal with the *Post-Dispatch*'s Joe Pulitzer to share profits and losses, the assumption was always that the chronically unprofitable *Globe-Democrat* would eventually fold. That would leave the *Post-Dispatch* to ride a monopoly to huge profits. But, for the time being, the *Post-Dispatch*'s profits were anemic. Costs were rising while advertising revenue remained stagnant. In 1969 the *Globe-Democrat* carried 25 million lines of advertising, and the *Post-Dispatch* carried 51 million. In 1978 the *Globe*'s advertising lineage had increased by only 3 million, to 28 million, and the *Post*'s had dropped by 5 million, to 46 million.

Shortly before Sam's death in 1979, Si had agreed to enter into a joint operating agency by which the *Post-Dispatch* would run the advertising and circulation departments for both papers. Only the papers' newsrooms would remain independent. (A casualty of the agreement was supersalesman Ben Magdovitz, who was marking his thirtieth year at the paper. Magdovitz ended up at the *Toledo Blade*. Its owner, Paul Block Jr., might not have cared personally for Sam, but he knew that Sam's advertising director would be the best in the business.) According to John Morton, "It was the only joint operating agency that was losing money, the only one in the country." Morton assigns the Pulitzers a share of the blame because "they insisted on publishing a...*New York Times*–type newspaper in a market that didn't want one, and they...had not done well in covering or penetrating the suburbs, which of course during the '60s and '70s is where all the newspaper business moved to." In addition, both papers had lost much of their grocery store advertising to suburban papers.

Sometime in the early 1980s, perhaps as late as 1983, Si met with Joe Pulitzer, and the two men negotiated another amendment to the agreement: Pulitzer would give the Newhouses half the profits that would surely accrue were the *Post-Dispatch* the only paper in town, in exchange for the Newhouses making that possible by closing the *Globe-Democrat*. In other words, says Ben Magdovitz, Pulitzer made Si an offer he couldn't refuse.

Just before Thanksgiving, 1983, Si informed Duncan Bauman that the time had come to close the paper. The last edition would be published on February 1, 1984.

The Newspaper Guild was permitted to bring in its own auditor to look at the books of both papers. The auditor confirmed that the agency that ran the papers had lost in the neighborhood of $12 million in one year. "This has been a bucket of red ink over there," the auditor told Robert A. Steinke, then executive secretary of the St. Louis Newspaper Guild.

The red ink is now just a bad memory. Magdovitz estimates a recent year's take for the Newhouses from the *Post-Dispatch*'s bottom line at about $14 million. Since Si agreed to shut down the *Globe-Democrat,* Magdovitz says, "they've taken out...maybe $40-50 million dollars." There is much more to come, as the agreement calls for the Newhouses and Pulitzers to share equally in the *Post-Dispatch*'s profits or losses for at least fifty years.

One executive on the *Globe-Democrat* observes that the Newhouses took the Pulitzers "like Grant took Richmond. When...you have the only Sunday paper in town and you settle for...having half the bottom line go to the other guy, I would say they made a pretty good deal with the Pulitzers." Every time he gets a report from the *Post-Dispatch,* says Robert Steinke, "I think, this is for absolutely nothing that [the Newhouses] get half the profit.... The last financial report I got I remarked to my wife how much money they took out for not having a newspaper or any businesses here."

Magdovitz and others believe fervently that Sam would never have let his favorite paper die.

Just as Si had not appeared at the *Long Island Press* but left Dave Starr to meet with distressed employees, so he stayed away from St. Louis, leaving Duncan Bauman to confront mounting bitterness. Unlike Long Island, where except for the most partisan old-timers, there was agreement that *Newsday* had outshone and out-reported the *Press,* in St. Louis the *Globe*'s staff fervently believed that Si was allowing the better paper to be buried. "We used the expression, 'We're number two, but we try harder,'" recalls *Globe* political editor, Jack Flach, a thirty-year veteran. "But all the sudden, here's the *Globe* picking up and picking up and there was...real talk among *Post* reporters and *Globe* staffers over at the local watering hole...that Newhouse would someday buy out Pulitzer and we would be the dominant newspaper and the *Post-Dispatch* would be gone." The news of the closing left the staff and many of the paper's readers stunned and saddened.

Edward O'Brien, chief of the *Globe*'s Washington bureau for almost thirty years, gentlemanly, discreet, loyal, was given no advance warning and was said to be humiliated when he learned the news on arriving at his office. Mitzi's brother Walter, so prone to feeling slighted, was given no advance warning by his nephew, and learned of the paper's death at the same time as his colleagues. His daughter Sue and his son Michael also became ex-employees of the paper. (Walter was offered the option of moving to Springfield but declined; Michael later landed at the Newhouse papers in Mobile, Alabama; Sue retired from the newspaper business.) Sue calls the closing "a complete and total shock.... We were just told one day that the paper was going to cease publication."

Before announcing the end, the Newhouses had secured Justice Department permission to close by documenting the joint operating agency's huge losses and the fact that the agency would immediately turn profitable if it were free of having to publish two newspapers a day.

But then there was a change of mind—perhaps the controversy and hand-wringing in Cleveland over the closing of the *Press* had something to do with it, perhaps the news of the profit-sharing deal, finally made public. Justice Department lawyers ordered the Newhouses to sell the paper. "Nobody in the newspaper industry thought anybody in their right mind would buy it," recalls Morton, "but along came this guy named Jeffrey Gluck." Gluck expressed confidence that he could save the money-hemorrhaging paper. Unfortunately, says editorial page editor Martin Duggan, Gluck "didn't have a nickel's worth of experience at running a daily newspaper." He ended up paying nothing for the paper but left unpaid bills and broken promises all over town. He was so short of funds that he had the building's air conditioning turned off and fed the staff salt pills. Some months later he sold to two local businessmen, who in turn held out a short time before the impossible finances forced them into bankruptcy and the paper finally was put to rest.[6]

For Si Newhouse, the decade of the 1980s would be one of acquisitions, of start-ups, of headline-making hiring and firing decisions. Reports of his alternately boneheaded and brilliant moves landed him in the media almost daily. Some would come to consider him the most powerful man in publishing.

Still, the words most frequently used to describe him were "weird" and "ruthless." But as he moved into his fifties, the phrase "Sam Newhouse's son" had finally been laid to rest.

15 | Si Goes Shopping

START UP AND LAUNCH were words that never existed in the father's vocabulary. They would become very much a part of his elder son's.

Si Newhouse was remarkably open to new ideas for magazines. When in the late 1970s a veteran *Glamour* editor named Phyllis Wilson pitched her idea to him, a conviction that women would buy a magazine focused on fitness and physical and emotional health, he listened. As she explained it, instead of Elizabeth Taylor offering tips for glowing skin, the magazine she had in mind would feature a dermatologist offering straight talk on how to improve the underlying health of the skin. Si quickly saw that Wilson had pinpointed a niche no other magazine was filling. He told her to develop a prototype.

The new magazine mogul's first launch, *Self,* hit the newsstands in 1979, the year of his father's death. Peter Diamandis, the publisher who commanded *Self,* recalls how clear and smart its mission was: "The next-generation *Glamour, Mademoiselle,* wasn't supposed to be cosmetics, it was supposed to be dermatology; it was supposed to be one step beyond the superficial."

The name, which many in the company considered the worst in magazine history, was said to have been coined by Si himself. In any case, he took credit for it because he wanted to be seen as the innovator. Besides, he did like the name and so, as it turned out, did the marketplace. "*Self* [took] off like a rocket initially," says Val Weaver, the former *Vogue* editor who had left Condé Nast but returned to become the magazine's first managing editor. It was an instant success. Women embraced it with unusual loyalty, and by 1980 *Self*'s circulation was inching above the 800,000 mark, having started at around half a million at launch. "It was really the first reader-friendly magazine," explains Kim Bonnell, then a young editor at *Glamour*, "that didn't address readers in a kind of imperial tone."

Self's quick and easy success prompted Si, his eye on Hearst's *Cosmopolitan*, to want to push *Self* into multimillion circulation, beyond its natural level. "Natural level"—the circulation numbers that a magazine's content and design could expect to draw in the absence of money-losing subscription gimmicks—was a concept that the owner did not yet understand. What made *Self* appealing and unique was that it spoke intelligently to an educated, sophisticated audience. Explorations on attaining peak health, fitness, and well-being would never attract as many readers as articles on sex and celebrities. But Alex Liberman knew what the boss wanted, and in an attempt to boost circulation, Liberman made a wrong turn, insisting on more glamour, celebrity, and sexiness—precisely the angle the magazine's readers said they didn't want. At around the same time editor Phyllis Wilson, who had been in remission from an earlier bout with breast cancer, suffered a recurrence that would soon kill her, and *Self*'s art director died of AIDS.

The magazine's circulation stalled at the million mark through the 1980s, and a restlessness and dissatisfaction set in among *Self*'s early and loyal readers who wondered what was happening to the magazine that had seemed so right for them. Still, in the decade's opening years *Self* appeared to be a winner, and Si's level of self-confidence inched upward.[1]

In 1979, the year *Self* was born, Si also acquired the company's first magazine for men—*Gentleman's Quarterly*, soon to be shortened to *GQ*. He bought *GQ*, then owned by Esquire, Inc., for $9 million from its chairman, Abe Blinder, who had sold *Esquire* to Clay Felker a couple of years before. David O'Brasky, a former publisher at *Esquire*, and at *GQ* before the sale to Si, calls that sum "the best $9 million Newhouse ever spent because instead of starting a men's magazine, he acquired one that he knew had vast potential."

By the time Si came on the scene, *GQ*, founded in 1957, had already begun to shed the gay image that had hobbled the magazine's numbers. In

1979 its circulation was 250,000; under Newhouse ownership it grew to exceed 700,000 and began to make money. Understanding that the magazine would never have major commercial success if it were perceived as having a gay readership, Si demanded that the process be sped up and insisted on the use of more women models. In 1980, he brought in *Esquire* advertising director Steve Florio, a rough-around-the-edges, macho salesman, to take care of the advertising side. Florio had worked for O'Brasky at *Esquire,* and it was O'Brasky who had recommended him for the *GQ* spot. In 1983 Si hired as the top editor a former *Newsweek* editor—coincidentally, he had also worked for one of the Newhouse papers in Harrisburg—named Arthur Cooper, who remains editor of the magazine today.

"The bottom line on *GQ*," says O'Brasky, "is that [Si] acquired it and did every single thing with it that needed to be done."[2] Right off the bat, Si seemed to have hatched two winners.

In 1980, as Si relished his successes with *Self* and *GQ*, he found weakness elsewhere, and he decided to change editors and to try to do the dirty work himself.

Edith Raymond Locke had arrived at *Mademoiselle* in 1949 as the assistant to the dress and millinery editor, had stuck with the magazine, and had risen to be its editor-in-chief. She had been in that position for eight years when, one morning in May 1980, she arrived at work to find a message from Si. He asked her to come to his office, and when she arrived, "He explained to me that he felt *Mademoiselle* had to go in a different direction, a new direction, and that he didn't think I could take it into that direction. And I asked why I wasn't given a chance to try...and he felt that that was counterproductive...and to see personnel for arrangements, etc., etc., etc." So uncomfortable was Si during this exchange, Locke recalls, that "he never looked up."

There was a second message waiting for her that day. It was from *Ladies' Home Journal* editor Lenore Hershey, who informed Locke that Si had already hired her replacement, a young woman named Amy Levin, then the *Journal*'s articles editor.

The firing of Locke, then fifty-nine, seemed to make Si aware that he had power to act for the good of the magazines—as he saw it—and thereafter he became a willing executioner. Others saw it in a different way. Grace Mirabella wrote in her memoir, *In and Out of Vogue,* that the manner of Locke's dismissal "sent shock waves through the magazine industry...and is still seen by many...as the blow that ushered in the new era of disloyalty, insecurity, and cutthroat competition that plagues the magazine world in our day."

Born in Vienna, Locke was from a family that had fled the Nazis and had arrived in the United States in 1939. "This woman lived and breathed this magazine," says Peter Diamandis, a former publisher of *Mademoiselle.* "A more hardworking...woman I have never met in my life." Before then, *Mademoiselle* had been edited since 1937 by one person, Betsy Talbot Blackwell. Blackwell was a woman who would not have considered appearing in public without a hat, and often wore one at her desk. Rumor had it that her maid ironed her stockings every morning.

Locke guided the magazine from a "white-glove" remnant of an era past—edited for college girls, but with a particularly Seven Sisterish cast—into something more democratic and modern and very much a reflection of Locke herself; lively, intellectual, classy. Starting under Blackwell, but accelerating under Locke, *Mademoiselle* became the place for serious fiction, nurtured by contributing editor Leo Lerman, who scouted such writers as Joyce Carol Oates and Truman Capote. Then-Random House chief Bennett Cerf told of signing up "an unknown writer called Truman Capote" after hearing about a story of his, "Miriam," that had been published in *Mademoiselle.* Mary Cantwell, once an editor at the magazine, described *Mademoiselle* as an "unlikely repositor[y] for some of the best American short stories. Everybody thinks those are in the *New Yorker.* They aren't. They're in *Mademoiselle.*"

Under Locke, *Mademoiselle* settled in at a circulation of around 650,000. That wasn't enough for Si. While he was naturally drawn to the highbrow aspect of *Mademoiselle,* he also wanted more people to buy it. He had taken to arriving at his office in the predawn hours to calculate the numbers himself. He saw that at *Mademoiselle* they were stagnant. Although the official circulation would be listed at a bit over 900,000 by 1980, newsstand sales—the key number, because subscriptions can be bought via deep discounting—were in dangerous decline. What Newhouse was after for *Mademoiselle* was numbers that matched *Glamour*'s, then at about 2 million, or better yet, that matched Hearst's *Cosmopolitan,* then at 2 million plus. Publishing for the college girl, he decided, was not the route to such numbers; aiming at secretaries, as *Glamour* and *Cosmo* did, was the ticket.

To veteran *Mademoiselle* editors such as Amy Gross, who had arrived at *Mademoiselle* in 1963 a week out of college, the notion of parroting *Glamour,* not to mention *Cosmopolitan,* was heresy. For Edie Locke the difference between *Mademoiselle* and *Glamour* was to be celebrated, not obliterated.... We always looked at *Glamour* as being intellectually below us."

As would occur time and again over the next decade and a half, Si assigned Alex Liberman to orchestrate the changes needed to get those millions for *Mademoiselle.* Suddenly, Alex was on the scene at a magazine to which he had previously paid little attention.

Liberman liked Edie Locke—he had pushed Si to name her editor—but then plotting to make *Self*'s cover girl look more sexy and less sweaty, he agreed that *Mademoiselle* needed to refocus. Alex's genius was for design, not editorial. Yet his grand title, editorial director, and Si's worshipful confidence in him meant that if he cared to, he could control both.

In the case of *Self,* Alex felt that women in all Condé Nast magazines should be drop-dead gorgeous, but how they got and stayed that way was not for publication. Exercise was slightly vulgar, best suited for the privacy of home or the gym. In the case of *Mademoiselle,* Alex argued that the stories were too serious. The magazine, he said, needed a good lightening up of editorial and design that would appeal to a younger, more culture-free audience. He gave Edie Locke his "suggestions," but subtly. "One does not have a disagreement with Alex," says Locke. It was always, "Darling, don't you think one should do such and so? This article was heavy, too sad, too serious. Why don't we lighten up the magazine?"

According to Peter Diamandis, Locke said no to what she felt would be only a temporary fix. Over the long term, Locke was confident that the magazine was right for its audience. The lesson to be drawn from her fate would be clear for her colleagues to see: one ignored Alex Liberman at one's peril.

It came to be that at Si's magazines, powerful editors-in-chief would bite their tongues while Alex sliced copy in half to facilitate the design.

Art directors became glorified assistants, meekly handing Liberman scissors and paste and stats of various sizes as he ripped apart layouts and covers to work his magic. "We used to have to wait for Alex to come down to look at layouts," recalls Locke, "sometimes late in the evening.... Alex would look at a bunch of layouts and say, 'Wonderful, it's exciting, it's lovely.' Next morning at 9:01 came the phone call, 'I thought about it in the middle of the night and it occurred to me that maybe we should...' and then the whole thing was out the door and redone."

The morning Si told her she was fired, Locke went looking for Liberman, who, as she expected, "was conveniently out that day because Alex hated confrontation." Had she seen him, she would have asked, "'How did this happen? Why wasn't I given a chance?' Alex probably would have said, 'All of these last few months, darling, I thought I let you realize that we wanted something else out of the magazine, and you didn't pick up on it.'"

Locke's successor, Amy Levin, then recently married to *GQ*'s Arthur Cooper, was altogether different. Sex was in, and the focus on the college girl was out, as was the college issue and the college guest editorship program that had brought to the magazine the likes of Sylvia Plath, Francine du Plessix Gray, and Joan Didion. Si hoped he had found a way to attract a mass readership to *Mademoiselle*, but in the meantime he had another purchase on his mind.[3]

Those on the lookout for Si's next move on the magazine front were stunned when, in 1980, he bought book publishing giant Random House. Founded by Bennett Cerf and Donald Klopfer in 1927, the year of Si's birth, the publisher was a giant not in size or profitability—like most book publishers, Random House's return on investment was minuscule compared to that generated by a monopoly newspaper—but in reputation. Random House, under Cerf, had published William Faulkner, James Joyce, Dr. Seuss, Eugene O'Neill, and Ralph Ellison. Encompassing such stellar imprints as Knopf—publisher of Willa Cather and Thomas Mann, among others—and Pantheon—publisher of Boris Pasternak and Jean-Paul Sartre—Random House was, and arguably remains, the most influential and prestigious of American book publishers.

Robert Bernstein, who came to Random House in 1957 as sales manager and would eventually run the place, describes the company that year as a seventy-employee, "happy" place. It was housed for a time on the parlor floor of the north wing of "Villard," a brownstone mansion designed by Stanford White, complete with a courtyard across from St. Patrick's Cathedral.

Wall Street took note when Cerf, who admitted that his dream was to be listed on the New York Stock Exchange along with U.S. Steel and du Pont, took his company public in 1958. One former Random House editor recalls the period as one in which "giant corporations [were] buying publishing companies and thinking that it was going to create all this synergy"—not to mention profit.

In 1966 one of those giant corporations, RCA, came calling, and Cerf sold out for $40 million in stock. He struck the deal with RCA chairman General David Sarnoff, after Sarnoff promised Cerf that RCA would never interfere with his decision to publish or not to publish any particular book. Sarnoff, who had founded NBC, then a division of RCA, diligently kept his word. After the deal closed, Bob Bernstein, who became head of Random House just at the time of the sale to RCA, sent him galleys of *Due to Circumstances Beyond Our Control,* a book on the television industry by the late Fred W. Friendly, a former president of CBS News, about to be published by Random House. Sarnoff returned the galleys with a note, "Please don't send me galleys of books, only finished books, because if people see galleys on my desk they will have the impression, which would certainly not be so, that I wish to express an opinion of the content of the book."

Interestingly, General Sarnoff and his men wanted Random House not so much for its glamorous trade division as for its unremarkable education division—a division that Cerf had always treated as an unloved stepchild. Cerf had acquired the L. W. Singer Company of Rochester, "a distinctly second-rate textbook publisher," says one former Random House executive, simply because other publishers were buying textbook houses—in the wake of the Soviet launch of *Sputnik*, the federal government was pouring money into textbook development—and he thought he'd best follow suit. At the time RCA saw educational publishing as a source of material for the software with which it hoped to fuel its growing computer division.

From the start, there was a clash of cultures between tweedy Random House and gray-flannel RCA. The top people at RCA came to resent Random House, to see it as an elite, pampered, unprofitable pipsqueak, and RCA withdrew into a kind of studied disregard of its tiny acquisition. Those at Random House felt both relief at being let alone and disdain for RCA's ignorance of the book business. "RCA didn't have a clue on how to manage Random House," says one of its top executives at the time, Alexander "Sandy" MacGregor III.

For all the interest RCA showed, Random House might as well have produced frozen chickens or rugs, and in fact RCA had purchased, along with Random House, companies that produced just those products. One former Random House editor recalls the amusement with which she and her colleagues viewed RCA's annual report: "RCA was a big defense contractor, and their graphs would be for jet planes and then there'd be TVs and the networks, and there was a little category called 'other' and it was us and Banquet Fried Chicken."

Anthony Conrad, who succeeded Sarnoff's son Robert as chairman—both David Sarnoff and Cerf died in 1971—was fascinated by publishing. "He read more of the books than I did," says one former Random House executive, but he landed in trouble with the IRS—he didn't file his income tax—and had to resign. His successor, Edgar H. Griffiths, was seen as much less friendly, and indeed, once he had determined that synergy was a pipe dream and that Random House's profit margins were too pathetically small to compensate, he decided to get rid of it as fast as he could.

Griffiths let Robert Bernstein, by then CEO of Random House, know that he wanted to sell, but gave him hardly any notice. Griffiths "called me and asked me to come over at one-thirty that day," Bernstein recalls, "and said that at two-thirty it was going out over the ticker tape that we were going to be for sale." Random House would be joined on the block, Griffiths added, by Banquet Foods, the chicken parts company.

"RCA peddled Random House around like a basket of rotten fruit," recalled the late James Michener, then and until his death in 1997 a Random House author. Hearst and Times Mirror were among several companies said to be interested. But it is literary agent Morton Janklow who takes credit for bringing Random House to his friend Si Newhouse's attention and persuading him to buy. "If you talk to Mort," says one former top executive, "he will tell you that he told Si, 'If you ever want to get into the publishing business, this is the opportunity you should not miss, once in a lifetime opportunity.'"

Si and Donald acted quickly. They invited Bob Bernstein to lunch at the Sky Club atop the Pan Am Building. The brothers' approach, Bernstein recalls, was "really perfect.... They said they'd like to buy [it] but really only if Random House wanted to be bought by them, and I should go back and take...whatever time was necessary and talk to...people, ...and then we'd have lunch again. And that's what I did." The Newhouses as owners were "okay" with his colleagues, who, Bernstein recalls, "sort of liked the idea of going private after RCA." (Because RCA was a public company, there was, recalls Sandy MacGregor, "continual pressure to do stupid things to get another penny of earnings per share in a given quarter.")

With his father likely up there nodding approval, Si paid $65 million in cash for Random House.

That Bob Bernstein and senior management took to the Newhouses was not surprising. Having been told of the family's hands-off stance with their newspapers, Random House people saw Si as heaven-sent. "The interesting thing," marveled James Michener, who later became a critic of Si's stewardship of Random House, "is that when Newhouse came on the horizon, he came on as a white knight.... They were a publishing family. I knew them." He said he felt good about them because he had "trusted the old man implicitly."

For Random House employees, who never felt comfortable under the thumb of a diversified corporation, Newhouse ownership seemed to signal a return to old values. "We were pleased to have been bought by someone who was at least in publishing," explains Seibert Adams, who ran the college department, "and understood the process and understood that the bottom line wasn't everything on a quarterly basis."

For Bob Bernstein, the change in ownership allowed him to shine. When he pushed RCA to buy a paperback house, a crucial ingredient in profitable publishing, RCA executives had insisted, "You can only buy a losing paperback house because if you buy a profitable one the FTC will be all over us." So Bernstein acquired a loser, Ballantine, and struggled unsuccessfully to turn it around. In 1981, a year after the Newhouses came in, Bernstein told Si he wanted to buy the paperback publisher Fawcett. Si told him to go ahead and never looked at the numbers. Bernstein bought Fawcett from CBS at a very low price, merged the two paperback lists, instantly acquiring a back list, and turned the paperback division from a drain into a moneymaker.

For George Rosato, who ran Random House's school division (books for elementary and high school students), Si Newhouse's arrival "provided me with the resources necessary to grow from $6 million to $32 million."[4]

For Si Newhouse, the quasi-intellectual, buying Random House, which published the writer he claimed as his favorite, Marcel Proust, was a thrill equivalent to that felt by an eight-year-old who suddenly discovers that his father owns F.A.O. Schwartz. When Si chose to talk, it was often about his favorite books and authors, and these were, by and large, serious writers.

Si was passionate about books long before he discovered art and film. His first wife, Jane Franke, recalled how much he loved to read, especially books about history. David Morgan, Si's friend from the time of his first marriage, remembers him always with a book in hand.

Joni Evans, later head of Random House's adult trade department, calls Si "shockingly well read" in philosophy, history, political science, science, and relatively difficult fiction. "He's crazy about Kazuo Ishiguro. He went on for weeks about him. [Ishiguro, author of the Booker Prize-winning *The Remains of the Day*, is published by Knopf.] He said to me, 'Oh, I'm really happy you're publishing Donald Barthelme.'" But Si once warned Bob Bernstein not to rely on his opinion in bidding on books: "I've never read a best-seller in my life."

Dinner with Si and Victoria always included plenty of talk about books, says Francine du Plessix Gray. "Si always questions me quite closely about what books I've read, how I've felt about some of the things he's published in the past year." His "cultural references," she says, are "quite extraordinary. He is an autodidact of all time who reads many, many, many books a week."[5]

"At first," says Sandy MacGregor, Newhouse ownership was "very, very positive." The sale had just closed when MacGregor and Bob Bernstein requested money to build a warehouse alongside the existing one. All it

took, MacGregor says, was a "ten minute phone call which was, 'Si, I really need to build this warehouse.'... He said, 'Fine, go ahead and start, send
me a memo.' There were no meetings with lawyers. It was a cost-justified
decision. I had the cost justification. I sent it to him, after the fact.... I
never heard another word about it. I just went ahead and built the warehouse.... He empowers the people who work for him."

Like his father, the elder son wanted to learn all he could about the
new business, which sometimes made Bob Bernstein a bit nervous. Twice
a year, accompanied by Bernstein and Sandy MacGregor, Si would visit
Westminster, Maryland, where most of the operations were located.

He also insisted on attending every sales conference, sitting
"through every minute of them," Bernstein remembers. He usually brought
with him his nephew, Steven Newhouse, Donald's firstborn and a graduate
of Yale, whom Si seemed to be grooming to run Random House. (Steven's
regular job at the time was at the undistinguished *Jersey Journal*.)

Sales conferences for book publishers are critical to a house's success. Twice or three times a year, the season's list is pitched by the editors
and marketing people to the sales force. The diminutive pair (Steven resembling Sam Newhouse with uncanny closeness), sat listening, learning,
rarely speaking, occasionally telling an editor, but only later in the corridor,
of a particular interest in one of his or her books. Nan Graham, then a young
editor at Pantheon, remembers her first sales conference—and, she suspects, Si's as well—at which Bob Bernstein slept through the editors' pre-
sentations while Si, seated next to Bernstein, acted like a "completely live
wire, paid attention to every single book that was presented." Later he
stopped Graham to ask about a book she had presented by Washington
artist Anne Truitt. "He'll come up to you after," recalls Joni Evans, "and
say, 'I really like the sound of that,' all excited like a little boy."

Steven Newhouse, while in the company of his uncle, remained mostly silent. But the younger editors seemed to like and respect him. Says a
Pantheon editor of the time, Wendy Wolf, when out of Si's gaze, Steve
"absolutely would mix. He would be very complimentary and always have
a book to talk to you about.... You got the feeling that he'd done his homework and he was paying attention."[6]

Si Newhouse had carved out a career that made him happy, and it seemed that he could not get to the office early enough. Picked up by a limousine service at his Seventieth Street house at four in the morning, Si arrived at the Condé Nast Building, before four-thirty. (Donald Newhouse kept the same schedule so he could be at his desk at the *Newark Star-Ledger* by four-thirty.) In working for Si, morning people had a definite advantage. He was known to call meetings for as early as 6:00 A.M.

And he was always ready for the day. "There is nobody who ever met with him, no matter how early in the morning," says David O'Brasky, "when he hadn't already read all the newspapers, all the trades, and didn't have three pages of notes. It was a very intimidating thing, especially Monday morning [when the trades came out]. He had *Ad Age, Ad Week, Media Industry Newsletter, Delaney,* the *Gallagher Report,* whatever was done in the industry, he had already read by seven Monday morning." Gael Towey, a former design director of *House & Garden,* says this voracious digestion of everything from the *New York Times* to *Publishers Weekly* is "the secret of Si's success."

Si's unpretentious suite on the fourteenth floor of the Condé Nast Building includes, besides his office, that of his secretary, Lillian Singer, a small conference room, a bathroom and adjoining exercise space, and an entrance foyer. Richard Penney explains that he designed the office to be "a very elegant editing or reading space for Si." Almost the entire periphery of the oversized room had ergonomically tilted reading counters so that Si "could stand in the morning and walk through and read whatever he chose during the day."

"Spartan," "straightforward," "modest," are the adjectives used to describe the office. The "nonshowiest guy I know," says Richard Kinsler, former *Mademoiselle* publisher.

On entering the office, the eye is first drawn to the oversize, custom-designed desk behind which sits Si, usually gulping iced tea. Extending around the office's periphery are identically framed Winsor McCay originals. Si's interest in film history made McCay especially appealing. In 1905 he created the newspaper comic strip *Little Nemo in Slumberland,* which in 1911 he adapted into the animated cartoon, *Little Nemo."*

Arriving in his office in those predawn hours, Si was dressed in his uniform of black slacks, a black or navy blue sweater or sweatshirt, a white shirt open at the neck—in warmer weather a polo shirt and khakis—and black, slipper-like loafers that he shed as he worked. The younger editors in his organization were always surprised to see this man of such wealth and power working in casual, worn-looking clothes and in his stocking feet.[7]

Lunch most days was at the Four Seasons, a publishing hangout, in the center booth, usually a business meal. For that Si changed in his bathroom into a coat and tie. He generally ate one baked potato. As he grew older, Si had become much more health-conscious. Gone was the college student who would wolf down cream cheese and jelly sandwiches and chain-smoke Lucky Strikes, or the young married man who, on his many visits to 21, favored the crab and eggs followed by a soufflé and punctuated by cigarettes. (He gave up smoking some years after he arrived at Condé Nast.) At dinner parties at Si's house, sometimes the guests would be served one thing and he another. Cooking for Si was an unenviable task.

After lunch, Si sometimes napped at his desk. Carolyn Sollis, an editor on *House & Garden,* remembers "one of our editors having to go in and wake him up and just being mortified seeing him with his feet up on his desk sound asleep." When not traveling Si would leave his office every afternoon around two o'clock for the gym at the Regency Hotel on Park Avenue. "He's a fanatic workout person," says one editor, who marvels that he uses a gym that "everyone else uses." One routine, always under the guidance of a personal trainer, consisted of an hour's worth of nothing but abdominal exercises. He walked to the gym alone. No bodyguard protected the billionaire dressed in a gray tracksuit and clutching an ordinary-looking canvas tote bag, packed not with gym clothes but with magazines and books.

Security did become an issue once, when then personnel head Pam van Zandt feared that an employee who had been fired might try to retaliate. She wanted to station a bodyguard outside Si's office, but he said no. He did take some precautions. When he exited the building for a destination requiring a car, he was never picked up in front. The driver retrieved him a block or two away, the idea being, presumably, that his routine remain unpredictable.[8]

His workout completed, Si returned home for a nap and some reading time before dinner and whatever was that night's activity. Then to bed and a few hours sleep before waking close by 3:00 A.M. for another day at the office.

When writer Iris Cohen Selinger interviewed Si for *Inside Media,* she described his office, with galleys and cover proofs everywhere in evidence, as looking like that of a working editor-in-chief. The difference was that Si's office looked as if it belonged to the man who was editor-in-chief of every magazine under the Condé Nast mast, and of all the competitors owned by Murdoch or Hearst or Hachette as well. Friends and employees report that Si reads every one of his own magazines, cover to cover, and reads much of the competition's. The result is scores of Post-its cluttering the pages. Gael Towey recalls the counters "piled high" with magazines lying flat and reaching up a foot and a half. "I asked him if he looked at them all, and he said yes."

He always took notes on yellow legal pads. As other media moguls embraced laptop computers, Si stuck with his yellow pads and blue Flair pens. His note taking would often generate memos, written in longhand. Diane Silberstein, who has worked on the advertising sales side of four of Si's magazines, remembers one note: "'Why aren't we getting this business? I see it running in,' and then he would list competitive magazines.... He longs for information, so you get him the information." When he was the editor of *House & Garden,* Lou Gropp remembers Si counting the pages to ascertain, "How does your editorial budget compare with—" and then he would name some competing shelter magazine.

For those on the receiving end of what was called, in-house, "yellow rain," whatever else was scheduled for that morning was put aside and Si's questions answered first. Richard Kinsler recalls, "I'd get a note from him that said, 'On page forty-six there's a little article about something that you wear in your hair and you have to write in to get it.... How did this pull?'" The notes, says Kinsler, typically contained one seemingly "simple question," which, he groans, "would take you nine years to answer."

Another Condé Nast publisher recalls receiving notes from Si that "I would have to have three people look up. Where the hell did that come from? And I would initially think to myself, 'God, doesn't he have anything better to do?' He'd ask me some question that I had no idea what he was even talking about.... 'How can we drop the bleed charge on the sixth of a page somewhere?' This is a guy who counts ads by hand, you get the first bound issue and he goes through and counts them by hand with his little calculator, and he wouldn't wait for somebody to give him the report on it."

On the editorial side Si was as avid a questioner, but somewhat gentler. One former high-ranking editor who during her long tenure at Condé Nast worked on two of the magazines recalls, "He often sends the magazine down with little stickies on the pages commenting on the pages, very detailed feedback. 'I think this is too crowded, maybe you should do more of this kind of picture.'" He was, she says, especially apt to question matters of design.

Si's files—"a manual follow-up system," Sandy MacGregor calls it— stored the old-fashioned way in folders and cabinets, were "startling.... It takes two people and like a twenty by twenty room full of file cabinets to run this system," MacGregor marvels. "And the files get thicker and thicker and thicker, so you can't not tell the truth because you're going to get caught."

It is difficult to imagine a Rupert Murdoch, perpetually airbound in pursuit of media deals, attending monthly print order meetings, but Si Newhouse did exactly that, and seldom missed one. At these meetings, scheduled just as the magazine was going to press and so named because that's when the print order for newsstand distribution is set, the editor-in-chief, armed with a dummy of the issue—a cover proof containing the crucial cover lines—previews the issue, page by page. In attendance, in addition to Si and the editor, are the chiefs of promotion, circulation, advertising—anyone who will have a role in pushing newsstand sales of a particular issue or, as Mary Jane Pool, former *House & Garden* editor-in-chief, puts it, anyone responsible for "delivering the magazine out to the world." The editor will describe the nature of the feature stories, and who the writers are. Si, says one former Condé Nast editor, would often pop up with a tough question, like, "Tell me about that study that was used to support the first point in the article."

A "grabby" cover line or article, says Edie Locke, might result in a larger print order. On the other hand, flat or uninspired cover lines might be flagged as a problem, discussed, and the editors expected to return to their offices to juice them up in a way that would attract the newsstand browser.

Unlike Sam Newhouse, who was most fascinated by the chase, the acquisition, the elder son is enamored by the properties themselves. He's "devoted to the magazines," says Richard Kinsler; "he nurtures them, he treats them like children." "It's not about money," says one magazine reporter. "It seemed hardly to be about money at all."[9]

Money and power, anyone who has ever hazarded a high school reunion knows, can transform the most unpopular boy in the class into the most attractive man in the grown up world. For Si Newhouse, the transformation never quite kicked in. What struck people first was not his money or power but his strikingly odd appearance. "The first time I saw him," says one Knopf editor, "I thought, 'God should never make anybody that ugly,' that it's too much to bear in life."

His mannerisms were even more peculiar than his looks. A magazine reporter who was granted a rare interview described him as one who "shuffles and has kind of bent-over shoulders and head down." She also noticed that he made a growling noise, punctuated by "Ahhhhhhhhh" and "Well, I, I, I" and long pauses. Pat Miller, a former Condé Nast editor-in-chief, says that Si's social awkwardness brought out the maternal in her: "It made you want to pat him on the head, kind of help him out. I was always trying desperately *not* to finish his sentences for him."

A conversation with Si is much more Samuel Beckett than William Shakespeare, one employee observed to a reporter. Sandy MacGregor, once stuck in a traffic jam with Si between exits on the Long Island Expressway, recalled that Si went to sleep rather than make small talk. Another executive stopped talking about his children to Si after repeatedly eliciting no response. "Si very rarely spoke about personal things to me."

Donovan Webster, then a young editor at *House & Garden,* would sometimes be called to Si's office to work out invoices for furniture Si had ordered for himself and billed through the magazine. "It was never friendly. He didn't want to know anything personal about me." Yet when Webster suggested to his mother that she write a letter to Si complaining about the change in focus of one of his magazines, "She wrote him this heartfelt letter about what he had done to her magazine." He responded with a "nice note," and, oddly, signed it, "Your friend, Si

Newhouse"—a show of warmth he could never muster with people he actually knew.

Many people, including his old girlfriend Geraldine Stutz and his first wife, Jane, insist that Si is not so much shy as he is reserved, a person who needs to put distance between himself and others. "It hasn't got to do with shyness," says Stutz, who characterizes it as "a desire to be the observer."

Writing in the *New York Observer*, Frank DiGiacomo described Si arriving at the Great Hall of the Metropolitan Museum of Art for the Costume Institute gala, joining such guests as Edgar Bronfman Jr., Richard Gere, Calvin Klein, Donna Karan, and Lee Radziwill. "Into this celebrity gridlock stumbled [Si Newhouse] as if he had unexpectedly arrived via a warp in the time-space continuum." He was, wrote DiGiacomo, "disoriented-looking," missing the receiving line, backing into another guest.

In certain situations and with certain people, Si can grin and mean it, and the grin can transform his face into something quite appealing. And for a man of such wealth and power to be so shy and self-effacing is attractive in itself. One newspaper reporter was surprised not only that Si granted her an interview but at how unaffected he seemed. This absence of pretension caught people off guard. "I was so prepared for him to be so weird that I found him quite fine.... I thought he was weirdly sweet. He would throw in a Yiddishism every once in a while.... He picked up the phone at one point because no one was answering [it].... It wasn't like he tried to play this, 'I'm worth five billion dollars,' very low key." What other people saw as weird speech mannerisms, she saw as simply deliberative. "He thinks about everything he says for quite a while before he says it." He was never chatty or expansive. Many questions ended with the answer, "No."

As angry as Marilyn Bobula was at Si for escaping scot-free from what she sees as a deliberate violation of the antitrust laws in the closing of the *Cleveland Press*, she admits that she couldn't help liking him. She found him "extraordinarily polite," even when he learned that he'd have to stay in Cleveland beyond the one day he had planned for his grand jury appearance. When her colleague Russell Twist, himself an art collector, engaged Si in a conversation about a painting that Si had just purchased, Si was eager to talk to him. "Newhouse lit up," recalls Bobula. "He wasn't snobbish about anything. He was very unassuming, very accommodating and polite, and he never acted resentful that he was kept over." (Bobula laughs that she bought him a cup of coffee in the courthouse snack bar because "he had no money on him. I thought, how ironic, the poor government attorney buying coffee for the billionaire.")

And there was that dry humor that Si displayed now and then. The late Bud Holland, a Chicago art dealer, was at a dinner party with Si at the apartment of dealer Harold Diamond. "Si, what kind of pictures do you have over there on Seventieth Street?" Holland asked him.

"Oh, you know," Si answered, "Pollock, Newman, Rothko, Lichtenstein, all the members of the B'nai Brith."

During Random House sales conferences Si liked to take the chosen few to restaurants that one former editor calls "funky places, nothing elegant"—for example, a diner decorated in 1950s style, with waitresses in poodle skirts and a menu heavy on meatloaf-type items. Si ordered a cup of chili and, says the editor, "inhaled" it while everyone else was being served. (She says that he has "dreadful" table manners and eats faster than anyone she has ever seen.) When the waitress next came around, Si asked, "Could I have another cup of chili?" "Another cup?" Bob Bernstein asked. Without skipping a beat, Si said, "It's only $3.95."

The humor is more than dry—sometimes it's sardonic. One book publishing mogul and rival of Si's stormed into lunch at the Four Seasons one day "in a rage," having just learned that Newhouse had conceded a major contract item to an agent—a concession that, this publisher feared, he and others would then also have to make. "It was a point which did not have to be given, it was given almost out of laziness.... It was a precedent and it would lower the profitability of the industry.... I realized I'm back to back in a banquette with Newhouse. I can't restrain myself and I turn around, 'Jesus Christ, how can you be so fucking stupid?'

"He just looked at me and said, 'Who ever told you I was so smart?'"10

16 | On the Prowl for Class: *Vanity Fair*

SI NEWHOUSE'S FONDEST DREAM, friends say, was to own the *New Yorker*. His father had tried to buy the celebrated magazine in 1961 from its then chairman Raoul Fleischmann and had failed. Mitzi was said to have urged Sam on. She wasn't a reader of the *New Yorker*—it was perhaps too esoteric for her. But she would have loved to have displayed it on her coffee table as hers. "I think Sam Newhouse wanted it to give to his wife as a present," says Jeanne Fleischmann, the wife of Raoul's son, Peter, who would take over as the magazine's chairman on Raoul's death in 1969. Jeanne remembers that when Sam Newhouse came calling, Raoul, who had backed editor Harold Ross in founding the *New Yorker* in 1925, "just said no." (Ved Mehta, a longtime staffer for the *New Yorker*, has written that Raoul responded to a phone call from Sam asking how much it would cost to buy the magazine by spitting out obscenities and slamming down the receiver.)

Now, thirty years later, the Newhouse son knew that were he to approach the Fleischmann son, he would have been similarly rebuffed; that, in the unlikely event that Peter were to sell, he would not sell to the likes of a Newhouse. The *New Yorker*'s own press critic, A. J. Liebling, had continued to pick on Sam. Writer Burton Bernstein, who joined the *New Yorker* staff in 1957 and knew Liebling personally, said that Liebling would often talk of Sam Newhouse's pernicious effect on American newspapers. "Liebling had a real loathing for the guy and everything he stood for."

With the *New Yorker* seemingly beyond his reach, Si decided to launch his own *New Yorker* by reviving the long defunct *Vanity Fair*, a Condé Nast title that had been born in 1913 and died in 1936. During twenty-two years of its first life, *Vanity Fair* had never made money—its circulation meandered around 90,000—but it had possessed the sort of élan that appealed to Si. It was, in its day, urbane, sophisticated—its contributors included Dorothy Parker, Robert Benchley, Aldous Huxley, Thomas Wolfe, e. e. cummings, André Gide, Gertrude Stein, Edmund Wilson, F. Scott Fitzgerald, Collette, D. H. Lawrence, Walter Lippmann, Man Ray, Picasso—witty, snobbish, the epitome of Condé Nast's motto, "Class, not mass." In describing what would today be called *Vanity Fair*'s target audience, its editor, Frank Crowninshield, explained that it was to be a magazine "that is read by the people you meet at lunches and dinners."

Crowninshield was a thoroughbred WASP who became a legend for his taste and hauteur. In remembering Crowninshield—the great uncle of former *Washington Post* honcho Ben Bradlee—Helen Lawrenson, a social critic who wrote for *Vanity Fair*, observed, "He never used a telephone directory and would say of someone, 'How will we ever get in touch with him? He's not in the Social Register.'"

In a conversation with Francine du Plessix Gray and her husband, Cleve, Si Newhouse explained that in resurrecting *Vanity Fair*, his goal was to publish a blend of the *New Yorker* and the *New York Review of Books*, with the addition of photographs, which had been abundantly displayed in Crowinshield's *Vanity Fair*.

To bring it off, Si decided that he needed an editor with the right intellectual credentials. Cleve Gray suggested a friend of his and Francine's, Richard Locke, then deputy editor of the *New York Times Book Review*. Alex Liberman interviewed him, and recommended him, and Si quickly offered Locke the job. Robert Gottlieb, who was then running Knopf for Si and had once worked with Locke at Simon & Schuster, seconded the recommendation. Perhaps most important, as Tom Maier reported in his biography of Si Newhouse, for all the affectionate references to the old *Vanity Fair*, Locke acknowledged that "the main target was the *New Yorker*."

Locke's appointment was announced in August 1981. The first issue did not appear until March 1983. Behind the scenes, Liberman, who had attempted to dissuade Si from reviving *Vanity Fair*, and Richard Locke were battling for the soul of a magazine that had yet to be published. Locke described his battle with Liberman as "a conflict between a magazine that

I believe I was asked to create, a magazine of writing and ideas, or a magazine of jazzy layout and bits and pieces. And jazzy layout won."

On the business side, harmony and unprecedented success reigned. An outsider, Joseph E. Corr Jr., who had headed distribution for Time, Inc. during the launch of *People* and ran the promotion department of *Life* during the glory days, was brought in as publisher. Doug Johnston, who had sold ads for *GQ* before Si bought it and who had come along with the sale to Condé Nast, was named ad director, and advertisers lined up to reserve space. Part of the response was to the hype and the romance of the old name, and part, says Johnston, given that for more than a year there was no actual magazine to show advertisers, to the reputation of Condé Nast. The first issue carried a then-record 168 pages of advertising. The mob of advertisers jockeying for space created a "buying frenzy," Johnston recalls. "For the first time in my career I had to actually call up people and tell them we couldn't take their ads."

Advertisers were made to jump through hoops to reserve space. Hotelier Leona Helmsley wanted the back cover. To get it, her ad agency people were told, she would have to buy an additional twelve pages inside to run sometime during the year. Doug Johnston pulled the number out of the air, hoping Leona and company would go away, but instead they said, "No problem." Johnston recalls potential advertisers "just smiling, looking at me, shaking their heads yes. I'd say, 'Don't you want me to tell you about this?' and they'd shake their head no." After so many years of trying to sell the pre-Condé Nast *GQ*, and facing "a war at every call," Johnston couldn't help but feel uneasy. "We'd gone out and created this idea that this was the greatest thing in the history of magazines, and the advertising community bought into it, and the fact that it was different and a little overintellectual, they didn't get it. But they had convinced themselves that it was supposed to be good, so therefore, it was."[1]

Members of the media understood it, saw next to nothing good in it, and venomously attacked the first few issues. "The anticipation was too great," Johnston explains. "No magazine could have lived up to it." But Johnston thinks he knows why reporters seemed to be lying in wait to eviscerate the magazine. When they had tried to interview Locke in those eighteen months before the first issue appeared, he refused. Johnston saw Locke's silence as insecurity, and in Johnston's opinion the insecurity was understandable. Locke had never been the top editor of any magazine, let alone a legend. When he was deputy editor of the *Times Book Review,* reporters had not stood in line to interview him, and now those same people saw Locke's reticence as arrogance. "He had rejected them and slammed the door in their faces," says Johnston, "so they were sitting there waiting. The press just tore the shit out of it." The *New Republic* put its six-page denunciation on the cover, featuring a Ralph Lauren ad and, inside, the contention by the late British writer Henry Fairlie that a twelve-page spread of Ralph Lauren ads was the sole item of worth in the entire issue. Fairlie called it "awful" and "ugly," a mindless celebration of celebrity that mistakes name dropping for culture.

Alex suggested to his biographers, Dodie Kazanjian and Calvin Tomkins, that the "vengeance" with which the press "pounced on the first issue...was perhaps more anti-Newhouse than anything else. I have never seen a magazine attacked so savagely."

Si had in a sense hit the big time, but not in the way he had hoped. He was, for the first time in his career, the center of media attention. Kazanjian and Tomkins observed that although Si had been an active head of Condé Nast for years, he had not yet put his "personal stamp" on Condé Nast "or established himself as a recognized presence in New York cultural circles. The new *Vanity Fair*...was his personal declaration of independence." To have it met with derision was painful.

Advertisers began to rethink their commitments. Only three issues of the revived *Vanity Fair* had been published when Si agreed with Liberman that Locke had to go. One former colleague of Locke's complains that he was "very badly used by Si.... He didn't know what magazine they wanted and they didn't know what magazine they wanted. It was a mess." Locke was trying to make the magazine intellectually stimulating, just what he thought Si wanted. The covers were black and white, the first an illustration of a centaur playing a flute, another featuring the writer Susan Sontag, and another the novelist Philip Roth with his finger up his nose. Typical of the pieces inside were an article by art critic Clement Greenberg and a novella by Gabriel Garcia Marquez.

After Locke was fired in May 1983, advertising, Johnston says, "took a dive." The June 1983 issue had twenty-two pages of ads, approximately one-eighth the number of pages of the premier issue.

Named as Locke's replacement was Leo Lerman, Si's mentor, friend, and inspiration. Everyone who had a line into Condé Nast, with the apparent exception of Lerman himself, knew it was an interim appointment. At age sixty-nine, Lerman's eyesight was steadily deteriorating, and his old taxi accident injuries had returned to cripple him. Even as Johnston was echoing the official company line by assuring advertisers that Lerman was there to stay—just as he had assured them that Si loved Richard Locke—the search was on to replace him.

Lerman, born within months of the old *Vanity Fair* and an avid reader of the magazine in his youth, had often said that his life's ambition was to be editor of a revived *Vanity Fair*. He was hurt but silent when Si gave the job to Locke. When he finally did get his hands on it, he thought he was in heaven. He didn't know that Si was using him as a means to buy time, that he had already approached a thirty-year-old British editor named Tina Brown.[2]

A graduate of Oxford, Tina Brown began her career as a reporter for *Punch* and was just twenty-five in 1979 when she became editor of the 270-year-old British society journal *Tatler*. As she would throughout her career, she threw over any traditions she cared to and turned *Tatler* into the most talked about magazine in London. She was utterly fearless in making *Tatler* fit her vision, and her vision was usually one that, if she weren't the first to have it, she was usually the first to have the guts to implement it.

Si Newhouse was so impressed that in 1982 he bought *Tatler*. About a year later, just as Leo Lerman was settling in as editor, Si asked Tina to come to America and run *Vanity Fair*. She declined. But Brown did agree to come to New York that summer of 1983, supposedly just to look around, serving for three months as a kind of behind-the-scenes consultant for *Vanity Fair*. Leo Lerman wouldn't talk to her. Still, for Tina it was a good summer. She inspired one important *Vanity Fair* story, and in the process, launched the magazine writing career of Hollywood producer Dominick Dunne, who later became *Vanity Fair*'s best-known byline. Seated next to Dunne at a dinner party—meeting him for the first time—she observed, "You're obviously not in the spirit of this party." He told her about his daughter Dominique, an actress in Hollywood who was murdered by her boyfriend. Dunne had just returned from the trial—the boyfriend was convicted on a charge of manslaughter and would serve just two and a half years in prison—and was devastated. Brown suggested that he write about it. He protested that he had never written in that genre. She pushed him to try. His tale of woe ran in the last issue before she officially took over. "*Vanity Fair*'s circulation," says one man high on the business side of the magazine, "was right down the tubes at that point, and people who had subscribed weren't reading it.... Helen Gurley Brown spotted it, read it, bought it, and reran it in *Cosmo* a year later."

The exit of Locke, the entrance of the ailing Lerman, and the rumors of a magazine in disarray had turned the unprecedented advertising success into something close to a failure. Publisher Corr was fired in November 1983, eight months after the first issue. According to Doug Johnston, Corr's final meeting with Si was "the fastest firing on record. It took about twenty seconds." Corr arrived at 8:00 a.m., the phone rang: "I've got to go upstairs," he told Johnston. "Three minutes after eight he's back. He calls me in his office. 'I just got canned.'" Si used the hoary "good news, bad news" routine—"The good news is I'm going to keep *Vanity Fair* alive," interrupting Corr's sigh of relief to add, "The bad news is you're fired."[3]

Si offered Corr's job to David O'Brasky, a veteran of ad sales at *Esquire*, *GQ* (before Newhouse), and *New York* magazine. O'Brasky had been lobbying Si for a job for two years. When Si bought *Gourmet* magazine that year, 1983, O'Brasky wrote Si a fan letter. He said he was sure that Si would "take the jewel that it was and polish it."

Si paid $26 million for *Gourmet*. The sale was all the sweeter because the *New Yorker* people also wanted it but dropped out when Si bid the price up to the point at which a public company like the *New Yorker* could not justify the expense. "When the Newhouses got involved with it," recalled the late J. Kennard Bosee, then the *New Yorker*'s treasurer, "all of a sudden the stakes changed and we couldn't compete with Sam's money." Si later confessed to a friend that he wanted the magazine so badly that he didn't check the financials as closely as he should have and probably overpaid. Winning *Gourmet* gave Si a huge boost of confidence. In the final bidding he was up against Malcolm Forbes and Rupert Murdoch, and he bested them both. (Later the three would appear on a panel sponsored by the Magazine Publishers Association. "Murdoch went on and on and on about how he tried to buy *Gourmet*," recalls one longtime employee of Si's. "Then Forbes played on the fact that the owner was a Scotchman, so he's telling the stories about how he had him over to the house and he had the boys and he all dressed in kilts and bagpipes and everything else to cajole this guy into selling it to them. Finally Si leaned forward and he said to Forbes and Murdoch, in so many words... 'There's only one problem here. You couldn't afford it.' He paid the top dollar; never mind the kilts.")[4]

Si was almost alone in thinking that O'Brasky could handle the publisher's job at *Vanity Fair*. Most opposed to the appointment was Condé Nast president Bob Lapham, who was said to detest the hypereffusive O'Brasky. Lapham advised the boss to forget O'Brasky, that he wasn't their kind of guy. But O'Brasky was a big talker. He held himself out as a rainmaker who would arrive on Monday, and on Tuesday the ads would start rolling back in. So desperate was Si to reverse the fortunes of this debacle that he believed him.

Meanwhile, O'Brasky and Johnston struggled to sell Lerman's version of the magazine. Lerman had announced that he would continue the magazine's literary focus, while adding "wit, irony and a look at life with humanity and richness." O'Brasky and others did worry that Lerman was giving *Vanity Fair* too pronounced a gay sensibility, but Lerman commissioned some intriguing pieces, including one by Francine du Plessix Gray on Nazi war criminal Klaus Barbie.

Tina Brown finally accepted Si's offer to run the magazine, and on New Year's Day, 1984, Si fired Leo Lerman. The revived *Vanity Fair* had been alive for under a year and already it was about to start on its third editor.

It was as gentle a firing as Si had ever done. He bestowed upon his friend the grand title of editorial advisor—a title invented for Lerman—to all the Condé Nast magazines. Leo was given an office, and any editor who had a question about taste, or anything cultural, knew whom to call. "His wisdom and experience became available to all his colleagues," Si would later say. "You could also say Leo became our guru."[5]

Tina Brown? Well, she was a mystery at the outset. "The general advertising person didn't know who Tina Brown was," says Doug Johnston. "All they knew was that we were bringing in our third editor, some British woman that no one has ever heard of and the bottom fell out.... We reached a point where our credibility was zip."

During that first year, 1984, before Tina found her footing, not even she could make Si forget how terribly disappointed he was with the magazine. Geraldine Fabrikant reported in the *New York Times* that "one executive who worked with Mr. Newhouse...recalls the mood at weekly meetings: 'It wasn't the money,' the executive said. 'It was painfully clear that for Si, it was an acute embarrassment. He kept saying 'This is a disaster.'"

O'Brasky had been running the business side of *Vanity Fair* for just four months when, in March 1984, at a meeting with Si and Bob Lapham, O'Brasky destroyed his future at Condé Nast by admitting that 1984 would not be the turnaround year. Instead, says Doug Johnston, O'Brasky explained to the assembled, "It's all going to happen in '85."

Si's manner turned ice cold, and the meeting ended abruptly. Si never again looked O'Brasky in the eye or addressed him directly. "From that time on," says Johnston, "David had no credibility with Newhouse."

Still, O'Brasky was working twelve to fourteen hour days trying to boost advertising. But chronic back problems, aggravated by stress, resulted in serious surgery and no sympathy from Si. "When I came out of surgery," recalls O'Brasky, "I was in the recovery room, I got on the phone to find out if Revlon booked a couple of pages." He could have hobbled out of bed, dressed, and made the pitch to Revlon in person, and Si would not have been impressed.

Having written off O'Brasky, Si asked his old friend and teacher, *Vogue* publisher Dick Shortway, to see if *Vanity Fair* was salvageable. He suggested that Shortway work with Doug Johnston. "I want to meet your staff," Shortway told Johnston. After spending ten minutes with them, Shortway concluded, "That's your problem. This staff doesn't look anything like *Vogue*'s staff."

"He was ready to just sweep the whole place clean," says Johnston, who suggested Shortway first accompany him on a few sales calls, "just to get a sense of what we're up against. And, to his credit, he did."

Their first call was to Shortway's good friend, the Italian jeweler Johnny Bulgari. "'Dick, Dick, how are you Dick? Good to see you. How are things at *Vogue*?' '*Vogue* is good, but that's not what I want to talk to you about. I want to talk to you about *Vanity Fair.*' 'Oh, no, no Dick. No *Vanity*, no. We talk *Vogue*, no *Vanity*.' And the net of it is," says Johnston, "we walk out with our tail between our legs. Dick is embarrassed. He's going to show me how to do it with his very close personal friend, and he can't even get into a conversation about it."

Then they visited Charles Jourdan, where Shortway's fourth wife, Kay, was the American director. It didn't help. No business. Shortway finally had to agree that it wasn't the sales force, it was the product, and that not even he, the best salesman in the history of magazines, could sell *Vanity Fair.*

Si desperately wanted Shortway to tell him that the picture was improving, and that all would be booming again soon. "Everyday he gets called up to Si Newhouse's office," recalls Johnston, "and he's saying, 'Is it fixed yet?'" Shortway would sometimes shade the truth. "He couldn't say he couldn't fix it," explains Johnston, so he'd tell Si, "'It's moving in the right direction'... to keep Si from getting anxious." The result, says Johnston, was that Shortway's dissembling "bought us time."

Shortway, then sixty, had good reason to try to pretty up the picture. He knew that Si could be mean, and quite capable of stabbing the messenger, especially if Si figured that the messenger was growing old and might soon have to be replaced. Some years before, Shortway had suffered a heart attack. He took a few weeks off and then returned to his workaholic routine. A recessionary period and a dip in *Vogue*'s ad revenue followed. While on a business trip to the West Coast, he received a call from Si: "Listen Dick, if you can't turn this thing in the next six months, you're out."

Shortway survived, but this man who had done so much for Condé Nast and for Si lived in a state of perpetual insecurity. Another Condé Nast publisher tells of a meeting with Si one morning in 1985, just at the time that Shortway was helping to resuscitate *Vanity Fair.* "*Vogue* was just coming off its biggest year, which was 1984," he says. "Dick Shortway was the king of all publishers at Condé Nast, and he and Si worked together years before that when they were kids at *Glamour,* so he was Si's most trusted publisher. And he's sitting on the edge of his chair and Si Newhouse has a copy of *Harper's Bazaar* and he's taking him through it and going, 'How come they have this one and we don't? How come they have this one and we don't?'"[6]

It was Johnston, sensing that Newhouse at any moment could close *Vanity Fair*, who called Si very early one morning to ask him to come down and look at the layout of the June 1984 issue. It carried forty-four pages of ads, no cause for boasting, but twice as many as the June 1983 issue. Si was down in forty seconds, recalls Johnston, "looked at it, smiled, said thank you very much, walked off."

One year later, at 8:00 A.M. as Johnston sat in his office still brooding that his boss was going to close the magazine, Si was upstairs firing O'Brasky. "Si came around from behind the desk," O'Brasky recalls. "He said, 'I've been giving a great deal of thought to *Vanity Fair*.' And I said, 'Yes?' He said, 'I've decided to stay with it for the long run.' I said, 'God bless you, sir.' He said, 'You don't understand. I want you to resign.' And my heart sank. I was fifty years old, I had just had a serious back operation, and my reputation was about to be destroyed. I apologized for losing his confidence." O'Brasky asked Si for a job on another of his magazines, even mentioning a specific title. Si said no. The transaction took all of five minutes.

O'Brasky was barely out the door when Si called Doug Johnston and asked him to come up. Newhouse was chuckling to himself as Johnston arrived. "I have good news and bad news. The good news is I've decided to make a long-term commitment to *Vanity Fair*. The bad news is you're going to be publisher." That was followed by a "forty-five-second pep talk.... 'We gotta hold the expenses down, we gotta get out and try to sell some ads.'"

"Wait a minute," Johnston protested, realizing that Newhouse had told him nothing. "I've got a thousand questions.... For openers, what's our goal here?" Si then talked about "the complexities of publishing, still saying nothing. Finally he says to me, 'We have to make progress, we have to do better tomorrow than we did today.'"

Shortly before, Kathy Leventhal, a standout among the *Vanity Fair* ad salespeople, had been moved over to *Glamour*, leading Tina Brown to believe that Si really did plan to close the magazine. But Leventhal was brought back and named Johnston's ad director. A hard-charging saleswoman, gutsy, smart, unstoppable, she became, in effect, the Ms. Outside; Doug Johnston, more introverted and contemplative, became Mr. Inside.

On the editorial side, Tina Brown retained Si's full confidence.

Just after Johnston became publisher, he went to Tina Brown to ask for help. He told her that the magazine had no "tagline," no catchphrase that explained what the magazine was, and that he needed one to help him sell. A meeting was held with the ad staff, Tina, her managing editor, Pamela McCarthy, and the cream of the writing, style, and photography crop—Marie Brenner, Dominick Dunne, Annie Leibovitz, Maria Schiano, Steven Shiff.

"The agenda," Johnston remembers, "was what do we have here? I knew that we were covering subjects that every other magazine was covering but somehow ours was different. Why was our article on Claus von Bulow [by Dominick Dunne with Helmut Newton's photos of von Bulow prancing about in leather while his wife lay comatose] different from every other? I wanted to hear that from the people who were actually doing it." Johnston recalls coming away from the meeting energized, knowing that "everything that went into that magazine went into it with intent. Everything had a purpose. It all fit together."

When asked, Tina would, as she had done with O'Brasky, accompany Johnston on "selected" sales calls. "She was our credibility," Johnston explains; "essentially, we would take her when we needed to make sure that somebody understood that what we were doing had a purpose."[7]

For all her aggressiveness, Brown was in fact quite shy. One woman who sold ads for *Vanity Fair* for nearly a decade says that "for a powerful and brilliant woman she was very insecure around strangers.... If you were ever in an elevator with her, she would never look at you, would never acknowledge who you were."

Although the shyness was natural, not feigned, it contributed to the legend that was fast growing around Tina Brown as the most powerful editor in New York. One prominent reporter profiled a presidential candidate at a time when it was clear that he was going to become the next president. She was later assigned to profile Tina Brown: "People were 40,000 times more forthcoming [about the presidential candidate] than they would be about Tina."

Very much a man's woman, Tina instinctively honed in on the man in the room who had the most power and money. One reporter noted that Tina

Brown as a child, at one of her father's parties—he was a movie producer, and her mother was Laurence Olivier's press agent and later a gossip columnist—could always be found on the lap of the star or producer or director who was at the very top of his game. One woman who freelanced for Tina was talking to a very important male writer when the editor in chief came over to talk to him, "and it was as if I wasn't there.... [He] had his arm around me, and Tina came and put her arm around him. I just thought, this is too weird, because she wasn't even acknowledging that I was present, and we were sort of physically linked."

Si Newhouse now absolutely approved of what Tina Brown was doing for *Vanity Fair* and thus for him, and he allowed her free rein. One former editor of *House & Garden* describes Tina as possessing "one of the signs of true power at Condé Nast"—the wherewithal to say, "Alex can't come and look at my cover." *Vanity Fair* became the hot magazine, a concoction of gossip, fawning movie star covers and profiles, and worshipful articles on the very rich and famous—especially the media and Hollywood elite— accompanied by the ubiquitous Annie Leibovitz photos. Pandering to advertisers of the stature of Ralph Lauren and Calvin Klein took the form of puff-piece cover stories masquerading as profiles.

Tina Brown's *Tatler* was known for its irreverence, but for the most part she left that attitude in London. In one of the most embarrassing episodes of her tenure at *Vanity Fair, Spy* magazine reporters reprinted Brown's obsequious letter to then Creative Artists Agency (CAA) chairman Michael Ovitz. Ovitz was routinely called the most powerful man in Hollywood because of the stars his agency represented. In her letter Brown promised Ovitz near total control were he to be so kind as to allow *Vanity Fair* writer Jesse Kornbluth to interview him. (Tina assured Ovitz that Kornbluth, also a screenwriter and thus compromised by potential con- flicts of interest, was "knowledgeably well disposed toward CAA.") From there she moved to flat-out flattery, telling Ovitz that the world thinks of him as a mere "agent" or, worse yet, a "packager," when in fact he is a "catalyst, activating creativity," the creator of "a consummate CAA cul- ture." Ovitz refused to cooperate on the profile.

Still Tina Brown's *Vanity Fair* was consistent; she had a formula, and it was working. By 1986 *Vanity Fair* began to catch on. By late 1987 it was on the move; by 1988 ad pages were up 56 percent for the first half; and by 1989, company officials claimed, the magazine was inching into the black. Just as she had done at *Tatler*, Tina Brown would quadruple *Vanity Fair*'s circulation.

Others insist that, even under Brown, *Vanity Fair* never made a nickel, that she slowed but did not stop the spill of red ink. Guesses as to *Vanity Fair*'s losses the first eight years of its revived life go as high as $100 million. But to Si that hardly mattered. *Vanity Fair*, by the late 1980s, had sizzle. While nearly every issue had a story or two of intellectual ambition, for the most part the magazine was *People* on better paper, written by expensive name writers. Si seemed hardly to notice how far *Vanity Fair* had veered from his founding vision. He was too busy noticing that, with a naked Demi Moore on the cover twice, once seven months pregnant and once not, *Vanity Fair* was receiving more press than any other magazine. Tina Brown was his find, and she had become the most famous magazine editor in America.

And it was Si Newhouse who had spotted Tina Brown and persuaded her to move to New York to edit what appeared to be a loser of a magazine. It was Si who secured her a green card, a wardrobe, a place to live; and it was Si who, to keep her in New York, gave her husband, Harold Evans, the former editor of the *Sunday Times* and the *Times* of London, the job of inventing and launching *Condé Nast Traveler*.

Harry Evans, who is twenty-six years older than his second wife—they were married in 1981 at the Hamptons summer home of Ben Bradlee and Sally Quinn—had been forced to resign as editor of the *Times* in 1982 after repeated arguments over editorial independence with the paper's new owner, Rupert Murdoch. So he was willing to follow Tina to the United States, but he grew tired of working in low-profile slots for Mortimer Zuckerman, the real estate mogul turned media mogul. Neither of his jobs, editor in chief of Zuckerman's Atlantic Monthly Press and editorial director of Zuckerman's *U.S. News and World Report*, could hold his attention, and Si feared that he'd persuade Tina to return with him to London.

In 1986 Si paid $25 million for *Signature*, a magazine sent to all Diner's Club card holders. He handed it to Harry Evans with instructions to spend what he needed to transform it into *Condé Nast Traveler*, the first issue of which appeared in September 1987. "I can spend what I want," Harry boasted to Patrick Reilly of the *Wall Street Journal,* with Reilly reporting that *Traveler*'s "editorial budget is one of the highest in Condé Nast's already high-priced stable of magazines." The magazine's distinguishing feature was that it substituted critical reporting for the usual boosterism of travel magazine writing. Harry Evans, who added the cover line, "Truth in Travel," paid all his reporters' expenses, overturning the long-standing practice of accepting complimentary airfare and hotel rooms in exchange, presumably, for favorable stories. Evans hired well-known writers and photographers—William Styron and Helmut Newton, for example—and, almost from the start, the magazine seemed hot.

Seemed hot. Hot does not mean profitable, as Harry's wife could have told him. According to a later report in the *Wall Street Journal,* more than nine years would pass before the company would claim that *Traveler* had turned a profit.[8] That detail aside, Si had plans for the husband that were almost as big as the plans he had for the wife—all designed to keep Tina happy and working for him in New York.

17 | Still on the Prowl for Class: The *New Yorker*

WHEN THE ELDER SON of Sam Newhouse was a high school student at Horace Mann, and, he said decades later, a regular reader of the *New Yorker*, one of its writers, his name since forgotten, came to speak to the boys about the magazine. Even at that time the *New Yorker*, not quite twenty years old, was the magazine that serious American readers couldn't wait to read, week after week. The adjective "legendary" seemed permanently affixed to its name. At that Horace Mann session, one of Si Newhouse's classmates asked the *New Yorker* writer if he would identify the person who wrote the then unsigned "Talk of the Town." As befitting the magazine's air of mystery and exclusivity, the writer wouldn't say.

The father having been rebuffed by the Fleischmann family when he tried to buy the *New Yorker* twenty-three years before, the son felt it was now time to go after the magazine of his aspirations. Si believed, for several reasons, that he could in 1984 acquire what he could not three years before. The *New Yorker*'s chairman, Peter Fleischmann, then sixty-two, was in poor health, having endured two operations for throat cancer and another for diverticulitis. Facing up to his mortality, Fleischmann began to fret about estate taxes and his fear that the enormity of the burden would force his survivors to sell the magazine. If he could sell it himself, he could exercise some control over who bought it.

Peter's son Stephen, then thirty-two, had worked on the business side of the magazine for a couple of years before quitting, and apparently was not considered as an heir apparent. Peter had long relied for day-to-day operations on George Green, then the magazine's president. Like Peter a Yale graduate, Green was, some say, the son Peter didn't have. Green's resignation early in 1984 deeply distressed Peter and weakened his resolve to carry on.

On the editorial side, William Shawn, who had started at the magazine in 1933 as a freelance "Talk of the Town" reporter and was only the second editor since the magazine's founding in 1925—he became editor in 1951 on Harold Ross's death—was seventy-seven, and had suffered a serious heart attack. Shawn had settled on neither a successor nor a plan for selecting one.

Hoyt "Pete" Spelman, then the magazine's marketing director, and one of the many whose lives were wrapped up in the Shawn/Fleischmann *New Yorker*—he had started at age twenty-two as a fact checker before moving over to the business side—claims that he had long warned Peter Fleischmann that the magazine was a sitting duck. In earlier years, Spelman had told Fleischmann that he should never have taken the *New Yorker* public and that he should revert to private ownership. With the family and its various trusts owning between 25 and 30 percent of the stock, Spelman argued, it was theoretically possible that the holders of the other 70 percent would decide to sell. "We've got to protect this thing somehow," Spelman warned, "or someday...somebody will make you an offer you can't refuse, or the other stockholders can't refuse." Spelman recalls ruefully that "Peter would respond in his usual way. He'd deflect the question and take another sip or another puff on his cigarette."

In 1984 Fleischmann recognized that he could procrastinate no longer, and word leaked out that he had cracked open the door a bit to buyers. At the same time board member Peter Messinger, who owned 13 percent of the company's stock, making him the second largest shareholder, signaled that he might sell his block. It was Messinger, said then *New Yorker* treasurer Ken Bosee, who "kind of put everything in motion."

Si Newhouse soon received a call from a magazine broker: "If you still want the *New Yorker*, it's for sale." Abe Blinder is said to have been the one to alert Si. Blinder (whose name, appropriately, rhymes with "finder), the founder and former chairman of *Esquire*, was the same man who served as the go-between in the sale of *GQ* to Si.

Peter Messinger considered the *New Yorker*'s executives complacent, timid, and wasteful. He met one of the magazine's writers, Nat Hentoff, at a party, and Hentoff told him that while William Shawn was the best editor he had ever had, he and other *New Yorker* writers shared a grievance: they would often turn in pieces and receive checks in payment, but the pieces never ran.

Equally wasteful, others thought, was Shawn's excessive patience with writers. The case of Joseph Mitchell, for example, was legend. A staff writer for the *New Yorker* since 1938, Mitchell came to work nearly every day until his death in 1996 but produced nothing for publication after 1965. In his obituary of Mitchell for the *New York Times,* Richard Severo wrote that "friends came to think of it as an exceptionally bad case of writer's block." Under Shawn it was not unusual for a writer to spend ten years working on a story.

Still, for all the magazine's and Shawn's complex idiosyncracies, the *New Yorker* had more prestige and more class than any other magazine published in America. "Never ever did any kind of marketing research idea enter into the conversation one would have with Shawn about what one wanted to write," recalls Suzannah Lessard, then a regular *New Yorker* writer.[1]

Soon after Si started prowling after the *New Yorker,* he invited Ken Bosee, a member of the magazine's board and recently appointed its president, to lunch at the Four Seasons. Struggling to make conversation as he watched Si "single-mindedly" stuff food in his mouth, Bosee asked Si to describe the kind of audience that each of his magazines reached for. Si looked up from his mad dash through his food and said simply, "All those magazines are like chickens. Only another chicken could tell the difference."

When he made that comment, Si was referring specifically to the women's magazines. He wanted to own a magazine that nobody would ever mistake for a chicken. That was the *New Yorker,* the Rembrandt of the magazine world.

Some close to the Newhouses felt that Si's drive to have the *New Yorker* was a way of avenging the rebuff of his father. Anti-Semitism was cited as a factor too in the snubbing of father and son by what seemed the very essence of a WASP enclave. The trouble with that theory, though, was that the Fleischmanns and Shawn were, nominally, Jewish. Raoul's uncles, Jewish immigrants from Vienna, had started the yeast business, and Raoul's immigrant father ran the family's bakery offshoot. Peter

Fleischmann was half Jewish and half Scotch Presbyterian and was raised in the latter religion. The *New Yorker*'s former president, George Green, was Jewish. Shawn was of Russian/Jewish roots. Peter Diamandis suggests that Si wanted to remove from the Newhouse name the "ragpicker" aspersion cast by the *New Yorker*'s Liebling. Acquiring the nation's most prestigious magazine would bestow on him and the Newhouse family "the literary stamp of approval."

Whatever his motive, Si went hard at it. In November 1984, at the first of several meetings at Peter Fleischmann's grand old apartment on East Sixty-sixth Street, Si explained that he had learned that a large block—17 percent—of *New Yorker* stock was available and that he would like to buy it. He volunteered—disingenuously—that he wanted nothing more than to be a "passive shareholder." Si was obviously interested in gauging Fleischmann's reaction, recalls Merrell "Ted" Clark, Peter Fleischmann's attorney and close friend—his schoolmate at Hotchkiss and Yale—who attended all meetings between Peter and Si. Fleischmann didn't object directly, "although," says Clark, "he certainly didn't say, 'I've been hoping you'd come along.'" Fleischmann later told his staff that he had not encouraged Si and that he indeed had hoped that Newhouse would simply go away.

Jeanne Fleischmann, Peter's second wife—she had been Shawn's secretary in 1948 when Harold Ross was still editor and Shawn his managing editor—says she was also present at the meetings to serve as a kind of interpreter for her husband. By that time, Peter had had cancer of the larynx and spoke through an electronic voice box. She could best understand him. Mrs. Fleischmann saw Si as "a very uneasy person," as verbally handicapped in his way as her husband was in his.

After that meeting, a joint statement was released by Peter Fleischmann and Si Newhouse. It read, in part: "Mr. Newhouse said that there were no plans to seek control of the *New Yorker* or to influence its management." The words "no plans to" should have set off red lights. Jeanne Fleischmann says her husband never believed that Si would stop short of owning the entire magazine.

Within a couple of days, there was a second meeting at which Si announced that he wanted to increase his stake. "Once again he said this block was available and he wanted to buy it," recalls Ted Clark, "and was there any objection and I think there was certainly no objection in the sense that Peter really had no right to object." Her husband could not have expressed his objection in a manner comprehensible to Si, insists Jeanne Fleischmann. "Peter was a gentleman, and when he said, 'I'd rather you didn't,' to Peter, that meant, 'Please don't.'"

At the third meeting Si dispensed with any niceties and proposed buying 100 percent and merging the magazine into his company, Advance Publications.

A weary and disheartened Peter Fleischmann, realizing that he was about to sell his prized family possession to a man with whom he would not care to share a meal, suggested that Newhouse talk to William Shawn to gauge his reaction. Peter knew what Shawn's reaction would be, and he hoped that its hostility would unnerve Si sufficiently to cause him to withdraw.

Ted Clark remembers the details of that meeting vividly. For secrecy's sake, it was held at Clark's apartment. "The meeting was sort of an effort by Shawn," recalls Clark, "to persuade Newhouse that he didn't want to buy the *New Yorker*, and an effort by Newhouse to persuade Shawn that Newhouse would be an acceptable owner."

Shawn told Si that the *New Yorker* was a "fragile thing, that few owners could understand it as the Fleischmann family did. He added that he himself would not want to work for anyone but the Fleischmanns." He explained to Si that the magazine did not and could not operate like a profit-making institution. "We would send a fact checker by the Concorde to London to check on a fact," Shawn told Si. "We would make a long-distance telephone call to an author in Los Angeles to ask his permission to change a comma.... We publish things that we think should be published, not because we think our readers will like them or even that many will read them, but that they're important. And no businessman," he added, "would put up with that."

Shawn had totally misjudged Si Newhouse, and his arguments had the opposite of their intended effect. "Every time Shawn said something like, 'Send the Concorde to England to check a fact,'" recalls Ted Clark, "you could see Newhouse saying, 'This is even better than I thought.'"

It was at this meeting that Shawn argued that the *New Yorker* should not be published by a profit-making company but by an eleemosynary institution or by a university. He mentioned the *Manchester Guardian* as a model. Newhouse argued the contrary: "One of the great strengths of the *New Yorker,*" he maintained, "and the reason people paid attention to it was because it did make a profit, ...and that added credibility to it and if you were just the *Christian Science Monitor,* being published by a eleemosynary institution, you wouldn't command respect in the same way that you would command respect if you were a terrific publication and also made money."

Later, as the *New Yorker* under Newhouse's ownership lost multimillions annually and Si's editors changed the magazine to stem the losses, many of these comments assumed a retrospective poignancy. But at that time they seemed sensible, and what Si thought was an excellent rejoinder gave him the confidence to let loose some flattery Shawn's way. According to Clark, who took detailed notes at the meeting, Si "went on to talk about his ambitions for the magazine, if he were so fortunate to own it.... He said that he hoped that twenty years from then he would be able to pick up the magazine and still see William Shawn as the editor and the quality would be just as good as it ever had been." Si elaborated for a reporter: "Just as I wouldn't change the name of the magazine, I wouldn't change Mr. Shawn."

In Clark's opinion, Si was sincere in his admiration for Shawn, who over the thirty-two years of his reign as editor in chief, had become a figure of near mythic proportions. At one point during the sales dance, "there was some question about whether Shawn would stay on if the magazine were sold and I remember Newhouse's lawyer calling me, 'What about this?... Si certainly does not want to pay all this money if he's not getting [Shawn] and the magazine is Shawn.'"

There were others, of course, who also coveted the *New Yorker*. CBS chief William Paley, for example, had made annual offers to buy the *New Yorker,* but gave up after a last try in 1963. Since the mid-1960s the Omaha investor Warren Buffett had been buying stock in the *New Yorker* and was viewed as interested in acquiring the magazine. During a meeting with Peter Fleischmann and Ted Clark in the early 1970s, Buffett had gracefully accepted Peter's refusal to sell him additional stock and had then sold the stock he owned. Buffett was a gentleman, says Jeanne Fleischmann, a man whom her husband liked very much. "He was their kind of person more than Si." If the magazine had to be sold, Jeanne adds, her husband "would rather have had somebody not quite so foreign as Si Newhouse to the *New Yorker,* somebody who would understand the *New Yorker,* which I think Peter felt Warren Buffett did and I don't think he thought that Si Newhouse would understand it or carry it on the way it had been carried on."

Buffett was more interested in the *New Yorker* than people knew. In 1971 he began to acquire stock in the Washington Post Company. When introduced to Katharine Graham he tried to persuade her to form a partnership with him to buy the *New Yorker,* explaining that he thought her company would be the perfect owner. She dismissed him and the idea. He was not discouraged. Within the next few years Buffett became a major stockholder in the Washington Post Company and an intimate personal and professional friend of Katharine Graham (and a member of her board). He again attempted to persuade Graham to buy the *New Yorker,* which he viewed as a savvy investment for her and thus for him. This time she took his advice. According to Ken Bosee, Kay Graham was "far more subtle and far more graceful" than Sam Newhouse had been. She and Peter Fleischmann met several times, "and she was trying to suggest to Peter that it would be a good idea if he sold it, but she wasn't going to start a war either, and I assume she decided that Peter said he didn't want to sell it and that was it."

After that initial meeting with Si Newhouse, Shawn told Ted Clark that if the magazine had to be sold to a publisher, perhaps Newhouse was "just about as good as you could get." But that moment of acceptance or optimism passed quickly, and Shawn made a last-ditch call to Warren Buffett, with whom he had become friendly, pleading with him to step up and save the magazine from Newhouse. Buffett didn't bite. He was known for buying cheap, or at the least, for buying at a reasonable price, not anywhere near the price that Si was willing to pay—a number that reflected his yearning for the magazine more than it did sound business judgment. Next Shawn called one of the Bass brothers. Ted Clark says that Shawn hoped that either of these multibillionaires would subsidize the magazine and create a nonprofit foundation to run it.

Ken Bosee, although he turned out to be no fan of Newhouse's, contends that Shawn would eventually have found fault with a Buffett or a Bass or any outsider. Bosee portrays Shawn as spoiled by having complete, unquestioned editorial control of the *New Yorker*. "For instance," Bosee recounts, "in 1960 we carried over 6,000 pages of advertising and we carried like 2,800 pages of editorial, and when the advertising had gone down to under 4,000 pages, our editorial had gone up to about 3,400 pages. So I talked to Shawn about this disparity." Shawn admitted that Bosee had a "convincing argument" and that he'd take it under consideration. As Bosee expected, Shawn said not another word about it. "In a normal type of business," Bosee explained, "the president wouldn't have to kind of go hat in hand to the editor to get him do something."

Finally recognizing that Newhouse would soon own the magazine, Shawn decided that it was "imperative" that he get from Newhouse a guarantee in writing that the independence of the editorial department would remain intact. So impenetrable had that wall been between church and state that Fleischmann was not allowed to step foot on the editorial floor, and the magazine designated its in-house lawyer, the late Milton Greenstein, as the sole liaison between the editorial and business departments of the magazine.

As the deal loomed closer, Shawn hired a lawyer and appointed a committee of editors—Lee Lorenz, *New Yorker* art editor since 1973 and cartoonist since 1958, among them—to help him draft clauses for the contract, which he hoped that Si, if he meant what he said about Shawn's importance to the magazine, would accept. Among the items Shawn requested—every one of which were his without question or complaint under Fleischmann—were total separation of church and state (i.e., editorial and business); the right to screen and veto advertising deemed by Shawn to be in poor taste; a say in the selection of a new company chairman or president; and total control over the selection of the next editor in chief. Si was noncommittal about all but the last item. Not surprisingly, Si declined to give Shawn the power to select his own successor. The final selection of an editor in chief, the contract read, would be made by

Advance (i.e., Si Newhouse), which "will consult with and seek advice and approval of a group of staff members to be selected and to function in a manner then deemed appropriate by the present senior editorial staff."

Just before Si took over, an unsigned "Notes and Comment" ran in the *New Yorker*. In it, Shawn proclaimed that what made his magazine special was the separation of its business and editorial sides, a division that meant that the magazine had "never published anything in order to sell magazines, to cause a sensation, to be controversial, to be popular or fashionable, to be 'successful.'" He argued that "the spirit of the *New Yorker*...has never been owned by anyone. It cannot be bought or sold." The implication was that the magazine, under Newhouse, might do all the above. As he wrote those words, Shawn must have realized just how completely the power had shifted. He had said that he would not work for a family other than the Fleischmanns; he had implied that he would leave if he didn't get all he wanted in the contract; but Shawn, as Si surely realized, had nowhere to go except retirement. For a man whose life was the magazine and its writers, that was no option.

John R. "Rick" MacArthur, publisher of *Harper's* magazine and a tireless critic of Si Newhouse's, was so alarmed by the news that Newhouse was about to take over the *New Yorker* that MacArthur telephoned Peter Fleischmann: "You can't do this. You're selling it to somebody who first of all probably doesn't read it and probably instinctively hates it.... This would be a terrible thing to do.' He obviously pressed the button on his voice box and said, 'I know what you mean, but it's too late.'"

According to Jonathan Schell, who among *New Yorker* writers was closest to Shawn, when Newhouse emerged as the buyer, he was "greeted with horror, absolutely with horror, because everybody could read *Vanity Fair* and his magazines and see what [they] were like and what was in store for the *New Yorker* if he acted true to form." A panicked buzz enveloped staff members as they contemplated what, Schell says, "seemed to be the likely end of the *New Yorker*." One editor at Knopf, an avid admirer of the magazine under Shawn, said that the shock and disillusionment resulted because Shawn and his people "had convinced themselves that they were working in an annex to heaven." Yet for all the loathing of S. I. Newhouse Jr., no one tendered his or her resignation.

In an effort to stem the fear that now seemed to border on hysteria, Si announced that he was placing the *New Yorker* directly under the parent company, Advance Publications; it would not be part of the dreaded Condé Nast. For some *New Yorker* people there was scant solace in being owned by a company named after a paper on Staten Island. Longtime *New Yorker* writer Calvin Trillin professes to have "liked the idea of being owned by the *Staten Island Advance*. I thought that was kind of revenge of the boroughs on the snotty *New Yorker*."

The bashing of Si Newhouse grew brutal among those on the editorial side, but on the business side there were at least a handful of employees who took heart at Si's imminent arrival. One who has since left the magazine, but who was there for years before and after the Newhouse acquisition, describes the Fleischmann/Shawn *New Yorker* as "as weird a place as you can possibly imagine, and many of us were pretty delighted that a professional guy like Newhouse was going to take over." He describes both the editorial and business staffs as "inbred and insular and aloof from the marketplace."[2]

The deal was consummated in May 1985 as Newhouse paid $168 million in cash for the *New Yorker*.

When Sam Newhouse bought Condé Nast, he knew that while his return would not be as high as what he was accustomed to on his newspapers, he could make quite a bit on the magazines. Si's motives were different, and Sam would not have approved. He was buying the *New Yorker* not because he thought "it was a good financial investment," confirms Ted Clark. "His interest was based on his admiration for the quality of the magazine."

Ken Bosee had valued the company at about $90 a share. When the magazine's board balked at Si's offer of $180 and its investment bankers recommended $200 a share, Si instantly agreed. "We figured that Newhouse was paying way more than the company was worth," said Bosee, and that the board's fiduciary duty to its stockholders required that his offer be accepted. Until Peter Fleischmann's dying day, recalls Ted Clark, he thought that "no sensible businessman would have paid as much money as Newhouse paid."[3]

The sale completed, the magazine's board met and voted in two new members of the board of directors—Si Newhouse and Steven Florio, who was then publisher of *GQ*.

Florio, whom Si immediately installed as *New Yorker* president, CEO, and publisher, was a face new to almost everyone at the magazine. Five years before, Si had given the thirty-year-old Florio the top business job at *GQ*. Si considered him a wunderkind who had turned *GQ* around from a magazine with a gay edge to one with a mainstream male readership. When Florio arrived at *GQ*, it carried fewer than 900 ad pages annually; when he left, it boasted 1,900 ad pages. He was Si's opposite in personality—outgoing, slick, street smart, hyperkinetic, flamboyant, hard charging, confrontational. Reared in the borough of Queens and proud of it, except for the conspicuously expensive pin-striped suits, he had the look of a bouncer in an upscale bar. How would he fare in the company of rumpled *New Yorker* ad salesmen who looked as if they had just left a squash game at the Harvard Club and who, according to Pete Spelman, "would come down the hall on a Monday morning having read the entire issue that weekend and discuss the merits of a William Trevor short story?"

To *New Yorker* writer, Burton Bernstein, Florio, with his bushy mustache and burly build, was one of a "dime-a-dozen hotshots, semi-educated, clawing their way up to the top anyway they can, bottom liners, anything goes so long as you can make the figures look good." To Pete Spelman, Florio was more complex: "He's a guy that in some ways I liked. He's funny, he could even be self-deprecating."

After the deal was done, Peter and Jeanne Fleischmann hosted a party in their apartment for Si and Florio and other Newhouse associates. Many of the guests were *New Yorker* staffers and executives. Jeanne remembers Si as "perfectly uneasy," and she had the impression that he "couldn't wait to leave. He was very quiet." She walked him to the door, and "it was difficult for me to talk to him."

Another guest at that party was Jonathan Newhouse, Norman's son, whom Si brought into the *New Yorker* as business manager and who looked to be the Newhouse whom Si was grooming to succeed him as head of the magazines. Jonathan was Si's first cousin but, at age thirty-two, more than a generation younger. Jonathan stunned the *New Yorker* people by assuring them, "There's nothing wrong with the *New Yorker* that we can't fix." The remark, says Robert Young, then the magazine's longtime advertising director and a member of its board, "was resented by everyone. The *New Yorker* was not something that had ever been referred to as fixable because you just don't come in and fix an institution. You can tailor it and massage it and do other things, tinker with it. But fixing. That got everybody's dander up."[4]

Si quickly called his new employees to a meeting. "If I wasn't intimidated by the *New Yorker* before," Si admitted to the assembled, "I am now!" This was only the second speech of his entire career, he confided, the first being the Magazine Publishers Association panel on which he had appeared with Murdoch and Forbes. "I'm no public speaker," Si admitted. "In fact I can't stand this.... But I'd like to share with you my thoughts about the *New Yorker*, why I'm so interested in [it], and have always been interested in [it]." According to Pete Spelman, "He gave a very convincing, somewhat rambling, unscripted account of the *New Yorker*, how long he'd read it, how much he loved it.... I was convinced he was sincere."

Spelman recalls it as "painful" to listen to Si because he was so uncomfortable, a reaction that, Spelman observed, was shared by Steve Florio, who could talk to anyone, anywhere, anytime. Si had introduced Florio as "the guiding light" and "the most dynamic young executive I've had at Condé Nast." But when it was Florio's turn to talk, his attempts at humor fell flat. According to Gigi Mahon, who wrote a book about the sale of the *New Yorker* to Newhouse, "[Florio] began by saying that when Newhouse asked him to take the job of publisher of *GQ* and later offered him the same title at the *New Yorker*, he had thought to himself, 'This guy Newhouse has got a hell of a training program for a young guy!' The remark jolted many listeners. Former European sales head Luis Dominguez recalls being astounded at its 'arrogance.'" Florio ended with another loser: "Incidentally, anybody from the Harvard Business School does not have to resign." When he asked for questions, there was an awkward silence. Every person in the room probably had questions, but nobody wanted to ask them of their new publisher. Florio was momentarily humiliated.

Despite the fact that he had supported the sale to Newhouse, Ken Bosee said he knew that once the papers were signed, his days were numbered. Whatever hopes he had of staying on—or, he says, at the least, of "some kind of graceful taking over"—were dashed when he went to Si's office to complain that Steve Florio had made a couple of decisions unilaterally, without consulting him. "So I said, 'What does this mean?' and Newhouse said, 'You can, you know, that's it, you're out.'" Bosee, who had worked for the *New Yorker* since 1948, had wanted to stay only through the end of the year, but Si asked him to vacate his office and be out by the end of the week.

Steve Florio eagerly moved into Bosee's office. (He had been working out of a converted storage closet—equipped with a rotary-dial telephone and a few pencils—given him, presumably, with malice aforethought.) He busied himself with assigning numbers to sales people—a 10 merited a forty-five minute meeting with Florio; those with lower numbers rated shorter meetings and the clear message that their services would not be required much longer. "People were terrified," recalls Bob Young. In the course of a few months, Florio fired at least a dozen salespeople.

In a letter to his staff at the time of the sale, Peter Fleischmann wrote of Si's promises, made during the negotiations, to keep on current personnel. Fleischmann also wrote that Si had asked him to stay on as chairman and that he had accepted. But staying on became meaningless and painful, says Jeanne Fleischmann, because "all of the sudden there wasn't any board, so Peter was chairman of nothing." (Si had promised in a meeting with the magazine's directors that he would retain the board intact.) Still Peter came to work every day, sat in his office, which had been his father's, and stared off into space. He decided to retire early, says his wife, after finding that he was "useless."

Bob Young, who as a member of the board had voted against the merger—he was concerned that Si's "portfolio" of magazines contained nothing like the *New Yorker*—was, like Pete Spelman, surprised at Si's seeming sensitivity in addressing his new employees. But then, says Young, Newhouse quickly began to "do all the things he said he wouldn't do."

Young had come to the magazine in 1962 as a salesman and worked his way up to a vice president's title, a seat on the board, and the position of advertising director. He very much wanted to keep his job. Florio asked him to fire several of his own colleagues, using him, in a sense, to do the dirty work. Four months into the new regime, Florio ordered Young to tell a fellow long-timer to clean out his desk. "You have fired eighteen or nineteen people," the man recalls admonishing Young. "Most of those people are people that you hired and that you trained."

"I never fired anybody that I didn't believe should be let go," Young replied. To his colleague that contention was "hypocritical, to say the least. And I told him then, 'Don't you realize that you're going to get yours sooner or later?'"

"No way, it's not going to happen." One month later, Florio unceremoniously fired Young.[5]

When Si Newhouse bought the *New Yorker* in 1985, it was profitable, but not as profitable as it had been twenty years before. In 1965, the *New Yorker* carried 6,092 pages of advertising, boosting it to number one among all magazines. And that was the same year, at the urging of William Shawn, that all cigarette advertising was banned from the *New Yorker*'s pages where it had previously appeared in abundance.

In 1966, the *New Yorker* boasted eleven capacity issues. Rather than expand its size to accommodate all comers, Shawn decreed that 252 pages would be the maximum number allowed because any more would be a burden on readers. The result was that advertisers were subjected to a wait list and their wares to the most stringent standards of class and taste. *Harper's* publisher Rick MacArthur calls Shawn "a business genius. He understood that exclusivity and snobbery worked to their advantage."

The *New Yorker*'s profits declined somewhat after 1966, but it never had a losing year. In 1984, the last full year of Fleischmann ownership, the *New Yorker* generated more than $60 million in advertising revenue from 3,529 pages sold, netting $5.5 million. And then Si and Steve Florio walked through the doors of the magazine's famously shabby offices at 25 West Forty-third Street. As one former *New Yorker* executive, who remains very high in the ranks of magazine executives, puts it, Steve Florio "took a profitable business and made it unprofitable."

Si and Florio's first move was to try to increase circulation. Subscriptions were hawked for as little as a money-draining $16 a throw or 32 cents an issue. The "bill me later" option was offered for the first time. While money was actually made on circulation during the Fleischmann years, Newhouse lost plenty because pushing up circulation totals by selling cheap subscriptions is very costly. (Florio's tactics included a 2-million-piece direct mail campaign, sent first class, and a $2.5 million ad campaign that included celebrity endorsements.) Plenty of money had to be spent to maintain the circulation at what was an unnaturally high level. Because, says Pete Spelman, these were not the natural readers who found the magazine on their own or were given a gift subscription, "You have to convince them over and over and over again to keep them."

The magazine under Fleischmann had such a phenomenally high renewal rate—a legend in the industry—that a single gentle reminder that one's subscription was about to expire was all the solicitation required. The old guard groused that Fleischmann's *New Yorker* would never have participated in such unseemly discounting of subscriptions.

The late Leo Hofeller arrived at the magazine in 1947, eventually becoming Shawn's executive editor and the person who first interviewed, encouraged, and then passed on to Shawn such writers as John Updike, John McPhee, and Jane Kramer. "The old *New Yorker* was put out on a very simple formula," explained Hofeller. "We published things that we thought were great.... We didn't think about readers.... Any time you put out something like that, you're limiting yourself to a certain growth.... There was never any objective to get circulation up.... It was virtually prohibited."[6]

When in 1985 Si Newhouse won the Magazine Publishers of America's Henry Johnson Fisher Award—honoring an individual for "significant and long-standing contributions" to the magazine business—he volunteered that the three biggest influences on his professional life were his father, whom he called "a giant, ...colossal intelligence, drive, and achievement"; the second was Alex Liberman; and the third was William Shawn, "precise, eloquent...and what the *New Yorker* is all about." The sentiment about Shawn was for the moment.[7]

Shawn had met with the editorial staff after the board voted to accept Newhouse's offer—a sad, anxious gathering that a tearful Shawn addressed from the top of the stairs. It was at that meeting that Shawn said, "The editorial staff was not a party to the negotiations. We were not asked for our approval, and we did not give our approval." Ted Clark calls that statement simply not true; Ken Bosee called it "charitably, a flat lie." Clark describes Shawn's "active participation during the negotiations, including his many phone conversations and meetings with me."

There were a few who saw that a man, and a sometimes selfish man, lived behind Shawn's deified image. Ken Bosee, for example, remembered being grilled by editorial employees, after the purchase by Newhouse, about why they were not given any restricted stock, which the sale to Si rendered extremely valuable. Bosee claimed that he had twice, pre-Newhouse, gone to Shawn, and that his predecessor as president, George Green, had gone once "to try to persuade him to let selected editors have pieces of restricted stock, but Shawn would have no part of it.... He said he couldn't decide how to allocate it."

Shawn may have been a liberal in cosmic matters, but he proved vigorously antiunion when the Newspaper Guild tried to organize in his own backyard. "There were no across-the-board ways of dealing in terms of pay," recalls former fact checker Patti Hagan, who was working to sign staffers up for the union. "It was all just whatever Shawn pulled out of his head and decided to bestow on someone." An in-house union, the employees' committee, was eventually established as a bargaining unit to deal with Shawn. Richard Sacks, then a fact checker, recalls that when the guild tried to organize in 1976, "Shawn used his aura and legend to beat that down, and what evolved after that was a kind of jury-rigged compromise whereby they allowed us to have an employees committee to petition the czar for redress and grievances. Of course the czar was Shawn."[8]

Si's desire to fire Shawn was complicated by the fact that Shawn had not selected, much less groomed, a successor. Over the years he had anointed one or another of his male subjects as the crowned prince, but something always got in the way of the actual investiture. Executive editor Robert Bingham was one rising star, but he died of a brain tumor. The other chosen men missed the mark for reasons less dramatic and more complex.

Jonathan Schell, a roommate at both Putney and Harvard of Shawn's son, Wallace, was first in Shawn's affections, but the staff loudly objected to his selection. A profoundly serious individual, a writer, not an editor,

Schell wrote pieces that shaped the magazine's strong anti–Vietnam War stance. His jeremiad on nuclear war, "The Fate of the Earth," was enormously influential. An oft-cracked joke was that Schell would make the magazine like the *Partisan Review* with cartoons. "What makes you think there would be cartoons?" was the rejoinder. Schell had many of Shawn's mannerisms—self-effacing, gentle, soft-spoken. He was dreamy, ethereal, at heart a philosopher. Like Shawn, he was also partial to the long, heavy fact pieces that some of his colleagues felt were making the magazine unappealing to younger readers. The fear, says Patti Hagan, was that Schell could "think up the ideas, but for somebody to actually bring the magazine out every week, it needed to be a more organized person, anchored person." By late 1976, Schell was no longer in line.

In June 1979 Shawn assured William Whitworth, then an associate editor, that there was a "strong possibility" that he would be the next editor. Shawn promised to slowly turn over some duties and began to do so. Whitworth says he wouldn't use the word groom to describe Shawn's approach, but insists it was "a slow-motion, ongoing process." Then, in late 1980, Mortimer Zuckerman offered Whitworth the editor in chief's job at the *Atlantic Monthly*. Whitworth told Shawn of the offer, looking for insight into the *Atlantic* and its owner and hoping for some signal. Shawn reportedly was so vague on the latter point that Whitworth decided to go. Whitworth disputes that, recalling that Shawn "advised me strongly against going." Yet Whitworth knew how difficult the transition would be, "a real hot seat," he says. Shawn was so accustomed to doing everything himself that he "would have been upset if I did something slightly different from the way he would have done it." Whitworth feared that the succession would amount to a "kind of tryout for me, and the minute I did something in a way he didn't want, that would be it."

Then, in 1982, came Bill McKibben, twenty-one years old, fresh from the *Harvard Crimson*, long on arrogance, a writer for "The Talk of the Town," and designated by Shawn as his successor. McKibben was another of Shawn's golden boys, who lacked the temperament and patience to be an editor. He tended not to edit pieces so much as to rewrite them, because he considered himself to be a superior writer. Once Shawn decided on a golden boy, explains Patti Hagan, "he would hear no evil, really didn't want to know the truth sometimes." But apparently Shawn recognized that his people would not accept McKibben, and the search for a successor resumed.

Next, at about the time that Si bought the magazine, came Charles "Chip" McGrath, a man of ambition and a titanic capacity for work, smart, an excellent editor, a company man who came to the magazine as night copy editor in 1973 straight out of Yale College and graduate school. McGrath, who would later carry the title deputy editor, had important duties at the magazine and was respected by most of his colleagues—some considered him too much a social register type who, predictably, seemed unsympathetic to the union—and by Shawn, but he was never quite chosen. "He was almost ready to move offices," says one editor. "It was really close." Lee Lorenz recalls that there was "a kind of understanding that yes, Shawn would leave and Chip would take over."

Shawn went so far as to actually put forward McGrath's name to Si, but nothing happened. According to one *New Yorker* writer who was edited by McGrath, Si took McGrath to lunch soon after he bought the magazine, to see for himself if McGrath might be the next Shawn. "At the end of that lunch," says this writer, "it was most apparent that Mr. Newhouse didn't think he was the right guy." This writer calls McGrath "the best magazine editor in America," but most agree that he didn't have the kind of personality that Si liked in his editors.

The candidates for successor were all current editors at the magazine, a factor considered essential because it was thought that nobody but an insider could possibly understand the peculiar *New Yorker* culture. But there was one outsider who was the subject of a conversation between Shawn and Fleischmann—Robert Gottlieb, the man who had run Knopf before and since Newhouse's purchase of Random House. Both men, Peter Fleischmann especially, were impressed by Gottlieb but, says Ted Clark, did nothing about acting on their hunch that Gottlieb might be a worthy successor. They worried about the staff reaction because Gottlieb was not "homegrown," and they also figured that Gottlieb would be reluctant to leave Knopf to come to the magazine as number two to Shawn—a "potential successor," says Clark, given that it might be years before Shawn retired.

Si also had his eye on Bob Gottlieb, who was not only Si's employee, but his friend, confidant, and fellow movie aficionado. Amy Gross, formerly of *Vogue,* recalls talking with Si about Gottlieb, and Amy could see in Si's expression "his tremendous admiration for Gottlieb, tremendous, his face lit up." The friendship reportedly started when Si's daughter Pamela expressed an interest in becoming a writer, and Si asked Bob to read her work. At Random House sales conferences, Si and Bob would often go off to dinner together.

Shawn was operating under the assumption that he had selected his successor, and it would be Chip McGrath. "It was all being done with Newhouse's blessing," says Jonathan Schell with certitude, or so Shawn thought until the day in 1987, two years after the purchase, when Si appeared in Shawn's office.

According to Schell, Newhouse showed up that afternoon and informed Shawn that he had asked Bob Gottlieb to come to the *New Yorker,* that Gottlieb had accepted, that Newhouse had announced this to the *New York Times,* and that he wanted Shawn to leave by a certain date. "So it was an absolute fait accompli, whereas previously Newhouse had said that Shawn could stay as long as he wanted."

There had been no consultation with Shawn, then seventy-nine. The promises that Si had made—that Shawn could stay until he died or voluntarily retired, and that the successor would be selected by Newhouse, but in consultation with *New Yorker* editors—were broken. Schell complains that "the succession that was underway was suddenly, abruptly severed, and Shawn was told to get out by date certain, and that somebody else whom neither he nor anyone else at the magazine had approved or wanted as the editor was abruptly brought in."

In a clumsy attempt to make the stricken Shawn feel better, Si told him that he and Bob Gottlieb had a quality in common—"charisma." Shawn strongly denied having any such quality. Shawn found it "such an odd word to apply to either of them," Lee Lorenz explains, "that I always felt that it wasn't quite the word [Newhouse] wanted. I think he meant that they were both media stars, that Shawn was a kind of legend here.... And Bob was a legendary figure in book publishing."

What Si said to Gottlieb in offering him the job is unknown; Gottlieb has declined to say. Schell, who knew Gottlieb because Gottlieb had been his editor at Knopf, talked to Gottlieb only once after Shawn's ouster. Gottlieb invited Schell to stay at the magazine. Schell declined, and became one of only three people—the others were Bill McKibben and a fiction editor, Gwyneth Cravens—to leave with Shawn.

Si apparently didn't understand that firing Shawn would be something different than firing any other editor, even Diana Vreeland. Losing Shawn, and to an outsider, sent the staff over the edge. Even those who didn't like Shawn realized that there would never be another like him.

Burt Bernstein recalls chatting one day with fellow *New Yorker* writer Bob Shaplen who had covered wars for the *New Yorker* since World War II. "I had just come back from covering a war in the Middle East, and we were trading war stories.... I was telling him about how I had tiptoed through a minefield in the Sinai Dessert and it suddenly occurred to me, 'What the hell am I doing this for? Why am I here? Why if I survive this am I going to go back home and stay up all night writing draft after draft of the piece to make it as good as I could possibly do it?' And then it suddenly dawned on me in the middle of the minefield, I'm doing it for Shawn."

The devotion to Shawn, says Perry Vandermeer, issue editor during the transition between Shawn and Gottlieb, was cultlike. "There was no masthead, you often labored for years in complete anonymity, no one knew who you were or what you were doing.... You really felt even if you were just sorting mail that you were part of a sort of an extended family, with a mission. Shawn knew everybody by name, down to each one of the messengers.... Everything was decided upon by [Shawn]. No newsbreak [end-of-column filler, usually a humorous aside] would go in without Shawn's passing okay of it." The final galley that the writer saw was called "the Shawn proof." His comments, says Burt Bernstein, were "always couched in very discreet, polite questions, and he'd say, 'Wouldn't it be better if we put the comma here and put the prepositional phrase over here, would that be alright?' and I'd look at it and say, 'Good Christ, why didn't I think of that?'" Bernstein was not alone in the opinion that "there was probably nobody who ever took pencil to paper who was a better editor."

Although Bob Gottlieb's name had come up in previous conversations, Shawn reacted as if Newhouse had just informed him that Tina Brown or Helen Gurley Brown or Bob Guccione was the new editor of the *New Yorker*. In fact, Bob Gottlieb was a thoughtful, interesting choice. Gottlieb was, after all, a real editor—some considered him the best book editor in town, a pencil and paper perfectionist with generally good taste—and he gravitated toward *New Yorker* writers. One former *New Yorker* editor who had left some years before to go to another magazine says that he watched the arrival of Gottlieb with some amusement. It was absurd, he thought, for the staff to greet Gottlieb as if he were "a barbarian," when in fact he was totally in tune with the magazine's values and had edited many of its writers.

Still, Bob Gottlieb was not wanted at the *New Yorker*. Even those like Richard Sacks, with his "intensely ambivalent feelings" toward Shawn, agreed to sign a letter asking Gottlieb not to take the job. Sacks signed it, he explains, because "the people I care for are signing it," naming in particular Calvin Trillin, respected for his skills as a writer and reporter and also for his honesty and levelheadedness.

Trillin served on the committee to produce and send the letter, even though, he says, he didn't agree with the idea that Shawn's successor must come from inside. "It made it sound sort of exclusive and snotty and that there was some sort of secret handshake that we all had to have." As to whether a letter would even work, "I didn't think that it would result in him not coming," says Trillin. "The only letter that could have had a result was not, 'Please don't take this job,' but, 'We won't work for you.' And that wasn't what the letter said."

Still, Trillin said, it was important to go on record, to protest not so much Gottlieb's appointment as Si's having broken two promises he had made in writing: "that we would not be part of Condé Nast and that he would consult with the editorial people before choosing a successor to Shawn, and it was pretty hard to see how he hadn't really reneged on both of those.... Somebody said to me at the time, 'Those promises are what's known as the usual Murdoch assurances,' which is to say that they don't mean squat. I said, 'Well then that's fine, but then they should be known as the usual Murdoch and Newhouse assurances.'"

Although some famous *New Yorker* names, such as John Updike, did not sign, probably the most famous name in the magazine's history, J. D. Salinger, did. Burt Bernstein, who says that Salinger "worshiped Shawn," recalls that Shawn himself, who talked to the exceedingly reclusive Salinger regularly, asked the author of *Catcher in the Rye* to sign.

While some signed the letter simply to make Shawn feel good, Suzannah Lessard signed thinking Gottlieb would read it and instantly change his career plans. "It was a typically quixotic *New Yorker* kind of an almost absurd thing in a way, but there was the hope that it would appeal to him as just a member of the literary world, the world of letters." Burt Bernstein, who couldn't wait to sign, says, "We all hoped to hell that this would turn off Gottlieb."

Rather than being swayed by the letter, or even offended, Gottlieb, who always said that there were three jobs he wanted, head of Knopf, head of the New York City Ballet, and editor of the *New Yorker*, found it, according to Perry Vandermeer, "charming in a certain way." Joni Evans says that both Si and Bob were "in love with the idea" of him taking over the magazine. Also, Gottlieb wanted out of Knopf. He was reportedly becoming "antsy" and "bored" there. Gottlieb was discouraged by the changes afflicting the publishing business, by the fact that authors' first allegiance was to their agents, not their editors, that they would hop among publishers in search of the fattest contract. "Bob said and correctly so," recalls Joni Evans, "that publishing was getting ugly and cheapened by money."

Many would note the irony that the person then most frequently cited for accelerating this change in the culture of book publishing was Si Newhouse, who would instruct his editors to bid whatever it took to corral a blockbuster and who encouraged editors at his own imprints to bid against each other.[9]

Turning out a monthly is difficult; turning out a weekly, much more so. During a very uneasy one-week transition, Shawn worked with Gottlieb. Chip McGrath, who became number two under Gottlieb and who might have been excused for feeling resentful, actually put the magazine out. "Bob really did not know how to get out a weekly magazine," says Lee Lorenz, "and Chip more than any other single person I think kept the thing going."[10]

Gottlieb had a lot to learn, and learn he did. But perhaps the most difficult lesson of all was that friendship with Si, even the closest of friendships like theirs, conferred no special treatment.

18 | All the Publisher's Women

IN 1981, SI NEWHOUSE fixed his gaze on a beloved fixture of the Condé Nast constellation, the eighty-year-old *House & Garden*. He was beginning to wonder if his only shelter magazine had become a bit dowdy and downscale. He was also worried about the competition from *Architectural Digest,* an upstart out of Los Angeles. Once a mere trade journal, it had been transformed by its owner, Cleon T. "Bud" Knapp, and its editor, the audacious Paige Rense, into something ultraslick and rich looking, and was beginning to outpace *H & G*.

It was Si's old friend and confidante, Mary Jane Pool, *House & Garden* editor in chief since 1970, who, according to one former editor, "put the bee in Si's bonnet" that their magazine needed a shot of style to contend with *Architectural Digest*. But Pool, Si decided, was not the one to do it. She was a no-nonsense editor who liked short, to-the-point copy and who didn't assign or accept a story until the question, What's in it for the reader? was answered to her satisfaction.

Apparently that wasn't enough for the owner, and he pushed Pool out of the magazine into early retirement. But it was done gently, and Pool left with no apparent resentment: "Si has taken care of me for the rest of my life, very nicely," she says.[1]

Louis Oliver Gropp was then editing the *House & Garden Guides*, newsstand magazines focused on architecture, decoration, and gardens, their material culled from the magazine. Gropp was surprised when Alex Liberman called to invite him to lunch at the Four Seasons. Gropp did not know Alex well because the older man had shown no interest in involving himself in what Alex likely regarded as pedestrian offshoots of the magazine.

"If you were going to change the magazine, how would you change it?" Alex asked Gropp.

"I would let *House & Garden* be *House & Garden* again," Gropp replied. He went on to say that the magazine, once the premier title in the shelter field, was trying too hard to compete with mass magazines such as *Better Homes and Gardens*. That magazine's circulation was pushing the 8 million mark, as compared to *House & Garden*'s not much more than 1 million. Gropp assured Liberman that the staff then at the magazine had "every ability" to create a much better magazine than *Architectural Digest*. Gropp felt that the *Digest* "was a rather superficial, shallow, admiration-of-the-rich kind of magazine, rather than a serious exploration of architecture and decoration." And Gropp challenged Alex: "There's no way Condé Nast would let *Vogue* be number two in the fashion field. Why are they doing that in the shelter field?"

The next day, the owner summoned Lou Gropp to his office and gave him his well-worn spiel: "Lou, I've got some good news and some bad news. We've decided to stop publishing the *House & Garden Guides*."

"That's pretty bad news," Gropp said. "I've been doing that for thirteen years. They're magazines that I like, and I work with a group of people that I like."

"But," Si said, his lips showing something that passed for a smile, "we want you to become the editor of *House & Garden*." Gropp accepted immediately.[2]

Two years later Si turned his attention to *Vogue*, where he and Alex Liberman installed the glamorous Anna Wintour with the title of creative director—an amorphous position created just for her. This move worried Grace Mirabella, then *Vogue*'s editor in chief, who later groused that Wintour had been fired from her first job in New York, at *Harper's Bazaar*, because she did not understand the American fashion market. At *New York* magazine, where Wintour went next, with responsibility for both interior design and fashion stories and a penchant for mixing the two, she caught the eye of Alex Liberman, who fell in love with her "youth and well-born British cool." Wintour's father was the former editor of the London *Evening Standard*; her mother, an American, was the daughter of a professor at Harvard Law School.

Mirabella, Newark-bred daughter of Italian immigrants, felt particularly vulnerable next to Wintour, who was brash, brainy, and so stylish that she made other *Vogue* editors, themselves over the top on the style scale, look frumpy by comparison, Anna Wintour was then thirty-three. Mirabella was fifty-four. In her memoir Mirabella remembered Wintour's arrival with irritation, describing the younger woman as "so sure she'd soon end up in my job that she considered me more of a momentary inconvenience than a person she might have to answer to or contend with."[3]

Vogue and *House & Garden* were the two Newhouse reclamation projects in those years, and soon he zoomed back on Lou Gropp. Si and Alex had concluded that while Gropp was moving *House & Garden* upscale, *Architectural Digest* still seemed to be attracting the attention of the sort that Si coveted. Si called Gropp to his office to inform him that they had decided "to bite the bullet," to cut circulation by 50 percent—from 1.2 million to 600,000—to upgrade the paper quality and the binding, to raise the cover price from $1.50 to $4.00, and to change the focus of the magazine. *Architectural Digest* was vulgar but to Si it seemed better than his own *House & Garden,* which enjoyed an audience fanatically loyal to its decorating tips and its tasteful and information-packed layouts, designed so that readers could adapt the details to their particular situations. Si hungered after the economically elite readership that preferred *Architectural Digest,* with its high-flown title, its disdain for the how-to or service approach of other shelter magazines, its celebration of the impossibly lavish homes of the very rich and powerful.

In retrospect, there was something of a failure of communication between Newhouse and Lou Gropp. Gropp was looking to raise *House & Garden*'s demographics by making it more elegant, more exquisitely written, more cutting edge, while maintaining its service approach. "Mausoleum Digest" was the name Gropp and his staff gave their rival. Si wanted *H & G* to mimic *Architectural Digest*. To him it was fresh, prestigious, something that younger people wanted to display on their coffee tables. He gave Gropp the assignment to move *House & Garden* in that direction, and he ordered Gropp to produce a prototype. Gropp did as he was told, with Liberman involved at every step, small and large, along the way. When Gropp showed the new *House & Garden* to Si, the owner said he loved it. "In the very first issue," Si wrote Gropp, "you have realized what we want to have happen with this magazine."

It was Lou Gropp's baby, but Alex Liberman became in effect the magazine's art director.[4] He took over so completely that the magazine's actual art director came to be known around the office as "paste-up boy."

In April 1986 Anna Wintour left *Vogue* for London and the editor in chief's job at *British Vogue*. Grace Mirabella was delighted to see her go. But she had another problem—a new competitor.

A year earlier, the American edition of *Elle* had hit New York with a bang, and for the first time in its recent history, *Vogue* seemed vulnerable. Nobody had expected this French import, half owned by Hachette and half by Rupert Murdoch, to do so well so fast. Diane Silberstein, then advertising manager of *Vogue*, later *Elle*'s publisher, remembers the "great fear and trepidation when *Elle* launched in '85, great concern about what was going to happen to *Vogue* and was *Vogue* ready for the next generation, the next era of fashion, had it gotten old and staid looking?" Next to *Elle*, with both content and graphics so hypercharged and highly colored, with text cut to a minimum, *Vogue* started to resemble a magazine one's mother might like.

Si Newhouse was not pleased. One former *Vogue* staffer told Gigi Mahon, reporting for the *New York Times Magazine*, that within days of *Elle*'s debut, Si and Alex were "scurrying around the halls at *Vogue* tearing up the book making changes." A former editor recalls the atmosphere as being so tense that "if you whispered the world 'Elle' in the halls, you looked around to see if anyone had heard you."

Vogue did manage to hold on to the number one spot, but *Elle* soon became—and would remain—number two, surpassing *Harper's Bazaar* in both advertising and circulation. One former Condé Nast publisher says that Grace Mirabella might not have wanted to recognize it, but "*Vogue* had hit the wall." Alex Liberman argued that that *Elle* had made *Vogue*'s "earnestness and nobility, its respect for art and for women's intelligence, look a bit quaint." Mirabella was told to "go young," as Amy Gross, then features editor at *Vogue*, later *Elle*'s editor in chief, puts it.[5]

While Mirabella struggled with an order that she felt she couldn't obey, Anna Wintour in London was unhappy. She and her husband, David

Shaffer, a child psychiatrist, had a one-year-old son who was with Anna in London while Shaffer practiced and did research in New York. Anna, then pregnant with their second child, issued Si an ultimatum: find her a spot in New York, or she would start returning some of the calls she'd been fielding from Si's competitors, *Elle* included, as well as an offer from one advertiser who wanted her to head a big cosmetics company, reportedly Clinique.

Newhouse immediately flew to London to have breakfast with Wintour. According to one report, she hoped he was going to offer her *Vogue*, whose editorship she had wanted since the day she stepped foot in its door in 1983, but she was willing to settle for *House & Garden*, and so said yes when Si offered it.

The consensus is that Si gave Anna *House & Garden* as a sort of practice run until he felt she was ready to take *Vogue*. That he already had a good editor in chief at *House & Garden* in Gropp was unfortunate, but Si wanted Wintour on board. He saw her as the next Diana Vreeland, but a Vreeland with a difference—a star whose defining characteristic, after style, was a hard-nosed business savvy rather than the eccentricity that defined Vreeland.[6]

Gropp was vacationing in California that summer of 1987, but he always checked in, and one day his secretary told him that Si Newhouse had been trying to reach him. When Gropp called him, his boss asked, "Lou, have you been reading *Women's Wear Daily* while you've been on vacation?"

"No," Gropp said, "I don't even tend to read it while I'm in New York." Then Si came to the point: "There have been a lot of stories in *WWD* that Anna Wintour is going to become the editor of *House & Garden*."

"Well, is that true?" Gropp asked.

"Yes," replied Si Newhouse.

When the two men later met in person, Si, almost apologetic, said to Gropp, "Perhaps, Lou, you put out too good of a magazine."[7]

Before Anna Wintour officially took over *House & Garden*, in September 1987, Gropp presided over the magazine's long-scheduled awards luncheon. Si had asked him to introduce Anna to the audience. One person who was at the luncheon remembers that when Si and Anna walked in together, there was a hush in the room and an electricity in the air. And he said he then understood that there was no way Gropp or any other editor, no matter how talented, could compete against Wintour, that Si seemed dazzled by this Brit of high accent and high style. The audience, however, was less dazzled, and gave Gropp a standing ovation.

Gropp philosophizes that he could never have been the kind of editor Si Newhouse wanted. "Condé Nast generally is very interested in having the current hot number as it is defined by a certain world. I was never that, will never be that."[8]

Gropp was right. Wintour set right out to make *House & Garden* hip. One of her first acts was to relieve the magazine of its straightforward title in favor of *HG*. Rooms and their furnishings, once the focus of the magazine's covers, gave way to celebrities or socialites or assorted moguls and moguls' wives photographed in their sitting rooms, media rooms, gardens. Anna Wintour "ruined" the magazine, says *Time*'s Bonnie Angelo, by changing its focus from design to celebrity. It seemed so much about celebrity and fashion that it was soon dubbed "Vanity Chair" or "House & Garment." "Things got published because they were celebrity homes," regrets Gael Towey, later *HG*'s design director, "not because they were good ideas."

Under Wintour, says Carolyn Sollis, Gropp's executive editor, the magazine was "visually chopped up so people felt they weren't getting what they wanted to see. If she photographed a house it was more in vignette form, so it was very stylish and the pictures looked great on the page, but people wanted to see a wide picture of the living room as opposed to a slice of a painting and a table and a piece of rug.... If you wanted to learn how to decorate, it was hopeless."

Complaints from *HG*'s readers were so vehement and numerous that a special toll-free line was established to take gripes and cancellations. But one person was delighted with Wintour's changes. That was Paige Rense, whose *Architectural Digest* continued to soar. She later told a reporter, "I just sent [Wintour] anonymous letters telling her, 'Keep up the good work!'"

While Wintour's remake was generally unpopular, to some it seemed brilliant. "She added spirit and light and fashion," says Anne Foxley, who had come to the magazine as an editor just two years out of college, "and she really was the first to try to mold *House & Garden* into a truly lifestyle magazine. And I think she was just three or four years too early." To Foxley those issues from 1988 are a source of inspiration because of Wintour's then-novel idea of using fashion photographers to shoot interiors.

Some might say that Wintour knew just what she was doing; that she was applying the American passion for celebrity to the shelter field; that she was following Paige Rense's lead, not so much advising readers how to design, decorate, or garden as fulfilling their voyeuristic urge to see how the rich do it. But Wintour was really missing even that market, which wanted its celebrities straight up, as *People* or tabloid TV or, for that matter, *Architectural Digest* delivered them. They didn't want an artsy presentation that might have caught the attention, for an issue or two, of some Manhattan designer. As Anna put her "fashion spin on what had become this sort of treasured magazine," says Lou Gropp with a touch of satisfaction in his voice, "people were furious and horrified and were falling away like flies."[9]

The working atmosphere at the magazine, always relatively pleasant, at least by Condé Nast standards, began to sour. Its editors, who had always prided themselves on being secure enough not to adopt the uniform of the day as did their Condé Nast sisters, suddenly found themselves taking six inches off their skirts and upgrading their wardrobes in an effort to avoid the disapproval of the chic and skeletal Wintour. One woman who had worked for two Condé Nast magazines observed that "riding up the elevator in the company of Anna Wintour can consume a year's worth of self-esteem."

A reign of terror ensued. One eccentric but brilliant older editor was kept around for a while, occasionally humiliated, and then sent to the fourteenth floor and given an office and a telephone and no work. Another older, extremely talented editor found herself not invited to meetings. She stuck around for two weeks before being asked to leave. Editors were summoned to Wintour's office one by one to explain themselves. She would allot each person, some employees of several decades, ten minutes to say what they did and why they did it. The experience was made even more unnerving by Wintour's refusal to remove her sunglasses. (It is said that she wore them indoors and out to disguise the thickness of her lenses.)

Nonetheless, Si Newhouse was happy and gave her carte blanche to run the magazine.[10]

In June 1988 Grace Mirabella's husband, William Cahan, a cancer surgeon, was at home in New York when a friend telephoned to tell him that Liz Smith was on the local evening news saying something about Grace. He turned on the television just in time to hear the gossip columnist report that Mirabella was out and Wintour was in at *Vogue*. "Don't ask me why Condé Nast would want to replace Grace Mirabella," Smith said. "*Vogue* is one of the healthiest, heftiest magazines in the Condé Nast chain. You know, if it ain't broke, don't fix it, but they're going to anyway." Nobody had bothered to tell Mirabella, who heard of her dismissal in a call from her shocked husband. She would later tell the *New York Times*, "For a magazine devoted to style, this was not a very stylish way of telling me."

Si Newhouse could have retired Mirabella with her share of honor and a hefty settlement, as he did in the past with others, but he didn't. Grace Mirabella was not the first and she would not be the last Condé Nast veteran to have her job, identity, and dignity snatched away with gratuitous rudeness.

After thirty-seven years at *Vogue*, seventeen as its editor, Mirabella worked out her compensation package herself and proposed it to Si, who agreed immediately. She later regretted that she hadn't asked for more, given the many years she had worked at *Vogue* for "relatively low pay," and given that Si did not offer to soothe the blow with a consulting editorship or some other corporate make-work job. "I was to finish my last issue and clear out."

Mirabella would later charge Si with panicking over *Elle* when he needn't have, and with failing to recognize the enormous strides she had made at *Vogue*, whose circulation was 400,000 when she took over from Vreeland in 1971 and grew to more than 1.2 million by the time she left in 1988. She points out that *Vogue*'s ad revenues were then $79.5 million, as compared to *Elle*'s relatively measly $39 million and *Harper's Bazaar*'s $32.5 million. Mirabella says that when she talked to her executioner after Liz Smith broadcast the news of her demise, Newhouse offered no explanation for her dismissal. She paints Alex Liberman as her friend, champion, and teacher, but in the end, cowardly and disloyal. "Alex absolutely adored

Anna," Mirabella writes in her memoir, *In and Out of Vogue*. "He loved her look, her glamour. He loved the intrigue of having her clicking around the office in her high heels trusted by and trusting no one except him."

Mirabella admits that she made a Faustian bargain when she took the editor in chief's job in 1971, by agreeing to "share power" with Liberman. "Share" is an understatement. She acknowledges that he controlled all the hiring and firing, so that Mirabella could not even select her own editors. Alex's biographers write that Mirabella had ceded to Alex responsibility for every area of the magazine except fashion coverage. He had "taken over the editing of *Vogue*'s nonfashion features," they add, because he felt that Grace's "grasp of cultural affairs" was not "sufficiently wide or deep."

Toward the end of her tenure at *Vogue* when in Mirabella's opinion, Alex's brilliance faded but his ego didn't, she began on occasion to talk back to him. "When I wanted to do a story on breast cancer, Alex told me, '*Vogue* readers are more interested in fashion than breast cancer.' I replied, 'Alex, I've been a woman longer than you, and they're interested in both.'" Usually, however, Mirabella swallowed her opinions and her pride. "You don't need to do another story about working women," he said. "Women are cheap labor and always will be."[11]

The day after Mirabella's ouster, Joni Evans, who had just joined Random House as an editor, was walking to lunch at the Four Seasons with Si and Bob Bernstein. "Si, how could you do that?" she asked him. "Why didn't you throw her a big party, and why didn't you just retire her, why wasn't this just a wonderful celebration?"

Si said, "I'm just not good at that."

"What do you mean you're not good at that? That's something that's very easy to be good at."

"No, I'm not good at that."[12]

To replace Wintour at *HG*, Si named Nancy Novogrod. Her first job after graduating from Mount Holyoke was at the *New Yorker* as a member of the typing pool. She worked her way up to become a reader in the fiction department. It was Wintour who hired Novogrod away from Clarkson Potter, a book publisher, to head *HG*'s decorating department. Novogrod was a much more traditional editor, a matron at home in Connecticut garden clubs who knew or aspired to know everyone who mattered. One *HG* editor calls her extremely "socially ambitious"; another calls her "a Rolodex with feet." According to Patti Hagan, then writing for the magazine, Novogrod's "main function was rainmaking, make the contacts with these people who had these fabulous homes." Novogrod was canny enough, says Hagan, not to balk when Liberman did what he wanted with the magazine's design.

One of Novogrod's editors watched an exchange between her boss and Liberman that left her with mixed feelings about Novogrod. An art editor had decided to use blue type instead of black on the opening page of one story. "This is blue type," Liberman said when he saw the layout, to which Novogrod replied, "Oh, yes, we were trying to do something different. Quite nice, isn't it?" "I don't like it," Alex replied. "Oh, you're right," Nancy agreed.

Gael Towey came to *HG* in 1989 as design director. Before that she had been art director at Clarkson Potter, where she had worked with Novogrod. Putting up with Alex, she says, was the toughest part of Novogrod's job, and by extension, of her own. Novogrod and she both admired a photograph of a mother playing with her child while lounging outside on an elegant red damask sofa. The sofa was placed on a patio in front of a pool. "It was this very sort of wild look, had a lot of style, and it had a kind of warmth." Novogrod agreed that it should run as a double spread. When Towey showed it to Alex, he was aghast. He hated the photograph, thought it was sentimental junk. "Well, if that's the way you feel about it, go ahead," he said coldly. Towey, naively thinking nothing of the exchange, ran excitedly to tell Nancy that Alex had given permission. "We published it, and he made my life miserable for three solid months," Towey recalls. "He never liked anything I did. Every single layout had to be done over." (Towey soon left for the start-up *Martha Stewart Living*.)[13]

After the the change in editors and names, *HG* began to lose circulation and ad pages. Lou Gropp had close ties to the furniture and fabric industries that were *House & Garden*'s natural advertisers. When he left, so did many of them. Some issues looked terminally thin, and as former *Mademoiselle* publisher Richard Kinsler puts it, "She [Wintour] sure gave it a shot of despair."

Anne Foxley does credit Anna with "a very good eye for interiors. But she just didn't respect the industry in the way that typical decorating magazine editors had respected it in the past." Carolyn Sollis, who worked under Pool, Gropp, and Wintour, calls Wintour "one of the most brilliant editors I ever worked for just because she had a such a vision and she was so decisive and she was given a direction to make *House & Garden* of the moment and she did, much to most peoples' horror. But she went right in there and changed the name and turned the look upside down overnight practically, and it scared lots of people away, but it also made a magazine that was very timely and relevant. I think had she had a little more time to be there, it might have been a real success."[14]

But Si needed her at *Vogue* and, some say, needed her in other ways. Not surprisingly, rumors soon circulated that the two were having an affair. Sex was, for some, the only way to explain how Wintour could be such an apparent failure at one magazine and then, instead of being fired or demoted, be rewarded with the most glamorous magazine title in America. Liz Smith originally reported the rumors, then telephoned Si to ask for a response. "He said that he was in love with his wife and his dog, and I went ahead and printed that, and as a result I think it all died down." Asked if he seemed upset by all the talk, she responds, "I've never seen him exhibit any kind of emotion," although she adds that he seemed to be flattered to be linked romantically to such a beautiful woman. "I think it was just a nasty story that started to circulate because people look at him from afar. They're afraid of him. They make up things about him. And he's so strange. Here he is one of the richest men in America and one of the most powerful, and he's this little sort of elf. He's not prepossessing."

But one longtime Condé Nast executive observes that no matter what Anna might have thought of him, he was obviously enamored of her: "You sit in a room and Anna Wintour walks in, and Si just lights up."

When Mirabella was editor, Si was rarely seen at *Vogue*. Once Anna arrived, Mirabella writes, "He was seen walking through the halls with baskets of jewelry, carrying things out for a run-through in Anna's office."

The demeanor that inspired the putdowns "Nuclear Wintour" and "Wintour of Our Discontent" seemed, at *Vogue,* to turn even icier. "Everybody starves themselves to look like Anna," says one former editor. "Everybody would get the Anna haircut [a page boy] or buy whatever shoes she was buying. It was the way to get ahead." For a time Wintour favored black tights with her stiletto heels. But then she took to going bare-legged, even in winter, leaving her poor imitators praying that she'd contract frostbite before they did. Robin Pogrebin of the *New York Times* would later report allegations that "Ms. Wintour's criteria for articles required that profile subjects be famous, rich or beautiful" and that she "has killed articles because the accompanying photographs showed unattractive people." Wintour denied doing any such thing, but one former editor insisted that Wintour has been known to say about a proposed profile subject, "Have you *seen* her? She's hideous."

Elle, the magazine that inspired Si Newhouse's machinations, changed too. Murdoch eventually sold his half interest in *Elle* back to Hachette. In 1988, the year of Mirabella's ouster, he backed a magazine for her and gave it her name. *Mirabella* briefly found its audience of older, more serious women, of the sort *Vogue* seemed to be abandoning, but the niche was not deep enough, and Murdoch killed the magazine in 1995. Hachette quickly bought it and placed it under the care of Amy Gross, who continued as top editor at *Elle*. Eventually Gross was fired from both magazines.[15]

Meanwhile, another Newhouse magazine, *Self*, began to falter, suffering from the illnesses and deaths of its editor, Phyllis Wilson, and its art director. Val Weaver, who succeeded Wilson and was true to Wilson's vision for the magazine, admits that her tenure included some rocky issues, but even then *Self*'s numbers remained healthy, and Weaver's last two issues hit a circulation of a million and a quarter.

But Si wasn't happy with those numbers. "Class, not mass," the Condé Nast motto, truly reflected the magazines' positions, most of which plateaued at circulations of around a million. But the ambitious owner wanted a mass magazine in his stable, one like Hearst's *Cosmopolitan,* and he'd hoped that one or another of his titles could fulfill that desire. For a time he thought *Mademoiselle* would be his vehicle, but that magazine was performing so poorly—"going to hell in a handbasket," says Weaver—that it hit the million mark and took a dive. *Glamour,* then with a circulation of about 2.3 million, was the closest thing to a mass title Si owned, but he wasn't going to touch Condé Nast's cash cow.

In 1934 Sam and Mitzi Newhouse set sail on a delayed honeymoon to Europe. (UPI/Corbis-Bettman)

Senator Joe McCarthy and his chief legal counsel, Roy Cohn, in 1954. A school friend and later best friend to Si Newhouse, Cohn would be blamed by some of the friends of Jane Franke, Si's first wife, for the breakup of the marriage in 1959. (UPI/Corbis-Bettman)

Donald Newhouse, 21, with his parents. Far more cheerful and emotionally sturdy than his older brother, Donald was serious, focused, and devoted to learning the family business. (AP/Wide World Photos)

Si Newhouse, 28, departing for an "Editors Tour of Europe," including Russia, Poland, Czechoslovakia, Yugoslavia, Turkey, and Greece. (UPI/Corbis-Bettman)

Sam and Mitzi at Syracuse's Hancock Field in 1964 to greet Lyndon and Lady Bird Johnson, in town to dedicate the first building of what was to become the Samuel I. Newhouse School of Public Communications at Syracuse University. When it was time to escort the president back to the airport, Sam told the university's president, "You take him over. I can't stand the SOB." (UPI/Corbis-Bettman)

Mitzi in 1964, the year she fulfilled one of her major ambitions—to appear in *Vogue*. The embarrassingly overheated text, under the headline, "People are Talking About," mentioned nowhere that she was the wife of the magazine's owner. (AP/Wide World Photos)

Portrait of Sam Newhouse, 1974,
by Gilbert Gordon Early.
(Gilbert Gordon Early)

Norman Newhouse in 1985.
(AP/Wide World Photos)

Ted Newhouse, eight years Sam's junior and intensely loyal
to him. Known as the family disciplinarian, his name sparks
few warm anecdotes or memories. (UPI/Corbis-Bettman)

Si and Donald escort their mother from Sam's funeral service in 1979. (AP/Wide World Photos)

Robert Gottlieb and William Shawn share a grim lunch at the Algonquin in 1987. Si Newhouse devastated Shawn with the news that he was being replaced by Gottleib as editor of the *New Yorker*. (Marina Garnier)

Si and his second wife, Victoria, an architectural historian previously married to a French count, enter New York's Museum of Modern Art in 1990. (Marina Garnier)

Si Newhouse and Steven Florio in 1993. Newhouse would soon appoint the bombastic and bullying Florio to head Condé Nast despite the fact that he had lost some $100 million while running the business side of the *New Yorker*. (Marina Garnier)

Si with James Truman.
(Marina Garnier)

Si confers with his younger brother Donald, who runs the newspaper and cable side of the business and makes money while Si, who presides over the family's glamorous properties, spends it. (Marina Garnier)

Jonathan Newhouse, Si's much-younger first cousin, is the Newhouse whom Si has designated his successor. (Marina Garnier)

Ron Galotti, boorish, profane, but a super-salesman and a favorite of Si's, was reportedly paid seven figures to leave Condé Nast and seven figures to return. (Marina Garnier)

Steven Newhouse, Donald's son, seems in line to take over his father's side of the business. (Marina Garnier)

Two of Si's most aggressive editors, Alexandra Penney (left) and Paige Rense. (Marina Garnier)

High-profile editors Tina Brown (left) and Anna Wintour in 1989, shortly after Si appointed the latter editor of *Vogue*. Rumors flew that she and Si were having an affair, but he denied it, saying that he was in love with his wife and his dog. (Marina Garnier)

Tina Brown, actor Harrison Ford, and Tina's husband Harry Evans at the *New Yorker*'s 70th anniversary party in 1995. (Marina Garnier)

Alex Liberman, a major figure at Condé Nast since 1961, became Si's mentor. (AP/Wide World Photos)

So he hit upon *Self*. "It was our turn," says Val Weaver. Because of the magazine's quick and stunning success, Si Newhouse believed that *Self* had the stuff to go mass market.

Alex Liberman, who until then had not been much involved with *Self*, decided that he had the formula for turning *Self*, the magazine of health and fitness, into Si's very own version of the sex-obsessed *Cosmo*. When Helen Gurley Brown, author of the best-seller *Sex and the Single Girl*, took over *Cosmopolitan* in 1965, the magazine was on the brink of collapse. She boosted circulation to 2.8 million via an unwavering focus on how to attract and keep a man by being good in bed. Sex sells was the message, delivered every month by cover models with skimpy clothes and substantial cleavage.

"What we need is something sexier, more personalities, more star power," Liberman told a meeting of *Self* editorial and business-side people. Every time a magazine hit a "blip," a man who was at the meeting says, Si would ask Alex what to do. "His answer was immediately sex and personality, one or the other, or both."

Newhouse called Val Weaver into his office in the spring of 1988. This time he didn't use his good news/bad news line. "You know we've been worried about *Self* and thinking about whether we should change its direction," Si told her. "If it's all right with you, we'd like to make a change in the editor in chief." He told Weaver that her replacement would be Elizabeth Crow, editor in chief of *Parents* magazine and director of magazine development for German-owned Gruner & Jahr USA Publishing. Weaver recalls feeling "shock," not that she was being let go but that Crow was "so mass." They wanted Crow, Weaver explains, because "she had taken *Parents* from a nothing to a phenomenon in a couple of years." Crow, whose husband, Pat, was a much-loved editor on the *New Yorker*, took the job, but at the last minute changed her mind when Gruner & Jahr offered her the position of president and chief executive of its U.S. operations. Weaver was called back to run the magazine for a couple of months until another editor could be found.

They thought they'd found her in Anthea Disney, a Brit who had worked as a reporter, editor, foreign correspondent, and columnist for the *London Daily Mail* and the *London Daily Express* and as editor of the

Sunday *New York Daily News*. Most recently she had been editor of *US* and had turned it around very quickly. Newhouse saw Disney as an editor who knew how to put out a celebrity-driven product, a woman who could double *Self*'s circulation to his goal of 2.5 million.

Disney says that she came to the magazine with a mandate to change it. "They needed to find a new way to position the magazine for both the reader and the advertiser that wasn't just, 'Let's lose weight, eat these vitamins, and you will feel great.' They asked me what my philosophy would be, and I said I thought there was a place in the market for a *GQ* for women that had intelligent articles but that, instead of coming from fashion as *GQ* does, would approach it from a health and a personal wellness standpoint.... That was the idea they signed on for." In fact, "*GQ* for Women" was soon the phrase used to sell the magazine.

Still Liberman's celebrity crutch was key, and when Disney told Weaver of her plan, Weaver warned her, "You couldn't get *Self* readers to read a celebrity piece to save your life.... If they wanted to read about celebrities, they bought *People,* and if they wanted to read about themselves, they bought *Self*." One woman who later became an editor at *Self* describes the magazine under Disney as "second-rate celebrities with big breasts."

But it worked. Newsstand sales, the most profitable part of a magazine's circulation, jumped right away. Unfortunately for Anthea Disney, Liberman was determined to be intimately involved with *Self*. (Until then Rochelle Udell had been playing the Liberman role by overseeing *Self*, and she and Disney worked well together.) The reason for his sudden interest, Disney maintains, were articles that ran in 1988 in the *New York Times* and the *Wall Street Journal* reporting that Disney had successfully repositioned *Self*. Alex Liberman's name was missing from the stories. Alex, says Disney, "started to feel that we had somehow taken the wind out of his sails."

That same year a cover story on Rochelle Udell, who had arrived at Condé Nast in 1972 as art director of *Vogue*, appeared in *Manhattan Inc.* Udell, who has moved gracefully between editorial, both words and design, and business, especially advertising sales and marketing, was widely considered Liberman's heir apparent as editorial director of all the magazines.

Newhouse himself had publicly praised her as a "wonderfully loose and unstructured talent." But after the admiring cover profile celebrating Udell's future appeared, her climb was unceremoniously halted.

In the summer of 1989, after only fourteen months on the job, Disney was on vacation at her home in Litchfield, Connecticut, when she received a telephone call from Si. He asked if he could stop by the next day en route to see Alex Liberman at his home, five miles away, in Warren, Connecticut. She told Si yes. She put down the phone, turned to her husband, and said, "I'm going to be fired tomorrow."

Disney describes her country house, a converted barn, as "truly rustic, in the middle of nowhere on a pond, a rural back road with a white picket fence." As Si Newhouse climbed out of a limousine, which filled the entire driveway, Disney's husband, Peter Howe, suddenly appeared carrying a chain saw he had used to chop down a dead tree. Si had never met Howe, but as Disney was about to introduce them, Si backed away as if he thought Disney's husband was going to "take his head off."

"So charming," Si said as they entered the house.

"Well, thank you," Disney said, "but I don't think you're here for *HG*, so why don't you tell me what it is you want."

"I don't think this is working," he said. "It's not comfortable with you and Alex."

She agreed that it was not comfortable. "Look, it's your magazine. It's your right to do what you want with it. Let's have no hard feelings. If there was a misunderstanding, there's no point in rehashing it. I would prefer it didn't become a shouting match at this point."

Disney, however, did remind Newhouse of a letter she had received the week before from Ralph Lauren, congratulating her on what she had done with *Self* and implying that he might soon become an advertiser. The news had no immediate effect on the owner. And Disney didn't know what more to say. She describes it as one of the most awkward moments of her adult life; once he fired her, what next? Was she to ask him to have a drink? Shoulders slumped, head down, hands in his pockets, Si mumbled good-bye and stumbled out of the house and into his waiting car.

Looking back at that time, Disney concludes that Alex never got it. "He just wanted to put out pretty young girls on the cover in workout clothes, and that's fine if that's what they wanted, but they shouldn't have hired me to do something else."

While bitter about Alex, Disney is not upset about her treatment by Newhouse. After his Connecticut drop-by, she gave no interviews. She says that she liked Si, calls their relationship "extremely cordial," and laughs recalling an earlier meeting with him at which she volunteered that she thought *Self* was "the worst title in the world for a magazine because it reeked of the seventies." He responded by smiling slightly and looking at his shoes. She learned later that the title was his.

Rupert Murdoch soon recruited Disney, eventually naming her editor in chief of *TV Guide*, which, with a circulation of 14 million, was the only billion-dollar-plus revenue producer in the magazine business, a feat for which she was credited. She continues to work for Murdoch as president and chief executive of his book publishing arm, HarperCollins, and as chairman and CEO of Murdoch's U.S. magazine, book, and on-line publishing divisions. (Murdoch sold *TV Guide* in 1998, thus exiting from the U.S. magazine market, in which he retained only one title, the small-circulation *Weekly Standard*.)[16]

Si's friend of thirty years, Alexandra Penney, became Disney's replacement. Penney had made her name and fortune seven years before on a best-selling book, *How to Make Love to a Man*, and on another called *Great Sex*. Robert Lang, who had helped her write *Great Sex* and whom Penney brought in as her assistant, describes the atmosphere when they arrived at *Self* in August 1989, as "Looney Tunes. Alexandra was firing people every five minutes; people were resigning every ten minutes." Lang tried to persuade her to keep some holdovers, but she insisted, "Oh, no, you can't trust them. You have to have your own people."

Long divorced from Richard Penney, Alexandra was best known among the Condé Nast cognoscenti for her skill in courting Si and Victoria as if her professional and personal life depended on it. (She managed to insert into every interview and many casual conversations her opinion of Si's brilliance.) One Condé Nast editor happened to catch a glimpse of Alexandra, who was then around fifty years old—she refuses to divulge her age—in Si's office: "She had a cup of coffee on the desk and not quite her feet up but that sort of body image, obviously very relaxed together.... She

behaved very differently than I behaved with the boss. I remember thinking that they obviously had a very intimate relationship."

Val Weaver insists that Si's decision to hire Penney came down to his
hunch that she was the person who could transform *Self* into a kind of
Cosmo, Condé Nast style. He saw her *How to Make Love to a Man* as a
"huge, mass best-seller. He felt that she knew how to tap into the mass
market. Celebrities hadn't worked. Health and fitness hadn't worked in
terms of multiple millions of magazines. Sex would work."

Immediately the magazine loaded up with stories on male/female
relationships, and, for the first time, covers featured men and women. And
now Alex Liberman had his woman in Alexandra, who framed his layouts
and hung them in her office. Veronique Vienne, whom Disney had hired as
art director shortly before she was fired, stayed on under Penney. Vienne
was instructed to alert Penney the moment she and Liberman completed a
layout. "She would enter the room and instantly dismiss me as a presence.
She would go toward the desk where the layouts were and she would say,
'Alex, ahhhh, ahhhh, ahhhh,' and he loved it.... And she would say, 'Oh,
you are,' and she would put both her hands on his hand and look deeply
into his face." Alexandra was, observes Veronique, following her own play-
book. She had advised the readers of one of her sex books never to forget
the two Ms—"move and moan."

Veronique Vienne realized immediately that she was the operating
room nurse assisting the surgeon. During work on a layout, one of her
assistants would stand next to her armed with scissors, knife, and loupe.
Another stood by the photocopier. Another stood at the door to "transmit
signals," and two "runners" waited at the ready, just in case. "I would have
every image stated in ten different sizes in every color," Vienne recalls. "I
was next to Alex supporting him while he was doing this layout. A couple
of feet behind me there was another assistant. 'Get me some red paper, get
me this or that.' There was another girl whose job was to put down the
Scotch Tape." One editor who was present at these sessions says that Alex
would often demand that a story be cut in half if doing so enhanced the
layout. He was never shy about making editorial suggestions. At one point
he decided that he detested the word *commitment*—a staple of women's
magazines—and that he adored the word *joy*, and would suggest, willy-

nilly, that the latter be substituted for the former. "But it isn't about joy," the editor would protest. Alex might drop the demand, but the editor would pay for her persistence in some other way.

Sex and *Self* turned out to be a losing combination. During the second half of 1990 newsstand sales dropped by 16 percent. In 1991 ad pages dropped by 27 percent. Publisher Marianne Howatson was fired after struggling "to resell the magazine with every changing look." She was replaced by Lawrence Burstein, who had been publisher of *Elle*. Penney then gave up on sex, returning *Self* to its roots as a health magazine, and its numbers started to improve—but, with circulation hovering about the million mark, not enough to satisfy the owner.[17]

At the same time that Si was trying to push *Self* into the mass market, he decided, in 1988, to buy the real thing. At the urging of then Condé Nast president Bernard H. Leser, he acquired his first blue-collar magazine, paying New York publisher Stanley Harris $10 million for the bimonthly, 500,000-circulation *Woman,* sold almost entirely on the newsstand.

The $10 million seemed almost beside the point. On the same day Si closed on *Woman,* he paid, at the top of the art market, $17 million for a Jasper Johns painting called *False Start*—a record price at auction for the work of a living artist. (For one week, it also held the record for the highest price ever paid for a twentieth-century work of art.) Johns's dealer, Leo Castelli, figures that Si, his long-time client, overpaid by at least $8 million; the "going price" at the time, Castelli says, was $8 or $9 million. Both the painting and the magazine turned out to be bum investments.

The Newhouse plan was to compete head-on at the grocery checkout counter with *Cosmopolitan* and also with Rupert Murdoch's fast-growing *New Woman*. Realizing its mass market potential, Murdoch had bought *New Woman* four years earlier and watched its ad pages multiply and its circulation hit 1.4 million.

To edit *Woman,* Si hired Pat Miller, who just happened to be editor and publisher of *New Woman,* and, before that, international director of Hearst, which owned *Cosmopolitan.* By selecting her, Miller says, Si "killed two birds with one stone," weakening *New Woman* by robbing it of its editor and at the same time giving Newhouse what he hoped would become a

Cosmo clone. Miller guesses that part of Si's motivation was to prove something to Murdoch. "He always had a sense of inferiority about Rupert."

She describes *Woman* at the time Si purchased it as "a very down-market little guttersnipe doing nicely." The typical Condé Nast editor and designer wanted to don latex gloves before touching its pages, almost every one of which, like *Cosmo,* had sex on or between its lines. Pat Miller didn't have to fight off Alex Liberman; he wanted nothing to do with *Woman.* At the first print order meeting Leo Lerman said to Miller, "Well, you may be only a woman, but we'll turn you into a lady yet." Personnel was "unloading [its] deadbeats on me," recalls Miller, people whom "nobody else wanted." The magazine became a dumping ground/resting place for displaced persons from the magazine's classier sisters.

Pat Miller was another Brit, from Manchester, who had arrived in New York via Fleet Street, had felt at home in the on-the-cheap Murdoch offices but never felt comfortable at Condé Nast. She describes her Condé Nast offices as "lavish, up-market, elitist, don't count the cost, fly Concorde, which decorator would you like for your office, and would you like a personal trainer or which health club would you like to join?" Under Murdoch, Miller would submit a budget, grit her teeth as it was cut, and live with it. At Condé Nast, there were no budgets. There was, she says, "absolutely no control there. I hated it."

Still, she had made the move and tried to make the best of it. "'Well,' I thought, 'I'd better move this magazine up-market pretty damn quick, so all these gurus will stop drawing their skirts aside.' Classic mistake—mine alone—that was to forget the reader and cultivate the corporate." When they took *Woman* to monthly publication, "circulation," Pat Miller said, "did not double, it halved. It was twice as much work, employed twice as many people, and cost twice as much to produce." Si would groan and ask Miller, "Why is it that as soon as Condé Nast takes over something, it becomes more expensive?"

After operating *Woman* for only sixteen issues, the owner decided it was not for him. He tried to sell it, but a magazine broker found no takers. It was Pat Miller who lobbied for simply closing it, realizing, she said, how embarrassing it was to Newhouse to hawk a magazine that he should never have bought and that nobody else wanted to buy. "I knew it was the first magazine Si had ever put up for sale. I suspect he was deeply embarrassed, and I thought a quick death was preferable to a proudly defiant hemorrhage." Si admitted to her that he had not carefully studied *Woman*'s financials before he bought it.

He would suffer another whopping loss when he tired of the $17 million Jasper Johns, sold it a couple of years later, and, estimates Johns's dealer, Leo Castelli, lost around $10 million on the transaction—roughly the purchase price of *Woman*. The Jasper Johns mistake was Si's loss only, and he might have claimed that two years of looking at the painting was worth $10 million. The closing of *Woman* had much wider ramifications for its employees and their families.[18]

If one went searching for the polar opposite of *Woman* in the Condé Nast stable, *Details*, which Si bought in 1988, the same year he bought *Woman*, was it. Founded in 1982, *Details* was a magazine covering the downtown club and fashion scene, devoid of any apparent ambition to go mainstream or national. It was relentlessly hip and hedonistic, given to cross-dressing fashion spreads, to coverage of body piercing and tattooing, and to attracting an audience of gay men, with an occasional bicycle messenger thrown in for good measure. Even locally, if anyone north of Fourteenth Street read *Details*, it was not because its editors tried to attract him.

Newhouse paid between $2 and $3 million for the magazine, whose circulation had yet to crack 100,000. Conventional wisdom holds that by agreeing to buy just one day after learning *Details* was for sale and by neglecting to study the magazine's books, Si overpaid. He closed the deal without ever meeting the magazine's founding editor, Annie Flanders.

But Newhouse had no intention of letting *Details* be *Details*. As he did at *GQ*, he ordered that the magazine be "recast"—this time into a younger version of *GQ*. To accomplish the makeover, he replaced Annie Flanders in 1990 with a young editor named James Truman—a shy, charming, boyish-looking Brit, a favorite of Anna Wintour's and soon a favorite of Si's. Wintour had brought James, as he was called, into *Vogue* in 1988 and named him arts editor and later features editor.

Truman had skipped college and worked, among other places, for a London rock music weekly called *Melody Maker*. Landing in New York in

1981, he became the American editor for the ultra-offbeat British style magazine the *Face,* and freelanced for various American magazines, including the early *Details.* (Si bought 40 percent of the *Face* and considered starting an American version, but decided to focus on *Details.*) Truman himself became a regular in publishing gossip columns, the subject of much speculation as to his sexuality—was he or wasn't he gay? He said no, others said yes. But he always described *Details* as being "sexually nondenominational."

Truman's charge was to turn *Details* into a general interest, national but still hip magazine for men in their twenties, the kind of magazine that would attract the fragrance and liquor advertisers that had until then kept their distance. Si wanted *Details* to have a little edge—Truman once ran a photograph of an electrocuted corpse—but not so much that advertisers would be confused or repelled; to have a patina of homosexuality, but not so much that the straight reader would be turned off. He wanted that sense of being offbeat, antiestablishment, hip, downtown maintained—for the time being, *Details* would keep its offices on lower Broadway in SoHo— but downtown in a style not so offbeat or antiestablishment that it would lose resonance with young men on the make and the advertisers who courted them. One writer described Truman's *Details* as "the Pearl Jam of the magazine world, the glittery showplace where rebellion, individualism, and nonconformity are conveniently packaged and paired with all of the correct accessories."

If *Woman* was a failure, *Details* appeared to be a success. By shifting the magazine's focus, Truman was credited with quadrupling *Details'* circulation to nearly 500,000. Advertising revenue grew apace. But *appeared* was again the operative word. In fact, when the *Wall Street Journal* assessed the Newhouse empire in early 1996, Si Newhouse admitted that *Details* was still losing money—not surprisingly, as he had spared no expense in retooling the magazine. Still, *Details,* larded with ads, had the appearance of success—one media reporter after another touted it as the magazine success story of the 1990s—and, for Si Newhouse, appearance was worth a lot.[19]

19 | Random Fire

AT THE TIME of the Newhouse brothers' purchase of Random House in 1980, Bob Bernstein's optimism was tempered somewhat when he and his wife attended a dinner given by Mitzi Newhouse in celebration of her sons' acquisition of the giant of American publishing. Helen Bernstein's dinner partner, a charmer from the evening's start to finish, was Roy Cohn.

Into the 1980s, Roy Cohn and Si Newhouse saw each other daily. "I encountered [Roy] almost every day in the office," says one former editor at *Vogue*, "and they were on the phone all the time.... I never had jury duty because every time I got a notice Si said, 'Give it to me. I'll give it to Roy.'"

In late 1984 Si Newhouse's closest friend was diagnosed as having AIDS. Until his death in 1986, Cohn, who had denied his homosexuality all his life, claimed that he was suffering from liver cancer. During Roy's illness, not a day went by when Si didn't call or visit. Si did another favor for his friend by reportedly insisting that Random House publish Cohn's memoirs. "If it wasn't for Si, I don't think Random House would have even looked at it," says one close friend of Roy's. "The reason they did is because Si told them to." The project was put in the hands of one of the house's most senior editors, Jason Epstein. When Cohn's manuscript arrived, the writing was so banal, so totally at odds with Cohn's personality, that Epstein brought in former *New York Times* reporter and Cohn crony Sidney Zion to make the book as interesting and outrageous as Cohn himself. Whenever Roy felt up to it—and at the end of his life he was often incoherent—Zion would rush to his side with a tape recorder.

Roy died before the memoir could be published, and at that point Si canceled it. (The book was later published by Lyle Stuart as *The Autobiography of Roy Cohn*.) Jason Epstein refused to be interviewed, but he insists that it was his decision alone to drop the Cohn memoir because Cohn's illness had rendered the material too thin to ever make an interesting book. Others contend that a close associate of Cohn's persuaded Si to cancel the book because there was something in the tapes that this man felt must be kept under wraps.[1]

Editors at Random House soon had other matters to worry about. During the late 1980s and most of the 1990s—Si announced early in 1998 that he planned to sell Random House—the new owner made changes that shook the industry to its nineteenth-century traditions. As a result, S. I. Newhouse—Donald continued to play no role in Random House—would become a controlling force on the book publishing scene.

The freckled, carrot-topped Bob Bernstein was a much different person than the man he now reported to, and the relationship between them was always pure business. They had agreed to have lunch every Tuesday at the Four Seasons, and whenever possible Bernstein would bring along one or another of his top people at Random House. Some observers suggested that Bernstein's height, six foot two, threatened Si. Others speculated that it was Bernstein's Harvard degree and his refined manner.

Bernstein was and remains deeply involved in human rights abroad. He is the chairman and founder of Human Rights Watch and while at Random House published books by, among others, Natan Sharansky, Jacobo Timmerman, Andrei Sakharov (from whom text was arriving while he was under virtual house arrest in Gorki), and Václav Havel (when Havel was in jail, before he became president of Czechoslovakia). Bernstein found out soon enough that Newhouse had no interest in human rights. According to André Schiffrin, who then headed the Pantheon imprint at Random House, Si "didn't like the crusading." Others recognized that Si was put off by Bernstein's habit of opening sales conferences with a human rights news update or sermon. (Bernstein says that he opened with the subject of human rights only when referring to a specific book on the list that he was involved with acquiring and launching.)

Still, in the early years of their relationship Bernstein was pretty much left alone to run the companies as he saw fit. Then, one day in the mid-1980s, Bernstein left town for a few days and returned to discover that Newhouse and Howard Kaminsky, who headed "Little Random" (so called to distinguish it from other Random House imprints such as Knopf and Pantheon) and who was very close personally to Si, had acquired Nancy Reagan's memoir. The price was huge, an advance—money paid the author up front and later deducted from royalties—estimated at $3 million. When Bernstein returned to his office, Newhouse presented the deal to him as a fait accompli. According to people close to the principals, Bernstein was shocked but merely said to Si, "I assume you wanted this." "Yes very much," Newhouse replied.

My Turn: The Memoirs of Nancy Reagan, written for her by William Novak, was a best-seller for more than three months but probably didn't earn out its advance. (One editor closely involved with the book insists that it did earn out, helped by rich paperback and first serial sales.)

Friends of Bernstein claim that what irritated him most, other than being bypassed altogether, was that it seemed to signal that the Condé Nast formula was being applied to Random House; that the venerable house would focus on celebrity books and the kind of commercial novels that had "best-seller" written all over them. It's not that Random House had avoided publishing such books over the years; but they weren't staples of the list. In addition, these people say, Bernstein didn't admire the Reagans. Random House, under Bernstein and Bennett Cerf before him, had stuck to the conceit that there were books worthy of the Random House name and books that were not. Nancy Reagan's book was not. (Bernstein points out that Random House and Knopf had always published celebrity and highly commercial books, that he had nothing against Nancy Reagan personally, and that his sole objection was to the price paid.)

Si disagreed with all objections to the Reagan book. Despite his own rarefied tastes, he wanted to publish big books; books that created the same sort of buzz as his hottest magazines; books that would make Random House a publisher in the news. It wasn't profit that the son sought so much as recognition—the very opposite of the father's approach.

The Nancy Reagan acquisition also further soured Bernstein's relationship with Howard Kaminsky. Kaminsky had been president and publisher of Warner Books before Si, with Bernstein's approval, brought him to Random House in 1984. Kaminsky and Newhouse had a lot in common. Besides being undersized, they shared an interest in movies—Kaminsky's cousin was Mel Brooks—and Kaminsky and his wife, Susan, were frequent guests of Si and Victoria in Palm Beach.

More significantly, Kaminsky agreed with his friend that Random House should go after the biggest, most commercial books and pay whatever was necessary to get them. Increasingly, Kaminsky, secure, almost cocky about his relationship with Newhouse, was treading on Bernstein's turf, even appropriating his title. "Howard in effect started reporting to Si and not reporting to me," recalls Bernstein. "It became more and more awkward." All editors had a cut-off sum of about $250,000, beyond which they were not allowed to acquire books without first talking to Bernstein. Kaminsky bought books above the cutoff and let Bernstein know later.

Finally, meeting with Newhouse in October 1987, Bernstein discussed his deteriorating relationship with Kaminsky, and Newhouse approved ending it. Kaminsky asked Bernstein if he would mind if he talked directly to Si. According to one former Random House editor, Kaminsky "went over to the Condé Nast building to have a conversation with the man he considered his very good buddy, and Si said, 'Nope, if Bernstein says you're out, you're out.'"

But Si Newhouse's terse reply to his friend Howard was far from a vote of confidence for Bernstein. It was rather perhaps a convenient way to get rid of Kaminsky, whom Si saw as having lost his touch. "Howard had overpaid for many projects that didn't work," explains a former head of a Random House imprint. Another veteran publishing figure—at Random House and elsewhere—says that Si would have made the other choice (i.e., fired Bernstein) had Kaminsky not been "failing."

Kaminsky went on to run Hearst's book publishing division, William Morrow, but he was pressured to resign in 1994. Oddly enough, Si and Howard have remained close. Kaminsky refused to discuss his Random House ouster, out of respect, he explained, for his friendship with Si.

Kaminsky's replacement at Random House was Joni Evans, former president of Simon & Schuster's trade division. Six weeks earlier,

Newhouse and Bernstein had hired her to run her own imprint at Random House, but with Kaminsky's ouster, they had new plans for her. Evans agreed reluctantly. She had already run the trade division at Simon & Schuster, and, she says, running Little Random "wasn't where my heart was…. The business was changing. It was all about money and too much money." She would not suffer long, as Si Newhouse, perhaps even then, had someone specific in mind to replace her.[2]

Bob Bernstein rid himself of Kaminsky, but he acquired another problem that year. Bob Gottlieb, moving to the *New Yorker* in 1987, handpicked Sonny Mehta to run Knopf.

Mehta, born in India and educated in England, was both commercial—he came to Knopf from mass paperback publishing—and literary in his approach to books. Considered by his employees and peers to be brilliant but difficult, he was prone to disappearing into black moods for days or even weeks at a time. He was vastly different from Gottlieb, who was available to his editors and authors at all hours.

Predictably, Mehta's first couple of years were rocky and by many accounts he and Bernstein did not get along at all. Bernstein reportedly tried to get Mehta to conform to certain company procedures, and Mehta resisted completely. Joni Evans was one who noticed that Bernstein disliked Mehta. Roger Cohen, then the publishing reporter for the *New York Times*, described relations between the two men as "fairly poisonous."

But it didn't much matter what Bernstein thought of Mehta. As evidenced by Mehta's salary, which one agent calls "huge," and perks, which included a spectacular Park Avenue apartment, Si Newhouse liked him—and liked him better each day as he racked up controversy, best-sellers, Pulitzer Prizes, and profits. Insiders say that Knopf was the only imprint within Random House that was making money.[3]

It was the acquisition of the Crown Publishing company in 1988, more than anything, that changed Random House, Inc., and created major problems for the company—problems that ten years later contributed to Si's decision to sell Random House.

For years Si Newhouse had wanted to buy Crown, a company founded by Nat Wartels in 1933. It was then called the Outlet Book Company, and it became rich by buying up remainders, books that hadn't sold out their print run and ended up piled on bookstore tables and cleared out, for their authors, at humiliatingly reduced prices. In 1936 Wartels published his first real book, *The Book of Furniture and Decoration,* and the legitimate publishing arm of his business was born.

By 1988 Crown was divided into three distinct parts, all of which, says Sandy MacGregor, then in effect Random House's chief operating officer, Newhouse thought would prove a "strategic fit." Outlet Books was one. The trade book division was another, with such highly commercial authors as Judith Krantz,* Jean Auel, Dominick Dunne, and Alex Comfort and his *Joy of Sex* guides. Third was Publishers Central Bureau, the mail order side of the business, the part that Si wanted most—an untapped gold mine, he thought, with the potential of turning the millions who read Condé Nast magazines and *Parade* and maybe even the newspapers into customers for Random House books and related products.

Alan Mirken, Nat Wartel's nephew, had started working part-time at Crown in 1943 and became president in 1979. Early one Friday morning in late spring 1988, Mirken called Si Newhouse. Seven years before, Bob Bernstein, at Newhouse's behest, had approached Wartels and Mirken to ask if Crown was for sale. They said no, not yet, but promised to call when they were ready to sell. This was the call.

After several meetings between the principals, Mirken announced to his employees, on August 15, 1988, the sale of Crown to Random House.

Wartels and Mirken had asked Newhouse for $200 million. They settled on an estimated $150 million. At first blush it seemed like a steal for Random House. But nobody, Si included, had looked closely enough at Crown's books. "Si never looked at the books," says Sandy MacGregor, "because there was nothing to look at." The mail order division proved terminally ill and in the end was sold off in pieces. The remainder division, critically ill, was eventually saved. The only relatively healthy part of the business was trade publishing.

---

*When agent Mort Janklow brought Krantz's first novel, *Scruples,* to Random House in the pre-Newhouse late 1970s, its editors reportedly refused to even consider it. It was published by Crown in 1978.

A former top Random House editor argues that the owners of Crown ran the place like the privately owned company it was. "The idea was to reward the principals as much as possible and not pay taxes. And a company that's run in that way doesn't do quarterly reports and doesn't allocate the overhead.... They didn't do their books the way a rational, modern company would do their books, but I don't think they cheated."

Bob Bernstein's warnings to the boss not to buy, or at least to "go much slower," only angered Si, whom, Bernstein says, had "a tremendous urgency in him...to acquire." In the end Si, with his brother Donald's approval, was following the lead of their father, who always put his profits into the purchase of another newspaper or two. "I always felt that they were reinvesting the monies that the business made," says Bob Bernstein, "and the government was paying half of it, and so for a private business it made sense to take the chances."

For the editorial people at Random House, the Crown acquisition was unwelcome; it was making the company bigger, less personal, and more downscale. "It changed the nature of the company," said one editor at Knopf.[4]

With Crown proving to be an excruciating headache, and Si so focused on the trade book part of the publishing business—that is, books sold to the general public in bookstores—he lost whatever little interest he might ever have had in another element of the company, college and school textbook publishing. He decided the same year that he acquired Crown, 1988, to sell the education division.

The decision baffled many in the business. Then–Simon & Schuster head Richard Snyder was buying textbook companies wherever he could, because textbooks yield a higher profit than do trade books. As Sandy MacGregor puts it, "[Si] made a decision to stay with trade publishing at a time when everybody else was running in the other direction."

Although Bob Bernstein insists that he would have held on to the education division, he too seemed to many to be not much interested in textbooks. Seibert Adams, who headed the college division at Random House, put on twenty sales conferences during his eleven years at the company. He remembers Bernstein as "obviously very bored" at the two he attended. Si never attended any. (Bernstein disputes this characterization, saying he was interested in the textbook division and attended "many" sales conferences.)

Still, Bernstein, like Bennett Cerf before him, understood the importance of school and college publishing and certainly felt that Random House should be doing it and doing it well. On top of obligation was the question of profit, and as Seib Adams insists, "Textbooks covered a lot of the expenses of the trade division. We were growing at a very rapid rate, and our overhead contribution to the company went up in relation to sales [which increased approximately sixfold between 1977 and 1988] rather than costs, so we were paying more and more toward the overhead of the corporation.... We were really subsidizing a Pantheon and a Knopf." (Given what followed—a decade of bleeding bottom lines—Si's decision to sell the education division seemed particularly ill-conceived, self-indulgent, and almost spoiled, one that a man who had had to make his fortune himself would never have made.)

Adams, who had come to Random House from CBS's textbook division, which, he says, "defined bureaucracy," found Random House under Newhouse wonderfully bureaucracy-free. "We set the goals," says Adams, "and if you met them nobody bothered you." At one point Adams decided he wanted to start from scratch a foreign language publishing program that would teach language the way a child learns it—by actually talking, rather than by memorization and drill. Adams produced a fifty-page proposal complete with market analyses. He showed it to Bernstein, who asked him, "Do I have to read it?" He never did, nor did Si, or anyone else at Random House. "You're head of the college division," Bernstein told him. "Do it."

Adams did, and that foreign language program today enjoys 30 percent of the world market.

Adams's only regular contact with the owner in this period was quarterly lunches at the Four Seasons. The lunches, Adams recalls, were "so stressful" because Si would wolf down his food while rapid-firing questions at Adams, most of them about lines of books with low profits or less-than-expected sales. (Adams, whose food would remain untouched, soon learned to grab a sandwich before going.)

In 1988 Si Newhouse canceled all three of their lunches, and Adams knew something was up. On the Wednesday morning after Labor Day, 1988, Adams was called into a meeting in Bernstein's office—Sandy MacGregor was also there—and informed that Newhouse had decided to sell the edu-cation division, that Si believed textbooks were an "incompatible business."

The investment bankers Newhouse hired to sell the division advised him that he could expect to get between $75 and $100 million. Adams knew this was a ridiculous underestimation, that he could do much better, and he wanted a chance to try his hand at it. According to Sandy MacGregor, Si's go-ahead was "grudging." And he insisted that Adams approach one company only; he didn't want the division shopped.

Adams had one publisher in mind—McGraw-Hill. The president of the college division of McGraw-Hill was an old friend who, like Adams, had started his career at Prentice-Hall. At lunch, Adams told him that it was possible he could get Random House's college division for him.

"He said, 'That would be really great because it would really fit with what we're doing at McGraw.'

"I said, 'All right, here's the deal. You can have an exclusive on the buyout for $200 million in cash, no negotiation, and we have to have a signed deal in seven days." With monumental chutzpah, offset by the cer-tainty that he had a valuable property to sell, Adams made another demand: "Every single employee at Random House has to be an employ-ee at McGraw-Hill, so if there's any cutback in people it has to be McGraw-Hill people."

Adams returned to the office. His friend at McGraw-Hill called at four that afternoon. "The chairman of the board of McGraw-Hill has approved the deal. We need a week to do due diligence, and the Jewish holidays are in there. Can we have eight days?" Adams, who got every-thing he asked for, replied, "Sure you can have eight days."

After receiving the news, Adams called Bernstein: "I think I have a deal for $200 million." Bernstein called Newhouse, who called the news "spectacular." And so the deal was signed, and Si and Donald Newhouse reaped more than twice what they thought the division was worth and more than three times what they had paid for all of Random House eight years before.[5]

On the first day of November 1989, Newhouse called in the sixty-eight-year-old chairman who had worked more than three decades at Random House "Look, Bob," he said, "I've made a change."

For Bernstein, who not long before had been quoted as saying, "I want to be publisher until I'm carried out," the news was devastating. "When I came to Random House in 1957 we were doing $4 million worth of business," he said in 1994, remembering that day. "In 1966 when I became head of it, we were doing $40 million. When I left we were doing $850 million."

All those numbers are accurate as far as they go; but at the time of Bernstein's ouster, Random House had reportedly stopped making money, and according to some accounts, including one in the *Wall Street Journal,* was losing quite a bit of money. (Bernstein disputes this characterization, calling Random House "as consistently profitable as any trade publisher from 1967 to 1990.") Shortly after firing Bernstein—Si called it a "retirement," Bernstein called it a "resignation"—Si told Roger Cohen of the *New York Times* that the company had become more "complicated" and would "require a different, less laid-back style of management." Si saw Random House as sprawling out of control, and blamed Bernstein's loose and decentralized operating style.

Joni Evans, while calling Si's treatment of Bernstein "shabby," also believes that Si was probably right to make the change. "I do think it was time for Bob to retire and the world was getting much larger and Bob was exhausted from Crown and he had done brilliant stuff with [Random House].... He had served his purpose, and he was really getting slightly outdated."

Yet she ponders again why Si didn't simply retire Bernstein with honors, make him chairman emeritus, throw him a lovely dinner, let him pursue his work for the Helsinki Watch Committee, give him a small office that he could use or not as he liked. Bernstein, with his A-list contacts, and what one former editor calls "enormous principle and values," certainly could have helped Random House land classy and coveted authors.

In 1991 Bernstein became publisher-at-large at John Wiley & Sons, which later gave him his own imprint, under which he published books on human rights, current affairs, politics, and history. He left Wiley in 1998.[6]

The first book that Si personally bought for Random House was Donald Trump's *The Art of the Deal*—an enormous success, with forty-eight weeks on the best-seller list. That was the kind of publishing that fit Si Newhouse, who had noticed that an issue of *GQ* with Trump on the cover had sold especially well. "I called Donald and suggested he do a book," Si told Geraldine Fabrikant of the *New York Times*. But Trump turned out to be a one-shot phenomenon. Trump's second book, *Surviving at the Top,* for which Random House paid an estimated $2 million advance, sold fewer than 200,000 of the 500,000 printed and lasted only seven weeks on the best-seller list. His third book, *Trump: The Art of the Comeback,* published in October 1997, had a smaller first printing—said to be 250,000—and lackluster sales. It made the *New York Times* list just twice.[7]

But Si Newhouse was not going to spend his time buying books. He needed someone he could trust to run the book publishing company. The early betting was on Joni Evans, who was still running Little Random and remained single, childless, tireless, and at least relatively speaking, friendly with Si—he testified for her during her acrimonious divorce from Dick Snyder. Other Random House people were also mentioned, but Newhouse wanted someone from the outside, and his choice was Alberto Vitale—born in Italy, reared in Egypt, then president and CEO of Bantam Doubleday Dell, part of the German publishing conglomerate Bertelsmann AG.

Under Vitale, diminutive in stature like Si, it appeared that Bantam Doubleday Dell was doing exceedingly well. It later emerged that it was losing money, but Si didn't know that, and neither, apparently, did anyone else. "Alberto was sort of the industry star at that moment," says a former Random House executive, and Si will always go after the star. Later, says one woman who worked for both Bob Bernstein and Vitale, "The rumor mill was that Alberto was tantamount to being thrown out of Bantam Doubleday Dell before he was hired by Si, that at that point it was just about ready to fall down around his ears." When this woman is asked why Si would hire someone who was allegedly such a failure at his last job, she answers in a tone that implies that the answer is obvious: "Why would Si buy Crown without looking at the books?"

Some people, Joni Evans among them, expressed optimism at Vitale's appointment because they thought he would be a decisive leader, a crisp manager. "He was very good at getting things done," says Evans, but she soon grew disenchanted. "I was not comfortable with his style of management."

According to one former Random House editor, "Alberto's prime way of getting people to do things is to get everybody to fight with everybody else, and to create Machiavellian, labyrinthine battlefields all over the company." Editors watched with dismay as collegiality gave way to hierarchy and trust and tradition to bureaucracy. Mail boys were outfitted in gray jackets so there could be no mistaking them for anything but mail boys. Editors drawing up invitation lists for book parties were told to include no one under the rank of vice president. Titles, office size, and location suddenly mattered.

To many editors, Vitale's oddest quality was that he didn't seem to have even the average person's interest in books, which he often referred to as "units." Wendy Wolf, then at Pantheon, was in London when she read an interview with Vitale in the *Financial Times* in which he said that he didn't have time to read books. During a meeting with Vitale on her return to New York, she asked him if the statement was accurate. "I'm a very busy man and...I trust my editors," he replied.[8]

It was a matter of weeks after the dismissal of Bob Bernstein and the arrival of Alberto Vitale that Newhouse turned his attention to Pantheon, the money-losing Random House imprint run by André Schiffrin.

The Pantheon that Bennett Cerf bought for a half million dollars in 1961 came with an illustrious history. Kurt and Helen Wolff, both refugees from Hitler's Germany, founded the house in 1942 in a Greenwich Village apartment. The couple, whose German publishing house had been "Aryanized" by the Nazis, arrived in New York penniless—they started Pantheon with a loan of $7,500—but already renowned. Kurt Wolff, among other accomplishments, had published Franz Kafka's first book. Jacques Schiffrin, André's father, who joined the Wolffs at Pantheon a year later, was equally respected, having founded one of the most distinguished publishing companies in Paris. Pantheon's list soon lengthened to contain such important European writers as Gunter Grass, Albert Camus, and André Gide.

André Schiffrin, born in Paris, had degrees from Yale and Cambridge, proficiency in six languages, and a studied intellectual manner. He joined Pantheon in 1962, and during his near-thirty-year tenure, most of it as head of the house, he brought to Pantheon such authors as Marguerite Duras, Anita Brookner, Jean-Paul Sartre, Simone de Beauvoir, Noam Chomsky, R. D. Laing, and Studs Terkel.

It was a prestigious list but not a profitable one. Pantheon's commercial successes—*Dr. Zhivago* by Boris Pasternak, *Gift from the Sea* by Anne Morrow Lindbergh, *Born Free* by Joy Adamson, *The Leopard* by Giuseppe di Lampedusa, *The King Must Die* by Mary Renault—were all acquired in the years before André arrived.

Bob Bernstein was always a supporter of Pantheon. "I always thought André was doing what I call very interesting publishing that should be done," says Bernstein. He characterizes Pantheon as "about $15 million [in annual sales] in an $850 million business, not exactly either a major loser or contributor." But numbers aside, Schiffrin insists, Pantheon "wasn't meant to be a source of enormous money. It was meant to be a source of experimentation and prestige."

Not for Alberto Vitale. "The first words Vitale said when he met me," Schiffrin recalls, "were, 'Ah, Pantheon, where all those marvelous books come from,' and it was only later that I realized it was an accusation." Vitale charged Schiffrin with losing "many millions of dollars over the past five years."

In early 1990 Vitale informed Schiffrin that Pantheon would no longer be allowed to run in the red. Schiffrin countered that, unlike most of the rest of Random House, Pantheon was a no-frills, low-expense operation, and that if the ink was red, it was only because Pantheon was charged with too much of Random House's huge overhead. Ironically, Pantheon was about to become quite profitable because it held contracts for the new *Simpsons* series by Matt Groening, a scarcely known cartoonist when Pantheon first published him.

Schiffrin considered that looming bonanza irrelevant; his fate at Pantheon, he contends, was more than a matter of dollars and cents. Schiffrin claims that Vitale ordered him to purge future lists not only of obviously unprofitable books but also of left-wing books. There was no room for misinterpretation, Schiffrin insists, quoting Vitale as saying, flat out, "'You should publish more right-wing books and not so many left-wing.' He said that directly to me in those precise words. And he denied it of course afterwards."

"Never, ever was political direction discussed by me or anybody," Vitale countered. "The statement that somebody wanted to balance the list with right-leaning books is pure misrepresentation of facts."

An editor at Knopf who is sympathetic to Schiffrin says that she doesn't believe the contretemps was "ideological." If Pantheon were making money, she argues, neither Newhouse nor Vitale would have cared how left-wing its books were. She adds, however, "Given the fact that it wasn't working out, it didn't help that he was running such a liberal house." More convincing is Schiffrin's argument that he and Newhouse/Vitale differed over the most basic philosophy of publishing: "We felt we should use the profits from the profitable books to pay for the not profitable books, which has been the way publishing has always worked. That's the ethos of publishing. That's how you kept serious books [in the marketplace], and Vitale wanted every book to make a profit, and a large profit, and those that didn't shouldn't be published."

Among Vitale's demands were that Schiffrin cut by two-thirds Pantheon's staff and its list: from 110 books—cloth, paper, and titles from the related imprint Schocken—to 40. According to Schiffrin, Vitale threatened to fire him "without any compensation whatsoever" should he fail to make the cuts.

Diane Wachtell, then Schiffrin's assistant, remembers her boss returning in despair from a meeting with Vitale, "This is never going to work. We don't speak the same language." She says that in dealing with Vitale, the "very genteel" Schiffrin "was out of his league." "How could I look myself in the face in the mirror every morning publishing the books I was publishing?" Schiffrin claims that Vitale asked him. "And he mentioned some of the books. The first one happened to be by a Nobel prize–winning novelist; the second was by Italy's leading historian, and he had no idea who these people were.... He just saw that the printing figures were too low, and therefore one ought to be ashamed of publishing a book of which one printed 5,000 copies."

Sandy MacGregor was in the room with Vitale and Schiffrin when Schiffrin, in effect, "forced a separation. Schiffrin went into a speech about how he won't make these cuts, he won't destroy the property." An editor at Knopf says—sadly, because she admires Schiffrin—that had he compromised at, say, sixty-five books, or even eighty, Newhouse and Vitale probably would have gone along.

When the news broke on February 27, 1990, that Vitale had forced Schiffrin's hand to the point that he felt he had no choice but to resign, an outcry arose—aimed squarely at Si Newhouse. It was as if by allowing Schiffrin to be fired, Newhouse was somehow hastening the decline and demoralization of American publishing.

To take Schiffrin's place, Vitale hired Fred Jordan, then editor in chief at the avant-garde Grove Press. On paper, Jordan had the right credentials. He had been editor of the literary magazine *Evergreen Review*, he had fought some of the century's major censorship battles, and at Grove he had edited such authors as Samuel Beckett, Jack Kerouac, Henry Miller, Eugene Ionesco, Václav Havel, and Bertolt Brecht. Still, Schiffrin partisans considered Jordan a "puppet."

If Vitale thought that Jordan could replace the revered Schiffrin in the hearts of Pantheon's editors and authors, he soon discovered how wrong he was, as both groups threatened to sever ties to Pantheon, especially after Vitale placed Pantheon under the supervision of Knopf head Sonny Mehta, proving their point that Jordan would be no more than a figurehead. The day after Schiffrin's ouster, four Pantheon senior editors—James Peck, Tom Engelhardt, Wendy Wolf, and Sara Bershtel—handed their resignations to Vitale. They also issued a statement explaining that they had "sought…to give voice to at least some of the victims of our age—and to expose those who abused their wealth and power."

Fred Jordan remembers his first day on the job. "Alberto came out of a meeting, and he was as pale as a sheet, and he said, 'They're all in there now and they're all resigning…. What should we do?'" Jordan advised him to persuade the editors to sleep on their decision. Vitale tried, but, Jordan adds, "Then, of course, everybody walked out."

Sonny Mehta would later step in to try to prevent the few holdouts from leaving. Diane Wachtell, a Harvard graduate who had started her career at Knopf at age twenty-one but found it "too mainstream for my tastes" and voluntarily, after only seven months, moved to Pantheon, was one of them. "How about this salary? How about this title?" Mehta and his appointees coaxed her. "Pick an office, any office. Want a bigger office looking over the East River?" (She had previously sat outside Schiffrin's door.) She soon followed Schiffrin to his new venture, a foundation-supported, not-for-profit publisher called the New Press.

The anger needed an outlet, and in the first instance anybody could remember of a publisher being the target of a protest, on Monday, March 5, some 350 authors—some published by Random House imprints, most not—editors, agents, and sympathizers gathered in front of the Random House building on Third Avenue and Fiftieth Street. Some editors who had Si's name on their paychecks also joined the picket line. One was Knopf editor Ann Close, another was her colleague at Knopf, Bobbi Bristol, who held a copy of *The Leopard,* as if she were at a wake. Demonstrators included Barbara Ehrenreich, Ariel Dorfman, Kurt Vonnegut Jr., Oliver Sacks, and Jill Krementz. With cameras and recorders going, the denunciations, mostly of Si Newhouse, flew. Studs Terkel, whose book *The Great Divide,* published in 1988, was said to have lost plenty of money for Pantheon, spoke to the crowd, calling the phrase "the bottom line" the "most obscene expression in the American vocabulary."

Fred Jordan, who was hanged in effigy, not surprisingly recalls the picket line as "very unpleasant. I thought that I had experienced it all at Grove Press during the sixties. I thought, what more can there be? I was wrong."

An embarrassing full-page ad decrying the "assault on editorial independence and cultural freedom" and signed by more than 120 authors, some published by Random House imprints, some published by Newhouse's *New Yorker,* appeared in *the New York Review of Books,* the very journal that Si had once claimed as a model for the relaunched *Vanity Fair.* Signers, most of whom Si would have enjoyed as dinner guests, included Martin Amis, Ken Follett, Alison Lurie, Susan Stamberg, Calvin Trillin, John Hersey, Isabel Allende, Elie Wiesel, Arthur Miller, Jessica Mitford, Amy Tan, Laurent de Brunhoff, Nadine Gordimer, William Styron, Russell Banks, Alice Adams, and Benjamin Spock, whose memoir, published by Pantheon in 1989, was also reportedly a money loser.

Si even took his lumps in *Publishers Weekly,* the trade magazine covering the publishing industry—a magazine that enjoyed much Random

House advertising and that one reporter called "normally mild-man-
nered." John F. Baker, then editor in chief, wrote a signed editorial head-
lining the loss of Schiffrin as "A Sad Day for André Schiffrin—and for
Publishing." Vitale allegedly called Baker and threatened, implicitly at
least, to withdraw Random House advertising from *Publishers Weekly.*

The embarrassment of the outcry would have been bad enough for Si
Newhouse were it limited to the industry, but it was multiplied by intensive newspaper coverage, most of it sympathetic to Schiffrin's and
Pantheon's plight. During the worst of the fury, Si reportedly flew to
Europe, where he found himself vilified as well. "Quality does not seem to
be the preoccupation of S. I. Newhouse," opined *Le Monde.* A writer for the
Times Literary Supplement described the founding of Pantheon by refugees
from the Nazis who set up the firm "to preserve a culture that Hitler was
trying to destroy. Now Si Newhouse has accomplished what the Nazis
could not. Displeased with the sort of books Pantheon brought out, ...he
has forced the resignation of André Schiffrin and decreed that Pantheon
will continue in name only."

For Newhouse and Vitale, the most alarming moment of all occurred
when a couple of Random House's most prominent and profitable authors,
E. L. Doctorow and James Michener, expressed unhappiness over
Schiffrin's treatment. Some ten days after Schiffrin's exit, Doctorow took to
the stage at the National Book Critics Circle annual award ceremony—he
was receiving the fiction prize for *Billy Bathgate*—to label the firing of
Schiffrin an act of censorship. He charged that his publisher had "disfig-
ured itself" by "behead[ing]" Pantheon.

Shortly thereafter, James Michener, then eighty-three, one of the best-
selling authors in Random House's history, who published thirty-three books
with Random House since 1950, issued a press release lamenting that a
publisher "perhaps the finest in the English-speaking world has been humiliated in public by acts primarily of its own doing." He mentioned Bernstein's
forced resignation and his replacement by Vitale, "an able number-crunch-
er, but not a man reared in the traditions of American publishing." He
threatened to take his best-sellers elsewhere. "I will have to detach myself
and try to find some small house, obedient to the old traditions."

In a frantic attempt to persuade him not to bolt, Newhouse and Vitale
flew to Washington, where Michener was attending a NASA advisory board

meeting, and met with him for four hours in his hotel room. "Gentleman, all three of us are in real trouble, and we're meeting here to see what can be done about it," Michener said as they settled in. He expressed his fear that young writers didn't stand a chance in the super-heated atmosphere that publishing in the 1990s had become. Si responded by promising that Random House "would plow back some of the royalties they made on my books into the development of younger writers." Michener said he had no idea if the promise was kept.

Si did most of the talking, Michener recalled. "He was angry at having had this come up. And he was very conciliatory." On the other hand, Michener added, Newhouse "sounded like a real tough-minded statesman concluding a deal." As for the mostly silent Vitale, Michener later told a reporter for the *New York Times* that the Random House chairman was "more bookish than I anticipated."

André Schiffrin claims that Newhouse offered Michener a lot of money to stay, and he is joined in that opinion by a top former Random House executive. People who knew Michener say that to suggest he was bought off is preposterous, that Michener gave much of his money away. "This man has given away over $100 million," says his agent, Owen Laster, who did not attend the meeting. "Something like that would have offended him. It just couldn't possibly be so." Michener himself said that the subject of money never came up except that they acknowledged that they had made a lot of money off of him and acceded to his demand that it be "plowed back into the system."

The truth, according to Michener, was much stranger. Michener was intent on leaving Random House, and instructed his agent to find him another publisher. "I had two manuscripts finished at that time, and incredible as it seems, I could not give them away.... I had no recourse but to stay [at Random House]," which subsequently published the books, one a novel and one nonfiction, both concerned with problems in the publishing industry.

The exodus of Pantheon authors, although not as serious as the exodus of a Random House author like Michener, was also alarming. Studs Terkel, whose first book, *Division Street: America,* published in 1967, was Schiffrin's idea, and whose book *The Good War* won the Pulitzer in 1985, was first out the door. "The barbarians have taken over at Pantheon, and they might as well be producing a detergent," he told the *Wall Street Journal*'s Meg Cox. Barbara Ehrenreich and Anita Brookner left as well, as did the Schell brothers, Jonathan and Orville.

But nothing alarmed Newhouse and Vitale more than the possibility that Matt Groening, creator of *The Simpsons,* might leave Pantheon in the wake of the resignation of his editor, Wendy Wolf. His contract contained an "editor's clause" allowing him to leave Pantheon should Wolf leave. To lose Matt Groening, whose *Love is Hell* and other cartoon books had sold more than a million copies, was something neither Vitale nor Newhouse could allow, and the courting of Wendy Wolf commenced. Bruce Harris, executive vice president of Random House trade publishing, with whom, Wolf says, she had previously exchanged barely two words, was suddenly calling her, inviting her to his office to rave about the Simpson calendar art. While she was chatting with Harris, Vitale wandered in, supposedly by chance, and after a few preliminaries, asked her, "Don't you think that people should have to pay their own way? Can't you imagine a smaller, streamlined [list] published beautifully, every year? Wouldn't that be wonderful?" "Wouldn't that require a reduction in our staff?" Wolf responded. He replied, vaguely, "Well, we'd have to make arrangements, things would happen."

On receiving Wolf's letter of resignation, Vitale quickly summoned her to his office. She had no history with the chairman, but, like Bruce Harris, Vitale was suddenly extremely friendly, explaining that he wanted to get to know her. "I like to think it was because I was a charismatic and brilliant editor, but it was also, I expect, because I was attached to what was about to become the most profitable property in the face of American culture, which was *The Simpsons.*"

"I'm very sorry to see you associated with this," Vitale told her in a paternalistic tone, "and I'm choosing to put this piece of paper aside.... I'm choosing to not act on your resignation." He offered her a raise, a promotion, and the title of executive editor.

The next day Wolf stayed home, having had her fill of the tension and despair in the office. Her assistant fielded several calls from Vitale, who when he eventually reached Wolf, told her "Just incidentally, it seems Si

Newhouse has expressed an interest in meeting you." When she replied that she'd have to think about it, Vitale asked, "Are you refusing to see him?" She repeated that she wanted to think about it. The next morning she called Vitale to say she'd be happy to meet "Mr. Newhouse." She compared the opportunity to "getting an invitation to go see the Wizard of Oz. You have to act on this when you can."

Ten minutes later the phone rang: "Hi, Wendy, it's Si. You want to come over for a chat?" He inadvertently gave her the wrong address, but she knew that he was in the Condé Nast building, so she found him anyway. He met her in the reception area, dressed in a designer sweatshirt—she was wearing green sneakers and casual clothes—and led her into his office. "He came around to the front of the desk, and we sat on two chairs. He went and got me a cup of coffee." It was all very informal and awkwardly friendly, with the emphasis on the awkward.

"Well, so, we have a bit a trouble here," he observed. "Everybody thinks things are so terrible."

"Look, Mr. Newhouse," Wolf replied, "this place is so broken. You don't have any authors, you don't have any editors."

"Well, everybody said I was going to ruin the *New Yorker*. I'd kill the *New Yorker*, and look how well it's doing." In fact, as he spoke, Newhouse was growing increasingly impatient with the slow pace of change under the editorship of Bob Gottlieb. "We can't afford to keep...bleeding money," Si explained to Wolf. And then he made a comment that she found "chilling." "We've let things go on too long," he said, adding that he regretted that he hadn't acted sooner. She had the strong impression that he was referring to Bob Bernstein, not Schiffrin.

The mention of the *New Yorker* reminded her of Newhouse's treatment of William Shawn and caused Wolf to decide, "This is one of those rare opportunities you have in the world to just kind of give him a piece of my mind, so I said, 'Look, I just should tell you since it's your company, you should know, if this is Alberto Vitale's idea of good crisis management, he's really screwing up. This has not been handled with any kind of aplomb or diplomacy or management negotiating skills, whatever.' He said, 'Oh, that's very interesting, that's very interesting.'" After chatting a bit about Winsor McCay, whose cartoons on Si's office walls

Wolf recognized and appreciated, she gave him another dose: "I think I should tell you, since we obviously are never going to meet again, that people are very unhappy [at Random House], that the quality of life is deteriorating there." The Random House at which people could expect to work for life had gone the way of Bob Bernstein. "That's very interesting," he repeated.

Although he was the one who had asked to see her, because of his lack of "conversational skills," she found herself doing all the work, "carrying the conversation forward and bringing up topics of conversation, suggesting questions he might ask me next, and then at a certain point he kind of looked at me, and I said, 'Well I guess that's about it. I guess I should be going now.' And he said, 'I'm sorry we can't do anything for you.'" He walked her to the elevator. "Tell Steve hello for me," she said, referring to Steven Newhouse, whom she knew from sales conferences and liked.

When she returned to her office, Fred Jordan had already been briefed on the failure of Si's mission, and Jordan, who had also offered her a raise if she would stay, ordered Wolf, who had worked at Pantheon for fourteen years, out of the office for good by five that afternoon. (Soon thereafter Jordan flew to California to woo Groening, who at about the same time accepted a multibook offer from Rupert Murdoch's HarperCollins. Wolf was hired as a consultant to oversee the projects, and about six months later went to work at HarperCollins full time.)

Si and Vitale had their defenders, of course, and the jockeying to publicize those views began. Erroll McDonald, then executive editor of Random House's paperback arm, Vintage Books, and one of the few blacks in the higher ranks of trade publishing in New York, wrote an op-ed piece that appeared in the *New York Times* some three weeks after Schiffrin's ouster. McDonald described as "pathetic" Pantheon's "welfare mentality." He described Studs Terkel as a man "who would never dream of publishing a book at a financial loss to himself." He denounced the "sense of entitlement to the Newhouse family's 'bottomless' fortune [that] informed the protesters' argument. As they would have it, poor performance in the pursuit of their own cultural and political passions should be subsidized by philanthropy; anything less than an open-ended license to lose someone else's money with impunity constitutes 'censorship.'" Some saw the hand of corporate PR in the piece and didn't hide their contempt for McDonald, who, they felt, had allowed himself to be used.

Soon thereafter McDonald was named Pantheon's executive editor, the position Vitale had offered to Wendy Wolf. Ex-Pantheonites considered McDonald's new title as nothing more than payment for his *Times* op-ed piece. "Erroll got his job through the *New York Times*," was the mordant joke making the rounds.

A news release, said to be conceived and written by Jason Epstein, and signed by thirty-nine of his colleagues at the various Random House imprints, lambasted Pantheon's editors for lacking "fiscal responsibility" and for not being willing to live "by the same fiscal rules as the rest of us at Random House." (Among those who signed were Joni Evans, Bruce Harris, Erroll McDonald, and Sonny Mehta.) Epstein, who acted as a spokesman for the group, later told a reporter for the *Wall Street Journal,* "We all feel we have to earn a profit in order to earn the right to publish the books we want. Why on earth André Schiffrin doesn't understand that is beyond me."

The forty Newhouse defenders were, predictably, ridiculed as toadies. In his own press release James Michener denounced the statement, which was signed by his own editor, as "perhaps the strangest public announcement in the history of American publishing. It was as if Julius Caesar had proclaimed in Rome: 'My wife Calpurnia is still virtuous.' And Bennett Cerf...must have turned in his grave." Vitale would insist in a letter to the *Times Literary Supplement* that the release was "issued entirely on their [the editors'] own."

Several Random House editors took it upon themselves to carry the letter around and ask editors to sign it. To some it began to seem like a kind of loyalty oath. Former Knopf senior editor Gordon Lish—fired in 1994, after eighteen years at Knopf, but for other reasons—refused to sign, as did Victoria Wilson, whom one of her former colleagues at Knopf describes as "very able and ambitious and is way up there in the hierarchy." (Wilson discovered Anne Rice at a writer's conference and has been her editor ever since.) Some among the forty signers, maybe many, honestly believed that Schiffrin's ouster was long overdue; that it had, as one former head of a Random House imprint put it, "more to do with a dated sort of pride in being anticommercial."

After the first year Fred Jordan was given the empty title of chairman, and the running of the company was officially switched to Sonny Mehta, who had in fact been running it since Schiffrin's dismissal. Two editors at Knopf, both admirers of Schiffrin's, have great praise for the Pantheon of today. But they agree that its list is "indistinguishable" from Knopf's.

For Si Newhouse to watch Schiffrin's humiliation required a special kind of resolve or insensitivity. André and his wife, Elena, had been social friends of Si and Victoria. They went to dinner and the theater together. It was on that friendship that Schiffrin drew when, as things became particularly "brutal" with Vitale, he, in desperation, called Si. Si did not return the call. That did not stop Victoria from calling Elena Schiffrin, with whom she had been particularly close, and suggesting that they go to the theater together, as they had in the past, as if nothing had happened. Elena declined. Unlike Howard Kaminsky, Schiffrin would not forgive and forget for the sake of preserving the friendship.

Two months after Schiffrin's ouster, a Pantheon title, *And Their Children After Them*, edited by Susan Rabiner—at first the only senior editor not to quit, she later joined her colleagues— won the Pulitzer Prize in general nonfiction. Hearing the news, Rabiner exclaimed, "What a vindication!" The book's author noted that Pantheon was the only publisher that had made an offer for the book.[9]

In 1990 even more than the usual load of rumors had Joni Evans about to lose her job as head of Little Random. Although Random House had eighteen best-sellers in 1990, Evans had signed and agreed to large advances for several flops, including Shana Alexander's book about Bess Myerson, and surprisingly, given Si's role in romancing Donald Trump, she was also blamed for the poor sales of the second Trump book.

"I kept going to him and saying, 'Si, if you want to hire somebody else, please do that,'" Evans recalls, adding that she told Si that she would be delighted to run her own imprint, the job she thought she was taking when she moved to Random House from Simon & Schuster in 1987. "No, no, no, no, no, you're the best, you're the greatest," she recalls Si assuring her.

The stream of compliments had barely ebbed when Si telephoned Joni to report that he'd found the "right person" to replace her—Harry

Evans, then editor in chief of *Condé Nast Traveler*, not related to Joni Evans but the husband of Tina Brown.

Si had big plans for Tina, then editing *Vanity Fair*, who was herself the subject of endless rumors. Some had unnamed movie moguls enticing Tina to Hollywood to run a studio; others had her returning with Harry to England.

Evans himself had, inevitably, grown bored with the travel magazine—he had, after all, been editor of the *Times* of London and, during fourteen years as editor of the *Sunday Times* of London, he had presided over such investigations as the Kim Philby spy scandal and the thalidomide scandal in Germany. Harry had reportedly told Si that he wanted out of the *Traveler*. He had been approached by ABC to work on a project about the end of the twentieth century, and he was close to saying yes. Si was toying with the idea of buying the *London Observer* "in order to provide Harry with something to do," says one agent who knows them both. It took Si longer than one might expect to make the connection that were Harry to go to London, Tina might follow.

And so, instead of buying Harry the *Observer*, Si bestowed upon him, in 1990, Joni Evans's job, one of the most desirable in American book publishing, president and publisher of Random House Adult Trade Books—all, some said, to keep Tina from abandoning a magazine that had become so identified with her that Si feared it could not survive her absence. Answerable only to himself and his brother, Si Newhouse seemed to have made one of the most risky personnel decisions of his reign. Harry Evans's book publishing experience was limited to five not very successful months as editor in chief of Mort Zuckerman's Atlantic Monthly Press. Still, says one agent, everyone who knew Harry knew he was "a quick study." One former head of a Random House imprint calls Evans "a man of just almost breathtaking imagination and verve."

As charming and canny as Harry Evans could be, he could not hide, in those early days, how little he knew about the book publishing business. One longtime editor at Knopf describes Harry as "like a child with his hand in the cookie jar, all the sudden it was open and he was just going to get in as fast as possible."

Among Harry's early buys was Marlon Brando's autobiography, for which Evans paid a reported $5 million. *Brando: Songs My Mother Sang*

Me, published in 1994 to awful reviews and sales, was short on revelation and insight. It was estimated that the ghostwritten book earned Brando more than $10,000 a page.

Negotiations for fashion photographer Richard Avedon's autobiography had been ongoing for nearly a year when Harry arrived at Random House. Joni Evans had offered Avedon's agent, Andrew Wylie, $1.1 million. "And then Harry came in," says one former Random House editor, "and one of his first acts was to come to me one day and he said he was going to triple the offer. I said 'Why? You'll be bidding against yourself. The offer's been on the table.... Andrew Wylie doesn't have anybody else in town who's going to give him anywhere near that money.'" Harry ignored her advice, and Avedon ended up with $3 million.

One former Random House executive describes Harry Evans on his arrival as impossibly arrogant, "acted like he knew everything about publishing," even though, she insists, he learned nothing from his "two minutes" at Atlantic Monthly Press. But "in the last two years," Sandy MacGregor says, "he has learned a lot, very bright man, and he's actually publishing books.... He's doing really well." The former head of a Random House imprint calls Evans "one of the most talented men I've ever known." She praises his energy and describes him as a "genius" and a "visionary."

Si Newhouse may have adored Evans, but Alberto Vitale reportedly felt quite differently. One former Random House editor explains that "Alberto resented Harry's personal relationship with Si," the sort he coveted for himself. Nobody would ever say that Si "adored" Vitale; socially Si barely tolerated him. But, says one longtime business-side veteran of Random House, Vitale was shrewd enough to know that as long as Si wanted Tina, Vitale was stuck with Harry. And, says this man, so politically savvy was Vitale that he knew that his job was to "coach" Harry and help him learn the job. When the rumor mill churned out predictions of Harry's imminent demise, anyone who really knew the score knew that Harry's job was safe just so long as Tina's was safe, or until such time as another job could be found for Harry—preferably one with some grand-sounding responsibilities—that would allow him to save face.

And for a time Evans would be considered a success, if in one way only—in drawing Random House into the news and, to the irritation of many of his underlings, in drawing attention to himself. Si Newhouse would continue for a while longer to ignore Random House's dismal earnings.[10]

Joni Evans was in effect fired on Halloween, 1990, and most humiliatingly, on the front page of the *New York Times*. But Newhouse gave her a consolation prize—her own imprint, Turtle Bay Books, located in a rented brownstone on East Fifty-first Street in the Turtle Bay section of Manhattan. In addition to her brownstone, Joni got an enormous amount of freedom, a staff of young, smart, attractive women, and a promised five years to nurture her baby into the black. Evans and her editors assembled an impressive list that included A. S. Byatt, Ann Beattie, Geoffrey Wolff, Michael Caine, Joan Rivers, and Erica Jong.

But everything about Turtle Bay rubbed Vitale the wrong way. He didn't like Evans or her editors, or the informal, collegial atmosphere, sans job titles and bureaucracy. He also didn't like the media attention that the start-up attracted. Some date Vitale's antipathy toward Joni Evans to his time running Bantam Doubleday Dell, when Joni declined his invitation to run its trade division. Others say she was too pushy, too difficult, too outspoken, too much in the news—too much, really, like Harry Evans. Vitale knew that he could pick on Harry only so much; and so, in classic bully style, he targeted Joni.

It soon became clear to Joni Evans that Vitale not only had no intention of honoring Si's five-year commitment but that his only intention was to shut down Turtle Bay. One former editor stresses that Vitale could not have made such a decision without Si's approval. Si Newhouse, she and others say, planned all along to let Joni play around at Turtle Bay for a couple of years and then to padlock the door. Giving Joni Turtle Bay, they contend, defused what could have turned into a variation on the Schiffrin uproar.

During its two years of operation, Turtle Bay published twenty books and produced no national best-sellers. Not even autobiographies by Michael Caine, Carol Matthau, and Joan Rivers made the national lists. Turtle Bay was further weakened by its high overhead—the rent, the cost of renovation—and the fact it had no backlist to offset front-list disappointments.

Alberto Vitale, some contend, was secretly pleased—until, says one former Random House executive, "It began to look as if they were going to make money on *Great Good Food,* the Julee Rosso [coauthor of the "Silver Palate" books] cookbook.... And Alberto [realized] that if Turtle Bay ever started making money, he would never have a chance to end it. So I think he seized the moment."

Turtle Bay was two years old in November 1992 when Joni Evans had lunch with Vitale. "It's going to take a long time for this little company to be in the black," Vitale told her. "Yes, it'll take about another two years," she replied. "I don't think it's a good idea. Come back within Random House." From that moment, she says, she knew Turtle Bay was a goner.

She didn't go to Si to remind him of his promise of five years, she says, because she knew that Vitale couldn't have wielded the ax without Si's permission. After Turtle Bay's closing in 1993, the Rosso cookbook went to Crown, where, with sales of 400,000, it outsold any title Crown published that year. Joni Evans has remained cordial with Si, has written for *Vanity Fair,* and in her new position as a literary agent and senior vice president of the William Morris Agency, has done business with Random House. "I just won't be close to him, that's all.... I just can't stand this monstrous part. And I would never work for this monstrous part again, knowing that loyalty doesn't mean a thing. Just knowing his way of doing things just keeps me at a distance from him."

The shuttering of Turtle Bay lacked the political overtones of the Schiffrin ouster that excited the troops in Berkeley, California, and Madison, Wisconsin. But it did resonate in Manhattan—too much, some thought. One editor remarked to a reporter for *New York* magazine, "You'd think Madame Curie was being denied a few more years to discover the cure for cancer."[11]

Random House under Si Newhouse and his chairman, Alberto Vitale, was a company fundamentally changed from the one that Bennett Cerf and Bob Bernstein ran. The changes, masterminded by Newhouse and implemented by Vitale, have spread not only through the various Random House imprints but through New York publishing as a whole. Feeding frenzies in search of the next sure thing have become the order of the day.

Vitale, with Si's encouragement, paid whatever it took to sign up the big book, the almost surefire best-seller. Colin Powell received a $6.5 million advance for his memoir. Pope John Paul II's advance, estimated at between $6 and $9 million, for *Crossing the Threshold of Hope,* was big news everywhere, and Si Newhouse was surely delighted when the *New York Times* carried the story on page one. Negotiating indirectly on the pope's behalf was agent Mort Janklow, who didn't get the $10 million he sought but easily topped the take he negotiated for his client Nancy Reagan. On the fiction side, both Joan Collins and Michael Crichton received advances estimated at $4 million.

Although Si Newhouse achieved market and media domination at Random House, he lacked a healthy bottom line because he acquired books by authors so famous that they demanded multimillions. Earning back a seven-figure advance is difficult, no matter how many weeks a book lasts on the best-seller lists. Even Colin Powell's book, with its million-plus copies in print, is thought to have merely broken even. For it to have made money, Powell would have had to have run for president or vice president.

Still, the attention that Powell's memoir brought to Random House was worth a lot to Si. "Si would like to own every book on the best-seller list," one former Random House executive said in exasperation.

While gross sales increased—up to $1.2 billion in 1996, first by a long shot among trade book publishers, as opposed to $850 million when Bob Bernstein was fired in 1989—operating profits reportedly had not risen since 1990, when Harry Evans arrived. The *New York Observer*'s Celia McGee described Random House in 1996 as "awash in red ink."

One editor at Knopf who was bitterly disenchanted with the new regime lamented, "We probably take many, many, many more returns than we've ever taken because we overprint, overpromote, and overpay, so everything comes home to roost." In an article about the sharp increase in returns afflicting publishers nationwide, the *New York Times* reported in August 1996 that while Alberto Vitale admitted that "returns are higher than we would like them," the "gossipy industry is rife with talk about books coming back to the publisher by the truckload." President Bill Clinton's *Between Hope and History* turned into an embarrassing bomb, with 500,000 copies printed and as many as 375,000 returned. (Random

House did not pay Clinton an advance or royalties, somewhat lessening the pain, and the book has done well in China, where the president is considered a hero almost of the stature of Richard Nixon.)

Vitale himself told a reporter for *Business Week* in early 1997 that the company had won "the publishing war" with many best-sellers, but had lost "the business battle." In late 1997 Vitale admitted to a reporter for the *New Yorker* covering the dismal state of trade publishing in the United States, "I don't make any profit here," although in the next breath he claimed "single-digit profit margins" for Random House.

For the time being, Random House would continue its open checkbook policy on certain books. One Random House editor was bidding on a proposal about a subject who was controversial and would have dominated the news. "Once we dropped out of the auction," she recalls, "Alberto walked by me in the hall and said, 'Chicken shit.'" She protested that the price had gone so high it would have been next to impossible to make any money. "Don't drop out unless I tell you to," Vitale warned her.

Si's rivals came to realize that so long as he owned Random House, it would always win the bidding war for the high-profile title; there was no limit on the amount he would spend for a book he wanted. Roger W. Straus, founder and president of Farrar, Straus & Giroux, the equal, at least, of Knopf in literary reputation and prestige—its authors have won ten of the last eighteen Nobel Prizes for literature—said in an interview that whenever his company competed in an auction, it was almost always bidding against Random House, and it always lost.

Straus exacted a sort of revenge when he sold his company to the German Georg von Holtzbrinck Publishing Group. Si reportedly wanted to buy Farrar, Straus and felt confident that Straus, formerly his next-door neighbor on Seventieth Street, would eventually sell it to him. But Straus resisted—despite an offer from Newhouse that was pegged at several million dollars higher than Holtzbrinck's—fearing it would take about twenty minutes for Farrar, Straus & Giroux to lose its identity in Random House.

Straus, who remains president, told of receiving a call from Vitale just as the deal was closing. "Roger, you can't do this without talking to Si and me." "That's not the direction I want to go in," Straus replied. "Roger, you don't understand. We are so powerful, we can do anything we want."

Straus claimed that when he was sick with cancer, Si "had one of his hatchet men calling here every day to see if I was going to make it."

When in September 1996, six years after the uproar over Schiffrin's ouster, Random House announced a change in direction for its imprint Times Books, there was barely a murmur of disapproval. Times had enjoyed a classy image as a publisher of public affairs books, and—until its acquisition by Si Newhouse—as the book publishing arm of the *New York Times*. The house had always published crossword puzzle, business, health, and consumer reference books, but they had resided in the background. No more. Their numbers would be increased, and they would be expected to turn the imprint into what Alberto Vitale called "a profit center." That Donald Trump's third book was published under the Times imprint—his first two were from Random House—may be seen as a dumbing down of the public policy side of the list.

Even Knopf, which combined profit and prestige as no other house could, found its grand image and mission altered. (Its founder, Alfred A. Knopf, once said, "I think that best-sellers should be abolished by law.") To some at Knopf it seemed sadly predictable when Simon & Schuster dropped Bret Easton Ellis's hyperviolent novel *American Psycho* and Sonny Mehta at Knopf, of all publishers, bought it and published it. But that was Mehta's way. The news that Sonny had signed Oprah Winfrey to write her memoir generated particular bitterness. One Knopf editor remembered an editorial meeting earlier on the same day the acquisition was announced. "One of the editors said, 'There's this wild rumor that we're going to publish Oprah Winfrey.' And Sonny, with a straight face, said, 'Well, it's a rumor.' And about two hours later there was a release in our mailboxes saying we had acquired it." (When it was announced, three months before scheduled publication, that Oprah had withdrawn her manuscript, applause and cheers erupted in various offices at Knopf.)

Although there had always been some competition between Random House imprints—especially Little Random and Knopf—Vitale encouraged cutthroat competition of the sort that previously existed between Random House and Simon & Schuster. The collegiality that in pre–Vitale and Newhouse days might have seen an editor at Knopf and his colleague at Random House decide which of the two would bid for a particular book was not the style of the Random House of the 1990s. The competition caused the characters of the various lists to flatten out until "in places," says one former Knopf editor, "we're indistinguishable from each other now."

While Si and Vitale encouraged competition between Harry Evans and Sonny Mehta, there was even competition within the Random House imprint itself. About a year before the O. J. Simpson trial ended, Random House signed, for a reported mid-six-figure advance, Jeffrey Toobin, who had covered the trial for the *New Yorker*, to write a book on the case. Toobin and his agent, Esther Newberg, were reportedly furious to learn that Harry Evans had signed another O. J. book, to be published shortly after Toobin's. The second book was by the controversial Larry Schiller, working with *Time* reporter James Willwerth. Schiller did his reputation, already checkered by a history of paying sources for information, no good by collaborating with Simpson on *I Want to Tell You*, his jailhouse claim of innocence.

At one point Esther Newberg, who had been promised that the Schiller book would appear on a later list, threatened to take Toobin to another publisher, to sue Random House, or to pledge never to bring another writer to Random House. When Newberg was asked if there were any similarities between the Schiller and Toobin books, she snapped, "They're both made out of paper."

Although both books made the best-seller list, the Schiller book, to the surprise of many because of its author's sleazy image, received strong reviews, at least a couple of which advised the reader, in effect, "If you're going to read one O. J. book, this should be it." Toobin must have had mixed feelings about his publisher when Schiller's book made the *Wall Street Journal*'s list, while his own book, published a month before, fell off. (Likewise, the second week of November 1996, Schiller's book held the number-one nonfiction spot at the *New York Times*; Toobin's book was off the list.) Had the people at Random House not broken their promise to Toobin, his book likely would have remained on the best-seller list for several weeks longer and would have sold another 25,000 copies or so.

Nearly as unhappy as Toobin was O. J.'s lead lawyer, Johnnie L. Cochran Jr., who had signed for an advance reported at $3.5 million with the Random House imprint of Ballantine and who, like Toobin, tried unsuccessfully to squash Schiller's book. Cochran, whose book, *Journey to Justice,* was published a couple of weeks after Schiller's and didn't do very well—50 percent of its initial print run was returned—would have preferred not to have faced competition within his own publishing house, and even worse, the Schiller book, which incidentally also lost money, contained derogatory information about Cochran. These writers would have been happier with a more conventional situation, in which a publisher did not force its own authors—and editors—to compete with one another for a limited amount of advertising, for promotion money, and for review and talk show attention.[12]

It was an odd way to do business, but under Si Newhouse, it had become the way.

20 | Bucking the IRS

IF THE NEWHOUSE FAMILY was unlikely to ever make the record books for editorial quality or daring, it would take first place in the annals of American business for generating what remains the largest estate tax dispute ever to reach the U.S. Tax Court.

In 1976, three years before the death of the senior S. I. Newhouse, a *Business Week* cover story on father and sons tried to explain the complex web that Sam and his accountant and lawyer wove in order to shrink Sam's tax bill. The reporter explained that Newhouse "spread ownership" among his properties, creating "a corporate labyrinth" in which the paper in Staten Island owned the paper on Long Island, which in turn owned the papers in Syracuse, which in turn owned those in Portland, which owned Jersey City and Newark. Newark owned Springfield, which owned Harrisburg. The Harrisburg company owned not only the *Cleveland Plain Dealer,* but also Condé Nast, and Condé Nast in turn owned part of the papers in Mobile, Alabama. The purpose was to keep surplus cash and thus Sam's tax liability down as low as possible. If a cash-poor company needed a new press, it borrowed from its parent company, which was by design cash rich. And so it went, an IRS agent's nightmare.

One person who worked for the Newhouse National News Service in Washington and has studied the company closely says simply that he always "regarded the Newhouse organization as a tax-avoiding device." He mentions a former bureau chief there telling him that all bureau expenses were billed to the individual newspapers, based not, in the usual way, on its circulation, but on the paper's profitability. The more profitable the paper, the more it paid.

331

The sons carried on the tradition, painstakingly guarding their books from the eyes of any Washington bureaucrat. In 1983 George Rosato, then running the school division at Random House, came to Si Newhouse with a request to spend $14 million for a computer company in California. As usual, Si was ready to give the go-ahead until he learned that the company had a contract with the U.S. Army and, says Rosato, "the contract would enable the Feds to get into Si's books." Si said no. Dick Snyder at Simon & Schuster later bought the company for $160 million.

When the Internal Revenue Service examined the estate tax return that Si and Donald, their father's executors, filed in May 1980, some nine months after Sam's death, agents decided the return deserved further scrutiny. That form valued Sam Newhouse's gross adjusted estate at $181.9 million. It valued Sam's common stock at $178.8 million and computed inheritance taxes due at just under $48.7 million. In May 1983 the IRS issued a notice of deficiency, informing the sons that their numbers were far too low. The IRS valued Sam's common stock at $1.2 billion and computed the tax bill at very close to $1 billion—$609 million in estate taxes, rather than $48 million, plus interest, plus a $305 million civil fraud penalty for so egregiously undervaluing Sam's holdings. The government charged that this was not an instance of innocent error or honest difference of interpretation, but rather a deliberate attempt to underpay.

Si and Donald did not put a check in the mail. In August 1983 the Newhouses' lawyers filed a petition with the U.S. Tax Court, characterizing the fraud charge as "preposterous"—an attempt to embarrass the Newhouses publicly so that they would pay taxes they did not owe.

A reporter for the *New York Times* described just how high the stakes were for Si and Donald: "Some industry experts think part of the Newhouse operations might have to be sold or that the company might have to make a public stock offering to raise the money if the government wins its case."

Those who didn't like the Newhouses, or their impact on magazines and newspapers, exulted at the family's woes. Writing in the *Village Voice*, Richard Pollak speculated that were the IRS to win the case, the brothers Newhouse might be forced to take the company public in order to generate enough cash. Doing so would not only force them to contend with pesky directors and shareholders, it would also open their books to examination by the SEC and other Washington busybodies. Pollak suggested that, alternatively, the Newhouses could raise cash by selling off properties—holding "media tag sales periodically, inviting their fellow barons to stop by and pick through the merchandise."

Though the Newhouse numbers and the IRS numbers had little in common, talk of a settlement was in the air. Most analysts predicted an out-of-court settlement—especially once the government retreated by dropping, in December 1986, the $305 million penalty for civil fraud, demanding "only" the $609 million plus interest.[1]

There was no settlement, and in January 1989 the Newhouses and the IRS met at trial in U.S. Tax Court in Washington. The presiding judge was B. John Williams Jr., who before his appointment to the tax court by Ronald Reagan in 1985 had worked for the IRS as special assistant to the chief counsel and for the Justice Department as deputy assistant attorney general, tax division. For a year before going on the bench, he had been a partner in the Washington office of the Philadelphia-based law firm Morgan, Lewis and Bockius.

Representing the government was IRS special trial attorney Robert J. Shilliday Jr., who contended that the Newhouses had tried to lower the estate tax bill by undervaluing the common stock—the voting stock—that Sam owned when he died. Other family members, Shilliday charged, owned preferred stock that not only had no voting rights but didn't even give its holders the right to look at the company's books. The Newhouses' numbers hinged on placing the same value on the common as on the preferred stock, whereas the IRS argued that the common stock was worth roughly seven times as much as the preferred. Shilliday maintained that until the patriarch's death, he controlled most of the empire's holdings because he held the only voting stock. Thus the estate tax bill should be for virtually the full value of the company, rather than the 22.2 percent that the sons' accountants used in arriving at the $48.7 million owed.

The Newhouses' chief trial lawyer, Albert H. Turkus, then of the Washington firm, Dow, Lohnes and Albertson, countered that while Sam Newhouse did indeed control the voting stock, he, his brothers Norman and Ted, and his sons Si and Donald were equal partners in running the company, making all decisions together in meetings or on the telephone.

Their stock, therefore, was equal in value to Sam's stock, and so they had properly computed the taxes on the 22.2 percent controlled by Sam.

Donald Newhouse, the first witness called, described the five men getting together, with none of them "dominating the discussions." A person who was there described Donald as "very forthright and strong-voiced, assertive, and confident of what he was saying." Si, who followed his brother to the stand, was just the opposite. He was predictably inarticulate, especially when pressed about how this consensus was reached among the father, with his voting stock, and the brothers and sons, with their nonvoting stock. "To put a formula on it almost destroys the concept," Si explained. "It is a very delicate concept. It depends on the tight working relationship and the good will that prevails among all of us.... It's a subtle process." When pressed about how a specific decision—to buy the Booth newspaper chain—was made, Si stumbled and finally gave up. "Well, it's a little like trying to describe love."

Si did describe the "five partners" as working "like demons," too busy to consider rank. He insisted that he could not remember his father ever "dictating business decisions. It was totally out of his nature."

It was surprising to the very few reporters who attended the trial—newspaper attention was sparse—how little Si and Donald knew about the company's numbers, a fact that would have seemed to support the government's contention that Sam called the shots. Si testified that he first learned in the early 1950s—when he was in his mid-twenties—that he owned stock in the company and that there were two classes of stock. The information came not from his father but from reading descriptions "in *Time* and some of the other magazines." He apparently didn't share this news with his brother, who testified that it was the mid-1960s before he learned that there were ten voting shares in the company and that his father owned all of them. Donald also testified that it wasn't until his father handed him a dividend check that he discovered he owned stock.

The second biggest surprise of the trial was the appearance, for the Newhouse side, of Rupert Murdoch. Murdoch and Si Newhouse, four years apart in age, were competitors, not close personally or professionally, circling each other warily and occasionally poaching each other's employees. They were very different in style, with Si attending to the tiniest detail of his magazines and approving clothing allowances that ran into the tens of thousands of dollars, while Murdoch took huge risks, scooping up potentially bankrupting satellite systems and running everything on the cheap. Still, they were sufficiently similarly situated that Murdoch presumably testified out of a kind of professional courtesy—one media mogul helping another—and self-interest, because he could easily imagine his heirs facing the same problem.

Murdoch insisted that the common stock on which the IRS was placing so high a value had, in the real world, little value. For all its voting rights, he explained, it didn't give its holder the right to sell the company, and so owning it would translate into a minority stake without any likely prospect of being able to take over the company. For him, Murdoch said, buying the common stock would be next to worthless because "we are not interested in buying minority stock in companies unless there is some strategic purpose, and one can see it as a stage to buying the whole of the company."

To some sitting in the courtroom, Judge Williams seemed obviously sympathetic to the Newhouses' position and openly hostile to the government's. He tore especially hard into two of the government's expert witnesses, both leaders in their fields—one a consultant to newspapers, the other to magazines.

James Kobak, a highly experienced and regarded magazine consultant and CPA, told Alison Frankel for an article she wrote on the trial for *American Lawyer* that he testified on behalf of the IRS because he thought the government was right. "We know who owned that company.... That was a trick [Sam] pulled." According to Kobak's reckoning, the fair market value of the Newhouse empire was $2.1 billion, nearly twice as much as the IRS's $1.2 billion. Unfortunately for IRS lawyer Shilliday, on cross-examination Kobak admitted to having made a $39 million error in his valuation of *Vogue*. "I will entertain a motion to strike this report and his testimony from evidence," Judge Williams said. The motion was forthcoming, and the evidence was struck. Kobak calls the $39 million number a "small error" in a 150-page report. "I could find a mistake the other way probably if I wanted to. This was just something for the judge to jump on. I don't think it was planned, but he found a way to get rid of all the experts that way."

"Is Mr. Morton going to be a little more credible than Mr. Kobak?" the judge asked as a second expert, John Morton, veteran newspaper analyst at Lynch, Jones and Ryan, took the stand. During his career, Morton had done some work for the Newhouses but then was on the other side, having been hired by the government to assign a value to the Newhouse newspaper properties. Morton, a longtime columnist for the *American Journalism Review,* has carved such a deep niche as the expert on the industry that his opinions and assessments appear in virtually every story about the sale or acquisition of newspapers and the general health of the industry.

Before long, Judge Williams lost patience with Morton. The judge blasted him both for making a mistake in evaluating the estate and for offering his own conclusion that the arguments made by the IRS's lawyers were the correct ones: "He is wrong on two counts. I am going to strike his whole report. His entire report is stricken! As a businessperson, that he would make a decision as to who's right and who's wrong among prominent and eminent legal experts, ...it is absolutely incredible to me that he could make that judgment."

Judge Williams blamed Shilliday for the alleged shortcomings of his expert witnesses. "[Mr. Shilliday], your lack of understanding in this case is exceeded only by your lack of preparation.... This is the worst performance I have seen on the bench—and for you to bring the [IRS] commissioner's case into here with this kind of testimony is absolutely beyond the bounds of reason."

That Shilliday made mistakes is beyond dispute. One of the most puzzling was his identification of Richard Meeker—a potentially promising witness for the government—as a former friend or associate of Sam's. Meeker, whose biography of Sam Newhouse was published in 1983, was decades younger than Sam, and the family despised the unauthorized book and withheld all cooperation from its author. On receiving a tongue-lashing from Judge Williams for that mistake, Shilliday instantly offered to drop Meeker as a witness.

John Morton and James Kobak were far more disheartened by Judge Williams's performance than they were by Shilliday's. "I found him to be very volatile for a judge," says Morton. "He calmed down some when some other tax court judges were sitting in the back, but when they left, off he went.... He tended to shout and pound and stuff like that. I've never seen a judge act like that before." By the time he testified, James Kobak remembers, Judge Williams "had been beating on [Shilliday] for six weeks, every single day apparently, and he was out of his head.... Every time he opened his mouth, while I was there at least, the judge would jump him, and so he wouldn't open his mouth. And a lot of the questions he should have asked me before the cross-examination, he never asked. You rehearse these things. It isn't as if you go in there spontaneously. He was useless."

In contrast, says Morton, Judge Williams never said a "cross word" to the Newhouses' lawyer. Kobak describes Judge Williams's tone in handling Albert Turkus as "like talking to your favorite son." "[Yours] was one of the best courtroom performances I've ever seen. It was really good."

The trial lasted seven weeks, and the transcript consumed twenty volumes.[2]

On February 28, 1990, Judge Williams issued his sixty-one-page opinion: a total victory for the Newhouses. Had they or their accountants and lawyers written the opinion, it could not have been more favorable. The judge estimated the value of Sam Newhouse's common stock at $176 million. Si and Donald would end up paying the $48.7 million the estate had declared in the first place a full decade earlier.

The crux of the judge's opinion was that just because the IRS believed that Sam Newhouse and his common stock absolutely controlled Advance meant neither that actual, as opposed to theoretical, buyers would agree, nor that they would accept the IRS's method of valuing the common stock. Judge Williams completely accepted the assertion that, while Sam was alive, the company was run by consensus. "Throughout Advance's history," he wrote, "all major decisions were reached by unanimous agreement after discussion in which all partook."

Anyone who spent any time in the courtroom could have predicted the judge's opinion. But what most caught their attention was the announcement—which preceded his filing of the opinion by three weeks—that Judge Williams, then only forty years old, was resigning from the tax court because, he said, "Although I had intended to devote my career to serving as a judge, my present circumstances would require my family to sacrifice their financial security to permit me to continue in my position." He returned as a partner to the Washington office of his old firm, Morgan, Lewis and Bockius.

A higher-up at the IRS observed that the proximity of the judge's resignation and the issuance of his opinion is "interesting." John Morton recalls plenty of speculation that Judge Williams or his firm, which doubled in size between the mid-1980s and mid-1990s to become the nation's fourth largest law firm, must have been promised some Newhouse business.

But nobody has produced a shred of evidence that there was any quid pro quo. In fact, one reporter who sporadically covered the case said that the chief clerk at the tax court had mentioned to him, when the case was first assigned to Judge Williams, that he is very tough on the IRS. Since that verdict, the judge's opinion has come to be respected by tax lawyers, and is often cited in comparable cases.

Coverage in the Newhouse newspapers of the estate's tax problems and the trial was sparse, to say the least. (Major papers such as the *New York Times* did cover it, but with brief reporting and little analysis or follow-up.) James P. Roper, who was then working part-time for the Newhouse Washington bureau and who had the tax court as part of his beat, covered the story carefully, as a freelance, for the industry trade magazine, *Editor & Publisher*. Roper requested permission to cover it for the Newhouse service as well, but the day before the trial was to begin, he was told by the bureau chief, who had his orders from above, that permission had been denied.

Richard Pollak, a persistent critic of the Newhouses, observed in 1985, as the case wended its way to trial, that the press "once again affirmed A. J. Liebling's dictum that 'newspapers write about other newspapers with circumspection.' Most dailies simply ignored the story when the court documents became available in the fall of 1983, and have done so since. A handful noted the case in a few paragraphs at the time, but not even the *Wall Street Journal* came back to it." Pollak complained that the few papers that did follow the case "seemed more in awe of the fortune Sam Newhouse had accumulated than in the implications of the whopping tax hustle the government alleges." Still, Pollak predicted—wrongly, as it turns out—that once the case went to trial it would be "the talk of the town."[3]

In using that phrase, Pollak was surely reminding his readers that had the Newhouses paid what the IRS claimed was their fair share of taxes, they might not have been able to afford to buy the *New Yorker*. Those who believe that the Newhouses pulled a huge and fast one will have to await the deaths of Si and Donald. Then, some say, the government will get its due and more.

21 | The Collector

SI NEWHOUSE BOUGHT Jasper Johns's painting, *False Start*, for $17 million in 1988, at the top of an overheated art market. Its history says something both about Si and about the contemporary art scene in America during the last half century.

The painting, an oil on canvas that measured approximately six feet by four and a half feet, was completed in 1959. In his book on Jasper Johns, Michael Crichton described it as a departure from Johns's earlier calm and dignified work; "explosive" and full of "riotous" color, "it seems to be blowing itself apart, in a kind of pyrotechnic display."

In 1960 Johns's dealer, Leo Castelli, had sold *False Start* for $3,150 to collector Robert Scull, who had made his money in the taxicab business. Scull, who with his wife, Ethel, would become one of the preeminent collectors of pop art in the 1960s, later sold *False Start* for somewhere in the six-figure range to François de Menil, the son of John and Dominique de Menil, heirs to the Schlumberger oil fortune. De Menil later consigned it to Sotheby's. Castelli figured, given the booming market, that the painting might sell for as much as $10 million, although it had been estimated to fetch "only" $8 to $9 million. Castelli, then eighty-two, had seen a lot since he opened his first gallery in Paris in 1939, but nothing like the scene in the main auction room at Sotheby's in Manhattan that November day in 1988.

Representing Si was Larry Gagosian, a young, brash, ruthless art dealer—"an ego the size of the Empire State Building," says one acquaintance. A Los Angeles native who started with a poster shop in Westwood Village, he left L.A. for New York with, at best, a mixed reputation. Writing in the *New Yorker*, critic Anthony Haden-Guest described Gagosian's "uncanny eye for art," but mentioned also that he is "surrounded by a shimmer of rumors of financial brinkmanship."

If Leo Castelli was an old-world gentleman, the soul of discretion and integrity, Gagosian, slick in his Comme des Garcons suit and vulgar in his language, had an image that was close to the opposite. But Si slowly switched his allegiance from Castelli to Gagosian, who had opened a gallery in New York in 1985.

One person who knows both men well says that Si was drawn to Gagosian in the same way that he was to Roy Cohn; and, further, that "Gagosian is a creature of Si's"—a kind of wholly supported subsidiary. At the start Gagosian was selling art both for Si and to Si—in the latter category, for example, a $10 million Mondrian called *Victory Boogie-Woogie*.* Then, after a reported disagreement, Si began using Sotheby's for sales and Gagosian for acquisitions.

Still, Gagosian played a role beyond that of the typical art dealer for Newhouse and other wealthy clients. "People tell [Gagosian] what they want and then he goes and finds it," says a reporter for the *Wall Street Journal* who followed the art scene. "He knows what's in whose collection and he calls up, 'I might be able to get Si Newhouse, I might be able to get X million for your this or that if you were interested in selling it.'"

Battling for *False Start* against Newhouse, who was with Gagosian in the auction room (earlier that evening Si bought Robert Rauschenberg's *Winter Pool* for $3.74 million), was Charles Saatchi. With his brother, he then controlled the biggest advertising agency in the world. Saatchi was bidding by telephone. Also bidding by phone was Hans Thulin, a real estate speculator from Stockholm and vintage automobile collector. The night before, at Christie's contemporary art auction, Thulin had paid $7 million for Johns's *White Flag*.

The bidding started at $3 million and went up quickly to $9 million. Saatchi dropped out at $10 million. When it resumed, it was Newhouse

---

*In late 1998, Si sold *Victory Boogie-Woogie* to the Dutch government for $40 million creating an uproar in Holland and triggering an investigation into whether taxpayers' money had been used "prudently." The Dutch Central Bank donated the money to buy the painting for the Hague Municipal Museum.

against Thulin, who, Leo Castelli says, couldn't afford the price but kept bidding. A slight bob of Si's head or "small gesture with his left hand," recalled Haden-Guest, gave Gagosian permission to make a quarter-of-a-million leap. Thulin dropped out after he realized that Si would not stop until the painting was his.

In victory, Si's expression remained impassive except for the start of a smile on his full lips. When Castelli telephoned Jasper Johns with the news that his painting had sold for $17 million, Johns exclaimed, "Good grief."[1]

Si never seemed satisfied with the art he acquired. He began collecting paintings of the color field artists—Barnett Newman, Morris Louis, Kenneth Noland. But then he seemed to lose interest in them and turned to abstract expressionists, pop artists, and others such as Robert Rauschenberg, Jasper Johns, Cy Twombly, Frank Stella, Roy Lichtenstein, Andy Warhol, Willem de Kooning, Franz Kline, Claes Oldenburg, and James Rosenquist. From there his eye caught the minimalist artists and then the postminimalists and some of the conceptualists. Si is a restless collector whose wealth has allowed him to follow his impulses.

Annalee Newman, the widow of Barnett Newman, who died in 1970, was close to Si and Victoria after her husband's death, but she was distraught over Si's decision to sell her husband's work. She was especially upset, as Alex Liberman's biographers Dodie Kazanjian and Calvin Tomkins report, when Si "sold Newman's magisterial *Chartres,* one of three rare triangular canvases, for a reported $3 million in 1990." Newman had been "reluctant to sell his paintings to people he did not know and trust." He explained that he sold to Si because he was "so passionate about my painting, I can't refuse him anything."

"Nobody knows exactly why at one point he gets tired of a certain number of artists that form a coherent group," says Leo Castelli, "and then goes on to another group, which again forms a coherent group." Castelli speculates that Si simply "doesn't get attached once he has acquired something that he wants very badly.... In the end he seems to lose interest." Castelli compares Si to a man who is passionate in his conquest of a woman, only to find his ardor waning once he has physically and emotionally possessed her.

In the early 1990s, at the bottom of the market, Si started to sell what Leo Castelli calls "some very good paintings." Among the gems that he has put on the block, says Castelli, is a "very important" Jasper Johns, one of the artist's largest, called *According to What?* (Finished in 1964, it measures more than seven by sixteen feet.) Si was likewise selling or planning to sell two very good Jackson Pollocks, some good early Rauschenbergs, some Lichtensteins, and some—according to Castelli—"very important" Andy Warhols.

(Si owned several Warhols, including the large *Marilyn*, which he had placed so that it faced his bed. In 1998, at another Sotheby's auction, Si paid $17.3 million—$300,000 more than he had paid for the Johns painting ten years before—for still another Warhol rendition of the movie star, this one called *Orange Marilyn*, completed in 1964, 40 by 40 inches, synthetic polymer and silkscreen ink on canvas. There are reportedly five Marilyns at precisely that size, the only difference among them the background color. It was the highest price ever paid for a Warhol, multimillions beyond the auction house's estimated take of $4 to 6 million. Si battled Las Vegas casino and resort magnate Steve Wynn in a telephone bidding war that ended when Wynn issued his final bid of $15.5 million.)

As Castelli was readying a Jasper Johns show in celebration of the artist's thirty-fifth-year showing at Castelli's gallery, Si told the dealer that he wanted to buy a particular Johns. "So I said, 'You're selling others that are just as good or better.' So he said, 'Well, I just want to buy the painting.' On this occasion I asked him, 'Why do you sell so many good paintings that you have?' 'Well,' he said, 'I can't say that I get tired of them, but I want to go on to new things.'" The Johns that Si wanted to buy, a large painting, was, says Castelli, obviously newer in date, but "it was not, I think, as good as the ones that he was selling."[2]

At about the time that Si was spending record sums on the Johns, he became interested in a smaller painting by Roy Lichtenstein, *Black Flowers*. The painting was then owned by Chicago architect Walter Netsch.

Starting in the 1950s, Netsch, then working in Chicago for Skidmore, Owings and Merrill, made regular trips to New York, where, holding himself to a strict budget, he bought art. He was said to have a wonderful eye, and one day in 1962 he was browsing in Leo Castelli's gallery when he saw a black-and-white painting by Roy Lichtenstein, then having his first show. Netsch guesses he was not an "impressive" enough looking person for Castelli to handle himself. He was turned over to Castelli's assistant, who sold Netsch *Black Flowers,* which Lichtenstein had completed that year, for $600.

Netsch derived far more than $600 worth of pleasure from the painting, which was eventually displayed prominently in the ultramodern home he designed himself and shared with his wife, Dawn Clark Netsch, a state senator with ambitions to be governor of Illinois.

In 1988 Dawn Netsch decided to run for state comptroller. She needed money for her campaign, and Netsch wanted to help her. So he listened when, one day that year, he received a call from a stranger who told him, quietly and politely, "I am a dealer in New York, and I'm offering for a client $2 million for the Lichtenstein.... You'll have three weeks to make up your mind because he has another painting in mind also.... And my name's Gagosian." (The painting had just been valued at $600,000 for insurance purposes.)

It was the height of the art boom, but Netsch was still floored by the offer. He quickly called a dealer in Chicago, who advised him, when told of Gagosian's involvement, "Get the check first."

Netsch told Gagosian that he might be interested in selling the painting. Gagosian said that his client, Si Newhouse, would come to Chicago to see the painting in person. Accompanied by Gagosian, Si arrived in a long white Cadillac at Netsch's house in the Old Town neighborhood of Chicago, an arty enclave that over the years has been home to many of the city's artists and writers. The collector sat in a chair, stared in silence at the painting for fifteen minutes, stood up, walked closer to it, shook Netsch's hand, and left.

He made no small talk and insulted Netsch by ignoring the other art that filled the soaring expanses and angles of a house that one reporter described as "sort of an art museum with bedrooms." (Netsch earlier designed the chapel at the U.S. Air Force Academy in Colorado Springs, and the influences are obvious.)

Gagosian called almost immediately to say that Si would buy the painting for $2 million. Netsch let it go with mixed feelings. "We held that painting for twenty-odd years," he says. "We don't sell paintings. We don't deal paintings. And I assumed it was going to another loving home, and then I heard it was in [Newhouse's] office. So I said to Dawn, 'Well, a lot of people are going to look at it.'"

In the meantime, Netsch gave his wife a large chunk to help finance her successful race for state comptroller. In 1994 he gave her nearly another million to help finance a winning gubernatorial primary campaign for governor. (She lost in the general election.)

That year, 1994, Netsch was at Sotheby's in New York talking to some friends. Suddenly, across the room, he saw *Black Flowers*. He was stunned. When the art market turned from boom to bust in 1990, Netsch figured that *Black Flowers* had lost 40 percent of its value. But there it was, uncrated in preparation for going on auction. It was estimated that it would sell for between $1.8 and $2.5 million.

At that auction, *Black Flowers* was accompanied to the block by two other pieces that Si Newhouse was selling—a 1983 untitled Jasper Johns that sold just under its low estimate, and a Claes Oldenburg wall relief that sold somewhat above its high estimate. As for the Netschs' beloved *Black Flowers*, according to Carol Vogel, writing in the *New York Times*, "There was barely a bid in the room, and no one was willing to go higher than $1.3 million." The *New York Post* illustrated its report on the auction with a photo of the painting, a "No Sale" banner superimposed on its top right corner.[3]

To Si Newhouse, these failures in the marketplace were somewhat embarrassing. The people whose opinions he valued read the *New York Times* and the *Wall Street Journal*, both of which covered the Sotheby's and Christies auctions closely, with lively reporting that featured a clear demarcation of the winners and losers. But in the end, Newhouse knew his properties would find a buyer. One thing was certain: the money simply didn't matter, which led people who followed the art market to the obvious next question.

Many wondered why Newhouse didn't give his collection of a particular artist or a school of painting to a museum—he was, after all, a Museum of Modern Art trustee—rather than sell it piecemeal and much of it at so great a loss. Why break up a collection that had taken such skill, energy, taste, money, connections, and influence to assemble? The answer is that this particular collector seems to lack that philanthropic bent without which museums would have to close their doors.

Leo Castelli sounds puzzled and disappointed as he compares Si Newhouse to other collectors who plan all along to donate their collections to museums. "Since [Si] has really any amount of money available, what he should have done is just set those paintings aside and then at one point given them to a museum."

Si seems willing to give art to a museum only when he has no choice, or when he has a strong desire to help an artist whom the museum might not otherwise have acquired. (He has, for example, given Alex Libermans to the Museum of Modern Art.) Castelli mentions "a wonderful large Lichtenstein" that Si was allowed to buy on the condition—imposed by the artist—that he give it to MoMA, where it now resides.

Si also differs from other collectors in his reluctance even to loan to museums, a regular and sacred practice of many serious collectors. (Walter Netsch, for instance, says that loaning paintings is a kind of civic responsibility to both the public and the artist.) Unless pushed and pushed hard, Newhouse simply refuses. A publisher of one of the Newhouse newspapers, then on Si's route, had to do just that with his boss until Si agreed to loan a Lichtenstein to an exhibit of the artist's work being organized by the local art museum.

A newer group of artists soon came to occupy Si's eye and ear— Eric Fischl, David Salle, Jeff Koons. Si owns one of Koons's stainless-steel rabbits. Referring to the prominent display Si gives to Koons's rabbit, an old friend says that one would not even have to ask if Si collected Koons. "I really think anybody who has been trendy, he usually has one of."[4]

Si's house, which had been his passion, lost his interest as well, and so the responsibility of overseeing it fell to Victoria. She hired a house manager but still hated the responsibility, even if it was only to make certain that the woman she hired was doing the job. The strained relationship with the house's designer, Richard Penney, had ended once Si retained other architects and designers to make changes. Even so, Penney would receive frequent phone calls from an agitated Victoria: "Victoria would call me in great angst trying to figure out why something was done the way it was so it could be repaired."

Looming largest was the problem of security. Si had always been concerned with trying to keep his home looking discreet, so as not to attract attention. But there were plenty of people who knew that a multibillionaire art collector lived there, and the number was growing. Husband and wife worried about break-ins.

According to Geraldine Stutz, who lived across Seventieth Street, the Newhouses were burgled twice; once while they were having dinner downstairs, and a second time "when they were away and came back and there was the place in shatters." They finally hired a twenty-four-hour-a-day guard who was stationed outside and another to live in the house, an arrangement that Victoria hated because it compromised her privacy. In 1988 the house underwent a major remodeling, including an upgrade of its security system.

While the work was under way, Si and Victoria moved into an apartment in United Nations Plaza, a large (some 240 apartments), impersonal, two-tower co-op, located at the corner of First Avenue and Forty-ninth Street. The buildings, which became known for strict attention to security—delivery people are not allowed beyond the back door; all deliveries are made by members of the house staff—are full of famous residents who feel they can live there anonymously and safely. (Residents have included Truman Capote, Robert Kennedy, Katharine Graham, Walter Cronkite, Mary Lasker, Johnny Carson, Gloria Vanderbilt, and Gordon Parks.)

Once settled in the apartment, with its spectacular views of the East River looking out toward Long Island City, the United Nations and its gardens, and the Queensborough Bridge, they, Victoria especially, found that they liked it. Victoria felt protected and free of the rigors of maintaining a house, and Si enjoyed the anonymity of high-rise life. They began to spend more and more time in the apartment.

No matter that the security was enhanced during the renovation of the Seventieth Street house: Victoria would never feel anything but exposed there. One Condé Nast editor who was planning a party for Victoria at the U.N. Plaza apartment went there one morning to see its physical layout. He expressed surprise when Victoria came to the door.

"Yes, I stay here when Si is out of town. I don't like to be at the townhouse alone." For a while they lived on Seventieth Street during the week and in the apartment on weekends, but eventually they sold the house.

Alex Liberman, Si's neighbor on Seventieth Street, followed him to U.N. Plaza and bought the apartment beneath his. One man who has been in both says that the color schemes and furniture—beige throughout—are almost identical. He describes both as looking "like an airport waiting room, ...absolutely institutional."

Having decided to stay in the building, the Newhouses bought the adjoining unit. To combine them, they hired architect Alexander Charles Gorlin, a Prix de Rome winner, who had received his first commission from Victoria when she hired him to design a garden gate for their Palm Beach house. In order to create more space to hang pictures in an apartment that has walls of floor-to-ceiling windows, Gorlin employed a museum design, creating cross walls on which art can be displayed on both sides.

Despite the cross walls, the walls of windows meant much less hanging space, and Si sold or put away more of his collection, giving precedence to young artists. Museum directors hearing of the move were surely hoping, but Si kept to his practice of selling art he no longer wanted.

Si, sans companion, much less bodyguard, was often seen by neighbors walking Nero, looking like the most ordinary of men. (He would reportedly try to sneak Nero through the front elevator when house rules required that he use the back.) "He's the only billionaire I know who eats in his living room," says one man in the book publishing business whom Si had invited to dinner parties. "It's quite extraordinary that a man of his wealth would live the way he does, which is basically from the point of view of a billionaire...in nasty circumstances."

Not everyone saw the U.N. Plaza five-bedroom apartment—estimated in 1997 by one man who follows the values of apartments in the buildings to be worth between $3 and $4 million—as such a hardship for two people to share.[5]

Si's need in the art market to search always for what one dealer calls the latest "taste sensation" was evident in the other passion in his life, his magazines—and nowhere more so than at the most prized of his possessions, the *New Yorker*. And that would cause no end of distress to those who thought "sensation" and the *New Yorker* should never occupy the same sentence.

22 | Ruthless

AT THE *NEW YORKER*, Bob Gottlieb was working nights and weekends to prove himself a worthy successor to Shawn and to stem the tide of red ink that started to flow in 1985 when Newhouse bought the magazine. While trying not to jar the sensibilities of the *New Yorker*'s staff and readers, Gottlieb did institute changes that made the magazine more modern. He tossed most of the huge bank of stories, many exceedingly long, that Shawn had paid for and accumulated. He brought in some new writers to cover rock and roll and Broadway musicals. He hired Jane and Michael Stern to write on American gothic, especially junk food. He snuck color into a stubbornly black-and-white layout. He used photography, though sparingly. He expanded and enlivened the "Goings On About Town" section by inserting drawings, caricatures, and capsule write-ups of actors and musicians. He allowed the use of four-letter words and descriptions of bodily functions and sex, all strictly prohibited by the uncompromisingly prudish Shawn.

But Gottlieb's reverence for the magazine caused him to make the changes gently, incrementally, so as not to damage its character. And some felt he wasn't going far enough, fast enough. Geraldine Fabrikant reported in the *New York Times* a comment heard around the *New Yorker* in those days: "Gottlieb is out-Shawning Shawn."

This approach wasn't to the liking of the man, his friend, who hired him. "When Bob came here," says Lee Lorenz, then the magazine's art editor, "Newhouse thought that was going to create a lot of excitement about the magazine." But it wasn't happening. Bob Gottlieb simply wasn't the star type.

Gottlieb didn't despair. He simply worked harder. If he could not make the transition from star book editor to star magazine editor, he would concern himself not only with putting out the best magazine he could, but also with improving the bottom line. "Gottlieb listened so much to [*New Yorker* president Steve] Florio and maybe even Newhouse about saving money that the magazine editorially suffered for it," says Perry Vandermeer, a former scheduling editor. Gottlieb worked closely with Florio, and once, after meeting with him, Gottlieb breathlessly told one writer that the magazine would have 40,000 new subscribers by the following June.

Gottlieb, with Newhouse and Florio, began studying the results of the response surveys so beloved by magazine publishers but so shunned by editors of the *New Yorker*. The old guard worried about Gottlieb's nod to the market. It also worried about his acquiescence to Si's bringing Condé Nast people over to influence the magazine. The boss was apparently reneging on his pledge to keep the *New Yorker* separate from Condé Nast, and Gottlieb was keeping quiet. For example, marketing guru Rochelle Udell came over from Condé Nast to help Gottlieb with design. "I think it was understood that she was there to bring the *New Yorker* into the Condé Nast fold," says Perry Vandermeer.

Still, Gottlieb, a superb line editor, very much a traditional *New Yorker*-type editor, became a respected and popular figure at the magazine, with the staff shifting from seeing him, says Vandermeer, as "this kind of occupying power," to winning people over by "his editing skills, his commitment to the writers."

In tennis shoes and T-shirt, Gottlieb was the antithesis of the famously buttoned-down Shawn, who wielded what former fact checker Richard Sacks calls "exquisite politeness" as a shield, and whose position as the patriarch brought with it elaborate rules of court. With Gottlieb, who in addition to an intense interest in movies and ballet had unconventional hobbies and a taste for kitsch that included a world-class collection of plastic handbags and pillows with messages on them, there were no apparent rules; his door was open to anyone. "He's the only boss I've ever had who I've told to fuck off without fear of consequences," says one *New Yorker* editor.

Despite Gottlieb's economies, the magazine continued to lose money. (In 1991 ad pages dropped by 18 percent for the year.) And Newhouse's eye fell not on its president, Florio, but on its editor, Gottlieb. It was that missing link again—*buzz*. "I think he heard people talking about other magazines," says Joni Evans, "and not the *New Yorker*, and he can't stand that people aren't talking about his magazine."

At one point, Gottlieb reportedly asked his boss directly, what wasn't he doing that Newhouse wanted him to do? According to Lee Lorenz, Bob never received an answer. Gottlieb later told Lorenz that in a series of conversations Si had expressed "a kind of vague dissatisfaction with the way the magazine was going, never really seemed to be able to say exactly what he thought Bob...should be doing." Publicly Newhouse expressed complete confidence in Gottlieb. Privately, he had grave misgivings.

According to Joni Evans, Newhouse eventually told Gottlieb that he had to jazz up the magazine even if it meant offending its aging and, most important, demographically undesirable readership. But Gottlieb wouldn't, because he knew that doing so would create a magazine that was something other than the one he loved. When the two men lunched together, according to one friend of Gottlieb's, "Si threw down the gauntlet, and Bob said, 'Fine. You're going to have to figure out how to get rid of me. If you've got to make the changes, I can't do that.'"

Late in the afternoon of Monday, June 29, 1992, word leaked of the imminent change of editors. Gottlieb was out, and his replacement was Tina Brown. One contributor to the magazine was awakened with the news at 2:00 A.M. by a friend, a *New Yorker* staff writer. "If this person had not been crying, I actually would have thought it was a joke because it seemed so unlikely."

Gottlieb was then in Tokyo, judging a translation contest. He had his own middle-of-the-night awakening by reporters seeking comment. Gottlieb later told Lee Lorenz that while he knew it was coming, it was not supposed to happen while he was away. It had been leaked to the press, Newhouse would explain to his friend, and so his people had to announce it.

Of his departure and Tina Brown's arrival, Gottlieb would proclaim, "I'm the happiest girl in the whole U.S.A.," a reference to a country-and-western hit by Donna Fargo. Few people believed him, but his ouster was no doubt cushioned by Newhouse's handing Gottlieb a parachute so gold-en—$400,000 a year for the rest of his life; in the event of his death, $200,000 a year for the rest of his widow's life—that its numbers have become legend within the company.

Gottlieb, then sixty-one, no longer needed the salary, but he did need something to do, and so part of the deal was that he could have an office at Knopf and edit the occasional book by one of his old writers, such as John Le Carre. (He also agreed to help Katharine Graham, long under contract with Knopf, write her memoirs.)[1]

And so Bob Gottlieb and Si Newhouse, to this day, remain friends.

Some insist that Newhouse had, from the day in 1985 when he signed the deal to buy the *New Yorker,* planned to install Tina Brown as its editor; that he would have done so in 1987 when he fired Shawn and put Gottlieb in his place, had he not feared that the staff would revolt en masse. It was too bold, too outrageously provocative a step to take then. But five years later, he reportedly figured, he could do it, and while he might lose a few fuddy-duddy writers and readers, so what? He'd have Tina, and she'd get people talking about the magazine. The advertisers would follow.

Si always saw Brown as a magazine genius and rescuer, and credited her with saving *Vanity Fair.* "Tina has done something miraculous," he said. Steve Florio told Si repeatedly that the *New Yorker* needed Tina. When the news broke that Newhouse had dumped Gottlieb and installed Brown, Florio exclaimed, tactlessly, "It's Christmas!"

"I loved Shawn, he was a brilliant man," Florio would later tell a reporter. "Gottlieb was fun every day, but working with Tina [at *Vanity Fair*] has been my life's experience, working with her every hour of every day."[2]

There was no meeting between Si Newhouse and his employees in 1987 when Shawn was fired and Gottlieb hired, but the staff was at its most feisty then, and the letter asking Gottlieb not to take the job was the result. "These *New Yorker* writers are really going to regret what they did to Gottlieb," Rick MacArthur of *Harper's* said at the time Gottlieb was fired. "He was Adlai Stevenson compared to Tina Brown."

With Steve Florio in tow, Newhouse arrived at the *New Yorker* on June 30, 1992, the day after the news of Tina Brown's appointment broke. As he had seven years before on buying the magazine, he faced a nervous and upset editorial staff. But there was a difference this time. It was Shawn's magazine then. Now it was Si Newhouse's. "The idea of the editor of *Vanity Fair* being made editor of the *New Yorker*," the irrepressibly critical Rick MacArthur told a reporter, "is like moving Trump Tower to the middle of the Brooklyn Botanic Gardens." One *New Yorker* writer describes the mood "as if we all realized that we had no power whatsoever. What were we going to do?"

During Gottlieb's tenure, the magazine had been moved from its famously shabby quarters to sleek white offices across Forty-third Street. The meeting of Newhouse, Florio, and the staff was held in the business conference room, rather than on the editorial floor—unthinkable under Shawn's strict separation of church (editorial) and state (business). A staffer assured *New York* writer Michael Gross that the choice of locations was deliberate; Si Newhouse saying, "This is where the *New Yorker* resides."

The gathering was not a dance for anyone. A couple of writers, Henry S. F. Cooper Jr. and Calvin Trillin, insisted on pressing Newhouse to say what exactly Gottlieb hadn't done that Newhouse wanted done. Instead of answering the question, Si paced and used and reused the word "evolution." (He sometimes switched to the word "evolvement," which grated on his audience's ears as much as another word he used, "intermingle.") Henry Cooper, later fired by Brown, persisted, asking if Gottlieb had been too slow in making changes. Newhouse avoided that question as well. Another writer kept repeating the same question in slightly different words, trying unsuccessfully to force the owner to answer.

"In a certain sense," says one *New Yorker* writer, "there was no way really for him to answer the concerns of the people there because we were speaking a different language." She mentions in particular that "Newhouse had this line about how it was still going to be a text-driven magazine, which for people who love language was a horrifying thing to say because if you really loved language you would never use an expression like text-driven." One editor describes Newhouse's responses as "dramatically bad, ...just semiliterate, he couldn't articulate much of anything." It was "painful" to observe, says Lee Lorenz. "There were long pauses while he tracked his thoughts. I just wanted to get out of that room."

Steve Florio, looking like his boss's bodyguard, hovered at Si's side. Perry Vandermeer recalls, "In the face of Trillin asking a very reasonable question, 'What do you really mean when you talk about the future evolution of the magazine?'... Florio protected him. Florio would speak up when Newhouse would pause or look down." When the questions came too fast and furious, Florio halted the interrogation.

Staff writer Burton Bernstein recalled Newhouse as being nonplussed in the face of "electricity of hatred.... Every pair of eyes in the room was on him, just loathing him. I've never been in a room like that before. This guy just went through it like he was addressing a family dinner. I thought, 'Jesus, if I were Si Newhouse standing up here, I would have turned to Florio and said, 'Look, you handle all this, I'm going home. I'm going out for a drink. I'm going to lunch. I'm not going to stand here and feel the incredible hatred.'" Asked if he didn't agree that this could be construed as a kind of courage, Bernstein replied, "You could call it courage. I would call it having the hide of a rhinoceros.... He has probably taken so much abuse, it doesn't matter to him anymore."[3]

In 1992, at the time the owner was replacing Bob Gottlieb with Tina Brown, he regarded *Vanity Fair* as a true phenomenon, along with *People*, one of the great magazine launches of the 1980s. That it had, according to one reporter for *Women's Wear Daily*, "never made a nickel, even under Tina," was not so important to this multibillionaire. What was important, says Peter Diamandis, was that "it was no longer a huge drain, and it was the darling of everybody in the press."

So now who would take Tina Brown's place? Si knew that he needed someone who could keep the magazine in the headlines and, he hoped, eventually even maneuver it into the black. He chose E. Graydon Carter, a Canadian—once a speechwriter for former prime minister Pierre Trudeau—who was then editor of the *New York Observer* and previously a founding coeditor of *Spy*.

Some contend that Graydon Carter had been Newhouse's first choice for the *New Yorker* job. According to an editor at the *New Yorker*, Tina caught wind of the offer and said, "Uh, uh, I want the *New Yorker*." But it is much more likely that Brown was Newhouse's first choice, although reportedly she, momentarily, hurt her chances and helped Carter's by hiring agent Morton Janklow to negotiate a $1 million salary and a piece of the profits. Cutting any outsider in on the profits was never the Newhouse way. Si said absolutely no to the demand, and she backed down.

Anyone who read *Spy* in its heyday or the *Observer* any week would probably have placed Graydon Carter at the bottom of Newhouse's list of candidates to run any of his magazines. Both publications, *Spy* especially, had been unusually cruel and personal in their attacks on Si. *Spy* took a kind of adolescent glee in making fun, in every issue, of his short stature—its editors called him a "dwarf"—and unengaging features. It also portrayed him as a man who has used "his enormous wealth to engineer proximity to all kinds of fascinating...people" and as a "billionaire monopolist" with "famous aversions to leisure and interaction with other human beings." None of this mattered to Si Newhouse. In this instance he apparently did have, as Burton Bernstein said, the hide of a rhinoceros. He felt that Carter was the man who could do the job, and that was that.

Tina Brown, herself a target of much derision in *Spy*, was reportedly very cool to the news of Graydon Carter as her successor. There was the embarrassment of the reprint in *Spy* of her smarmy letter to CAA chairman Michael Ovitz, the one that seemed to encapsulate all that was wrong with *Vanity Fair* and its habit of cozying up to Hollywood. In *Spy*'s pages, Tina was the "bosomy Oxford coed with a facility for cultivating close friendships with influential older men in the publishing world"—Harry Evans, in particular, whom, *Spy* claimed, Tina relentlessly pursued until he left his wife and three children to marry her.

Tina Brown was surely the hardest and hottest act to follow in journalism, and Graydon Carter weathered some rough patches in his early days at *Vanity Fair*. When Brown left the magazine and for two years thereafter, advertising went into a free fall as the buzz followed her to the *New Yorker*. But the decline slowed, and by 1996 advertising had rebounded to almost the 1992 level. Circulation reached a new high of 1.1 million, and publishing experts speculated that *Vanity Fair* would earn about $5 million that year. The first half of 1997 was even better, with an increase of nearly 100 pages over the year before. The April 1997 issue was so fat, the size of a small telephone book, that the cover bannered, "Our Biggest Issue Ever!" By mid-1997, a reporter for the *New York Daily News* claimed for the magazine earnings of $10 to $15 million a year.[4]

Tina Brown arrived at the *New Yorker* in September 1992, with much media fanfare. In her wake came her publicist, Maurie Perl, her managing editor, Pamela Maffei McCarthy, and several writers, editors, and designers, all from the dreaded *Vanity Fair*. While still at *Vanity Fair*, Tina Brown had written in her editor's column her version of what a magazine should be, or not be: "Once in a while...I run into a flabby old cliché about what constitutes a 'serious' magazine. It's the mealymouthed idea that visual excitement is somehow at odds with intellectual content, and that reading material can be deemed worthwhile only if it is presented as a wad of impenetrable text with a staple through the side." She later characterized the typical old *New Yorker* story as "the 50,000-word piece on zinc." She said that she had no intention of being the "curator" of a "stuffed bird."

Indeed, as she found her bearings at the *New Yorker*, Brown bore no resemblance to a curator. But she didn't exactly seem an editor either. She was more a grand scheduler, who was once quoted as saying that she would view it as an indulgence if she could take a blue pencil to paper.

As Tina Brown began to gather force, it was obvious that for her, timeliness was everything. And so the *New Yorker* quickly became all that Shawn's magazine was not and did not want to be. She noted on her arrival that the *New Yorker* was not a "visually driven" magazine, and that while she would miss working with "some of the great photographers of our time, that particular visual expression is not going to be appropriate." Before 1992 was out, she hired Richard Avedon as the magazine's first staff photographer. Next came *Vanity Fair* photographer Annie Leibovitz, noted for her shots of movie stars. (Believing that there was nothing that could not be described in words, the magazine's founder, Harold Ross, prohibited photographs, and Shawn agreed completely.) Then she started assigning stories about the media, particularly profiles of the men on top. Barry Diller, who has run Hollywood studios and television networks, a friend of both Brown's and Newhouse's, showed up so often in Tina's *New Yorker* that Calvin Trillin told a reporter if he could ban two words from the magazine, they would be "Barry Diller." Ken Auletta, whom Tina recruited, wrote so many media mogul profiles, and so similar were they in their adulatory tone and content, that a parody of the Auletta treatment—"Awestruck" by "Ken Fellata"—appeared in the *New Republic*.

In a practice perfected at *Vanity Fair*, Brown ordered the magazine delivered to the homes of movers and shakers in New York, Los Angeles, and Washington on the Sunday night before its Monday release. As an attention- and advertising-grabbing device, she started special issues—on fashion, on cartoons, on the home, on black America, on women, on love, on politics, on crime, on Hollywood, on California, on Broadway, on fiction—and they did attract advertising. The Hollywood issue, timed to the presentation of the Oscars, sold eighty-eight pages of ads, compared to thirty-seven for the same issue the year before.

They also attracted plenty of criticism. Even the seemingly innocuous fiction issue, which contained plenty of interest to read, hit a raw nerve among the growing ranks of critics of the magazine. David Streitfeld wrote in the *Washington Post Book World* that "the *New Yorker* itself would never be satisfied with merely being interesting. It wants at all costs to be talked about." He called the fiction issue "typical of the magazine's all-consuming demand for publicity.... It wants to be celebrated for doing once a year what it used to do without fuss every week." (Pre-Tina, the *New Yorker* typically carried two stories per issue; during her regime, some issues carried one story and others none.)

The fashion issue prompted the most ridicule. One former *New Yorker* contributor described it as seeming "almost like a trade magazine that you would hand out at a trade fair to flatter the people who had exhibitions there." *Newsweek* lambasted it as "a 248-page wet kiss to designer royalty." Brandishing a newspaper photo of Tina Brown and Harry Evans dancing at the party to celebrate the fashion issue and to boost fashion advertising, Rick MacArthur lamented, "There's Tina and Harry dancing on the grave of the *New Yorker*."

The focus on fashion, on the media, on the latest movie, on celebrity, blurred the lines between the *New Yorker* and *Vanity Fair*. A photo spread by Annie Leibovitz that celebrated the principals in the O. J. Simpson case—including Nicole's dog, Kato Kaelin sans shirt, and Paula Barbieri sans pants—seemed the very essence of *Vanity Fair*, except that it ran in the *New Yorker*.

Brown went whole hog on the Simpson case, assigning Jeffrey Toobin—a writer she hired in 1993—to cover the trial and running his dispatches regularly. One week "Talk of the Town" contained three takes on the case. After twenty-eight years writing for the *New Yorker*, George W. S. Trow left in 1994 in disgust over the pile of O. J. coverage: "For you to kiss the ass of celebrity culture at this moment that way," Trow wrote Brown, "is like selling your soul to get close to the Hapsburgs—in 1913."*

Before Brown, the *New Yorker* was a magazine that many readers scanned for the cartoons and advertisements and saved for a long plane ride or a week in the country, and if the issues were six months old, it didn't matter because the articles, as well as the cartoons, had a timelessness to them. One editor of a magazine that today competes with the *New Yorker* admits that he reads more of it now than he used to because, being in the business, he feels he needs to read the latest profile of the hottest media mogul. But he misses the magazine as it was. "The problem with the magazine now," he says, "is that it's like every other magazine, and all the articles you read in it you can read anywhere."

Some of the pieces in the magazine smacked of press agentry. Tina Brown ran a profile of Sharon Stone to coincide with the opening of the remake of *Diabolique*. To add to the hype, gossip columnists picked up news of the actress' argument with Richard Avedon after Stone refused to wear a transparent dress, in which Avedon wanted her to pose. To coincide with Oliver Stone's movie *Natural Born Killers*, Brown ran a profile of the director by Stephen Schiff—one of several *Vanity Fair* writers whom she brought with her to the *New Yorker*—accompanied by full-page celebratory photos by Richard Avedon. She ran a David Remnick profile of radio

*After Harry Evans signed Larry Schiller—O. J. Simpson's collaborator on *I Want to Tell You*—to write a book about the O. J. trial, Tina Brown was seen urging Schiller to write for the *New Yorker*. His first piece, on the murder of six-year-old beauty queen JonBenet Ramsey, appeared in the January 19, 1998, issue.

"shock jock" Howard Stern that hit the stands just as Stern's movie, *Private Parts,* hit the screens. (Shawn had so bridled at the slightest hint of promotion or topicality that when Mel Brooks was being interviewed for a *New Yorker* profile and he asked if the piece could be published to coincide with the release of his new movie, the very notion repulsed Shawn: "We could never do that," one editor recalls Shawn saying, "and if the movie is coming out, we'll have to delay publication by six months.")

If Bob Gottlieb opened the *New Yorker* to relatively discreet mentions of sex, Tina Brown opened it to almost anything. Susan Faludi's "The Money Shot" described men "waiting for wood" (i.e., a sustained erection) in the San Fernando Valley's pornography industry. The story was illustrated by photos, including one of John Wayne Bobbitt, whose wife, in a rage, cut off his penis. Readers were offered the news that "people wanted to gaze upon [Bobbitt's] recapitated dick," and so they were watching his film, *JWB Uncut.* A series of Annie Leibovitz photographs of Las Vegas topless dancers entitled "Showgirls"—apparently inspired by the movie of the same title—had text by Stephen Schiff, who wrote of the women's backgrounds in ballet, of one speaking five languages and taking correspondence courses in Dutch law. Two of the dancers were pictured topless, one holding her topless young daughter. Also published in the *New Yorker* was an embarrassing piece by Daphne Merkin about her until-then secret desire to be spanked. (Brown later named Merkin the magazine's film critic.)

Then there was Richard Avedon's 26-page fashion spread, timed for Halloween, featuring supermodel Nadja Auermann, posing with a male skeleton, carrying the anorexic look of high fashion to new extremes and seeming to celebrate necrophilia. Among the poses were Nadja and the skeleton having sex, and Nadja nursing the skeleton's baby.

Before long Tina took on the magazine's most sacred institution, the cartoons. She started a special cartoon issue. She urged cartoonists to make their jokes more topical and their characters look "like the people you actually meet." Critics of the new regime worried that cartoons had become "so dependent on the moment" that anyone looking at them several years or even one year later wouldn't see the humor. (In the wake of the public disgrace of network sportscaster Marv Albert, Brown ran a drawing of a middle-aged woman trying on a bra and garter belt as the sales clerk looked on approvingly. "It's absolutely *marv*," read the caption. During the week when allegations exploded that President Clinton had had sex in the White House with a twenty-one-year-old intern, a cartoon showed one man asking another, presumably his guide, "How long has the Oval Office had a mirror on the ceiling?") They also complained that the quality of the drawing had declined as message became all, leaving style to fend for itself.

With the goal of boosting newsstand sales and thus advertising— advertisers shun magazines whose newsstand sales are declining or flat— *New Yorker* covers, selected by Tina, in consultation, until his retirement, with Lee Lorenz, grew deliberately provocative. Before Brown, says Lorenz, neither he nor anyone else on the editorial side thought much about newsstand sales, which, to Lorenz's surprise, for some issues barely reached 10,000. Under Brown, some issues sold as many as 60,000. "We selected covers not to grab people by the lapel when they went by the newsstand," Lorenz explains, "but to be part of people's homes for a month or so while they were browsing through the magazine." The new covers seemed designed to grab browsers by both lapels and shake hard.

For the Valentine's Day, 1993, cover, cartoonist Art Spiegelman drew a side-curled Hasidic Jew kissing a dreadlocked black woman. He later drew, for a Christmas cover, Santa Claus urinating on a wall in the shape of a Christmas tree, which, to Spiegelman's surprise, Tina Brown vetoed. But she did run his Easter cover featuring the Easter Bunny being cruci-fied on a IRS tax form, the pockets of his business suit emptied.

Perhaps the biggest shocker was the update on Eustace Tilley, the top-hatted Regency fop engaged in inspecting a butterfly through his mon-ocle. It had been drawn by the magazine's first art director, and graced the *New Yorker*'s cover every February since its founding in 1925—until 1994, when Brown substituted a Robert Crumb drawing of a pimply teenage punk wearing chin stubble, an earring, a reversed baseball cap, and a stoned expression, and reading a flyer for a triple-X-rated Times Square porn shop. Tina dubbed him Elvis Tilley and explained that he was Eustace's grandson. In subsequent years he appeared as a woman in a low-cut dress and as a detective. In 1998 Eustace Tilley didn't appear at all.

The issue that normally would have featured him, the magazine's publicist explained, was the special double issue on California.

Even Jimmy Breslin, the very antithesis of snobbishness and effeteness, took Tina's *New Yorker* to task: "Once, the magazine was a church. It wasn't quite my denomination, but it was still a church. Suddenly, it is nothing more than a cheap booth on a boardwalk.... Dear Lord is she over-rated, and her magazine so tasteless and boring."

There were some moments under Tina that were so wacky as to seem almost surreal—such as her appointment of the television sitcom star Roseanne as a consulting editor—or, as a spokesman for the *New Yorker* put it, a "collaborator"—for the double issue on women. Roseanne was pictured in a full-page Annie Leibovitz photograph holding her naked baby, Buck. The *Washington Post*'s gossip writers labeled it "part of the once-highbrow mag's growing crush on Hollywood." Ian Frazier, since 1974 a *New Yorker* writer, quit in a huff over the very idea of Roseanne. "I think the goal is to scorch the outrage back to nothing so that you can't be outraged anymore," Frazier told a reporter.* Defending herself and Roseanne, Brown explained, "I mean, she's had a much greater range of experiences than most of the people who you can find who are editors and writers walking around the *New Yorker*."[5]

In an interview with Patrick Reilly of the *Wall Street Journal* two weeks after taking over the *New Yorker*, Tina Brown promised, "Yes, there will be a blood change," and that was one promise she kept. Tony Hiss, James Lardner, Burton Bernstein, and Michael Arlen were eventually shown the door. Nat Hentoff found his story ideas routinely rejected. Milton Viorst, who covered the Middle East; John Newhouse (no relation to Si), who wrote the "Annals of Diplomacy" column for twenty years; Elizabeth Drew, who covered Washington for the magazine for nineteen years; and Raymond Bonner, who wrote a two-part, 40,000-word piece on Indonesia and who covered war and famines, were also pushed out. (Brown cut way back on

*Frazier bemoans "the fact that Shawn's glorious career should end with this guy [Newhouse].... The collision of the two was one of the real tragedies of American letters, that such a crass company should end up with such a good magazine."

the foreign affairs stories, many about decidedly unglamorous places and issues, but a staple of the magazine under Shawn and even more so under Gottlieb.) She would later claim to have hired twenty-eight new writers and lost thirty-three of the old. "We kept all the ones I wanted to keep."

Eventually, some of the best of the old editors also left, including Charles "Chip" McGrath, who had shown enormous loyalty and hard work in assisting both Gottlieb and Tina Brown, neither of whom knew how to put out a weekly magazine. McGrath was pushed from editing major fact pieces, as they're called at the *New Yorker*, back from whence he came as editor of the diminished fiction department. He took the job of top editor of the *New York Times Book Review*. Daniel Menaker, a *New Yorker* veteran of twenty-six years, most of them in the fiction department, saw his request to Brown for the job of fiction editor refused, and he accepted an offer from Tina's husband, Harry, to become a senior editor at Random House.

Only one person quit directly over Tina's appointment—Garrison Keillor, host of public radio's *Prairie Home Companion*, who has continued to publicly blast Newhouse and Brown: "If some ditzy American editor went to London, took over the *Spectator* and turned it into, say, *In Your Face: A Magazine of Mucus*, there would be a big uproar.... Here, a great American magazine falls into the clutches of a Staten Island newspaper mogul who goes out and hires a British editor who seems to know this country mainly from television and movies, and nobody says much about it."

But many veteran *New Yorker* writers are still there, including Calvin Trillin, Roger Angell, Lillian Ross, John Updike, Pauline Kael, Philip Hamburger, Janet Malcolm, Arlene Croce, and John McPhee. McPhee, though, an elegant writer on "small" subjects, was said to be in a "tailspin" on hearing Tina say that the magazine would no longer publish the old-style *New Yorker* pieces: "We're not going to have any long stories about archeology anymore." (She put a stop to the practice of paying writers by the word, which, she said, "just encourages verbosity.")

Others from the Shawn era would quit in protest over some perceived cheapening of the magazine. The late Veronica Geng, a gifted parodist and a favorite of William Shawn's, resigned soon after Brown's arrival. Staff writer Jamaica Kincaid, who happened to be Shawn's daughter-in-law, left in a huff in 1996—she had joined the *New Yorker* twenty years before—decrying the magazine's "coarseness" and "vulgarity." In fact, Tina Brown had run pieces of Kincaid's that Shawn would have considered nothing if not vulgar, including one autobiographical sketch in which she described lying in the bathtub giving herself a coffee enema. "Once the coffee was too hot and I burned my bottom all the way up," she wrote.[6]

Tina Brown, especially, has shown a tin ear for the inevitable conflicts of interest that arose because while she was running what remains the nation's most prestigious magazine, her husband was running the nation's most prestigious book publisher. She had barely taken the reins from Bob Gottlieb when the British novelist, John Le Carré, then Gottlieb's writer at Knopf, publicly denounced her. The reason was a "Talk of the Town" item that was harshly critical of a biography of Rupert Murdoch written by Le Carré's friend, William Shawcross. The "Talk" item's author had already bashed Shawcross's book in reviewing it for a British journal.

In the biography, Shawcross, who had worked as an investigative reporter for Harry Evans at the *Sunday Times*, wrote unflatteringly of Evans's short stint as editor of the Murdoch-owned *Times* of London. Murdoch fired Evans in 1982. In Shawcross's rendition, Harry, who claimed that he was fired because he would not brook Murdoch's interference in editorial matters, was both not up to the job and fawning for Murdoch's approval. (To counter Evans's charges, Murdoch released a note from Evans in which he pleaded with the mogul to guide him as he covered Margaret Thatcher's new budget.)

Le Carré, who charged that bashing Shawcross's book was Brown's way of protecting her husband's reputation, called the *New Yorker* item "one of the ugliest pieces of partisan journalism that I have witnessed in a long life of writing." He argued that Tina should have revealed her conflict of interest. Tina labeled Le Carré's complaint sexist and denied that she was "banging some drum for Harry."

Evans and Brown insisted that they gave no special consideration to the other. Still, Random House and its imprints—there were then thirty-five under its umbrella—seemed to capture the lion's share of reportage, review, and excerpt attention in the *New Yorker*, as well as in *Vanity Fair* and other Condé Nast titles, although it's hard to know if they would have anyway, even if the ownership of all the above were not the same.

In an issue from November 1997, three of the four "Talk of the Town" items featured writers published by Random House imprints. The first described another feud involving John Le Carré (Knopf), this time with Salman Rushdie (Random House, Knopf, Pantheon).* The second featured *Vanity Fair* writer Dominick Dunne and his book about the O. J. Simpson trial, *Another City, Not My Own,* just out from Crown. The third was a valentine to Anna Wintour and *Vogue* food writer Jeffrey Steingarten, whose book *The Man Who Ate Everything,* a collection of his columns for *Vogue,* was just out from Knopf. In describing the book party Wintour hosted for Steingarten at Le Cirque 2000, *New Yorker* senior editor Hendrik Hertzberg so effusively praised both the book—"worth celebrating, so well prepared, so expertly seasoned, and so full of flavorsome surprises"—and Wintour that it seemed that somewhere, if only parenthetically, it should have been noted that Knopf and the *New Yorker* and *Vogue* shared the same owner, and perhaps even that Hertzberg and Steingarten knew each other at Harvard, where they received their degrees in the same year.

When Harry Evans agreed to pay President Clinton's former top political adviser, Dick Morris, $2.5 million for his memoir, it made big news. The deal, with its huge advance, disgusted many people because Morris had been forced to resign after the news broke that he had consorted with a prostitute in a hotel suite close to the White House that was paid for by Clinton's campaign committee. Morris, who was married, resigned on the day Clinton was to give his acceptance speech at the Democratic National Convention in Chicago.

Evans had made the deal with Morris five months before, but had increased the size of the advance *after* a supermarket tabloid broke news of the scandal. It was later reported that Morris and his wife had met with Harry Evans and Tina Brown for lunch in their apartment. It was, apparently, a lunch to celebrate the book deal, but Tina's presence led to speculation that she had struck a deal to buy an excerpt to run just before the book's publication. Harry denied that the *New Yorker* had an interest. Tina

---

* Le Carré severed ties with Knopf, his publisher of thirty years, in mid-1998.

promised that she would not excerpt from the book or run an article by Dick Morris. She did not promise not to run an article about Morris and the book, which she did at the time of the book's publication.

Two days later, Dick Morris, at Tina's invitation, came to breakfast at the *New Yorker*'s offices to entertain the magazine's advertisers and to be questioned politely, and incredibly, off the record, by the magazine's political staff. Harvard professor Henry Louis Gates moderated.

For Random House to recoup what it paid for the Morris book, at least a half million copies would have had to be sold. But Morris, like Marlon Brando, did not tell the public what it wanted to know. His agent insisted that Random House had paid a $2.5 million advance for a book about political strategy. "This is not a book about a call girl," Harry Evans agreed early on, "but the governance of America and the White House and other important subjects." The book, predictably, flopped. According to one report, only 81,000 copies were sold, for a loss to Random House of $1.5 million.

Harry Evans was also the publisher of the best-selling *Primary Colors*, written by "Anonymous." The plot about the campaign for the presidency by the governor of a small southern state, beset by insatiable appetites for women, power, food, and adoration, was obviously written by a Washington insider, but who? Eventually *Newsweek* writer Joe Klein, who continued to cover the White House while he denied to his colleagues and to the public that he had written the novel, was snagged by a handwriting expert and forced to confess. His embarrassed editors at *Newsweek* demoted him. Klein, thanks to Tina Brown, recovered nicely. Some months later, Brown hired him to be the *New Yorker*'s top political reporter.

One former *New Yorker* writer suggested that it could have been worse. She could have offered the job of writing "Letter from Washington" to another of Harry's authors, Dick Morris. A couple of weeks later, *New York Post* gossip columnist Richard Johnson described Dick Morris as having "a book deal with Random House and a column in the *New Yorker*." The next day Johnson issued a correction: "We mixed up our disgraced political pundits yesterday when we reported that Dick Morris is writing a column for the *New Yorker*. It's Joe Klein who was hired by Tina Brown. Morris is the campaign consultant who had to quit the Clinton-Gore team after he got caught with a call girl. Klein is the political columnist who...was caught lying that he wasn't the 'Anonymous' who wrote *Primary Colors*. Both are Random House authors for Brown's husband, Harry Evans."[7]

And so it went, back and forth at Si Newhouse's properties. For dueling Manhattan gossip columnists, it was a windfall. For serious readers, it was something else again.

In May 1997, in an effort to slow the losses, Harry Evans, who insisted that Random House turned a record profit in 1995 and had made money every year but one since he was placed in charge, was relieved of most of his responsibility for day-to-day operations, including budgets. Two former underlings, Ann Godoff and Walter Weintz, were promoted to handle those jobs, with Evans, while claiming to still be in charge, demoted to being the company's public face, his authority significantly diminished.

The charade ended in November 1997 with the announcement that Harry Evans would leave Si Newhouse's employ to return to Mortimer Zuckerman's, as editorial director of the real estate mogul's three print properties—the *New York Daily News, U.S. News & World Report,* and the *Atlantic Monthly*. Evans's replacement, Ann Godoff, some twenty years younger than Harry (and the acquiring editor of such best-sellers as John Berendt's *Midnight in the Garden of Good and Evil*), had for months been running the editorial side anyway. Two titles that had belonged to Harry Evans, president and editor in chief, were bestowed upon Godoff, along with praise from a delighted Alberto Vitale, who called her "probably the best editor in the business." When Vitale was asked to gauge the impact of Harry's departure, he replied, "None."

Harry, then sixty-nine, engaged in some frantic but ultimately futile spinning about how he was reluctantly leaving for a better job, even threatening to sue his home-country newspaper, the *Spectator,* for describing him as having been pushed out of Random House. He had apparently faced the choice of getting out or accepting the role of figurehead. (Tina's status with Si made it impossible for him to actually fire Harry.) Doreen Carvajal reported in the *New York Times* "stories" that Evans had been asked to assume an emeritus role and to take offices some twenty floors above the editorial department. Evans vigorously disputed that angle, but few disputed that a belt-tightening was underway at Random House; that Godoff would cut back on spending, on self-promotion, and on the money-losing celebrity titles so favored by Harry Evans. It was noted in the *Times* that Godoff would not be inheriting one of Harry's many Random House perks—his chauffeur-driven car.

Then came speculation that Evans would be little more than a figurehead in the Zuckerman operation; that the job was a face-saving favor from Zuckerman, the godfather to one of Harry and Tina's children. Indeed, six months into the new job, he was calling himself "the invisible man." Had he not concocted the designation, the reporters and editors working for the Zuckerman properties would have done so for him. When in late June 1998 Zuckerman fired James Fallows, editor of *U.S. News*, Zuckerman insisted, to much derision and disbelief, that Harry had done the deed. The coverage of the beheading of Fallows was full of embarrassing jabs at Harry. The *Times* led with the news that Zuckerman had fired Fallows, and quoted one editor as calling Harry "a papier-mâché boss...frantically trying to look like he's not taking orders from Mort." Evans insisted to *Washington Post* media reporter Howard Kurtz, "I have not been known simply to be a lapdog," sounding a bit like Richard Nixon insisting that he was not a crook.

The inevitable conflicts of interest did not end with Harry Evans's departure because Si Newhouse continued to own both the *New Yorker* and Random House. And a new conflict loomed for Tina's media-obsessed *New Yorker*. How could it fairly cover Zuckerman and his properties, especially the *New York Daily News*, when the husband of the *New Yorker*'s editor oversaw them, and when, as he was quick to boast on accepting Zuckerman's offer, he would own a piece of the company? (Zuckerman soon clarified that Harry would have an "equity stake" only if Zuckerman took the company public.)[6]

If Gottlieb had pinched pennies in a fruitless effort to please Newhouse and Florio, Brown had no such inclination. Her editorial budget was reportedly $35 million a year, as compared to $10 million for Gottlieb and $5 million for William Shawn during their respective last years. Brown handed out the $100,000-and-way-up—some say as much as $200,000 a year—multiarticle contracts common at *Vanity Fair* to the more splashy writers she recruited. (She also started a contributors' page featuring photographs of that issue's writers.) She double-staffed by retaining the current staff, at least temporarily, while recruiting an overlay of new. According to Perry Vandermeer, Tina would just keep "adding people on top, so your job just disappeared after a while, because there were four people doing what one person did before." And, typical of Condé Nast, anyone in a position of even the most modest authority was given an assistant or two. A staff that under Gottlieb was streamlined became bloated; the size, says Vandermeer, tripled or quadrupled.

Brown killed pieces she had bought—she acquired twice as many articles as she needed—to make room for others that, typically, were tied to some breaking scandal or merger or election. She bought excerpts from books, paid the writers five-figure fees, and then routinely killed them. The excerpt "gets lost in the shuffle," explains Perry Vandermeer, "because it was last week's stroke of genius."

In addition to Brown's extremely high salary, she reportedly received a housing allowance, a clothing allowance, and a tuition allowance for her children's schooling. She also spent lavishly on parties, once reportedly flying silverware from New York to Chicago for a party there. Then there was $250,000 for a pre-Oscar bash at the Hotel Bel-Air, attended by Barbra Streisand, Michael Ovitz, Steven Spielberg, and company. Next came $500,000 to care for 150 media honchos, among them Diane Sawyer, Michael Eisner, Barry Diller, and Steve Martin, Tina's guests at a conference at the Disney Institute in Florida to discuss "the future of entertainment." (Vice President Al Gore attended as well, and his travel expenses—the cost of getting him there and back on Air Force Two—were also compliments of Si Newhouse.) To mark the publication of her California issue, Tina hosted a party in Los Angeles at the fashionable Coco Pazzo in the fashionable Mondrian Hotel and attracted the likes of Robert Altman, Oliver Stone, Ted Danson, Mary Steenburgen, George Stephanopoulos, Angelica Huston, Steve Martin, again, Michael Eisner, again, Helmut Newton, Dennis Hopper, and David Hockney. It was all for the cause of promotion and publicity—the guests were for the most part not even potential sources of advertising—and giving Si what he wanted, a magazine with media buzz.

While Gottlieb's *New Yorker* lost money, Tina Brown's hemorrhaged it. "The cost of acquiring that editorial is so high," says one former *New Yorker* executive, "that from a business point of view it's a disaster.... The efforts at circulation are so heavily discounted that there's no revenue.... When you don't have a circulation revenue stream to offset it, you're in trouble."

Lack of advertising was the biggest problem. By the end of 1993, the number of ad pages sold had slipped to 2,253, a bit more than a third the number during Shawn's heyday. Confirmed reports found even that number inflated, as Florio was going off the rate card—extending special deals to auto makers, for example—and "giving it away." (Pete Spelman, formerly the magazine's marketing director, maintains that in the years before Newhouse, "When the *New Yorker* published a rate card, it lived by the rate card. After Mr. Newhouse bought it, the rate card was made out of rubber.") In 1994 ad pages fell seven percent. In 1996 ad pages were off 4.4 percent from the year before.

The *New Yorker,* under Si Newhouse, has yet to have a profitable year. Energetic attempts have been made to put a positive spin on that bleak reality. In a *New York Times* article published late in 1996, an official of the magazine was quoted as saying that he expected it to be in the black by the next year, which matched a prediction by Newhouse that the magazine would turn a profit in 1997. That same official, interviewed by *Advertising Age* in October 1995, had predicted a profit in 1996. Back issues of the *Times* and other newspapers are full of predictions of profitability—from Steve Florio and Tina Brown and Si Newhouse—that have never been realized. More recent estimates have boosted the annual loss to near a million a month and probably closer to $15 million annually. Late in 1997, Brown gave an interview to a writer for the *New York Daily News.* The article was full of good news—circulation up 27.2 percent since her arrival five years before; ad revenue up more than 50 percent during the same period; a deal with Mercury Records to put *New Yorker* fiction on audiotape and CD; an all-photography issue on tap to include thirty pages of Avedon shots—but also the hint that 1997 might not be the turnaround year. Later predictions from West Forty-third Street then had the magazine breaking even or turning a profit in 1998. By January 1998 Steve Florio predicted profitability in eighteen months to two years. Ten days later he dropped the eighteen months and promised profitability in two years. Circulation figures for the first six months of 1997, released around the same time, showed a drop of 8 percent.

Jonathan Schell, who so intensely opposed Newhouse's buying the magazine, seems to take no pleasure in its woes. "The tragedy here," Schell says, "is that as far as I can tell Newhouse himself can't decide whether writing is remarkable or beautiful or distinguished or outstanding. He has to rely on the judgment of others. He sees that others say that the *New Yorker* is great, and he buys it. But then he's the one in charge of it, and has to make decisions about its basic editorial direction. But he has no more clue how to do this than how to paint a Jasper Johns painting. He cannot continue the *New Yorker's* traditions in any shape or form. It's a pitiful waste. And when you add the fact that he has lost money on the scale of Pentagon overruns, it all becomes too sad and ridiculous to think about."

Given that the *New Yorker* was losing so much of the Newhouse brothers' money, it might have occurred to the elder son, or to Donald, to take the ultimate revenge on A. J. Liebling and shut it down. Si didn't, in part because the magazine under Brown brought him the kind of attention he craved. Also, killing the *New Yorker* would have meant admitting to an unbearable failure. What Si would probably do is what he has always done—change editors.

Indeed, one Friday afternoon in February 1998, media insiders were trafficking in rumors that Tina was about to be dismissed. Si denied any such plan, explaining to a reporter for the *New York Times* that of course "the new *New Yorker*," as he called it, was losing money because he viewed it as, essentially, a start-up. "It was practically a new magazine," Si explained. "She did what we would have done had we invented the magazine from scratch." (Coming from a man who had vowed on buying the *New Yorker* to honor its traditions, that was some admission.)

Surely Tina Brown understood that, as much as her boss praised her, she hadn't much job security. She was safe in her job, insisted one *New*

Yorker editor, only so long as the magazine was talked about. "The day that [Si] goes to a certain kind of cocktail party and discovers that people are talking about how the *New Yorker* has just become like every other week- ly, without even the resources of a *Time* or *Newsweek* to get the real story, that'll be it for Tina Brown."

Still, it was a mistake to count Tina Brown out too soon. The almost- all-Diana—including the cover—rush-job issue that hit the stands in September 1997, just after the death of the Princess of Wales, seemed to drag the magazine about as far as possible from the Shawn version. (For the first time in the magazine's history, it was published on Friday instead of Monday to take advantage of the Saturday funeral.) To Brown's critics, her bylined piece describing a lunch the previous June at the Four Seasons with Princess Diana and Anna Wintour said it all—and none of it good. But the issue created the buzz of her boss's dreams—it didn't hurt that Brown coanchored NBC's coverage of the princess' funeral—and newsstand sales soared 175 percent, the highest in 30 years.*

Items that had earlier popped up in the gossip columns about Tina Brown and Harry Evans returning to England seemed premature, espe- cially after Harry changed jobs. Speculation from the *Times* of London that newly elected prime minister Tony Blair would offer the arts ministry to Tina Brown seemed unlikely, as did another gossip item that had Blair

---

*When Shawn met with members of the magazine's advertising staff in 1970, he delivered a sermon summarized by one of those present: "We have to decide whether we're going to publish a magazine to satisfy agency people and clients or to satisfy ourselves and our readers. It would be a terrible mistake to put covers on the magazine that would obviously create greater newsstand sales for the sake of creating newsstand sales.... [We] must not write articles for the sake of gaining a greater circulation. We must continue to write and edit...in the way we always have, which is to do it in the way that they, the writers and editors, want to write the magazine, not the way the outside commercial world wants us to. Our position in the publishing world has been one of uniqueness.... The moment we lose that, we are out of business altogether." To Ian Frazier, the dilemma faced by Si Newhouse and Tina Brown was sadly predictable: "What the *New Yorker* under Shawn had to sell was integrity; the fact that it was this magazine of unimpeach- able integrity made people believe in it, believe the ads in it. That was its busi- ness niche."

offering Brown the job of ambassador to Washington, as did another that had Harry landing the ambassador's job. Liz Smith quoted a story making the rounds that "the British government wants to make Harry a cultural czar in England, a kind of André Malraux for beefeaters." (Malraux was named France's first culture minister by General Charles de Gaulle.) Next came a report that the prime minister would name Harry to the post of chairman of the Arts Council.

The gossips were right in describing Evans and Brown as avid backers of the young prime minister. He, and most things British, were an exception to Brown's distaste for coverage of foreign affairs, and she assigned many stories—too many, some veteran readers of the *New Yorker* believe—on the dynamic, attractive leader and on the affairs and mores of her home country. More and more the *New Yorker* seemed dominated by British writers, self-consciously Anglophilic, striving after a tone decidedly British and sometimes tabloidesque.

Liz Smith went on to dismiss the rumors of Tina and Harry's departure and to quote a Condé Nast employee as saying, "All I know is if they are going, they'll have to take Si along with them. He couldn't bear it without both of them!"[8]

That cheery prediction lost its punch when Harry Evan lost his job. And for Tina, even bigger news—news that would land her, photograph included, on the front page of the *New York Times*—was on the way.

23 | The Bumbler

WHEN SI NEWHOUSE HANDED the top job at *Mademoiselle* to Amy Levin, he knew he might have a problem should she fail to boost its stagnant circulation of 922,000 to the couple of million he wanted. Levin's husband was Art Cooper, the top editor at *GQ*. Cooper was very successful there; the numbers for *GQ* looked so good, in the late 1980s especially, that Si was reluctant to upset the balance at one of his company's star performers. So he did nothing.

Although Levin heeded Newhouse's and Alex Liberman's directions to cut down on the intellectual tone and make *Mademoiselle* "sex-driven," the bottom line remained anemic. In 1991, when *Mademoiselle*'s ad pages were off by 16 percent, its publisher, Richard Kinsler, figured that he had better get out. A year later he jumped ship, to *New York* magazine. Newhouse, recognizing that sex wasn't working, kept complaining to Liberman that something else must be tried to draw the female masses to *Mademoiselle*. Just as Liberman had suddenly appeared at *Mademoiselle* during Edie Locke's waning days as editor in 1980, so he reappeared, pushing Levin to change her formula. She resisted, and it was Alex who told Si to get rid of her.

After watching *Mademoiselle* struggle for twelve years of Amy Levin's tenure—circulation had grown to 1.2 million by the second half of 1992, but ad pages had dropped from 1,500 in 1980 to 1,296 in 1992—Si finally fired her. He compensated, in the years to come, by showering Levin's husband with perks and favors that were outsized even by Condé Nast's special standards for star editors. Newhouse reportedly loaned Cooper $1.2 million to buy a country house in Litchfield County,

Connecticut, and later forgave the loan. He also, reportedly, bestowed upon the then-fifty-eight-year-old Cooper a guarantee of either his job or his full salary until he turned sixty-five.

Art Cooper stayed put, and *GQ* came to dominate the men's magazine field. In recent years, however, intense competition from other, more service-oriented or more daring men's magazines has hurt *GQ*, which never reached the numbers of the late 1980s. (Under publisher Michael Perlis and his successor, Richard D. Beckman, known as "Mad Dog Beckman" for his aggressive selling techniques, *GQ* did shake off its main rival, *Esquire*, in both ad pages and circulation. Under Beckman, *GQ* boasted double-digit ad page increases in 1996, 1997, and 1998. While in 1997, *GQ* had more than three times as many ad pages as *Esquire*, a year later, under a new editor, Cooper's former number two, *Esquire* enjoyed an ad surge of more than 50 percent.)

Seeming to have learned little from his outing with Levin, Si took the recommendation of Anna Wintour and gave the top spot at *Mademoiselle* to Gabe Doppelt. Then thirty-two years old, Doppelt is South African, a protégé of Wintour's who had worked for her at *Vogue* and at *British Vogue*. She had also trained under Tina Brown at the *Tatler* and was said to be "best friends" with *Details* editor James Truman. Most important, she was as hip, as cutting edge, as anyone at Condé Nast, and her mandate was to make the magazine relevant to women in their twenties.

Doppelt was generally well liked around the shop, but Newhouse could not have made a more inappropriate appointment. According to Richard Kinsler, Doppelt's tenure was "a disaster immediately. Advertisers ran away. The circulation was no good, nobody understood the book." (Estée Lauder, Maybelline, and Revlon were among the advertisers to cut back or pull out.) Doppelt's *Mademoiselle* came to be known in the company as *She-Tails*. Doppelt would run articles about lesbianism ("Young Lesbians—They're Fresh, They're Proud"), masturbation, the thrill of shoplifting, how to rent a pornographic movie, the legalization of marijuana. And newsstand sales plummeted.

Doppelt lasted a year—she went on to MTV—and Newhouse's next move was to the opposite extreme. He hired Elizabeth Crow, most recently the president and chief editorial director of Gruner & Jahr U.S.A.

Publishing and the woman he had once tried to hire to head *Self*. She was also a middle-aged wife and mother who had driven up the circulation of *Parents* magazine. She had overseen the relaunch of the teen magazine *YM*, which in three years grew in circulation from 835,000 to 1.9 million. Crow, then forty-seven, seemed so stodgy, so middle American, especially next to Doppelt, that some on the staff took to calling her "old crow." But she gave *Mademoiselle* a mainstream freshness. Cover models no longer looked as if they had spent the summer in a crack den. And newsstand sales rose sharply; circulation grew to 1.3 million in the first half of 1994. Crow kept the gains coming. For 1996, *Mademoiselle* enjoyed the biggest increase in ad pages of any of the Newhouse women's magazines—11.2 percent—while *Vogue, Self,* and even *Glamour* all posted gains under three percent. (*Glamour*'s drop was temporary, and in 1997 ad page numbers surged 17 percent over the year before.)[1]

By the fall of 1992, staffers at *HG* knew that their magazine was in trouble. Its editor, Nancy Novogrod, had not been able to bring back to health the magazine, then ninety-one-years-old, that Anna Wintour and her bold experiments had so weakened.

But the problem wasn't only the radical makeover Wintour gave the magazine in 1987 when she changed its name from *House & Garden* to *HG* and its focus from practical decorating to fashion and celebrity. The recession that started in 1989, a year after Wintour left *HG* for *Vogue*, had hit shelter magazines particularly hard. *HG* was losing money at a rate of between $3 and $5 million a year, according to reliable estimates. At the same time its main competitor, *Architectural Digest*, published in Los Angeles by Knapp Communications, had overtaken *HG* in numbers of advertising pages sold and in circulation.

Having inherited the mess left by Anna Wintour, Nancy Novogrod had seemed at first overwhelmed and indecisive. She was not helped, says Carolyn Sollis, then the magazine's decorating director, by the "confusion about the Condé Nast corporate point of view about what *HG* should be at that point. I think her directions changed practically weekly." Should *HG* ape *Architectural Digest*'s focus on the homes of the rich and famous, or should it return to its roots as a reliable source of design and decoration ideas? One editor recalls the constant calls to Novogrod from Si, who would offer one suggestion after another.

Still, numbers aside, the news for Novogrod and her editors was not all bleak. One of the seeming best pieces of news was that Alex Liberman had withdrawn from the magazine. Because he had suffered a heart attack, it was said, he had to husband his energy. By the fall of 1992 Rochelle Udell had more or less taken his place and, with Novogrod, was shepherding the magazine back to the practical and accessible. In reality, Alex withdrew not for health reasons but because he had no interest in that kind of magazine. He had liked Wintour's arty version, but a return to the old *House & Garden*'s decorating tips and tricks of the trade left him cold. Alex's new enthusiasm was for *Allure,* a Condé Nast beauty magazine launched in March 1991 that had become a favorite of Si's.

But hope soon evaporated when, later in 1992, the news hit that Newhouse was looking to buy Knapp Communications, whose magazines *Architectural Digest,* or *AD,* as it was called for short, and *Bon Appetit* were up for sale. Si was not alone in wanting *AD,* but he wanted it more than anyone else because he hated the fact that *HG* was perceived as lagging behind it. The quickest way to regain the top spot among shelter magazines, Si decided, was to buy it.

He also was set on hiring *AD*'s editor, Paige Rense, who had run the magazine out of Los Angeles since 1970. Under her stewardship, *AD* increased its circulation from 40,000 to 650,000. Rense was as closely identified with *AD* as Helen Gurley Brown was with *Cosmo.* Sixty-three at the time, Rense was a high school dropout, but she was smart, brassy, bold, and extremely well connected. She had no desire to move to New York and risk the supervision of Alex Liberman. Had she been willing to make the move, Si would likely have hired her to run *HG,* to turn it into a clone of *AD,* and with time, to grab back the lead.

While *HG* editors considered Paige Rense's *AD* impossibly vulgar and unintentionally hilarious, the boss considered it the country's most elite shelter magazine. Competing with Si to buy *AD* and *Bon Appetit* were the New York Times Company, Hearst, Cahners, Hachette Filipacchi, and K-III. But Si offered the most, and his bid included a promise of 10 percent over the highest bid. In March 1993, for $175 million in cash, Si won the magazines.

On the very day that he consummated the deal for *AD* and *Bon Appetit*, he announced his decision to close *HG*. He explained that the decision was strictly business; that having acquired *AD*, it no longer made economic sense to keep *HG*; that there wasn't enough advertising to feed both. One of the first people he informed was an ecstatic Paige Rense. Nancy Novogrod was further down the list.

The next morning, a stricken Novogrod, who had reportedly expected that the acquisition of *AD* would mean further changes in *HG*'s approach but had never expected Si to close it, sat in her office calling her people, many of them still at home, to tell them to go immediately to the *HG* conference room. One editor had just sat down at his desk when Novogrod and Rochelle Udell appeared in his doorway. "There were tears running down Nancy's face, and I just assumed that someone was deathly ill or her child had been hit by a car. I didn't have an inkling."

HG editors and designers, seated in rows of chairs, faced Si Newhouse—dressed for the occasion in a double-breasted Italian suit—Condé Nast president Bernard Leser, and personnel chief Pam Van Zandt, all standing in the front of the room. Leser opened the meeting by saying, according to Denise Martin, then an *HG* features editor, "how sorry they all were and...introduced Mr. Newhouse who...gave this extremely dry, unemotional little talk about how this was a business decision and when they bought *AD* they had thought that this would be a good combination, but after more careful study it's not going to be possible. Thank you for all your good work and so on and then he stopped and there was absolute silence." According to Martin, "No one made a move to relieve it, to make it anything but dead silence." Not a single question was asked, not even the one on most people's lips: "If only one shelter magazine can survive at Condé Nast, why not close *Architectural Digest*?"

Anne Foxley, then *HG*'s decorating editor, recalls Si as speaking, without any emotion, "really awkwardly and really, really slowly, like one word every seven seconds. It became that much more intense. We started crying, tears rolling out of our eyes." He seemed oblivious, she says, to the anguish in the room. "He didn't look at us. He looked at his shoes, hands in his pockets, he looked very awkward, very small." One editor, who describes himself and his colleagues as "stunned," recalls the brevity and the lack of detail in Si's remarks and the closer, "'People from personnel will be calling each of you to discuss the people problem.' That was the only reference to the unfortunate situation that most of us were thrust into." They were told to close the July issue and to clear out in ten days.

Bernie Leser had promised that efforts would be made to find slots at other magazines for *HG* people. "Then when we had our individual meetings with personnel," recalls Anne Foxley, "there was zero encouragement that there were any jobs at other magazines." In fact, only two people took jobs elsewhere in the company.

Anne Foxley was asked, along with a few of her colleagues, for a résumé, which Pam van Zandt would take to Los Angeles and give to Paige Rense for consideration. "She quickly learned," says Foxley, "that Paige Rense didn't want any of us." Not a single person on *HG*'s editorial staff was offered a job at *AD*. Nancy Novogrod was given a make-work corporate title. She promptly left to become editor in chief of *Travel & Leisure*.

Rense surely knew how disdainful the *HG* crowd was of her and her splashy, celebrity-obsessed magazine. "We thought it was lifestyles of the rich and famous," said Anne Foxley. That's precisely the attitude Rense had in mind when she told the *Times*' Deirdre Carmody, "People are much too concerned about having good taste. I mean, it's not a character flaw if you don't have good taste."*

Rense explained that she hired no one from *HG* because there were no openings on her spare staff of thirty—a staff that she did not intend, she added, to expand. That was a not-so-subtle dig at the spendthrift ways of Condé Nast. "I learned to do things with very few people because I didn't have the money," she told a reporter, "and by the time I did have the money, I realized that I didn't need all those people."

As *HG* editors scattered to different magazines, they had one bit of solace: the unanimous opinion, as one editor puts it, of "endless people afterwards...[who have] expressed their amazement that he closed the wrong [magazine]."

---

*Rense regularly features the houses of Hollywood stars. In one issue devoted entirely to the subject ("Hollywood at Home!"), she ran a piece on the home of producer Joel Silver, a friend of Si Newhouse. Silver is best known for the *Lethal Weapon* series. The tribute to Silver's restoration of a Frank Lloyd Wright house in the Hollywood Hills was written by Victoria Newhouse.

Lou Gropp, who after being forced out of Condé Nast became founding editor of *Elle Decor* and then editor of *House Beautiful,* where he remains today, describes Condé Nast as "a very reactive company." In this case, he suggests, a little bureaucracy—a board of directors or some shareholders—might have prevented Si from making what is widely perceived as a mistake. "Sometimes bureaucracy slows things down in a positive way."[2]

Carolyn Sollis, who had come to the magazine just out of college in 1971, decided that she would not leave as ordered without letting Si see that there were human faces behind the casualties of his decision. She made an appointment to see him. She describes him as "very gracious and...sad about what happened in his own little way." She told him that he probably didn't know how long she had worked for the magazine, and that she had come to *House & Garden* through her great-aunt, Margaret Ingersoll, who for many years had been the fabric editor of *Vogue.* Si acknowledged that Margaret had been one of his "great friends" and that he had relied on her counsel when he arrived at Condé Nast more than thirty years before. He told Sollis that closing the magazine was "the toughest decision I ever had to make."

During that meeting, she also told him that he had made a terrible mistake; that the group of people he was disbanding was smart and well respected in the industry; that the magazine he was closing had "nothing to do with *Architectural Digest* and how different the two really were and we understood that it was a business decision but in fact we all think it's going to come back. We're waiting."[3]

Sollis, who became executive editor of *House Beautiful* under her old boss, Lou Gropp, did not have to wait long. In March 1995, just two years after Si Newhouse closed *HG,* came the announcement that he was reopening it under the title *Condé Nast House & Garden.* What was going on here?

Reporters speculated that Newhouse must have noticed that magazines such as the upstart *Elle Decor*—its ad pages up 54 percent between December 1993 and 1994 and its circulation more than doubled—were doing very well. The *Wall Street Journal*'s Susannah Patton wrote that

"Condé Nast...doesn't want to be left behind when almost every other major magazine publisher is diving into a rejuvenated home-magazine market. With ad pages and circulation numbers soaring, advertisers and publishers can't seem to get enough of the home magazines that crowd newsstands."

Once again Si Newhouse had badly miscalculated, in two ways: one, when he failed to see where the country was moving; and two, when, as he did with the book publisher Crown, he overestimated the charms of *Architectural Digest. AD,* it turned out, was not the cash cow Newhouse had hoped it would be. In fact, a good argument could be made that its numbers, even in the couple of years before he bought *AD,* were headed in the wrong direction. At the end of 1991, for example, ad pages were down 534 pages. Between 1993 and 1994, ad pages dropped 21.3 percent. And it was even worse for *AD*'s running mate, *Bon Appetit.* Ad pages were down 58.8 percent. Could it be that again Si hadn't studied the books closely enough?

In the first quarter of 1994, one year after Newhouse bought *AD,* it was superseded by Lou Gropp's *House Beautiful.* "The joke may be," says Gropp, "that Si got *AD* after *AD* was over." *AD* was, Gropp explains, "a very eighties magazine where too much is never enough."

One former Condé Nast publisher attributes *AD*'s disappointing numbers to ads sold for less than the stated rate, and Newhouse and his people failing to take that into account. Condé Nast president Bernie Leser later confirmed that in part when he said that the magazine, before its acquisition by Condé Nast, had given advertisers "enormous discounts," as much as 50 percent, which had been discontinued after the Newhouse acquisition.

Newhouse admitted his blunder in closing *HG* when he told Robin Pogrebin of the *New York Times,* "We are sensitive to a greater interest in the home than was the case even as recently as three years ago."

But in jumping back into the field, Newhouse was beset with a new array of problems. All those fabulous demographic trends notwithstanding, the relaunched *House & Garden* had to contend with the growing clout of some ninety competitors including *Country Home, Traditional Home, House Beautiful, Metropolitan Home, Garden Design, Home Garden,*

Country Living Gardener, Country Living, Colonial Homes, Martha Stewart Living, and *This Old House.* (The publisher of *Garden Design* has a high-end shelter magazine in the works.) The *Wall Street Journal*'s Paul Reilly quoted one expert as observing, "It's a very crowded field of magazines all chasing a fairly small pie of ad dollars." The group publisher of the company that puts out *Elle Decor* told a reporter in the summer of 1996, "The bad news is, we're probably at the top of the market right now."[4]

In 1994 Paige Rense married the noted artist Kenneth Noland, causing some to wonder whether she might retire. But she showed no sign of easing her dedication to the magazine that had been the center of her life for twenty-five years. And she showed as much feistiness as ever when she responded to the rebirth of *House & Garden* by boasting to a reporter, "I killed it once, I'll kill it again."

The first issue of the new *HG,* which appeared in mid-August 1996, was crammed with 207 ad pages, a record for what the *Wall Street Journal* termed a launch but the *New York Times* more accurately termed a "second debut." But subsequent issues were skinnier. The second issue, October 1996, had 102 ad pages; November had 115; December, 70, just a bit over one-third of the number in the first issue. Writing in the *New York Observer,* Michael M. Thomas referred to *Condé Nast House & Garden* by the acronym *ISM,* which, he explained, stands for the *Incredible Shrinking Magazine.* (The magazine put on a bit of weight in 1998, with ad pages for the first half up 27 percent over the same period a year earlier.)

Right off, there was dissension in the ranks at *House & Garden.* Patti Hagan, who wrote about gardening for the *Wall Street Journal* and had contributed to the magazine when it was *House & Garden* and then *HG,* became the restart's first gardening columnist. In that capacity, she was assigned a column addressing the question of whether gardeners should or should not wrap trees during winter in order to protect them from cold, wind, and wildlife. When the "Dig It" column was set in type and the galleys returned to Hagan for proofing, she noted that three consecutive paragraphs on Martha Stewart, comprising almost one-third of the column, had been cut. (Not another word in the piece had been touched.) Stewart, unlike Hagan, is a pro-wrapper, and Hagan harshly criticized Stewart's position, as articulated in her book on gardening published by Random House imprint Clarkson Potter: "Just reading the unexpurgated details of Martha Stewart's garden wrapping exhausts me. What real gardener...has time for this 'fidgety-tidy way.'" She suggested that "sensible novice gardeners...trade in" *Martha Stewart's Gardening* for *The Ruth Stout No-Work Garden Book*.

A note to Hagan from executive editor Betsy Pochoda called the cut in Hagan's copy a "judgment call having to do with the wisdom and manners of a fledgling magazine attacking the leader in the field." But it was also true that Si Newhouse published Martha Stewart's books—twenty-two so far, the first, *Entertaining*, in its thirtieth printing—and although he had initially passed on her magazine because he mistakenly believed it lacked the potential to attract a mass audience, he had become interested again in trying to buy it. (By 1997 the magazine claimed a circulation of 2.3 million, and its ad revenue had jumped 97.1 percent. "It was not one of the decisions I'm most proud of," Newhouse was quoted as saying.)

Hagan balked. Pochoda and the editor, Dominique Browning, refused to restore the paragraphs or to comply with Hagan's demand that the column not run without the paragraphs restored. Hagan hired a lawyer. In a letter to Browning, the lawyer called the cuts "censorship." (Hagan attempted a compromise by condensing the three paragraphs to one, but still the editors would not allow any mention of Stewart.)

Hagan's contract was not renewed, and her wrapping piece never ran. (It later ran in the *Wall Street Journal*.) It was replaced by a homogenized piece that carried no byline, made no mention of Martha Stewart, and mostly weighed in on the pro-wrapping side, referring to anti-wrappers as "the humorless, the obsessed and the deeply cuckoo."[5]

Hagan was replaced as gardening columnist by Tom Christopher, whose first "Dig It" column appeared in March 1997. Its tag line identified him as coauthor, with Marty Asher, of the just-published book *The 20-Minute Gardener*. Not mentioned was the fact that the book was published by Random House and that Asher is editor in chief of Vintage, a Random House imprint.

The next month, April, Christopher's "Dig It" appeared again, along with the debut of Christopher and Asher's column, "The 20-Minute Gardener," and—in various spots in the magazine, including a line on the cover—five plugs for *The 20-Minute Gardener*. Later in 1997 Christopher wrote a glowing "Dig It" about landscape architect James van Sweden, whose *Gardening with Nature* was just out from, natch, Random House.

Christopher, who with Marty Asher is currently writing *The 20-Minute Fruit and Vegetable Gardener* for Random House, insists that there was no "great corporate plan" for any of the above—both "Dig It" and "The 20-Minute Gardener" and blurbs galore continue to run—and doubts that there is any organized communication between the magazine and the book publisher. He claims that when *House & Garden* editors approached him to take over the Hagan column in the fall of 1996, they had no idea that he had a book coming from Random House, and that the idea to turn his and Asher's column into an adaptation of and, indeed, a recurring monthly advertisement for the book, was his agent's.

But Patti Hagan points to the magazine's multiple hypes for Christopher and Asher's book, and cites a letter to her from Christopher describing pressure from Random House publicists to sign on for the column as a means to boost the book. Some call this synergy but others call it a lowering of standards. Patti Hagan calls it a conflict of interest.

24 | The Bully Boys

IN 1994 BERNIE LESER had worked for Condé Nast for thirty-five years, the last seven as president. Leser had started the Australian edition of *Vogue* in 1959, the year Sam Newhouse bought the company. The elder son learned to depend on Leser, who became one of his closest advisers. Leser also tended to the people in the company in a manner that was well beyond the scope of S. I. Newhouse's personality. Although Leser was unable to stop the boss's abrupt dismissals, and in some cases presumably agreed with Si's decisions, he was considered a tempering influence. "Many more heads would have rolled," says one former publisher, were it not for Leser, who was said to be particularly appalled by Si's clumsy dismissal of Grace Mirabella.

Leser in 1994 was sixty-eight years old, and no one had to remind Si Newhouse that the powers at Condé Nast, himself included, were pushing seventy—the seemingly irreplaceable Alex Liberman was eighty-one—and that a new generation of leaders would have to be put in place. So Leser's eventual retirement had been discussed, but in general terms. Newhouse knew that Leser, a tremendously gregarious man, loved the people, the pace, the business, too much to retire voluntarily any time soon. In an interview in late 1991, Leser happily pointed to the Condé Nast tradition of executives working well into their eighties as a precedent for his staying on.

Leser was in Tokyo in January 1994 when he received a phone call from his boss. "You'll be very upset," Si said in his characteristically goofy manner when he was about to have someone's head. "There's a story in *Advertising Age* that Steve Florio is taking over and you're going."

Bernie laughed nervously and said, "Oh, well, we've heard that before, you know."

"Well," Si said, delivering his punch line, "this time it's true."

"You shit!" was Leser's enraged reply as he banged down the phone.

Leser's friends, rallying behind him, felt the same way. "You don't have to fire Bernie Leser on an airplane," says one publishing CEO who knows both men well. But Si did, and Leser was forced to rush home from Japan and, a few days later, to submit to what must have been an unbearable interview with the *New York Times'* Deirdre Carmody.

Surely much to the delight of the Condé Nast public relations people, Carmody missed the undertext and reported the Condé Nast line that Leser, a native Australian, was happily heading home to Sydney with the important title of chairman, Asia-Pacific, and the charge to expand the magazine group throughout the Pacific. Leser talked of plans to develop a Japanese version of *Vogue*, which would join the already-existing Japanese *GQ*.[1] On the surface it all sounded okay, but that job title had previously belonged to one of his own underlings. And in his new position he would be reporting to Si's young cousin, Jonathan Newhouse, then running the international division.

If his colleagues were surprised to see Bernie Leser so brutally axed, they were shocked at the choice of his successor, Steve Florio, then forty-four years old. President of the *New Yorker* since Newhouse's purchase of the magazine in 1985, Florio had seen it lose millions every year of his stay, for a total of some $100 million. Why reward him with the top job in the company? And given the magazine's sorry numbers, which included a 28 percent drop in ad pages, why wasn't Florio fired?

Pete Spelman, whom Florio fired from the *New Yorker*, has a simple theory—that Florio "will do anything" that Si asks him to do, and that very rich men need someone like Steve Florio. Others claim that it was a matter of chemistry. Si was attracted to Florio's personality—boisterous, loud, pushy, "a bullshitter," says Richard Kinsler—because it was so different from his own. Newhouse himself once observed to a reporter that Florio's "energy level is huge.... Somebody said to me, 'He fills a room.' I don't think [the speaker] was talking about Steve being overweight. I think he was talking about Steve's personality." It was the same kind of larger-than-life presence that the short and wiry Roy Cohn had. And Si Newhouse always seemed to be looking for a new Roy Cohn to be part of his life.

That Steve Florio knew how to play Si was obvious. As one former publisher put it, "Florio...did every little manipulative thing he could to get Si to see in him something that Si didn't have." The package included befriending and courting Si's older son, Sam, with whom Florio shared a love of boating.

When Newhouse explained to Meg Cox of the *Wall Street Journal* why he had selected Florio to head his company, there was something downright Orwellian in the top-to-bottom exaggeration. During Florio's nine years at the top of the *New Yorker*'s business side, Newhouse told Cox, Florio had done a "brilliant job."

But Cox's colleague at the *Wall Street Journal*, Joanne Lipman, gave a different angle to Florio's appointment. When Si called Florio to his office at 6:00 one January morning in 1994 to tell him he had the job, he also handed him a profit-and-loss statement. It was the first the burly publisher had ever seen, and, Lipman wrote, Si considered it so confidential that "few individuals outside the family ever see it." The "shock," Lipman added, was that the magazines were losing money. With help from people "familiar" with the company, Lipman estimated that for the fiscal year ending January 31, 1994, Condé Nast had lost between $15 and $20 million. (*New York Daily News* business writer Keith Kelly would later peg the loss for 1993 at $30 million.)

Lipman reported that of thirteen Condé Nast titles, nine were in the red, and specified that the losers included *Mademoiselle, GQ, Condé Nast Traveler, Details, Self, Vanity Fair,* and *Allure*. (With the addition of *Condé Nast House & Garden* and the newer *Condé Nast Sports for Women*, there are now fifteen Condé Nast magazines. The *New Yorker*, which on its own was said to have lost well over $10 million annually—$30 million for 1993 alone—would not have appeared on the statement because it was not yet officially part of Condé Nast.)

Florio took on his new job with gusto. During his first year, he changed publishers at nine of the magazines. As of early 1997, only one publisher of the group Florio had inherited from Bernie Leser—Alexandra Golinkin at *Allure*—remained in place.

Florio's good fortune continued. He was allowed to choose his own successor as president and CEO of the *New Yorker,* and that person turned out to be his younger brother, Tom Florio. Tom happily gave up his post as publisher of *Condé Nast Traveler,* one of the loser publications. Those who had dubbed Steve Florio Pinocchio were not surprised when he insisted that he had nothing at all to do with the promotion of Tom; the company line was that he was Tina's first choice.

Tom Florio, who earlier in his career had sold ads at *Vanity Fair,* was said to be a smart enough fellow, but he proved a chip off the older block when it came to turning the numbers around at the *New Yorker.* By late 1996 some issues of the magazine were so thin that one week it arrived in this writer's mailbox stuck inside the pages of the *New Republic.* With ad pages estimated to have declined more than 3 percent for 1996, Tom Florio predicted that things would be much better the next year: ad pages and revenue, he promised, would grow "significantly." For the first half of 1997, ad pages were down 3.4 percent from the same period the year before.

Around the same time, a reporter for the *Wall Street Journal* revealed that Tom Florio, with the "wary blessing" of Tina Brown, had instituted a policy of warning some fifty companies on a "sensitive advertiser list" when editorial material to appear in an upcoming issue might prove offensive. Florio argued that the church and state divide that once informed the magazine was no longer operative; "ecosystem," he explained, best described the relationship between editorial and advertising.

The paucity of advertising was reflected in still another special double issue that contained a full-page ad for a new collection of *New Yorker* cat cartoons, a smaller ad hawking a poster adapted from the cover of the special cartoon issue, and a two-pager, front and back, advertising *"The New Yorker* goes to sea," the Crystal Symphony's around-the-world cruise, each segment to feature talks by a *New Yorker* writer, editor, or cartoonist. The staffers' services were offered in exchange for a promise that Crystal would buy six pages of advertising in the magazine during 1998. The outcry from those who didn't like the deal resulted in a promise that the names of the staffers selected to entertain the ship's passengers, in exchange for an all-expense-paid cruise for two, would not be used in the ads. They were used, however, in Crystal press releases that promised that "the wit, wisdom and style of the *New Yorker* magazine will be showcased aboard Crystal Cruises." (The American Society of Magazine Editors [ASME] quickly blasted Tom Florio, complained that the deal violated its guidelines, and protested to the Publishers Information Bureau, which audits ad sales in magazines. ASME is lobbying to have the six pages of advertising remain uncounted in the *New Yorker*'s total.)

The younger Florio found his name in the gossip and news columns in late 1997 when Diane Silberstein, whom he had hired as the magazine's publisher in October 1994 and fired in March 1997, slapped him, Si Newhouse, and Advance Publications, Inc. with a lawsuit charging wrongful discrimination on the basis of her pregnancy. Silberstein claimed that when she announced that she was pregnant with her second child, Tom Florio was obviously unhappy and advised her of the difficulties of juggling a job and two children. Silberstein had arrived at *Glamour* in 1978 and had worked for three of the Newhouse magazines before leaving Condé Nast to become publisher of *Elle*. It was from that position that Tom Florio coaxed her back to the fold. Florio denied all of her claims. The suit is pending. Some nine salespeople have reportedly left the company, unhappy with Tom Florio's management.[2]

"It's just interesting to watch that Condé Nast is becoming a top-heavy company of bully boys," says one woman who left the Newhouse empire for another magazine company. She was referring to Steve Florio, but also to Ron Galotti. Before becoming publisher at *Vanity Fair*, where he replaced the soft-spoken, earnest Doug Johnston, Galotti held the publisher's job first at *Mademoiselle* and then, as founding publisher, at *Condé Nast Traveler*.

Johnston had prided himself on his sales force, on having the lowest turnover rate of any Condé Nast publisher. Advertisers knew his people, trusted them, and knew whom to call with a question or complaint. Those advertising people also delivered. In 1985, when Johnston became publisher, 429 ad pages were sold; by 1989, his last full year in the job, that number stood at 1,487. (Johnston stands out among former publishers in showing no bitterness. What he appreciated about Si Newhouse, he says, "was that he gave me the time and space to allow me to figure things out for myself. As long as it got done, he left you alone." He calls the nine years he spent on *Vanity Fair* "a great gift, an incredible education in publishing.")

Then Galotti arrived in late 1990 and fired everybody. In his two and a half years at *Vanity Fair*, there was a turnover of thirty-five people.

With his slicked-back hair, his perpetual tan, his large cigar, his sleek suits and Ferrari, his screaming fits of profanity, and his boorish approach to managing his staff, Galotti, then in his early forties, came to represent the dark side of Condé Nast. But Newhouse didn't seem to care. He "was enamored of Ron Galotti," Richard Kinsler, among many others, observes. Galotti struck many as a Roy Cohn type, but not as nice. His employees watched with amused disdain while maintenance men moved conference room furniture so Galotti, dressed in a "little leotard," could kick-box with his private trainer.

One saleswoman, on business with Galotti in Paris, had taken a hired car and driver for a meeting with an advertiser. When she returned to the Ritz Hotel, the meeting having run longer than expected, she was greeted by Galotti screaming across the lobby, "Where the fuck have you been?" During that same trip, she brought Galotti along to lunch with a very important advertiser, the head of a major fashion house. Over lunch, which the advertiser hosted, he raved about this woman. As they left, his praise ringing in her ears, Galotti remarked, "That man wants to sleep with you." She reported the comment to personnel, but nothing happened. She guesses that "because *Vanity Fair* was doing so well, their philosophy was, 'I know that Ron's a tough guy, but the numbers talk and he's producing.'"

Newhouse liked Galotti so much that he was seen for a time as a good bet to succeed Bernie Leser. Florio disliked Galotti for obvious reasons, but Bernie Leser despised him. "Ron was bragging that he was going to be the next president," says a woman who worked for him. Loudly and in public places, Galotti would volunteer that he hoped that Bernie Leser was run over by a bus.

Galotti did produce. A woman who worked unhappily for him describes him as "an exceptionally intelligent man. He makes it his business to really, really understand the business, which very few publishers do. He knows everything about the magazine from circulation to little innuendoes of selling. And when he is into selling, he's exceptional." Another ex-employee marvels that Galotti would "never go out on a business lunch without knowing where that client's business is in the competition." Most publishers, she says, just go to the lunch and don't bother with that kind of detail.

Another person who worked for Galotti and grew to detest him admits that "Galotti had a tremendous track record at Condé Nast. He built business. He laid the foundation for magazines, and Si Newhouse, I guess, didn't care how he did it. He built the *Traveler*.... He definitely brought business back to *Mademoiselle* when it was suffering."

Galotti had been Tina Brown's publisher at *Vanity Fair*, and she, like Newhouse, saw him as a winner. Si had originally slated Galotti to be publisher of *Vogue*, but had acceded to Brown's pleas that he be sent to *Vanity Fair*.

Brown and Galotti grew so close that in 1992, when she told her staff at *Vanity Fair* that she was leaving for the *New Yorker*, she dissolved into tears and into the arms of Ron Galotti. Galotti felt like crying too; he instantly realized that, without Tina and with a sales force that would have revolted if it felt it had any power to do so, *Vanity Fair* would become a much harder sell. Galotti desperately wanted to follow Tina to the *New Yorker* but guessed correctly that this was one wish that Si would not grant because Steve Florio already had that job.

The rivalry between Galotti and Florio intensified after Brown left and Graydon Carter took over at *Vanity Fair*. Galotti was not happy with the choice, believing that Carter didn't have the stuff to keep *Vanity Fair* hot. When, early in Carter's reign, the numbers started to go bad at *Vanity Fair*, Galotti became vulnerable. (Ad revenue dropped 20 percent in 1993, the first full year under Carter's command.) On top of that, says David O'Brasky, it was difficult to find anyone who would work for Galotti; six sales jobs remained open at *Vanity Fair*, and few first-rate people applied. "Every time someone walked into the personnel office," says a woman who had worked for Galotti, "they'd say, 'I'd love to work for this company but not *Vanity Fair*.'"

By May 1993 Galotti was unemployed. "Ron's style was tolerated while he was producing," explains a former Condé Nast publisher. "The minute the magazine's numbers turned sour, that...level of management that had been so alienated by him moved on him. They went to Si Newhouse and said, 'Hey, look, this isn't working anymore.' They convinced Si to get rid of him." Galotti was out of work for eight months before returning to Hearst in January 1994—he had worked there earlier as the launch publisher of *Country Living*—as publishing director of *Esquire* and *Esquire Gentleman*.

In March 1994, with Bernie Leser at the time still officially president but powerless, Si decided to bring Galotti back. Florio, who would have preferred to see Galotti hired as publisher of *Siberian Life*, could do nothing but pretend that the decision was his. Galotti came back in style. He was named publisher of *Vogue* and given the added title of senior vice president of Condé Nast. Galotti snidely referred to his short time out from Condé Nast as "my little exile." He was all smiles, not surprisingly: it was reported that on top of the $2 million Galotti received as severance pay, Si gave him $1 million to return—in the form of a signing bonus. But Newhouse was said to have cautioned Galotti to check his temper and his brutal style of management. Indeed, a clause in his new contract reportedly required him to treat people with respect.[3]

Ron Galotti's appointment as publisher of *Vogue* created another problem for the owner and Steve Florio, in the person of the sitting publisher, Anne Sutherland Fuchs. Then forty-six, Fuchs was highly regarded throughout the Newhouse organization. In 1990 Si and Bernie Leser had hired her away from *Elle* in an attempt to damage the new competition. (Before *Elle*, she had been publisher of *Woman's Day*.) In an apparent attempt to soften the nasty public relations that resulted, Steve Florio promptly announced that Fuchs would be joining his "executive management team," with the title of senior vice president, director international. In other words, she was administered a kick upstairs.

Anne Fuchs wasn't a member of the Florio "executive team" for long. In August 1994 she was hired by Hearst as senior VP-group publishing director, with operating responsibility for *Harper's Bazaar, Town &*

Country, and *Marie Claire.* She persuaded three important *Vogue* staffers to follow her.

Vogue was a struggle for Galotti. Ad pages fell 6 percent in the last half of 1995 when compared with the same period in 1994. Galotti blamed the decline on the slump in the fashion and beauty industries. Others blamed the decline on Galotti's continued abusive treatment of his staff. One woman who is delighted to no longer to work for Galotti says, "Look at *Vogue* today. Nobody wants to go work there." Still, Galotti has shown that, for all his faults, he has the right stuff. By 1996, Galotti was doing about 3 percent better at *Vogue* than he did in 1995. In 1997 he was ahead by 19 percent over the year before. The September 1997 issue, Condé Nast flacks claimed, was so stuffed with ads—563 pages—that it weighed more than the Manhattan telephone directory. In late 1997, Robin Pogrebin would declare in the *New York Times* that, under Wintour, *Vogue* had reached "a whole new blockbuster level as the bible of fashion" and that, under Galotti, it had enjoyed its "best financial year" in its 105-year history.[4]

Galotti's replacement at *Vanity Fair* was Kathy Neisloss Leventhal, who had worked at *Glamour* and then at *Vanity Fair* as Doug Johnston's ad director. David O'Brasky calls her "one of the smartest salespeople I've ever worked with." She had left *Vanity Fair* before Galotti's arrival to become the launch publisher of *Allure.* (On her mother's side, Leventhal is a member of the Gertz department store family, once the most important advertiser in Sam Newhouse's *Long Island Press,* a fact, she says, that never came up in any of her many meetings with Si Newhouse.)

Having read in the newspapers that Condé Nast was starting a beauty magazine, she knew what the boss had in mind when he called her to his office one Friday morning in 1990. "We're thinking of doing this beauty magazine, and we're going to need a publisher," he told her. "He never said, 'We want you to be the publisher,'" Leventhal recalls. "Then he described Linda Wells [then beauty editor of the *New York Times,* formerly a beauty editor at *Vogue*], who he wanted very much to be the editor.... 'Perhaps she'll be the editor.' I left his office.... On Monday I was the publisher."

Kathy Leventhal had only ten weeks to sell *Allure*. The first issue, dated March 1991, carried seventy-four pages of advertising. The magazine ended its first year with only 290 ad pages.

While the title, *Allure*, was said to be Alex Liberman's—he was closely involved in the magazine, appearing in its art department daily— the concept was Newhouse's. He wanted a magazine that would focus on straightforward, practical beauty advice rather than on fashion. Leventhal describes the magazine's "mission" as a "journalistic magazine for intelligent, urban-minded women about the subject of beauty, ...sort of a complete antithesis of what beauty magazines had been about." It would be full of information, but it would not preach to women, and it would never treat them like "idiots." Diane Silberstein, who was then the magazine's advertising director, says it was "a sign of the [recessionary] times that people were spending much less money on fashion and it was certainly a lot easier to get a quick fix from a $20 Chanel lipstick when you could no longer afford a $3,000 Chanel suit."

Still, *Allure* was not easy to sell. "You would tell the advertising community that mission statement," Leventhal recalls, "and I would say 99 times out of a hundred, the look that we experienced was that of a dog that hears a piercing noise. People cocked their heads and said, 'What?'"

But once she settled in, Leventhal was a success at *Allure*, a magazine that one former publisher described as "a charismatic newcomer" for Condé Nast. Advertising pages quintupled. Circulation increased 83.9 percent between the second half of 1991 and the second half of 1992. And by the early mid-1990s, *Allure* was touted as one of Condé Nast's top performers, one of the few titles that had double-digit ad gains. By the end of 1995 *Allure* had a circulation of 700,000 and 1,322 ad pages, making it the fastest-growing launch in Condé Nast history. In the numbers of cosmetic/beauty ads, it outscored all other magazines, including *Vogue*.

That said, *Allure*'s circulation stalled at 700,000, and between 1996 and 1997 its newsstand sales dropped by 9 percent. It was among the magazines mentioned in the *Wall Street Journal* as losing money. (Actually, Si Newhouse disputed the claim that nine of his magazines were losers. He insisted that only two were, *Details* and *Allure*. Two years later, in early 1998, Si admitted that *Allure* and *Details* continue to lose money.)

Still, Leventhal saw the magazine as eventually inching into the black, and she and *Allure* seemed well positioned—no one disputed that she had been as good a launch publisher as any—when Newhouse called her to his office. This time he asked her to return to *Vanity Fair*. She told him that she loved *Allure* and would prefer to stay there. Si told her that he needed her at *Vanity Fair*. So in May 1993 she returned, unhappily. Her situation was complicated by a difficult pregnancy that left her bedridden for the final two months.

Things at *Vanity Fair* were not good that year. Not only were ad pages down steeply in 1993, but during the first four months of 1994 they declined by 28 percent. While Leventhal could survive the profit and loss bumps at *Vanity Fair*, she could not survive the ouster of Bernie Leser, who had been her mentor. Steve Florio was not a Leventhal fan—some thought, that she, like Anne Fuchs, threatened him. Leventhal resolved to hang on. As rumors spread of her impending dismissal, she insisted that she had Florio's confidence—he had assured her that she did—and would go, "only if carried out feet first."

When Steve Florio fired her in June 1994, she was furious, particularly because, she says, Florio lied to her. "He told me I was a superior executive," Leventhal recalls, "but that I was like a plant that needed to be repotted." He informed her that she would be going to the fourteenth floor to evaluate new magazine ideas with the title of corporate director of special projects. Florio told the *New York Post* that the corporate job was a "step up" for Leventhal, then thirty-eight years old.

Leventhal didn't believe him. She went to see the boss. "'Steve tells me that there are a lot of ideas that are going to be evaluated for launches.' Si Newhouse's eyes glazed over, and he said, 'I don't want to do any launches right now.' So I realized rather immediately that I had been moved out to pasture and misled by the new guy. So I said, 'Life is too short. Why should I sit here and make lunch dates and manicure appointments. I'm outta here.'" She left the magazine business.[5]

In 1994, when Alex Liberman's health was noticeably declining, the rumor mill ran double-time handicapping his successor. The consensus was that Rochelle Udell was out of the running, having too clearly shown her eagerness to take his place. The odds were on Tina Brown, who, some thought, would love to extricate herself honorably from the burden of putting out a magazine every week that lost money almost every week; and Anna Wintour, who was perceived as having performed poorly at *Vogue*. Wintour, who three years later would be deified in the *New York Times* as an "icon," a "star,"and a "persona," then found herself contending with pesky rumors that she would be returned to Europe to take a job with Condé Nast International while Linda Wells, the editor of the hot if unprofitable *Allure*, would take her place at *Vogue*.

But in late January 1994, just two weeks after Newhouse made the switch from Bernie Leser to Steve Florio, he announced that Liberman, then eighty-one, was, more or less, retiring—he would keep his office and his access to Si—and that his replacement would be *Details'* James Truman, then thirty-five. Truman had no background in design, and his only leadership role was as editor of a money-losing magazine.

The selection of Truman, a Brit born in Nottingham, at a high six-figure salary, was a shocker. Many thought that Newhouse would hire a woman, but not the insiders who understood the Condé Nast hierarchy. While women had, practically from the founding of Condé Nast, been editors in chief and, as the years passed, had even become publishers, all of the important jobs seemed reserved for men. On the corporate side—in the genuine power jobs, not the make-work jobs—for years, the only woman was Pam van Zandt, who as personnel chief and dispenser of tissues to tearful, terminated employees had held a job that traditionally belonged to women, and who in any case had taken over from another woman, her boss, Mary Campbell.

Alex Liberman was frank, if politically incorrect, when he remarked to Rebecca Mead, then a reporter for *New York* magazine, "I think it is better for a man to be in this job, because you deal with other men. You know, the business side is all male, and you deal with the engravers, printers, all those things. And I think the women editors are more receptive to something from a man, and there may be female resentment, jealousy."

Then there was the issue of age. Nobody would have looked at Tina Brown or Anna Wintour, both mothers of young children, and thought of them as aging, but in the Condé Nast culture they were middle-aged. James

Truman was not much younger than either of them—Tina was then forty and Anna forty-four—but seemed to the boss and Liberman to be fresh and full of attitude. Neither Brown nor Wintour could ever have what James had, a boyishness, an awkward, unstudied charm, a naughtiness that appealed to both Si and Alex. A former Condé Nast art director speculates that Alex was intimately involved in the selection of Truman, that he "saw something of himself in James," a "sort of asexual, charming man."

Some of the older editors in chief—among them, Art Cooper of *GQ* and Ruth Whitney of *Glamour*—were unenthusiastic about Truman's promotion. On the day that his appointment was announced, Cooper told Meg Cox of the *Journal*, "I haven't worked with anybody for eight years. Ruth Whitney has a similar independence. The magazines that work successfully independently will continue to do so." Si soon had to warn Cooper to moderate his opinions.

Paige Rense was much less diplomatic in her reaction to Truman. "If he starts telling me what to do," she told a reporter, "I am going to spank him and send him to bed without his dinner." "I am running *Architectural Digest*. Flat out. I am," she insisted to another reporter. Next she volunteered that while she'd take advice from Alex Liberman or Si Newhouse, "It's difficult for me to imagine taking suggestions from someone who has no real track record or a very limited track record."

Truman soon replied, "I look forward to working with the next editor of *Architectural Digest*." Later, in an interview with a reporter for *Women's Wear Daily* in which he denied an assortment of rumors about himself, he joked, "I am not going to be Paige Rense's seventh husband." Relations between the two grew so poisonous that speculation had it that the restart of *Condé Nast House & Garden*, Truman's first big project, was Truman's idea, and that the entire point was to raise Rense's blood pressure. (Steve Florio denied the revenge theory, insisting that it was he, Florio, who first suggested to Si that the magazine be revived.)

Ruth Whitney, who was nearing her thirtieth year as editor of *Glamour*, characteristically issued no public comment or warning. Whitney was known for her dedication to keeping attention focused not on her but on her magazine. She didn't have to send signals that James should keep his distance—or so went the conventional wisdom that nobody at

Condé Nast would dare to fool with a woman, then in her late sixties, who although neither young nor glamorous made millions for the company. Florio, in a rare burst of honesty, would later say, "Without *Glamour*, I don't even want to think about what the bottom line of this company would look like.... It's the original 300-pound gorilla." As things would turn out, even Ruth Whitney should have been watching her back.[6]

Liberman continued to keep his hand in the magazines for a while, but it would never be anywhere near the same again for him. The inimitable Tatiana had died in 1991, and Alex remarried Melina Pechangco, the Filipino nurse who had tended to Tatiana. His friends explained that, after decades of nursing Titiana's physical and emotional ups and downs, Alex wanted someone to take care of him.

A couple of days before Truman officially took over for Alex, a reporter who was profiling the new editorial director called the main number at Condé Nast and asked for Alex Liberman. The woman who answered, a proper-sounding Brit, paused and said, "Can you spell that?" Not finding the name, she asked, "Do you know which department or magazine he works on?"

"He's the editorial director," the reporter blurted in exasperation. In her confusion, the young woman's accent degenerated from "posh" to "ordinary working class."

That Si Newhouse was extremely attached to Alex and did everything he could for him is beyond a doubt, but as Alex aged, the power in the relationship inevitably shifted to Si. He had outgrown Alex on subjects of all sorts, including art. "I think Alex in many ways follows Si now in his artistic taste," says one friend who knows both men well, "He'll declare that Jeff Koons is a genius."

By early 1995 Liberman was suffering further bouts of poor health and became increasingly reclusive, spending more time at his home in Florida.[7]

Another long-termer, Leo Lerman, died on August 22, 1994, at age eighty, and so Si Newhouse was orphaned from his two great father figures. He was stricken by Lerman's loss. Si had always treated Lerman with great kindness. Speaking shortly before Lerman's death, Francine Gray called it "an example of the extraordinary generosity Si has towards people who have lost all material, pragmatic use for him." She was speaking of the great care with which Si arranged for limousines, for home nursing, all to allow Leo to stay in style in his own apartment. "And that has to be taken into account along with all the alleged ruthlessness.... There are these deeply felt areas of tenderness and loyalty." Lerman's companion, Gray Foy, says of Si, "I have never, ever known anybody who was as kind and as concerned about a friend."

Newhouse was first on a long list of speakers at Lerman's memorial service on November 7, 1994, in the auditorium of the Museum of Modern Art. He recalled visiting "Leo's inner sanctum [which] became a mystic experience. The walls of his office were covered with photographs of friends and heroes, men and women who exemplified creativity and beauty of spirit, softly played classical music in the background, the plentitude of books piled high, the largesse of Leo's space and Leo's life." He told the crowd that Leo Lerman considered magazine journalism to be "high culture" and the editors at Condé Nast to be "guardians of a great tradition and responsibility."

Newhouse was followed by Julie Harris, who between sobs told the story of Leo calling the young producer of *The Glass Menagerie* and suggesting Harris for the role of Amanda Winfield. Her speech was achingly beautiful, from her recitation of a poem by Emily Dickinson to the "jonquil" speech from *The Glass Menagerie*.[8]

Lerman's death confirmed for some the end of an era. One former editor on *Vogue,* an old-timer who was there when Newhouse first arrived, insists that today at Condé Nast, "loyalty is a word that doesn't exist." On the editor/publisher level, she adds, the only person Si has ever been completely loyal to is Dick Shortway: "He has taken care of Dick all his life." (Not quite all. Shortway was first "retired" from *Vogue,* but kept in the company. Si sent him to England and then to Los Angeles as a sort of ambassador for Condé Nast, a make-work job, but a job nonetheless. That lasted until 1997, when Si told him, "It's over," and severed him from the company payroll and expense account.)

One Condé Nast publisher who moved to a rival company describes his former colleagues as feeling more insecure than ever: "I would sit at a lunch...and there were all these nervous jokes about whether I'll be here tomorrow. I sat next to an editor whose magazine was soaring, and I asked this person where she was going for Christmas. She prefaced her answer with, 'If I'm still here.'" Steve Florio sounded proud of the new tone when, in a speech before the Advertising Women of New York, he boasted, "Today it's a blood sport, and you better be...sharp enough if you want to play."

David O'Brasky, who was fired as publisher of *Vanity Fair*, recalls being impressed with a generous publishers' pension plan at Condé Nast until a fellow publisher pointed out that in the company's history under Newhouse ownership, only one publisher—Elliot Marion at *Bride's*—ever retired. The rest, to a man and woman, were fired, quit, kicked upstairs, or in a few cases, actually promoted.

One of the first casualties of the James Truman administration was Alexandra Penney, who since 1989 had been editor in chief of *Self*. Having so tirelessly flattered Alex Liberman, she could not have been happy at his departure. But the resourceful, political Penney rose to the occasion, and proved second to none in fawning over James Truman.

It didn't work. Newhouse stood at Alexandra's side in July 1994 as he told her staff of her "resignation" in order to assume the important new corporate position of director of media development. Deirdre Carmody reported that this was "the first time that Mr. Newhouse...had made such an appearance, ...a way for him to underscore his long-time friendship with Ms. Penney and the fact that in her new job, she would report directly to him." Insiders could only figure that Penney was Carmody's source. In fact, Penney had been given one of those graveyard slots, and she knew that it mattered not whether she reported to Si or to Si's dog, Nero, the next time she entertained him and his canine friends.

Penney, then an estimated fifty-six years old, insisted that the resignation had been her very own idea, but Meg Cox of the *Wall Street Journal* quoted others at the company who insisted that the move had "the fingerprints" of Truman all over it. Word on the street was that Newhouse wanted Ellen Levine, then editor of *Redbook*, to replace Alexandra at *Self*. Levine reportedly responded to the offer by saying that she'd take *Glamour*, but not *Self*.

In the face of that rejection came, six days later, a reprieve for Penney; really a kind of holding pattern imposed by the boss until he could find a star like Ellen Levine to accept the offer. Penney was busily putting her own spin on the news. "When we started to discuss my successor," she told Meg Cox, "the candidates were terrific, but I started to feel, I started this momentum, let me carry it on. I've gotten this magazine in great shape, and I want to enjoy it."

It did seem puzzling to insiders why Penney was dethroned in the first place when the magazine, aside from a worrying slump in newsstand sales early that year, seemed to be prospering. Its circulation stood at 1.3 million, which, while not the mass magazine that Newhouse wanted, was among Condé Nast titles second only to *Glamour*. It also had the largest percentage increase in advertising pages—18 percent—through the first six months of 1994.

In fact, the bottom line was rocky. So sky-high were expenses that even Newhouse had begun to question them. Veronique Vienne, when she arrived as art director of *Self*, asked Rochelle Udell, "'What's the budget?' and Rochelle looked at her pained and she said, 'We don't do budgets here,' like 'We don't do windows'; like, 'If you ask the price you can't afford it.'" Vienne remembers one photo shoot that ended up costing $100,000 and resulted in one published photo—cropped, at that.

"We were told," says one former editor, "'Just spend what you think you have to spend in order to put out a good magazine.' So we did." Then suddenly things changed, and a budget of sorts was imposed. Penney, accumulating complaints from Si, was beginning to warn her editors, "We're spending too much money." The word came down, this editor says, that *Self* was 600 percent over budget. There was shock in the editorial offices: "We didn't even have any idea until that point of where the limit was or if there was a limit."

Then in 1995, as expenses continued north, revenues headed south. More narrowly focused magazines, such as *Shape* and *Fitness,* were proving to be competition. In 1995 ad pages were flat; during the first half of 1995 circulation fell by 5 percent from the year before, while newsstand sales slipped by 10 percent.

At the same time, Penney's relationship with James Truman did not improve, and according to one report, the November and December 1994 issues "bear the scars of the continuing power struggle between [them]." Truman reportedly insisted that half of the November issue be reshot. He went over Alexandra's head to move her creative director to another magazine, and he let it be known that the December issue needed work.

In late August 1995, a bit more than a year after her reprieve, Penney resigned a second and final time, offering the unlikely explanation: "It has something to do with boredom, I suppose. But I want to include both genders and more of the general culture into my working life." In an effort, presumably, to keep her options open and to protect her social life, she claimed that her experience with Si Newhouse at *Self* had been "the best learning experience of my life, outside of sex." For good measure, she directed a truly zany compliment the way of Steve Florio, who, she volunteered, had "eliminated...the Machiavellian quality" at Condé Nast. On the subject of Truman, not even Alexandra Penney could muster a tribute. Wisely, she said nothing.

Rochelle Udell, having been left without a job when *HG* was shuttered, had been named to the next-to-no-profile job of president of CondéNet, charged with developing sites on the World Wide Web for selected magazines. It was from there that the woman who for so long had been seen as the next Alex Liberman was asked to take over at *Self*. That was rather like a man who had been president of the United States becoming governor of Mississippi. On the other hand, Rochelle Udell had loved *Self* from its birth, and although she was then an art director, she couldn't help inserting herself into editorial decisions. Now she would be free to tinker all she wanted.

In 1996 *Self*'s ad pages were flat, and the search continued for a new direction. It seemed unlikely that Newhouse would kill it. *Self* was the first magazine he had "started from scratch," as former managing editor Linda Rath puts it. She recalls how important it seemed at the time for him to take credit for the magazine's initial success. "He wanted to be seen as the innovator, that under his watch a new magazine was created." Making a success of *Self* remained to Si Newhouse a matter of pride, crucial to his still, after all those years, shaky sense of self.

By late 1997 it appeared that Udell's take was working, with ad pages through September up 18 percent from the year before.[9]

In 1997 Si increased his book publishing holdings in England by buying from Reed Elsevier the imprints Heinemann, Secker & Warburg, Methuen, Sinclair Stevenson, Mandarin, and Minerva. The deal brought to the Newhouses such backlist authors as Umberto Eco, Graham Greene, and George Orwell. The *New York Observer* commented that the sale means that Si "took a few more steps...toward becoming the publisher of every writer in the history of the world."

So it came as a shock, even to those in the upper reaches of Random House, when on March 23, 1998, the news broke that Si and Donald Newhouse had decided to sell their publishing house to the German media conglomerate Bertelsmann AG. Determined to stick with the *New Yorker,* despite its million-dollar losses, Si apparently had acceded to the concerns of his brother, who was said to have suggested gently but repeatedly over the course of 1997 that keeping one money loser was tolerable, but that keeping two was not. When faced with an excessively rich offer from Bertelsmann's chief executive elect, Thomas Middelhoff, Si agreed reluctantly to jettison Random House, with its eroding profits, flat sales, and gloomy outlook. (Nineteen-ninety-seven profits were reportedly a mere million on sales of one billion; for the same year, Simon & Schuster's trade division generated $67 million in profits on sales of $550 million.)

Selling Random House was not a decision Si would have reached on his own. He reportedly wanted to hang on and, in an attempt to boost Random House's bottom line, had considered buying Rupert Murdoch's HarperCollins.

In the States from Germany to improve his English and his knowledge of the American publishing market with an eye toward acquisition, Middelhoff, then forty-four, had approached Si on his birthday, November 8, 1997. "If you're ever thinking about selling Random House, we'd be interested in talking," Middelhoff told him. According to one report, Middelhoff's approach was casual, and he was stunned when Si replied, "Give me a week to think about it." Later that month, Si contacted Middelhoff, and negotiations began in earnest and in secret. (To preserve secrecy, meetings were held in the Lazard Freres offices of the Newhouses' investment banker Steven Ratner, and negotiations were dubbed "Project Black," with Si sporting the designation of "Black No. 1." The Bertelsmann players were known by various denominations of "Blue.")

According to the *New York Observer*'s Warren St. John, family members had concluded that "synergy is crap" and that nothing much had come of trying to promote Random House books through the magazines or of trying to convert magazine articles into profitable books. In Los Angeles for the Oscars on that Monday morning when the sale was announced, Si explained that the family would focus on managing and expanding the "core business," which he later defined as newspapers. "We are planning our future," he told the *New York Times'*, Geraldine Fabrikant, noting that he was seventy and his brother sixty-eight. He stressed that the inevitable bite of inheritance taxes lurked, but that the family intended to keep Advance private. He implied that the sale would help the family stick to that plan.

And so he agreed to sell out to a German behemoth that had entered the U.S. book publishing market in 1977 with its purchase of Bantam. In 1986 Bertelsmann bought Doubleday, Dell and Delacorte. At the time it put its bid in for Random House, Bartelsmann was the fourth largest American publisher—as compared to Random House, which was first.

Because both companies are privately held, the price paid was not made public, but insider estimates ranged from $1.2 to $1.6 billion in cash, with $1.4 the most oft-cited number.

Founded in the small German town of Gutersloh in 1835 as a publisher of religious tomes and Brothers Grimm stories, Bertelsmann was at the time of the announcement the world's third biggest media company—its size exceeded only by Time Warner and Walt Disney. It had operations in more than fifty-five countries and 57,200 employees worldwide in the business of book publishing, magazine publishing (the German newsweekly *Stern*, majority stake in Gruner & Jahr, which publishes *Family Circle* and *McCall's*), newspaper publishing, audio publishing, book clubs (almost 25 million members worldwide), on-line services (in partnership with America Online, the biggest on-line provider in Europe), book sales (aiming to become the world's largest on-line bookstore), music (the Arista and RCA record labels), video, radio, three German national television networks, digital television, television production and broadcasting.

On closing, the new company, which would be known as Random House, would claim an estimated 25 percent share of the U.S. consumer book market. The Authors Guild, which a month later, in an attempt to block the sale, filed a formal complaint with the Federal Trade Commission, claimed that the combined company would command more than 36 percent of the adult trade book market. A spokesman for the Bertelsmann side countered that the correct number is about 11 percent.

Those who bemoaned the increasing consolidation in the book business hoped that the deal would not withstand scrutiny by the Justice Department's antitrust unit or by the Federal Trade Commission. The response among writers—twenty-six of whom, including Kurt Vonnegut, Joyce Carol Oates, and Anne Tyler, wrote an open letter urging the FCC to block the deal—editors, and agents was a sinking feeling that this was yet another blow to American publishing. Books with blockbuster potential would not only continue to push aside serious fiction and nonfiction but would do so at an accelerated pace.

The Authors Guild complaint, along with another lodged by the Association of Authors' Representatives, presumably gave the FTC pause, at least temporarily, and Bertelsmann, faced with the prospect of intense scrutiny by the Feds in search of antitrust violations that the merger might create, withdrew its application on April 30 and refiled it the next day, this time including more precise figures from which an evaluation of anticompetitive aspects could be determined. The maneuver was intended to avoid a "second review phase," under which the Feds would have had unfettered access to the merging companies' financials and executives. The prospect of FTC officials deposing executives and subpoenaing corporate documents was a one that the privately held Random House and Bertelsmann wanted to avoid at all costs. On May 29 an FTC spokeswoman announced that the agency had closed its investigation and that the merger could continue without further FTC scrutiny. The deal closed on July 2.

No one disputed that the new company would encompass all divisions and imprints of Random House and Bantam Doubleday Dell in the United States and abroad, making it far and away the United States' and the world's largest publisher of commercial books in English. It would be more than twice the size of its nearest rival, Penguin Putnam.

"Full editorial independence" was promised for all, although, ominously, the press release announcing the sale noted that "until the closing, each company will continue to operate independently," implying that, after the closing, mingling of operations would occur.

Many at Random House were not happy with the company under Newhouse/Vitale control, but they despaired of the giant combine that the acquisition would forge. They feared loss of jobs (there was "overlap," a top Bertelsmann official conceded, between the lists of Little Random and Doubleday, and "economies of scale" was a much-heard phrase), independence, status, perks, prestige, and the cancellation of contracts for books that lacked best-selling potential. Bertelsmann reportedly would insist on profit margins of 15 percent—4 or 5 percent has been more like it for most publishers—taking the attitude that book publishing needn't be less profitable than any other sector of the media business.

But if there was one happy note, it was the humiliation of the widely reviled Alberto Vitale, who would lose his titles of chairman and CEO to forty-seven-year-old Peter Olson, a one-time banker who had run, in a low-profile manner, Bertelsmann's North American book operations. Vitale, sixty-five, would become chairman of the combined company's "newly created Supervisory Board." In other words, he'd likely be retired as soon as possible. Peter Olson described the board as a forum for "senior executives...[to] come together on, say, a quarterly basis to discuss strategy." No member would have any operating responsibilities.

Reporters speculated that neither of the key players in the next generation—Steven, Donald's son, or Jonathan, Si and Donald's much-younger first cousin—had been interested in running Random House. But those who knew Steve Newhouse knew the pleasure he seemed to draw from Random House. More likely, Jonathan and Steven were not seriously consulted.

For his uncle Si, whose pursuit of prestige had not slackened—on signing the deal to sell, he called Random House "the most...prestigious trade publisher in the world"—the decision could be seen as an embarrassing admission of failure. That he had made money and a lot of it on the transaction was indisputable, but also indisputable was that he had taken a venerable publisher and stripped it of its values and its intellectual tone. The company he was selling was a Random House far different from the one presided over by Bennett Cerf and Bob Bernstein.

While American book people fretted about the growing foreign influence in U.S. publishing—only three of the major houses are still American-owned—German book people countered that there was little literary left of the Newhouse-owned Random House anyway; that by 1998, like other mega-American publishers, it had become largely a purveyor of blockbusters.[10]

Some at Condé Nast have complained that James Truman has turned out to be a rather aloof and limp-willed leader. In a front-page *New York Observer* story published late in the summer of 1997, Lorne Manly reported that Truman, by then drawing an annual salary of just under a million dollars, is considered effete and lazy. While he held sway at *Condé Nast House & Garden* and at *Self,* he was largely ignored by the big-foot editors at *Vanity Fair, GQ, Glamour,* and *Architectural Digest.* That freed up time for sessions of yoga and boxing. The big fear among those on the editorial side of the magazine was that Truman's loss was Florio's gain, and that the dreaded salesmeister would soon start to poke about uninhibitedly in editorial. The first step in that direction came when Florio began to boast that not only did all Condé Nast publishers report to him, but that he had also managed to take over a duty—controlling compensation of all editors in chief—that should have been Truman's. Truman reportedly merrily gave up that power perch, offering no struggle whatsoever.

No one suggested that James Truman should fear for his job, for they noted that Newhouse still seemed in love with James and that he could do or not do as he pleased and Si would still find him wonderful. (At the 1997 Condé Nast holiday party Si again dubbed James "a young Alex.") So in awe was the boss of Truman's innate "taste and judgment" that he put his editorial director in charge of overseeing the interior decoration of a new office building for the company.

In May 1996 Si had announced Condé Nast's move from the Madison Avenue building that Sam Newhouse had bought into a building on Times Square slated to open in 1999. The planned forty-eight-story building, at the northeast corner of Broadway and Forty-second Street, was previously the site of Nathan's Famous Hot Dogs. Si's magazines will occupy eighteen floors, and the building will carry the Condé Nast name. Si demanded and received $10.75 million in tax breaks from the city and state by threatening to move 650 back-office jobs—of a total payroll of 1,570—out of the city. Calling Newhouse greedy and a liar, critics complained that Condé

Nast is the one company so identified with Manhattan that there seemed no danger at all that it would flee the city for, say, New Jersey or, as Steve Florio later threatened, South Carolina.

Early reports had it that the *New Yorker* would be exempt from the move, allowed to remain in its offices on West 43rd Street and to adhere to, at least on paper, the promise that Si Newhouse had made when he bought the magazine—that the *New Yorker* would remain separate from Condé Nast. But by late summer, 1997 word had leaked that the *New Yorker* would be expected to move into the Condé Nast building. Tom Florio claimed that just because the *New Yorker* would be rooming with the likes of *Self* and *Allure* did not mean that it would be officially placed under the Condé Nast masthead. Both Florios insisted that the *New Yorker* would remain independent.

In January 1998, *New York Daily News* business writer Keith Kelly reported that Si Newhouse had asked Tom's brother Steve to see what he could do about stanching the *New Yorker*'s flow of red ink. Steve described himself as a "consultant" to the magazine, which until then was run on the business side by his younger brother. When Si was asked if that new arrangement meant formally merging the *New Yorker* into Condé Nast, he replied, "We haven't decided yet." Ten days later he announced that not only would the *New Yorker* move to Times Square—and the design and decor of its offices would be no different from that of every other Condé Nast magazine—but that it would also join the others under the Condé Nast umbrella.

Overseeing the merger was Steve Florio, to whom Tom now reported and who began to review Tina Brown's editorial budgets. Tom claimed to feel just fine about what many others saw as a humiliating demotion. Tina was reportedly initially apprehesive but then claimed to feel "confident" about it. In fact, word was that Tina was lobbying to have Tom replaced by someone who could sell more ads.

Inevitably the tabloids picked up on the story. Under the headline, "The Fighting Florios: Brothers' Battle is Turning Condé Nasty," the *New York Post*'s Paul Tharp quoted one source as saying, "Tom feels Steve is walking all over him and making Tom look bad just so Steve looks good to Si." Friends of Tom's complained that when he took over the publisher's role at the *New Yorker* from Steve in 1994, the magazine was a mess, losing more than twice as many millions a year as it does under Tom, and that it was Tom who cut the losses. Tharp reported that Steve was trying to undermine his own brother by whispering to Tina Brown that Tom was hurting what she was working so hard to accomplish. When the *New York Times'* Robin Pogrebin finally picked up the story nearly a month later, she described the elder Florio's manipulations in terms that seemed less than brotherly. Tom was furious at Steve for describing himself as riding to the magazine's rescue and threatened Steve that if he fed that line to a reporter again, Tom would go to the *Wall Street Journal* with numbers showing Steve's gargantuan losses during his years at the *New Yorker's* helm. Instead, according to one of Pogrebin's sources, Steve himself went to the *Journal,* and a story soon ran, again portraying Steve as Si's guy to wipe out the red and disipline the troops, Tom principal among them.

On the eve of Memorial Day weekend, 1998, timed to minimize press coverage, came the announcement that Tom Florio was out. He'd be returning as publisher from whence he came, to the money-losing *Traveler.* David Carey, publisher of the money-losing *House & Garden,* would be the new *New Yorker* publisher, and *Traveler's* publisher, Lisa Hughes, would take over at *House & Garden.* So Steve Florio, with Si's approval, had ousted his own brother (albeit with a pay boost of some $200,000). Press speculation had it that Steve was worried that Tom might finally be cutting the losses and, given Steve's own nine-year run of spectacularly large losses at the *New Yorker,* did not care to see his younger brother credited with turning things around. (Once it is under the Condé Nast umbrella, the *New Yorker's* fortunes will probably improve because it can then be offered to advertisers as part of a group buy.)

Tina Brown, while claiming to have had no hand in the coup, had reportedly lobbied for *Business Week* publisher David Ferm and was angry about Carey's selection, on which she had not even been consulted—a puzzling slight because spiking his brother was supposed to have been Steve Florio's attempt to keep Tina Brown on board and happy. Various names, including Graydon Carter's, were suggested as a replacement for Brown, whose contract expired on July 1, 1998, without her signing a new one. (She continued to be represented by Mort Janklow.)

The *Times'* Robin Pogrebin reported that some felt that Tom Florio lacked the ability to market the *New Yorker* as the "'cachet sell' it once was—when advertisers fought for space in the intellectually formidable magazine." Not mentioned was that while many phrases could be used to describe Tina Brown's *New Yorker*, "intellectually formidable" was not one of them. Pogrebin then quoted Steve Florio, to whom Carey would now report, as predicting profitability in 1999. Three days later, Florio said profitability might be two or more years away. And so it goes.

Steve Florio appeared again to have emerged more powerful than ever, even if the vanquished was his own brother. But the publication of a *Fortune* story some five weeks later wounded Steve by branding him an inept manager who lost even more millions during his tenure as head of the *New Yorker* than Tom lost during his. Worse yet, *Fortune*'s Joseph Nocera and Peter Elkind pegged Condé Nast's performance under Steve as sluggish—under 8 percent, as opposed to the 15 to 20 percent margins common at other magazine companies—and that dismal performance didn't even reflect the fortune lost by the *New Yorker*. They claimed that *Cosmopolitan* made nearly as much in 1997 as all the Condé Nast titles combined. To finish him off, the *Fortune* reporters called Florio a liar who falsely claimed to have served in the military, to have earned an MBA, to have played minor league baseball, and to have played football at NYU. But most damning, perhaps, was the charge that in his interview with the *Wall Street Journal*'s Joanne Lipman for her page-one story, Steve Florio overestimated Condé Nast revenue for 1994 by some $273 million. Si responded to the killer article by throwing a party for Florio, calling the piece "nonsense" and his CEO "a man of intelligence and great heart,... my kind of guy."

Meanwhile, Si's most powerful and pampered editors, now including Tina Brown, were jockeying for position over which would win the biggest corner office on the most desirable floor with the best view. Lorne Manly described James Truman, then fussing over the building's cafeteria and its private dining rooms rather than the look and content of the magazines, as indisputably "the prince of Condé Nast."[11]

And he was, in a sense, but several other princes, princes by blood, were also waiting to take the throne.

III | The Family and the Future

25 | The Princes

IN 1997 SI NEWHOUSE turned seventy, and with Donald younger by two years, the matter of succession became a pressing question. But in one area there was no question. Si might assure James Truman that he is the Alex Liberman for the 1990s and beyond; Steve Florio might believe that he'll be Si's guy forever; but all knew that one day the magazines, the newspapers, the cable operation—the whole organization—would be run by someone of their generation whose last name was Newhouse.

The personalities, the potentials of the third generation of Newhouses are the subject of much speculation, especially because none of Si's or Donald's children have much of a public personality. But that is the way it is supposed to be in the tightly knit family. By temperament, training, and tradition, Newhouses avoid the spotlight.

While the third generation of many financial dynasties has typically been weak and wavering, the Newhouse children seem energetic and focused. Donald Sterling, formerly of the *Oregon Journal* and the *Oregonian,* marvels at the strength of the younger generation, which he describes as full of capable, hardworking, and earnest potential successors to Si and Donald. Some, of course, seem better than others.

S. I. Newhouse III, the firstborn of Sam's grandchildren, is the eldest, at forty-five, of the three children of Si and his first wife—and the only one in the business. Like his father, Sam, as he is called, attended Syracuse University and dropped out. His first job was as a trainee at the *New Orleans Times-Picayune.* He is currently publisher of the *Jersey Journal,* one of the weakest of the Newhouse papers, unusual among the family's newspaper properties for being a money loser. In the family tradition, he is expected to visit other newspapers, and travels regularly, for example, to the *Oregonian,* first in the company of his great-uncle Ted and later with his uncle Donald.

No one describes Sam as brilliant or as a visionary or a leader. "Competent" is about as good as the adjectives get. Like his father, he often appears quiet, withdrawn, and averse to small talk.

Sam has hewed to the family tradition of keeping costs down. When a reporter for the *Wall Street Journal* profiled the Newhouse family in 1982, he described Sam as being "as thrifty as his grandfather.... He rents out some of the newspaper's space in Jersey City to a doctor to raise an extra $850 a month."

Sam dresses informally, again like his father, but quirkily too, tending, one observer said, toward "T-shirts, red suspenders, and hiking boots." He looks "like a bigger version of Si," says a veteran of Condé Nast, taller by several inches and stockier, with close-cropped hair. A former editor on *Self* describes Sam as looking "almost exactly" like his father, having "that same kind of simian look that his father has."

After Sam married Carolyn in 1977—they would later have two sons, one of them S. I. IV—they moved to a large loft on Franklin Street in TriBeCa, complete with a roof garden. They retained Si's designer, Richard Penney, who recalls that the son showed little of the father's interest in design. Sam's passion was for such grown-up toys as model helicopters, which he flew off the roof garden, and for a model train that circled the roof. Lou Gropp was once seated next to Sam at a dinner and asked him why he chose to live in a loft. "I like to roller-skate," he replied. His love for boating continues, as does an intense interest in scuba diving.

Carolyn Newhouse was a different sort altogether. One man who knew her before and after her marriage to Sam and who also knew Sam well describes the couple as "dramatically different, ...absolute opposite poles." He thought highly of Carolyn, whom he calls "a very competent person" who, before her marriage to Sam, operated a horticulture business in SoHo, supplying trees and plants to corporate clients.

Furthermore, says this observer, Carolyn has a strong personality, "a very clear point of view and independence, which she exercised with regularity." She did not share Sam's enthusiasm for his various hobbies, and he did not share hers in the arts and in her desire to mix with people in interesting Manhattan social circles. Slightly older than Sam, she was more cultured and well rounded. During the process of designing their loft, it was Carolyn who met with Richard Penney. One man who worked closely on the loft with Carolyn praises her good taste and recalls "having very interesting conversations with her, whereas with Sam if you weren't talking about the things that interested him, you just weren't talking to him."

Friends deny that Sam is shy or particularly quiet. When a subject hits home for Sam, he can, says one man, "talk a blue streak" and become extremely "hyper." According to George Rosato, who headed Random House's school division, it was Sam, in the mid-1980s, who took an avid interest in pushing the company into software publishing. Sam is also currently involved with the Condé Nast New Media Department in an attempt to move the notoriously computer-averse company into the interactive age.

Most who know Sam Newhouse predict that he'll remain removed from the center of power. Whatever role Sam ends up playing in the company, it will likely be on the newspaper, not the magazine, side.

After Sam and Carolyn divorced, with Carolyn obtaining custody of their sons, he married Ellen Breslow, a former editor at *Vogue* and beauty editor at *Self*, currently working on the corporate side of Condé Nast to improve the company's data base. Breslow began to date Sam in 1988 when she was still at *Self*, although she married him after leaving the magazine. Short, with dark, wavy hair, Breslow, a bit plump but curvy and sexy looking, is not the typical Condé Nast fashion and beauty editor, who tends to be blond and rail-thin. The couple have no children together.[1]

The most private of Si's children is Wynn, known as Wynnie, the middle child, smaller than his older brother and physically a dead ringer for his father. Wynn, who also attended Syracuse and left before graduation, started in the business as a "gopher" at the Condé Nast Studio on East Forty-fifth Street near the United Nations, where sets were built and then photographed for such magazines as *House & Garden, Bride's,* and *Glamour.* One *HG* editor describes Wynn as a person who "worked hard and helped everybody out." He next went to Condé Nast in Paris as a photographic technician.

In 1974, when he was twenty and working at the *Staten Island Advance,* he caught his arm in a press, severely mangling the arm and hand. The hand was nearly severed, and was reattached in one of the early applications of microsurgery. Reconstructive surgery followed, and the hand is said to be partially functional.

Wynn left the business after the accident, moved to Boston, where he worked as a programmer for a computer software company, and in 1992 married Catherine, a nurse. They keep an apartment on Beacon Street in Boston and a summer house on Martha's Vineyard. The latter sits on a bluff on the edge of the water overlooking Edgartown's inner harbor and is decorated in a nautical motif that reflects the couple's love of sailing. They have a Siamese cat named Edgar, but no children. (So grandly traditional is the house in design and decoration that it was recently featured in the magazine *Traditional Home.*)

Carol Loomis wrote of Wynn that he was "considered by family members a man who will do almost anything except what you want him to." But family friend Gray Foy sees another side, describing Wynn as "like an angel, sweet and gentle and very bright, really like a visitor from a much nicer world." Another friend of the family's who during the 1970s was close to Si and his children feels great affection for Wynn, especially when compared to Sam. He calls Wynn "more outgoing and forthcoming than Sam, a little bit more logical, ...more grounded."

Of Si's children, Wynn is the most independent, and he tends to be peculiarly detached from the ins and outs of the family empire. One former editor at Random House remembers Wynn coming to a party at her apartment with a friend of hers whom he was then dating. "He looks around and says, 'Gee, you sure have a lot of books.' I said, 'Well, I'm in the book publishing business.' He said, 'Oh,' looking mildly interested. And I said, 'Random House.' He says, 'Ohhh.' 'Your father owns it.' He says, 'Oh, right.'"

Wynn now suffers from multiple sclerosis and uses a wheelchair. He is a partner in a Boston-based company that manufactures lightweight wheelchairs as well as other specialty chairs for racing and even skiing. Catherine is active in an organization that works to educate the public on issues related to wheelchair use.[2]

The youngest of Si's children and his only daughter, Pamela, has also avoided the family business. Joni Evans once asked Si why this was so, and he responded that in the Newhouse family the business passes to the sons. Pamela's mother, Jane Franke, calls that statement ridiculous. "My ex-husband would have been just thrilled if Pam had wanted to be involved." She had no interest in it, Jane said. "It certainly was her choice." (It is curious, though, that Donald's only daughter, Katherine, is not in the business; both her brothers are. Two of Norman Newhouse's sons are in the business, but his only daughter, Robyn, is not.)

Richard Penney calls Pamela "very supportive of Si and very loving, interested in what he was interested in." Gray Foy, a big fan of Pamela's, describes her as "very close" to her father, the child with the most natural rapport with him, and his intellectual peer.

She is also her father's protector. When this writer asked Pamela for an interview, she took offense at the very idea: "I feel it is a violation of the respect people owe one another to publish the biography of an unwilling subject." The concept of a public figure, of the importance of examining the lives of people who are influential in politics or academia or the arts or media, seemed a notion that had yet to cross her mind. If the values of journalism had ever been discussed over the Newhouse dinner table, Pamela's mind had obviously been elsewhere. Then again, chances are that the subject never came up—that it is one to which Si himself hasn't given much thought. How else to explain his rejection of a request for an interview by *Fortune*'s Carol Loomis, with the sentence; "My brother and I feel this goes against all our principles." That several of his magazines would have to shut down were story ideas scrapped because subjects were unwilling is a concept that seems conveniently beyond the scope of both father and daughter.

Pamela, who is outspoken and, relative to other Newhouses, colorful and flamboyant, was once a serious pianist. She later switched course and studied to become a nurse.

Her marital history has been as unconventional as she is. In November 1980 she married Verne Hendrick and, two weeks later, gave birth to Jacob Henry Newhouse Hendrick. "As an heiress to one of the world's great fortunes," writes Tom Maier, "Pamela asked her husband— whose annual income at the time was ten thousand dollars—to sign a prenuptial agreement the day before they married. Under the legal arrangement, Hendrick waived any future claim to the Newhouse fortune, agreeing to keep their financial affairs separate. The couple also agreed that Pamela would care for and support any children from their marriage in the event of a divorce." Four months later, in March 1981, the two were divorced in the Dominican Republic. Hendrick moved to Michigan, and Pamela was granted permission to drop his name from the baby's. She, the baby, and a nanny lived in a building downtown.

Pamela is now married to architect/artist Steve Mensch. After living in Paris with Mensch, who earned degrees in fine arts and architecture at Cornell, where he had once served on the design faculty, she moved with her first child and a child she had with Mensch to New Hope, Pennsylvania. Mensch visited there on some weekends, sporadically, reports one person who knows them, and usually via helicopter.

Mensch was otherwise to be found in Greenwich Village, where he had overseen a "gut rehab" of his nineteenth-century house, once a warehouse and scenery-painting school. That house was featured in *HG* of March 1993, the very month that Si announced that he was shutting the magazine down. The pressure to include the house, which several of *HG*'s editors disliked intensely, reportedly came from Victoria Newhouse in a telephone call to *HG* editor in chief Nancy Novogrod. The shortcomings of Mensch's house and his art, which filled nearly every wall, were beside the point, and Nancy Novogrod, who even hyped the piece in her editor's column, felt obliged to go along. Nowhere in the eight pages of text—by Pilar Viladas, then *HG*'s architecture editor—and photographs is it mentioned that this house and art belong to a close relative of Si's.*

In the piece, Mensch reveals a lot about himself and, inadvertently, about his relationship with Pamela. The house served as both his studio and

---

*Victoria did not always have to ask. *HG* editors, for example, always included a book from Victoria's Architectural History Foundation in their holiday roundup. "No one said you have to review this," explains one editor, "just that we definitely knew we had to review it." When Victoria's second book, *Towards a New Museum*, was published in 1998, *Vanity Fair*'s Elissa Schappell hyped it in her "Hot Type" column as "insightful." *Architectural Digest*'s Paige Rense did *Vanity Fair* one better when she ran an excerpt from the book without mentioning the relation between Victoria and the magazine's owner.

a retreat, he said, where he could find sanctuary and "serenity"; it was a perfect expression of himself, he added. "For an architect to do a building only for himself, to suit every idiosyncrasy, is great." Then there are the paintings—all by Steve Mensch. The article even featured a photograph of Mensch working on a large self-portrait. As the designer who laid out the piece recalls, "You could tell that this person had an inflated view of himself." Mensch's subjects are mostly athletes and bodybuilders, "gleaming flesh and muscle," Viladas writes, glorifying the male form. One painting of a sumo wrestler dominates a living room wall. (While teaching at Cornell, Mensch had designed a house for himself in Ithaca. Carl Sagan and his wife later bought it, had it demolished, and built their own house on the site.)

Mensch recently completed a home for his family atop a waterfall in the Hudson River valley near Rhinebeck, New York. That house was featured in October 1998 in his father-in-law's other shelter magazine, *Architectural Digest*. The writer was the respected architectural critic and *AD* contributing writer Suzanne Stephens, who is also a friend and colleague of Victoria Newhouse. (Stephens sits on the board of Monacelli Press which published Victoria's latest book.) Neither that connection nor the much more important one—that Mensch is Si's son-in-law and "Pam," whose name and opinions appear throughout the text, is Si's daughter—was mentioned anywhere.

Stephens writes that Mensch, Pam, and "their friend Greg Patnaude" share the house, along with the Menschs' two teenage sons. For Pam, who has resumed the study of piano, there is a studio in which she practices on her baby grand; for Steven there is a painting studio; and for Greg there is a gardening shed and a dovecote for his carrier pigeons. The sons were given their own cottage. (Taking nepotism to a new excess, the same issue of *Architectural Digest* carried a celebration of a house designed by Dutch architect Rem Koolhaas. The writer was Victoria Newhouse. Neither the relationship between Si and Victoria, nor the friendship between Victoria and Koolhaas, a favorite of Victoria's and a frequent guest at U.N. Plaza dinner parties, was mentioned.)

Gray Foy describes Pamela as "just brilliant in whatever she does." In that assessment he agrees with Bob Gottlieb, who has reportedly pronounced her by far the smartest of the children.[3]

Donald and Susan Newhouse reared their children in the Park Avenue co-op below Sam and Mitzi's. They are reportedly loving, attentive parents who have actively participated in their children's lives, their school lives especially. Susan was an energetic volunteer at the Collegiate School, and at Temple Emanu-El, a member of committees and boards. Both parents are known as unassuming, generous, and, given their wealth, remarkably accessible. Their three children led conventional, secure lives and grew into unspoiled adults.

Donald's firstborn, Steven O. Newhouse, is a graduate of the Collegiate School in Manhattan and of Yale College, where he was known as a serious and diligent student. Eager early on to join the family business, Steven started in the classified section of the *Newark Star-Ledger* while still in high school. During his Yale years, he interned on the *Staten Island Advance*. After college he worked at the *Oregonian* for a summer, and, while still in his early twenties, he was assigned to the *Springfield* (Massachusetts) *Union-News*, where he worked as a copy editor and reporter and was trained in all aspects of editorial by Dave Starr.

Worried that the staff in Springfield would see him as the pampered son of the owner, Steven went out of his way to prove himself a hard worker who accepted no special treatment. "He volunteered to work the night shift," wrote a reporter for the *Wall Street Journal*, "and once offered to chase fire engines at a warehouse fire in the middle of the night, even though he was home in bed at the time." Robert Miraldi remembers Steven, during his stint at the *Advance,* as "very likeable, he listened, one always had the feeling that he was embarrassed to be a Newhouse, that [others would think] he was there just because of his name." Steven never threw his weight around, Miraldi adds, never said, "Well, I'm a Newhouse, I'm an owner here, do what I tell you." From Springfield, Steven went to *Parade* as a copy editor, and from there, in the early 1980s, to Jersey City, where he remains editor in chief of the *Jersey Journal.*

Rapidly balding and even a bit shorter than his father and his uncle Si, Steven looks very much like his father and his grandfather, Sam. A Washington bureau chief for one of the Newhouse papers watched Steven and his cousins at a reception for the news service in Washington: "They look like plants that haven't had enough sunshine. They all have this sort of wan, pale look, ...odd-looking bunch."

Steven is married to Gina Sanders, currently publisher of *Gourmet*—before that publisher of *Details*—who has recently given birth to the couple's first child. Former *Vanity Fair* publisher David O'Brasky describes her as "short, dark, bright, perky, and cute." She lends her sparkle to Steven in the same way that his mother, Susan, enlivened and energized Donald.

Those who know Sanders say she is sufficiently competent to have qualified for a Condé Nast publisher's spot even without marriage to Steven. Still, Steve Florio apparently figured he was cementing his ties to the Donald side of the family when, at a meeting for Condé Nast publishers in Florida, he introduced the new publishers and said, with a straight face, "It wasn't until after I hired her that I found out that she was Donald's daughter-in-law. I just found out about it the other day."

A markedly unassuming man, Steven Newhouse often takes the subway to his office in Jersey City and a subway and a bus to Newark Airport. A former employee saw Steven "zoom by" on the subway platform. He stopped to talk long enough to explain that he was hurrying home to feed the baby. Steven's office at the *Jersey Journal* has been described as "just a little bit better than a dump." He doesn't seem to mind. When a reporter from *American Journalism Review* came to interview him, he met her in the lobby, and they walked up several flights to his office. When she requested a cup of coffee, they walked down again and into a deli next door, carrying their Styrofoam cups back up the stairs. He refused to be photographed for the article.

A Washington bureau chief for one of the Newhouse papers wonders "how somebody who's in a family with such wealth can be so understated." But he calls Steven's underwhelming presence deceiving: "For baseball pitchers there's a description called sneaky fast, and Steve is kind of sneaky quick mentally. He's quiet, quiet, quiet, and then—bang—he hones in on the subject. He's a lot more impressive than your first impression of him."

Steven was popular and respected among young reporters at the *Jersey Journal,* many of whom he hired. Typical was Jeff Pundyk, a graduate of Columbia whom Steven hired in 1983, along with several other Ivy Leaguers. The new reporters were interested in investigating, not befriending, the local politicians and businessmen who had previously enjoyed a

cozy relationship with the powers at the paper. Steven encouraged and supported his staff, even when reporters investigated corruption in the top layer
of the city's political machine. "He always stood by me," Pundyk recalls. "I
never encountered a situation where I couldn't write what I wanted to write."

Steven, who reads voraciously and, next to Pamela, is the closest to
an intellectual that the Newhouse brothers have produced, was learning
the business of Random House, and people there were convinced that he
would eventually oversee the book publishing arm of the empire. Most of
them thought that would be good for the company and were not happy
when the sale of Random House to Bertelsmann was announced.

Steven attended all Random House sales conferences, and talked to
the editors about books of theirs that he admired and actually read. But
while meetings or sales conferences were in progress, he studiously avoided offering opinions about books or even asking a question. He just listened. Joni Evans was so puzzled by Steve's dedication to attending every
event while holding to a monastic silence, that she once asked him, "Steve
you're at these four thousand lunches. Do you ever say anything?"

"My family believes I'm not to talk," he replied. "I'm just to learn."

By the late 1980s, Steven also gradually took over for Dave Starr as
supervisor of the Newhouse National News Service in Washington, a
stepchild property that has recently been more indulged and seems to be
gaining a bit in stature.

It is Steven who has prompted his father to begin putting money into
the newspapers. No dispassionate judge would call the Newhouse chain
high quality, but certain of the papers, the *Star-Ledger* in Newark and the
Times-Picayune in New Orleans in particular, have improved.

Of Donald's two sons, Steven definitely seems the one to watch. After
the sale of Random House was announced, the informed betting was that
Steven would fill his father's shoes, running the newspaper and cable businesses. Donald's other son, Michael A. Newhouse, is general manager of
the *Trenton Times,* and keeps an even lower profile than that of his elder
brother's. The exception was a published report late in 1997 that he had
purchased for $4.5 million a thirteen-room co-op, once home to the
Woolworth family, at 655 Park Avenue.[4]

Besides Si and Donald's progeny, the sons of Norman Newhouse, Si's first cousins, although a generation younger than he, are playing major roles in the company. In fact, Si has publicly announced that Jonathan, the third of Norman's four sons, will follow him as head of Condé Nast. "When time catches up with me," Si told the *Wall Street Journal*'s Joanne Lipman in 1996, the chairman's job will pass to Jonathan.

Jonathan Newhouse is forty-six years old, as short as Si but better looking. He is smart, funny, and for a Newhouse, almost gregarious. And he seems less eccentric than others in the family. He loves sports, baseball especially, and knows the standings, the subtleties of the game.

Reared in Great Neck until his father, Norman, was dispatched to New Orleans to run the papers there and in the region, Jonathan worked summers at the *Long Island Press,* when his father was editor. He quit Yale in his junior year and went to work in the composing room of the *Springfield Union.* Because he was small and young, he was occasionally asked to crawl inside the presses and clean them.

In the mid 1970s he was sent as a reporter to the *Staten Island Advance,* where he loved to cover blood-and-guts stories. "What a character he was," recalls then-*Advance* reporter Terry Golway. Jonathan covered the police beat and, says Golway, "was a terrific reporter, a lot of enthusiasm.... There was a flood in Staten Island, and he was called to duty, and I just remember him walking around the newsroom with no shoes and socks, frantically reporting the story." Like Si when he used the pseudonym Si Mason while reporting for the Syracuse University paper, Jonathan was uncomfortable using the Newhouse name and bylined his stories "Ned Houseman." Later, says Golway, Jonathan "put on a jacket and tie, and he was helping Dick Diamond, *Advance* publisher, with the business end of things."

Jonathan openly agonized about whether he had done the right thing in leaving Yale. Beyond that, he told a colleague on the city desk one night, he wondered if he really wanted to commit himself to the family business: "Was it the kind of thing that would really make him happy?.... Did he want to be simply another Newhouse-in-the-business, whether he deserved it or not?"

Jonathan was sent to St. Louis to continue his training, but on the business side. While there, he was also given the assignment of visiting the papers in Harrisburg with his cousin Donald. Adhering to the family value of listening instead of talking, Jonathan too avoided expressing opinions directly. Saul Kohler, retired editor of the *Harrisburg Patriot-News,* remembers one visit by Donald and Jonathan. Because computer spell checkers were then so expensive, Kohler suggested that every reporter be given "the best spell checker in town," a *Random House Dictionary.* "Of course they own Random House, so I thought we'd get it free, that's why I said it." Donald said nothing, Kohler recalled, and Jonathan "made notes like it was going out of style." Three days later Kohler received a call not from Jonathan but from his father Norman, who offered "twelve reasons why they couldn't send me seventy-three dictionaries, but suggested that I might know a bookstore that sold them."

Because Steven and Jonathan were considered the standouts of their generation of Newhouse men, Si and Donald decided to be clear about the younger men's territories. Rivalry and gamesmanship had not been part of Si and Donald's portfolio, and they wanted the same for their progeny. Although Jonathan's heart was with the newspaper business, he was moved in 1980 to the magazine side. As a kind of orientation, he was sent first to the Condé Nast circulation department. One man for whom Jonathan later worked called it "like a summer intern program." When *Vanity Fair* was revived, Jonathan was sent there as business manager, and soon a pattern developed. In 1983, when Si bought *Gourmet,* he sent Jonathan there in the same job. In 1985, when Si bought the *New Yorker,* he sent Jonathan, again as business manager, although the honorific vice president was added. In 1988, when Si bought *Details,* he dispatched Jonathan downtown, but with a promotion. At *Details* Jonathan was the boss, and his title was publisher.

Jonathan was also expected to keep his hand in the newspapers. While at *Vanity Fair* and *Gourmet,* for example, he went, many Thursdays, to visit the *Cleveland Plain Dealer.* Like Si, Jonathan read every word of every magazine; but even after moving to the magazine side, he was still expected, like Donald, to read all the Newhouse newspapers. One man for whom Jonathan worked at *Vanity Fair* recalls seeing Jonathan every day plowing through a stack of the family papers. (He was also assigned to look after maintenance of the Sam Newhouse family mausoleum at the Baron Hirsch Cemetery on Staten Island.)

At the magazines, Jonathan's role, to some degree, was to be his cousin's eyes and ears—a member of the family in the magazine's inner circle—but those who worked with him at *Vanity Fair* say that they never saw him as a snoop or a spy. "He fit in," says one coworker. "It wasn't like anyone thought you've got to watch what you say because he'll repeat it to Si. I would say almost the opposite. He was like part of the team"—so much so that he and several of his colleagues ran together in the 1984 New York Marathon.

People who work with Jonathan like, trust, and respect him. One former publisher calls him "analytical," with a real understanding of the business and a willingness to work hard. Robert Young, then the *New Yorker's* advertising director, says Jonathan was diametrically different from Steve Florio, "subdued" in his manners, focused on circulation and on the relationship between the business and editorial departments.

One person close to the scene says it wasn't long before Si's golden boy Florio, then president of the *New Yorker*, and his successor Jonathan, then the magazine's business manager, "locked horns." This man calls Jonathan "absolutely straightforward while Steve is highly devious and political." Jonathan would see the *New Yorker's* troubling numbers and interpret them honestly; Florio would see the same numbers and twist them into fabulous news. Florio feared that Jonathan "might inhibit his spin" and cause Si to recognize just what a mess the magazine was. So when *Details* entered the family constellation, Florio grabbed his chance and persuaded Si to put Jonathan there, in what was seen, after all, as a promotion. Florio being Florio, has bragged to underlings that he "fired" Jonathan. Florio presumably understands that when Jonathan takes over, Florio's job will be in some jeopardy.

Jonathan's next assignment, in 1990, was more complex and challenging—to Paris and then to London as chairman of Condé Nast International. As of May 1997 there were forty-one editions of Condé Nast magazines published internationally, an increase of eleven in the last thirteen months. But Hearst, the dominant player internationally (under former *New Yorker* president George Green, current president of Hearst Magazines International) publishes nearly 100 magazines internationally, thirty-three editions of *Cosmopolitan* alone and twenty-six of *Marie Claire*.

The reason for the discrepancy in numbers, Jonathan told a reporter, is that Condé Nast has no desire to publish in third-world countries. "Our advertisers are interested in richer developed countries," he explained, showing a streak of foolishness, not in Latin America and Central America, where Hearst has magazines. Jonathan would soon eat that statement. In 1998 *Glamour en Espanol* began publishing in twenty Latin American countries, as Latin America emerged as the growth area in the twenty-first century for American publishers.

The other reason that Condé Nast lags behind Hearst is that Condé Nast, then with only two magazines in Asia, has been slow to penetrate that market. It was Jonathan's charge, with presumably a great deal of help from Bernie Leser in his role as chairman, Asia-Pacific, to speed things up there and to turn Condé Nast into a contender. (Leser left the company in 1997 to launch a headhunting firm to place people in the upper reaches of magazine mastheads.)

In late 1995, with the only Asian edition of *Vogue* published in Singapore, Jonathan announced a South Korean edition, which would compete with the already established *Elle* and *Harper's Bazaar*. In 1997 he launched *Vogue* in Japan and *Glamour* in South Korea and predicted growth in Asia to match the European division, which then accounted for one-third of the company's business. He promised a big push especially into China, which he called the biggest market in the world. He had earlier announced plans to start Condé Nast China to publish Chinese-language editions of *GQ* and *Vogue* in Taiwan, where competitors *Elle, Cosmopolitan, Harper's Bazaar*, and *Marie Claire* are available. (Late in 1997 an edition of *Condé Nast Traveler* was introduced in Britain, and in 1998 *Condé Nast House & Garden* came to South Africa.) In early 1998 Jonathan promised at least seven magazine launches in the next year, including a Russian *Vogue* (which developed in the midst of the ruble's collapse), an Italian *Condé Nast Traveler*, an Australian *GQ*, and an *Architectural Digest* for Taiwan.

In her memoir Liz Tilberis, currently the editor in chief of Hearst's *Harper's Bazaar*, formerly the top editor at British *Vogue*, offers a rare harsh assessment of Jonathan. She had worked for the Newhouses at *British Vogue* for twenty-two years, rising from intern to editor in chief. In 1991, when rumors hit that she would leave London for New York to take over *Harper's* and to try to revive the competition with *Vogue* that had existed before 1962 when Si and Alex lured Diana Vreeland away from *Bazaar,* Jonathan demanded she meet him for breakfast at Claridge's. He offered her a raise, writing the amount on a linen napkin. Then he offered two warnings: "You wouldn't like New York. There are beggars on every corner, AIDS is rampant, it's a bad place for kids, and if you go to the country, there are ticks and you get Lyme disease." When the waiter refused to let Jonathan sign for the meal on the house account, he threw a tantrum. After confirming his credit, he delivered the second warning: "If you do go, you will never work for Condé Nast again." (She grabbed the *Harper's Bazaar* job after making an appointment to see Si Newhouse in New York. Her purpose was to draw from Si some sort of endorsement of the work she had done at *British Vogue.* When he responded to her torrent of words with "I see" and "Right," she realized that it was time to move. "If he had just dropped his habitual inscrutability for one moment to give me and *British Vogue* a vote of confidence, I would have happily stayed on.")

Jonathan's personal life has been more turbulent than those of his cousins. One man who worked with Jonathan on the *Advance* calls it "always in tatters." He married Debra Wollens in 1983, and they had two daughters. The couple was, this man says, a "very poor match." They lived in an apartment on the Upper West Side and were part of a conspicuously intellectual group. According to one former Condé Nast publisher, Debra was somewhat "eccentric," made much of her antipathy to "money and power," and was in a constant struggle "to figure out what she wanted to do," to resolve her "personal issues." Although she did not have a career of her own, she reportedly had little enthusiasm for the role of corporate wife and the entertaining that went with it. She was said to have particularly resented the move to Paris.

Jonathan was reportedly so miserable in his marriage that he visited a clairvoyant in Paris. Madame Favrot told him that he would find perfect happiness in a new marriage. Soon the news hit the gossip columns that Jonathan was involved with Ronnie Cooke—then the creative director of the ultra-upscale Barney's, formerly the fashion editor of *Details,* whom he had met when he was the magazine's publisher. As *New York* magazine's gossip writers put it, Jonathan "power-coupled" with Cooke, and, it was noted, he even flew to New York from Paris to attend an "intimate birthday party" for her. The two later married, with Debra keeping custody of the children, and Ronnie and Jonathan moving to London. She soon took the creative director's position at Calvin Klein's in-house advertising agency, and splits her months between New York and London, commuting via the Concorde.

One reporter for a London newspaper noted that, while married to Debra, Jonathan "looked ill at ease at fashion shows and attended jamborees with all the appearance of misery, every inch the poor little rich boy." In his second marriage, the reporter added, Jonathan "was visibly changed—he smiles, he chats and he's better dressed." Jonathan called his second wedding day "the most wonderful thing that has ever happened to me." The two share a Victorian townhouse in Notting Hill Gate. (In 1998 they bought a five-story house on West Twelfth Street in Greenwich Village to use while in New York.)

Jonathan has easily outdistanced his older brother Mark, the first-born of Norman's sons. A Yale graduate, said to be bright and decisive, Mark, four years older than Jonathan, is better looking and taller than the run of Newhouses and since 1980 has been the vice president and general manager of the *Newark Star-Ledger*. Former *Long Island Press* reporter Karl Grossman covered the 1972 Democratic National Convention with Mark, when he was serving a stint on the *Press*' editorial side. "He was not using his connections.... There were no airs to him." There may, however, be a bit of bitterness: Yale alumnus David O'Brasky recalls his first meeting at the *Star-Ledger* with Mark, whose opening line was, "I'm the one who graduated from Yale."[5]

That Si would select as his successor a cousin rather than a son or a nephew does make a statement about the brothers' quest for excellence in the succession. But there are those who feel the succession is still hardly solid, that, particularly, the leadership role at the newspapers, *the* money-making division, is still an open question.

One publishing rival of Si Newhouse contends that no member of that generation, Jonathan and Steven included, has the stuff to run the newspaper side *or* the magazine side. He calls the situation facing the family "the peril of nepotism.... They're not necessarily the best people for the job."

Of course it will be some years before Jonathan is put to the test. It is highly unlikely that Si will retire anytime soon, because his work is his life. "I kid Jonathan," says Dick Shortway, "and say 'Mr. Chairman Elect,' and he says, 'Yeah, twenty years from now.'" (Recently Si issued a memorandum to his top staff that Steve Florio's several-week absence from the office resulted from illness, not from Jonathan's return from London to run the American operation.) In his seventieth year, Si told a reporter, "I'm hoping they carry me out of here." His health appears to be good. An avid exerciser, he looks to be in his late fifties.

Si and Donald's relationship remains warm. The brothers are said to talk every day, as often as four or five times—"morning, noon, and night," says one former Condé Nast publisher. No one can remember their ever having had an argument—at least not as adults and business partners.

Their relationship seems remarkably sweet. One publisher of a Newhouse paper recalls the time his Washington bureau chief arranged for him to sit at the head table with President Reagan during the annual Gridiron dinner. Much as the publisher would have enjoyed the experience, he decided, "What the hell sense does this make? I'm sitting at the head and the Newhouses are down here on the floor." So he called Si: "'You're going to sit at the head table with the president.'... Well, he just was tickled at that." But then Si had second thoughts. "About a week later he called me," the publisher recalls, and said, "Would it be possible if Donald and I would trade places at the Gridiron dinner? I'll sit there half the time, and Donald comes up there and sits there the other half." And that's exactly how the evening went.

Decisions involving large expenditures of Newhouse money are not made until both brothers sign off, but then it's each to his own. In the case of the Random House or the *New Yorker* acquisition, for example, the brothers had to agree to proceed, but once the deal was done, these were Si's babies. On matters relating to the newspapers or cable, Donald holds sway. The decision in late 1993 to put $500 million behind Barry Diller's hostile, and ultimately unsuccessful, takeover attempt of Paramount Communications was Donald's.

For all their closeness in business, if Si and David weren't brothers and business partners, they would have little in common. The adjectives often used to describe Donald are "sweet," "uncomplicated," "approachable," "nice." Donald is far warmer than Si, with a normal personality— many multiples more outgoing than Si's—and interests that are far more conventional than Si's. Donald has been known, for example, to take his son to a Knicks game. Returning to Syracuse for a homecoming football game, Donald was seen on a commercial flight wearing a bright orange sweater with holes in both sleeves.

Donald has a sense of humor, a personal touch that has endeared him to many of his employees. On the day Saul Kohler became editor of the *Harrisburg Patriot-News*, the accident at Three Mile Island occurred. On the day Kohler retired and took a job as director of media relations with Bell Telephone of Pennsylvania, he received a handwritten note from Donald: "I remember when you came as editor, Three Mile Island happened. Now I suppose since you're with the phone company, we'll have to lay in a supply of homing pigeons." When John Baum, the publisher of the Harrisburg papers, died, Donald called Kohler in tears. "I wanted a quote from him, but he said, 'I can't now. Give me an hour. I'll call you back,' and he did."

Most Sunday nights the two men and their wives—no children—dine together at Sette Mezzo, an Upper East Side restaurant, where they are said to avoid entirely the subject of business.[6]

In the end, though, there is something unequal about the relationship, rendered even more unequal when the Newhouse brothers, in deciding to sell Random House, excised a major piece of Si's portfolio. "Donald makes the money and Si spends it" is a comment heard often. Donald's profit centers are the newspaper and cable properties. The former constitutes the largest privately held chain in the United States, with twenty-eight newspapers and a combined circulation of more than 3 million. (Until 1997, there were twenty-nine papers. Donald made a move that Sam would have applauded. He closed the family's afternoon *Mobile Press*, leaving open its morning *Register* and thereby cutting costs and raising profit margins.) The cable business, in a partnership with Time Warner, Inc., boasts 1.8 million subscribers, estimated as the second largest cable TV company in the United States. In a joint venture with Time Warner, the Newhouses also own Road Runner, a high-speed cable-modem service charged with vastly speeding up home Internet connections via use of a broadband as opposed to a telephone line connection.

Typical for the Newhouse papers are profit margins of 25 or even 30 percent. Shortly after his father's death, Si himself pronounced everything aside from the newspapers as "peripheral" to the profitability of the company. And that, over the years, has largely remained true. Sam's biographer, Richard Meeker, concluded that the newspapers "fund everything else." David O'Brasky speculates that just one Newhouse newspaper, the *Staten Island Advance*, which is far from the most profitable in the chain, probably makes as much as all the Condé Nast magazines combined. In the ranking of the richest billionaires, *Forbes*, in 1998, describes the magazines as "barely profitable" and the newspapers as a "fat cash cow."[7]

Si's recognition of where the money comes from has not yet discouraged him from embracing the magazines and lavishing money on them. But by the mid-1990s, the Condé Nast magazines and the *New Yorker*, with their multimillion-dollar losses, were no longer merely peripheral to the company's profits. They had become an actual drain—some more so than others.

By February 1997, James Truman was trying to move *Details* in a different direction, a sure indicator that the magazine was in trouble. "I have an intuition that downtown is dead as a subject," Truman declared, "and that sex, drugs and rock 'n' roll is not really a very contemporary focus for a young men's magazine. It feels quite passé to me." Behind Truman's "intuition" that *Details* should go mainstream, with articles on grooming and fitness, is circulation that has stagnated at just under 500,000 since 1994 and declining sales at the newsstand—down by an alarming 10 percent for the first half of 1997.

In May 1997, Truman's handpicked editor in chief for *Details,* Joe Dolce, quit after learning that Truman had ordered a headhunter to interview other candidates for his job. Dolce's replacement is Michael Caruso, a former articles editor at *Vanity Fair,* most lately the deposed editor of *Los Angeles* magazine. Truman reportedly ordered Caruso, who plans for the first time to cover sports, to boost circulation by 40 percent over the course of his three-year contract. *Details*, it was announced, would be moved from its downtown location to the new building in Times Square, where it would share quarters with *House & Garden*. The first half of 1998 passed with *Details'* performance, as measured by the sale of ad pages, flat.

The *New Yorker* especially, because of the high price paid for it and the continued losses, is often described as "the ultimate indulgence" for Si. As former *New Yorker* art editor Lee Lorenz says, "It's very hard to put all this together with the Sam Newhouse tradition, which is essentially to buy cheap and just let the money roll in." One veteran *New Yorker* editor agrees that the newspapers are money machines that make it possible for Si to play with the *New Yorker*. "Even so," he says, "there must be some kind of understanding about how much money he can lose. They don't just keep handing and handing it to him." In fact, in the case of the magazines, handing it to him is precisely what Donald has done.

The losses at the *New Yorker* are one thing, but Si for years also went along with losses at most of the other magazines. "None of us ever knew if we were making money," says one former editor. "It was never an issue."

Lately, it seems to have finally become an issue. Those who watch Condé Nast closely insist that the brothers have agreed that the losses must be reversed, or at the least slowed. That's the reason Steve Florio was put in charge of the magazines—to force down the profligate spending, the culprit, most believe, in the bleeding bottom lines at the majority of the magazines. In his usual noisy way, Florio has rubbed out some of the excesses—$30 carryout lunches, flights on the Concorde, ulimited car service—with the truly elite, of course, excepted.

Still, while perks are not as free-flowing as before, personal trainers and clothing allowances—the latter said to be $500 a week for every fashion editor, twice as much for top editors, perhaps as much as $100,000 for Anna Wintour—and rent stipends and lunches at the Royalton Hotel's restaurant 44 (a. k. a. Cafe Condé Nast or the Condé Nast Canteen, where the Condé Nast mantra is "Let Si get this"), BMWs with leather seats, and luggage Federal Expressed to a star editor's destination so he or she is freed of the task of carrying it, and double staffs for star editors, and fees and advances for writers far in excess of the competition's, are alive and well. Si's latest interest-free loan, reportedly nearly $2 million, was to Harry Evans and Tina

Brown to use as a down payment on a $3.7 million triplex co-op on East Fifty-seventh Street. He had years earlier loaned $2 million, interest free, to *Vanity Fair* chief Graydon Carter to purchase an apartment in the Dakota.

But Florio continues to target red ink, and for the first time in anyone's memory he has instituted budgets for every one of the Condé Nast magazines. By the close of 1997—a strong year for ad sales for magazines in general—Condé Nast was thought to have turned a profit. Whether Tina Brown was also saddled with a budget was unclear, although *New Yorker* editors reported that she no longer was assigning twice as many pieces as she had space to run. And in mid-1998 she saw her page width narrowed by an eighth of an inch, for an annual savings of half a million dollars a year. On a more modest scale, *Vogue*'s managing editor issued an edict that while the company encouraged in-office celebrations of employees' birthdays, it would no longer foot the bill.[8]

Driven by the newspapers and cable, the worth of Advance Publications—still the country's largest privately held media conglomerate—has, by one estimate, more than tripled since Sam left it to his sons. In 1997 writers for the *Nation* estimated 1995 revenues at $5.3 billion. In addition to the newspapers and the magazines and cable, Si and Donald own television and radio stations, part of a pulp mill, real estate that includes an airport in Massachusetts, Lifetime and the Learning Channel, 24 percent of the Discovery Channel, and assorted other properties here and abroad.

While the Newhouse brothers' fortune is often described as the largest in private hands in America, the numbers and the players remain as elusive as they were in Sam's time. As Carol Loomis wrote eight years after Sam's death, their "wealth is a staggering total for two men many Americans have never heard of. Each controls more than any du Pont or Rockefeller or Ford." Today, Si's piece of the pie is estimated by *Forbes* at $4.5 billion; his brother's the same.[*][9]

---

*On the most recent Forbes 400 list of the richest Americans, the brothers rank behind Bill Gates, Warren Buffett, and several of the Waltons; but they outrank Rupert Murdoch, Walter Annenberg, Sumner Redstone, Edgar Bronfman, the Lauder brothers, any of the Rockefellers, and Larry Tisch. [10]

That Si's part of the business is not so wonderful has not dampened his and Steve Florio's enthusiasm for starting or buying more magazines. In September 1997 came a monthly for women who participate in active sports, *Condé Nast Sports for Women*. But it entered an already crowded field. First came *Jump*, a sports magazine for teenage girls. Time Warner tested two issues of *Sports Illustrated Women/Sports*, an offshoot of the original, and will test several additional "special" issues in 1999. Another in the mix was *Women Outside*, a sports and outdoor magazine launched in the fall of 1998 by the company that owns *Outside*. With so many new contenders, the owner of *Outside* wondered out loud, "How many women's sports magazines should be in the marketplace?"

Four months before the first issue of *Condé Nast Sports for Women* was to appear, its publisher was fired and replaced by the publisher of *TV Guide*—a sign that advertising was slow in arriving. (One report had it that the original publisher had argued in vain for rejecting cigarette advertising.) That Newhouse spent $40 million to launch it is not surprising, given that a staff of twenty-two had been in place for a year before the magazine, which was scheduled to debut in spring 1997, appeared. (While the first issue was a thick 212 pages, the second was only 138 and newsstand sales were disappointing.)

In January 1998 Si bought for a reported $5 to $7 million the monthly *Women's Sports & Fitness*, announced that *Condé Nast Sports for Women* would become *Condé Nast Women's Sports & Fitness* and that publication would be cut from monthly to bimonthly. The consensus among media reporters is that Si and Steve Florio goofed; unlike the publishers of *Jump*, which has plenty of lifestyle stories and still has an uncertain future, the Condé Nast brass failed to understand that there are not enough women interested in reading about pure sports. In February 1998 a new executive editor was hired and charged with bringing big doses of fitness, nutrition, and beauty news to the magazine.

In early 1998 came news of *Condé Nast Currency*, a personal finance magazine for both sexes, said to be in the works for a year and developed by members of the business, not the editorial, staff. It was mailed to all subscribers of all Condé Nast titles in April 1998 and then evaluated for possible publication on a regular schedule.

In May 1998, for approximately $85 million Si Newhouse bought the technology magazine *Wired,* in which he already held since 1994 a 12 percent stake. One magazine consultant explained the purchase of the techno-geek *Wired,* based in San Francisco and started in 1993 for Internet aficionados, as the realization that "they've pushed the envelope as far as they can go with beauty and fashion magazines, so they're stretching for new ideas." They were also stretching for a new market, with a magazine that is about as different as possible in its soul from *Vogue* and *Vanity Fair.* Si promised *Wired'*s editors that their magazine could stay in San Francisco, although some worried when, in a speech to employees after the sale, Steve Florio suggested that they "think of us as your rich uncles in New York."

In addition to the possibility of bringing out another traditional men's magazine, Si and Florio are exploring some potential commercial off-shoots—a weekly television show tied somehow to *Architectural Digest,* which reportedly has reached the development-of-a-pilot stage, and not as far along in planning but possibly in the offing, television shows based on *Bon Appetit, Gourmet, Condé Nast Traveler, Self,* and *Vogue.* There are also plans to join with the Los Angeles talent agency International Creative Management to sell articles appearing in Condé Nast magazines to Hollywood. Florio also told a reporter for *Advertising Age,* "We're exploring *GQ* sunglasses as a brand, but you won't see a *GQ* fragrance. We won't become competitors to our advertisers."[11]

Sunglasses? It's all a long way from the world of Sam Newhouse, who believed in buying newspapers, making plenty on them, and plowing the profit right back into buying newspapers.

That formula is not much in evidence today. The only daily the Newhouses have bought since Sam's death is the *Trenton Times.* In 1995 Donald Newhouse paid $268.9 million for the Charlotte, North Carolina–based American City Business Journals Inc., which bills itself as the nation's leading publisher of weekly business newspapers. The papers cater to local businesses in such cities as Atlanta, Dallas, Denver, Baltimore, and Miami. In addition to twenty-eight weekly newspapers, with a combined paid circulation of 330,000, the company includes three auto-racing magazines—

On Track is the best known—and an advertising firm. Less than a year later the Newhouses added Citymedia, a Minneapolis-based publisher of six weekly business journals, to American City. In late 1997 the Newhouse brothers bought SunMedia Corp., a chain of twenty-three weekly newspapers in suburban northeast Ohio. In early 1998 they announced the start of *Sports Business Journal,* a national weekly magazine that, one reporter noted, "aims to become the *Variety* of the American sports business."

But Donald has found the pickings of profitable or potentially profitable daily newspapers slim. As John Morton explains, "There are only a handful of...mid-sized dailies left that aren't already owned by chains." He estimates the number as some ten newspapers in the entire country that have what it takes to be of interest to Donald Newhouse, "and you've got every big newspaper company in the country camping on their doorsteps." When Disney put up for sale in 1997 four newspapers, including the *Kansas City Star* and the *Fort Worth Star-Telegram,* John Morton speculated that Newhouse would try to buy them, but instead Knight-Ridder paid $1.65 billion for the papers, and Newhouse reportedly was not in the running as a bidder. Nor was it in the bidding later that same year, when Cowles Media with its flagship, the *Minneapolis Star Tribune,* went for $1.4 billion—the most ever paid for a newspaper company—to the medium-sized McClatchy Newspapers, like Newhouse, family-owned, but a rapidly expanding chain.[12]

As Steven prompts his father and uncle to funnel money into the dailies they already own in an effort to create papers that the family can be proud of, and that might even win a prize or two—goals that Sam Newhouse would have dismissed as muddy-headed and unbusinesslike*—is the family reaping a return on its investment?

The *Newark Star-Ledger* had been run since 1963 by Newhouse in-law Mort Pye. Before arriving at the paper in 1957, Pye had worked, since 1941, at the *Long Island Press.* At the *Star-Ledger,* Pye took the word *parochial* to new heights of absurdity. Not only did the paper expend next

*When the *Oregonian* won a Pulitzer in 1957, Sam Newhouse, its owner of seven years, remarked, "For a Newhouse newspaper to get a Pulitzer Prize, that's something."

to no resources on national, international, and even regional news, but local coverage tended to be unreadable, unreliable, and unwaveringly boosterish to such local institutions as the corruption-riddled city hall and the public school system, and to big building projects—the interstate highway and the Meadowlands sports complex, for example—that Pye believed would help the state of New Jersey.

Editorial columns were used routinely "to settle scores or to be unduly solicitous to top public officials," in the words of Jim Warren, a former *Star-Ledger* reporter.

Mort Pye was seventy-six when he was finally retired in December 1994—he died three years later—and was replaced by a journalist of an entirely different caliber, Jim Willse, the former editor of the *New York Daily News*. A year into Willse's tenure, the *New York Times'* press reporter, William Glaberson, pronounced the *Star-Ledger* so improved as to be barely recognizable. The old *Star-Ledger*, Glaberson wrote, "was known for a special timidity." No longer. It has taken on Mayor Sharpe James in, "for the *Ledger*, an unprecedented investigation into [local] patronage." Glaberson called the changes Willse brought to the paper perhaps "the most ambitious effort to revitalize a large newspaper under way anywhere in the country." Besides new sections and more color printing, several dozen new journalists were hired. The Newhouses, Glaberson speculated, were pouring millions into the paper.

By mid-1996 Terry Golway, who covers local politics for the *New York Observer*, lives in New Jersey, and regularly skipped the *Star-Ledger*, claimed to read it every day: "It's a night and day transformation." The Newhouses, he explains, are investing heavily in a paper that is already one of the most profitable in the world; they are doing so for the sake of good journalism; not because the bottom line demands it. Willse was able to hire reporters and editors away from New York dailies, Golway said in disbelief. One new, fearless hire was assigned to Newark City Hall and was soon evicted. The politicians "just don't know what to make of it because they've never been confronted by it before."

Golway was especially impressed with the *Star-Ledger*'s new editorial page editor, Rich Aregood, whom Willse brought to the paper from the *Philadelphia Daily News*, where he had won a Pulitzer Prize. Aregood said publicly that a key reason for his move was that at Knight-Ridder, the public company that owns the *Philadelphia Daily News,* there was far too much pressure to produce a profitable bottom line. He complained that newspapers "are falling prey to the quarterly profits disease."

Mike Greenstein, a long time observer and critic of the *Syracuse Herald-Journal* and *Post-Standard* and a former teacher at the Newhouse school, argues that those papers too have improved. Previously, he says, they were "pathetic" and "Neanderthal." He sees now, with the ascension of the younger Stephen Rogers—the son of the Newhouse hand who had long run the papers and who had himself become a major power in Syracuse— "a turnaround.... They hired more reporters.... They did more in-depth stories.... They dragged themselves into the twentieth century finally."

In New Orleans, the *Times-Picayune* has moved from being a joke in the sort of journalism circles that Sam ignored to being a darling. In 1996 a reporter for *American Journalism Review* applauded its multipart investigations on such subjects as corruption in legalized gambling, Medicaid billing abuses, and nepotism in a legislative scholarship program. A year and a half later the same magazine published an all-out valentine to the paper, cheering its vast improvement and its winning two Pulitzer Prizes in 1997, outdoing the *Washington Post* and the *New York Times,* which won one apiece. (The *Times-Picayune* won for a series analyzing the environmental, commercial, social, and political threats to the world's supply of fish. The paper's Walt Handelsman also won for his editorial cartoons. One cartoon, which Handelsman flagged as a favorite, was certainly inspired by the Random House $2.5 million advance to Dick Morris. Two bloated politicians are seen from behind. "I lied, I cheated, I betrayed my wife, my boss, my friends. I sullied my reputation.... I'm the lowest of the low," says one. The other replies, "Who's your publisher?"[13]

If Steven Newhouse is the engine behind these changes, it should also be noted that some of the Newhouse papers remain beyond his influence and stuck in a rut of mediocrity and worse. Looming largest among them is the *Cleveland Plain Dealer*—a paper that Steven knows better than any other member of his generation because it is on his route and because, for years, he visited it every month with his father. It is the biggest paper in Ohio and the one with the most clout. "The big bully of

Ohio journalism," one publisher of another daily in the state calls it. It produces profits beyond the wildest fantasies of most publishers, but it is also, because of a certain sense of corruption and ties to powerful interests in the state, perhaps the most relentlessly reviled paper in the country.

For a time, it looked as if things were set to improve at the *Plain Dealer*. At the instigation not of Steven but of then-publisher Tom Vail, the stubbornly independent William J. Woestendiek was hired as editor. Although an unlikely choice for Vail, Woestendiek had been editor of two newspapers that had won Pulitzer Prizes, and he was hired to win one for the *Plain Dealer*.

Woestendiek raised the quality of the paper's editorial. But forces beyond his control made the improvements short-lived. In 1990 Tom Vail was removed as publisher and his assistant, Alex Machaskee, took over. Machaskee had been Leo Ring's right-hand man, strongly antiunion when he was in charge of labor relations. (Ring retired in December 1993 and died a year later.) Among reporters and editors, Machaskee was despised—routinely referred to as "Alex the snake."

Machaskee had once worked for a small newspaper and liked to think of himself as a reporter, but he lacked journalistic values, reporters say, and the most basic knowledge of international and domestic affairs. Former *Plain Dealer* Washington bureau chief Rick Zimmerman remembers when Tom Vail wanted to visit China and ordered Machaskee to plan the trip. Machaskee called Zimmerman: "'I've been trying to get the embassy out in Washington, and I looked under Communist China and Red China.' I said, 'Just to begin with, Alex, it's People's Republic of China, and not only that, they don't have an embassy here. You'll have to go up to Ottawa.'" If Vail and the stubborn and outspoken Woestendiek were hardly made for each other, Machaskee and Woestendiek were a brawl ready to happen. One former editor recalls that when he traveled to Cleveland for a job interview, relations between the two had so soured that they weren't speaking to each other and used the dumbfounded applicant as a go-between.

Woestendiek lasted six years. He says that he and Machaskee "agreed to disagree." Others say Machaskee shoved him out the door.

Their "quarrels," Woestendiek explains, were "about the role of advertisers and the independence of the newsroom." According to then–*Plain Dealer* reporter Gary Webb, "Woestendiek had a reputation of telling the business side of the newspaper to get fucked, which is like the kiss of death at the *Plain Dealer*. Of all the newspapers I've worked for, that is the most bizarre operation, where the business side essentially runs the newspaper."

Woestendiek left Cleveland in 1988. He was replaced by Thomas H. Greer, who, according to Webb, was "widely viewed as a flunky for Machaskee." The *Plain Dealer* didn't win any Pulitzer Prizes under Woestendiek or his successor. Good reporters and editors tended to leave and to win their Pulitzers elsewhere—Walt Bogdanich, for example, won his at the *Wall Street Journal,* Daniel Biddle won his at the *Philadelphia Inquirer,* and Gary Webb, on a team with five colleagues, won one for the *San Jose Mercury News.*

But even at the *Plain Dealer,* change may be in the air. Tom Greer was kicked upstairs into a seemingly work-free vice presidency in 1992, and his replacement was David Hall, formerly editor of the *St. Paul Pioneer Press,* the *Denver Post,* and the *Hackensack* (New Jersey) *Record.* Hall was said by some to be Machaskee's choice, but also Steven Newhouse's. According to one source, Hall, who is close to Steven, has protection from Machaskee: "When push comes to shove every once in a while, he goes to Steven for protection." (Critics of Hall's tenure say they can't imagine why he'd need Steven's help, because he has turned the paper into a fluffy, advertising-friendly product that must totally satisfy Machaskee.)[14]

How this most recalcitrant of the Newhouse papers fares in the next several years will be the surest sign of the kind of stamp Steven Newhouse is going to put on the Newhouse newspapers.

More widely disparaged than any Newhouse newspaper is the family's national news service—"the laughingstock of Washington," says one of its former reporters. There Steven's influence, as he took over for Dave Starr, was obvious. It was Steven who, in 1990, presided over the sacking of the bureau chief, Robert Fichenberg, and the hiring of his replacement, Deborah Howell, editor of the *St. Paul Pioneer Press* during a period when the paper won two Pulitzer Prizes. (One source claims that Steven first offered the *Plain Dealer* editorship to Howell, but she turned him down.)

After stints at Gannett and then Hearst—he had been fired as executive editor of Hearst's *Knickerbocker News*—Fichenberg landed at Newhouse compliments of Dave Starr, with whom, during World War II, he had shared a foxhole or a tent, depending on who provides the details. He had no Washington experience and is remembered by reporters for behaving like "a martinet," for his poor news judgment, and for his sexist and coarse treatment of women reporters.

But most remembered are such loony antics as his demanding that reporters supply their own coat hangers, and that they ask their sources to agree to dutch treat lunches. And then there was his obsession about cleanliness. "Every Friday afternoon we'd have to clean everything off our desk," says one former reporter, "not one scrap of paper on our desk." One man who was famous for his messy desk came to work one morning and noticed that his paper piles were shorter. A colleague had observed Fichenberg, early that morning, throwing the reporter's notes into the trash can.

The atmosphere in the bureau, says Paula Schwed, who has worked for UPI, for Gannett News Service, and is currently at the *Atlanta Constitution*, was "a reign of terror." "Working for this man was to me a living hell," agrees former NNNS reporter Mick Rood.

In selecting Deborah Howell, Steven Newhouse has put a woman in a place where none has tread before—at the head of a major news bureau. Some gripe that Howell is a world-class self-promoter, but she has also brought a great deal of attention to the bureau. Fichenberg behaved like a tyrant in the bureau, but the rest of the journalistic community in Washington largely ignored him or never heard of him. Howell, almost alone among Newhouse employees, is quoted and consulted and celebrated.

On arriving she quickly cleaned house, firing about half the national staff. She went on the road, visiting the papers and asking, "How are we doing? What are we doing right? What are we doing wrong?" She had, says a Washington bureau chief for one of the papers, "the full backing of the Newhouses," which showed itself in the opening of a new office with greatly expanded space on Connecticut Avenue across from the Mayflower Hotel, and in Howell's $250,000 salary.

In 1996 the Newhouse National News Service won its first Pulitzer Prize, although it was awarded not for writing and reporting but for feature photography. The winner was a twenty-two-year-old free-lancer who captured on film a female circumcision rite in Kenya.[15]

Sam and Mitzi Newhouse have their names on two major institutions—Sam the journalism school at Syracuse, Mitzi one of the theaters at Lincoln Center. (In 1973, for a gift of one million dollars, what had been the Forum Theater at Lincoln Center was renamed the Mitzi E. Newhouse. She gave the money—earmarked to make the New York Shakespeare Festival a permanent part of Lincoln Center—to producer Joe Papp at a time when he desperately needed funds to meet operating expenses.) There have been no such monuments so far from the sons, and Si continues to make almost no mark on American philanthropy. When friends talk about his philanthropic activities they mention that he gives generously to a movie house in Manhattan that plays the obscure, grade-C movies of the 1940s and 1950s that he so adores.

Donald and Susan Newhouse are more visibly and conventionally charitable, through their work for such staples of the Manhattan rich as the New York Public Library. Donald, who has been a trustee of Syracuse University, takes care of the family's continuing support of the Newhouse School. (Si has never served as a trustee of Syracuse or any other school.) The university's current chancellor, Kenneth Shaw, reports that almost all his contacts are with Donald.

Donald directed enough money the university's way to make its top official wary of doing anything to displease him. When Chancellor Tolley's daughter suggested that this writer peruse her father's papers at the Syracuse University library, a librarian checked "with channels," as she put it. According to the librarian, Donald Newhouse was asked by Chancellor Shaw if the files could be opened to a woman writing a book about Si Newhouse, and Donald said no.

When Sam died, he left nothing in his will to charities, but he did set up a charitable foundation that the sons administer, generally, as their father did, targeting causes that are connected to the cities in which they own newspapers.

Others, such as Alan Mirken, who sold Crown to Si, claim that Si is generous in his contributions, he just does so quietly and prefers no public recognition. Through the $50.4 million Samuel I. Newhouse Foundation, Si and Donald give to the United Jewish Appeal (UJA)—in 1994 just under $1 million.[16]

In the art world, Si continues to be seen as a man sorely lacking in philanthropic instincts. A controversy at the Barnes Foundation underscored that impression.

The Barnes Foundation was established in 1922 by Albert C. Barnes, who was both a physician and a manufacturer of patent medicines, including an antiseptic used to fight eye infections in infants. When Barnes died in an auto accident in 1951, he left an incomparable collection of impressionist masterpieces, including 180 Renoirs, 69 Cézannes, 60 Matisses, and 45 Picassos, as well as works by Van Gogh, Seurat, Gauguin, Toulouse-Lautrec, Monet, and an array of African tribal sculpture. But along with the art, Barnes left a will riddled with restrictions on how the art could be shown—only by appointment, only in the house in Merion, Pennsylvania outside Philadelphia where he had carefully and eccentrically arranged it and ordered that every piece must hang precisely as he had left it. (Barnes did not allow labels to identify the paintings' titles.)

Barnes also decreed that the collection could not tour, that no painting could be sold or lent, and that no color photograph could be taken of any painting because he believed that photography distorted the original. The son of a butcher, Barnes despised the art and museum establishment, which he considered snobbish and elitist, and so he insisted that his collection be operated not as a museum but as a school at which working people would be taught how to view art.

Barnes's wishes seemed to have meant little to Richard H. Glanton, an attorney who became the president of the Barnes Foundation. Glanton reportedly had no particular interest in art. His path and the Barneses' crossed because he was counsel and a trustee of Lincoln University, a predominantly black school in Pennsylvania. Dr. Barnes had been a major backer of the college—he had a great interest in black culture, as attested to by his assemblage of African sculpture—and he had left Lincoln in control of his entire collection. After allegedly maneuvering Lincoln trustees onto the Barnes board, Glanton was, his critics charge, able to assume control.

Before long, the Barnes Collection was open to the public on a limited schedule—Glanton is currently fighting for the museum, as it is now aptly described, to be open six days a week—and plans were afoot for a major and worldwide tour. Glanton's plans to make the Barnes immensely profitable, and in the process to enrich Lincoln University, were soon slowed by threatened and actual lawsuits. Nonetheless, Glanton pursued the publication of a catalog, which, he understood, would be a major moneymaker, and that's where Si Newhouse came in.

In 1991 Susan Ralston, an editor at Knopf who specialized in art books, tipped Si to a publishing opportunity that he should not miss. As Glanton recalls it, it was art dealer Richard Feigen, a Lincoln trustee, who recommended Si and Knopf. In any case, Newhouse and Ralston were soon meeting with Glanton. In 1990, several prominent publishers had been asked to and did submit proposals for the rights to publish the catalog.

Paul Gottlieb, CEO, president, and editor in chief of Harry N. Abrams, Inc., the leading art book publisher in America, had been called early on by Esther Van Sant, the Barnes Foundation's director of education. She informed Gottlieb that the foundation was contemplating the publication of a catalog and invited him to see the collection and to make a proposal. He did both. Then Gottlieb began to deal with Glanton. The proposal Gottlieb submitted was "fairly well developed," he recalls, but, he claims, Glanton asked him to leave out a specific advance and insert in its place the phrase "a substantial sum." The number would be filled in later. (Glanton denies making such a request.) As Glanton worked out the details of a worldwide tour of the collection, he presumably realized that the value of the rights to publish the catalog would vastly increase.

When Si Newhouse met with Glanton, he offered a specific amount—an advance of $750,000 to be paid to the Barnes. He also sweetened the pot considerably by offering to have his Newhouse Foundation give a grant of $2 million to Lincoln University. There was no way that any other publisher could match such a proposal. "The next thing one knew,"

Gottlieb says, "Random House had the publishing rights. I was furious. I tried to get some kind of response and some answer to my own proposal." Once he learned about the high-six-figure advance and the $2 million to Lincoln University, Gottlieb understood why, suddenly, his calls and letters went unanswered.

According to Gottlieb and others, a rival publisher was said to have offered more, and at least two houses other than Abrams and Knopf made serious proposals, but Glanton wanted Si Newhouse. The $2 million for Lincoln University was said to be one reason. Another publishing executive might have paid a higher advance than Si did, a much higher advance, but that money would have gone to Barnes, not Lincoln.

Glanton's political aspirations were said to be another reason. When the $2 million was given to Lincoln, it was handed over not by Si but by the publisher of the Newhouse papers in Harrisburg. Glanton, who has admitted ambitions to run for the U.S. Senate from Pennsylvania, may have been swayed not only by the $2 million grant to Lincoln University but also by the fact that Newhouse owns both papers in the state capital. Glanton, Gottlieb says, assured his board that he had properly evaluated all proposals—a claim that Gottlieb maintains cannot possibly be true, because Gottlieb's proposal did not contain a specific dollar advance. Gottlieb insists he was ready to specify the amount but was never asked to do so.

Among participants in the competition for the catalog, there was anger and resentment and a feeling that Si had acted in an underhanded manner. "We weren't about to make any $2 million donation to anybody," says Michael Loeb, who then worked for Harry Abrams and who also knew both Newhouse brothers at Horace Mann. "I think in this case [Newhouse] really used [his foundation] to acquire for Random House something that Random House could not have acquired itself.... We were just shut out."

Paul Gottlieb, like Si, is on the board of the Museum of Modern Art. Gottlieb also sits on the board of the New York Studio School. With the latter in mind, he wrote to Si, "congratulating him on his coup and on his generosity [to Lincoln University]. And I said, 'It sure would be nice to see some of your generosity falling closer to home. How about something for this school?'" He sent a "very nice" contribution to the school's scholarship fund, Gottlieb reports.[17]

26 | The Queen of Buzz Buzzes Off

WHEN TINA BROWN told her staff on Wednesday morning, July 8, 1998, that she was stepping down as editor of the *New Yorker*, she sent Manhattan's media mavens reeling. The expectation—and it was certainly Si Newhouse's and Steve Florio's—was that she would sign her contract and continue to preside over a magazine that, in turn, would continue to bleed both money and prestige. But Tina Brown had other plans, and that those plans involved Hollywood surprised no one who read *Vanity Fair* and the *New Yorker* under her direction and noted how often they celebrated Hollywood stars, Hollywood money men, and Hollywood hype.

The night before, she had summoned her staffers via fax to a meeting at ten-thirty the next morning. On the agenda: the special "NEXT" issue planned for October. A conference, this one in Las Vegas, would be spun off, and assorted movie and media moguls, such as her close friend, Disney chairman Michael Eisner, would attend, just as they had her last NEXT conference in Orlando. When her staffers filed in, Tina was already talking—but about herself, specifically what was next for Tina Brown.

She explained that she had signed a contract the night before to launch a new "media venture" with Harvey Weinstein, the man who, with his brother Bob, had his start promoting rock concerts and operating a second-run theater in Buffalo before moving up to distribute low-budget movies that nobody else wanted. So successful were the brothers that in 1993 they sold their company, Miramax, to Disney. They continued to run a booming concern that not only distributes movies but also makes them— some schlocky horror and sci-fi titles, but others critically acclaimed works such as *The Piano, Sex, Lies and Videotape, Good Will Hunting, The English Patient, My Left Foot, The Crying Game, Pulp Fiction,* and *Trainspotting.*

When Tina appeared in Si's office at 9:00 A.M. that same Wednesday—an hour and an half before she met her staff—to tell him that she would not sign the five-year deal he had proposed, she presented him with a stunner of a problem. (Si was completely surprised. Both Tina and her agent, Mort Janklow, had led him to believe that she would sign. At lunch with Si two days earlier, she had mentioned nothing.) The company had been wounded by the *Fortune* article that depicted Steve Florio as a loser and a liar, and the magazine Tina ran as the deepest money pit in the business. Now she was jumping ship, just as advertisers were digesting what surely should count as among journalism's most brutal attacks on a person and a company—made worse because the magazine was the sober *Fortune,* not *Spy,* or even the media-obsessed *New York Observer* or *New York* magazine.

For Si, the bad news was twofold. Not only was she leaving, but Tina was taking Ron Galotti with her, so Si was also losing the publisher of *Vogue,* who had set things on the ups at the company's flagship magazine. More important, Galotti had filled for Si the bullyboy role that Roy Cohn had left vacant and that Steve Florio, whose image had morphed from bully to blowhard, had flubbed.

A few among Tina's brood reportedly wept as she described her new job, shed a few tears herself, and told them how much she loved them. She would be chairman, and Galotti president, of a "multimedia unit" under the auspices of Miramax, itself under the auspices of Disney, whose center would be a magazine. Its raison d'être would be to assign and nurture pieces to be spun off into television, via Disney's ABC, and film productions, via Miramax. Tina and Ron, although they would not share in equity, at least initially, would reap part of any profits that the magazine or the television/film offshoots might generate. She repeatedly referred to herself and Galotti as owners and explained that since the death of her mother a week before, she had decided she needed a new and fun challenge, and that it was time to be an owner, not merely an employee. When she looked at the five-year contract and the multimillions offered by Si, she explained, "I couldn't stand the thought of getting married for five more years."

The response from her colleagues, some of whom were already angling for her job and others who were presumably planning ahead to contribute to Tina's "movie magazine," as a *New York Times* editorial writer dismissed her new venture, was praise soaring out of proportion to her record. Michael Kinsley, a seasoned editor at several magazines who wanted Tina's job, was quoted as calling her "the best magazine editor alive" and the *New Yorker* "the hottest magazine being published." (*Times* columnist Maureen Dowd, typically, offered a more cynical view, predicting that "money-hungry writers [would] shape their journalism into movie pitches, the kind you find in publications like *Spec, Script Marketplace* and *Spec Screenplay.*")

A rash of similarly cynical reportage about Harvey Weinstein—he had been assiduously courting Tina since reading that her contract would soon expire and had dispatched his lawyers to meet Mort Janklow—brought matters back to earth. Anyone who worked with Harvey Weinstein—sloppy-looking and fat, a college dropout from Queens, coarse, profane, a tightwad and a screamer, who promised publicly that he would never scream at Tina—and experienced how cheap he could be knew that he wouldn't for a second have stomached the losses that Si Newhouse blithely accepted at the *New Yorker.* His movies didn't cost much to make, and he insisted that they stay within budget. It was also pointed out that Tina and Ron would have to have every project approved by Weinstein, that they would pocket a piece of the profits only if there were any, and that—given Tina's tenure at *Vanity Fair* and the *New Yorker*—profits might prove elusive. It began to seem as if the pair would be joining the hordes of slick operators prowling the lots with development deals. Then there were the less-than-promising statistics: out of 160 films made in America the year before, only three traced their start to magazine articles. Still, Harvey Weinstein seemed euphoric, calling the magazine "a pipeline for ideas" and declaring, "It's all about content." Tina echoed his words when she disavowed any responsibility for the losses at the *New Yorker,* explaining that it was the publisher's job to bring in advertising. "My job is to bring in content, to bring in talent."

Buried in the hype was the most likely reason for Tina's exit: she had lost the battle for control of the *New Yorker* to Steve Florio. He had wanted the *New Yorker* brought under the Condé Nast umbrella; she hadn't. He had wanted the *New Yorker* to room with its sibling magazines in the new tower then being built on Times Square; she wanted to stay put in her own quarters. (She was heard to say after announcing her departure, "At least I won't have to move to that hellish building."*) Steve Florio and Tina had agreed on Tom Florio's ouster, but Steve had selected his brother's successor without even consulting Tina. She had also run into opposition when she wanted to launch other media ventures under the *New Yorker* imprimatur. Her contract was said to be not as rosy as Tina described, but rather to require certain concessions and tighter financial controls, to be implemented by the elder Florio—a dilution of her freedom and access to Si. On his own, or at the insistence of Donald, Si had refused, as he had when he hired her in 1992, to give her the profit-sharing she wanted. (Liz Smith presented Tina's side, claiming that she was offered a "substantial salary increase, plus a big retirement package," and that the job was offered "'unconditionally,' with no budget restrictions.")

On Thursday, July 9, Si, dressed in a black T-shirt, accompanied by Steve Florio, again found himself at a crisis meeting of *New Yorker* writers and editors. But by the summer of 1998 so many of the old-timers who longed for the days of good taste and William Shawn had been purged or retired that the boss's reception lacked that element of disdain so palpable

---

*The remark proved eerily prescient when, two weeks later, a twenty-story construction elevator shaft with attached scaffolding collapsed, hurling a fifty-foot girder through the roof of a subsidized residence for the elderly poor across the street and crushing to death one woman. Twelve people were injured in what the city's building commission labeled the worst construction disaster of the decade. Times Square, paralyzed for days to come, was described as resembling the set of a disaster movie, as huge hunks of twisted steel rained on terrified people below. One day later, twenty-five-stories' worth of scaffolding dangled precariously from the building's side. With buildings and stores closed, loss of income soared, as did the misery index for the 300 senior citizens whose home was heavily damaged, and others in the area, including AIDS patients. It was the fourth major construction accident at the forty-eight-story site, and the second death. One man told a reporter for the *New York Times* that in eighteen years as a sheet metal worker, he had never seen so many accidents at one construction site; "It seems like it's a bad luck job."

at earlier Newhouse appearances. Still rampant, however, was fear. Whatever they thought of Tina—and many were, after all, her hires—they worried more about who might replace her. Roger Angell, an old-timer who, in the minds of some, had joined the enemy by working so apparently harmoniously with Tina, urged Si to reassure them that he had no plans to bring in a cost-cutter or an "efficiency expert." He had no such plans, he promised. Within the week he would announce Tina's successor, he added, and that person would be someone who would make him "comfortable and excited" and who would "turn a light on in my head." So chastened and beaten was the staff that no one asked the obvious question: Why should we believe you when you have broken most, if not all, of the promises you made at previous meetings? The meeting lasted fifteen minutes. Si and Tina exchanged what was described as an "awkward" embrace.

Tina left for lunch with her new partners, Harvey Weinstein and Ron Galotti. Their destination was Si's usual restaurant, the Grill Room at the Four Seasons. They were the center of attention and the target of a mad scramble of other media types to offer congratulations.

Florio's first task was to find a new publisher for *Vogue,* and he quickly announced that Richard "Mad Dog" Beckman, then publisher of *GQ,* who had steeply boosted ad pages at that magazine, would take the post. Si's choices to replace Tina were less obvious. In the old days, Alex Liberman would have been at his elbow to guide him. James Truman, the touted "new Alex," was vacationing in Greece and declined to interrupt his idyll. With the *New Yorker* just shoved under the umbrella of Condé Nast, Truman's territory, he should have been neck-deep in the decision. But he was hosting a dinner party for thirty a couple of days hence, he explained, so how could he possibly return?

The *New York Times* ran news of Tina's exit on the front page above the fold, reflecting coverage, especially in the print media, that seemed loonily excessive. With a circulation of some 808,000, then slightly on the decline—advertising was also down slightly—the *New Yorker,* in the scheme of things, was not only a small player but a money-losing one at that.

Names mentioned as potential successors to Tina included Peter Kaplan, editor of the *New York Observer;* Kurt Anderson, a founding editor of *Spy* and the fired editor of *New York*, who wrote the "Culture Industry" column for the *New Yorker;* Sonny Mehta, head of Knopf, now working for Bertelsmann; Steven Swartz, founding editor of *Smart Money;* and Dominique Browning, whose own magazine, *House & Garden*, was faring so poorly that she or one of her acolytes must have tossed her name into the mix. (She was the only woman whose name appeared in speculation.)

The real candidates seemed less enamored of the chance to take over. James Truman was said to be under serious consideration, but either he didn't want it—this was a job in which he would actually have to edit—or he wasn't quick enough to recognize that if he did, he should have hurried back to New York. Graydon Carter was reportedly offered the job and turned it down, not wishing once again to be stuck following in Tina's footsteps and having to repair her horrific finances. Art Cooper was said to have turned it down, but while most believed it had actually been offered to Carter, fewer believed that Cooper had been given the opportunity to say no.

It was Tina who claimed that she lobbied Si for her favored writer, David Remnick, a prolific producer who had worked for the *Washington Post* before entering Tina's stable in 1992. Graydon Carter would also take credit for bringing the thirty-nine-year-old to Si's attention, claiming that when Si and Florio appeared in his office the day of Tina's resignation to offer him her job, he had proposed Remnick, a man he admitted he barely knew. But Remnick, who was soon described by any and all who hoped to win his favor as the consummate intellectual, a man of gravitas who cared about ideas and shunned buzz, who preferred a seminar at the Council on Foreign Relations to any cocktail party, was his own most canny promoter. A look at his career showed someone who knew how to befriend people who could help him, who knew whose apple to polish. He had written glowing profiles of his mentor, John McPhee—the man who recommended him for his job at the *Post*—and of Tina's husband, Harry Evans. That weekend, when Si was saddled with the selection—he wanted the announcement made the next Monday—Remnick faxed Si a 3,000-word description of his vision for the magazine.

In the meantime Si had asked Michael Kinsley, editor of the Internet magazine *Slate* and formerly editor of the *New Republic*, to hurry to New

York from Redmond, Washington, where *Slate* was headquartered in the bosom of its parent company, Microsoft. Kinsley chatted with Si at his apartment on Saturday, July 11, had lunch with him that day at a restaurant, and had dinner with Si and Donald, their wives, and the brothers' eldest sons that Sunday night at Sette Mezzo, Si and Donald's usual Sunday-night haunt, where, Kinsley reported, the conversation steered clear of business. When Kinsley left the restaurant, he thought he had the job—and for good reason. Si had offered it to him on Saturday, and although he seemed disappointed that Kinsley asked for forty-eight hours to think it over, Si seemed willing to indulge him. Kinsley was to call Si at seven-thirty the next morning, just to confirm that he would accept the job. They had agreed that Kinsley would accompany Si to a meeting that next morning with Tina and David Remnick, and that their mission would be to persuade Remnick to stay on even though he would not be editor.

On returning to his hotel, Kinsley found a message to call Si, who explained that he sensed the editor's reluctance. Kinsley tried to reassure Si that he would enthusiastically accept, but simply wanted to sleep on the decision; he had also promised his bosses at Microsoft that he would inform them before announcing his departure from *Slate*. To Kinsley's astonishment, Si then withdrew the offer. Within minutes of hanging up, Kinsley e-mailed a group of friends, colleagues, and the biggest boss of all, Microsoft chairman Bill Gates, and described what he considered to be Si's weird, nasty, unprofessional, and dishonorable behavior. The message was soon forwarded to editors and writers nationwide. Si had behaved like a jerk, Kinsley wrote, adding that he would never work for him, and that he considered Si's retreat from his word to be a lucky escape.

Si withdrew the offer from Kinsley because he had decided, that Sunday night, to select Remnick. The next morning Si called Remnick to offer him the job. He faced *New Yorker* staffers once more, again with Tina Brown in attendance, to introduce the new editor, whose appointment was greeted with applause and gushing praise by everyone who wanted a sinecure, or at the least, an assignment. Gore Vidal was alone in calling it "crazy" to give the job to someone whose only editing in chief experience was on his high school newspaper in New Jersey. (Perhaps the most shameless suck-up was committed by *Nation* writer and MSNBC contrib-

456 | Citizen Newhouse

utor Eric Alterman, who said that when people talk about Remnick, "it is with a kind of awe." Remnick, understandably nervous because his day had been tarnished by the much juicier news that Kinsley had been Si's first choice, promised, oddly, to infuse the magazine with "hilarity." Although not even Si Newhouse could have been intimidated by the thoroughly docile staff, Si closed by saying, "I hope I don't have to come back here again." Remnick said disingenuously, "Until the morning, I was delighted to be a writer at the *New Yorker*."*

And so in the course of a wild eight months, Tina's husband Harry had been shoved out of the ill-performing Random House; four months later Si announced the sale of Random House; and nearly four months after that Tina Brown exited, explaining that she was leaving at the right time because the right time was when the magazine was perfect. In fact, by leaving, she had drawn attention to just what a mess the magazine had become under the ownership of Si Newhouse.

In her wake Brown left renewed fears that Donald Newhouse, with whom Si consulted the minute Tina bolted, would force his brother to sell the *New Yorker*, and that Si would have to go along. That the free-spending days would be over was everybody's guess. And although Jonathan Newhouse, the designated heir, was not on the scene, it was soon reported that he was in the growing camp of those who felt that the only way the *New Yorker* could make sense financially was to go biweekly. Si promised he would never do that. Those who had been around the publishing business

---

*Remnick's honeymoon was tainted by the *New York Post*, which reminded readers of an ugly accusation. The author of a book on Hasidic Jews, Jerome Mintz, and his publisher, Harvard University Press, had complained that Remnick, in writing a piece on the Hasidim in Crown Heights, had appropriated material without crediting its source. Jeanette Walls, who broke the story in *New York* magazine in August 1993, wrote that Mintz and his publisher had been unsuccessful in seeking an apology or an acknowledgment. Walls characterized Mintz's complaint as a seeming "appropriation of Mintz's analysis, structuring, and marshaling of facts." Walls also wrote that editors at the magazine twice offered to review the book favorably. Tina at the time denied all, as did Remnick in an angry conversation with Walls. Unfortunately Mintz, a professor of anthropology at Indiana University, died in the spring of 1998. His editor at Harvard, Margaretta Fulton, refused to comment, although she did not refute any of the details in the Walls item.

for more than five minutes knew that he was not a man who kept his promises. Michael Kinsley had learned that lesson the hard way.[1]

The summer of 1998 held still another shocker. Tina Brown's exit was barely a month old when Si Newhouse shoved into retirement *Glamour* editor in chief Ruth Whitney, age seventy, the woman whom Steve Florio had, in effect, called the savior of Condé Nast's bottom line. *Glamour*'s circulation had slipped a bit to 2.1 million, but it continued to be touted as Condé Nast's "cash cow." In collaboration with James Truman, finally back from vacation, and Steve Florio, Si hired Bonnie Fuller, editor of Hearst's *Cosmopolitan* for just eighteen months and the person credited with boosting the magazine's circulation to 2.7 million.

Although the wooing of Fuller reportedly took some weeks, Si didn't bother to let Whitney, *Glamour*'s top editor for thirty-one years, know what was afoot. When he called her to his office on August 6, he informed her that she was retiring and that Fuller had already been offered and had accepted the job. If Whitney couldn't continue to be editor herself, she would have wanted her executive editor to take over. She was reportedly humiliated and angry, and when Si made the announcement of the change in editors to *Glamour*'s staff, Whitney was not at his side. She saw *Glamour* as a much more serious magazine than *Cosmo*. She had made money for Si Newhouse, increasing circulation by a million copies during her tenure, while regularly publishing issue-oriented articles. Fuller, who had succeeded the legendary Helen Gurley Brown, had improved *Cosmo*'s numbers, not only in circulation but in advertising revenue and newsstand sales, by adding more articles about beauty, fashion, and celebrities. Fuller lacked Whitney's zeal for educating her young readers. By selecting Fuller, Whitney told a reporter, Si Newhouse was saying that "only numbers matter and that women's magazines are just commodities."

Si claimed that he hadn't asked Ruth Whitney to resign, and that during his meeting with her, "she said to me she realized it was time," as if the changing of the guard was Whitney's idea.[2] So different was her take on the situation from Si's that to Condé Nast watchers his statement sounded as if it had come directly from the lips of Steve Florio.

27 | Hearst, Luce, Murdoch— Newhouse?

JUST AS SECOND-TERM presidents obsess about their place in history, so do presidents of universities, CEOs, editors, publishers, and media moguls.

Sam Newhouse was different. He never cared much about how he was viewed by outsiders, his peers in the media included. And he certainly did not care to put his newspapers in the service of promulgating his own views, which he kept so close to his vest that most of his employees had no idea what they were.

Others who built newspaper empires and whose careers overlapped the Newhouse patriarch's were made of radically different stuff. William Randolph Hearst, thirty-two years Sam's senior, was the son of a mining prospector who struck it very rich in Nevada. George Hearst bought a newspaper in San Francisco, and, some said, a U.S. Senate seat from California. The son attended Harvard but dropped out and, a few years later, in 1887, took over his father's ailing *San Francisco Examiner*. He turned it into a moneymaker and began to buy papers in New York and other cities until he owned a chain of forty-two dailies. He was so successful that on Sundays nearly a quarter of the newspapers sold in the United States were Hearst papers. (He also owned magazines, a wire service, radio stations, and two movie companies.)

Henry Luce, three years Sam's junior, was the son of missionaries who did their proselytizing in China. He was also a Yale and Oxford man, who with a college classmate raised the money to start *Time*, which became the most profitable and influential of popular magazines.

Both Hearst and Luce were men of ideas, of political beliefs to which they held fast and which they ordered their publications to both reflect and promote. Hearst saw his newspapers and Luce his news magazine not as properties but as tools to publicize, to push their viewpoints. Hearst used his papers to agitate, to arouse the public to demand war with Spain in 1898. Luce, a dogmatic Republican, used his news magazine as a bulwark against communism, and a supporter of such conservative favorites as Nationalist China. The late Richard Clurman, once *Time*'s chief of correspondents, called Luce "a journalistic and corporate evangelist" whose publications were "missions," never products.

William Randolph Hearst, whose employees called him "the chief," served two terms in Congress, lobbied to be president in 1904, and for the rest of his career crowned himself a kingmaker. In 1932, for example, Hearst ordered his candidate for the presidential nomination, Speaker of the House Cactus Jack Garner, to release his delegates from California to Franklin Roosevelt. Garner ended up on the ballot as FDR's running mate. Hearst and Luce expected to have the ear of whomever occupied the White House or his scalp if the president's politics veered too far to the left. Sam Newhouse didn't mind escorting Mitzi to state dinners, but he minded very much the expectation that he would push any of his employees to endorse a particular president or a policy.

Both Luce and Hearst were publishing geniuses. In founding *Time*, Luce invented the news magazine, and in subsequent launches he was nearly as prescient in giving the public *Life*, *Fortune*, and *Sports Illustrated*. While other moguls practiced yellow journalism, Hearst perfected it.

That Sam Newhouse might as easily have owned laundromats as newspapers shows how different a breed he was from Luce or from Hearst, who routinely wired instructions to his editors about which stories to play on page one and how to slant them, and paid so little attention to the bottom line that he nearly went bankrupt in the 1930s. "Local autonomy," Sam's catchphrase, was not one that would have even occurred to a Hearst or Luce. Richard Clurman recalled the time in the 1950s when Luce scribbled across a business-related story scheduled for publication, "I resent the fact that these men are fighting for a huge chunk of the 'national estate' without there seeming to be any point to the fight. None seems to stand for a damn thing. This is the sort of thing that turns one against capitalism. I resent having these great companies owned by pointless men like these." Although Luce never said, it is a fair guess that he would have considered Sam and his sons to be "pointless men."

Sam could enter the newsrooms of his own papers without anyone recognizing him or even realizing he was there. Hearst, the model for Charles Foster Kane in Orson Welles's *Citizen Kane,* was a subject of endless public fascination. Hearst's spectacular castle at San Simeon and his affair with actress/showgirl Marion Davies helped feed the larger-than-life press lord image. Henry Luce married the writer, congresswoman, and diplomat Clare Boothe. With her movie-star beauty, her brilliance, her ideas, and her determination to succeed in a man's world, Clare Boothe Luce was a standout, and she and Henry were among the most renowned of American couples. Mitzi Newhouse's ideas did not extend beyond her closet door, and outside a certain slice of Manhattan, she was virtually unknown.

When Hearst died in 1951 and Luce in 1967, their empires passed to professional managers. Their sons had limited roles, although Hearst's son and namesake carried the title editor in chief and became a real journalist, sharing the Pulitzer Prize for international reporting in 1956. But he did not run the corporation. William Randolph Hearst Jr. would later lament, "I lived in my father's shadow all my life." Today the Hearst corporation is a huge operation that emcompasses fifteen magazines (among them *Cosmopolitan, Redbook, Harper's Bazaar,* and *Good Housekeeping,* the last with a 5 million circulation), ten daily newspapers, six television and six radio stations, hard and softcover publishing houses, 50 percent of the Lifetime cable channel, 50 percent of A&E, and 20 percent of ESPN. Time Inc., since merged with Warner Communications, Inc., is a colossus of a conglomerate, the largest media and entertainment combine in the world, covering the business of movies, book publishing, cable, newspapers, and of course magazines.

Sam Newhouse had a different idea. He was not out to change the way that Americans received and digested their news. If Luce and Hearst sought political power, Sam Newhouse sought profit and an empire to build for his sons so that they in turn could pass it to their sons. In 1962 Sam told Calvin Trillin, then a reporter for *Time*, "I'm very hard-boiled about the boys. I've built this thing up, and I'm not going to let it go to pieces."

And so it fell to Si and to Donald. Donald has run things pretty much in his father's style. Sam would have approved. Si has been a different story altogether.

Hearst and Luce, bellicose and towering, drew attention to themselves via their opinions, their genius, and their chutzpah. The American public was their audience, their target, and they never stopped trying to stamp their views on it. Si likewise seeks attention, but his target consists of the movers in Manhattan, in the Hamptons, the Vineyard, the politically attuned in Hollywood, even, lately, in the flashier precincts of Harvard Yard. He reaches this elite not by making pronouncements but by acquiring prestigious properties. Si lives for the attention, the social cachet. *Vogue*, the *New Yorker*, Knopf, and Random House have opened doors for the tongue-tied multibillionaire that would otherwise have slammed shut in his face.

How else would Katharine Graham, who fled in disgust from the advances of Si's father and is known for her impatience with the homely and the halting, find herself as Si's guest of honor at a book party at the Four Seasons celebrating the publication of her memoir? Where else but to Knopf would the regal Graham have turned for a publisher? And so in the *New York Times* society pages ran a shoulder-to-shoulder photograph of Kay Graham and Si Newhouse. (Next to it is a photograph of two other guests at Si's party for Kay, David Rockefeller and Brooke Astor, the latter a woman who also rejected the advances of Sam Newhouse when he sought in 1961 to buy *Newsweek*, then controlled by the Astor Foundation. Brooke opted instead for Kay's husband, Phil Graham, charismatic, attractive, and WASPy.)

In that insatiable need for social acceptance and status Si differs too from William Randolph Hearst's most direct descendant, Rupert Murdoch, four years Si's junior, whose mantra for his $10 billion high-tech, global communications behemoth is power, pure and simple, prestige be damned. Like Hearst, Murdoch is a buccaneer, a risk taker, a mogul determined to conquer, to control the world's media, to own all sources of programming so that he can beam his product to homes around the world. He claims that he will soon reach more than three-quarters of the wired world, and who would think of disputing that?

Such domination allows Murdoch to influence the business climate on the six continents on which he owns vehicles of communication, among them newspapers (more than 130), magazines, book publishing houses, satellite and cable television, Fox Broadcasting—a fourth and surprisingly successful network that the experts insisted would never work—and the Hollywood movie studio Twentieth Century Fox. Murdoch is not so much interested in imposing his conservative politics on government as in influencing presidents, prime ministers, and politicians at all levels to give him the breaks he needs to expand, to make the next deal, to gamble and to win.

It likely surprised no one who knew him that Murdoch killed a memoir about to be published by his book publishing arm, HarperCollins. He did so after learning that its author, Chris Patten, the last British governor of Hong Kong, took a harsh view of China's human rights abuses and its antidemocratic policies in Hong Kong, which reverted to Chinese control in 1997. Murdoch has extensive business interests in China, including his satellite service, Star TV, and part ownership of an Asian satellite TV company, and plans to expand there. Harsh experience—in 1994, at the request of Chinese authorities who did not like a special the BBC aired about Mao Tse-tung, Murdoch cut the BBC World Service from his satellite broadcasts into China—had taught him to avoid irritating Chinese government officials.

To influence politicians in New York—Murdoch is said to have "created" Ed Koch—and thus to provide a better backdrop for the expansion of his empire there and beyond is surely the reason Murdoch bought the problem-plagued *New York Post*. In both its news columns and its editorials, the *Post* has energetically boosted Mayor Rudolph Giuliani. Murdoch's critics charge that multimillions in tax breaks and incentives have followed. One critic has charged recently that the *Post* can be counted on to dole out similar favors to New York governor George Pataki, in exchange for Pataki's support of a $13 million economic development grant. The money will help Murdoch build a color printing plant in the Bronx.

In England Murdoch put his papers behind Margaret Thatcher, and she repaid him with breaks and policies—easing of regulations and monopoly oversight—that helped him to expand his base there. Later, disillusioned with Thatcher's successor, conservative John Major, Murdoch put his media muscle behind Liberal party leader Tony Blair. (Blair was soon accused by his political opponents of lobbying the prime minister of Italy on behalf of Murdoch, who was attempting to buy a controlling interest in an Italian media company.) "If you are in newspapers and magazines, you fight very hard for your beliefs," Murdoch was recently quoted as saying.

Although the Australian-born Murdoch is himself an Oxford graduate and the son of a prominent and knighted journalist from whom he inherited a small newspaper, Murdoch delights in offending members of the cultural elite. Unlike Si Newhouse, but like Hearst, Murdoch has the common touch. He understands that the straphanger wants to be amused more than informed, that he prefers his prejudices and opinions confirmed rather than challenged. While Murdoch owns the *Times* and the *Sunday Times* of London, he also owns a couple of the crassest tabloids—*The Sun* and *News of the World*—in a country infamous for crass tabloids. In the United States one of Murdoch's prized properties is the *Star*, a deliberate ripoff of the *National Enquirer*, featuring the same mix of ugly scandal, Hollywood scuttlebutt, diet tips and quackery for the downscale. Although Murdoch has since sold most of his magazines, he has owned *Soap Opera Digest,* the *Daily Racing Form,* and *TV Guide*. These are not publications to send Si's acquisitive juices flowing.

Rupert Murdoch is happiest in the air en route to making another multibillion, heartstopping, potentially ruinous deal, or in the unlikely event that a deal is not in the offing, to spending a private evening with his children. He will eventually hand the empire over to one of the three children from his second marriage.

Si takes his pleasure from a venue quite different.

Giorgio Armani was in Manhattan in September, 1996, to open two boutiques on Madison Avenue. He dined at Si Newhouse's U.N. Plaza apartment. Liz Smith described the setting as stuffed with "priceless contemporary art" and with "super sophisticated and smart" guests—David Salle and Eric Fischl, Lee Radziwill, and an assortment of Si's employees, including Anna Wintour and Tina Brown. In a toast to his guest of honor, Si compared the Italian fashion designer's opening of two new shops to Caesar's declaring in Asia Minor, "Veni, vidi, vici."[1]

He might have intended the tribute to be tongue-in-cheek, but it came out sounding silly. No matter. S. I. Newhouse Jr. has finally climbed high enough that he can say or do whatever he pleases. And all those who depend on him for their current or future prospects may think him vacuous and self-indulgent, but they keep those feelings to themselves. To his face, they take him seriously indeed. Standing on his family's billions, he has been able to indulge his passion for the fashionable, his need to be the master of the "class" of Manhattan's most glitzy media.

Notes

IN THE NOTES THAT FOLLOW, an asterisk preceding a name indicates that that person was interviewed by the author. In instances in the text in which a direct quote or paraphrase is not credited to its source by name, the reader should assume that the source has requested anonymity. The abbreviations below are used throughout:

AJR American Journalism Review
AP Associated Press
CJR Columbia Journalism Review
E&P Editor & Publisher
FOIA Documents obtained under the Freedom of Information Act
MIN Media Industry Newsletter
NY New York magazine
NYDN New York Daily News
NYO *New York Observer*
NYP New York Post
NYT *New York Times*
NYer the *New Yorker*
PW Publishers Weekly
VV Village Voice
WSJ Wall Street Journal
WJR Washington Journalism Review
WP Washington Post

Chapter 1—THE SELF-MADE MAN
1. *Lee Lorenz.
2. Joanne Lipman, "How S. I. Newhouse Jr. Is Leading Makeover of Condé Nast Empire," *WSJ*, January 4, 1996; LaVerne M. Hagan, "Condé Nast Pashas," *WSJ*, February 13, 1996.
3. Richard H. Meeker, *Newspaperman: S. I. Newhouse and the Business of News* (Ticknor & Fields, 1983), 8, 10, 20; Anne Chamberlin, "America's Unknown Press Lord," *Esquire*, August 1959; *Calvin Trillin; Dodie Kazanjian and Calvin Tomkins, *Alex: The Life of Alexander Liberman* (Knopf, 1993), 214; "The Newspaper Collector," *Time*, July 27, 1962; "America's Most Profitable Publisher: Seat-of-the-Pants Management That Works," *Business Week*, January 26, 1976; William Pearson Tolley, *At the Fountain of Youth: Memories of a College President* (Syracuse University Press, 1989); Thomas Maier, *Newhouse: All the Glitter, Power, and Glory of America's Richest Media Empire and the Secretive Man behind It* (St. Martin's Press, 1994), 20; Alison Frankel, "The Six-Year Tax Case against the Newhouse Estate," *American Lawyer*, May 1990.

4. Philip Hochstein, *If It Please Their Honors* (News Book, 1988); Tolley, *At the Fountain;* "The Newspaper Collector"; Jefferson Grigsby, "Newhouse, after Newhouse," *Forbes,* October, 29, 1979; *Margot Hentoff; "Samuel I. Newhouse Dies at 84," *NYT,* August 30, 1979; *Calvin Trillin; "America's Most Profitable Publisher"; *Karl Grossman; Maier, *Newhouse,* 19; James Barron, "Norman Newhouse Is Dead at 82; Executive with Newspaper Chain," *NYT,* November 7, 1988.

5. Chamberlin, "America's Unknown"; FOIA, U.S. Dept. of Justice, FBI, March 29, 1962; UPI/Corbis/Bettmann, caption, July 4, 1978; "America's Most Profitable Publisher"; Carol J. Loomis, "The Biggest Private Fortune," *Fortune,* August 17, 1987; "Samuel I. Newhouse Dies"; *Calvin Trillin; "The Newspaper Collector."

6. Daniel Machalaba, "Newhouse Chain Stays with Founder's Ways, and with His Heirs," *WSJ,* February 12, 1982; Grigsby, "Newhouse, after Newhouse"; "Newspaper Collector"; Barron, "Norman Newhouse Is Dead"; Maier, *Newhouse,* 20; *Mel Elfin; "'Nachas' for Sam," *Newsweek,* August 17, 1964.

7. George Garneau, "Billion-Dollar Disagreement" and "Newhouse Tradition: Management by Discussion," *E&P,* January 14, 1989; Chamberlin, "America's Unknown."

8. *Terry Golway; *Jane Franke; *Calvin Trillin; "Newspaper Collector."

9. *Sally Obre; *Miki Denhoff; *Ruth Spaet; Maier, *Newhouse,* 30; Meeker, *Newspaperman,* 42, 183; Chamberlin, "America's Unknown."

10. Meeker, *Newspaperman,* 57; Maier, *Newhouse,* 30; *Ruth Spaet.

11. Meeker, *Newspaperman,* 58.

12. *Calvin Trillin; Meeker, *Newspaperman,* 123–24, 86–87; Christopher Mason, "West of Eden," *NY,* September 2, 1996; *NY,* November 6, 1995.

13. "Newspaper Collector"; "America's Most Profitable Publisher"; "Samuel I. Newhouse Dies"; Machalaba, "Newhouse Chain Stays with Founder's Ways"; *Robert Lewis.

14. Meeker, *Newspaperman,* 124; Richard Pollak, "The $1 Billion Misunderstanding: The IRS vs. the Newhouse Empire," *VV,* November 5, 1985; *Elaine Reiner; *Sally Obre; *Ray Josephs; Enid Nemy, "Patricia Mason, 71, Is Dead; Greenwich Village Broker," *NYT,* May 19, 1997; Michael Gross, "Social Life in a Blender," *NY,* February 2, 1998; *Jane Franke; "Newspaper Collector"; *Ruth Spaet; *Sue Spoto; *James Michener; Kazanjian and Tomkins, *Alex,* 216.

15. Meeker, *Newspaperman,* 124; *Paul Keil.

16. *Sue Spoto.

17. *Calvin Trillin; Loomis, "Biggest Private Fortune"; *Richard Penney; Chamberlin, "America's Unknown."

18. *Joseph Bernstein.

Chapter 2—THE EDUCATION OF THE HEIR
1. *Arthur Sprung; Harold J. Bauld and Jerome B. Kisslinger, *Horace Mann-Barnard: The First Hundred Years* (n.d.); *Robin Lester; *Joseph Bernstein; Daniel Rose, "The Forties," photocopied clipping; *Larry Lowenstein; Nicholas von Hoffman, *Citizen Cohn: The Life and Times of Roy Cohn* (Bantam, 1988); Ann Charters, *Kerouac* (St. Martin's, 1994).

2. Rose, "The Forties"; *Robert Carneiro; *Joseph Bernstein.

3. *Samuel Heyman; *Robert Carneiro; letter to author from Robert Carneiro, April 16, 1997.

4. *David S. Maimin, Jr.; *Bill Green; *Arthur Sprung; *Gary P. Marcus; Sidney Zion, *The Autobiography of Roy Cohn* (Lyle Stuart, 1988), 24.

5. *Allan J. Newmark; *Arthur Sprung; *Michael Loeb; "Q & A: John Kennedy and *National Enquirer* Editor Emeritus Iain Calder," *George*, August 1996; *Robert Carneiro; Lowenstein Papers, #4340, ser. 1, fol. 14, Southern Historical Collection, University of North Carolina Library, Chapel Hill; *David S. Maimin Jr; Zion, *Autobiography*, 62.

6. *Paul Haberman; *John Haldenstein; also, *Samuel Heyman; *Bill Green, *Robert Carneiro; *Dottie Dicintio; Thomas Maier, *Newhouse: All the Glitter, Power, and Glory of America's Richest Media Empire and the Secretive Man Behind It* (St. Martin's Press, 1994), 28–29; Lowenstein Papers; *William H. Chafe; *David S. Maimin Jr; William H. Chafe, *Never Stop Running: Allard Lowenstein and the Struggle to Save American Liberalism* (Basic Books, 1993), 22–23; Rose, "The Forties"; *Joseph Bernstein; *Lionel Spring.

7. *John Haldenstein; *Paul Haberman; *Margot Hentoff; *Walter Goodman; Lowenstein Papers; *Allan J. Newmark; *Jim Carleton; Maier, *Newhouse*, 34.

8. *William Pearson Tolley; *Katryn Tolley Fritz; *Frank Piskor; *Jim Carleton; *Dottie Dicintio; Chafe, *Never Stop Running*, 29; *John Haldenstein.

9. *Louis C. Pulvermacher; *Sandy Gluck: *Arthur Sprung; *John Haldenstein; *Paul Sack; Lowenstein Papers; note to author from Dr. Ira H. Kaufman, November 1995; *Bernard Futter; *Dottie Dicintio; Bauld and Kisslinger, *Horace Mann–Barnard;* *David S. Maimin Jr.

Chapter 3—COLLEGE, MARRIAGE, AND A PARK AVENUE CO-OP

1. Carey Goldberg, "William Tolley, 95, Is Dead; Syracuse Chancellor for 27 Years," *NYT*, January 28, 1996; William Pearson Tolley, *At the Fountain of Youth: Memories of a College President* (Syracuse University Press, 1989); Lowenstein Papers, #4340, ser. 1, fol. 14, Southern Historical Collection, University of North Carolina Library, Chapel Hill; *Murray Raphel.

2. *William Pearson Tolley; Lowenstein Papers; *Paul Keil; Thomas Maier, *Newhouse: All the Glitter, Power, and Glory of America's Richest Media Empire and the Secretive Man Behind It* (St. Martin's Press, 1994).

3. *Murray Raphel; Lowenstein Papers; *Paul Keil; *Bob Shogan; *Walter Goodman; *Donna Cole; *Leonard Zweig; *Mel Elfin.

4. *Dottie Dicintio; Lowenstein Papers; *Paul Keil.

5. Lowenstein Papers; *Jane Franke; *Shirley Schine; *Margot Hentoff; *Donna Cole.

6. *William Pearson Tolley; Tolley, *At the Fountain;* *Frank Piskor; *Jane Franke.

7. *Bob Shogan.

8. *Margot Hentoff; "Jane Franke Bride of Publisher's Son," *NYT*, March 12, 1951; *Shirley Schine; *Elaine Reiner; *Jane Franke; *Ruth Spaet.

9. Lowenstein Papers; William Randolph Hearst Jr. with Jack Casserly, *The Hearsts: Father and Son* (Roberts Rinehart, 1991), 301–3; Richard Weiner, *Syndicated Columnists* (Richard Weiner, Inc., 1979), 83, 144; W.A. Swanberg, *Citizen Hearst* (Scribner's, 1961), 299, 306; "Jane Franke Bride."

10. *Jane Franke; *Paul Keil; "America's Most Profitable Publisher: Seat-of-the-Pants Management That Works," *Business Week*, January 26, 1976; *Geraldine Stutz; Irwin Molotsky, "Trial Begins on Newhouse Tax Issue," *NYT*, January 14, 1989; Maggie Mahar, "All in the Family: How the Newhouses Run Their Vast Media Empire," *Barron's*, November 27, 1989; *David Morgan; *Ray Josephs; *Peter Diamandis.

11. *Jane Franke; *Leonard Zweig; *Milton Jaques.

12. *Robert C. Notson.

13. *Jane Franke; Nat Brandt, "Confessions of a Young Reporter," *Silurian News*, May 1995; *Gene Mater.

14. *Jane Franke; *Ray Josephs; *Robert Hochstein; *Jules Witcover; Ray Josephs Papers, Syracuse University, Archives and Records Management, November 18, 1958; Richard H. Meeker, *Newspaperman: S. I. Newhouse and the Business of News* (Ticknor & Fields, 1983), 226.

15. *Jane Franke; *Ray Josephs.

Chapter 4—ROY COHN TAKES CENTER STAGE
1. *David Morgan; *Jane Franke; *Shirley Schine.
2. *Shirley Schine; *David Morgan.
3. *Jane Franke; *Monte Sideman.
4. *Jane Franke.
5. *Donna Cole; *Elaine Reiner; *Ray Josephs; *David Morgan.
6. *Jane Franke; *Sally Obre; *Ray Josephs; *Harriet Burket Taussig; *Elaine Reiner; *Chessy Patcevitch; Richard H. Meeker, *Newspaperman: S. I. Newhouse and the Business of News* (Ticknor & Fields, 1983), 183–84; Dodie Kazanjian and Calvin Tomkins, Alex: *The Life of Alexander Liberman* (Knopf, 1993), 216.
7. *Martin Duggan; Ray Josephs Papers, Syracuse University Archives and Records Management, November 18, 1958; *John Robinson Block.
8. *Chessy Patcevitch; *Elaine Reiner; *Geraldine Stutz; *Neil Walsh.
9. *Jane Franke; *Ben Magdovitz; "The Newspaper Collector," Time, July 27, 1962.
10. *William Denis Fugazy; *Jane Franke; *Sally Obre; *Neil Walsh; *Robert Hochstein; Sidney Zion, *The Autobiography of Roy Cohn* (Lyle Stuart, 1988), 81–82, 179, 299; *Terry Golway; *Nicholas von Hoffman; *Tom Corbally; *Richard Meeker; *Erwin Knoll; Nicholas von Hoffman, *Citizen Cohn: The Life and Times of Roy Cohn* (Bantam, 1988); Meeker, *Newspaperman;* *Leonard Zweig; Thomas Maier, *Newhouse: All the Glitter, Power, and Glory of America's Richest Media Empire and the Secretive Man Behind It* (St. Martin's Press, 1994), 96; Ronald Kessler, "A Rough Dealer: Control of the Newsstands Gives Henry Garfinkle Power over Publishers," *WSJ*, July 3, 1969; *Gary P. Marcus.
11. *Sally Obre; *Geraldine Stutz; *Neil Walsh; Zion, *Autobiography*, 296; "Dropping By the Stork: The Mob in the Back as the Stars Lined Up," *NYT*, July 2, 1996; *Jane Franke; William Denis Fugazy; *David Morgan; *Gary P. Marcus.
12. *David Morgan.
13. *Robert Hochstein; *Taki Theodoracopulos; *Peter Diamandis; *David Morgan; *Elaine Reiner; *Sally Obre; *Geraldine Stutz.
14. *Jane Franke.
15. Patricia Felmar, secretary to Louis Nizer, Phillips, Nizer, Benjamin, Krim & Ballon, letter to author, June 27, 1994.
16. *Jane Franke.
17. *Geraldine Stutz; *Joni Evans; *Robert C. Notson; *Harriet Burket Taussig; Meeker, *Newspaperman*, 227; *Jane Franke.

Chapter 5—"WHAT MAKES SAMMY RUN?"
1. *Robert C. Notson.
2. "America's Most Profitable Publisher: Seat-of-the-Pants Management That Works," *Business Week*, January 26, 1976; *Mel Elfin; "Samuel I. Newhouse Dies at 84," *NYT*, August 30, 1979; James Barron, "Norman Newhouse Is Dead at 82; Executive With Newspaper Chain," *NYT*, November 7, 1988; Richard H. Meeker, *Newspaperman: S. I. Newhouse and the Business of News* (Ticknor & Fields, 1983); *Leo Meindl; "Irving Newhouse: Printing Specialist, 70," *NYT*, February 20, 1994; *Saul Kohler; *James Roper; Iver Peterson, "Mort Pye, 79, Longtime Newark Editor, Dies," *NYT*, December 2, 1997.

3. "Newhouse Is Now Owner of New Orleans Papers," *E&P*, June 9, 1962; FOIA.

4. *James Warren; *Robert Miraldi.

5. Thomas Maier, *Newhouse: All the Glitter, Power, and Glory of America's Richest Media Empire and the Secretive Man Behind It* (St. Martin's Press, 1994), 154–55; "America's Most Profitable Publisher"; *Estate of Samuel I. Newhouse, Deceased, Samuel I. Newhouse, Jr. and Donald E. Newhouse, Executors, Petitioner, v. Commissioner of Internal Revenue, Respondent,* docket no. 23588-83, filed February 28, 1990; *Ray Josephs; *Calvin Trillin; Carl Spielvogel, "Advertising: A Builder in the Fourth Estate," *NYT*, March 29, 1959; "The Newspaper Collector," *Time*, July 27, 1962.

6. "America's Most Profitable Publisher"; *Newhouse v. Commissioner of Internal Revenue*; *Robert C. Notson; *Donald Sterling.

7. *Robert C. Notson; Carol Loomis, interview with Ray Josephs for *Fortune;* *Robert Lewis; *James E. Sauter; *Jane Franke; *Ray Josephs; Loomis/Josephs interview; Jennifer Dunning, "New Careers for Dancers, as the Body Begins to Know Its Years," *NYT*, December 28, 1996.

8. *Leo Meindl; Barron, "Norman Newhouse Is Dead"; *John Maher; *Jackie Gebhard; *Paul Keil; *Ruth Knowles; FOIA, U.S. Dept. of Justice, FBI, memorandum, April 20, 1953; *Mel Elfin; "America's Most Profitable Publisher"; Maier, *Newhouse;* *Murry Frymer.

9. *Jane Franke; *Ben Magdovitz.

10. *Sue Spoto; *Ben Magdovitz; *Morton Mintz.

11. *Erwin Knoll; letter to author from Nathan H. Brandt Jr., May 30, 1995; Philip Hochstein, *If It Please Their Honors* (News Book, 1988); "An Abrasive Position," *Newsweek*, April 27, 1967; *Elaine Reiner; *Bonnie Angelo; *Donald Bacon; *Florence Selden.

12. Daniel J. Leab, *A Union of Individuals: The Formation of the American Newspaper Guild, 1933–1936* (Columbia University Press, 1970); 154; Meeker, *Newspaperman*, 96–98; *James A. Michener; Michael O. Allen, "The Big Fix in Jersey: A Brighter Star-Ledger," *CJR*, May/June 1995; Meeker, *Newspaperman*, 89–93.

13. *Robert Hochstein; Hochstein, *If It Please;* *Ben Magdovitz; *Bill Howard; "An Abrasive Position"; *Paul Keil; *Bonnie Angelo; *Erwin Knoll; *Milton Jaques; *Robert Hochstein; *Ben Magdovitz; "Abrasive Position"; Hochstein, *If It Please.*

14. *Robert Hochstein; *Ben Magdovitz; Anne Chamberlin, "America's Unknown Press Lord," *Esquire*, August 1959.

15. *William Denis Fugazy; Zion, *Autobiography*, 278–81; *Sally Obre.

Chapter 6—BUILDING THE EMPIRE

1. *Robert Hochstein; *Calvin Trillin; *Robert C. Notson.

2. *Robert Hochstein; Richard H. Meeker, *Newspaperman: S. I. Newhouse and the Business of News* (Ticknor & Fields, 1983), 217.

3. *Robert Hochstein.

4. *Robert Hochstein.

5. *J. Kenneth Beaver; *Saul Kohler; Meeker, *Newspaperman*, 89–90, 140–42.

6. *J. Kenneth Beaver; *Milton Jaques; Anne Chamberlin, "America's Unknown Press Lord," *Esquire*, August 1959;

7. Meeker, *Newspaperman*, 208–12; *Ben Magdovitz; "Retired publisher Cook dies," *Springfield Union-News*, August 25, 1987; "Sidney R. Cook, a memory now," *Springfield Union-News*, August 25, 1987.

8. FOIA, U.S. Dept. of Justice, FBI, memoranda, April 20, 1953, February 11, 1958; *Ray Josephs; Carol Loomis, interview with Ray Josephs for *Fortune*.

9. FOIA, memoranda, November 1958, February 2, 1949, and April 10, 1951; Curt
Gentry, *J. Edgar Hoover: The Man and the Secrets* (Norton, 1991), 46, 462–63; FOIA, mem-
oranda, April 20, 1953, April 24, 1953, February 11, 1958, March 29, 1962, May 8, 1958,
April 30, 1958, March 29, 1962, March 28, 1962, April 10, 1962, April 16, 1964, April
24, 1964, April 21, 1953, and November 20, 1956; Herbert Mitgang, *Dangerous Dossiers:
Exposing the Secret War Against America's Greatest Authors* (Donald I. Fine, 1988), 152;
George Seldes, *Witness to a Century* Ballantine, 1987, 331, 361, 370–72; FOIA, memorandum, February 11, 1958.

Chapter 7—NEWSPAPERMAN?
  1. *Robert Miraldi; *Calvin Trillin.
  2. *Erwin Knoll; Walter Johnson, ed., *Selected Letters of William Allen White*
(Greenwood, 1968), 253; Richard Kluger, *The Paper: The Life and Death of the New York
Herald Tribune* (Knopf, 1986), 208–15.
  3. *Erwin Knoll.
  4. *Saul Kohler; *Mona Mills.
  5. *Calvin Trillin; *Paul Keil; *Leo Meindl; *Ray Josephs; "Samuel I. Newhouse Dies
at 84," *NYT,* August 30, 1979; *Robert C. Notson; "The Newspaper Collector," *Time,* July
27, 1962; "America's Most Profitable Publisher: Seat-of-the-Pants Management That
Works," *Business Week,* January 26, 1976; *Jack Flach; *Milton Jaques; *Estate of Samuel
I. Newhouse, Deceased, Samuel I. Newhouse, Jr. and Donald E. Newhouse, Executors,
Petitioner, v. Commissioner of Internal Revenue, Respondent,* docket no. 23588-83, filed
February 28, 1990; Maggie Mahar, "All in the Family: How the Newhouses Run Their Vast
Media Empire," *Barron's,* November 27, 1989; *Ben Magdovitz.
  6. "America's Most Profitable Publisher"; Mahar, "All in the Family"; Carl Spielvogel,
"Advertising: A Builder in the Fourth Estate," *NYT,* March 29, 1959; *Martin Duggan;
*Ben Magdovitz.
  7. *Paul Keil; Donald Bacon.
  8. Lowenstein Papers, #4340, ser. 1, fol. 14, Southern Historical Collection, University
of North Carolina Library, Chapel Hill; Philip Hochstein, *If It Please Their Honors* (News
Book, 1988); Maggie Mahar, "All in the Family: How the Newhouses Run Their Vast Media
Empire," *Barron's,* November 27, 1989; "America's Most Profitable Publisher"; *Ben
Magdovitz.
  9. *Robert C. Notson; Daniel J. Leab, *A Union of Individuals: The Formation of the
American Newspaper Guild, 1933-1936* (Columbia University Press, 1970), 43, 141,
144–46; *Robert Miraldi; *Jackie Gebhard; Richard H. Meeker, *Newspaperman: S. I.
Newhouse and the Business of News* (Ticknor & Fields, 1983), 86–87.
  10. *Robert Miraldi.
  11. *Robert Miraldi; *Robert F. Keeler.
  12. *Harry Selden; *Florence Selden; flyer from *Long Island Daily Press* chapter of the
Newspaper Guild of New York; *Newspaper Guild Bulletin,* July 11, 1934; *Bill Howard;
*May Spencer Vecsey; Leab, *Union of Individuals,* 138–39, 141; *Reporter, Newspaper Guild
of New York,* no date; letter to author from Josephine Phillips, February 1, 1995; *Jackie
Gebhard.
  13. *Karl Grossman; *John Maher; *Peter Gianotti.
  14. *Leo Meindl; *Terry Golway; *Robert Miraldi; Paula Schwed.
  15. *Jack Flach; *J. Kenneth Beaver; *Ben Magdovitz; Meeker, *Newspaperman,* 167,
192–93; "Newspaper Collector"; *Robert A. Steinke; *Erwin Knoll; Daniel W. Pfaff,
Joseph Pulitzer II and the Post-Dispatch: A Newspaperman's Life (Pennsylvania State

University Press, 1991); Peter Phipps and Dan Cook, "Plain Dealer Offered Coles $14.5 Million to Fold Press," *Akron Beacon Journal*, January 16, 1984; Dan Cook with Stan Crock, "Did Si Newhouse Conspire to Kill the Cleveland Press?" *Business Week*, July 1, 1985.

16. *Morton Mintz; *Ben Magdovitz.

17. Meeker, *Newspaperman*, 194–95; *Robert C. Notson.

18. Meeker, *Newspaperman*, 235; Alana Baranick, "Leo Ring, Plain Dealer Labor Negotiator," *Cleveland Plain Dealer*, December 18, 1994; *Gary Webb; FOIA, U.S. Dept. of Justice, FBI; Jim Neff, "How Jackie Presser Got the Plain Dealer to Play His Tune," *WJR*, December, 1989; *Bob Samsot; *Jim Neff; *William Woestendiek; Roldo Bartimole, *Point of View*, no. 22, February 10, 1990; *Tom Andrzejewski; *Murry Frymer; *H. Michael Rood; *Paula Schwed; *Herbert Kamm.

Chapter 8—THE SECRETS OF SAM'S SUCCESS

1. Daniel Machalaba, "Newhouse Chain Stays with Founder's Ways, and with His Heirs," *WSJ*, February 12, 1982; Mark Lisheron, "Big Time in the Big Easy," *AJR*, July/August 1997; *Erwin Knoll; Nat Brandt, "Confessions of a Young Reporter," *Silurian News*, May 1995.

2. *Richard Meeker; *Mel Elfin; *Jules Witcover.

3. *James Warren; *Robert Miraldi; *Erwin Knoll.

4. *Bill Howard; *Paul Keil.

5. "America's Most Profitable Publisher: Seat-of-the-Pants Management That Works," *Business Week*, January 26, 1976; *Ben Magdovitz; *Robert Hochstein; *Paul Keil.

6. *Ray Josephs; Machalaba, "Newhouse Chain Stays with Founder's Ways"; Richard H. Meeker, *Newspaperman: S. I. Newhouse and the Business of News* (Ticknor & Fields, 1983), 129, 184; *Calvin Trillin; "The Newspaper Collector," *Time*, July 27, 1962.

7. Philip Hochstein, *If It Please Their Honors* (News Book, 1988); *Jules Witcover; *Erwin Knoll; *Bonnie Angelo; "An Abrasive Position," *Newsweek*, April 27, 1967.

8. *H. Michael Rood; *Donald Bacon; *Bonnie Angelo; "An Abrasive Position"; *James Roper; *Erwin Knoll; *Jules Witcover; *Robert C. Notson; *Bill Howard; *Katherine Kahler.

9. *Donald Bacon; *Karl Grossman; *Robert Miraldi.

10. *Ray Josephs.

11. Hochstein, *If It Please Their Honors;* *Calvin Trillin.

12. *John Robinson Block.

13. Katharine Graham, *Personal History* (Knopf, 1997); Howard Bray, *The Pillars of the Post: The Making of a News Empire in Washington* (Norton, 1980), 189; *Clark Clifford (for the author's biography of Graham, Carol Felsenthal, *Power, Privilege and the Post: The Katharine Graham Story* [Putnam, 1993]).

14. Felsenthal, *Power, Privilege*, 179-180, 226; Graham, *Personal History*, 279.

15. Mark Lisheron, "Big Time in the Big Easy," *AJR*, July/August 1997; Michael Hoyt and Mary Ellen Schoonmaker, "Onward—and Upward?—with the Newhouse Boys," *CJR*, July/August 1985; *Donald Sterling; *Milton Jaques; Meeker, *Newspaperman*, 139–45, 238; *William Block; William Glaberson, "New Editor Tries to Write 'The End' to Star-Ledger of Past," *NYT*, March 20, 1995; *Ben Magdovitz.

16. "Newhouse Purchases Two Alabama Dailies," AP, December 2, 1955; "The Newspaper Collector"; "America's Most Profitable Publisher."

17. *James E. Sauter; "America's Most Profitable Publisher"; "Samuel I. Newhouse Dies at 84," *NYT*, August 30, 1979; "The Newspaper Collector"; "All in the Family";

Jonathan Friendly, "Newhouse's Private Empire," *NYT,* October 12, 1983; "IRS Says S. I. Newhouse Estate Owes More Taxes," *E&P,* October 1, 1983.

18. FOIA, U.S. Dept. of Justice, FBI, memoranda, March 17, 1951, April 12, 1962, February 12, 1968, and October 10, 1969.

19. "America's Most Profitable Publisher"; Felsenthal, *Power, Privilege,* 297; *AJR,* January/February 1996; "IRS Says S. I. Newhouse"; *Peter Diamandis.

Chapter 9—THE LAST HURRAHS
1. *Ben Magdovitz.
2. William Pearson Tolley, *At the Fountain of Youth: Memories of a College President* (Syracuse University Press, 1989); *Frank Piskor; *William Pearson Tolley.
3. Letter to author from David M. Rubin, Dean, S .I. Newhouse School of Public Communications, May 2, 1995, with historical documents enclosed; Richard H. Meeker, *Newspaperman: S. I. Newhouse and the Business of News* (Ticknor & Fields, 1983), 216.
4. *Frank Piskor; *I. M. Pei; Witold Rybczynski, review of *I. M. Pei: Mandarin of Moderism,* by Michael Cannell, *Washington Post Book World,* November 19, 1995; *Jim Carleton; letter and documents from David M. Rubin.
5. *William Pearson Tolley, *Katryn Tolley Fritz; Tolley, *At the Fountain.*
6. *Edgar Allen Poe; *Robert Gettlin.
7. *Donald Bacon; *William Denis Fugazy; Jack Valenti, *A Very Human President* (Norton, 1975), 166–68.
8. Philip Hochstein, *If It Please Their Honors* (News Book, 1988).
9. Carl Spielvogel, "Advertising: A Builder in the Fourth Estate," *NYT,* March 29, 1959; letter and documents from David M. Rubin; *Ben Magdovitz.
10. Syracuse University Archives, audio tapes of dedication of Newhouse School, WSYR Radio; *William Pearson Tolley; Michael R. Beschloss, *Taking Charge: The Johnson White House Tapes, 1963–1964* (Simon & Schuster, 1997), 504–5.
11. *Calvin Trillin; "The Newspaper Collector," *Time,* July 27, 1962; Anne Chamberlin, "America's Unknown Press Lord," *Esquire,* August 1959; "Samuel I. Newhouse Dies at 84," *NYT,* August 30, 1979.
12. Audio tapes of dedication of Newhouse School; letter and documents from David M. Rubin.
13. *Robert C. Notson; *William Pearson Tolley; letter to author from George E. Reedy, May 2, 1995.
14. *William Pearson Tolley; *Martin Duggan; *Jack Flach; *Ben Magdovitz; *Robert C. Notson; *Donald Sterling.
15. Joseph A. Califano Jr., *The Triumph and Tragedy of Lyndon Johnson* (Simon & Schuster, 1991), 307–17.
16. *Robert Lewis; *James E. Sauter; *John Morton; Maggie Mahar, "All in the Family: How the Newhouses Run Their Vast Media Empire," *Barron's,* November 27, 1989; *Ben Magdovitz; "Samuel I. Newhouse Dies"; Linda Sandler, "Reading, Writing and Borrowing: Famed Cranbrook School and Others Turn to Wall Street," *WSJ,* May 6, 1998.
17. *Ben Magdovitz; *Gilbert C. Early.
18. *Donald Sterling; *Ben Magdovitz; *Jane Franke; *Saul Kohler; *Florence Shientag; "Samuel I. Newhouse Dies"; "Colleagues Eulogize S. I. Newhouse," *E&P,* September 8, 1979.
19. *Frederick W. Hughes; Pat Hackett, ed., *The Andy Warhol Diaries* (Warner, 1989), 244.

20. *Ray Josephs.
21. Jeffrey Hogrefe, *O'Keeffe: The Life of an American Legend* (Bantam, 1994), 212, 265–67; *Joni Evans.

Chapter 10—SI FINDS A HOME
1. *Ben Magdovitz; *Peter Diamandis; *Ray Josephs; *Elaine Reiner; Dodie Kazanjian and Calvin Tomkins, *Alex: The Life of Alexander Liberman* (Knopf, 1993), 217.
2. *Ray Josephs; "America's Most Profitable Publisher: Seat-of-the-Pants Management that Works," *Business Week*, January 26, 1976; Carl Spielvogel, "Advertising: A Builder in the Fourth Estate," *NYT*, March 29, 1959; *Jo Pulvermacher; *Kathleen Casey Olds.
3. Grace Mirabella with Judith Warner, *In and Out of Vogue* (Doubleday, 1995); *Audrey Nichols; Kazanjian and Tomkins, *Alex*, 214; John Homans, "Fall of Grace," *NY*, October 2, 1995.
4. Kazanjian and Tomkins, *Alex*, 109–10; Helen Lawrenson, "The First of the Beautiful People," *Esquire*, March 1973.
5. *Edith Raymond Locke; *Louis Oliver Gropp; Kazanjian and Tomkins, *Alex; *Gray Foy; *Francine du Plessix Gray.
6. *Kathleen Casey Olds.
7. *Edith Raymond Locke; Kazanjian and Tomkins, *Alex*, 242; Lawrenson, "The First of the Beautiful People"; Mirabella, *In and Out*, 61–62; *Nancy White.
8. *Valorie Griffith Weaver; *Edith Raymond Locke; *Elaine Reiner.
9. *Chessy Patcevitch; Richard H. Meeker, *Newspaperman: S. I. Newhouse and the Business of News* (Ticknor & Fields, 1983), 183.
10. *Jane Franke; *Peter Diamandis.
11. *Ben Magdovitz.
12. *Martin Duggan; *Peter Diamandis.
13. Kazanjian and Tomkins, *Alex; Meeker, *Newspaperman*, 178; "'Street & Smith's' Gets a 'USA Today' Makeover," *MIN*, February 10, 1997; Mary Cantwell, *Manhattan, When I Was Young* (Penguin, 1995), 109; *Edith Raymond Locke; "America's Most Profitable Publisher."
14. *Harriet Burket Taussig; *Kathleen Casey Olds.
15. *Harriet Burket Taussig; Kazanjian and Tomkins, *Alex*, 274.
16. *Kathleen Casey Olds; *Mary Jane Pool.
17. *Miki Denhof.
18. *Peter Diamandis; *Chessy Patcevitch.
19. *Barbara Slifka; Mirabella, *In and Out*, 104–105; Calvin Tomkins, "The World of Carmel Snow," *NYer*, November 7, 1994; Nancy Franklin, "Empress of Excess," *NYer*, September 16, 1996; *Nancy White; Kazanjian and Tomkins, *Alex*, 198, 236–38; Cathleen McGuigan, "The Divine Madame V.," *Newsweek*, September 4, 1989; Diana Vreeland, *D.V.* (Da Capo Press, 1997).
20. *Nancy White; Polly Mellen biography from Ted Kruckel, Inc., New York.
21. *David O'Brasky; *Pat Miller; *Sally Obre; *Anthea Disney.
22. *Sally Obre; *Geraldine Stutz; Cantwell, *Manhattan*, 83; *Harriet Burket Taussig; *Valorie Griffith Weaver.
23. *Mary Jane Pool.
24. *Sally Obre; audio tapes from "A Celebration of Leo Lerman," memorial service, November 7, 1994.
25. *Peter Diamandis; *Valorie Griffith Weaver; *Richard Shortway.

26. *Mary Jane Pool; *Louis Oliver Gropp; *Miki Denhof.

27. Mirabella, *In and Out*, 131; *Louis Oliver Gropp.

28. *Valorie Griffith Weaver; *Kimberly Bonnell.

29. *Ray Josephs; *Sally Obre; Peter Slatin, "Si's Condé Nast H.Q. Sale Could Fetch $70M," *NYP*, January 27, 1998.

Chapter 11—SI FINDS AN IMAGE

1. *André Emmerich; *Calvin Trillin; *Sally Obre; Richard H. Meeker, *Newspaperman: S. I. Newhouse and the Business of News* (Ticknor & Fields, 1983), 184; Dodie Kazanjian and Calvin Tomkins, *Alex: The Life of Alexander Liberman* (Knopf, 1993), 279.

2. *Jane Franke; *Geraldine Stutz; *Miki Denhof; Kazanjian and Tomkins, *Alex*, 279.

3. *André Emmerich; *Peter Diamandis; *Sally Obre; Grace Mirabella with Judith Warner, *In and Out of Vogue* (Doubleday, 1995), 220; *Francine du Plessix Gray; *Mary Jane Pool; Kazanjian and Tomkins, *Alex*, 280; *Richard Penney; *Bud Holland; *Leo Castelli.

4. *Robert Lang; Holly Brubach, "A Movable Salon," *NY*, January 1, 1995; *Amy Gross; Joan Juliet Buck, "Leo's Lair," *Vanity Fair*, November 1994; Gray Foy; audio tapes from "A Celebration of Leo Lerman," memorial service, November 7, 1994; Trip Gabriel, "Leo Lerman Remembered for Buoyant Style, Wit and Elegance," *NYT*, November 7, 1994.

5. "Art Everywhere You Look," *House & Garden*, 1969; *Jo Pulvermacher; *Richard Shortway.

6. *Geraldine Stutz; Sidney Zion, *The Autobiography of Roy Cohn* (Lyle Stuart, 1988); *Sally Obre; Neal Gabler, *Winchell: Gossip, Power and the Culture of Celebrity* (Knopf, 1994); *Peter Diamandis.

7. *Thomas Maier; *Peter Diamandis; *Frederick W. Hughes; *David Morgan; *Tom Corbally; *Gary P. Marcus; *Nicholas von Hoffman; *Liz Smith; *Taki Theodoracopulos; *Geraldine Stutz; *Sally Obre.

8. *Nancy White; *Edith Raymond Locke; *Sally Obre; *Geraldine Stutz; "S. I. Newhouse Jr. to Wed an Editor," *NYT*, October 29, 1962.

9. *Jane Franke; *Dottie Dicintio; *Francine du Plessix Gray.

10. *NYT*, April 6, 1966; Thomas Maier, *Newhouse: All the Glitter, Power, and Glory of America's Richest Media Empire and the Secretive Man Behind It* (St. Martin's Press, 1994), 40–41; Richard H. Meeker, *Newspaperman: S. I. Newhouse and the Business of News* (Ticknor & Fields, 1983), 227; Enid Nemy, "When the Bachelor Goes Home," *NYT*, April 6, 1966; *Valorie Griffith Weaver; *Chessy Patcevitch.

Chapter 12—THE MAN ALMOST IN CHARGE

1. Dodie Kazanjian and Calvin Tomkins, *Alex: The Life of Alexander Liberman* (Knopf, 1993), 189, 277–78, 281 n; *Florence Shientag; *Peter Diamandis; *Harriet Burket Taussig; *Richard Penney.

2. *Richard Penney; *Amy Gross; *Louis Oliver Gropp; *Geraldine Stutz; *Leo Castelli; *Seibert Adams; *Peter Diamandis; *Edith Raymond Locke; *Wendy Wolf.

3. Grace Mirabella with Judith Warner, *In and Out of Vogue* (Doubleday, 1995), 130–31; Kazanjian and Tomkins, *Alex*, 281, 284.

4. *Valorie Griffith Weaver; Mary Cantwell, *Manhattan, When I Was Young* (Penguin, 1995), 86–87.

5. *Valorie Griffith Weaver; Kazanjian and Tomkins, *Alex*, 285.

6. Mirabella, *In and Out*; *Valorie Griffith Weaver.

7. Kazanjian and Tomkins, *Alex*, 281–82; Mirabella, *In and Out*.

Chapter 13—VICTORIA AND NERO
  1. "Samuel I. Newhouse Jr. Weds Mrs. Victoria de Ramel Here," *NYT*, April 15, 1973; *Gray Foy; *Francine du Plessix Gray; *Jane Franke; *Taki Theodoracopulos; *Robert Lang; *Franz Schulze; *Anne Foxley; *Mary Jane Pool; *Peter Diamandis; *Sally Obre; *Margaret Thalken.
  2. *Thomas Maier; *Francine du Plessix Gray; *Gray Foy; "Liz Smith," *NYP*, November 10, 1996.
  3. Christopher Simon, "When a Star's Dog Is Ailing, This Veterinarian Jets In," *WSJ*, October 9, 1997; *Francine du Plessix Gray; *Joni Evans; Joanne Lipman, "How S. I. Newhouse Jr. Is Leading Makeover of Condé Nast Empire," *WSJ*, January 4, 1996; *Kathy Neisloss Leventhal; *Amy Gross; *Anthea Disney; Carol J. Loomis, "The Biggest Private Fortune," *Fortune*, August, 17, 1987; *Jane Franke; Richard Johnson, "Page Six," *NYP*, October 22, 1996; Simon, "When a Star's Dog"; Neal Travis, "Barneys' Bubblybash," in "Neal Travis' New York," *NYP*, February 23, 1998.
  4. *Paul Gottlieb; *Richard Penney; Edward Vernoff and Rima Shore, *International Dictionary of 20th Century Biography* (New American Library, 1987); Victoria Newhouse, *Wallace K. Harrison, Architect* (Rizzoli, 1989); *Franz Schulze; Herbert Muschamp, "Designing Museums: Often Not a Lively Art," *NYT*, June 28, 1998.
  5. *Francine du Plessix Gray; *Gray Foy; *William Denis Fugazy; *Joni Evans; *Miki Denhof; *Franz Schulze; *Leo Castelli; *André Emmerich; *Louis Oliver Gropp; *Mary Jane Pool.
  6. *Richard Penney.
  7. Lipman, "How S. I. Newhouse Jr. Is Leading"; *Nicholas von Hoffman; Travis, "Barneys' Bubblybash"; *Francine du Plessix Gray; *Jane Franke; *Edith Raymond Locke; *Alexander MacGregor III; *Taki Theodoracopulos.

Chapter 14—DOING THE DIRTY WORK
  1. Maggie Mahar, "All in the Family: How the Newhouses Run Their Vast Media Empire," *Barron's*, November 27, 1989. *Peter Diamandis; *Karl Grossman; Richard H. Meeker, *Newspaperman: S. I. Newhouse and the Business of News* (Ticknor & Fields, 1983), 244–45; *Erwin Knoll; *Robert F. Keeler; *William Woestendiek; *Leo Meindl; *John Maher; *Jackie Gebhard; *Mike Greenstein; Anne Chamberlin, "America's Unknown Press Lord," *Esquire*, August 1959; Karl Grossman, "How New York Newsday Died—and Why It Didn't Have To," *Extra*, January/February 1996; *Barney Confessore; Damon Stetson, "The Long Island Press Shuts Down," *NYT*, March 26, 1977.
  2. *Ben Magdovitz; *Robert F. Keeler; *Mel Elfin; *Donald Bacon; *H. Michael Rood; *Martin Duggan; *William Woestendiek; *Milton Jaques; *Estate of Samuel I. Newhouse, Deceased, Samuel I. Newhouse, Jr. and Donald E. Newhouse, Executors, Petitioner, v. Commissioner of Internal Revenue, Respondent*, docket no. 23588-83, filed February 28, 1990; *Robert C. Notson.
  3. Carol J. Loomis, "The Biggest Private Fortune," *Fortune*, August 17, 1987; "All in the Family."
  4. *John Ettorre; FOIA; *Herbert Kamm; Michael Hoyt and Mary Ellen Schoonmaker, "Onward—and Upward?—with the Newhouse Boys," *CJR*, July/August 1985; Peter Phipps and Dan Cook, "Plain Dealer Offered Coles $14.5 Million to Fold Press," *Akron Beacon Journal*, January 16, 1984; *Howard Metzenbaum; "Report of the Office of Professional Responsibility," Department of Justice, March 30, 1987; Douglas Frantz, "Former Plain Dealer Publisher Back in Court over Press Mess," *Chicago Tribune*, July 10, 1985; "The

Biggest Private Fortune"; Peter Phipps and Dan Cook, "Owners Saw Small Profit from Press," *Akron Beacon Journal*, July 1984; Thomas Petzinger Jr., "Newhouse Conspired To Form Monopoly, Judge Suggests," *WSJ*, March 21, 1985; John Funk, "Attorney for Ex-Owner of Press Testifies in Probe of Paper's Sale," *Akron Beacon Journal*, March 5, 1985; *John Morton; Gigi Mahon, *The Last Days of The New Yorker* (McGraw Hill, 1988); staff and wire reports, "Press Closing to Be Probed by U.S.," January 20, 1984; Andrew Radolf, "Investigation in Cleveland," *E&P*, February 4, 1984; John Funk, "Court Throws Out Printers' Suit over Failure of Cleveland Press," *Akron Beacon Journal*, March 21, 1985; Bill Kapner; "Press Grand Jury Probe Picks Up Steam," *Crain's Cleveland Business*, April 22, 1985; Roldo Bartimole, "Say It Isn't So, Joe," *Point of View*, March 2, 1985; *Richard Meeker; Dan Cook and Peter Phipps, "Newspaper Probe Ends until January," *Akron Beacon Journal*, December 13, 1984; "Grand Jury Recesses Temporarily in Probe of Newspaper's Closing," *Akron Beacon Journal*, March 7, 1985; *C. Russell Twist; *Marilyn Bobula; "All in the Family"; Mahon, *Last Days*, 296; "Justice Department Drops PD-Press Antitrust Probe," June 17, 1987; John Funk, "Ex-U.S. Attorney Sues over Dismissal," *Akron Beacon Journal*, November 25, 1986; *James Neff; Fred McGunagle, "U.S. 'Stop the Press' Case Moribund," *Elyria Chronicle-Telegram;* Ken Myers, "Ex-Prosecutor's Suit Illuminates Probe of PD, Press," *Akron Beacon Journal*, March 20, 1987; Mike Casey, "PD-Press Investigators Clashed," *Crain's Cleveland Business*, April 6, 1987; John Funk, "Ex–U.S. Attorney Sues over Dismissal," *Akron Beacon Journal*, November 25, 1986; "Metzenbaum to Probe Role of Ginsburg in Press-close," Knight-Ridder, November 2, 1987; Margot Hornblower, "Si Newhouse, the Talk of the *New Yorker*," *WP*, May 7, 1985; FOIA, report of Office of Professional Responsibility; *Richard G. Zimmerman; Sidney Zion, *The Autobiography of Roy Cohn* (Lyle Stuart, 1988), 180; Nicholas von Hoffman, *Citizen Cohn: The Life and Times of Roy Cohn* (Bantam, 1988), 406–7; Roy Cohn, "You Can Beat the IRS," *Parade*, April 3, 1983; Kitty Kelly, *Nancy Reagan: The Unauthorized Biography* (Simon & Schuster, 1991); Zion, *Autobiography*, 272–73; "Senate Members Vow Ginsburg Probe," AP, November 3, 1987; "Metzenbaum to Probe Role of Ginsburg in Press-close," Knight-Ridder, November 2, 1987; Suzanne Garment, *Scandal: The Culture of Mistrust in American Politics* (Times Books, 1991), 263; Dan Cook, with Stan Crock, "Did Si Newhouse Conspire to Kill the Cleveland Press?" *Business Week*, July 1, 1985; *Mary Rose Oakar; "A Chronology: The Demise of the Cleveland Press," *E&P*, March 30, 1985; *Ben Magdovitz.

5. James Neff, "How Jackie Presser Got *The Plain Dealer* to Play His Tune," *WJR*, December 1989 (excerpted from Neff's *Mobbed Up* [Atlantic Monthly Press, 1989]); *James Neff; Hoyt and Schoonmaker, "Onward—and Upward?"; *Bob Samsot; *Gary Webb; "Vail: 'No Apology, No Retraction,'" *WJR*, December 1989; *Ben Magdovitz.

6. *Ben Magdovitz; *John Morton; Jefferson Grigsby, "Newhouse, after Newhouse," *Forbes*, October 29, 1979; *Robert A. Steinke; Daniel W. Pfaff, *Joseph Pulitzer II and the Post-Dispatch: A Newspaperman's Life* (Pennsylvania State University Press, 1991); *Martin Duggan; Phipps and Cook, "Plain Dealer Offered Coles "; *Jack Flach; *Mona Mills; *Sue Spoto.

Chapter 15—SI GOES SHOPPING

1. *Mary Jane Pool; *Peter Diamandis; *Robert Lang; *Linda Rath; *Valorie Griffith Weaver; *Steven Cohn; *Kimberly Bonnell.

2. Rachel Urquhart, "Voyage to the Bottom of the Newsstand," *Spy*, November 1990; John Blades, *Chicago Tribune*, April 12, 1990; *David O'Brasky; Dierdre Carmody, *NYT*, April 13, 1995; Gigi Mahon, *The Last Days of The New Yorker* (McGraw Hill, 1988), 297–98.

3. *Edith Raymond Locke; Grace Mirabella with Judith Warner, *In and Out of Vogue* (Doubleday, 1995), 218; *Peter Diamandis; Mary Cantwell, *Manhattan, When I Was Young*

(Penguin, 1995), p.138; Gigi Mahon, "S. I. Newhouse and Condé Nast: Taking Off the White Gloves," *NYT Magazine*, September 10, 1989; Bennett Cerf, *At Random: The Reminiscences of Bennett Cerf* (Random House, 1977), 223; Cantwell, *Manhattan*, 63; *Steven Cohn; *Amy Gross; Linda Hall, "The Writer Who Came In from the Cold," *NY*, September 2, 1996.

4. *Susan Kamil; Roger Cohen, "Changing Spirit at Random House," *NYT*, March 19, 1990; Cerf, *At Random*, 189–90; Jason Epstein, "Ink," in "The Talk of the Town," *New Yorker*, April 6, 1998; *Robert Bernstein; *George Rosato; *Alexander MacGregor, III; Daniel Machalaba, "Newhouse Chain Stays with Founder's Ways, and with His Heirs," *WSJ*, February 12, 1982; *Seibert Adams; *James A. Michener; *Owen Laster; Richard Pollak, "The $1 Billion Misunderstanding: The IRS vs. the Newhouse Empire," *VV*, November 5, 1985; "Newhouse Will Buy Random House," AP, February 7, 1980.

5. *At Random*, 99–100, *Jane Franke; *David Morgan; *Miki Denhof; *Joni Evans; *Francine de Plessix Gray.

6. *Alexander MacGregor III; *Robert Bernstein; *Nan Graham; *Joni Evans; *Wendy Wolf.

7. *Neil Walsh; Geraldine Fabrikant, "Si Newhouse Tests His Magazine Magic," *NYT*, September 25, 1988; Carol J. Loomis, "The Biggest Private Fortune," *Fortune*, August, 17, 1987; Linda Fibich, "A New Era at Newhouse," *AJR*, November, 1994; *Robert Young; *David O'Brasky; *Gael Towey; *Richard Penney; *Diane Silberstein; *Richard Kinsler; *Carolyn Sollis; *Frederick W. Hughes; *Louis Oliver Gropp; *Wendy Wolf; John S. Bowman, ed., *The Cambridge Dictionary of American Biography* (Cambridge University Press, 1995); Edward Vernoff and Rima Shore, *International Dictionary of 20th Century Biography* (New American Library, 1987); Mahon, "S. I. Newhouse and Condé Nast"; Iris Cohen Selinger, "Si Speaks," *Inside Media*, December 4–17, 1991; *Donovan Webster.

8. *Robert Lang; *David Morgan; *Louis Oliver Gropp; *Francine du Plessix Gray; *Carolyn Sollis; Mahon, "S. I. Newhouse and Condé Nast"; *Ben Magdovitz; *Kathy Neisloss Leventhal.

9. Selinger, "Si Speaks"; *Frederick W. Hughes; *Gael Towey; *Diane Silberstein; *Louis Oliver Gropp; *Richard Kinsler; *Edith Raymond Locke; *Alexander MacGregor III; *Mary Jane Pool.

10. *Pat Miller; *Alexander MacGregor III; *Robert Bernstein; *Donovan Webster; *Jane Franke; *Geraldine Stutz; Frank DiGiacomo, "Careerist Glitzmongers Hijack Bluebloods' Ball," in "The Transom," *NYO*, December 11, 1995; *Marilyn Bobula; *Bud Holland.

Chapter 16—ON THE PROWL FOR CLASS: *VANITY FAIR*
1. *Jeanne Fleischmann; Ved Mehta, *Remembering Mr. Shawn's* New Yorker: *The Invisible Art of Editing* (Overlook, 1998); Bruce Lambert, "Peter Fleischmann, 71, Who Led the *New Yorker* into the 1980's," *NYT*, April 18, 1993; *George Green; *J. Kennard Bosee; *Robert Young; *Burton Bernstein; *Edward A. Kosner; Helen Lawrenson, "The First of the Beautiful People," *Esquire*, March, 1973; Sylvia Jukes Morris, *Rage for Fame: The Ascent of Clare Boothe Luce* (Random House, 1997); Henry Fairlie, "The Vanity of 'Vanity Fair,'" *New Republic*, March 21, 1983; Veronique Vienne, "Make It Right Then Toss It Away: An Inside View of Corporate Culture at Condé Nast," *CJR*, July/August 1991; *Francine du Plessix Gray; Wilfred Sheed, *Clare Boothe Luce* (Berkley, 1984), 60; Thomas Maier, *Newhouse: All the Glitter, Power, and Glory of America's Richest Media Empire and the Secretive Man Behind It* (St. Martin's Press, 1994), 232–33; *Perry Vandermeer; Dodie Kazanjian and Calvin Tomkins, *Alex: The Life of Alexander Liberman* (Knopf, 1993), 306; Curtis Prendergast with Geoffrey Colvin, *The World of Time Inc.: The Intimate History of a Changing Enterprise, 1960–1980* (Atheneum, 1986), 439; *G. Douglas Johnston.

2. *G. Douglas Johnston; Fairlie, "The Vanity of 'Vanity Fair'"; Kazanjian and Tomkins, *Alex,* 305–6; *Edward A. Kosner.

3. *David O'Brasky; *G. Douglas Johnston; Gigi Mahon, *The Last Days of The New Yorker* (McGraw Hill, 1988); "Dunne's Simpson Novel," *NYT,* November 7, 1997.

4. *J. Kennard Bosee; Geraldine Fabrikant, "Si Newhouse Tests His Magazine Magic," *NYT,* September 25, 1988.

5. *G. Douglas Johnston; Kazanjian and Tomkins, *Alex,* 306; *David O'Brasky; Grace Mirabella with Judith Warner, *In and Out of Vogue* (Doubleday, 1995); audio tapes from "A Celebration of Leo Lerman," memorial service, November 7, 1994.

6. *G. Douglas Johnston; Fabrikant, "Si Newhouse Tests"; *David O'Brasky.

7. *G. Douglas Johnston; *David O'Brasky.

8. "Flattery Will Get You Ten Pages...Maybe: The Tina Brown–Mike Ovitz Correspondence," *Spy,* August 1990; Fabrikant, "Si Newhouse Tests"; Iris Cohen Selinger, "Si Speaks," *Inside Media,* December 4–17, 1991; Gigi Mahon, "S. I. Newhouse and Condé Nast: Taking Off the White Gloves," *NYT Magazine,* September 10, 1989; Elizabeth Kolbert, Soul of the Buzz Machine, *NYT Magazine,* December 5, 1993; *Lisa Lockwood; *George Green; *Peter Diamandis; Patrick M. Reilly, "Travel Magazine of Condé Nast Cuts Boosterism," *WSJ,* October 1, 1990; Joanne Lipman, "How S. I. Newhouse Jr. Is Leading Makeover of Condé Nast Empire," *WSJ,* January 4, 1996.

Chapter 17—STILL ON THE PROWL FOR CLASS: THE *NEW YORKER*

1. *Samuel Heyman; Margot Hornblower, "Si Newhouse, the Talk of the *New Yorker,*" *WP,* May 7, 1985; *James Kobak; *Peter Slusser; Gigi Mahon, *The Last Days of The New Yorker* (McGraw Hill, 1988), 116–17, 127, 134–35; letter from Peter Fleischmann to the staff of the *New Yorker,* April, 19, 1985; *Merrell Clark; letter to author from Merrell Clark, October 14, 1994; *Robert Young; *John MacArthur; *Leo Hofeller; *Hoyt Spelman; *J. Kennard Bosee; *David O'Brasky; Phil H. Dougherty, "Advertising: Catechizing the *New Yorker,*" *NYT,* March 29, 1972; letter from Charles Schwartz Jr. to stockholders, March 14, 1972; *Nat Hentoff; *Suzannah Lessard; Richard Severo, "Joseph Mitchell, Chronicler of the Unsung and the Unconvetional, Dies at 87," *NYT,* May 25, 1996; "Postscript, JM, Three Generations of *New Yorker* Writers Remember the City's Incomparable Chronicler," *NYer,* June 10, 1996; Jim Windolf, "Off the Record," *NYO,* September 14, 1992.

2. *J. Kennard Bosee; *André Emmerich; *Merrell Clark; Mahon, *Last Days,* 63, 248, *George Green; *JUF News,* June 1993; *WP,* June 20, 1993; *Peter Diamandis; *Jeanne Fleischmann; Mahon, *Last Days,* 248; Hornblower, "Si Newhouse"; Carol Felsenthal, *Power, Privilege and the Post: The Katharine Graham Story* (Putnam, 1993), 321, 397; *Jonathan Schell; letter to Merrell Clark from William Shawn, February 11, 1985; Michael Gross, "Tina's Turn: The *New Yorker*'s Head Transplant," *NY,* July 20, 1992; Michael Hoyt and Mary Ellen Schoonmaker, "Onward—and Upward?—with the Newhouse Boys," *CJR,* July/August 1985; *John MacArthur; *Calvin Trillin.

3. Gross, "Tina's Turn"; Mahon, *Last Days;* letter to author from Merrell Clark, October 14, 1994; *Merrell Clark; *J. Kennard Bosee.

4. Mahon, *Last Days;* *Richard Kinsler; Joanne Lipman, "How S. I. Newhouse Jr. Is Leading Makeover of Condé Nast Empire," *WSJ,* January 4, 1996; Joseph Nocera and Peter Elkind, "The Buzz Factory," *Fortune,* July 20, 1998; *Hoyt Spelman; *Burton Bernstein; *Jeanne Fleischmann; *Robert Young.

5. *Hoyt Spelman; Mahon, *Last Days,* 287–89; *Ken Bosee; Peter Stevenson, "S. I. Newhouse's Fabulous Florio Boys Leave Jones Beach for Corner Offices," *NYO,* July 20, 1992; *Robert Young; letter from Peter Fleischmann to the staff of the *New Yorker,* April

19, 1985; "Agreement and Plan of Merger," with letter to stockholders, April 9, 1985; *Jeanne Fleischmann.

6. *Hoyt Spelman; *Robert Young; *John MacArthur; Edwin Diamond, "Caught in the Buzz Machine," *Nation,* January 2, 1995; *J. Kennard Bosee; Elizabeth Kolbert, "Soul of the Buzz Machine," *NYT Magazine,* December 5, 1993; *George Green; Jim Windolf, "Brown's Two Years at the *New Yorker:* 'I Finally Think We've Got It Right,'" *NYO,* October 3, 1994; *Edward A. Kosner; Gross, "Tina's Turn"; Mahon, *Last Days,* 36; *Leo Hofeller; Robin Pogrebin, "What Do the Changes at the *New Yorker* Mean for Tina Brown?" *NYT,* June 1, 1998.

7. News release, Magazine Publishers of America, December 20, 1994; *George Green; Carol J. Loomis, "The Biggest Private Fortune," *Fortune,* August 17, 1987.

8. Hoyt and Schoonmaker, "Onward—and Upward?"; Hornblower, "Si Newhouse"; letter to author from Merrell Clark, October 14, 1994; *J. Kennard Bosee; Mahon, *Last Days,* 278; *Patti Hagan; *Richard Sacks.

9. *Leo Hofeller; Gross, "Tina's Turn"; Mahon; *Last Days,* 105, 333–343; *Richard Sacks; *Patti Hagan; *William Whitworth; *Lee Lorenz; Michael Coffee, "*PW* Interview with Bill McKibben," *PW,* November 13, 1995; *Perry Vandermeer; "McGrath of 'New Yorker' to Head 'NYTBR,'" *PW,* November 21, 1994; Jim Windolf, *NYO,* September 7, 1992; *Donovan Webster; *Merrell Clark; Philip H. Dougherty, "Advertising: *New Yorker* Meets," *NYT,* March 27, 1974; *Alexander MacGregor III; *George Rosato; *Wendy Wolf; *Perry Vandermeer; *Amy Gross; *Jonathan Schell; Hornblower, "Si Newhouse"; *Burton Bernstein; *Calvin Trillin; *Suzannah Lessard; *Nat Hentoff; *Joni Evans; *Robert Bernstein.

10. *Perry Vandermeer; *Lee Lorenz.

Chapter 18—ALL THE PUBLISHER'S WOMEN
1. *Carolyn Sollis; *Louis Oliver Gropp; *Mary Jane Pool.
2. *Mary Jane Pool; *Louis Oliver Gropp; *James Kobak; Thomas Jaffee, "The Corn Is Green," *Forbes,* December 4, 1995; "Ink," *Los Angeles Times,* January 30, 1997.
3. *Anne Foxley; Grace Mirabella with Judith Warner, *In and Out of Vogue* (Doubleday, 1995), 215; Dodie Kazanjian and Calvin Tomkins, *Alex: The Life of Alexander Liberman* (Knopf, 1993), 310.
4. Amanda Vaill, "The Only Dame in Town," *NY,* February 21, 1994; *Louis Oliver Gropp.
5. Iris Cohen Selinger, "Si Speaks," *Inside Media,* December 4–17, 1991; *Diane Silberstein; Gigi Mahon, "S. I. Newhouse and Condé Nast: Taking Off the White Gloves," *NYT Magazine,* September 10, 1989; Robin Pogrebin, "Anna's World," *NYT,* November 17, 1997; Kazanjian and Tomkins, *Alex,* 316; *Amy Gross.
6. Kazanjian and Tomkins, *Alex,* 313; *Amy Gross; *Louis Oliver Gropp.
7. *Louis Oliver Gropp.
8. *Louis Oliver Gropp.
9. *Anne Foxley; Geraldine Fabrikant, "Si Newhouse Tests His Magazine Magic," *NYT,* September 25, 1988; *Bonnie Angelo; *Gael Towey; *Carolyn Sollis; Vaill, "The Only Dame"; *Louis Oliver Gropp.
10. *Denise Martin; *Carolyn Sollis; Veronique Vienne, "A Culture of Abuse at Condé Nast," *Journal of Graphic Design* (American Institute of Graphic Arts) 9, no. 1 (1991); *Harriet Burket Taussig; *Donovan Webster; *Denise Martin; *Patti Hagan; *Louis Oliver Gropp; *Anne Foxley; Liz Tilberis with Aimee Lee Ball, *No Time to Die* (Little Brown, 1998).

11. Mirabella, *In and Out*, 10, 12, 200, 203–4, 218, 222, 224; Kazanjian and Tomkins, *Alex*, 311–12, 316; N. R. Kleinfield, "Heads Have a History of Rolling at Newhouse," *NYT*, November 2, 1989.

12. *Joni Evans.

13. William Norwich, "Style Diary," *NYO*, October 28, 1996; *Anne Foxley; *Patti Hagan; *Gael Towey.

14. *Miki Denhof; *Richard Kinsler; *Anne Foxley; *Carolyn Sollis.

15. *Liz Smith; Mirabella, *In and Out*, 224; Pogrebin, "Anna's World"; Paul Tharp, "Mirabella Leaves No Grace for Gross," *NYP*, April 3, 1997. *Valorie Griffith Weaver; *Anthea Disney; Pat Miller, "Flips, Failures and Honest Mistakes: Magazines That Didn't Make It," Magazine Publishers of America conference, October 10–13, 1993; *Peter Diamandis; Paul Tharp, "Bertelsmann Buys 7 Times Magazines," *NYP*, June 17, 1994; *Val Monroe; Mahon, "S. I. Newhouse and Condé Nast"; "Newhouse's Grim Trip to Disney Land," in "Intelligencer," *NY*, September 11, 1989; Selinger, "Si Speaks"; Deirdre Carmody, "A Former TV Critic Is Selected as Editor in Chief of *TV Guide*," *NYT*, June 30, 1995; Patrick M. Reilly, "News Corp. Names Its Internet Editor, Anthea Disney, CEO of HarperCollins," *WSJ*, March 4, 1996; Geraldine Fabrikant, "Murdoch Sets *TV Guide* Sale For $2 Billion," *NYT*, June 12, 1998.

17. *NYT*, August 30, 1995; *Robert Lang; *Veronique Vienne; *Meg Cox; *Pat Miller; *Valorie Griffith Weaver; Vienne, "A Culture of Abuse"; Selinger, "Si Speaks"; Joanne Lipman, "How S. I. Newhouse Jr. Is Leading Makeover of Condé Nast Empire," *WSJ*, January 4, 1996; *Kimberly Bonnell.

18. Pat Miller, "Flips, Failures and Honest Mistakes"; Mahon, "S. I. Newhouse and Condé Nast"; "Power Struggle: Keith Rupert Murdoch vs. Samuel I. Newhouse, Jr." *Manhattan Inc.*, September 1989; *Pat Miller; Anthony Haden-Guest, *True Colors: The Real Life of the Art World*, Atlantic Monthly Press, 1996; Edmund White, "Moma's Boy," *Vanity Fair*, September, 1996; *Leo Castelli.

19. Mahon, "S. I. Newhouse and Condé Nast"; Fabrikant, "Si Newhouse Tests"; *Richard Kinsler; Maggie Mahar, "All in the Family: How the Newhouses Run Their Vast Media Empire," *Barron's*, November 27, 1989; Selinger, "Si Speaks"; Rebecca Mead, "The Truman Administration," *NY*, May 23, 1994; Lisa Lockwood, "The Truman Doctrine," *Women's Wear Daily*, July 29, 1994; John Cassidy, *NYP*, May 20, 1994; Judith Levine, "The Man in the Mirror," *CJR*, March/April 1994; Patrick M. Reilly, "Condé Nast's Bad Boy Puts Up His Dukes," *WSJ*, November 18, 1994; Keith White, "How Details Magazine Turned Me into a Rebel Consumer," *Washington Monthly*, April 1994; *Marshall Loeb; Deirdre Carmody, "Condé Nast's Auteur to Step Down," *NYT*, January 26, 1994; Meg Cox, "James Truman Gets Star Status at Condé Nast," *WSJ*, January 26, 1994; Meredith S. Tcherniavsky, "Truman Era Begins at Condé Nast," *AJR*, March, 1994; *NYT*, February 21, 1994; Lipman, "How S. I. Newhouse Jr. Is Leading"; Celia Brady, "La Dolce Vita at *Details*," in "Magazine Heaven," *Spy*, holiday issue 1996.

Chapter 19—RANDOM FIRE

1. *Robert Bernstein; Sidney Zion, *The Autobiography of Roy Cohn* (Lyle Stuart, 1988), 11; *Neil Walsh; *Alexander MacGregor III; *Wendy Wolf; *André Schiffrin; Thomas Maier, *Newhouse: All the Glitter, Power, and Glory of America's Richest Media Empire and the Secretive Man Behind It* (St. Martin's Press, 1994), 194; letter to author from Jason Epstein, August 18, 1994.

2. N. R. Kleinfield, "Heads Have a History of Rolling at Newhouse," *NYT*, November 2, 1989; *Robert Bernstein; *NYT*, May 5, 1993; Roger Cohen, "Changing Spirit at Random

House," *NYT*, March 19, 1990; *André Schiffrin; Edwin McDowell, "New Publisher Named in Shift at Turbulent Random House," *NYT*, October 31, 1990; Karen Freifeld, "Lunch Hour of Rage," *Newsday*, March 5, 1990; *Alexander MacGregor III; "Hearst's Kaminsky Resigns as President of the Book Group," *WSJ*, April 27, 1994; Geraldine Fabrikant, "President of Hearst Book Group Resigns," *NYT*, April 27, 1994; Maureen O'Brien, "Kaminsky Quits Hearst for 'Personal Reasons,'" *PW*, May 2, 1994; *Joni Evans.

3. *Robert Bernstein; *Susan Kamil; *NYT*, January 26, 1994; *Joni Evans; Roger Cohen, "Lots of Words, but Are They True?" *NYT*, October 15, 1990.

4. *Alan Mirken; Alexander MacGregor III; Maggie Mahar, "All in the Family: How the Newhouses Run Their Vast Media Empire," *Barron's*, November 27, 1989; Cohen, "Changing Spirit"; Edwin McDowell, "The New Role of Random House," *NYT*, May 5, 1985.

5. *George Rosato; *Alexander MacGregor III; *Seibert Adams; Mahar, "All in the Family."

6. Cohen, "Changing Spirit"; *Joni Evans; *Robert Bernstein; *WSJ* reference in Roger Donald, "Taking Issue with the Random 40," in "My Say," *PW*, April 20, 1990; Rich Turner, "Media," *NY*, June 17, 1996; Edwin McDowell, "Random House Publisher a Human-Rights Activist," *NYT*, August 6, 1987; Calvin Reid, "Bernstein to Leave John Wiley," *PW*, May 11, 1998.

7. Roger Cohen, "Briefly at the Top, Book by Trump Is Fading," *NYT*, October 10, 1990; Geraldine Fabrikant, "Si Newhouse Tests His Magazine Magic," *NYT*, September 25, 1988; Edwin McDowell, "New Publisher Named in Shift at Turbulent Random House," *NYT*, October 31, 1990; *Joni Evans; *Robert Bernstein; Richard Johnson, "Page Six," *NYP*, April 16, 1998; "Best Selling Books," *WSJ*, November 26, 1997; "Best Sellers," *NYT*, December 7, 1997; "Best Sellers," *NYT*, December 14, 1997.

8. *Joni Evans; *George Rosato; Dierdre Carmody, "Condé Nast's Auteur to Step Down," *NYT*, January 26, 1994; *Alexander MacGregor III; Mary B. W. Tabor, "Publisher Chooses New International Chief," *NYT*, April 6, 1995; Michael M. Thomas, "Why It's Crunch Time for Big Publishers of Books," *NYO*, March 26, 1990; *Wendy Wolf.

9. *Wendy Wolf; *André Schiffrin; Edwin McDowell, "Chief of Pantheon Is Said to Have Been Asked to Quit," *NYT*, February 27, 1990; David Streitfeld, "Pantheon and the War of Words," in "Book Report," *WP Book World*, March 18, 1990; "Helen Wolff, Publisher of Translated Books, Dies at 88," *NYT*, March 30, 1994; *PW*, March 1990; Martin Walker, "Pantheon Buried by Profit," *Manchester Guardian*, April 1, 1990; Bennett Cerf, *At Random: The Reminiscences of Bennett Cerf* (Random House, 1977); Tom Englehardt, "Books You'll Never See," *Mother Jones*, January/February 1991; *PW*, April 20, 1990; Henry Kisor, "Bottom-line Reef Snags a Fine Publisher," *Chicago Sun-Times*, March 4, 1990; Doug Ireland, "The Fall of the House of Pantheon," *VV*, March 13, 1990; press release, Random House, February 27, 1990; *Robert Bernstein; Madalynne Reuter, "Protests Mount over Events at Pantheon," *PW*, March 16, 1990; letter from Alberto Vitale responding to Stuart Klawans, "The Silencing of Pantheon," *Times Literary Supplement*, March 16–22, 1990; "At Pantheon, Closed Books," *NYT*, March 8, 1990; *Diane Wachtell; Cohen, "Changing Spirit"; Edward McDowell, "250 Protest Resignation at Pantheon," *NYT*, March 6, 1990; *Alexander MacGregor III; Jack Miles, "Pantheon Is Dead, Long Live Pantheon," *Los Angeles Times Book Review*, March 18, 1990; "Newhoused," *Nation*, March 19, 1990; *Fred Jordan; press release from James Michener, March 19, 1990; "Words of Protest at Random House," *NYP*, March 6, 1990; Deirdre Donahue, "Authors Protest at Random House," *USA Today*, March 6, 1990; *Newsweek*, March 19, 1990; John Leonard, "Cultural Shock," *Newsday*, March 8, 1990; *New York Review of Books*, April 12, 1990;

NYT News Service, March 3, 1990; "Editors Who Submitted Resignations Are Sacked Ahead of Time," *Newsday,* March 5, 1990; Freifeld, "Lunch Hour of Rage"; "Random House Officials Back Pantheon Dismissal," *WSJ,* March 13, 1990; Edwin McDowell, "More Protests of Pantheon Resignation," *NYT,* March 2, 1990; John F. Baker, "A Sad Day for André Schiffrin—and for Publishing," *PW,* March 9, 1990; Stuart Klawans, "The Silencing of Pantheon," *Times Literary Supplement,* March 16–22, 1990; Roger Cohen, "Top Random House Author Assails Ouster at Pantheon," *NYT,* March 9, 1990; Edwin McDowell, "Michener Threatens to Quit Random House in Protest," *NYT,* March 20, 1990; Edwin McDowell, "Book Notes," *NYT,* March 21, 1990; Edwin McDowell, "Michener Talks," in "Book Notes," *NYT,* March 28, 1990; *James Michener; *Owen Laster; Norman Oder, "Studs Terkel: Curiosity Hasn't Killed This Cat," interview, *PW,* July 28, 1997; Meg Cox, "Four Editors Quit at Random House over Aide's Firing," *WSJ,* March 1, 1990; Erroll McDonald, "At Pantheon Books, 'A Welfare Mentality,'" *NYT,* March 20, 1990; press release, March 12, 1990, "A Statement from Editors and Publishers of Random House, Inc."; "And They Un-Died Happily Ever After," "Intelligencer," *NY,* December 19–26, 1994; Doug Ireland, "Press Clips," *VV,* May 1, 1990; David Streitfeld, "Nonfiction Prize a Victory for Pantheon's Ex-Publisher," *WP.*

10. Meg Cox, "Random House Taps Condé Nast Editor," *WSJ,* October 31, 1990; *Joni Evans; Deirdre Carmody, "Busy Pair with Time for Family," *NYT,* October 31, 1990; Suzanne Andrews, "The Trouble with Harry," *NY,* July 7, 1997; David Streitfeld, "Life at Random," *NY,* August 5, 1991; *André Schiffrin; McDowell, "New Publisher Named"; *Bonnie Angelo; Patrick M. Reilly, "Random House Is Stacking Up Hit after Hit," *WSJ,* September 27, 1995; *Robert Bernstein; James Reginato, "Literary Lion: Roger Straus Is America's Most Outspoken Publisher," *W,* March, 1996; Richard Johnson, "Page Six," *NYP,* September 3, 1994; Richard Johnson, "Marcia; the Next Big-Bucks Bomb?" in "Page Six," *NYP,* April 2, 1997; Alexander MacGregor III; G. Bruce Knecht, "Evans Leaves Random House for Zuckerman," *WSJ,* November 26, 1997; Robin Pogrebin, "Harold Evans to Be Editorial Czar of Zuckerman Publishing Empire," *NYT,* November 26, 1997.

11. *Joni Evans; Esther B. Fein, "Random House Shuts Turtle Bay Books," *NYT,* February 11, 1993; Phoebe Hoban, "A Random Killing at Turtle Bay," *NY,* March 1, 1993; Cox, "Random House Taps."

12. Sarah Lyall, "A Different Role for the Pope: Author with a Big Price Tag," *NYT,* July 14, 1994; *NYO,* February 15, 1996; Daisy Maryles, "Bestsellers 95, Winning Combinations," *PW,* January 1, 1996; Daisy Maryles, "What a Week for Random Inc.," in "Behind the Bestsellers," *PW,* October 2, 1995; Mary B. W. Tabor, "At Powell's Publishing House, Some Regrets," *NYT,* November 9, 1995; Alexander MacGregor III; Patrick M. Reilly, "Random House Is Stacking Up Hit after Hit," *WSJ,* September 27, 1995; Geraldine Fabrikant, "Evans at Random House: Big Spender, Big Sales," *NYT,* March 8, 1993; Celia McGee, "At Dick Morris' Random House, Time Is Up for the Old Times," in "Publishing," *NYO,* October 14, 1996; "Bill's Book Sales Are Hope-less," *NYP,* December 6, 1996; Erik Eckholm, "China Agog at Clinton Visit (He's a Hero Akin to Nixon)," *NYT,* June 24, 1998; Doreen Carvajal, "The Summer of No Reading," *NYT,* August 1, 1996; Katherine Gazella, "Most Readers Turn Away from Books by Politicians," *Chicago Sun-Times,* March 17, 1997; Judy Quinn, "They Shall Return," *PW,* April 7, 1997; Sarah McBride, "Sellers' Market for Books on Washington Dries Up," *WSJ,* August 29, 1997; Hardy Green, "Superstores, Megabooks—and Humongous Headaches," *Business Week,* April 14, 1997; Ken Auletta, "The Impossible Business," *NYer,* October 6, 1997; Celia McGee, "Publishing," *NYO,* October 6, 1997; Tom Wolff, "Roger & Me," *Vanity Fair,* 1996; Reginato, "Literary Lion"; Stephan Herrera, "Where's Holtzbrinck?" *Forbes,* June 1,

1998; G. Bruce Knecht, "Peter Osnos Resigns from the Top Post at Times Books," *WSJ*, September 19, 1996; Doreen Carvajal, "Times Books Head Leaving to Start a New Imprint," *NYT*, September 19, 1996; Paul Tharp, *NYP*, September 19, 1996; McGee, "At Dick Morris' Random House"; "New Publisher Named for Times Books," *NYT*, November 15, 1996; Dinitia Smith, "Peter Osnos Plans to Publish Nonfiction by Public Figures," *NYT*, May 29, 1997; Gayle Feldman, "'Intensity' Plan Shows Publishing's Big Profit Hunt," *NYT*, January 22, 1996; "Knopf: Mega-Selling Author Jumps to Bantam," *NYP*, December 10, 1996; "Koontz Switches Publishers," *PW*, December 16, 1996; *Owen Laster; *Robert Bernstein; *André Schiffrin; Maureen O'Brien, "Media Ink!" *NYP*, May 26, 1996; Sarah Lyall, "Book Notes," *NYT*, August 3, 1994; Paul Galloway, "Sticky Situations," *Chicago Tribune*, December 6, 1996; David Margolick, "O.J.'s Ghost," *Vanity Fair*, November 1996; *NYT Book Review*, November 10, 1996; "Tina Takes Out a Contract on Toobin," in "Intelligencer," *NY*, December 2, 1996; Frank Digiacomo, "The O.J. Canon: More Shots Fired," in "The Transom," *NYO*, September 30, 1996; Johnson, "Marcia"; G. Bruce Knecht, "Book Superstores Bring Hollywood-like Risks to Publishing Business," *WSJ*, May 29, 1997; Judy Quinn, "The Case That Just Won't Die," *PW*, August 26, 1996; Deirdre Carmody, "Publishers Lining Up a New List of Memoirs," *NYT*, October 4, 1995; Doreen Carvajal, "Media," *NYT*, September 30, 1996; "New O.J. Titles, Fact & Fiction," *PW*, March 14, 1997; "Page Six," *NYP*, April 7, 1997; Dinitia Smith, "An Empire with Modest Beginnings," *NYT*, March 24, 1998.

Chapter 20—BUCKING THE IRS
1. James P. Roper, "IRS Closer to Settlement with Newhouse Estate," *E&P*, April 25, 1987; "America's Most Profitable Publisher: Seat-of-the-Pants Management That Works," *Business Week*, January 26, 1976; *George Rosato; Maggie Mahar, "All in the Family: How the Newhouses Run Their Vast Media Empire," *Barron's*, November 27, 1989; Alison Frankel, "The Six-Year Tax Case Against the Newhouse Estate," *American Lawyer*, May, 1990; Gigi Mahon, *The Last Days of The New Yorker* (McGraw Hill, 1988), 293; "IRS says S. I. Newhouse Estate Owes More Taxes," *E&P*, October 1, 1983; Jonathan Friendly, "Newhouse's Private Empire," *NYT*, October 12, 1983; Richard Pollak, "The $1 Billion Misunderstanding: The IRS vs. the Newhouse Empire," *VV*, November 5, 1985.
2. Michael Hoyt and Mary Ellen Schoonmaker, "Onward—and Upward?—with the Newhouse Boys," *CJR*, July/August 1985; Roper, "IRS Closer to Settlement"; Irwin Molotsky, "Trial Begins on Newhouse Tax Issue," *NYT*, January 14, 1989; Mahar, "All in the Family"; *James Roper; Frankel, "The Six Year Tax Case"; George Garneau, "Billion-Dollar Disagreement" and "Newhouse Tradition: Management by Discussion," *E&P*, January 14, 1989; *James Kobak; *John Morton; *Richard Meeker.
3. Frankel, "The Six Year Tax Case"; *Estate of Samuel I. Newhouse, Deceased, Samuel I. Newhouse, Jr. and Donald E. Newhouse, Executors, Petitioner, v. Commissioner of Internal Revenue, Respondent*, docket no. 23588-83, filed February 28, 1990; press release, U.S. Tax Court, February 5, 1990; *James Kobak; *John Morton; *James Roper; *Robert Lewis; Dean Starkman, "Can a Law Firm Be Its Partner's Keeper?" *WSJ*, January 7, 1997; Roper, "IRS Closer to Settlement"; *David S. Maimin Jr.; Pollak, "The $1 Billion Misunderstanding"; Mahon, *Last Days*, 275–276.

Chapter 21—THE COLLECTOR
1. Michael Crichton, *Jasper Johns* (Harry N. Abrams, 1977); Anthony Haden-Guest, *True Colors: The Real Life of the Art World* (Atlantic Monthly Press, 1996), 168–75; Jill Johnston, *Jasper Johns: Privileged Information* (Thames & Hudson, 1996); *Nan Graham;

*Bud Holland; Anthony Haden-Guest, "Of Dealers and Players," in "Talk of the Town," *NYer*, October 2, 1995; "Purchase of $40 Million Painting Triggers Uproar," *Korea Times*, September 4, 1998; *Diane Wachtell; *Meg Cox; *Paul Gottlieb; *Leo Castelli, *André Emmerich; Richard Johnson with Jeane MacIntosh, "Casino King Aced Out on Warhol," in "Page Six," *NYP*, June 26, 1998; David Ebony, "Mixed Bag at Spring Auctions," *Art in America*, July 1998; *Sotheby's Contemporary Art Catalog*, part 1, May 14, 1998.

2. *Leo Castelli; *Gray Foy; Dodie Kazanjian and Calvin Tomkins, *Alex: The Life of Alexander Liberman* (Knopf, 1993), 281.

3. Mark Brown, "Dawn's Quixote," *Chicago Sun-Times*, May 15, 1994; *Walter Netsch; Carol Vogel, "Are Happy Days Here Again for the Art World?" *NYT*, April 29, 1994; Carol Vogel, "Cracks Still Deep in Contemporary-Art Market," *NYT*, May 5, 1994; Claudia Carpenter, "Art Giants Bomb in Sales Bloodbath," *NYP*, May 6, 1994.

4. *Leo Castelli; Miki Denhof; *Frederick W. Hughes; *Walter Netsch; Johnston, Jasper Johns; *André Emmerich.

5. *Richard Penney; *Geraldine Stutz; *Richard Kinsler; Martin Filler, "The Architect of a Master Builder's Store of Art," *NYT*, June 2, 1996; *Francine du Plessix Gray; *Ray Josephs; *Leo Castelli; *Louis Oliver Gropp; *NYO*, March 9, 1998; Deborah Mitchell, *NYO*, March 23, 1992; *Robert Lang; *André Emmerich; Monique P. Yazigi, "Say What You Like but It's Still Really Nice Over Here," *NYT*, October 21, 1997.

Chapter 22—RUTHLESS

1. *Burton Bernstein; *Calvin Trillin; *Lee Lorenz; Michael Gross, "Tina's Turn: The *New Yorker*'s Head Transplant," *NY*, July 20, 1992; *Perry Vandermeer; *John MacArthur; *Richard Sacks; Iris Cohen Selinger, "Si Speaks," *Inside Media*, December 4–17, 1991; Edwin Diamond, "Caught in the Buzz Machine," *Nation*, January 2, 1995; *Joni Evans; Gigi Mahon, "S. I. Newhouse and Condé Nast: Taking Off the White Gloves," *NYT Magazine*, September 10, 1989; *Donovan Webster; Deidre Carmody, "Tina Brown to Take Over at the *New Yorker*," *NYT*, June 30, 1992; Jim Windolf, "Tina Brown's Debut: Oct. 5 *New Yorker* has Vanity Flair," in "Off the Record," *NYO*, September 14, 1992; *Jane Bernstein; *André Schiffrin.

2. Mahon, "S. I. Newhouse and Condé Nast"; *Perry Vandermeer; *Lee Lorenz; Michael Gross, "Tina's Turn"; Peter Stevenson, "S. I. Newhouse's Fabulous Florio Boys Leave Jones Beach for Corner Offices," *NYO*, July 20, 1992.

3. *John MacArthur; Stuart Elliott, "Tongues Wag Over Shift at New Yorker," *NYT*; *Perry Vandermeer; Michael Gross, "Tina's Turn"; *Burton Bernstein; *Calvin Trillin; *Suzannah Lessard; *Lee Lorenz.

4. *Lisa Lockwood; Hilton Kramer, "The Browning of America," in "Media Watch," *NYP*, September 24, 1996; *Edward A. Kosner; *Richard Kinsler; *Peter Diamandis; Deirdre Carmody, "Spy Magazine Can't Find Buyer, and Closes," *NYT*, February 19, 1994; *Terry Golway; David Yelland, "Tina Brown: New Yorker Near Profit," *NYP*, August 14, 1996; George Rush and Joanna Molloy, "Rush & Molloy," *NYDN*, September 6, 1996; *NY*, July 20, 1992; Lisa Anderson, "Now He's Fair Game," *Chicago Tribune*, September 29, 1993; "Flattery Will Get You Ten Pages...Maybe: The Tina Brown–Mike Ovitz Correspondence," *Spy*, August 1990; Suzanne Andrews, "The Trouble with Harry," *NY*, July 7, 1997; *Thomas Maier; Paul Tharp, "Publisher Is Ousted at Vanity Fair," *NYP*, June 19, 1994; *John MacArthur; *George Green; *William Whitworth; *Donovan Webster; Geraldine Fabrikant, "Making Money, Not Waves, at Vanity Fair," *NYT*, September 9, 1996; Keith J. Kelly, "He's Fair-ing Pretty Well," *NYDN*, May 1997; G. Bruce Knecht, "Guide Raises Selection, Disclosure Issues," in "Advertising," *WSJ*, August 22, 1997.

5. *NYP,* December 27, 1995; Patrick M. Reilly, "Changes Imminent, but Not Immense, as Brown Takes Over at the New Yorker," *WSJ,* September 21, 1992; *Advertising Age,* July 6, 1992; Gigi Mahon, *The Last Days of The New Yorker* (McGraw Hill, 1988), 145; Elizabeth Kolbert, "Soul of the Buzz Machine," *NYT Magazine,* December 5, 1993; Joanne Weintraub, "How Good Is Tina Brown's New Yorker?" *AJR,* April 1995; *Perry Vandermeer; *Burton Bernstein; Linton Weeks, "Daddy Dearest," *WP,* June 15, 1996; Richard Turner, "Media Mogul Madness," in "Media," *NY,* September 18, 1995 (parody of Ken Auletta's "Annals of Communications" is "Awestruck," by Ken Fellata; parody written by Malcolm Gladwell and Jacob Weisberg); Diamond, "Caught in the Buzz"; Jim Windolf, "Brown's Two Years at the *New Yorker:* 'I Finally Think We've Got It Right,'" *NYO,* October 3, 1994; *Lee Lorenz; David Streitfeld, "Book Report," *WP Book World,* September 10, 1995; John Blades, "Waiting for the Snow," in "Books/Authors," *Chicago Tribune,* November 7, 1994; Deirdre Carmody, "From Magazines, Flashes of Fiction," *NYT,* June 20, 1994; *Suzannah Lessard; *John MacArthur; Maureen Dowd, "A Hip-Hop New Yorker," in "Editorial Notebook," *NYT,* April 17, 1995; Terry Golway, "Wise Guys," *NYO,* August 29–September 5, 1994; Frank DiGiacomo, "It's a Bit Chilly in Here! (Notes on Tina Fest '95)," in "The Transom," *NYO,* February 20, 1995; *Edward A. Kosner; George Rush, and Joanna Malloy, "Throwing Stones," in "Rush & Malloy," *NYDN,* February 7, 1996; Richard Johnson, "One Too Many," in "Page Six," *NYP,* February 2, 1996; David Remnick, "The Accidental Anarchist," *NYer,* March 10, 1997; "The Money Shot," *NYer,* October 30, 1995; Michael Shain, "Media Ink," *NYP,* September 24, 1997; William Powers, "The Magazine Reader," *WP,* February 27, 1996; George Rush and Joanna Malloy, "Gianni, We Hardly Knew Ye: Versace Lookin' Good at Show," in "Rush & Malloy," *NYDN,* October 31, 1995; Richard Johnson, "Page Six," *NYP,* November 1, 1995; *Lee Lorenz; Deirdre Carmody, "New Yorker's New Editor Sees the Future in the Past," *NYT,* September 24, 1992; cartoon by P. Steiner, *NYer,* October 31, 1997; cartoon by P. Steiner, *NYer,* February 2, 1998; *Hoyt Spelman; Eric Utne, "Tina's New Yorker," *CJR,* March/April 1993; *NYer,* February 15, 1993; Jay Stowe, "Spiegelman, Tina Brown Feud Over O.J. Cop-out," in "Off the Record," *NYO,* October 30, 1995; *AJR,* January/February, 1994; *NYer,* April 17, 1995; Bill Hoffmann, "New Yorker Cover of Sailors Kissing Starts Another War," *NYP,* June 10, 1996; *NYT,* February 16, 1996; letter to author from Patti Hagan, February 20, 1994; "No Tilley Cover at New Yorker," *NYT,* March 26, 1998; Jimmy Breslin, *New York Newsday,* July 1994; "Yikes, the New Yorker," *NY,* September 11, 1995; Annie Groer and Ann Gerhart, "Roseanne the Editor," in "Reliable Source," *WP,* September 8, 1995; Jay Stowe, "New Yorker Staff Heckles Tina's Roseanne Folly," *NYO,* September 11, 1995; *Ian Frazier.

6. Reilly, "Changes Imminent"; *Burton Bernstein; *Richard Sacks; Utne, "Tina's New Yorker"; *Nat Hentoff; Nat Hentoff, *Speaking Freely: A Memoir* (Knopf, 1997); Robert Sam Anson, "Will Joe Klein Rescue the New Yorker?" *NYO,* October 28, 1996; Charles Trueheart and Howard Kurtz, "Elizabeth Drew Out at New Yorker," *WP,* August 14, 1992; *Raymond Bonner; Keith J. Kelly, "Subscribing to the Era of Tina Brown," *NYDN,* September 22, 1997; *Lee Lorenz; *Patti Hagan; Garrison Keillor, "An Institution Gone to the Dogs," *New York Newsday,* April 10, 1995; Jay Stowe, "Off the Record," *NYO,* January 22, 1996; "Putting Myself Together," *NYer,* February 20–February 27, 1995.

7. Windolf, "Brown's Two Years at the New Yorker"; Andrews, "The Trouble with Harry"; Deirdre Carmody, "Tina Brown Accused of Misusing the New Yorker," *NYT,* October 15, 1992; David Handelman, "His & Her Power," *NY,* April 17, 1996; Richard Johnson, "Page Six," *NYP,* January 6, 1997; Ken Auletta, "The Impossible Business," *NYer,* October 6, 1997; Vanessa Friedman, "Fax from London," in "The Talk of the Town," *NYer,* December 8, 1997; Rebecca Mead, "Ink," in "The Talk of the Town," *NYer,*

December 8, 1997; Hendrik Hertzberg, "Dept. of Hoopla," in "The Talk of the Town," *NYer,* December 8, 1997; Michael Shain, "Le Carré Departs Knopf after Cold War with Rushdie," *NYP,* June 17, 1998; George Rush and Joanna Molloy, "Carré On!" *NYDN,* June 17, 1998; G. Bruce Knecht, "Dick Morris Sees Cash in Scandal, Gets Book Deal," *WSJ,* September 5, 1996; Doreen Carvajal, "Adviser Had Secret Deal for Book," *NYT,* September 6, 1996; Maureen Dowd, "Literary Lion," *NYT,* September 8, 1996; David Streitfeld and Peter Baker, "Dick Morris Maneuvered to Hide His Book Plans," *WP,* September 11, 1996; James Bennett, "For Fallen Clinton Aide, Forum for Ethics Lecture," *NYT,* September 13, 1996; Doreen Carvajal, "It Takes Nerve to Bet Millions on a Disgraced News Maker," in "Media," *NYT,* September 30, 1996; Joe Klein, "The Consultant," in "Letter from Washington," *NYer,* January 27, 1997; Michael Shain, "Revealed! Inside Morris's Book," in "Media Ink," *NYP,* December 22, 1996; David Streitfeld, *WP,* January 10, 1997; Michael Wines, "Successful Political Books," February 17, 1997; Katherine Gazella, "Most Readers Turn Away from Books by Politicians," *Chicago Sun-Times,* March 17, 1997; G. Bruce Knecht, "Book Superstores Bring Hollywood-like Risks to Publishing Business," *WSJ,* May 29, 1997; Sarah McBride, "Sellers' Market for Books on Washington Dries Up," *WSJ,* August 29, 1997; Anson, "Will Joe Klein Rescue"; Richard Johnson, "Page Six," *NYP,* November 12, 1996, and November 13, 1996; Lorne Manly, "Can Mort Rescue the Amazing Harry?" *NYO,* December 8, 1997; Sherryl Connelly, "His Prints Are All Over the Place," *NYDN,* February 21, 1996; Andrews, "The Trouble with Harry"; "Weintz Leads New Random Unit; Godoff to Be Trade Ed.-in-Chief," *PW,* May 19, 1997; Knecht, "Evans Leaves Random House"; Pogrebin, "Harold Evans to Be Editorial Czar"; Michael Shain, "Evans Help Us," *NYP,* November 26, 1997; Mary Huhn, ". . . But who is Harold Evans?" *NYP,* November 26, 1997; Lorne Manly, "Harry Evans Leaves Random House for Zuckerman's Shop," *NYO,* December 1, 1997; Doreen Carvajal, "A Quick Changing of the Editors," *NYT,* December 1, 1997; Celia McGee, "Publishing," *NYO,* October 6, 1997; Robin Pogrebin, "After 6 Months, Harry Evans Still 'Invisible Man,'" *NYT,* June 15, 1998; Robin Pogrebin, "*U.S. News & World Report* Decides to Replace Its Editor," *NYT,* June 30, 1998; G. Bruce Knecht, "Amid Slump in Ad Pages, U.S. News Fires Its Editor," *WSJ,* June 30, 1998; Howard Kurtz, "James Fallows Fired after Stormy Tenure at U.S. News," *WP,* June 30, 1998; Mary Huhn, "Fallows Exits U.S. News," *NYP,* June 30, 1998.

8. Kolbert, "Soul of the Buzz"; Carmody, "Tina Brown to Take Over," *NYT,* June 30, 1992; Utne, "Tina's New Yorker"; Jay Stowe, "S. I. Newhouse Lumps New Yorker in with Condé Nast Glossies," *NYO,* September 8, 1997; *NYer,* September 22, 1997; Mary Huhn, "Is New Yorker's Tina Brown Casting About for a New President?" *NYP,* February 2, 1998; *Ian Frazier; *Perry Vandermeer; *Richard Sacks; *Robert Young; *Franz Schulze; David Plotz, "Let Si Get This," *Slate,* December 5, 1997; Liz Smith, "Felix and Oscar Redux," *NYP,* February 17, 1998; Richard Johnson, "Page Six," *NYP,* February 23, 1998; Anson, "Will Joe Klein Rescue"; Windolf, "Brown's Two Years at the New Yorker"; "The New Yorker Goes Hollywood II," in "Intelligencer," *NY,* June 6, 1994; Richard Johnson, "Diane Slapped over Jackson Puff Job," in "Page Six," *NYP,* October 17, 1997; Liz Smith, *NYP,* October 12, 1997; *J. Kennard Bosee; Geraldine Fabrikant, "Changes at New Yorker among Its Top Editors," *NYT,* February 7, 1995; *Hoyt Spelman; Robin Pogrebin, "The New New Yorker: The Talk of the Town, Except on Madison Avenue," *NYT,* October 14, 1996; Constance L. Hays, "Award Puffs Magazines' Egos but Fails to Bolster Ad Sales," *NYT,* April 28, 1997; David Yelland, "Newhouse to Post; I'm Making a Mint," *NYP,* September 27, 1996; *NYO,* October 21, 1996; *John MacArthur; Reilly, "Changes Imminent"; letter to author from James Kobak, February 6, 1995; *NYT,* February 7, 1995; Joanne Lipman, "How S. I. Newhouse Jr. Is Leading Makeover of Condé Nast Empire,"

WSJ, January 4, 1996; *Richard Kinsler; Kelly, "Subscribing to the Era"; Keith J. Kelly, "Getting a Fix on New Yorker," *NYDN*, May 26, 1998; Paul Tharp, "Is the New Yorker a Not-for-Profit Business?" *NYP*, May 26, 1998; *Jonathan Schell; Robin Pogrebin, "The Year of the Pointing Fingers at the New Yorker," *NYT*, February 16, 1998; Lorne Manly, "Off the Record," *NYO*, December 22, 1997; Michael Shain, "Media Ink," *NYP*, September 3, 1997; Tina Brown, "A Woman in Earnest," in "Manhattan Chronicles," *NYer*, September 22, 1997; *Robert Young; Lorne Manly, "Off the Record," *NYO*, November 3, 1997; Keith J. Kelly, "Red Ink Still Flows at Tina's New Yorker," in "Scene & Heard," *NYDN*, January 20, 1998; "Patrick Reilly, "Newhouse Acts to Stem New Yorker's Red Ink," *WSJ*, January 30, 1998; Keith J. Kelly, "New Chapter for Mag," *NYDN*, February 3, 1998; Robin Pogrebin, "New Yorker to Become Part of Condé Nast's Ad Package," *NYT*, February 4, 1998; Mary Huhn, "Editors Green with Envy over Tina's $35M budget," *NYP*, February 9, 1998; "Would 'TNY's' Tina Brown go to 'Blair House' to Shed a Few 'Pounds'?" *MIN*, April 28, 1997; Richard Johnson, "Short List," in "Page Six," *NYP*, June 1, 1997; Andrews, "The Trouble with Harry"; Liz Smith, "A British Exodus?" *NYP*, November 4, 1996; Richard Johnson, "Page Six," *NYP*, October 6, 1997; George Rush and Joanna Molloy, "Rush & Molloy," *NYDN*, October 21, 1997; Alan Riding, "Malraux Joins the Greats in the Pantheon as the French Exult in the Pride of Image," *NYT*, November 25, 1996.

Chapter 23—THE BUMBLER

1. *Steven Cohn; *Kimberly Bonnell; *Richard Kinsler; *Amy Gross; *Edith Raymond Locke; Joanne Lipman, "How S. I. Newhouse Jr. Is Leading Makeover of Condé Nast Empire," *WSJ*, January 4, 1996; "Publisher Is Out of a Job at New York Magazine," *New York Newsday*, August 5, 1994; Paul Tharp, "Giving Condé Nest Eggs: Interest-free Loans Buy Newhouses for All," *NYP*, June 12, 1997; Richard Wilner, "Old House Back in the Newhouse Empire," *NYP*, October 16, 1997; Maureen O'Brien, "GQ Editor Gets Unusual Lifetime Contract," *NYP*, August 21, 1996; Patrick M. Reilly, "New Men's Magazines Seek Winning Mix," *WSJ*, March 12, 1996; Jay Stowe, "Off the Record," *NYO*, March 11, 1996; Deirdre Carmody, "Condé Nast Makes Shifts After Exit by *GQ* Publisher," *NYT*, November 30, 1995; Deirdre Carmody, "Early Signs Are Promising for George Magazine," *NYT*, January 29, 1996; Geraldine Fabrikant, "Top Editor Departing Esquire Magazine," *NYT*, May 20, 1997; Robin Pogrebin, "Has Esquire Gone Out of Style?" *NYT*, July 1, 1996; Patrick M. Reilly, "*Gear*, New Men's Magazine," *WSJ*, July 24, 1998; Mary Huhn and Paul Tharp, "How 5 New Editors Fared Freshman Year," *NYP*, July 5, 1998; Warren St. John, "Off the Record," *NYO*, March 16, 1998; Robin Pogrebin, "The Publisher as Impresario," *NYT*, November 9, 1997; Paul Tharp, "Condé Nast Plans Men's Sports Magazine," *NYP*, March 11, 1997; Meg Cox, "Mademoiselle's New Editor Is Guiding Magazine's Return to the Mainstream," February 7, 1994; Patrick M. Reilly, "Magazine Forsakes Grunge to Engineer a Comeback," *WSJ*, August 3, 1994; Deirdre Carmody, "New Makeover for Mademoiselle," *NYT*, March 21, 1994; Rebecca Mead, "The Truman Administration," *NY*, May 23, 1994; Pam Hunter, "Magazine Heaven," *Spy*, July/August 1994; Robin Pogrebin, "The Long-Term Low Profile Behind the Buzz at Glamour," *NYT*, September 8, 1997; Patrick M. Reilly, "In Boom, Magazines Vie for Top of Heap," *WSJ*, December, 1997.

2. Sally Clark, "A Chill in the Corridors of Taste," in "Washington Home," *WP*, September 30, 1993; Deirdre Carmody, "Maverick Editor Gets a New Home at Condé Nast," *NYT*, October 25, 1996; Deirdre Carmody, "House & Garden to Rejoin a Rich Club," *NYT*, April 17, 1995; *James Kobak; *Carolyn Sollis; Paul Tharp, "The Test of Dominique Browning," *NYP*, October 14, 1996; *Louis Oliver Gropp; Amanda Vaill, "The Only Dame in Town," *NY*, February 21, 1994; *Denise Martin; *Richard Kinsler; Susannah

Patton, "Condé Nast to Revive House & Garden As Home-Magazine Sales Bloom Again," WSJ; Robin Pogrebin, "House & Garden Reappears on a Crowded Stage," NYT, July 30, 1996; Keith J. Kelly, "Condé Nast Old Guard Is Marching Out," Advertising Age, February 6, 1995; *Kimberly Bonnell; *Patti Hagan; *Anne Foxley; William Norwich, "Style Diary," NYO, October 28, 1996; Victoria Newhouse, "Joel Silver: The Producer's Frank Lloyd Wright House in Los Angeles," Architectural Digest, April, 1998.

3. *Carolyn Sollis.

4. Carmody, "House & Garden to Rejoin"; Patton, "Condé Nast to Revive"; *George Green; Vaill, "The Only Dame"; John Cassidy, "Condé Nast's Empire Is Stumbling Badly," NYP, April 12, 1994; *Louis Oliver Gropp; Deirdre Carmody, "Another Pacific Passage for a Condé Nast Soldier," NYT, January 17, 1994; Pogrebin, "House & Garden Reappears"; Patrick M. Reilly, "From Soup Ladles to Hamptons Spreads, Condé Nast Bets Big on Nesting Yuppies," WSJ, July 30, 1996; Deirdre Carmody, "Magazines Follow Baby Boomers into the Garden," NYT, February 6, 1995; Lorne Manly, "Off the Record," NYO, August 18, 1997.

5. William Norwich, "Style Diary," NYO, September 9, 1996; Pogrebin, "House & Garden Reappears"; Reilly, "From Soup Ladles"; Tharp, "Test of Dominique"; Michael M. Thomas, "The Midas Watch: The Face in the Mirror Causes the World's Grief," NYO, November 25, 1996; Patrick M. Reilly, "Steven Florio Gets Top Business Post at New Yorker, Succeeding His Brother," WSJ, May 26, 1998. *Patti Hagan; Jerry Oppenheimer, Martha Stewart: Just Desserts (Morrow, 1997); Robin Pogrebin, "At Struggling Time Warner, Time Inc. is Money," NYT, February 3, 1997; Geraldine Fabrikant, "Martha Stewart Is Said to Seek a Break With Time Warner," NYT, April 10, 1996; Patrick M. Reilly, "Martha Stewart Cooks Up a Threat: She May Leave Time Warner," WSJ, April 10, 1996; Paul D. Colford, "People Grabbed Top Ad Revenues," in "Ink," Newsday, January 30, 1997; "Martha Stewart to Buy Her Company," NYT, February 5, 1997; Patrick M. Reilly, "Martha Stewart Takes Over Control of Her Empire in Split with Time, Inc.," WSJ, February 5, 1997; Lorne Manly, "Off the Record," NYO, February 10, 1997; "Dig It," Condé Nast House & Garden, November 1996; *Tom Christopher; Tom Christopher, "The Natural Canvas," Condé Nast House & Garden, December 1997; letter from Tom Christopher to Patti Hagan, February 14, 1997; press releases from Random House, January 1997; Robin Pogrebin, "Master of Her Own Destiny," NYT, February 8, 1998.

Chapter 24—THE BULLY BOYS
1. Deirdre Carmody, "New President and Publishers at Condé Nast," NYT, January 13, 1994; Meg Cox, "Condé Nast Names Steven T. Florio To Be Its President," WSJ, January 13, 1994; "Changes Seen at Condé Nast," NYT, January 12, 1994; Paul Tharp, "Magazine Slugfest: Condé Nast, Hearst Duke It Out Overseas," NYP, May 14, 1997; *Pat Miller; *Richard Shortway; Iris Cohen Selinger, "Si Speaks," Inside Media, December 4–17, 1991; *Marshall Loeb; *Alexander MacGregor III; Deirdre Carmody, "Another Pacific Passage For a Condé Nast Soldier," NYT, January 17, 1994.

2. *Richard Kinsler; *Hoyt Spelman; Keith J. Kelly, "Condé Nast Old Guard Is Marching Out," Advertising Age, February 6, 1995; Cox, "Condé Nast Names"; Joanne Lipman, "How S. I. Newhouse Jr. Is Leading Makeover of Condé Nast Empire," WSJ, January 4, 1996; Keith J. Kelly, "Condé Nast CEO Faces Hard Juggling Act," NYDN, January 18, 1998; Robin Pogrebin, "The Year of the Pointing Fingers at the New Yorker," NYT, February 16, 1998; *David O'Brasky; Keith J. Kelly, "Condé Nast's Florio Reveals New Launches, Brand Extensions," Advertising Age, January 13, 1997; Carmody, "New President and Publishers"; Scott Donaton, "Florio Takes Charge at Condé Nast,"

Advertising Age, January 17, 1994; Peter Stevenson, "S. I. Newhouse's Fabulous Florio Boys Leave Jones Beach for Corner Offices," *NYO*, July 20, 1992; "New Yorker Shifts Ad Executive Posts, Cuts Publisher Title," *WSJ*, November 25, 1996; *Steven Cohn; G. Bruce Knecht, "Magazine Advertisers Demand Prior Notice of 'Offensive' Articles," *WSJ*, April 30, 1997; Warren St. John, "Off the Record," *NYO*, May 4, 1998; *NYer*, April 27 and May 4, 1998; Warren St. John, "Off the Record," *NYO*, May 11, 1998; "Fired New Yorker Publisher Sues Magazine for Sex Bias," *WSJ*, October 23, 1997; Cindy Adams, "After a Pregnant Pause, Fired Chief Fighting Mad," *NYP*, October 21, 1997.

3. "Hearst Names Galotti to New Esquire Post," *WSJ*, January 28, 1994; Deirdre Carmody, "Ex–Condé Nast Publisher Is Hired for Post at Esquire," *NYT*, January 28, 1994; *G. Douglas Johnston; Lipman, "How S. I. Newhouse Jr. Is Leading"; Bagher Hossein, "The Two Biggest Assholes in Publishing," *Spy*, March/April, 1997; Ruth G. Davis, "Central Park Place," *NY*, September 25, 1995; *Richard Kinsler; Selinger, "Si Speaks"; *David O'Brasky; Kelly, "Condé Nast Old Guard"; Carmody, "Ex–Condé Nast Publisher Is Hired"; Michael Gross, "Tina's Turn: The *New Yorker*'s Head Transplant," *NY*, July 20, 1992; Meg Cox, "James Truman Gets Star Status at Condé Nast," *WSJ*, January 26, 1994; Keith J. Kelly, "He's Fair-ing Pretty Well," *NYDN*, May 1997; *Diane Silberstein; *Kathy Neisloss Leventhal; Paul Tharp, "It's War! Vogue Battles Harper's," *NYP*, March 10, 1994; "Condé Nast's Florio Names Fuchs, Kliger Sr. VPs," *WSJ*, March 10, 1994; *Kimberly Bonnell.

4. Donaton, "Florio Takes Charge"; *Richard Kinsler; Selinger, "Si Speaks"; "Condé Nast Officials Shift," *NYT*, March 10, 1994; Tharp, "It's War!"; Lisa Lockwood, "The Truman Doctrine," *Women's Wear Daily*, July 29, 1994; *Diane Silberstein; Kelly, "Condé Nast Old Guard"; *Steven Cohn; Lipman, "How S. I. Newhouse Jr. Is Leading"; "Candace's Mr. Big Weds Another," in "Page Six," *NYP*, November 28, 1996; Paul Tharp, "Condé Nast Plans Men's Sports Magazine," *NYP*, March 11, 1997; Richard Johnson, "Size Counts," in "Page Six," *NYP*, August 22, 1997; Robin Pogrebin, "Anna's World," *NYT*, November 17, 1997; Patrick M. Reilly, "In Boom, Magazines Vie for Top of Heap," *WSJ*, December, 1997; Lane L. Levere, "Advertising," *NYT*, March 5, 1998.

5. *David O'Brasky; *Kathy Neisloss Leventhal; Selinger, "Si Speaks"; *Diane Silberstein; Jim Windolf, "Details Man Must Solve a VF Paradox," *NYO*, June 20, 1994; Pat Sloan, "Numbers Tell Pretty Story for Allure," *Advertising Age*, March 1, 1993; Michael Shain, "A More Allure-ing Redo," in "Media Ink," *NYP*, November 19, 1997; Robin Pogrebin, "Magazines Multiplying as Their Focuses Narrow," *NYT*, January 2, 1997; Paul Tharp, Gregory Zuckerman, and Farhan Memom, "Toward 2000! The Young Media Elite," *NYP*, March 4, 1996; Deirdre Carmody, "Magazine Circulation a Mixed Bag in '93," *NYT*, February 21, 1994; Lipman, "How S. I. Newhouse Jr. Is Leading"; "Details, Vanity Fair Get New Publishers," *Chicago Sun-Times*, June 9, 1994; Robin Pogrebin, "The Year of the Pointing Fingers at the New Yorker," *NYT*, February 16, 1998; Patrick M. Reilly, "Condé Nast Taps a New Publisher to Lift Vanity Fair," *WSJ*, June 9, 1994; Paul Tharp, "Publisher Is Ousted at Vanity Fair," *NYP*, June 19, 1994; Paul Tharp, "An Axman Cometh at Condé Nast," *NYP*, June 10, 1994.

6. Pogrebin, "Anna's World"; Cox, "James Truman Gets Star Status"; Tharp, "It's War!"; Keith J. Kelly, "Hearst Strikes Back with Raid on Condé Nast," *Advertising Age*, September 5, 1994; Meredith S. Tcherniavsky, "Truman Era Begins at Condé Nast," *AJR*, March, 1994; Jim Windolf, "Off the Record," *NYO*, August 22, 1994; Paul Tharp, "At Condé Nast, It's Getting Nasty," *NYP*, November 21, 1994; *Kimberly Bonnell; *Anthea Disney; Lockwood, "The Truman Doctrine"; Pam Hunter, "Party Days at Condé Nast," in "Magazine Heaven," *Spy*, September/October 1994; Linda Stasi, "Condé Nast-y Rumors,"

in "Hot Copy," *NYDN*, July 17, 1994; Rebecca Mead, "The Truman Administration," *NY*, May 23, 1994; Lipman, "How S. I. Newhouse Jr. Is Leading"; *Veronique Vienne; Jim Windolf, *NYO*, July 4–July 11, 1994; Dierdre Carmody, "Condé Nast's Auteur to Step Down," *NYT*, January 26, 1994; John Cassidy, "The Remarkable Rise of a Condé Nast Brit," *NYP*, May 20, 1994; *Robert Lang; *Chicago Tribune*, February 13, 1994; Patrick M. Reilly, "Condé Nast's Bad Boy Puts Up His Dukes," *WSJ*, November 18, 1994; Lockwood, "The Truman Doctrine," Patrick M. Reilly, "Condé Nast Picks Browning as Editor of House & Garden," *WSJ*, April 14, 1995; "Why is Newhouse Reviving the Dead," in "Intelligencer," *NY*, February 10, 1995; Robin Pogrebin, "The Long-Term Low Profile Behind the Buzz at Glamour," *NYT*, September 8, 1997.

7. *Francine du Plessix Gray; letter to author from Francine du Plessix Gray, February 25, 1995.

8. *Francine du Plessix Gray; *Gray Foy; audio tapes from "A Celebration of Leo Lerman," memorial service, November 7, 1994.

9. *Diane Silberstein; "Dead-Serious Business," in "Neal Travis' New York," *NYP*, June 1, 1997; *David O'Brasky; Carol J. Loomis, "The Biggest Private Fortune," *Fortune*, August, 17, 1987; Meg Cox, "Editor Is Out at Condé Nast's Self Magazine," *WSJ*, July 13, 1994; Deirdre Carmody, "Top Editor at Self Magazine Named to Condé Nast Post," *NYT*, July 13, 1994; *Pat Miller; "Call Her Miss Moneypenney," in "Intelligencer," *NY*, December 4, 1995; *Liz Smith; Paul Tharp, "Condé Nast Puts Udell in at Self," *NYP*, September 12, 1995; Paul Tharp, "Self Magazine Editor Penney Steps Down," *NYP*, July 13, 1994; "James Truman Fiddles with Self," in "Intelligencer," *NY*; Jeffrey A. Trachtenberg, "Condé Nast Self Goes 'Interactive' with July Issue," *WSJ*, June 8, 1994; Paul D. Colford, "Condé Nast Excels at Musical Chairs," in "Ink," *New York Newsday*, July 21, 1994; Rebecca Mead, "The *Self*-Actualization of Alexandra Penney," *NY*, August 1, 1994; Hunter, "Party Days at Condé Nast"; *Veronique Vienne; Meg Cox, "Self's Editor Changes Mind; Will Keep Job," *WSJ*, July 19, 1994; *Veronique Vienne; *Robert Lang; Patrick M. Reilly, "Alexandra Penney, the Editor in Chief of Condé Nast's Self Magazine, Resigns," *WSJ*, August 30, 1995; Patrick M. Reilly, "Condé Nast's Udell Succeeds Penney as Editor of Self," *WSJ*, September 12, 1995; "The Latest Self Flagellation," in "Intelligencer," *NY*, October 24, 1994; Anthony Ramirez, "Self Magazine Editor Resigns; Calls Decision Firm This Time," *NYT*, August 30, 1995; *Linda Rath; Paul Tharp, "Health Magazines Are Good Business," *NYP*, March 7, 1997; *Steven Cohn.

10. Press release from Bertelsmann, Advance Publications, Inc., March 23, 1998; press release from Alberto Vitale, Random House, March 23, 1998; Doreen Carvajal, "German Media Giant Will Buy Random House for $1.4 Billion," *NYT*, March 24, 1998; Edmund L. Andrews, "Hansel & Gretel Inc.," *NYT*, March 24, 1998; Geraldine Fabrikant, "'Planning Our Future,' Newhouse Brothers Say," *NYT*, March 24, 1998; Michael Shain, "Germans Buy Random House," *NYP*, March 24, 1998; Michael Shain, "Si Closes Book At Random House," *NYP*, March 24, 1998; Michael Shain, "It's Hard to Make Book with Books," *NYP*, March 24, 1998; Jon Elsen, "Middelhoff Builds Publishing Giant," *NYP*, March 24, 1998; Paul Tharp, "Condé Nast Heir Expanding Global Affairs," *NYP*, March 24, 1998; Keith J. Kelly, "Deals Book at Random," *NYDN*, March 24, 1998; Keith J. Kelly, "What Will Si Do with Money is 1.2B Question," *NYDN*, March 24, 1998; Doreen Carvajal with Geraldine Fabrikant, "Random House Sale Shakes Up Literary World," *NYT*, March 25, 1998; "Remaindered," *NYT*, March 25, 1998; Martin Arnold, "Much Rumbling about a Merger," in "Making Books," *NYT*, March 26, 1998; Warren St. John, "So Why Did Newhouse Sell Random House to Bertelsmann?" in "Off the Record," *NYO*, March 30, 1998; Edmund L. Andrews, "American Pop Culture, Foreign-Owned," *NYT*, March 29, 1998; Keith J. Kelly,

"Authors Seek to Put Book Merger on the Shelf," *NYDN*, March 25, 1998; Porter Bibb, "In Publishing, Bigger Is Better," *NYT*, March 31, 1998; I. Jeanne Dugan, "Boldly Going Where Others Are Bailing Out," *Business Week*, April 6, 1998; John F. Baker and Jim Milliot, "Bertelsmann to Buy Random House," *PW*, March 30, 1998; Michael Maren, "Random Outcomes," *NY*, April 6, 1998; Eric Alterman, "Random Violence," *Nation*, April 13, 1998; Geoff Shandler, "Bertelsmann's Online Blitzkrieg," *Salon*, April 7, 1998; Nora Rawlinson, "The Random House Acquisition: An Interview with S. I. Newhouse," *Bookwire*, April 3, 1998; Daniel Johnson, "Springtime for Bertelsmann," *NYer*, April 27 and May 4, 1998; Doreen Carvajal, "Authors Guild Tries to Block Proposed Merger of 2 Publishers," *NYT*, April 27, 1998; André Schiffrin, "Eyes on the Bottom Line," WP, April 30, 1998; Doreen Carvajal, "Bertelsmann Hits a Snag In Acquisition," *NYT*, May 2, 1998; G. Bruce Kencht, "Random House Refiling to FTC May Stall Approval," *WSJ*, May 4, 1998; Michael Shain, "No Backtracking on Bertelsmann Deal," *NYP*, May 4, 1998; "The Business Observer," *NYO*, May 4, 1998; John F. Baker, "BDD/Random Merger Gets Extra Scrutiny in Washington," *PW*, May 11, 1998; David Margolick, "The German Front," *VF*, June 1998; Geraldine Fabrikant, "New Deal May Loom for Simon & Schuster," *NYT*, May 19, 1998; Keith J. Kelly, "Heavyweight Authors Take Punch at Merger," *NYDN*, May 20, 1998; Felicity Barringer, "F.T.C. Clears Merger Path for Publishers," *NYT*, May 30, 1998; James Surowiecki, "The Publisher's Curse," in "The Capitalist," *NYT Magazine*, May 31, 1998.

11. Lorne Manly, "By Newhouse's Decree, James Truman Plays Prince of Condé Nast," *NYO*, August 18, 1997; Julie V. Iovine, "Moving Day Angst at the Citadel of Chic," *NYT*, February 26, 1998; Richard Johnson, "Nice Guy," in "Page Six," *NYP*, December 12, 1997; Ann Marie Kerwin and Scott Donaton, "Condé Nast Loses Another Exec VP as Clinton Quits," *Advertising Age*, August 25, 1997; "Si Newhouse Builds His Condo Nest," *NYO*, May 20, 1996; Jay Stowe, "S. I. Newhouse Lumps New Yorker In with Condé Nast Glossies," *NYO*, September 8, 1997; Maureen O'Brien, Paul Tharp, and Peter Slatin, "Condé Nast Fired Backroom Staff Despite City Cash," *NYP*, May 9, 1996; Thomas J. Lueck, "Condé Nast to Move Its Headquarters to New Times Square Tower," *NYT*, May 8, 1996; Herbert Muschamp, "Smaller Is Better: Condé Nast Meets Times Sq.," *NYT*, May 18, 1996; Peter Slatin and Paul Tharp, "Condé Nast Seals $11 M Tax Deal for Times Square Move," *NYP*, May 7, 1996; David Yelland, "The Inside Story: How Si Really Got the $10.75M," *NYP*, May 9, 1996; Charles V. Bagli, "Times Sq. Giveaway Grants Newhouse a Giant Tax Break," May 20, 1996; Michael M. Thomas, "S. I. Newhouse Jr. Loves That Suck-Up Literati," *NYO*, June 10, 1996; Peter Grant, "Critical of Condé"; Gersh Kuntzman, "Condé Nast's Moving Story," *NYP*, May 13, 1996; Peter Grant, "Condé Nast Joins New 42nd St.," *NYDN*; Peter Slatin, "Work Starts at 'Condé Towers,'" *NYP*, August 2, 1996; Peter Slatin, "A Groundbreaking Review," *NYP*, August 2, 1996; Devin Leonard, "Durst and Klein Risk the Wrath of Disney with 42nd Street Plot," *NYO*, December 9, 1996; "Chow Deluxe," in "Page Six," *NYP*, August 13, 1997; Liz Smith, "Tony & Talented," May 8, 1998; Kelly, "Condé Nast CEO Faces"; Keith J. Kelly, "Red Ink Still Flows at Tina's New Yorker," in "Scene & Heard," *NYDN*, January 20, 1998; Patrick Reilly, "Newhouse Acts to Stem New Yorker's Red Ink," *WSJ*, January 30, 1998; Mary Huhn, "Is New Yorker's Tina Brown Casting about for a New President?" *NYP*, February 2, 1998; Keith J. Kelly, "New Chapter for Mag," *NYDN*, February 3, 1998; "Off the Record," *NYO*, February 9, 1998; Paul Tharp, "The Fighting Florios," *NYP*, February 9, 1998; Pogrebin, "The Year of the Pointing Fingers at the New Yorker"; Warren St. John, "Off the Record," *NYO*, March 9, 1998; Robin Pogrebin, "New Yorker's Top Executive Is Replaced," *NYT*, May 23, 1998; Michael Shain, "New Yorker's Florio Gets Brown-Bagged,"

NYP, May 23, 1998; Patrick M. Reilly, "Steven Florio Gets Top Business Post at New Yorker, Succeeding His Brother," *WSJ,* May 26, 1998; Keith J. Kelly, "Getting a Fix on New Yorker," *NYDN,* May 26, 1998; Paul Tharp, "Is the New Yorker a Not-for-Profit Business?" *NYP,* May 26, 1998; Keith J. Kelly, "For Brown, Carey not a Ferm Choice," *NYDN,* May 29, 1998; Warren St. John, "Off the Record," *NYO,* June 1, 1998; Mary Huhn, "'Ta-Ta' Time for Tina?" *NYP,* May 28, 1998; Keith J. Kelly, "*Ms.* Editors Close to Buyout Deal," *NYDN,* June 9, 1998; Paul Tharp, "Liar, Liar: Mag Flays Florio as Fibber & Financial Failure," *NYP,* June 30, 1998; Joseph Nocera and Peter Elkind, "The Buzz Factory," *Fortune,* July 20, 1998; Keith J. Kelly, "Newhouse Looking to Deal," *NYDN,* July 2, 1998.

Chapter 25—THE PRINCES

1. *Donald Sterling; Carol J. Loomis, "The Biggest Private Fortune," *Fortune,* August, 17, 1987; "America's Most Profitable Publisher: Seat-of-the-Pants Management That Works," *Business Week,* January 26, 1976; *NYT,* April 9, 1995; *Jim Flanagan; Daniel Machalaba, "Newhouse Chain Stays with Founder's Ways, and with His Heirs," *WSJ,* February 12, 1982; *Robert C. Notson; *G. Douglas Johnston; *Robert M. Greenberg; *Jane Franke; *Val Monroe; *Richard Penney; Thomas Maier, *Newhouse: All the Glitter, Power, and Glory of America's Richest Media Empire and the Secretive Man Behind It* (St. Martin's Press, 1994); *Anthea Disney; *Louis Oliver Gropp; *George Rosato; *Thomas Maier; *Richard Shortway; *Val Monroe.

2. *Jane Franke; Maier, *Newhouse;* *Carolyn Sollis; "America's Most Profitable Publisher"; Loomis, " Biggest Private Fortune"; *Margot Hentoff; *Richard Penney; *Peter Diamandis; *Gray Foy; Pamela J. Wilson, "Ode to Ease," *Traditional Home,* July 1997; *Pamela J. Wilson.

3. Loomis, " Biggest Private Fortune"; *Richard Shortway; *Joni Evans; *Jane Franke; last will and testament of Sam Newhouse, signed November 8, 1976; *Richard Penney; *Gray Foy; *Richard Meeker; *Amy Gross; letter to the author from Pamela Mensch, December 18, 1994; Maier, *Newhouse;* *Denise Martin; Pilar Viladas, "Advanced Geometry," *HG,* March 1993; Elissa Schappell, "Hot Type," *Vanity Fair,* May 1998; "Towards a New Museum: A Provocative Book Assesses Recent Experiments in Exhibiting Art" (excerpt from Victoria Newhouse, *Towards a New Museum*), *Architectural Digest,* July, 1998;*Anne Foxley; *Thomas Maier; *Robert Bernstein; Suzanne Stephens "New York River Dance: An Architect's Family Compound Straddles a Dam," *Architectural Digest,* October 1998; Victoria Newhouse, "Rem Koolhass in Bordeaux," *Architectural Digest,* October 1998.

4. *John Robinson Block; Linda Fibich, "A New Era at Newhouse," *AJR,* November, 1994; Machalaba, "Newhouse Chain Stays"; *Robert Miraldi; last will and testament of Sam Newhouse; Loomis, "The Biggest Private Fortune"; *James Roper; *John Robinson Block; *Jane Franke; *Jeff Pundyk; *David O'Brasky; *Sue Spoto; Patrick M. Reilly, "Condé Nast Picks Several Corporate, Magazine Aides," *WSJ,* September 29, 1994; *MIN,* November 14, 1994; *MIN,* February 10, 1997; *G. Douglas Johnston; *Alan Mirken; *Wendy Wolf; *Robert Bernstein; *Joni Evans; William Glaberson, "New Editor Tries to Write 'the End' to Star-Ledger of Past," *NYT,* March 20, 1995; N. R. Kleinfield, "Heads Have a History of Rolling at Newhouse," *NYT,* November 2, 1989; "Barbara Goldsmith Leaves the Woolworth Apartment; A Newhouse Steps In," *NYO,* December 15, 1997.

5. Jefferson Grigsby, "Newhouse, after Newhouse," *Forbes,* October 29, 1979; Rebecca Mead, "The Truman Administration," *NY,* May 23, 1994; Joanne Lipman, "How S. I. Newhouse Jr. Is Leading Makeover of Condé Nast Empire," *WSJ,* January 4, 1996; "Forbes

400," *Forbes*, October 16, 1995; *Robert Young, *Louis Oliver Gropp; *George Green; *Richard Kinsler; *G. Douglas Johnston; Gigi Mahon, *The Last Days of The New Yorker* (McGraw Hill, 1988); *Terry Golway; *David O'Brasky; *Robert Miraldi; *Ben Magdovitz; *Saul Kohler; *WSJ*, April 11, 1996; Sarah Mower, "Wish You Were Her?" *Telegraph Magazine*, April 19, 1997; Paul Tharp, "Magazine Slugfest: Condé Nast, Heast Duke It Out Overseas, *NYP*, April 14, 1997; Constance L. Hays, "Even Titles Are Flexible as U.S. Magazines Adapt to Foreign Ways," *NYT*, August 4, 1997; *WSJ*, July 5, 1996; Robin Pogrebin, "Changing of Guard at Cosmo," *NYT*, January 13, 1997; Richard Wilner, "Fuller Fills Six Slots at Cosmo," *NYP*, December 13, 1996; Fara Warner, "Cosmopolitan Girl Is Dressing Up for Summer Debut in Indonesia," *WSJ*, April 9, 1997; Deirdre Carmody, "Magazines Find Green Pastures Abroad," *NYT*, March 20, 1995; James Brooke, "American Publishers Add Readers in Booming Latin America," *NYT*, May 11, 1998; Fara Warner, "Condé Nast Plans Vogue's Introduction to Korean Women," *WSJ*, November 3, 1995; *NYT*, April 11, 1996; Fara Warner, "Condé Nast Opts to Make Taiwan Its First Stop in Asian Campaign," *WSJ*, May 1, 1996; "Publishing Firms Set South African Venture," *WSJ*, June 30, 1997; Paul Tharp, "Condé Nast Heir Expanding Global Affairs," *NYP*, March 24, 1998; Wendy Bounds, "Condé Nast to Russians: Let Them Read Vogue," *WSJ*, September 4, 1998; Liz Tilberis, with Aimee Lee Ball, *No Time to Die* (Little, Brown, 1998); "Unhappy Family, the Newhouse Way," in "Intelligencer," *NY*, August 8, 1994; "Newhouse of Love," *NY*, June 20, 1994; "Newhouse's New House," *NY*, November 28, 1994; "Jonathan's New Home Amid Condé Nast's Starlets," *NYO*, August 31–September 7, 1998; *Karl Grossman; Paul Tharp, "Pick of the Litter," *NYP*, March 29, 1998.

6. *Richard Shortway; "No More Rumor at the Top for Si," in "Intelligencer," *NY*, October 27, 1997; Keith J. Kelly, "Condé Nast's Florio Reveals New Launches, Brand Extensions," *Advertising Age*, January 13, 1997; *Peter Diamandis; Geraldine Fabrikant, "Si Newhouse Tests His Magazine Magic," *NYT*, September 25, 1988; Iris Cohen Selinger, "Si Speaks," *Inside Media*, December 4–17, 1991; Grigsby, "Newhouse, after Newhouse"; *Alexander MacGregor III; *Robert Bernstein; *Joni Evans; *David Morgan; *Mel Elfin; *Edward A. Kosner; *David O'Brasky; *George Green; *Ray Josephs; *Richard Kinsler; *Edith Raymond Locke; Loomis, "The Biggest Private Fortune"; *Donald Sterling; *Saul Kohler.

7. *Edward A. Kosner; "Forbes 400," *Forbes*, October 14, 1996; "Forbes 400," *Forbes*, October 16, 1995; Tim Jones, "For Newspapers, a Bundle of Woes," *Chicago Tribune*, October 29, 1995; Mark Crispin Miller, "The Crushing Power of Big Publishing," *Nation*, March 17, 1997; preface and afterword to paperback edition of Maier, *Newhouse* (Johnson Books, 1997); Lawrence M. Fisher, "Microsoft and Compaq to Buy 10% Stakes in Road Runner," *NYT*, June 16, 1998; Saul Hansell, "Technology," *NYT*, June 29, 1998; Suzan Revah, "Bylines," *AJR*, March, 1997; *WSJ*, August 7, 1995; Loomis, "The Biggest Private Fortune"; Mower, "Wish You Were Her?"; Grigsby, "Newhouse, after Newhouse"; *Richard Meeker; *David O'Brasky; *Forbes*, July 6, 1998.

8. Lipman, "How S. I. Newhouse Jr. Is Leading"; Paul Tharp, "Condé Nast Plans Men's Sports Magazine," *NYP*, March 11, 1997; Peter Slatin and Paul Tharp, "Condé Nast Seals $11 M Tax Deal for Times Square Move," *NYP*, May 7, 1996; Lorne Manly, "Off the Record," *NYO*, February 17, 1997; Constance L. Hays, "Condé Nast Makes High-Level Changes at Two Magazines," *NYT*, May 5, 1997; Patrick M. Reilly, "U.K. Magazine Queues Up to U.S. Men," *WSJ*, March 26, 1997; Lorne Manly, "After Declaring Death of Downtown, James Truman Ousts Details Editor," "Off the Record," *NYO*, May 5, 1997; Mary Huhn, "For New Yorker, Narrower Is Better," *NYP*, May 21, 1998; "Editor Named at Details," *NYT*, May 21, 1997; Paul Tharp, "Devil's in Details: Condé Nast Bets on

'Swashbuckler,'" *NYP*, May 16, 1997; Liza Featherstone, "Boys Will Be Girls," *CJR*, May/June 1998; Keith J. Kelly, "Some Floored by New Condé Nast Offices," *NYDN*, May 5, 1998; Mary Huhn and Paul Tharp, "How 5 New Editors Fared Freshman Year," *NYP*, July 5, 1998; Robin Pogrebin, "The Year of the Pointing Fingers at the New Yorker," *NYT*, February 16, 1998; Lorne Manly, "Off the Record," *NYO*, June 23, 1997; Keith J. Kelly, "Details to Draw on Artist," in "Scene & Heard," *NYDN*, September 30, 1997; *Lee Lorenz; Pam Hunter, "Party Days at Condé Nast," in "Magazine Heaven," *Spy*, September/October 1994; Mead, "The Truman Administration"; David Plotz, "Let Si Get This," *Slate*, December 5, 1997; Cindy Adams, "After a Pregnant Pause, Fired Chief Fighting Mad," *NYP*, October 21, 1997; Paul Tharp, "Giving Condé Nest Eggs: Interest-free Loans Buy Newhouses for All," *NYP*, June 12, 1997; Paul Tharp, "Vanity Fair Editor Moves to Digs in 'Dead' Downtown"; *NYP*, June 26, 1997; Richard Wilner, "Old House Back in the Newhouse Empire," *NYP*, October 16, 1997; Keith J. Kelly, "Condé Nast Old Guard Is Marching Out," *Advertising Age*, February 6, 1995; *Richard Sacks; Keith J. Kelly, "Condé Nast CEO Faces Hard Juggling Act," *NYDN*, January 18, 1998; Huhn, "For New Yorker"; Warren St. John, "Off the Record," *NYO*, July 13, 1998.

9. Richard Pollak, "The $1 Billion Misunderstanding: The IRS vs. the Newhouse Empire," *VV*, November 5, 1985; Geraldine Fabrikant, "Si Newhouse Tests His Magazine Magic," *NYT*, September 25, 1988; Miller, "The Crushing Power"; Mower, "Wish You Were Her?"; Maggie Mahar, "All in the Family: How the Newhouses Run Their Vast Media Empire," *Barron's*, November 27, 1989; George Manners, "Web Site First to Spawn TV Show," *NYDN*, December 11, 1997; "Forbes 400," *Forbes*, October 14, 1996; "Reed Elsevier to Sell Book Unit to Random House," Dow Jones, *NYT*, February 1, 1997; "Reed Elsevier to Sell Adult Trade Division to Random House," *WSJ*, February 3, 1997; "Heard on the Bloomberg, the Business Observer," *NYO*, February 10, 1997; Gigi Mahon, "S. I. Newhouse and Condé Nast: Taking Off the White Gloves," *NYT Magazine*, September 10, 1989; Loomis, " Biggest Private Fortune"; "200 Billionaire Profiles," *Forbes*, July 28, 1997; "Forbes 400," *Forbes*, October 13, 1997; Leslie Cauley, "Discovery and BBC Agree to Launch New TV Channels," *WSJ*, March 19, 1998.

10. "Forbes 400," *Forbes*, October 13, 1997.

11. Lipman, "How S. I. Newhouse Jr. Is Leading"; *NYDN*, January 31, 1996; Constance L. Hays, "Advertising," *NYT*, April 14, 1997; "Women Are Good Sports," *NYP*, November 25, 1996; Paul Tharp, "Women's Sports Magazine War Heats Up," *NYP*, January 7, 1997; "Condé Nast Plans Women's Sports Magazine for 1997," *WSJ*, January 31, 1996; Patrick Reilly, "Will Women's Sports Magazines Be Hits?" *WSJ*, June 26, 1996; Keith J. Kelly, "Condé Nast Women's Sports Title Delays Its Rookie Season," *Advertising Age*, August 26, 1996; Keith J. Kelley, "Polly Perkins Picked A Fight & Lost," *NYP*, October 7, 1998; Jay Stowe, "A Publisher Targets Steve Florio; Saying Condé Nast Ripped Her Off," in "Off the Record," *NYO*, July 22, 1996; "Media City," *NYP*, October 27, 1997; Hays, "Condé Nast Makes High-Level"; Lorne Manly, "Off the Record," *NYO*, May 5, 1997; Robin Pogrebin, "Adding Sweat & Muscle to a Familiar Formula," *NYT*, September 21, 1997; Keith J. Kelly, "Time Warner Exec's off to New Brill Media Mag," *NYDN*, December 12, 1997; Robin Pogrebin, "Condé Nast Buys a Magazine; Will Alter Sports for Women," *NYT*, January 13, 1998; Mary Huhn, "Condé Nast Revamps Women's Sports Mag," *NYP*, January 13, 1998; *WSJ*, "Publishing," January 13, 1998; Keith J. Kelly, "Women Outside on Horizon," *NYDN*, January 15, 1998; Patrick M. Reilly, "Time Out for Women's Sports Magazines," *WSJ*, January 19, 1998; Keith J. Kelly, "SI Puts New QB in Lineup," *NYP*, January 28, 1998; Keith J. Kelly, "For Top Editor, the Time-ing's Right," *NYP*, December 8, 1997; Firestone, "Boys Will Be Girls"; Mary Huhn, "Condé Nast Mag Tries to Shape Up," *NYP*,

June 8, 1998; Keith J. Kelly, "Condé Nast Joins High-Finance Crowd," in "Scene & Heard," *NYDN*, January 16, 1998; Mary Huhn, "Condé Nast Is Spending Cash for Currency," *NYP*, March 3, 1998; "Condé Nast is Buyer of Wired Magazine for Over $75 Million," *WSJ*, May 8, 1998; Mary Huhn, "Wired Gets a Newhouse," *NYP*, May 9, 1998; Amy Harmon, "Digital Culture Pioneer Sold to Condé Nast," *NYT*, May 11, 1998; Warren St. John, "Before Newhouse Sailed In, Failed I.P.O. Sunk Wired," *NYO*, May 18, 1998; Amy Harmon, "Chief of Condé Nast Solicits Ideas for Wired," *NYT*, July 27, 1998; Patrick Reilly, "Newhouse Acts to Stem New Yorker's Red Ink," *WSJ*, January 30, 1998; Kelly, "Condé Nast CEO Faces"; Lorne Manly, "Off the Record," February 3, 1997; Kelly, "Condé Nast's Florio Reveals."

12. "Publisher to Buy Magazine Group," *NYT*, June 25, 1996; *John Morton; Patrick M. Reilly, "Disney May Sell ABC's Papers And Magazines," *WSJ*, January 29, 1997; Geraldine Fabrikant, "Disney to Sell Capital Cities Publications," *NYT*, January 29, 1997; Patrick M. Reilly, "Disney to Keep Fairchild Magazines after Proposed Sale Draws Big Interest," *WSJ*, February 7, 1997; Joseph B. Treaster, "Knight-Ridder to Buy 4 Newspapers from Disney for $1.65 Billion," *NYT*, April 5, 1997; Nikhil Deogun and Bruce Orwall, "Knight-Ridder Inc. Returns to Its Roots with Pact to Buy 4 Disney Newspapers," *WSJ*, April 17, 1997; *NYT*, August 5, 1995; *WSJ*, August 7, 1995; "Bloomberg Business News," *NYP*, August 5, 1995; "Advance Publications to Acquire SunMedia," *WSJ*, December 1, 1997; Robin Pogrebin, "ESPN Rivals Set for Fight as Magazine Debut Nears," *NYT*, January 19, 1998; Iver Peterson, "Is McClatchy Bid for Cowles Too Rich?" *NYT*, November 17, 1997; "All in Another Family," in "Bylines," *AJR*, December 1997.

13. Anne Chamberlin, "America's Unknown Press Lord," *Esquire*, August 1959; *James Warren; *James Roper; Glaberson, "New Editor Tries to Write 'The End'"; William Glaberson, "Media," *NYT*, December 25, 1995; Iver Peterson, "Mort Pye, 79, Longtime Newark Editor, Dies," *NYT*, December 2, 1997; Iver Peterson, "1996 Pulitzer Prize Form a Snapshot Portrait of Journalists in the Workaday World," *NYT*, April 10, 1996; *Terry Golway; William Glaberson, "The Media Business," *NYT*, April 10, 1995; William Glaberson, "Philadelphia Editor Going to Newark," *NYT*, February 18, 1995; Alicia C. Shepard, "Love and the Editorial Page," AJR; *Mike Greenstein; Art Kramer, "Big Projects, Big Payoffs in the Big Easy," *AJR*, January/February, 1996; Iver Peterson, "20 Pulitzer Prizes Are Announced with a Theme of Personal Impact on Lives," *NYT*, April 8, 1997; "Journal Reporters Win Pulitzer Prize for Chronicling New AIDS Therapies," *WSJ*, April 8, 1997.

14. Linda Fibich, "A New Era at Newhouse," *AJR*, November, 1994; *John Robinson Block; *William Woestendiek; *John Ettorre; *Richard G. Zimmerman; letter from Richard Zimmerman to William Woestendiek, May 7, 1985; *Bob Samsot; Roldo Bartimole, "Pee Dee Dark Ages: Machaskee Moves in," *Point of View*, February 10, 1990; Michael Hoyt and Mary Ellen Schoonmaker, "Onward—and Upward?—with the Newhouse Boys," *CJR*, July/August 1985; *Gary Webb; *Robert Lewis; *Herbert Kamm; *Tom Andrzejewski.

15. *Bob Rast; *AJR*, June 1994; *John Ettorre; *James Roper; *Katherine Kahler; *George Hager; *H. Michael Rood; *Jim Flanagan; *Richard G. Zimmerman; *Paula Schwed; *Milton Jaques; Peterson, "1996 Pulitzer Prizes."

16. Syracuse University Archives, audio tapes of dedication of Newhouse School, WSYR AM and FM; *Ray Josephs; Loomis, "Biggest Private Fortune"; *Kenneth Shaw; telephone conversation with Amy Doherty, Syracuse University Library; *Alan Mirken; "America's Jewish Billionaires: How Rich! How Charitable?" *Moment*, December 1996.

17. *Alex O. Osford Kostman; *Michael Loeb; *Paul Gottlieb; *Richard Glanton; Carol Vogel, "An Art Tour Comes Home, Its Fortune Made," *NYT*, November 19, 1995; *Petition of the Students of the Barnes Foundation for Recusal of the Attorney General of Pennsylvania as Representative and Parens Patriae for the Barnes Found*, Orphans' Court Division, June 1994; opinion, Orphans' Court Division, July 10, 1995; memorandum from S. Gordon Elkins, December 16, 1992, attorney for the de Mazia trustees; *Barnes Watch*, April 1993; *Barnes Watch*, January 1995; Anne Higonnet, "Whither the Barnes?" *Art in America*, March 1994; "Barnes Storm," *Vanity Fair*, August 1991; Roger Kimball, "Betraying a Legacy: The Case of the Barnes Foundation," *New Criterion*, June 1993; Hilton Kramer, "Calling Dr. Barnes: Commence Spinning," *NYO*, May 10, 1993; Michael Kimmelman, "The Barnes Foundation: No Longer a Recluse," *NYT*, November 24, 1995; Lee Rosenbaum, "Masterpieces Back Home, Hung in Same Weird Way," *WSJ*, November 28, 1995; Iver Peterson, "Times-Mirror Seeks Buyer for Publisher of Art Books," *NYT*, September 5, 1996.

Chapter 26—THE QUEEN OF BUZZ BUZZES OFF

1. Patrick M. Reilly and Wendy Bounds, "Tina Brown Quits the New Yorker for New Venture," *WSJ*, July 9, 1998; Janny Scott and Geraldine Fabrikant, "Editor of the New Yorker Leaving for New Venture," *NYT*, July 9, 1998; Bernard Weinraub, "A Match Made in Hollywood: The Marriage of Razzle and Dazzle," *NYT*, July 9, 1998; Keith J. Kelly, "A Short List of Likely Successors," *NYDN*, July 9, 1998; Mary Huhn and Paul Tharp, "'Brownout' on a Dark Day at the New Yorker," *NYP*, July 9, 1998; Neal Travis, "Her Job Finished at the New Yorker, Tina Took the Money and Ran," *NYP*, July 9, 1998; Mary Huhn and Paul Tharp, "Stable of Big Names in New Editor Horse Race," *NYP*, July 9, 1998; Paul Tharp and Cathy Burke, "Tina's Power Outage," *NYP*, July 9, 1998; Liz Smith, "Don't Cry for Talented Tina Brown," *NYP*, July 9, 1998; James Poniewozik, "Brown and Out in New York," *Salon*, July 9, 1998; Bob Minzesheimer, "Tina Brown, Ready for the Next Big Thing," *USA Today*, July 9, 1998; Jonathan Mahler, "Tina Goes to Hollywood," *Slate*, July 9, 1998; Susan Lehman, "Buzzing about the Buzz Machine," *Salon*, July 9, 1998; David Firestone, "New Yorker Staff Takes Deep Breath," *NYT*, July 10, 1998; John J. Goldman, "Newhouse Meets with Nervous Staff," *Los Angeles Times*, July 10, 1998; Neal Travis, "Tina's in Hostile Territory," *NYP*, July 10, 1998; "Talk of the Town: Tina Brown's Successor," in "The Reliable Source," *WP*, July 10, 1998; Mary Huhn and Paul Tharp, "After-Brown Countdown," *NYP*, July 10, 1998; Beverly Beyette, "New New Yorker is 'Absolutely Tina,'" *Los Angeles Times*, July 10, 1998; Keith J. Kelly, "Pundits Ponder Pick for New Yorker," *NYDN*, July 11, 1998; Maureen Dowd, "TINA!" in "Liberties," *NYT*, July 12, 1998; Paul Tharp, "Brown's Real Role with Miramax Is in Development," *NYP*, July 13, 1998; Marjorie Williams and Timothy Noah, "The Breakfast Table," *Slate*, July 13, 1998; Mary Huhn and Paul Tharp, "Two More on Tap to Trail Tina," *NYP*, July 13, 1998; Bruce Handy, "Buzz Buzz Buzz," *Time*, July 20, 1998; Richard Turner, "A Life after the New Yorker," *Newsweek*, July 20, 1998; Felicity Barringer with Geraldine Fabrikant, "Tina Brown Edits Her Career to Match the Zeitgeist," *NYT*, July 13, 1998; Robin Pogrebin, "Staff Writer Named Editor at New Yorker," *NYT*, July 14, 1998; Warren St. John, "Tina Goes Cheek to Cheek with Miramax," *NYO*, July 20, 1998; Patrick M. Reilly, "Amid Shouts and Murmurs, Remnick Is Talk of the Town," *WSJ*, July 14, 1998; "Don't Call It Journalism," *NYT*, July 14, 1998; Fred Kaplan, "New Yorker Wishes upon a Star," *Boston Globe*, July 14, 1998; Marjorie Williams and Timothy Noah, "The Breakfast Table," *Slate*, July 14, 1998; Mary Huhn, "Insider Takes Helm at New Yorker," *NYP*, July 14, 1998; Paul Tharp, "Remnick Gets the New Yorker," *NYP*, July 14, 1998; Michael Shain, "New Editor:

A Mix of Old and New, with a Little Less Buzz," *NYP,* July 14, 1998; Mary Huhn, "Kinsley: Si Courted Me to Run It All," *NYP,* July 14, 1998; Fred Bruning, "Tina Brown, Talk of the Town," *Newsday,* July 14, 1998; Tom Carson, "She, Tina," *VV,* July 14, 1998; James Ledbetter, "Kinsley—for a Day," in "Press Clips," *VV,* July 14, 1998; Eric Alterman, "Good News about Journalism," *MSNBC,* July 14, 1998; Maureen Dowd, "How About Our Needs?" in "Liberties," *NYT,* July 15, 1998; Richard Grenier, "Does Tina See What Is Coming?" *Washington Times,* July 17, 1998; Franklin Foer, "The Weinsteins: Moguls of the Old School," *Slate,* July 18, 1998; Robin Pogrebin, "Losing Vogue's Publisher Could Hurt Condé Nast as Much as Tina Brown's Departure," in "Media," *NYT,* July 20, 1998; Belinda Luscombe, "Kinsley is King For a Day," in "People," *Time,* July 20, 1998; Jeannette Walls, "Harvard U. Press Takes Tina to Task," *NY,* August 23, 1993; Steven Greenhouse, "Elevator Scaffold Falls, Killing Woman and Paralyzing Times Sq.," *NYT,* July 22, 1998; Bill Hutchinson, "Lethal Rain Falls on 43rd," *NYDN,* July 22, 1998; Tracy Connor, "Traffic Turmoil for Times Sq. Area," *NYP,* July 22, 1998; Tracy Connor, "Frightened Folks Ran for Their Lives," *NYP,* July 22, 1998; Owen Moritz, "A Tragic History Plagues Tower," *NYDN,* July 22, 1998; Tracy Connor, "Times Sq. to Take Off Rest of the Week," *NYP,* July 23, 1998; Tara George, Michael Finnegan, and Bill Hutchinson, "Officials Eying 3 Possible Causes," *NYDN,* July 23, 1998; David W. Dunlap, "1 1/2 Acres of Netting to Enclose Damaged Scaffold," *NYT,* July 23, 1998; Dan Barry, "Manhattan Tries to Cope with Accident Aftermath," *NYT,* July 23, 1998.

2. Felicity Barringer, "Advertising," *NYT,* August 11, 1998; Patrick M. Reilly, "Condé Nast Lures Cosmopolitan's Fuller to Be New Editor at Glamour Magazine," *WSJ,* August 11, 1998; Phyllis Furman, "A Glamour Job: Cosmo Editor Joins Condé Nast," *NYDN,* August 11, 1998; Keith J. Kelly, "Si Fills Spot with Fuller," *NYP,* August 11, 1998; Keith J. Kelly, "The Truth about Ruth: She Hates Glamour's Pick," *NYP,* August 11, 1998; Paul Colford, "Top Guns and Bottom Lines," *Newsday,* August 13, 1998; Richard Turner and Yahlin Chang, "Styles and Substance," *Newsweek,* August 24, 1998; Ginia Bellafante, "A Rival Takes the Reins," *Time,* August 24, 1998.

Chapter 27—HEARST, LUCE, MURDOCH—NEWHOUSE?

1. Richard H. Meeker, *Newspaperman: S. I. Newhouse and the Business of News* (Ticknor & Fields, 1983), 88; "The Newspaper Collector," *Time,* July 27, 1962; Edward Vernoff and Rima Shore, *International Dictionary of 20th Century Biography* (New American Library, 1987); Richard M. Clurman, *To The End of Time: The Seduction and Conquest of a Media Empire* (Simon & Schuster, 1992), 30–31, 36; "Heir to Newspapers Wm. R. Hearst Jr.," *Chicago Tribune,* May 16, 1993; Bruce Lambert, "William Randolph Hearst Jr., 85, Journalist, Dies," *NYT,* May 16, 1993; *WSJ,* August 1, 1997; Susan Orenstein and Jay Stowe, "Hearst CEO Ends Veronica's Hobby," *NYO,* April 29, 1996; Michael Shain and Richard Wilner,"Redbook Readying Publisher Shakeup," *NYP,* August 18, 1997; George Rush and Joanna Molloy, "Rush & Molloy," *NYDN,* February 9, 1997; "Evening Hours, No Time for Winter's Gloom," *NYT,* February 9, 1997; "In Cyberia No One Can Hear You Scream," *NYO,* January 8, 1996; Sarah Lyall, "Murdoch Blood, Murdoch Empire," *Vanity Fair,* July 1997; Ken Auletta, "The Pirate," in "Annals of Communication," *NYer,* November 13, 1995; "The New Establishment 50: Leaders of the Information Age," *Vanity Fair,* October 1995; *Anthea Disney; Geraldine Fabrikant. "Murdoch Bets Heavily on a Global Vision," *NYT,* July 29, 1997; Paul Farhi, "Murdoch, All Business," *WP,* February 12, 1995; Michael Lewis, "Rupert Murdoch, Conqueror! What Does This Man Want?" *NYO,* June 16, 1995; James Ledbetter, "Rupert's Failure," in "Press Clips," *Village Voice,* July 22, 1998; Robert Frank, "Britain's Blair is Criticized for Role in Murdoch Bid for

Italian Broadcaster," *WSJ*, March 30, 1998; Helene Cooper and John Lippman, "Harper Collins Won't Publish Patten Memoirs," *WSJ*, February 27, 1998; Warren Hoge, "Murdoch Halts a Book Critical of China," *NYT*, February 28, 1998; Barbie Dutter, "Publisher Drops Book Ripping China," *Chicago Sun-Times*, February 28, 1998; Robert La Franco, "Rupert's on a Roll," *Forbes*, July 6, 1998; Russell Baker, "Murdoch's Mean Machine," *CJR*, May/June 1998; Liz Smith, "Armani's Twofer," *NYP*, September 11, 1996; Amy M. Spindler, "A New Armani Conquers a New World," *NYT*, September 17, 1996.

Index